Masterplots

2,010 Plot Stories & Essay Reviews
from the World's Fine Literature

Revised Edition

Including the Four Series
and Further Critical Evaluations

Edited by
FRANK N. MAGILL

Story Editor
DAYTON KOHLER

Volume Three
CRO - ESS
1223 - 1836

SALEM PRESS
Englewood Cliffs, New Jersey 07632

LIBRARY OF CONGRESS CATALOG CARD NUMBER 76-5606

REVISED EDITION
First Printing

PRINTED IN THE UNITED STATES OF AMERICA

LIST OF TITLES IN VOLUME THREE

LIST OF TITLES IN VOLUME THREE

LIST OF TITLES IN VOLUME THREE

LIST OF TITLES IN VOLUME THREE

THE CROCK OF GOLD

Type of work: Novel
Author: James Stephens (1882-1950)
Type of plot: Fantasy
Time of plot: Any time
Locale: Irish countryside
First published: 1912

Principal characters:
THE PHILOSOPHER
THE THIN WOMAN, his wife
SEUMAS AND BRIGID, two children
ANGUS OG, an early Irish god
CAITILIN, his mortal wife

Critique:

This tale of adventure and philosophical discussions is a modern classic in its field. Stephens is most successful in his attempt to bring old Irish legends to life in the pages of a delightful book. The philosophic discussions abound with a delightful humor, and the seriousness of some of the observations in no way lessens the magic quality of the story. The tale is a wandering one, containing many elements and telling many stories. All of them are entertaining to read, and most of them are perfect in execution.

The Story:

In the center of a very dark pine wood lived the two old Philosophers and their wives, the Grey Woman of Dun Gortin and the Thin Woman of Inis Magrath. One couple had a little boy named Seumas, the other a little girl named Brigid. Both were born on the same day.

When the children were ten years old, one of the old Philosophers decided that he had now learned all he was capable of learning. This conclusion depressed him so much that he decided to die. It was unfortunate, as he pointed out, that at the time he was in the best of health. However, if the time had come for him to die, then die he must. He took off his shoes and spun around in the center of the room for fifteen minutes until he fell over dead. So grieved was the Grey Woman that she, too, killed herself, but as she was much tougher than her husband she spun for forty-five minutes before she died. The Thin Woman calmly buried the two bodies under the hearthstone.

The people who lived on the edge of the pine wood often came to see the Thin Woman's husband when they needed advice. One day Meehawl MacMurrachu came to the Philosopher to learn who had stolen his wife's scrubbing board. The Philosopher, after much questioning, finally decided that the fairies had taken it. He advised Meehawl to go to a certain spot and steal the Crock of Gold that the Leprecauns of Gort na Gloca Mora had buried there. For years the Leprecauns had been filling their Crock of Gold by clipping the edges of gold coins that they found in men's houses at night. They needed the gold to ransom any of the little people caught by human beings.

Losing their gold to Meehawl made the Leprecauns angry, and they tried to make Meehawl bring it back by giving him and his wife all kinds of aches and pains. Next they came stealthily and lured Brigid and Seumas down into a little house in the roots of a tree, but fear of the Thin Woman was on them and they set the children free. Then they sent the Great God Pan, the god of the beast which is in every man, to lure away Caitilin, Meehawl's daughter, with the music of his pipes.

When Meehawl came with his tale of

sorrow, the Philosopher sent Brigid and Seumas to tell Pan to let the girl go. But Pan refused to answer their questions. When they told the Philosopher, he became so angry that he ordered his wife to bake him some cakes to eat on the way, and he started off by himself to visit Pan. But none of the Philosopher's arguments could persuade Pan to free Caitilin, and the Philosopher went off to get the help of Angus Og of the old gods.

Angus Og himself went to see Pan and the girl in their cave and forced the girl to choose between them. Caitilin, who had learned the true meaning of hunger and pain with Pan, did not know how to choose. Angus Og explained to her that he was Divine Inspiration, and that if she would come and live with him and be his wife, he would show her peace and happiness. By several signs he proved that he was the favorite of the gods of the earth and had more power than Pan. Caitilin sensed that true happiness, which she had never known, would be found with Angus Og, and that only hunger could be found with Pan. So she chose to leave Pan and go with Angus Og. Thus she was saved from the beast in man.

The Philosopher, on his way back home, delivered several messages from the god. One message he gave to a young boy, a promise from Angus Og that in time the old gods would return, and that before they did the boy would write a beautiful poem in their praise. Cheered by the news that the gods would soon come back, the Philosopher finally arrived home, where he greeted his wife with such affection that she decided always to be kind to him and never again to say a cross word.

Unknown to them, the Leprecauns had informed the police in the village that there were two bodies buried under the hearthstone in the Philosopher's house. One day the police broke into the house, found the bodies, and accused the Philosopher of murder. Meanwhile Brigid and Seumas were playing in the woods, and quite by chance they happened to dig a hole and find the Crock of Gold where Meehawl had buried it. They gave it back to the Leprecauns, but the return of the gold was not enough to set matters right. The police kept the Philosopher in jail. Then the Thin Woman baked some cakes and set out to find Angus Og, dragging the children behind her and saying the worst curses there were against the police. The first gods she met were the Three Absolutes, the Most Beautiful Man, the Strongest Man, and the Ugliest Man. By her wisdom the Thin Woman was able to answer their questions and save herself and the children from their frightful powers. When they had passed these gods, they found the house of Angus Og. He was waiting for someone to come and ask him to aid the Philosopher, for it is impossible for the gods to help anyone unasked.

Calling all the old gods together, Angus Og and his wife led a great dance across the fields, and then they went down into the town with all the gods following. In the town their merry laughter brought happiness to all who saw them except the most evil of men. The charges against the Philosopher were forgotten and he was free to go back to his house in the pine woods and dispense wisdom once more. Then the gods returned singing to their own country to await the birth of Caitilin's and Angus Og's child and the day when the old Irish gods could again leave their hidden caves and hollows and rule over the land with laughter and song.

Further Critical Evaluation of the Work:

James Stephens was a minor member of the Irish literary renaissance which began toward the end of the nineteenth century. Like such major figures as

W. B. Yeats, John Synge and Sean O'Casey, Stephens embodies the wit, imagination, and satiric vein that distinguishes the movement. Another of its identifying characteristics was its intense Irish patriotism, which discovered a focus in the rebellion against England and the campaign for home rule. This nationalism founds its way into the literature in the form of the celebration of the ordinary people—the peasants and the urban proletariat—and their history, including the myths of the ancient Irish gods.

Like all fables, Stephens' *The Crock of Gold* can be read on a number of levels. Much like *Alice's Adventures in Wonderland,* it is a delightful story in itself and can be enjoyed for Seumas' and Brigid's humorous adventures among such mythical creatures as the Leprechauns and the Greatgods, Pan and Angus Og. Yet one would be amiss if he overlooked Stephens' political and moral intention and his call for Irish unity.

At the beginning of the story the Irish people are hostile to one another. When matters are brought to a boil with the theft of the crock of gold and the arrival of Pan, the Philosopher, who is responsible for the upheaval, is unable to bring order. Representing Ireland's intellectuals, he has lost touch with his own people. Realizing his impotence, however, he seeks out Angus Og. It is in this turning toward ancient wisdom that the gold as well as harmony are restored. At the end the people are promised that Caitilin's and Angus Og's child will come to return Ireland to its rightful rulers. Following the same path, Stephens suggests, the Irish will be able to arrive at its true Renaissance and gain its freedom from English tyranny.

CROME YELLOW

Type of work: Novel
Author: Aldous Huxley (1894-1963)
Type of plot: Social satire
Time of plot: 1920's
Locale: England
First published: 1921

Principal characters:
HENRY WIMBUSH, owner of Crome
ANNE WIMBUSH, his niece
DENIS STONE, a young poet
MR. SCROGAN, a man of reason
GOMBAULD, an artist
MARY BRACEGIRDLE, a victim of repressions
JENNY MULLION, a keen-eyed observer

Critique:

Aldous Huxley has written an amusing satire on the ill-fated love affair of a sensitive young poet. Using the plot as an excuse for bringing together all sorts of interesting and unusual facts and stories, he holds the reader's interest by an almost continual shift of emphasis. We learn of each of the guests at the house party, their faults, interests, and virtues. As in all of Huxley's novels, there is much philosophical discussion. No particular ideas are set forth as correct, but a precise picture of the early twenties as Huxley saw them is presented to the reader with wit and dexterity.

The Story:

Denis Stone, a shy young poet, went to a house party at Crome, the country home of Henry Wimbush and his wife. He went because he was in love with Wimbush's niece, Anne. Anne looked down on Denis because he was four years younger than she, and treated him with scorn when he attempted to speak of love.

Mr. Wimbush was interested in little except Crome and the histories of the people who had lived in the old house. Mrs. Wimbush was a woman with red hair, probably false, and an interest in astrology, especially since she had recently won a bet on a horse with her star-given information. Other guests at the party included Gombauld, an artist who had been invited to paint Anne's picture; the diabolically reasonable Mr. Scrogan; deaf Jenny Mullion; and Mary Bracegirdle, who was worried about her Freudian dreams. Denis and Anne quarreled, this time over their philosophies of life. Denis tried to carry all the cares of the world on his back, but Anne thought that things should be taken for granted as they came. The quarrel cost Denis his first opportunity to tell Anne that he loved her.

Mary Bracegirdle discussed with Anne her dreams and repressions. Having decided to secure either Gombauld or Denis for a husband, she chose the wrong times to talk with both men. Gombauld was busy painting when Mary came up to him. Denis was smarting with jealousy over the time Anne and Gombauld spent together.

Ivor Lombard arrived for the party. Ivor, a painter of ghosts and spirits, turned his attentions toward repressed Mary, and secretly visited her one night in the tower. He went away without seeing her again.

From time to time Mr. Wimbush called the party together while he read stories of the early history of Crome. These stories were from a history at which Mr. Wimbush had worked for thirty years. Denis often wondered if he would ever get a chance to tell Anne that he loved her. Walking in the garden after a talk with Mr. Scrogan, whose cold-blooded ideas about a rationalized world annoyed him, he found a red notebook in which Jenny had been writing for the past week. In it he found a collection of sharply satirical cartoons of all the people at the house party. Jenny had drawn him in seven attitudes which showed up his absurd jealousy, incompetence, and shyness. The cartoons deeply wounded his vanity and shattered his conception of himself.

He was further discouraged by the fact that there was nothing for him to do at a charity fair held in the park outside Crome a few days later. Mr. Scrogan made a terrifying and successful fortune-teller; Jenny played the drums; Mr. Wimbush ran the various races; and Denis was left to walk aimlessly through the fair as an official with nothing to do. Gombauld made sketches of the people in the crowd, and Anne stayed by his side.

The night after the fair Denis overheard part of a conversation between Gombauld and Anne. Without knowing that Anne had repulsed Gombauld, for she had made up her mind to accept Denis if he ever got around to asking her, Denis spent hours of torture thinking of the uselessness of his life. At last he decided to commit suicide by jumping from the tower. There he found Mary grieving because she had received only a brisk postcard from Ivor. She convinced Denis that both their lives were ruined, and advised him to flee from Anne. Convinced, Denis arranged a fake telegram calling him back to London on urgent business. When it arrived, Denis realized with dismay that Anne was miserable to see him go. The telegram was the one decisive action of his life. Ironically, it separated him from Anne.

Further Critical Evaluation of the Work:

Even an early work like *Crome Yellow* shows traces of the novels which were to make Huxley into one of the major voices of his generation. Autobiographical, the novel is almost entirely taken from his early life. Written around the theme of a sensitive young poet's unsuccessful love, it is more, however, than the exegesis of his own unrequited love. Huxley uses the plot to bring together a wide variety of characters. The most interesting feature for the reader familiar with Huxley's best-known novel, *Brave New World,* is the introduction of Scrogan, whose personality undergoes a metamorphosis in the course of the book. Originally a mere house guest, though a malignant one, Scrogan gradually becomes the voice which Huxley adopts later in *Brave New World.* His function in the book is the voice of the devil, whose mad theories of the herd and the elite will blossom completely in Huxley's later social satire.

Given the idiocy and banality of those gathered at Crome, it is not difficult to imagine Scrogan's philosophy coming into existence. Like Mary Bracegirdle (a name of singular significance), all the house guests are shut off from their own feelings and obsessed by their own worlds and themselves. Like Mr. Wimbush who subjects them to his reading of the ridiculous history of Crome—to which no one listens—they all speak *at* one another, never *to* anyone. The essence of the comedy, then, arises from their failure to understand and to communicate; the pathos of the situation emerges from missed connections and, finally, from missed opportunities of love. Because Denis Stone (again an apt and telling name) fails to confront Anne, he loses her love. Only Jenny Mullion sees accurately and truly; it is an absurd world which deserves our ridicule if not our pity. And it certainly deserves Mr. Scrogan.

CROTCHET CASTLE

Type of work: Novel
Author: Thomas Love Peacock (1785-1866)
Type of plot: Comedy of manners
Time of plot: Nineteenth century
Locale: England
First published: 1831

Principal characters:
EBENEZER MAC CROTCHET, a country squire
YOUNG CROTCHET, his son
LEMMA CROTCHET, his daughter
SUSANNAH TOUCHANDGO, loved by young Crotchet
MR. CHAINMAIL, an antiquarian
CAPTAIN FITZCHROME, a young army officer
LADY CLARINDA BOSSNOWL, loved by Fitzchrome

Critique:

In *Crotchet Castle,* as in his other novels, Peacock ridicules the excesses and exaggerations in human behavior. His satire is never unkind; rather, it is the product of a mind that is tolerant of weaknesses but vexed by an overabundance of those weaknesses in an imperfect world. The plot is almost non-existent, and the people are caricatures; but in spite of these apparent defects the book gives a fairly accurate picture of nineteenth-century English country life.

The Story:

The squire of Crotchet Castle had descended from Scotch and Jewish ancestors, but he tried to hide this ancestry under the guise of an English country squire. His background having given him the ability to make money readily, he used his wealth to buy a manor and a coat of arms. His wife was dead, his son in London, leaving the squire alone with a daughter. Young Crotchet, who had inherited his father's love for money, had taken his father's gift of a large sum and turned it into enormous profits. His business dealings were shady, and many thought his day of reckoning would come. For the present, however, he was riding on a crest of success. He had been engaged to Miss Susannah Touchandgo, the daughter of a great banker, but when that gentleman had absconded with the bank's funds, leaving his daugh-

ter almost penniless, young Crotchet had deserted his love without a backward glance. Susannah had retreated into Wales, where in simple surroundings she taught a farmer's children for her livelihood.

Squire Crotchet's daughter Lemma had assumed some of the facial characteristics of her ancestors, a fact which was compensated for in the eyes of local swains by the size of her father's fortune. A suitor had not yet been selected for her, but there would be no problem in choosing one from the many who sought her hand and her purse.

Crotchet Castle was a gathering place for philosophers and dilettantes picked at random by Squire Crotchet. These would-be intellectuals engaged in long and tiresome disputes on all branches of philosophy and science. One of them, a Mr. Chainmail, longed for a return to the customs and morals of the Middle Ages, for he believed that the present was decidedly inferior to the past. He was violently opposed by others of the group who worshipped mammon. No one of the philosophers ever changed his views; each found much pleasure in expounding his own pet theory.

While strolling through the grounds one day, some of the gentlemen came upon a young army officer, Captain Fitzchrome. The captain, invited to join the group, accepted readily, for he was in

1229

love with one of the guests, Lady Clarinda Bossnowl. Lady Clarinda obviously loved the captain, but she had been promised to young Crotchet. The match was purely a business arrangement; he would exchange his money for her title. The captain pleaded with her at every opportunity, but she silenced him and her own heart by ridiculing his lack of funds. Lemma Crotchet, in the meantime, was pledged to Lady Clarinda's brother. The four young people spent many hours together, much to Captain Fitzchrome's sorrow.

One day the squire took his guests on a river voyage down the Thames. They visited places of learning and culture, but saw little of either except the buildings supposed to house those virtues. During the trip the captain finally gave up his hopes of winning Lady Clarinda, and he left the party without notifying anyone. He settled in a village inn, where he was later joined by Chainmail, the antiquarian, who had left the party in order to study a ruined castle in the neighborhood. Since the captain knew the way to the castle, he offered to guide Chainmail, but he was called back to London on business before they could undertake their expedition. Chainmail went on alone.

During his researches Chainmail caught a glimpse of a nymph-like creature who fascinated him so much that he could not rest until he had made her acquaintance. After many false attempts, he met her and learned that she was Susannah Touchandgo, the lady betrayed by young Crotchet. Chainmail found her perfect in every way but one. He knew she would share the simple, old-fashioned life he loved, but he had determined to marry a lady of gentle birth. Susannah, ashamed of her father's theft, would tell him nothing of her family background. In spite of her reluctance in this respect, Chainmail loved her and spent many happy hours at the farmhouse in which she lived.

Captain Fitzchrome returned. Learning of his friend's plight, he encouraged Chainmail to ask for the lady's hand, but the antiquarian could not change his views on his need for a wife of gentle birth. The situation was brought to a climax when they saw in the paper an announcement of the approaching marriage of Lady Clarinda and young Crotchet. Susannah was temporarily overwrought by the news, and in trying to comfort her Chainmail inadvertently proposed. Then Susannah told him of her father's crime. Chainmail could overlook that fact in his joy over the discovery that Susannah was of good blood. In a few days the two were married.

The following Christmas most of the friends gathered again at Crotchet Castle. Lemma Crotchet had married Lord Bossnowl, but Lady Clarinda Bossnowl had not yet married young Crotchet. The young man was a little dismayed at seeing Susannah married to Chainmail, for he still held her in affection. Lady Clarinda cast longing glances at the captain, even to the point of singing a song that was obviously intended for him. There was no sorrow in her heart, consequently, when young Crotchet disappeared. His firm had failed and he was penniless. It was assumed that he had crossed the Atlantic to join forces with Susannah's father, who had set up business there; the two rogues would make good partners.

Lady Clarinda would not again be put up for sale. She gladly accepted Captain Fitzchrome and his smaller but more stable fortune.

Further Critical Evaluation of the Work:

Born and educated in the eighteenth century, Peacock carried the ideas and ideals of the Century of Reason into the nineteenth century and the age of Victoria. Although ostensibly set in the first half of the nineteenth century, the scenes of *Crotchet Castle* might more easily be from the comedies of Sheridan or Goldsmith. Artificiality reaches the point of absurdity. The scenes at the country villa might almost be out of paintings by Watteau—or even Boucher. The influence of Voltaire and the rationalists and satirists of the previous century on Peacock is well known. At one moment the exchanges of Captain Fitzchrome and Lady Clarinda are worthy of Shakespeare's Beatrice and Benedict, then the scene abruptly changes to pseudophilosophic discussions that might have been taken from *The Satyricon* of Petronius. Peacock's writing always makes the reader think of something else, because it is based on previous creations rather than upon nature and direct observation of humanity. Quotations and exclamations in Greek, Latin, French, and other languages stud the dialogue like spangles on a ballgown, glittering but at times affected and gaudy.

The word "fashion" is the be-all and end-all of the characters' existence. Only money is more important than the pursuit of the fashionable; and, in fact, often they seem to be inextricably intertwined. Even as Peacock satirizes snobbery, the reader feels that Peacock is nevertheless a genuine snob, himself; his sharpest barbs are for the *nouveau riche* Jews trying to buy their way into the gentry. Peacock looked dubiously upon the changing times, particularly upon the growth and development of science during the first half of the nineteenth century. In novels such as *Crotchet Castle,* he satirizes the coming industrial age and the new-found riches of certain classes rising on the wave of change, and glorified that leisurely age when people had the time and inclination to sit around eating and drinking and talking . . . especially talking.

THE CRUISE OF THE CACHALOT

Type of work: Pseudo-factual account
Author: Frank T. Bullen (1857-1915)
Type of plot: Adventure romance
Time of plot: Late nineteenth century
Locale: At sea
First published: 1898

Principal characters:
FRANK T. BULLEN, the narrator
MR. JONES, fourth mate
ABNER CUSHING, a sailor
MR. COUNT, first mate
CAPTAIN SLOCUM, of the *Cachalot*

Critique:

The Cruise of the Cachalot was for some years a favorite with boys, because of its dramatic picture of life aboard an American whaler during the last century. There is no plot and almost no character analysis; indeed the author made no pretense at writing a literary work. The chief value of the book lies in its full descriptions of whale hunting. As natural history the book must seem inexact to a modern reader; and the author's unquestioning acquiescence in the many needless hardships of the common sailor is indicative of an uncritical approach.

The Story:

By a strange combination of circumstances, Frank Bullen found himself in New Bedford, Massachusetts, looking for a ship. He was only eighteen at the time, but already he had spent six years at sea.

He was strolling down a street in New Bedford, intent on a possible berth aboard any ship, for his pockets were empty, when he was hailed by a scraggy Yankee with the inevitable tobacco juice dribbling down his whiskers. Asked if he wanted to ship out, he accepted eagerly without knowing the type of craft or any of the conditions of employment. He accompanied the sharp-featured Yankee to a small, dirty hall where he joined a group of men all bound for the same ship. When he saw the motley crowd of greenhorns, he felt doubts about joining the ship, but there was little chance to back out. After hastily signing the ship's articles, he went with his mates to the docks.

All of the crew were carefully kept together until they were safe in the small boat. On the trip out into the harbor Bullen saw with many misgivings the *Cachalot*, which would be his home for three years. He deeply regretted signing on, for the *Cachalot* was a whaler and whalers were notoriously the worst ships afloat. The *Cachalot* did not compare favorably with the trim English whalers with which he was more familiar. She was small, a three hundred and fifty tonner, dirty and unpainted, and quite dumpy-looking because she had no raised bow or poop.

Once on board, Bullen's worst fears were realized. The officers were hard and mean; they carried lashes with them and a clumsy or slow sailor often felt the sting of a lash on his back. The men needed a great deal of discipline, however, to do a halfway decent job. Of the twelve white crew members, Bullen was the only one who had been to sea before. The hands were beaten and cursed, and they were not even allowed to rest while they were seasick.

Along with the white greenhorns, there were a score of Portuguese, all experienced whaling men. There were also four mates and Captain Slocum. The captain was a hard driver and a foul

THE CRUISE OF THE CACHALOT   by Frank T. Bullen. By permission of the publishers, Appleton-Century-Crofts, Inc.

talker. The first mate, Mr. Count, was an older man, the only decent officer aboard. The fourth mate, Mr. Jones, was a giant Negro.

Because of his past experience, Bullen escaped most of the abuse meted out to his fellows. After the ship had been scrubbed and polished, and the men had been licked into shape, he became almost fond of the ship. That feeling was heightened when he learned the *Cachalot* was, in spite of her lines, seaworthy.

The ship was heading toward Cape Verde, to the delight of the Portuguese. At last the first whale was sighted. Bullen was put into the boat of the first mate and told to mind the sail. The boat came up almost on top of the whale before Louis, the harpooner, threw his great hook. When the whale sounded, the hands paid out over two hundred fathoms of line. Then the whale began to rush away at full speed, towing the boat in his wake. When he slowed down, the boat was brought close enough for the harpooner to use his lance. After a final flurry, the whale died and was towed alongside.

After some months at sea, Bullen had an unpleasant picture of ship's discipline. Abner Cushing, a Yankee sailor, tried to make some beer in the forecastle. Needing some potatoes for his brew, he stole a few from the officers' galley. One of the Portuguese reported the theft to the captain and, as punishment, Abner was strung up by the thumbs and lashed vigorously by one of the harpooners until he fainted. When his punishment was over, he was not allowed to go below, but was forced to turn to immediately. The cruise was an ill-fated one for Abner. He was in a small boat when a whale unexpectedly turned and bore down on the frail craft. The line was hurriedly pulled in. Then the whale sounded, and as the line was paid out Abner's neck caught in a loop. The weight of the descending whale severed his head neatly.

Mr. Jones, after the *Cachalot* had been at sea over a year, became greatly depressed. He recalled a fortune-teller's prediction that he would die in a fight with a white man and finally decided that Captain Slocum was destined to cause his death. Deranged, he went on the bridge, wrapped his huge arms around the captain, and jumped with him into the sea. When Mr. Count assumed command, he promoted Bullen to Mr. Jones' vacant post.

Once Bullen nearly met his end when a harpooned cachalot suddenly turned sidewise and with his mighty tail smashed a boat to bits. His foot tangled in the wreckage, Bullen went under. When he came up, nearly exhausted, he caught blindly at a rope and hauled himself along until he came to the inert whale. He clambered aboard and clung to the harpoon in the side of the dead whale. But the whale suddenly came to life. When the other boats came alongside after the whale had finally died, Bullen had a dislocated thigh and severe rope burns on each arm.

At last, after three years, the *Cachalot's* barrels were full, and the ship headed home around Cape Horn. In good time the lookout sighted Cape Navesink. With every flag flying, she came into New Bedford. The cruise of the *Cachalot* was ended.

Further Critical Evaluation of the Work:

Frank Bullen's childhood was cruel. Like Charles Dickens, he was a homeless waif and child laborer in London who lacked schooling. He was adopted briefly by a kindly aunt and began to read Milton's *Paradise Lost* at five years of age; but the aunt, his solitary childhood friend, died when Bullen was eight, and he was cast into the street. Alone in the world, with "no-one caring a straw for me," he trusted God and was signed on an English vessel when he was twelve years old. Bullen spent the next six years at sea. He landed in New Bedford, Massachusetts, when he was eighteen and secured a berth on a sailor's nightmare, a whaler, in this case the "Cachalot," a venerable tub "as leaky as a basket."

The Cruise of the Cachalot is a combined autobiographical/fictional narration which gives an account of a South Sea whaler from a seaman's standpoint. Bullen also described the methods employed, the dangers met, and the woes experienced by whalers, using a clear style in order not to weary the reader. He scorned padding, sought accuracy of detail, and penned a tersely thrilling story of a voyage around the world that lasted for years. Its many fascinating passages include a description of a cyclone off the remote Seychelles Islands, storms at sea, the vast face of the sea and the sky, a passage through the Sargasso Sea, labors, landings, harpoonings, beatings, and a brush with the Confederate raider "Alabama," among other adventures. All this was done while pursuing cachalots, or sperm whales, which yielded by-products such as spermaceti and ambergris, mentioned by Shakespeare and Milton. The book's minor inaccuracies are the inevitable ones produced by its fast pace and man-of-action approach.

Bullen was at first puzzled as to how to write The Cruise of the Cachalot but decided to write it as if he were simply spinning a yarn to a single friend. When this approach met with difficulties, he offered his rich materials to the famous Rudyard Kipling, assuming that the latter could do it literary justice. Kipling declined the material and encouraged Bullen to handle it by himself. After reading Bullen's manuscript, Kipling wrote a Foreword to it that has since been carried in every edition of The Cruise of the Cachalot. Kipling's foreword describes the book as "immense" and unequaled in sea wonder and mystery. Praising the manner in which Bullen depicted whaling through fresh and realistic sea pictures, Kipling commented that Bullen must have discarded enough material to write five books.

CRY, THE BELOVED COUNTRY

Type of work: Novel
Author: Alan Paton (1903-   )
Type of plot: Social criticism
Time of plot: Mid-twentieth century
Locale: South Africa
First published: 1948

Principal characters:
THE REVEREND STEPHEN KUMALO, a Zulu clergyman
GERTRUDE, his sister
ABSALOM, his son
MSIMANGU, his friend
MR. JARVIS, his white benefactor

Critique:

In South Africa today there is racial unrest more bitter than any now known in our own country. *Cry, the Beloved Country* is a beautiful and tragic story of that unrest, told with poetic loveliness. It is a story of personal tragedy, as well as a story of a national tragedy. This distinguished novel by a South African minister has quickly, and rightly, found a permanent place in twentieth-century literature. Dramatized, the story has been equally compelling as a play.

The Story:

The letter brought fear to the hearts of the Reverend Stephen Kumalo and his wife. To a Zulu, letters were rare and frightening. Once opened, they could never be closed again, their contents forgotten. Kumalo waited until he could control his fear before he opened the letter from Johannesburg telling him that his sister was a sick woman and needed his help. The trip would be costly for a poor Zulu clergyman, but he must go. Perhaps there he could also find their son Absalom, who had never been heard from since he left the village. They knew in their hearts that in Johannesburg Absalom had succumbed to the evil resulting from the white man's success at breaking up the tribes and compelling black men to work in the mines.

Taking their small savings, Kumalo journeyed to the city. He went first to the mission and met Msimangu, who had written the letter. Msimangu was a clergyman also, working for his people in the city as Kumalo worked in the country. He sorrowfully told Kumalo that his sister Gertrude was a prostitute and a dealer in illegal liquor. She and her child were in want, even though she had once made much money from her trade. Kumalo located Gertrude, with the help of Msimangu, and found her willing to go with him to the temporary rooms he had found with a good woman. When his business was finished, she and the child would go with him to his home, away from temptation.

Before looking for his son, Kumalo visited his brother John, a successful merchant and a politician who was under surveillance by the police for his ability to stir up the blacks. But John was discreet; he took no chance of being arrested and losing his business. Many of the black leaders sacrificed everything to help their people, but not John. Expediency was his only thought. He had left the church and turned a deaf ear to his brother's pleas that he return to the good life.

Kumalo began his search for Absalom. With Msimangu, he searched everywhere, each place visited adding to his fear, for it was obvious that the boy had been engaged in stealing, drinking, and worse. Often they walked for miles, for the black leaders were urging their people to boycott the buses in order to get the fares reduced. Kumalo learned that Absalom had been in the company of his brother John's son, both of them in and out of trouble. The trail led to a reformatory, but the boy had been dismissed shortly before because of his good behavior. The white teacher of the reformatory joined Kumalo in his search because the boy's behavior reflected on his training. Kumalo found next the girl who, soon to bear Absalom's child, waited to marry him. The old man knew at once that should Absalom not be found, the girl must return to the hills with him and make her home there.

At last he found Absalom in prison. In company with John's son and another boy, Absalom had robbed and killed Arthur Jarvis, a white man who had befriended the blacks. Broken-hearted, the old man talked with his son. He could tell that the son did not truly repent but only said the right things out of fear. His one ray of goodness was his desire to marry the girl in order to give his unborn child a name. Kumalo wept for his son. But he wept also for the wife and children, for the father and mother of the slain man.

At the trial Absalom was defended by a lawyer found by Kumalo's friends. The plea was that the murder was not planned, that the boy had shot in fear. The judge, a good man, weighed all the evidence and pronounced a verdict of guilty; the punishment, death by hanging. John's son and the other boy were acquitted for lack of evidence. The verdict was a gross miscarriage of justice, but John was more powerful than Kumalo.

Before Kumalo left Johannesburg, he arranged for the marriage between his son and the girl. Then he started home, taking the girl and Gertrude's child with him. Gertrude had disappeared the night before they were to leave, no one knew where. She had talked to him of becoming a nun, but Kumalo feared that she had gone back to her old life; Gertrude liked the laughter and fun.

At home, the people welcomed their minister, showering love and blessings upon him. The crops were poor that season and people were starving. Kumalo prayed for his people and worked for them. Knowing that they must learn to use the land wisely, he was helpless to guide them. He went to their chief to ask for coöperation, but the chief was concerned only for himself and his family.

Hope came to the people in the form of a child. He was the grandchild of Mr. Jarvis, father of the man Absalom had murdered. Mr. Jarvis had always helped the black people, and after his son's death he gave all his time to the work started by the murdered man. He sent milk for the children and brought to the people an agricultural demonstrator who would help them restore fertility to the soil. Mr. Jarvis built a dam and sent for good seed. His grandchild became Kumalo's friend, and through him the white man learned of the needs of the people. Kumalo, whose son had killed his benefactor's son, was at first ashamed to face Mr. Jarvis. When they met, few words were exchanged, but each read the heart of the other and understood the sorrow and grief there.

The bishop came and told Kumalo that it would be best for him to leave the hills and the valley, to go where his son's crime was unknown. Kumalo grieved and stood silent. Before the bishop left there came a letter from Mr. Jarvis, thanking Kumalo for his friendship and offering to build his people a new church. The bishop felt ashamed. How little he understood this man and his people.

When the day came for Absalom's execution, Kumalo went into the mountains. There he had gone before when struggling with fear. Mr. Jarvis, knowing the torment that was in his soul, bade him go in peace. When the dawn came, Kumalo cried out for his son. He cried too for his land and his people. When would dawn come for them?

Further Critical Evaluation of the Work:

As in the novels of André Malraux, *Cry, the Beloved Country* combines a perfect blending of action, philosophy, moral indignation, and sensitive character portrayal. This is a novel which impresses its message upon the reader on many different levels. First and foremost, it is a human tragedy, a narrative which has the power to exalt the reader in the same manner as did the classic tragedies of antiquity. The Reverend Stephen Kumalo is one of the great figures of twentieth century literature. He is not rich or grand in station, although he is the spiritual leader of his people; he is a plain little man, but he possesses a great soul and magnificent courage. His story is one that could have been treated in merely political terms, but Paton saw beyond this level and penetrated to the real tragedy of the human condition.

Human values are at question in *Cry, the Beloved Country*. How can human beings treat one another in this way? How can God allow people to do such things? The events that catapult the Reverend Kumalo from his quiet village to urban Johannesburg force him to confront and question all of the basic values that he has lived by. He sees, at an advanced age, a totally different side of human existence, but he is not destroyed by what he discovers. Those whom he loves the most suffer the most, and finally are destroyed. But Stephen Kumalo comes through—stronger than ever, although never to be the same.

Mr. Jarvis, the rich white patrician, also is changed by the tide of catastrophic events which sweep along all the major characters. One feels at the end of the book that there is hope, if all human beings will learn to love one another. Through this way, each individual can save himself, and, in turn, perhaps humanity as a whole can be saved. Paton emphasizes in *Cry, the Beloved Country* that the fundamental issues which plague humanity are beyond mere political control.

CUDJO'S CAVE

Type of work: Novel
Author: John Townsend Trowbridge (1827-1916)
Type of plot: Historical romance
Time of plot: 1861
Locale: Tennessee
First published: 1863

Principal characters:
PENN HAPGOOD, a Quaker schoolmaster
MR. VILLARS, a blind clergyman
VIRGINIA, and
SALINA, his daughters
LYSANDER SPROWL, Salina's estranged husband
AUGUSTUS BLYTHEWOOD, a planter
MR. STACKRIDGE, a Unionist farmer
CARL, a German boy, friend of Penn
OLD TOBY, a freed slave
CUDJO, and
POMP, runaway slaves
SILAS ROPES, a bully

Critique:

Written during the Civil War, *Cudjo's Cave* mingles elements of propaganda with its historical setting and romantic theme. Because the novel displays deep sincerity, however, and a considerable degree of literary skill, it has enjoyed a popularity outlasting by many years the political issues which gave it birth. The book presents clearly and forcefully the problem of the rural population in Tennessee during that difficult time of decision at the beginning of the Civil War period. In that particular time and place the problem was peculiarly acute because Tennessee was a border state and its citizens had many reasons for indecision when faced by the realities of conflict between North and South. The writer, working close to actual history, dramatized effectively the guerrilla warfare fought among the people of Tennessee and Kentucky.

The Story:

In 1861, Penn Hapgood, a young Quaker, was the schoolmaster in the small Tennessee town of Curryville. Because he made no effort to conceal his anti-slavery convictions, he was unpopular among the hot-headed Secessionists of the community. The Unionists, on the other hand, had offered him a commission in the militia unit they were secretly organizing. Penn refused the commission offered him on the grounds of his religious faith.

His unpopularity grew after he aided Dan Pepperill, a poor white flogged and ridden on a rail because he had befriended a whipped slave. Penn's friend, a kindly young German named Carl, offered him a pistol to use in self-defense if he were attacked, but the schoolmaster saw no need to arm himself. A short time later a party of ruffians seized Penn and tarred and feathered him. Carl, unable to save his friend, searched for some Union sympathizers to defend Penn, but by the time the rescue party arrived at the schoolhouse the young teacher was not to be found. It was learned, however, that he had gone to his boarding-house, where his landlady, Mrs. Sprowl, had refused to let him in. She had acted on the orders of Silas Ropes, the leader of the mob.

Penn had found shelter in the home of a blind clergyman, Mr. Villars. The minister's household was made up of his two daughters, Virginia and Salina, old

Toby, a freed slave, and Carl, the young German. Old Toby and Farmer Stackridge, a stanch Unionist, tended to Penn and put him to bed in the clergyman's home. While he was still resting, Augustus Blythewood, a planter in love with Virginia, appeared at the house. Although she was little attracted to her suitor, Virginia entertained him graciously in order to conceal the fact that the fugitive was hidden nearby. Another caller was Lysander Sprowl, the son of Penn's landlady. Salina, the older sister, and young Sprowl were married, but they had separated some time before.

Sprowl, having learned Penn's whereabouts, promised to lead the villagers to the schoolmaster's hiding place. The aroused townspeople accused Mr. Villars of hiding an Abolitionist. While they were threatening the old man, Penn disappeared from the house under mysterious circumstances.

A mob, aroused by Blythewood, seized old Toby and prepared to flog him in an effort to learn Penn's whereabouts. Carl managed to cut the Negro's bonds before the mob could carry out its threat. Toby, escaping, ran into Blythewood and recognized him. The planter then called off the mob and went to the minister's house, where he pretended great indignation at what had happened.

Penn, meanwhile, was safe in Cudjo's Cave, a hide-out known only to runaway slaves. Having heard the angry townspeople threatening Mr. Villars, he had in his half-delirious condition fled into an adjoining field before he fainted. When he came to, he found himself beside a fire in a cavern, with Cudjo and Pomp, two escaped slaves, ministering to his wants. They had befriended Penn because of the help he had given Pepperill several weeks before. Pomp, in particular, was a magnificent old fellow, almost heroic in his dignity and spirit. Both slaves had suffered at the hands of Blythewood and Ropes, the town bully. Through the two Negroes Penn sent word to Mr. Villars that he was safe. The clergyman

sent Penn's clothes and food to the hiders.

When he was able to travel, Penn decided to set out for the North. Near Curryville he fell into the hands of a small detachment of Confederate soldiers. Convicted at a drumhead trial, he was sentenced to be hanged unless he joined the army. He refused. Carl, who had helped his friend before, volunteered to enlist in Penn's place. Set free, Penn was again in danger from a group of townspeople led by Ropes and Sprowl, but with the aid of Farmer Stackridge he managed to elude his pursuers. Blythewood, hearing of his escape, was furious that Penn had slipped through his fingers.

Penn did not go far, however, for he was unwilling to leave the Villars family without protection. His fears were justified. When he returned secretly to the minister's home, he learned that Mr. Villars had been seized and carried off to prison. Penn himself was captured a short time later, and among his fellow prisoners he found the blind clergyman. Because Carl was one of the soldiers detailed to guard them, he and the minister were able to make their escape. Stackridge was guiding them to a place of safety in the mountains when they were again captured. As the soldiers were about to run Penn through with their bayonets, one of their number dropped dead. The others ran away. Pomp and Cudjo appeared and led the fugitives to Cudjo's Cave.

Augustus Blythewood proposed to Virginia Villars, but she, realizing his dislike for Penn, would have nothing to do with the young planter. Meanwhile Stackridge and a party of his Unionist friends were skirmishing with the Confederate soldiers in the woods nearby. Virginia, while searching for Penn, was captured by a Confederate soldier, but she was relieved when she discovered that her captor was Carl. Before the young German could lead her out of the forest, set afire by the skirmishers, he himself was captured by Ropes' men. After she had climbed to a rocky ledge, the fire having cut off her escape on both sides, she was rescued from her predicament by Penn and Cudjo, who conducted her to the cave. That night rain put out the forest fire. In the morning old Toby appeared at the cave. He was overjoyed to discover that his mistress and her father were both safe.

Lysander Sprowl, in the meantime, had taken possession of Mr. Villars' house and forced Salina to serve him there. When Toby returned with a note to tell Salina that her sister and her father were safe, the Negro tried to deceive Sprowl as to the fate of the fugitives, but Salina, who still loved her worthless husband, incautiously showed him Virginia's note. Sprowl brutally ordered Toby flogged in order to learn where Mr. Villars and Penn were hidden. Angered by Sprowl's cruelty, Salina set fire to her father's house and under cover of the confusion helped old Toby to make his escape.

Sprowl, encountering Carl, demanded that the young German lead him to the cave. Carl pretended to agree, but along the way he managed to hit the bully over the head with a stone. While Sprowl was still unconscious, Carl dragged him to the cave, where he was securely bound. Meanwhile old Toby and Salina made their way to the cave, and they arrived about the time Carl appeared with the wounded Sprowl. Pomp had also conducted to the cave the band of Unionists led by Stackridge. They prepared to turn their quarters into an underground fortress.

Before long a party led by Silas Ropes discovered the location of the cave. He and his men guarded the entrance in the hope of starving the occupants into submission.

Salina, ever changeable, loosened Sprowl's bonds so that he was able to escape. He went at once to the troops under Blythewood and arranged to have a squad of men sent to attack the cave. When Sprowl, at the head of the attacking force, reached the entrance of the cave, he found it defended by his wife. She fired at her husband, wounding him fatally, and was herself bayoneted by one of the Confederate soldiers. Virginia and her father were captured and taken before Blythewood.

The planter again pleaded his suit with Virginia, but she received his offers with contempt. While they argued, apart from the camp, Pomp suddenly appeared and told his former master that any sudden move would mean his death. Carl and Penn were covering Blythewood with their guns, and he was taken a prisoner to the cave. There Pomp compelled his former master to sign a safe conduct pass for the defenders and an order for the attackers to cease the fight.

Under safe conduct, the defenders left the cave. Mr. Villars, Virginia, Penn, and Pomp set out for Ohio. They left behind them in the cave the body of Salina, as well as those of Cudjo and Ropes, who had killed each other during an earlier attack. Pomp returned long enough to free Blythewood before joining his friends on their way to safety.

Penn and Carl went from Ohio to Pennsylvania, where they enlisted in the same regiment. Pomp served the Union as a colored scout. In many battles of the war Penn did heroic service, earning for himself the nickname of "The Fighting Quaker."

Further Critical Evaluation of the Work:

Trowbridge used a dramatic and often moving story as a vehicle to put across his anti-slavery message. At times, the plot comes close to melodrama, but the narrative strength and the skill of many characterizations manages to raise the action to a higher level. Although the book is not great art, it is well crafted and enjoyable. In addition, it is of genuine historical interest for the picture it draws of the emotions and attitudes of the Civil War period.

The villains in the tale are the least convincing characters; most of the time they are no more than sketches, without depth or subtlety. No doubt many men committed such vile acts, but the reader is given no insight into their deeper instincts or motivations. Another flaw in the book is the dialogue, which is at times stilted and unrealistic. In particular, Old Toby's black dialect and Carl's German accent are both unconvincing, falling perilously close to stereotypes. Cudjo's speech and actions also on occasion slip into stereotypical patterns.

Pomp, however, is a character at once noble and believable. Although on the surface he seems almost too perfect to be true, the reader comes to feel an affection for this extraordinary black man. The author penetrates Pomp's personality and creates in him one of the two best characters in the novel. Penn Hapgood, the Quaker schoolmaster, is the other character who lifts the book above the ordinary. The abolitionist Penn is shown to be an idealist of subtle feelings and courage, a man willing to risk his life for what he believes. His speeches against the system combine propaganda with genuine emotion. He shows his wisdom when he declares that "education alone makes men free," and acknowledges that many white men might be considered slaves. Pomp's testimony to the joys of freedom, however precarious, is a moving and powerful statement. Throughout the long novel, Penn and Pomp stir the reader's interest and sympathies.

CULTURE AND ANARCHY

Type of work: Social criticism
Author: Matthew Arnold (1822-1888)
First published: 1869

In *Culture and Anarchy,* Matthew Arnold sought a center of authority by which the anarchy caused by the troubled passage of the Reform Bill of 1867 might be regulated. At its best his style is clear, flexible, and convincing, but Arnold wrote in such a complicated mood of indignation, impatience, and fear that his style and his argumentative method are frequently repetitious and unsystematic. Still, the book is a masterpiece of polished prose in which urbane irony and shafts of ridicule are used to persuade the Victorian middle class that it must reform itself before it can reform the entire nation.

Writing as a so-called Christian Humanist, Arnold primarily directed his criticism against the utilitarianism of the followers of Jeremy Bentham and John Stuart Mill and against the various movements of liberal reform. Disturbed by the social and political confusion, by Fenianism and the Hyde Park Riots of 1866, and by the inability of either the Church or the government to cope with the growing unrest both in England and on the Continent, Arnold attempted to describe an objective center of authority that all men, regardless of religious or social bias, could follow.

This center of authority is culture, which he defined on the level of the individual as "a pursuit of our total perfection by means of getting to know, on all matters which most concern us, the best which has been thought and said in the world." Because this authority is internal, it is a study of perfection within the individual, a study which should elevate the "best self" through a fresh and free search for beauty and intelligence. By following "right reason," the disinterested intellectual pursuits of the "best self," Arnold foresaw a way to overcome the social and political confusion of the 1860's

and to prepare for a future in which all men could be happy and free. With this basically romantic view of man as a means and human perfectibility as the end, Arnold turned to social criticism, carefully showing that no other center of authority was tenable. The ideal of nonconformity, the disestablishment of the Church, led to confusion or anarchy because it represented the sacrifice of all other sides of human personality to the religious. The ideal of the liberal reformers also led to anarchy because it regarded the reforms as ends rather than means toward a harmonious totality of human existence.

Arnold clarifies his definition of culture by tracing its origin to curiosity or "scientific passion" (the desire to see things as they really are) and to morality or "social passion" (the desire to do good). Christianity, as he saw it, was like culture in that it also sought to learn the will of God (human perfection) and make it prevail; but culture went beyond religion as interpreted by the Nonconformists in that it was a harmonious expansion of all human powers. In even sharper terms, culture was opposed to utilitarianism which Arnold considered "mechanical" because it worshiped means rather than ends. In fact, anything—materialism, economic greatness, individual wealth, bodily health, Puritanism—that was treated as an end except that of human perfectibility was to Arnold mere "machinery" that led to anarchy. Only culture, the harmonious union of poetry (the ideal of beauty) and religion (the ideal of morality), saw itself as a means that preserved the totality of the individual. Culture looked beyond machinery; it had only one passion—the passion for "sweetness" (beauty) and "light" (intelligence) and the passion to make them prevail. With such a passion it sought to do away with social classes and religious bias to make the best that has been thought and known in the world ("right reason") the core of human endeavor and institutions.

After establishing his definition of culture in terms of the individual, Arnold turned toward the problem of society. He saw the characteristic view of Englishmen toward happiness as the individual's desire "to do what he liked," or freedom, but he also saw that each class had its own opinion as to what it liked to do. In other words, there was a strong belief in freedom but a weak belief in "right reason" which should view freedom disinterestedly. This misplacing of belief was to Arnold one of the chief causes of anarchy; it was the mistake of acting before thinking. Ideally, "right reason" should precede action, and the State should be the disinterested union of all classes, a collective "best self." In reality, the State was being led toward anarchy by class interests because the aristocracy, or "Barbarians," were inaccessible to new, fresh ideas; the middle class, or "Philistines," had zeal but not knowledge; and the working class, or "Populace," was raw and untrained. Because culture alone could join the two sides of the individual, culture alone could overcome the narrow views of the three classes since it was disinterested and sought only the perfection of all men. Members of the different classes possessed the same human nature and saw happiness as freedom; also, the "best self" was common to all classes. Therefore, since authority could be found neither in religion nor in politics, it could be found only in individuals who, by following "right reason" rather than class bias, could assert their "best selves" in a harmonious union that sought the best for everyone. The major impediments to such a state were what Arnold called "Atheism," the outright denial of such a thing as "right reason," and "Quietism," the utilitarian belief that reason was the result of habit. These impediments Arnold rejected on the basis of intuition and faith. Ethics can be known intuitively, and by building faith on the individual's intuition the spirit of culture could overcome the present anarchy.

The enlargement of his terms from the individual to the State naturally led Arnold to consider the historical development of the social and political confusion that he confronted. In the famous chapter titled "Hebraism and Hellenism," Arnold accounted for the very ground and cause out of which actual behavior arises, by distinguishing between (1) the energy in human affairs that drives at practice, the obligation of duty, self-control, and work (Hebraism) and (2) the energy that drives at those ideas which are the basis of right practice (Hellenism). Like the "scientific passion," Hellenism's chief function is to see things as they really are, and like the "social passion," Hebraism seeks proper conduct and obedience. In other words, what Arnold earlier analyzed as the opposing drives in the individual, he now enlarges to a historical context, all human endeavor in the Western World being associated with either the one or the other drive. Both drives aim at human perfection or salvation, but their means and ideals are sharply different. Hebraism, or "strictness of conscience," inculcates a sense of sin, but Hellenism, the "spontaneity of consciousness," teaches what Arnold has called culture.

The rise of Christianity marked the great triumph of Hebraism over Hellenism, but the Renaissance marked the resurgence of Hellenism. The anarchy of the 1860's Arnold saw as the result of Puritanism's reaffirmation of Hebraism in the seventeenth century, a reaffirmation that was against the currents of history. The problem was intensified by the Puritan belief that duty was an end in itself, whereas in reality both great drives are no more than contributions to human development. Thus, in England there was too much Hebraism, so much, in fact, that religion and politics had become mechanical. As a solution, Arnold suggested that

Hellenism be imported. In Hellenism, which ultimately is a synonym for culture, the ideals of internal harmony, or the unity of the total man, and of harmony with things overcome the one-sidedness of Hebraism. The other drive, however, should not be excluded, for Hellenism alone leads to moral relaxation. There should be a harmony of both sides, a union from which would come the awakening of a healthier and less mechanical activity.

After analyzing culture in terms of the individual, the State, and history, Arnold turned to the particular issues before Parliament at the time he wrote. He directed his wit and some of his most vivacious ridicule against the four political reforms that were at the heart of liberalism—the disestablishment of the Irish Church, the Real Estate Intestacy Bill, the Deceased Sister's Wife Bill, and Free Trade—and showed that the liberal reformers lacked disinterestedness, displayed a remarkable absence of reason, and unconsciously led to anarchy. By leaving the issues that were uppermost in his mind to the last, he dramatically illustrated that culture alone could lead to perfection. For him the four bills were examples of the disbelief in "right reason" and the Philistine endeavor to act without thought. Thus, he warned that without "right reason" there could be no society and without society there could be no perfection. Only "right reason," the disinterested search for the best that has been thought or done regardless of class interests, could defeat anarchy by establishing the way to happiness through harmony.

CUPID AND PSYCHE

Type of work: Classical myth
Source: Unknown
Type of plot: Allegory of love
Time of plot: The Golden Age
Locale: Ancient Greece
First transcribed: Unknown

Principal characters:
PSYCHE, daughter of a Greek king
CUPID, the god of love
VENUS, the goddess of beauty

Critique:

Cupid and Psyche is the simple but moving story of the union of a mortal, Psyche, and the god Cupid. In this ancient mythological tale a beautiful maiden achieved immortality because her love and faith triumphed over mistrust.

The Story:

Psyche, daughter of a Greek king, was as beautiful as Venus and sought after by many princes. Her father, seeking to know what fate the gods might have in store for her, sent some of his men to Apollo's oracle to learn the answer.

To the king's horror, the oracle replied that Psyche was to become the mate of a hideous monster, and the king was ordered to leave his daughter to her fate upon a mountaintop, to prevent the destruction of his people. Psyche was led, clad in bridal dress, to a rocky summit and left there alone. The weary girl soon fell into a swoon.

Venus, jealous of Psyche's beauty, called her son Cupid and ordered him to use his arrows to turn Psyche's heart toward a creature so hideous that mortals would be filled with loathing at the sight of Psyche's mate. But when Cupid saw his victim asleep he fell in love with her and decided that she should be his forever. While Psyche slept, Zephyrus came at Cupid's bidding and carried her to the valley in which Love's house stood. There she awoke in a grove of trees in which stood a magnificent golden palace. She entered the building and wandered through the sumptuously furnished rooms.

At noon Psyche found a table lavishly spread. A voice invited her to eat, assured her that the house was hers, and told her that the being who was to be her lover would come that night.

As she lay in bed that night a voice close beside her told her not to be afraid. The voice spoke so tenderly that the girl welcomed her unseen suitor and held out her arms to him. When Psyche awoke the next morning, her lover had gone, but he had left behind a gold ring and had placed a circlet on her head.

For a time Psyche lived happily in the golden palace, visited each night by the lover whose face she had not seen. But at last she became homesick for her two sisters and her father. One night she asked her lover to permit her sisters to visit her the next day. He gave his consent, but he warned that she was not to tell them about him.

Zephyrus carried the sisters to the valley. Overjoyed to see them, Psyche showed them the beauties of the palace and loaded them with gifts. Jealous of her good fortune, they tried to make her suspicious of her unseen lover. They suggested that her lover was a serpent who changed into the form of a youth at night, a monster who would at last devour her. To save herself, they advised her to hide a lamp and a knife by her bed so that she might see him and slay him as he slept.

Psyche did as they had suggested. That night, as her love lay asleep, she lit the lamp and brought it close so that she might look at him. When she saw the handsome young man by her side, she was powerless to use her knife. As she

1245

turned, sobbing, to extinguish the flame, a drop of burning oil fell on Cupid's shoulder. Awaking with a cry, he looked at her reproachfully. With the warning that love cannot live with suspicion, he left the palace. Psyche tried to follow, but fell in a swoon at the threshold.

When she awoke, the palace had vanished. Determined to seek her lover, she wandered alone across the countryside and through cities hunting the god. Meanwhile Cupid took his vengeance on her sisters. To each he sent a dream that she would become his bride if she were to throw herself from the mountaintop. Both sisters, obeying the summons, found only the arms of Death to welcome them.

No god would give the wandering Psyche shelter or comfort, or protect her from the wrath of Venus. At the temples of Ceres and Juno she was turned away. At last she came to the court of Venus herself. Warned by her heart to flee, she was nevertheless drawn before the throne of the goddess. Venus decided that Psyche should be kept as a slave. She was to be given a new task to do each day and was to live until she once more began to hope.

Psyche's first task was to sort a huge pile of mixed seeds and grain into separate heaps, with the warning that if there were so much as one seed in the wrong pile she would be punished. But by dusk she had separated only small heaps of grain. Cupid so pitied her that he commanded myriads of ants to complete the task for her.

Next day Psyche was ordered to gather the golden fleece of Venus' sheep. Obeying the advice of a reed at the edge of the river, she waited until the animals had lain down to sleep and then collected the wool which had been left clinging to the bushes.

Psyche's third task was to fill a jug with the black water which flowed down a steep mountain into the rivers Styx and Cocytus. This task she was able to complete with the aid of a bird who carried the jug to the stream, collected the water, and brought it back to her.

On the fourth day Psyche was given her most difficult task; she was to go to the land of the dead and there collect some of the beauty of the goddess Proserpine in a golden box. If she succeeded, Venus promised, she would treat Psyche kindly thereafter. But to visit Proserpine and to return was an almost impossible achievement. In despair, Psyche determined to cast herself from a tower, but as she was about to kill herself a voice called to her and told her how she might fulfill her mission.

Following instructions, Psyche traveled to Proserpine's realm. There she might have stayed on forever if she had not thought suddenly of her love. On her way back, she had almost reached the daylight when envy seized her. She opened the box, thinking she would have whatever it contained for herself, but no sooner had she lifted the lid than she fell into a deep sleep filled with nightmares.

She might have lain that way forever if Cupid, going in search of her, had not found her. He awoke her with one of his arrows and sent her on to his mother with the box. Then he flew off and presented himself before Jove with his petition that Psyche be made immortal. Jove, after hearing his pleas, sent Mercury to conduct Psyche into the presence of the gods. There she drank from the golden cup of ambrosia Jove handed her and became immortal. So she and Cupid were at last united for all time.

Further Critical Evaluation of the Work:

Although the allegorical theme of Cupid's love for Psyche (or at least a maid) was known by Hellenistic times, the one known literary source for this complete tale is the *Metamorphoses* of "Lucius" Apuleius (A.D., second century). Better known as the *Golden Ass,* this Latin "novel" deals with the transformation of Lucius into an ass, his year-long journey and checkered adventures, his ultimate restoration to human shape, and his devotion to the Egyptian goddess Isis. At the center of this eleven-book work (4.28-6.24) is couched the story of Cupid and Psyche, as told by an old crone to a beautiful girl. This "pleasant tale and old wives' story," as the old woman put it, belongs to the genre of *Märchen,* or folk-tale, and throughout Europe, Scandinavia, Africa, Asia, and Indonesia are known variations on this theme, which includes an enchanted lover, jealous sister, mystery, mistrust, search, tasks, and happy reunion. Apuleius' readers would have immediately recognized the character Psyche as typical of the heroines of Greek "novels" or "romances": she is, of course, lovely and in love, but she is also timid, pious, naïve, and curious. This last characteristic, her most serious fault, Apuleius uses to relate Psyche to Lucius, the central figure of the novel. Both, because of *curiositas,* were violently thrown into a life of suffering and despair; both overcame their trials and achieved true happiness by devotion to a deity.

Cupid and Psyche has through the years been recognized for its allegorical possibilities, since after all Cupid ("Desire," Eros in Greek) is one of the oldest allegorical divinities, and Psyche does mean "Soul." That Apuleius intended symbolic reflection of the larger work is hardly debatable, but that he saw the story as a vehicle of teaching *Christian* virtue is unfounded. Nevertheless, the universal charm of the story prompted Fulgentius Planciades (A.D., sixth century) to allegorize thus: the city is the world, Psyche's father is God, her mother is matter, her sisters represent flesh and the will, Venus is lust, and Cupid is "cupidity"; Fulgentius, however, is unable to perfect his allegory with satisfactory consistency. Calderon (seventeenth century) saw the three daughters as paganism, Judaism, and the Church, the last of whom was wedded to Christ. The Platonists, who no doubt recognized echoes from Plato's *Phaedrus,* saw the sisters as the tripartite soul: desire and spirit are overcome by sure reason, and the ultimate acceptance of the rational soul among the gods symbolized freedom from the Orphic cycle of death and re-birth. Jungians see Psyche as the psychic development of the feminine; Venus symbolizes fertility, and the marriage to Cupid is sexual bondage.

In this story Cupid is considerably more mature than the familiar Hellenistic winged archer-cherub, and his beauty is emphasized; nevertheless, he is still mischievous and his mother's minion. Venus, however, is an outright burlesque; she seems to have grown more vain with age and motherhood, and her jealousy of the beautiful young virgin Psyche is painful. Still, such a characterization is necessary if Venus is to be given the role of the folk-tale witch who sets the apparently impossible tasks, which are also appropriate to Venus' role as mother-in-law, since the wool, grain, water, and beauty are Psyche's symbolic *Brautproben,* or dowry, representing wifely abilities and virtues.

Tasks and journeys are traditional themes in heroic tales, especially when they are punishments for some sacrilege. Psyche's crime, despite her original guilelessness, is twofold: she has offended Venus and she has violated her husband's trust. It is interesting to observe how in Apuleius' version Psyche, who was so *simplex* that she could not even lie to her sisters about her husband, loses her innocence as soon as she is persuaded by them to kill the "monster." Thereafter it is she, not Cupid, who lures her sisters to their deaths. Psyche, therefore, loses innocence, but she gains knowledge and a chance to regain happiness—eternally. This again is the theme of the larger work, the *Metamorphoses,* in which Lucius is initiated into the Isiac mysteries and becomes the priest of Isis, forsaking the evils of a world of asses in men's flesh.

Another addition to the synopsis above must be included. Apuleius has Cupid warn Psyche that if she keeps secret the strange nature of their marriage, the child she is bearing will remain divine. Apuleius ends his story with the birth of a child who is fittingly called Voluptas, or "Joy." Thus the eternal union of love and the soul does result in the soul's divine, that is, immortal, joy.

As a product of the classical age, *Cupid and Psyche* is full of familiar classical literary and mythological illusions. The "labors" motif, which has been mentioned, includes the traditional *catabasis,* or journey to the underworld (cf. Herakles, Orpheus, Odysseus, Aeneas). The deserted Psyche recalls the despair of Ariadne, Andromeda, and of course Dido. The theme of the opened container recalls Pandora. Psyche's apotheosis, or deification, finds precedent especially in the myth of Herakles. As for the gods, their portraits become near parodies of Homeric models, in that they act with stereotypical predictability. Later versions of *Cupid and Psyche* are found in Boccaccio's *Genealogy of the Gods* and in Walter Pater's *Marius the Epicurean;* besides Calderón, other writers who have handled the theme are Molière, Corneille, Thomas Heywood, and Joseph Beaumont.

E. N. Genovese

THE CUSTOM OF THE COUNTRY

Type of work: Novel
Author: Edith Wharton (1862-1937)
Type of plot: Social criticism
Time of plot: Late nineteenth century
Locale: New York, Paris
First published: 1913

Principal characters:
UNDINE SPRAGG, a predatory woman
ELMER MOFFATT, her first husband
RALPH MARVELL, Undine's second husband
PAUL, son of Undine and Ralph Marvell
RAYMOND DE CHELLES, her third husband
PETER VAN DEGEN, her lover
ABNER E. SPRAGG, her father

Critique:

This novel traces the development and refinement of a woman's ambition. Undine Spragg is a heartless creature whose striking beauty has led her to believe that the sole aim of society is to provide diversion and security for its women. However deeply Edith Wharton may incriminate the heroine, there is an even greater incrimination of the society that produced her, for Undine is the purest exponent of a world motivated by the desire for power and status. The well-constructed story is carried along by a direct, unornamented prose style.

The Story:

Undine Spragg, who came from Apex City with her parents, had been in New York for two years without being accepted in society. Her opportunity came at last when she was invited to the dinner given by Laura Fairford, whose brother, Ralph Marvell, took an interest in Undine.

Ralph, although his family was prominently established in social circles, had little money. Moreover, he was an independent thinker who disliked the superficiality of important New York figures like Peter Van Degen, the wealthy husband of Ralph's cousin, Clare Dagonet, with whom Ralph had once been in love.

About two months after their meeting Undine became engaged to Ralph. One night they went to see a play. Undine was shocked to find herself sitting next to Elmer Moffatt, a figure in her past whom she did not want to recognize in public. She promised to meet him privately in Central Park the next day. When they met, Moffatt, a bluntly spoken vulgarian, told Undine that she must help him in his business deals after she married Ralph.

Moffatt also went to see Undine's father and asked him to join in a business deal. Moffatt threatened to make Undine's past public if Mr. Spragg refused.

Ralph and Undine were married and Ralph was happy until he realized that Undine cared less for his company than for the social world. Mr. Spragg, having made the business deal with Moffatt, had thus been able to give Undine a big wedding. Ralph soon began to realize the ruthlessness of Undine's desire for money. Her unhappiness and resentment were increased when she learned that she was pregnant.

In the next several years Moffatt became a significant financial figure in New York. Ralph, in an attempt to support Undine's extravagance, went to work in a business to which he was ill-suited. Undine, meanwhile, kept up a busy schedule of social engagements. She had also accepted some expensive gifts from Peter Van Degen, who was romantically interested in her, before Peter left to spend the season in Europe.

One day Undine saw Moffatt, who wanted to meet Ralph in order to make a disreputable business deal. The business deal succeeded and Undine went to Paris to meet Peter. Before long she had spent all her money. She then met the Comte Raymond de Chelles, a French aristocrat whom she thought of marrying. In the face of this competition Peter frankly told Undine of his desire for her and said that if she would stay with him he could give her everything she wanted. At this point Undine received a telegram announcing that Ralph was critically ill with pneumonia and asking her to return to New York immediately. Undine decided to stay in Paris.

Ralph recovered and, after four years of marriage to Undine, returned to the Dagonet household with his son Paul. He began to work hard at the office for Paul's sake and on a novel which he had begun.

Undine, after an uncontested divorce from Ralph, lived with Peter Van Degen for two months. Peter, however, was disillusioned when he learned that Undine had not gone to see Ralph when he was critically ill; he left her without getting the promised divorce from his wife Clare.

Ralph, meanwhile, was concerned only with his son and his book. Then he learned that Undine was engaged to Comte Raymond de Chelles and badly needed money to have her marriage to Ralph annulled by the Church. Undine agreed to waive her rights to the boy if Ralph would send her one hundred thousand dollars to pay for her annulment. Ralph borrowed half of the needed sum and went to Moffatt to make another business deal. As Undine's deadline approached, with the deal not yet concluded, Ralph went to see Moffatt, who told him that the matter was going more

slowly than expected and that it would take a year to go through. Moffatt told Ralph that he himself was once married to Undine, back in Apex City, but that Undine's parents had forced the young couple to get a divorce. After hearing this story Ralph went home and committed suicide.

Undine, now in possession of her son, married Raymond de Chelles. She was very happy in Paris, even though Raymond was strict about her social life. After three months they moved to the family estate at Saint Désert to live quietly and modestly. When Raymond began to ignore her, Undine became bored and angry at her husband's family for not making allowances for her customary extravagance.

One day she invited a dealer from Paris to appraise some of the priceless Chelles tapestries. When the dealer arrived, the prospective American buyer with him turned out to be Moffatt, now one of the richest men in New York. Over the next several weeks Undine saw a great deal of her former husband. When the time came for Moffatt to return to New York, Undine invited him to have an affair with her. Moffatt told her that he wanted marriage or nothing.

Undine went to Reno, where she divorced Raymond and married Moffatt on the same day. Moffatt gave Undine everything she wanted, but she realized that in many personal ways he compared unfavorably with her other husbands. The Moffatts settled in a mansion in Paris to satisfy Undine's social ambitions and her husband's taste for worldly display. When Undine learned that an old society acquaintance, Jim Driscoll, had been appointed ambassador to England, she decided that she would like to be the wife of an ambassador. Moffatt told her bluntly that that was the one thing she could never have because she was a divorced woman. Still dissatisfied, Undine was certain that the one thing she was really meant for was to be an ambassador's wife.

Further Critical Evaluation of the Work:

The Custom of the Country, one of Edith Wharton's most successful novels, was published midway through her productive 1905-1920 period, which culminated in a Pulitzer Prize. The novel reflects not only her overwhelming concern with American cultural inadequacies and her contempt for the values of the newly moneyed and growing middle class, in which she resembles her contemporary, Henry James, but also her interest in the issue of woman's role in society.

By the time Wharton wrote *The Custom of the Country,* the way had been paved by writers such as Theodore Dreiser and Robert Grant for the portrayal of self-serving, cold-blooded, and unsympathetic heroines. The battle which was fought at the turn of the century between those who insisted on realistic female characters and those who still clung to traditional idealized presentations of women had, by 1913, definitely been decided in favor of the realists. Thus the public had been conditioned sufficiently to accept a heroine like Undine Spragg, who is the epitome of amoral materialism. Through her character, Wharton is able to deal with both the cultural issue and the women's issue simultaneously, since Undine has been molded into her present ugly form by the forces of the grasping, unprincipled, and uncultured new commercial class. She is vain, crude, and opportunistic; she is intellectually and aesthetically, as well as spiritually, empty.

The problem in the novel is that Wharton cannot bring herself to absolve Undine of guilt for becoming what society has made of her—in fact, the author increasingly despises her heroine. Unable to remain objective toward her creation, Wharton allows Undine to become an inhuman abstraction; in so doing, she sacrifices the chance to subordinate individual characterization to a broader indictment of social conditions, as she did so successfully in *The House of Mirth.* The novel is thus marred not only by her loss of objectivity toward the heroine, but also toward some of her minor characters; Wharton is less harsh than she might otherwise have been in her judgment of such characters as Abner Spragg and his wife, simply because their vulgarity is never allowed to triumph as is Undine's. But the deeper reason for the author's intolerance of Undine Spragg lies in the fact that her sin of vulgarity is compounded by that of pretentiousness and lack of self-understanding— to Wharton, the worst sin of all.

THE CYCLOPS

Type of work: Drama
Author: Euripides (c. 485-c. 406 B.C.)
Type of plot: Satyr play
Time of plot: Remote antiquity
Locale: Mt. Aetna in Sicily
First presented: Fifth century B.C.

Principal characters:
ODYSSEUS, King of Ithaca
THE CYCLOPS
SILENUS, aged captive of the Cyclops
CHORUS OF SATYRS
COMPANIONS OF ODYSSEUS

Critique:

By purely aesthetic standards, the *Cyclops* cannot be considered a valuable or important play, but it otherwise has a twofold interest as the only complete satyr play preserved from ancient Greece and as a dramatization of an episode from Homer's *Odyssey*. Euripides has kept the main line of Homer's tale, but for the sake of enhanced humor has added the character of old Silenus and, of course, the Chorus of Satyrs. Furthermore, the exigencies of stage presentation have made it necessary for him to change Homer's ingenious escape device to a mere slipping through the rocks past the blind Cyclops. The light tone of the play must have been a welcome relief to the Greek audience, for it followed three somber tragedies presented in succession.

The Story:

As he raked the ground before the cave of his master, the Cyclops, old Silenus lamented the day he was shipwrecked on the rock of Aetna and taken into captivity by the monstrous, one-eyed offspring of Poseidon, god of the sea. About Silenus gamboled his children, the Chorus of Satyrs, who prayed with their father to Bacchus for deliverance. Suddenly Silenus spied a ship and the approach of a group of sailors obviously seeking supplies. Odysseus and his companions approached, introduced themselves as the conquerors of Troy, driven from their homeward journey by tempestuous winds and desperately in need of food and

water. Silenus warned them of the cannibalistic Cyclops' impending return, urged them to make haste and then began to bargain with them over the supplies. Spying a skin of wine, the precious liquid of Bacchus which he had not tasted for years, Silenus begged for a drink. After one sip he felt his feet urging him to dance. He offered them all the lambs and cheese they needed in exchange for one skin of wine.

As the exchange was taking place, the giant Cyclops suddenly returned, ravenously hungry. The wretched Silenus made himself appear to have been terribly beaten and accused Odysseus and his men of plundering the Cyclops' property. Odysseus denied the false charge, but although he was supported by the leader of the Chorus of Satyrs, the Cyclops seized two of the sailors, took them into his cave, and made a meal of them. Horrified Odysseus was then urged by the satyrs to employ his famed cleverness, so effective at Troy, in finding some means of escape.

After some discussion, Odysseus hit upon a subtle plan: first they would make the Cyclops drunk with wine; then, while he lay in a stupor, they would cut down an olive tree, sharpen it, set it afire, and plunge it into the Cyclops' eye. After that escape would be easy.

When the Cyclops emerged from his cave, Odysseus offered him the wine, and the giant and Silenus proceeded to get hilariously drunk. So pleased was the monster with the effects of the Bacchic fluid that Silenus without much trouble persuaded him not to share it with his fellow giants but to drink it all up by himself. The grateful Cyclops asked Odysseus his name (to which the clever warrior replied "No man") and promised that he would be the last to be eaten. Soon the Cyclops found the earth and sky whirling together and his lusts mounting. He seized the unhappy Silenus and dragged him into the cave to have his pleasure with him.

As the Cyclops lay in a stupor, Odysseus urged the satyrs to help him fulfill the plan they had agreed upon, but the cowardly satyrs refused and Odysseus was forced to take his own men for the task. Soon the agonized Cyclops, shouting that "no man" had blinded him, came bellowing out of the cave. The chorus mocked and jeered him for this ridiculous charge and gave him false directions for capturing the escaping Greeks. The berserk giant thrashed about and cracked his skull against the rocks. When the escaping Odysseus taunted him with his true name, the Cyclops groaned that an oracle had predicted that Odysseus would blind him on his way home from Troy, but he told also that the clever one would pay for his deed by tossing about on Poseidon's seas for many years. The satyrs hastened to join the escape so that they could once more become the proper servants of Bacchus in a land where grapes grew.

Further Critical Evaluation of the Work:

Since the average length of a Euripidean tragedy is about twice the 709 lines of this satyr play, we might well have expected its relatively uncomplicated plot, its straightforward, undeveloping characterization, and its reliance on the traditional trappings of such plays, namely the chorus of lustful, uncouth, undisciplined satyrs. Until the early part of this century such characteristics had to be assumed for all satyr plays, but with the discovery of considerable papyrus fragments of Sophocles' satyr play, the *Ichneutae* ("Trackers"), we may now be all but certain that so little satyric drama survived simply because it lacked variety. As comic relief it was serviceable, but as classic drama it lacked much; and it is quite likely that we have the *Cyclops* only because the ancients judged it the most worth saving.

As we might deduce from the surviving titles of other satyr plays, the *Cyclops* has several common motifs and devices: slapstick buffoonery, reversal of fortune for the hero and the villan, theft, and satyric mischief (drunkenness and lechery).

Satyr plays, like practically all Greek tragedies, were drawn from mythology, but the playwright was always free to modify the story and characters. In the *Cyclops,* Odysseus is essentially the same person as in Homer: he is brave but sensible and shrewd; he does not become the unpopular ruthless figure of Euripides' *The Trojan Women* or Sophocles' *Philoctetes*. Amid the coarse satyrs he maintains his heroic dignity and in contrast with the lawless, beastly Cyclops, he is selfless and urbane. The Cyclops, however, lacks the depth of Homer's character. The brutal punishment for his haughty violation of Zeus' law of hospitality is turned into a comic incident of the bully getting his just dessert. Euripides is able to divert our horror or pity for the monster by sublimating some of the Cyclops' disgusting personality into the more human character of Silenus; for while Silenus is himself unfit for civilized society, he is still an endearing Falstaffian rascal. Furthermore, though a thorough coward, his old age has brought him a cleverness equal to that of Odysseus.

CYMBELINE

Type of work: Drama
Author: William Shakespeare (1564-1616)
Type of plot: Tragi-comedy
Time of plot: First century B.C.
Locale: Britain, Italy, and Wales
First presented: 1609

Principal characters:
CYMBELINE, King of Britain
THE QUEEN, Cymbeline's wife
CLOTEN, the queen's son by a former husband
IMOGEN, Cymbeline's daughter by a former marriage
POSTHUMUS LEONATUS, Imogen's husband
PISANIO, servant of Posthumus
IACHIMO, an Italian braggart
BELARIUS, a banished lord
GUIDERIUS, and
ARVIRAGUS, Cymbeline's sons, reared by Belarius
CAIUS LUCIUS, a Roman ambassador

Critique:

Shakespeare apparently drew upon a number of sources for the plot of *The Tragedy of Cymbeline*. All historical accuracy of the play is debatable and actually unimportant. Cymbeline himself was a mythical character of tribal legend. The details of relationship among the characters are to be found in other romantic writings which appeared prior to Shakespeare's time and which were apparently adopted to clothe the skeletal international aspects of the story. *Cymbeline* presents a plot of political intrigue—both domestic and international—and personal emotional involvement. That the personal well-being of the characters takes precedence over military and political details gives the play its human-interest appeal. The apparition of Posthumus has the richness of detail found in similar scenes in *Macbeth*.

The Story:

Gullible Cymbeline and his conniving queen planned to have Imogen, his daughter, marry his stepson Cloten. Instead, Imogen chose the gentle Posthumus as a husband and secretly married him. Banished by the king in a fit of anger, Posthumus fled to Italy after promising that his loyalty and fidelity to his bride would always be above reproach. As a token of their vows Imogen gave Posthumus a diamond ring that had belonged to her mother, and Posthumus placed a bracelet of rare design upon Imogen's arm.

In Rome Posthumus met Iachimo, a vain braggart who tried to tempt Posthumus by appealing to his sensuality. Posthumus, not to be tempted into adultery, told Iachimo of his pact with Imogen and of the ring and bracelet they had exchanged. Iachimo scoffingly wagered ten thousand ducats against Posthumus' ring that he could seduce Imogen.

Iachimo went to Britain with letters to which he had forged the name of Posthumus. Because of these letters Imogen received him. Then Iachimo, by ambiguities and innuendo, played upon her curiosity regarding the faithfulness of her husband. Failing to win her favor in that way, he gained access to her bedroom in a trunk which, he had told her, contained a valuable gift, bought in France, intended for the Roman emperor; he had asked that the trunk be placed in her chamber for safekeeping. While Imogen slept, he noted the details of the furnishings in the room, took the bracelet from her arm, and observed a cinque-spotted mole on her left breast.

Back in Italy, Iachimo described

Imogen's room to Posthumus and produced the bracelet, which he said Imogen had given him. Incredulous, Posthumus asked Iachimo to describe some aspect of Imogen's body as better proof of his successful seduction. Iachimo's claim that he had kissed the mole on Imogen's breast enraged Posthumus, who swore that he would kill Imogen. He sent a letter to Pisanio, commanding that the servant kill Imogen. He also sent a letter to Imogen asking her to meet him in Milford Haven. Pisanio was to kill Imogen as they traveled through the Welsh hills.

On the journey Pisanio divulged the real purpose of their trip when he showed Imogen the letter ordering her death. Unable to harm his master's wife, Pisanio instructed her to dress as a boy and join the party of Caius Lucius, who was in Britain to collect tribute to the Emperor Augustus and who was soon to return to Rome. Then Imogen would be near Posthumus and could ultimately disprove Iachimo's accusations against her. Pisanio also gave Imogen a box containing a restorative, entrusted to him by the queen in case Imogen became ill during her trip. The contents, presumed by the queen to be a slow-acting poison, had been procured from her physician, who, suspecting chicanery, had reduced the drug content. The medicine would only induce long sleep. Taking leave of his mistress, Pisanio returned home.

Dressed in boy's clothing, Imogen, hungry and weary, came to the mountain cave of Belarius, who, banished from Cymbeline's court twenty years before, had kidnaped Guiderius and Arviragus, Cymbeline's infant sons. In Wales the two boys had been brought up to look upon Belarius as their father. Calling herself Fidele, Imogen won the affection of the three men when she asked shelter of them. Left alone when the men went out to hunt food, Imogen, emotionally spent and physically ill, swallowed some of the medicine which Pisanio had given her.

Cymbeline, meanwhile, had refused to pay the tribute demanded by Rome, and the two nations prepared for war.

Cloten, infuriated by Imogen's coldness to his attentions, tried to learn her whereabouts. Pisanio, thinking to trick her pursuer, showed him the letter in which Posthumus asked Imogen to meet him at Milford Haven. Disguised as Posthumus, Cloten set out to avenge his injured vanity.

In Wales he came upon Belarius, Arviragus, and Guiderius as they hunted. Recognizing him as the queen's son, Belarius assumed that Cloten had come to arrest them as outlaws. He and Arviragus went in search of Cloten's followers while Guiderius fought with Cloten. Guiderius cut off Cloten's head and threw it into the river. Returning from their search, Arviragus found Imogen in a deathlike stupor. Thinking her dead, the three men prepared for her burial. Benevolent Belarius, remembering that Cloten was of royal birth, brought his headless body for burial and laid it near Imogen.

Imogen, awakening from her drugged sleep, was grief-stricken when she saw close by a body dressed in Posthumus' clothing. Still sorrowing, she joined the forces of Caius Lucius as the Roman army marched by to engage the soldiers of Cymbeline.

Remorseful Posthumus, a recruit in the Roman army, regretted his order for Imogen's death. Throwing away his uniform, he dressed himself as a British peasant. Although he could not restore Imogen's life, he would not take any more British lives. In a battle between the Romans and Britons, Posthumus vanquished and disarmed Iachimo. Cymbeline, taken prisoner, was rescued by Belarius and his two foster sons. These three had built a fort and, aided by Posthumus, had so spurred the morale of the fleeing British soldiers that Cymbeline's army was victorious.

Failing to die in battle, Posthumus identified himself as a Roman after Lucius had been taken, and was sent to prison by Cymbeline. In prison he had a vision in which Jove assured him that he would yet be the lord of the Lady Imogen. Jove ordered a tablet placed on Posthumus' chest. When Posthumus awoke and found the tablet, he read that a lion's whelp would be embraced by a piece of tender air and that branches lopped from a stately cedar would revive. Shortly before the time set for his execution, he was summoned to appear before Cymbeline.

In Cymbeline's tent, the king conferred honors upon Belarius, Guiderius, and Arviragus and bemoaned the fact that the fourth valiant soldier, so poorly dressed, was not present to receive his reward. Cornelius, the physician, told Cymbeline that the queen had died after her villainies. Lucius pleaded for the life of Imogen, still dressed as a boy, because of the page's youth. Pardoned, Imogen asked Iachimo to explain his possession of the ring he wore. As Iachimo confessed his dastardly cunning and lying to win the ring from Posthumus, Posthumus entered and identified himself as the murderer of Imogen. When Imogen protested against his confession, Posthumus struck her. Pisanio then identified Imogen to keep Posthumus from striking her again.

The truth disclosed, Belarius understood his foster sons' affinity for Imogen. Posthumus and Imogen, reunited, professed lifelong devotion to each other.

After Guiderius had confessed the murder of Cloten, Cymbeline ordered him bound, but he stayed the sentence when Belarius identified himself and the two young men. Cymbeline then blessed his three children who stood before him. A soothsayer interpreted Jove's message on the tablet left on Posthumus' chest. The lion's whelp was Posthumus, the son of Leonatus, and the piece of tender air was Imogen. The lopped branches from the stately cedar were Arviragus and Guiderius, long thought dead, now restored in the king's love. Overjoyed, Cymbeline made peace with Rome.

Further Critical Evaluation of the Work:

Cymbeline, together with *The Winter's Tale* and *The Tempest,* belongs to Shakespeare's final period of writing. These last three plays are marked by their mood of calmness, of maturity, and of benevolent cheerfulness; a kind of autumnal spirit prevails. This is certainly not to say that *Cymbeline* lacks its villains, its traumatic events, or its scenes of violence—the play contains all these elements—but that the overall tone is serene in spite of them. *Cymbeline* may be classified as a tragi-comedy to distinguish it from its more dazzling predecessors among Shakespeare's comedies, such as *Love's Labour's Lost* or *Twelfth Night,* with their roguish heroes and heroines, their dialogues filled with witty and sparkling repartee and their plots abounding in mischievous scheming and complications. The main characters in *Cymbeline,* by contrast, are remarkable for their virtue rather than their cleverness, wit, or capacity for mischief; Posthumus is a model of earnestness and fidelity, while Imogen is the picture of purity and wifely devotion. The text is memorable not for the brilliance and sparkle of its dialogue, but for its passages of moving poetry such as "Fear no more the heat o' th' sun." Likewise, much of the plot is composed of the trials and sufferings of the good characters brought on by the scheming of the bad ones—even though the play ends as comedy must, with the virtuous happily rewarded and the wicked duly punished.

In the plot of *Cymbeline,* Shakespeare combined two lines of action: the political-historical storyline of the British king preparing for war with Rome, and the love story of Imogen and Posthumus. For the former, Shakespeare once again used as his source Holinshed's *The Chronicles of England.* However, finding the reign of *Cymbeline,* a descendant of King Lear, too dull and uneventful to make an interesting drama, he took the liberty of assigning to that king the refusal to pay the Roman tribute, which action Holinshed attributed to Cymbeline's son Guiderius. In this way he was able to enliven the plot by introducing a war and resolving it in a peace treaty at the end. Fortunately, however, this portion of the play's action—which remains rather uninteresting despite the coloring of the accounts—is very minor in comparison to the story of Imogen, which provides the central interest in *Cymbeline.* The love story is based on a wager, between a cunning villain and a devoted husband, regarding the faithfulness of the absent wife; for this story Shakespeare was indebted to one of the tales in Boccaccio's *Decameron.* In addition to the two main storylines, *Cymbeline's* plot contains numerous instances of characters traveling in disguise and cases of mistaken identity, including the subplot (Shakespeare's invention) of Belarius' abduction and subsequent rearing of the king's infant sons in Wales. Such elements tend to make the plot of *Cymbeline* seem extravagant even to the point of parody when it is read; but when one sees the play performed, its action appears more unified, if still somewhat confusing.

Cymbeline bears many resemblances to previous plays of Shakespeare. The figure of the gullible king influenced by his wicked queen reminds one of *Macbeth,* as does the scene of supernatural intervention in the form of Zeus, the ghosts of Posthumus' family, and the tablet bearing a prophecy—although in this play the prophecy device is weak and extraneous to the plot, and believed to have been inserted by a coadjutor. Iachimo, while he does not approach Iago in malignancy, nevertheless calls to mind Othello's tormentor through his cunning strategies and his cultivation of Posthumus' capacity for jealousy. Likewise, the scenes of Imogen's travels disguised as a boy and her eventual reunion with her lost brothers are reminiscent of Viola's similar adventures in *Twelfth Night.* Perhaps most important, however, is not the affinity of *Cymbeline* to Shakespeare's earlier work, but rather its own unique merit, as well as the relation it bears to that final masterpiece which was to follow, *The Tempest.*

THE CYPRESSES BELIEVE IN GOD

Type of work: Novel
Author: José María Gironella (1917-)
Time: 1931-1936
Locale: Spain
First published: 1953

Principal characters:

MATÍAS ALVEAR, a telegraph operator in Gerona
CARMEN ELGAZU DE ALVEAR, his wife
IGNACIO,
CÉSAR, and
PILAR, the Alvear children
MARTA MARTÍNEZ DE SORIA, sweetheart of Ignacio
MATEO SANTOS, a Falangist organizer and the sweetheart of Pilar
COSME VILA, a Communist leader
DON JORGE DE BATILLE, a wealthy Catalan landowner
AGUSTÍN, an anarchist
JULIO GARCIA, the friend of Matías, chief of police in Gerona
ERNESTO ORIOL, the friend of Ignacio
LUIS COMPANYS, a Catalan lawyer and politician
JOSÉ ANTONIO PRIMO DE RIVERA, founder of the Falange Española
GENERAL FRANCISCO FRANCO BAHAMONDE, later head of the Spanish
State

The Cypresses Believe in God possesses qualities, both historical and social, that command a measure of critical respect in keeping with the compassion and high seriousness of its theme. Part of the book's importance lies in its subject, the drift of the Spanish people into bloody and disastrous civil war. Señor Gironella's plan is ambitious and impressive. This novel tells the story of Spanish life and history from the founding of the Republic in 1931 to the outbreak of the Civil War in July, 1936. The second part, *One Million Dead,* deals with the actual fighting of the war.

The Spanish Civil War has already received extensive treatment in Hemingway's *For Whom the Bell Tolls* and Malraux's *Man's Hope,* but these were tourist books and not conceived on so vast a scale. Gironella, on the other hand, tells the story as it shaped itself in one man's lifetime and experience. This complex and crowded novel, published in Spain in 1953, makes the reader understand why the Spanish Civil War holds its own unique place among the wars of our troubled century: it was a conflict whose

issues were both peninsular and universal, and like the American Civil War it was a tragic drama creating against a seething background of history its own spiritual climate of turbulence and anguish.

That agony is peculiarly Spanish, the national *mystique* of a proud and melancholy people. In a brief preface written for the American edition of *The Cypresses Believe in God,* Gironella declared that it is difficult to consider Spain with detachment. Legends grow: Spain of legend and folklore, of tragic history, of folklore, of the fiesta and the bullfight. Yet he was prepared to defend the complexity of his ancient and unhappy land: to him it represented the possibility of a thousand ways of life.

In Spain, when the novel first appeared, it was called implacable. The term very well describes the nature of Señor Gironella's performance. At the same time it must be admitted that the novel's acceptance by the present regime in Spain leaves it open to political questioning. Gironella himself was a young Falangist, nineteen years old at the be-

1259

ginning of the Civil War, but the book gives the impression that he himself went through a period of indecision and confusion similar to that of his own Ignacio before choosing sides in the conflict. He is therefore able to preserve a point of view which is on the whole admirably objective when dealing with events and personalities for whom there was in actual history no middle ground. Also, the novel is saved from becoming a completely partisan work by the fact that Gironella, as a Roman Catholic, is also a writer in that great Christian tradition. In spite of his tendency to overplay the role of the Communists in the events leading up to the military uprising against the Republic, his generous and full understanding of men and their motives saves him from a too doctrinaire point of view. His allegiance to the traditional order of Church and State is no more extreme than that of Ernest Hemingway, for example, in support of the Loyalist cause.

In the opening pages of the novel the writer presents his people against their background with the beautiful precision and rather flattish realism characteristic of the Spanish novel. The focusing center of the story is a typical middle-class family, the Alvears, who live in the provincial capital of Gerona in Catalonia, a prosperous region of northeastern Spain which during the Civil War became a Loyalist stronghold. Matías Alvear is a telegraph operator who has moved to Gerona from Madrid. A man of even disposition, he likes to fish in the river beneath his apartment windows and play dominoes in his favorite café of an evening. He has Socialist and Anarchist relatives in Burgos and Madrid, but he himself believes that with some brains and a little honesty the Republicans will survive. His wife, Carmen Elgazu de Alvear, has inherited the stanch Basque Catholic reverence for authority and tradition. They have three children. Ignacio, the oldest, had been intended for the priesthood, but he discovers that he has no real religious vocation and becomes a teller in

a bank. César, the second son, is a seminarian; completely without political interests, he is his devout mother's pride. Pilar is the daughter, convent-educated and attracted to the young leader of the Gerona Falangists.

Gironella begins with a family, but like the expanding waves of a stone dropped into a deep pool his novel gradually widens to enclose a picture of a city, a whole society, a nation. Yet in the coming conflict of Socialist-Republican-Anarchist forces on the one hand and Catholic-Monarchist-Nationalists on the other it is still the individual who counts for most. Ignacio is the person through whom the ambiguities and agonies of the Civil War are most clearly revealed. He has absorbed his father's liberal views as well as his mother's religious beliefs. He begins as a believer in the Republican formulas, strengthened by his knowledge of ancient abuses man has suffered under the authority of Church and State, but his growing skepticism of other abuses sanctioned in the name of progress keeps him from whole-heartedly accepting the new political and social creeds. He assures himself that he will fight when he is able to see clearly. At the end of the novel he is still torn between his distrust of the old prejudices and injustices and his dislike for the new fanaticism and violence, but he is slowly turning toward the Falangist party because, in spite of its chauvinism, it stands for Catholic tradition and a program of order.

For César, the sixteen-year-old priest, there is no such conflict. His end is martyrdom before a firing squad in one of the flaring episodes of violence that were dividing Spain into two passionate halves. He is killed for his efforts to save the Blessed Sacrament from destruction while wild Republican mobs are burning the churches. By that time the failure of a military uprising in Gerona and the reprisals that follow point to the inevitable outbreak of civil war and the hatreds and cruelties it will soon engender. But Señor Gironella never loses sight of the human predicament and the single man who finds himself a party to mass movements.

Out of small details Señor Gironella traces out the complexities and uncovers the deeper reality of *The Cypresses Believe in God*. His novel makes one thing clear. The Spanish Civil War was not a conflict, with issues plainly drawn, between liberals and reactionaries, beween laborers and bourgeoisie. It was a struggle in which men of innocence and virtue on both sides were corrupted by forces of modern ideologies and made to serve ignoble and vicious ends. In this powerful novel the author shows us the schizophrenia of modern history itself.

CYRANO DE BERGERAC

Type of work: Drama
Author: Edmond Rostand (1868-1918)
Type of plot: Tragi-comedy
Time of plot: Seventeenth century
Locale: France
First presented: 1897

Principal characters:
CYRANO DE BERGERAC, poet and soldier
ROXANE, with whom Cyrano is in love
CHRISTIAN DE NEUVILLETTE, a clumsy young soldier

Critique:

Considered by many the most popular play of the modern French theater, *Cyrano de Bergerac* is also a perennial favorite with American audiences. Cyrano is more than a hot-tempered swordsman who gets into trouble because he resents people who make fun of his nose, and his name is more than a symbol for physical ugliness. Cyrano de Bergerac symbolizes magnanimity, unselfishness, beauty of soul.

The Story:

In the theater hall of the Hôtel de Burgundy, a young soldier named Christian de Neuvillette anxiously waited for the beautiful Roxane to appear in her box. Christian had fallen passionately in love with this girl whom he had never met. While he was waiting for her arrival, Christian became increasingly upset because he feared that he would never be able to summon sufficient courage to address her, for he believed she was as brilliant and as graceful as he was doltish and clumsy.

Also in the audience, waiting for the curtain to go up, was one Ragueneau, a romantic tavern-keeper and toss-pot poet, whose friends praised his verses to his face while behind his back they helped themselves to the pastries that he made. Ragueneau inquired of another poet concerning the whereabouts of Cyrano de Bergerac. The actor Montfleury, Cyrano's enemy and one of Roxane's suitors, was to star in the play, and Cyrano had threat-

ened him with bodily injury if he appeared for the performance. Cyrano, however, had not yet arrived.

At last Roxane appeared. The play began, and Montfleury came out on the stage to recite his lines. Suddenly a powerful voice ordered him to leave the stage. After the voice came the man, Cyrano de Bergerac, one of the best swordsmen in France. The performance was halted abruptly.

Another of Roxane's suitors tried to provoke a fight with Cyrano by ridiculing de Bergerac's uncommonly big nose. Cyrano, sensitive about his disfiguring nose, became the insulter instead of the insulted. Words led to a duel. To show his contempt for his adversary, Cyrano composed a poem while he was sparring with his opponent, and when he had finished the last word of the last line, Cyrano staggered his man. Le Bret, Cyrano's close friend, cautioned the gallant swordsman against making too many enemies by his insults.

Cyrano confessed that he was exceptionally moody lately because he was in love with his lovely cousin Roxane, despite the fact he could never hope to win her because of his ugliness. While Le Bret tried to give Cyrano confidence in himself, Roxane's chaperone appeared to give Cyrano a note from his cousin, who wanted to see him. Cyrano was overcome with joy.

The place selected for the meeting between Cyrano and Roxane was Ragueneau's tavern. Cyrano arrived

CYRANO DE BERGERAC by Edmond Rostand. Translated by Brian C. Hooker. By permission of the publishers, Henry Holt and Co., Inc. Copyright, 1923, by Henry Holt and Co., Inc. Renewed, 1951.

early, and, while he waited for his beautiful cousin, he composed a love letter which he left unsigned because he intended to deliver it in person. When Roxane appeared, she confessed to Cyrano that she was in love. Cyrano thought for a moment that she was in love with him. But he soon realized that the lucky fellow was not Cyrano himself, but Christian. Roxane asked Cyrano to take the young soldier under his wing, to protect him in battle. Cyrano sadly consented to do her bidding.

Later, when Christian dared jest with Cyrano concerning the latter's nose, Cyrano restrained himself for Roxane's sake. When he learned that Cyrano was Roxane's cousin, Christian confessed his love for Roxane and begged Cyrano's help in winning her. Christian was a warrior, not a lover; he needed Cyrano's ability to compose pretty speeches and to write tender, graceful messages. Although his heart was broken, Cyrano gave the young man the letter he had written in Ragueneau's tavern.

Cyrano visited Roxane to inquire about her love affair with Christian. Roxane, who had recently received a letter from Christian, was delighted by his wit. Cyrano did not tell her that he was the writer of the letter.

Shortly afterward Christian told Cyrano that he now wanted to speak for himself in his wooing of Roxane. Under her balcony one evening Christian did try to speak for himself, but he became so tongue-tied that he had to ask the aid of Cyrano, who was lurking in the shadows. Cyrano, hidden, told Christian what to say, and Roxane was so delighted by these dictated protestations that she bestowed a kiss on Christian.

A friar appeared with a letter from the Count de Guiche, commander of Cyrano's regiment, to Roxane. The count wrote that he was coming to see her that night, even though by so doing he was deserting his post. Roxane deliberately misread the letter, which, she said, ordered the friar to marry her to Christian. Roxane asked Cyrano to delay de Guiche until after the ceremony, a request which de Bergerac effectively carried out by making the count think that Cyrano was mad. After learning that Roxane and Christian were already married, the duped de Guiche ordered Christian to report immediately to his regiment.

In a battle which followed, Cyrano and the other cadets were engaged against the Spanish. During the conflict Cyrano risked his life to send letters to Roxane through the enemy's lines, and Roxane never suspected that the author of these messages was not Christian. Later Roxane joined her husband, and to him she confessed that his masterful letters had brought her to his side.

Realizing that Roxane was really in love with the nobility and tenderness of Cyrano's letters, Christian begged Cyrano to tell Roxane the truth. But Christian was killed in battle shortly afterward, and Cyrano swore never to reveal Christian's secret. Rallying the cadets, Cyrano charged bravely into the fight, and under his leadership the Spanish were defeated.

Fifteen years passed. Roxane, grieving for Christian, had retired to a convent. Each week Cyrano was accustomed to visit Roxane. But one day he came late. When he arrived, he concealed under his hat a mortal wound which one of his enemies had inflicted by dropping an object from a building on Cyrano's head. While talking about her dead husband, Roxane recited to Cyrano Christian's last letter, which she kept next to her heart. With Roxane's permission, Cyrano read the letter which he himself had written, even though it had grown so dark that neither he nor Roxane could see the words.

Suddenly Roxane realized that Cyrano knew the contents of the letter by heart, that he must have written it. With this realization came her conviction that for fifteen years she had unknowingly loved the soul of Cyrano, not Christian. Roxane confessed her love for Cyrano, who died knowing that at last Roxane was aware of his love and that she shared it with him.

Further Critical Evaluation of the Work:

Edmond Rostand's family was wealthy, and he never seemed to need to be commercial. He worked at a slow and sure pace and chose his themes as they came to him. His canon includes one volume of poetry, *Les Musardises* (1890), and the dramas: *Les Romanesques* (1894), *La Princess lointaine* (1895), *La Samaritaine* (1897), *Cyrano de Bergerac* (1897), *L'Aiglon* (1900), and *Chantecler* (1910).

In keeping with his image as an individualistic writer, Rostand leaves a body of work which defies the often-held view of the late nineteenth century as an age of somber, morbid, and usually unintelligible works of art. Several parallels with Shakespeare's *Romeo and Juliet* can be traced in *Cyrano de Bergerac;* and Rostand's *Les Romanesques* is a satirical treatment of the *Romeo and Juliet* theme. Dramatic invention, the use of splendid and spectacular settings, the presence of an eloquent, witty, and adventuresome hero, the conflict of love versus honor, the recklessness and self-sacrifices of the characters, and the point of honor upon which the whole play turns—all are elements of the romance tradition and are present in *Cyrano de Bergerac.*

Motion picture and television adaptations as well as several successful stage revivals of *Cyrano de Bergerac* over the years demonstrate that Rostand's popular turn-of-the-century verse play has the earmarks of a classic. Written just before the beginning of the twentieth century, *Cyrano de Bergerac* reflects the themes and symbols of late nineteenth century romanticism, with its emphasis on the heroic individual (appropriately, one who feels he has failed), its story of ill-fated lovers and wasted lives, and its symbolic moon as mother-and-home of the hero. Considered in its historical perspective, *Cyrano de Bergerac* is the culmination of a romantic revival in French literature.

But in tone the play charts a drastically different course from the "decadent" products that filled the theaters during the same period. In creating Cyrano, Rostand reached into the seventeenth century for his character. The real Cyrano was a little-known writer who lived in France from 1619 until his death in 1655. The bearer of an unusually large nose, he wrote about it in his books—books which have come down to us as the early ancestors of the science fiction genre.

It is tempting to speculate that Rostand also found his proper tone in the seventeenth century, for *Cyrano de Bergerac* is a play based on certain Renaissance-like assumptions, such as the reality of honor and the drama it can create when confronted with a passion like love. The theme of the play —"the making of a style out of despair"—also has affinities with seventeenth century values. Men who lived three hundred years ago in Europe were still experiencing the flowering of heroic individualism: the exhilarating belief that man can, with courage, strength, and intellectual ability, will into being— create—his world as he chooses. It remained for Rostand's age to turn the two-sided coin from "man is everything" to "man is nothing." An underlying assumption of *Cyrano de Bergerac* is the presence of despair, but Rostand handles it lightly, and it is the style which a man can create within this framework of despair that interests him. Rostand's word for style becomes "panache"—literally "white plume" but a word with broad symbolic connotations in the play. The word signifies something of a swashbuckling quality. It conveys a sense of superiority, courage, pride. A man with "panache" would virtually swagger, and, like Cyrano, he is almost bound to have enemies.

In spite of its evident stage popularity, *Cyrano de Bergerac* has taken its share of critical abuse from reviewers, who have panned it as insincere, mere shallow, bustling physical activity, and a study in useless sacrifice. The extravagance of the play, in terms of setting, language, and action, and its improbabilities also clash with the expectation of critics more accustomed to realism. But Cyrano is a poet, like his author. And Rostand uses this play, as he does all of his works, as a vehicle for his own lyric voice.

This important point brings up a related problem the play offers to those who cannot read it in the original French. Those unfamiliar with French must depend upon translations, and although there are several English ones from which to choose, all suffer to some extent because of linguistic and cultural differences which accompany language barriers. Rostand uses the Alexandrine couplet, which gives the language of the play a weighty balance of rhyme and rhythm. But rhyming couplets in French are simply easier on the ear than they are in English. French has more rhyming endings and more acceptable combinations of its rhyming words than have proved possible in English. Out of five readily accessible English translations, three attempt to retain the poetic tone by using blank verse or rhymed verse. The other two avoid the restrictive nature of Rostand's perferred rhyme scheme. One is unrhymed, but a close literal translation; the other uses various rhyme schemes freely and attempts to find English or American parallels for Rostand's witty references to French life and history, providing a lengthy introduction to explain why the changes were made. Regardless of what translation is used, the high lyrical style of the play is evident. One translation focuses on the concept of "panache" by using the French term in different contexts throughout the play. It helps define this last word of Cyrano's which serves as a key to the play's meaning. For example, early in the play at the Pont Nesle battle, Cyrano declares that he came alone except for his triple-waving plume, this "proud panache." Later, in the debate with de Guiche over whether it was honorable for the latter to throw off his white scarf to escape, Cyrano argues that the white plume is a man's panache, a manifestation of his very soul, not to be bartered or squandered but to be preserved as a sign of contempt for his enemies.

Finally, at the end of the play and the end of his life, Cyrano describes the leaves as falling with a certain panache: they float down like trailing plumes of fading beauty, masking their fear of returning to the inevitable ashes and dust of Biblical prophecy; they fall gracefully, with style, as though they were flying. Truly, *Cyrano de Bergerac* is about style created out of despair.

Jean G. Marlowe

CYROPAEDIA

Type of work: Fictional biography
Author: Xenophon (c. 430-c. 354 B.C.)
First transcribed: Fourth century B.C.

Principal personages:
CYRUS THE GREAT
CAMBYSES, his father and king of the Persians
MANDANE, his mother, the daughter of Astyages
ASTYAGES, King of Media
CYAXARES, Astyages' son and Mandane's brother
ARASPAS, Cyrus's comrade from youth
PANTHEIA, the wife of Abradatas
ABRADATAS, an Assyrian noble
CAMBYSES and
TANAOXARES, the sons of Cyrus

Among the surviving authors of ancient Greek literature, Xenophon has the distinction of being the first who wrote in a variety of prose genres, forms which deal with an even greater variety of subject matter. Most of the early prose writers of Greece devoted themselves with notable single-mindedness to either history, the philosophic or scientific treatise of a given sort, dialogue, or rhetoric. But Xenophon wrote in nearly all of these forms. What is more, one of his latest works is a composition which even now is essentially *sui generis*. The *Cyropaedia,* or *Education of Cyrus,* has been called a historical romance. The name may be convenient, but there is in fact no adequate classification for the work. "Didactic-romantic-political-fictional-biography" might come closer.

Xenophon has incorporated in the *Cyropaedia* some treatment of nearly all the topics which he developed separately in his more restricted works. Of his historical interests, despite the title and ostensible subject, there is only a slight trace: the historical and geographical reliability of Xenophon's tale is minimal. The *Hellenica,* covering Greek history from the point where Thucydides left off, in 411 B.C., to the death of Epaminondas in 362 B.C., and the *Anabasis* remain his only strictly historical creations. The latter, a famous account of the author's participation as a young man in a Greek merce-

nary army expedition deep into the Persian Empire, is probably his best work. The *Cyropaedia* "resumes" some of the romance of expert generalship in exotic terrain. The extensive discussions of Cyrus' wise arrangements in military, political, social, and economic order recall the concerns reflected in Xenophon's *Constitution of Sparta, Agesilaus* (on the Spartan king, here treated as a model leader), *Hiero,* and *Oeconomicus.* The account of Cyrus' education and the portrait of his personal virtues and world-wisdom which culminates in his death-bed discourse to his sons on the soul— these continue in their way the philosophical writings of Xenophon which are centered on Socrates, chiefly in the *Memorabilia.* The attention devoted to horsemanship, hunting, and conviviality ("Cyrus at Banquet," as it were) are vestiges of still other works of his. As a final seasoning for the whole, Xenophon includes the first love romance in Western literature, the story of Pantheia and Abradatas.

This topical cross section presents a complex of matters from which a writer of genius might well have woven an absorbing tapestry comprising an intellectual and cultural summary of the age, an encyclopedic *Bildungsroman* like *Wilhelm Meister's Apprenticeship* or *The Magic Mountain.* Xenophon failed to do so. The quality of the product can be assessed after the following summary:

Book I: Cyrus the Great is born of Cambyses, King of Persia, and Mandane, the daughter of Astyages, King of Media. Reared until his twelfth year in Persian simplicity and discipline, he then visits Media for five years. There he learns to ride a horse and hunt, and he wins the friendship and admiration of the Medes by his virtues. He returns home and completes his training under his father's guidance. When Media is threatened by an Assyrian invasion, Cyaxares, the son of the now deceased Astyages, asks aid of the Persians. Cyrus is sent in command of the Persian forces. Book II: In Media, Cyrus reorganizes his army and prepares it physically and psychologically for combat. The King of Armenia, a vassal to Cyaxares, revolts. Book III: Cyrus reconquers him by brilliant strategy and recovers his allegiance to Cyaxares by equally brilliant diplomacy. He executes a similar feat with the Chaldeans, the neighbors of the Armenians. Cyaxares and Cyrus then advance together to meet the Assyrians, and, thanks largely to Cyrus' generalship, the Assyrians are defeated in a first engagement at the border. Book IV: Cyaxares becomes jealous of Cyrus' reputation and decides to stay behind with his own army, allowing Cyrus to move ahead as he pleases. Cyrus, however, persuades most of the Median army to accompany him as well. He wins over to his side the Hyrcanians, a subject people of the Assyrians. After a second defeat of the Assyrians he provides the Persians with a cavalry force of their own. Cyaxares in growing vexation orders that the Median "volunteers" with Cyrus be sent home. Cyrus sends a message in justification of his non-compliance. Gobryas, a vassal of the Assyrian king, defects to Cyrus. Book V: Cyrus advances to the walls of Babylon but postpones an assault on the city. Three more subject peoples accede to the Persians. Cyrus returns to the border of Media and there confronts the spleen and chagrin of Cyaxares with such dexterity that his uncle is publicly reconciled to

him. Book VI. Further military preparations are carried on in winter quarters. Pantheia, the wife of a noble subject of the Assyian king, had been earlier captured and given into the keeping of Araspas, a Median officer in Cyrus' entourage. Araspas now attempts to seduce her. She appeals to Cyrus and is protected. In consequence, her husband Abradatas is won over to Cyrus. Book VII: A massive army of Assyrians and allies under the command of Croesus, King of Lydia, is defeated. Before the battle Pantheia takes pathetic leave of Abradatas, who dies a hero's death in the fighting. Pantheia kills herself over his body. Croesus, captured after the siege of Sardis, is generously treated by Cyrus. After several other campaigns, Babylon is taken by stratagem and victory is complete. Book VIII: Cyrus organizes his empire, marries the daughter of Cyaxares, and after a long reign holds a final edifying discourse on his deathbed. A surprising postscript sarcastically details the degeneration of the Persians since the time of Cyrus.

On the very face of it the arrangement is unpromising. The action advances without complication except for such essentially irrelevant episodes as those involving Pantheia. And in no other fashion is there sufficient human richness to sustain the objective material. Xenophon's political and moral concerns, to be sure, are worked in by a superabundant series of dialogues and speeches, devices which Thucydides had employed with brilliant effect. (The Magic Mountain again provides some parallels.) But for Thucydides the issues and personalities of the Peloponnesian War were problematic and many-sided to an overwhelming degree. Xenophon's Cyrus, by contrast, is so mercilessly idealized that no counterforce can be set up to provide enough tension to launch issues or personalities. The nearest thing to such a confrontation lies in the theme of the growing jealousy of Cyaxares. Thucydides would have been capable of presenting in Cyaxares a potent distillate of everything vital in

Spartan and Athenian culture which opposed that particular composite of Athenian-Spartan ideals read by Xenophon into the figure of Cyrus. But Xenophon's Cyaxares is a pathetic also-ran who is graciously manipulated by his hero-gentleman nephew.

The didactic material is not simply embedded in the inorganic framework of successive events without human complication; a lapidary could still have made the segments memorable. But for the most part, when Xenophon settles into a discourse or dialogue, he produces a run of facile, repetitious, platitudinous elegance. (Skill in specious conversation was clearly part of the Greek ideal of the gentleman, as it has been of the later European permutations.) In this fashion he managed to stuff out his stick-figure design to some four hundred pages.

One obvious moral to be drawn, then, is that the *Cyropaedia* should never be read straight through except in Greek, since it is only the grace of its style which gives some salt to many a dull page. But it should in justice be admitted that a wisely condensed English version would be worth its reading time. Anecdotes possessed of point and humor, moments with some vividness of situation and character, do occur. (For example, some country-bumpkin rookies in training are told that they must march behind their lieutenant. When the lieutenant is by chance sent on a postal errand, the entire platoon obediently runs off behind him.) And at times the practical wisdom has its interest. Cambyses to Cyrus on how to manage his men: When encouraging them by hopes which are not certain to be fulfilled, one should not personally suggest these doubtful hopes; get someone else to act as mouthpiece.

More important, however, some rapid acquaintance with the text of the *Cyropaedia* will always be worthwhile because of the position this book occupies in the development of the ancient political imagination. Both Xenophon and another Socratic enthusiast gave their minds much to the problem of the inadequacy of existing Greek political systems. Plato's *Republic* in its artistry and profundity transcends Xenophon beyond all compare. But Plato never conceived of a satisfactory political order larger than the city-state, and the times were leaving him behind: until our own days of uncertain world government, *empire* was henceforth to be the chief ideal for international political order, and from Alexander the Great to Stalin that empire was to be predominantly monarchical. Xenophon, a half-century before Alexander, is the first literary exponent of monarchical empire.

DAISY MILLER

Type of work: Novelette
Author: Henry James (1843-1916)
Type of plot: Psychological realism
Time of plot: Mid-nineteenth century
Locale: Vevey, Switzerland, and Rome
First published: 1878

> *Principal characters:*
> DAISY MILLER, an American tourist
> WINTERBOURNE, an American expatriate
> GIOVANELLI, Daisy's Italian suitor

Critique:

As in most of James' work, there is practically no plot in *Daisy Miller*. Rather, James is interested in a conflict between European and American customs and ideals. The crudities and touching innocence of Daisy Miller are revealed against a background of European manners and morals, and both are shown from the point of view of an expatriate American who has lived abroad too long. The special point of view makes *Daisy Miller* an ironic study of contrasts.

The Story:

Winterbourne was a young American who had lived in Europe for quite a while. He spent a great deal of time at Vevey, which was a favorite spot of his aunt, Mrs. Costello. One day, while he was loitering outside the hotel, he was attracted by a young woman who appeared to be related to Randolph Miller, a young American boy with whom he had been talking. After a while the young woman exchanged a few words with him. Her name was Daisy Miller. The boy was her brother, and they were in Vevey with their mother. They came from Schenectady, Winterbourne learned, and they intended to go next to Italy. Randolph insisted that he wanted to go back home. Winterbourne learned that Daisy hoped to visit the Castle of Chillon. He promised to take her there, for he was quite familiar with the old castle.

Winterbourne asked his aunt, Mrs. Costello, to meet Daisy. Mrs. Costello, however, would not agree because she thought the Millers were common. That evening Daisy and Winterbourne planned to go out on the lake, much to the horror of Eugenio, the Millers' traveling companion, who was more like a member of the family than a courier. At the last moment Daisy changed her mind about the night excursion. A few days later Winterbourne and Daisy visited the Castle of Chillon. The outing confirmed Mrs. Costello's opinion that Daisy was uncultured and unsophisticated.

Winterbourne made plans to go to Italy. When he arrived, he went directly to the home of Mrs. Walker, an American whom he had met in Geneva. There he met Daisy and Randolph. Daisy reproved him for not having called to see her. Winterbourne replied that she was unkind, as he had just arrived on the train. Daisy asked Mrs. Walker's permission to bring an Italian friend, Mr. Giovanelli, to a party Mrs. Walker was about to give. Mrs. Walker agreed. Then Daisy said that she and the Italian were going for a walk. Mrs. Walker was shocked, as young unmarried women did not walk the streets of Rome with Italians. Daisy suggested that there would be no objection if Winterbourne would go with her to the spot where she was to meet the Italian and then walk with them.

Winterbourne and Daisy set out and eventually found Giovanelli. They walked together for a while. Then Mrs. Walker's carriage drew alongside the strollers. She beckoned to Winterbourne and implored him to persuade Daisy to enter her carriage. She told him that Daisy had been ruining her reputation by such behavior; she had become familiar with Italians and was quite heedless of the scandal she was causing. Mrs. Walker said she would never speak to Winterbourne again if he did not ask Daisy to get into the carriage at once. But Daisy, refusing the requests of Mrs. Walker and Winterbourne, continued her walk with the Italian.

Mrs. Walker determined to snub Daisy at the party. When Winterbourne arrived, Daisy had not made her appearance. Mrs. Miller arrived more than an hour before Daisy appeared with Giovanelli. Mrs. Walker had a moment of weakness and greeted them politely. But as Daisy came to say goodnight, Mrs. Walker turned her back upon her. From that time on Daisy and Giovanelli found all doors shut to them. Winterbourne saw her occasionally, but she was always with the Italian. Everyone thought they were carrying on an intrigue. When Winterbourne asked her if she were engaged, Daisy said that she was not.

One night, despite the danger from malarial fever, Giovanelli took Daisy to the Colosseum. Winterbourne, encountering them in the ancient arena, reproached the Italian for his thoughtlessness. Giovanelli said that Daisy had insisted upon viewing the ruins by moonlight. Within a few days Daisy was dangerously ill. During her illness she sent word to Winterbourne that she had never been engaged to Giovanelli. A week later she was dead.

As they stood beside Daisy's grave in the Protestant cemetery in Rome, Giovanelli told Winterbourne that Daisy would never have married her Italian suitor, even if she had lived. Then Winterbourne realized that he himself had loved Daisy without knowing his own feelings, that he could have married her had he acted differently. He reasoned, too late, that he had lived in Europe too long, that he had forgotten the freedom of American manners and the complexity of the American character.

Further Critical Evaluation of the Work:

In *Daisy Miller*, James represents the conflicts between American innocence and independence and the rigid social conventions characteristic of the American colony in Rome. While Daisy deliberately flaunts convention by her unorthodox behavior, Mrs. Costello and Mrs. Walker make appearance their only basis for moral judgment. Winterbourne, troubled by the ambiguity in Daisy's character, seeks some objective basis for making a judgment.

Daisy realizes that the other Americans have no interest in her as an individual. Living in a world of moral judgments based entirely upon social conventions, they are only concerned to preserve the appearance of morality through "proper" behavior. Determined to be accepted on more meaningful grounds than these, Daisy asserts those freedoms she would be allowed in America, but which are clearly out of place in Rome. Confident in her own innocence, she refuses to conform to the restrictions her compatriots would place upon her.

Innocence and crudity are the terms characterizing Daisy, and these conflicting qualities are the source of Winterbourne's confusion about her. He, like his aunt and Mrs. Walker, has a tendency to make judgments on the basis of superficial appearances. Daisy, however, seems innocent to him in spite of her unconventional behavior, so he cannot fit her into a neat category as he would like. But discovering Daisy in a seemingly compromising position with Giovanelli in the Colosseum gives Winterbourne the evidence he needs, and with some relief he declares Daisy morally corrupt. In so doing, he places himself solidly among the other Americans who, like himself, have lived too long abroad to appreciate the real innocence which underlies Daisy's seeming moral laxity. Too late Winterbourne realizes at the graveside that his formulation of Daisy has been unjust.

DAMAGED SOULS

Type of work: Biographies
Author: Gamaliel Bradford (1863-1932)
Time: 1737-1893
Locale: America, England, Europe
First published: 1923

> Principal personages:
> BENEDICT ARNOLD
> THOMAS PAINE
> AARON BURR
> JOHN RANDOLPH
> JOHN BROWN
> PHINEAS TAYLOR BARNUM
> BENJAMIN FRANKLIN BUTLER

Though the reviews of the time were not unmixed, *Damaged Souls* remains as the best book by Gamaliel Bradford and unique in the history of letters: a contribution to American history, biography, and literature. Although Taine is supposed to have originated the term, Bradford was the most active "psychographer." His biographical studies are not so much life stories as spiritual silhouettes.

The introductory essay, applauded as a new departure, the model for interviews in depth, suggests that the souls of Bradford's subjects are not damned, that each has a unique quality offset by a flaw. While H. L. Mencken suggested that only the first five are worthy of the sympathetic treatment, Barnum and Butler having insufficiently developed or callously overthrown souls, most critics accepted Bradford's carefully documented verdicts on the minds and hearts he explores.

Bradford, admitting to prejudice, likens Arnold's manly though misguided vigor and Burr's personal though selfish charm to Paine's and Barnum's blatant and zealous natures. But in all those selected some kind of spiritual flaw appears to explain, even though it does not justify, the stigma that has determined the public reputations of these personages. Bradford's main purpose, however, was not to stress the stigma but to show his people in their rounded and more human characters. Thus of Benedict Arnold, who abandoned the unfortunate Major André, who blackened his reputation for valorous, unselfish deeds, the reader gains an insight into his quixotic nature, his anger and feeling of slight, his physical needs, and his despair. The most telling irony concerns a meeting with Talleyrand in which Arnold dared not reveal himself.

Thomas Paine's character was formed in rebellion, Bradford believes, and his restless nature and brilliant verbal insights formed a platform for vigorous action. His work was inspired by love of humanity rather than by the egoism so marked in his exterior. There is no reason why he did not advance in the cause of the poor and the downtrodden, though rebellion was his method and violence often the result. His exterior appearance, his slovenly habits and lack of cleanliness, his addiction to drink in a drinking age, only illumine his lack of selfish concern and his higher loyalties.

Aaron Burr, by contrast, had no ideals, but exhibited a most joyful, forthright nature. He indulged himself in the pleasures of companionship, especially that of women whom he found irresistible, and he lived off those who were drawn into his confidence and bewitched by his charm. His strange projects are to this day inexplicable, perhaps not even realized in the planning, though his "villainies" seem to be the result of lack of consideration. Burr's love for his daughter and her tender but open-eyed concern for him form a kind of redemption. He carried no grudges, he gave generously if indiscriminately, and he looked to eternity and a god whom he believed kinder than most people give him credit for.

God's angry man, John Brown, seems to Bradford the most complex of all since right is on both sides where Brown's motives and actions are concerned. His intense and fanatical enthusiasm formed the glory and caused the damage. Barnum was the product of his age who honestly believed that humbug was a commodity, though he himself preferred the high things and practiced a warm-hearted cordiality. John Randolph, on the other hand, was the noblest of these flawed personages; his noble qualities of mind and spirit were undone by bad temper and exacerbated nerves, so that he had little influence for good. Benjamin Franklin Butler, the least engaging of the group as well as the most self-righteous, felt, in summation, that he had performed only good acts and those continually.

Gamaliel Bradford remains a persuasive advocate of restrained judgment, leaving to God the final decisions, as he whimsically suggests we must. To read deeply *pro et contra* was his technique, his formula to seek and display motive and drive; and his rhythm was that of his subject's pulse. The result is Bergson's *élan vital* brilliantly projected. Bradford's gallery of portraits, finally, included whole and mended as well as damaged souls, and his books will remain in our relativist age as models.

DAME CARE

Type of work: Novel
Author: Hermann Sudermann (1857-1928)
Type of plot: Domestic romance
Time of plot: Nineteenth century
Locale: Germany
First published: 1887

Principal characters:
>PAUL MEYERHOFER, a simple farmer
>MAX MEYERHOFER, his father
>FRAU ELSBETH, his mother
>ELSBETH DOUGLAS, a neighbor girl

Critique:

This novel, which has enjoyed widespread critical acclaim, is frequently read in language classes. It is an outstanding example of German romanticism. The three hallmarks of its epoch are the style colored by a kind of world-sadness, its completely rural setting, and its sentimental tone. *Dame Care—Frau Sorge* in the original—covers a wide span of years in its action, but it is gracefully concise without being abrupt. Sudermann exhibits a paternal sympathy for his characters; perhaps his greatest gift is his understanding of all classes of people.

The Story:

About the time their third son, Paul, was born, the Meyerhofers lost through forced sale their country estate, Helenenthal. Meyerhofer tried to keep his wife, Frau Elsbeth, in ignorance of what was going on, but she was so uneasy in her bed that at last he told her that a family named Douglas had bought his property.

Meyerhofer was a violent man, given to grandiose schemes to make wealth and endowed with a martyr complex. It suited him to move his family to a humble farm, within sight of Helenenthal, where they would be constantly reminded of their lost prosperity. Frau Elsbeth, who was a docile woman, shuddered at the prospect.

Mrs. Douglas, a kind-hearted woman, came to see the mother and her baby. She assured Frau Elsbeth that she could stay on at Helenenthal as long as the family wished. The two women became good friends. Mrs. Douglas acted as godmother for Paul, and Frau Elsbeth was godmother for Elsbeth, a daughter born to the Douglases a short time later. In spite of their friendship, however, Meyerhofer took offense at a fancied slight and moved his family in bleak November to their farm on the moor.

In those poor surroundings Paul led a secluded childhood. His mother, sensing his retiring disposition, was kind to him; his father was brutal. He continually ridiculed his son by comparing him unfavorably with his two lively older brothers. Paul was frequently beaten by his heavy-handed father, and after the beatings his mother would comfort him. She often told him stories; the one he remembered best was a frightening tale. It was about Dame Care, a gray woman who laid great burdens on poor people. Some years after they moved, Frau Elsbeth had twin daughters, Katie and Greta.

About the time Paul was learning to whistle, bad times came to the farm. The mortgage was due and there was no money to pay it. Day after day Meyerhofer drove into town and came back very late, usually drunk. In spite of the awe she felt for her husband, Frau Elsbeth determined to seek help. She took Paul with her to Helenenthal on a memorable visit. There she explained her husband's dislike for the Douglas family and asked for their help. The amiable Mr. Douglas gave her the money to pay the mortgage. Paul played with Elsbeth while the grownups visited.

At school Paul did not succeed easily. He had to study a long time to get his work done and he had to memorize all the answers to problems. But his handwriting was very good. The Erdmann brothers, wild-eyed and saucy, made his life miserable for years. They often beat him, stole his lunch, and threw his clothes into the river.

The Meyerhofer property was surrounded by a peat bog. Always too busy to pay attention to his farm, Meyerhofer bought a used steam engine to harvest peat. He gave half his harvest as down payment to Levy, a sharp trader, and hired an engineer whom Levy had recommended. But the old engine would never run, and Meyerhofer learned that the supposed engineer was only a tramp hired by Levy for a few days' imposture. That winter, when Levy came to collect the other half of the harvest, the duped Meyerhofer drove him off with a whip. Levy, a shrewd man of business, went to a lawyer. Meyerhofer was compelled to give up his harvest and, in addition, pay a heavy fine.

After the older brothers had been sent away to school there was no money to educate Paul, who was sent to confirmation classes. He saw Elsbeth there, even sat near her. She was kind to the boy and went out of her way to speak to him. The Erdmann brothers teased them about the friendship and said that Paul was sweethearting. Hating ridicule, Paul seldom spoke to Elsbeth.

For five years Paul, toiling on the farm, got little help from his father. Once when he was out seeding a distant field, Paul saw Elsbeth. Delighted to see him again, she gave him a book of Heine's poetry, and she was impressed with his ability to whistle whole symphonies. Once after she had been abroad for a long time, a party was given on her return and Paul and his family were invited. The rest of the Meyerhofers went early in the day, but Paul went after dark so that no one would see his shabby clothes. He watched his two sisters having a merry time, and saw his father talking grandly with Mr. Douglas.

Out of sympathy for Paul, Mr. Douglas agreed to go in with Meyerhofer on one of his schemes. On the strength of Douglas' endorsement, Meyerhofer borrowed money recklessly. When he heard what was going on, Mr. Douglas came to the farm and told Meyerhofer to stop. Meyerhofer set the dog on him, but Mr. Douglas, though bitten, choked the savage beast. While Paul was apologizing to his neighbor, Meyerhofer attacked a servant, Michel, who had watched the scene. Michel picked up an ax. Paul took it away from him and threw it down a well. Then he carried his struggling father into the house. From that day on Paul was master in the household.

While Paul was wandering late one night near Helenenthal, he saw brilliant flames shooting from his farm buildings. Michel had fired the barn. Paul was able to save the house, the livestock, and the old steam engine, but everything else was lost.

Beaten in spirit, Frau Elsbeth died a lingering death. At the funeral Paul saw Elsbeth again. Since her own mother was incurably ill, she felt a strong bond of sympathy for Paul. Later Paul, with the aid of books on mechanics sent by his remote brothers, began to rebuild the steam engine which had been his father's folly. He worked so hard that he had little time to look after his sisters. One night he overheard them in the meadow with the Erdmann boys and learned that his sisters' honor had been smirched by his old enemies. Waiting in a deserted road for them at night, he forced them at pistol point to swear they would marry Katie and Greta.

Finally getting the old steam engine to work, Paul began to cut and market peat. As his trade increased he became a man of substance and traveled about Germany. He heard of Elsbeth from time to time and knew she planned to marry her cousin.

One night, eight years after their barn burned, Paul suspected Meyerhofer's intention to burn the Douglas barn. To distract his father from his mad deed, he set fire to his own house and barn and was seriously burned in the flames.

Paul was taken to Helenenthal. The searchers had found Meyerhofer dead of a stroke near the Douglas barn, a broken pot of petroleum by his side. Although it was Elsbeth's wedding day, she insisted on staying by Paul's bed. The vicar was sent away, and her cousin left. For many weary days Elsbeth watched over Paul. After his recovery Paul was tried for the deliberate burning of his own house. Admitting his guilt, he blamed himself for always having been so timid and withdrawn. Now that he had lost everything, he felt himself free at last. Dame Care, who had been his nemesis all his life, had been routed.

Paul was sentenced to two years in prison. On his release Elsbeth and Mr. Douglas met him to take him home. Both Helenenthal and Elsbeth would be his.

Further Critical Evaluation of the Work:

Dame Care is an extraordinary study of a human being who becomes trapped by circumstances into sacrificing his life to his family. The gradual development of the conviction in Paul's mind that his life must be this way is portrayed with great subtlety and psychological penetration. Paul longs to be selfish, but never can bear to shirk responsibility. He knows that people take advantage of him, but he cannot deny help to those who need him. Sudermann poignantly describes the plight of this conscientious young man, carefully avoiding sentimentality or falseness of tone. The author perfectly captures the right sympathetic note as he writes about Paul. At all times, the style is even and restrained, allowing the events to produce the emotional reaction.

Fairy tales form a background for the story of Paul's growing up and subsequent bondage. They are the only frame of reference young Paul has, as he tries to comprehend the dark and mysterious world. It is natural that he should think of Elsbeth in the White House as a fairy princess far above him. The subtle, tender, slowly maturing relationship between Paul and Elsbeth is related by the author with a mastery of nuance and suggestion; the mutual pain that the two young people experience is never made melodramatic or false, although their situation might seem to be that of a romantic melodrama.

The power of selfishness is hauntingly dramatized in the book, as Paul's family convinces him that he must live apart from the joys of ordinary mortals. All he can do, he tells Elsbeth, is watch over the happiness of others and to make them as happy as possible. But, after the final catastrophe, he realizes that nobody has appreciated his sacrifices, nobody has noticed that he has given away his own happiness. People who take do so without concerning themselves about those who must do the giving.

Sudermann shows as much skill with scenes of action as he does with psychological analysis. The dramatic moment when Paul saves his father's life and establishes himself as master of the farm is brilliantly rendered; the two fires that destroy the farm both are described with vivid, vigorous prose. The countryside around the farms and village is pictured clearly, with concise, yet poetic, descriptions. Sudermann is as successful at bringing to life the minor characters as he is the major ones; Paul's selfish and self-centered brothers and sisters and guilt-tormented, half-mad father are particularly well done. Frau Elsbeth, Paul's mother, might have become a cliché figure, the long-suffering wife, but she is portrayed with a sensitive and subtle understanding that makes her a genuine human being; her suffering is completely understandable and thereby pitiable. Many of the characters are unlikable, and often the story is painful to read, but it is, thanks to the author's great skill, completely engrossing from beginning to end. *Dame Care* presents a stark, but realistic, view of human nature, alleviated only by the decency of a few rare individuals.

THE DAMNATION OF THERON WARE

Type of work: Novel
Author: Harold Frederic (1856-1898)
Type of plot: Social criticism
Time of plot: The 1890's
Locale: New York State
First published: 1896

Principal characters:

THERON WARE, a young Methodist minister
ALICE WARE, his wife
FATHER FORBES, a Catholic priest
CELIA MADDEN, a rich young Irish-Catholic girl
DR. LEDSMAR, Father Forbes' friend
MR. GORRINGE, a trustee of Theron's church

Critique:

The Damnation of Theron Ware was one of the first novels to deal with the problems of an American clergyman. While the book was in part an indictment of the hypocrisy of a particular denomination, it was not meant to be wholly so. The author intended to show that any individual was bound to fall who was not given a moral bulwark on which to lean in adversity. The novel condemns the minister's denomination only in so far as it did not prepare him to meet the beliefs of others and accept them, while still holding to the beliefs in which he had been trained. It is the training, not the denomination, which is taken to task.

The Story:

Theron Ware had gone to the annual statewide meeting of the Methodist Episcopal Church with great expectation of being appointed to the large church in Tecumseh. He was greatly disappointed, therefore, when he was sent to Octavius, a small rural community.

To the minister and his wife, the town and its citizens did not appear formidable at first, but a hint of what was to come occurred the first morning after their arrival. A boy who delivered milk to Mrs. Ware informed her that he could not deliver milk on Sunday because the trustees of the church would object. Shortly afterward the trustees told the new minister that his sermons were too dignified and that Mrs. Ware's Sunday bonnet was far too elaborate for a min-

ister's wife. Theron and his wife were depressed. Unhappy in his new charge, Theron decided to write a book about Abraham.

One day Theron assisted an injured Irish-Catholic workman and went home with him to see what help he might give. At the man's deathbed Theron observed the parish priest and a pretty young red-haired girl, Celia Madden, who assisted him. Upon becoming acquainted with these two, the minister was surprised to find that his earlier hostility to Catholics and the Irish was foolish. These people were more cultured than he, as he learned a few evenings later when he went to the priest for some advice in connection with his proposed book.

At the priest's home he met Dr. Ledsmar, a retired physician interested in Biblical research. Both the priest and the doctor knew a great deal about the actual culture of Abraham and his people. They tried to be tactful, but the young minister quickly saw how wrong he had been to think himself ready to write a religious book on any topic; all he knew was the little he had been taught at his Methodist Seminary.

Upon leaving Father Forbes and the doctor, Theron walked past the Catholic church. Hearing music within, he entered to find Celia Madden at the organ. Later he walked home with her and discovered that she was interested in literature and art as well as music. Once again that evening Theron was made to realize how little he actually knew. He went home with the feeling that his own small world was not a very cultured one.

Three months later there was a revival at Theron's church. Mr. and Mrs. Soulsby, two professional exhorters, arrived to lead a week of meetings which were designed to pay off the church debt and put fervor into its members. The Wares, who entertained the Soulsbys, were surprised to find that the revival leaders were very much like insurance salesmen, employing very much the same tactics. During the revival week Theron was non-plussed to discover what he thought were the beginnings of an affair between his wife and one of the trustees of his church, Mr. Gorringe.

In a long talk with Mrs. Soulsby, Theron told her that he had almost decided to give up the Methodist ministry because of the shallowness he had discovered in his people and in his church. Mrs. Soulsby pointed out to him that Methodists were no worse than anyone else in the way of hypocrisy, and that all they lacked was an external discipline. She also reminded him that he was incapable of making a living because he lacked any worldly training.

Theron's life was further complicated when he realized that he was beginning to fall in love with Celia Madden. Because of her interest in music, he had asked her advice in buying a piano for his home, and she had, unknown to him, paid part of the bill for the instrument. He also found time to call on Dr. Ledsmar, whose peculiar views on the early church interested him. He disgusted the old doctor, however, with his insinuations of an affair between Father Forbes and Celia.

In September the Methodists of Octavius had a camp meeting. Its fervor did not appeal to Theron, after his more intellectual religious reading and his discussions with Celia and Father Forbes, and he went off quietly by himself. In the woods he came upon a picnic given by Father Forbes' church. At the picnic he met Celia and had a long talk with

her, kissed her, and told her of his unhappiness in his double bondage to church and wife.

Soon afterward he alienated Celia by telling her that he was afraid of scandal if he were seen talking with her. He also offended Father Forbes by reports that Dr. Ledsmar had spoken slightingly of Celia. The priest told his housekeeper that he was no longer at home to Theron Ware.

One day Theron openly confronted his wife with his suspicions about her and Mr. Gorringe. She denied the charges, but her very denial seemed to speak against her in her husband's mind. In his unhappiness he went to see Celia. She was not at home, but her brother, who was dying slowly of tuberculosis, saw him. With the license of the dying he said that when Theron arrived in Octavius he had the face of an angel, full of innocence, but that in the eight months the minister had spent in the little town his face had taken on a look of deceit and cunning. Celia's brother continued by warning the minister that he should stay among his own people, that it was bad for him to tear himself from the support which Methodism had given him.

Leaving the Madden home, Theron learned that Celia was going to New York City. It occurred to him that Father Forbes was also going to the city that evening and perhaps they were traveling together. He went home and told his wife that urgent business called him to Albany; then he went to the station and boarded the train unseen. In New York he saw the priest and Celia meet, and he followed them to a hotel. After the priest had left the hotel, he went upstairs and knocked at Celia's door. She told him that she was busy and did not wish to see him, adding that she had noticed him following her earlier in the journey. While he pleaded with her, Father Forbes came in with some other gentlemen and informed Theron that they had come to New York to get another brother of Celia's out of a bad scrape.

Dismissed, Theron stumbled down the stairs. A few days later he arrived at the Soulsby house at dawn. He told an incoherent story of having tried to commit suicide, of stealing money from the church at Octavius, and of wandering alone about the city for hours while he tried to drink himself to death.

The Soulsbys took him in and sent for his wife. He was ill for months. After his recovery both he and his wife realized that he was never meant for the ministry. Through the Soulsbys, Theron was finally able to make a new start in a real estate office in Seattle. Theron knew he would make a successful real estate agent. Or if that failed, he could try politics. There was still time enough for him to be in Congress before he was forty.

Further Critical Evaluation of the Work:

In the nineteenth century and the early twentieth century, a great deal of religious debunking took place in American literature, both journalistic and imaginative, fueled—at least in part—by the muckraking temperament of the times. Contributions ranged from Nathaniel Hawthorne's "The Minister's Black Veil" (1836) and *The Scarlet Letter* (1850) to Sinclair Lewis' *Elmer Gantry* (1927). Harold Frederic's *The Damnation of Theron Ware* added another example to the debate. And a debate it was: clerical ethics and integrity as well as those of institutionalized religion are, in fact, still being hotly contested. Thus, Frederic's novel was meaningful in its own time and still has contemporary relevance.

From this unique position, the novel takes on a significance not usually accorded it by critical consensus, for the book has generally been viewed as a one-of-a-kind indictment of religious hypocrisy rather than as an element in the mainstream of a literary trend. Theron Ware's confusions, for example, were and are viewed in inappropriate nineteenth century terms of self-denial and sacrifice. The emotional problems of Theron Ware have thus been wrongly analyzed: the Reverend Mr. Ware, so the conventional interpretation goes, is simply trying to assert his latent creativity by attempting to write a book and expand his cultural horizons. But, this interpretation notwithstanding, Ware does not succeed, although his attempts cost him his ministry, alienate his friends, and threaten his marriage. And questions remain: "Why did Theron Ware fail? Why was Theron Ware damned?"

First of all, Ware is an extraordinarily immature person, a condition engendered largely by the narrowness of his religious upbringing and his ministerial training which left him unequipped to cope with the realities of life. Second, Ware's understanding of sexuality is, at best, adolescent, for he cannot see beyond the virgin or whore dichotomy and hence is unable to develop a mature relationship with any woman—Alice, Celia, or Mrs. Soulsby. Third, Ware has virtually no insight into himself. He knows nothing of his capabilities, his needs, or his desires; indeed, he seems, at times, hardly to be aware of his own existence. Consequently, Theron Ware is an emotional cripple, blocked from meaningful relationships with himself, with women, and with society at large, including its cultural heritage. That religious training should prove so emotionally debilitating is a severe damnation of such training. Yet the person thus afflicted is equally damned, but in another, more profound way. For Theron Ware, even with the opportunity for a new career in real estate, shows at the end of the book no more promise of succeeding than he showed at the beginning.

THE DANCE OF DEATH

Type of work: Drama
Author: August Strindberg (1849-1912)
Type of plot: Psychological realism
Time of plot: Late nineteenth century
Locale: Sweden
First presented: 1901

Principal characters:
EDGAR, a captain in the Swedish coast artillery
ALICE, his wife
JUDITH, their daughter
CURT, Alice's cousin
ALLAN, Curt's son, in love with Judith

Critique:

The dramatic works of Strindberg have seldom been translated or produced in English-speaking countries, although his plays are known throughout Europe. Strindberg was especially interested in establishing a Swedish dramatic literature comparable to that of Ibsen in Norway. This particular play was written in two parts, in the way that Shakespeare wrote *Henry IV* in two parts; it is, in essence, a double play, the first part dealing with the mature adults and the second with their children. European critics have often referred to *The Dance of Death* as Strindberg's greatest dramatic achievement. The characters are real to the reader, shockingly so. And yet, beyond the intense realism, there is a fabric of symbolism, the meaning of which is nothing less than the vast sum of human relationships.

The Story:

For twenty-five years Edgar, a captain in the Swedish coast artillery, and his wife Alice had lived an unhappy existence. Their unhappiness was caused by Edgar's contempt for everyone else in the world; he thought of himself as a better being than others, even his wife, and he had made their marriage a tyranny. They lived on an island off the coast, where Edgar was the commanding of-ficer of the artillery detachment. Living in an old prison, they avoided the other people of the island as well as officers of the post and their wives. Indeed, Alice was virtually a prisoner in her home. The only means of communication she had with the mainland was through a telegraph key, which she had taught herself to operate. Her skill she kept a secret, for her husband did not want her to have any means of communication with the outside world.

Alice's only hope of release from her husband's tyranny lay in the fact that he was ill and might die at any time. On their silver wedding anniversary Curt, Alice's cousin, arrived on the island to officiate as the quarantine officer. On his first visit to Edgar and Alice he learned about the life which they led, when Edgar suffered an attack and Alice gloated over her husband's illness. Curt, who had been divorced by his wife, also learned that Edgar had caused the divorce and persuaded the court to award the custody of the children to Curt's wife.

During the two days that Edgar lay ill, grave changes took place in the three people. Alice turned gray-haired; feeling that the time had come when she should admit her age, she had stopped tinting her hair. She also became an object of distrust to Curt, for she tried

THE DANCE OF DEATH by August Strindberg, from PLAYS BY AUGUST STRINDBERG. Translated by Edwin Bjorkman. By permission of the publishers, Charles Scribner's Sons. Copyright, 1912, by Charles Scribner's Sons. Renewed, 1940, by Edwin Bjorkman.

to make love to her cousin while her husband lay ill. Curt, unable to understand her actions, could not fully realize how much she hated her husband and how much she had suffered during the past twenty-five years. Edgar himself resembled a corpse after his illness; but he immediately tried, upon his recovery, to dominate the others.

On the third day after his attack the captain told his wife he was going to divorce her. In retaliation, she tried to have him convicted of the embezzlement of government funds, of which he was innocent. She also embraced her cousin Curt in her husband's presence, at which time Edgar tried to kill her with his saber. After that incident, both husband and wife subsided emotionally, admitting they had tortured each other enough. They both said they hoped that they could get along with each other peaceably, if not happily.

A few months later Curt's son Allan, a cadet stationed with Edgar's artillery company, fell in love with Judith, the daughter of Alice and Edgar. The parents, failing to realize the youngsters were serious in their affair, thought that Judith was making game of Allan at her father's request, for Edgar hated Allan because he was Curt's son. At the time Edgar was trying to arrange a marriage for Judith with a major in the regiment, a man older than Edgar. The lovers' quarrels of the two young people only served to heighten the illusion under which the three grownups labored.

Edgar, meanwhile, was also busy undermining Curt's position as quarantine officer. After gleaning information from Curt, he then published articles about quarantine management in periodicals and thus gained a reputation for himself in a field in which he was actually ignorant. After his retirement, the result of his illness, he planned to run for the national legislature, in opposition to Curt, who had expected to try for an office. Edgar completely discredited Curt with the voters by taking up a subscription

for his rival, who, acting on Edgar's advice, had lost a great deal of money in an unwise investment. With deliberate malice, Edgar did everything he could to discredit Curt in the eyes of the world and to reduce him to abject poverty and dependence.

After Curt had lost his money, Edgar bought his house and its furnishings and then left the house exactly as it was, in order to make the loss more poignant to Curt. Then Edgar was made an inspector of quarantine stations, an appointment which made him Curt's superior in employment. Curt, accepting his reverses calmly and stoically, refused to lose his head, even though Alice tried to make him seek revenge. Alice still hoped that her ailing husband might die quickly, before he could completely ruin the lives of Curt, his son Allan, Judith, and Alice herself.

In the meantime the captain continued his plan to marry Judith to a man who could help to fulfill Edgar's ambitions. Instead of marrying her to the major, he arranged a marriage to the colonel of his old regiment, notwithstanding the fact that the colonel was more than forty years older than the girl. So far as anyone could suppose, the marriage was to take place; Judith herself seemed to be agreeable to the match. Alice made one last attempt to spoil the plan, but a letter she had written was intercepted by Edgar and returned by him to his wife.

Judith herself ruined Edgar's scheme by revealing her true love to Allan. To prevent the marriage, she called the colonel on the telephone, insulted him, and broke off the engagement. Then, with her mother's aid, she arranged to go to Allan at the military post to which Edgar had sent him. The failure of his plan was too much for Edgar. He suffered an apoplectic stroke, much to the delight of his wife, who saw revenge at last for all that she and the other members of the family had suffered at the sick man's hands. Unable to control her delight at

Edgar's approaching death, she taunted him on his deathbed with the fact that he was hated and that his evil plans were finally going awry. His only answer, since he had lost the power of speech, was to spit in her face.

After Edgar's death, which occurred within a few hours, both his wife and her cousin admitted that death had changed their attitudes toward the dead man. Alice said she must have loved him as well as hated him, and she hoped that peace would rest with his soul.

Further Critical Evaluation of the Work:

Strindberg's specialty in his plays was the stripping bare of "that yawning abyss which is called the human heart," as one of his characters calls it. Perhaps only Dostoevski in modern literature has penetrated equally to the depths of psychological torment. His characters say things that most people feel at times, but which they restrain themselves from expressing or even admitting to their consciousnesses. All of his life, Strindberg was obsessed with the dual nature of the human brain, with the contrast between inner feelings and their outer expression. The power, and horror of, *The Dance of Death* comes from this expression of the normally suppressed thoughts of the characters. This startling honesty seems to shatter moral and social conventions, and to leave both characters and audience vulnerable and exposed. "It's horrible," says one of the characters in one of Strindberg's later plays, "don't you find life horrible?" And the reply is, "Yes, horrible beyond all description." But the endurance of both Strindberg and his characters in the face of madness and violence suggests that he saw, in spite of everything, that there was no acceptable alternative.

From the first lines of *The Dance of Death,* one is struck by the intensity of the speeches. Alice and Edgar are caught in the midst of a duel, or, rather, in the last and brutally final stages of a duel. When the play opens, the conflict is only verbal, but it soon becomes more passionate and more violent. At times, the dialogue seems to be on the verge of becoming no more than an insane ranting, and yet there are moments when Strindberg rises above his fury and sums up the tragedy of life in a few sentences—and the play thus achieves greatness.

It is vital to understand the intimate relationship between Strindberg's life and work to comprehend fully his dramas, particularly *The Dance of Death.* Essentially pessimistic, August Strindberg lived a tortured existence, from a childhood of poverty and insecurity to years as both ministry and medical student, to a period as a free lance journalist. His first major play, a historical drama, was rejected by the Swedish Royal Theatre. He became famous with the publication of his first novel, *The Red Room,* but he continued writing plays. The conflict between the sexes inspired some of his most intense dramas, including *The Father* and *Miss Julie,* and, ultimately, *The Dance of*

Death. Married three times, the central relationship of his life was his violent and tormented first marriage. Like D. H. Lawrence, Strindberg was obsessed with the idea of the lower-class male, himself, marrying the aristocratic lady and then bringing her down to his own level. This obsession is reflected in *Miss Julie* and in the relationship between Alice and Edgar in *The Dance of Death.* The disaster of his marriage and the loss of his four children drove him into an alcoholism which had threatened before to possess him, and, despite his growing fame as a writer, he became a lonely and unhappy man, unable to find steady employment.

In his later plays, Strindberg combined the techniques of naturalism with his unique vision of psychology. These bold dramas, with realistic dialogue, highly wrought symbols (such as the wedding ring, the fortress, the wreaths, and the piano in *The Dance of Death*), and stark settings, brought about a revolution in European drama. One of his last and greatest plays, *The Dance of Death* reflects both his first marriage and the collapse of his life afterwards. All of his work possessed extraordinary vitality, but in *The Dance of Death,* Strindberg transformed essentially autobiographical material into a drama of exceptional power; this and other late works, such as *A Dream Play* and *Ghost Sonata,* influenced modern playwrights such as Elmer Rice, Eugene O'Neill, Luigi Pirandello, and later, Edward Albee, whose drama *Who's Afraid of Virginia Woolf?* was directly influenced by *The Dance of Death.*

Strindberg has been accused of hating his female characters, and no character has prompted this statement more than Alice in *The Dance of Death.* Were Strindberg's greatest plays the product of a dangerous and intense misogyny? Is this what gives his brilliant psychological dramas their peculiarly perverse power? No doubt he did suffer from a persecution mania brought on by his intense problems, and his writing does suggest in places paranoiac tendencies. The women in the plays, such as Julie and Alice, tend to be strong and vengeful creatures, who deliberately try to lead men to destruction. But the power of *The Dance of Death* and other dramas of this late period must be due, also, to a deep introspective analysis of his sufferings, for, between his bouts of madness, Strindberg was able to examine his mental disturbance and to make use of the knowledge he gained from such examinations. From a reckless, Bohemian existence, he emerged, in his last years, into a guilt-ridden form of Christianity, Swedenborgian mysticism, and a Schopenhauerian pessimism according to which the real world exists outside human reality. His third marriage, to the young actress, Harriet Bosse, dissolved after less than three years and he discovered that he had inoperable cancer. Then, suddenly, the Swedish people recognized his greatness and began speaking of a Nobel Prize for him. "The anti-Nobel Prize is the only one I would accept," he retorted. When his first wife died in 1912, he collapsed, although he had not seen her for twenty years. Three weeks later, he was dead. Thirty thousand people came to his funeral. The battle of the sexes, for him, at least, was finished.

Some critics have said that both Edgar and Alice are monsters battling to the death, like a pair of dinosaurs clashing in some ancient burial ground, but the fact is that they are not monsters any more than the characters of *The Father* or *Miss Julie* or any other of his plays. They are two trapped individuals struggling desperately to survive, but not knowing what to do; every frantic gesture that they make only wounds them that much more. They tear at their own flesh, like half-mad beasts, in a terrified frenzy, but they are not evil. They are, perhaps, two of the most pitiful human beings in modern literature. The scenes in which Alice plays the Hungarian dance on the piano and Edgar performs the violent jig with his jangling spurs and in which Alice hurls her wedding ring at Edgar are excruciatingly painful, cutting beneath the layers usually left by more conventional playwrights. Alice and Edgar are bound together by a love-hate relationship that neither can escape, except into death. As Strindberg himself knew, even distance and time cannot release a man or woman from certain types of bondage. At the end of the First Part of the play, Edgar realizes how hopelessly he and his wife are bound, and laughs that they might as well celebrate their silver wedding anniversary. "Let us pass on," he cries. Somehow, they endure, and that, perhaps, is the message of the play. And Alice, when Edgar dies at the end of the Second Part, finally understands that she loved Edgar, as well as hated him, and she prays for peace for him. And, by implication, she prays for herself, for all either of them ever craved was peace.

Bruce D. Reeves

A DANCE TO THE MUSIC OF TIME

Type of work: A trilogy of novels
Author: Anthony Powell (1905-
Time: 1921 to 1932
Locale: An English public school, London, Oxford, and some country houses
First published: A Question of Upbringing, 1951; A Buyer's Market, 1952; The Acceptance
World, 1955

Principal characters:
NICHOLAS JENKINS, the narrator, a novelist
CAPTAIN GILES JENKINS, his uncle
PETER TEMPLER, Nick's friend, later at work in London
MONA, his wife
JEAN, his sister
CHARLES STRINGHAM, a friend of Nick and Templer
KENNETH WIDMERPOOL, an older schoolfellow of Nick
MR. LE BAS, the housemaster at Nick's school
MR. SILLERY, an Oxford don
EDGAR DEACON, a painter and antique dealer
RALPH BARNBY, an increasingly successful young painter
GYPSY JONES, a young Communist
E. ST.-JOHN CLARKE, a successful, unfashionable novelist
MARK MEMBERS, a poet and critic
J. G. QUIGGIN, a literary journalist
BARBARA GORING, a debutante
MILLY ANDRIADIS, a society hostess

Anthony Powell's great series of novels is a unique project today, with twelve books planned. The style and subject matter are traditional and each volume can be appreciated in isolation. As is consistent with the major theme, Powell moves forward and back in time unfolding his plot. There are no innovations of form in the books. Nevertheless, these novels are regarded as probably the most original and stimulating fiction appearing in England at the present time.

The first three books, which cover the period from the early 1920's to the early 1930's, form a complete social history of the period expressed through the experience of Nick Jenkins, his friends, colleagues, and their families. A Question of Upbringing and A Buyer's Market are in four parts; The Acceptance World is in five.

The evocative power and subtle, arresting brilliance of Powell's style are immediately apparent in the descriptive opening sections. All the elements are there: high-seriousness, near-bathos controlled

with wit, metaphors from the arts, and an astringent nostalgia. This talent for meaningful juxtaposition of phrase is also important in Powell's delineation of character. In the first section of A Question of Upbringing, Kenneth Widmerpool with his aggrieved expression takes concrete form in Nick's mind: his appearance is plain, stiff, and Widmerpool moves in a like manner out of the fog-like air. Nick's vision of Widmerpool as an individual remains with him, and their lives are to be linked erratically for the next thirty years.

Widmerpool feels moral disapproval of Nick's closest friends, Charles Stringham and Peter Templer. Stringham, who reminds Nick of Veronese's Alexander, belongs to the class also castigated by Nick's Uncle Giles, who is a wealthy man. Templer, Widmerpool feels, is a poor influence on the members of the house, and he becomes almost physically distressed at young Templer's experiments with pipe-smoking, alcohol, and women. Widmerpool leaves school a year before Nick, although in a typically economical illustration of his farcical intrusion on Nick's life and of his latent power his name remains on the house-list through an oversight of the housemaster, Le Bas.

Nick and Widmerpool next meet in France—this episode forms the third section of the book—whence Nick has gone trying to solve the problem of being more mature than a boy, but not yet an adult male.

Powell uses hyperbole so accurately and incisively that one or two sentences reverberate throughout a chapter and control the reader's emotional response. Witty and unlabored, this account and another on Widmerpool place the two boys at a precise point in their adolescence. The economy with which such analyses are effected enables Powell to write largely on actual happenings: here, the social environment of a Tourraine house party for paying guests.

The second section of *A Question of Upbringing* is more closely concerned with society in its limited sense and deals also with the family and early love relationships of Nick, Stringham, and Templer. This chapter opens with a consideration of one's judgment of other people which is a commentary also on Powell's own blend of comic and tragic incident. Powell has an exact eye for significant detail and a virtually absolute selectiveness of words and metaphor. Each phrase in his extremely descriptive books interprets the mood, place, or character described. This stylistic ability gives to the novels an absorbing, almost gripping power.

At a family lunch Nick discovers Stringham's reservations about Templer, whom Nick had always regarded as Stringham's closest friend. Stringham feels that Templar does fit in with the idea of home life. Stringham's "home life" includes a stepfather, Buster Foxe, whose personality is cold and chilling; his mother, a thrice-married beauty, rich and overpowering; and Tuffy Weedon, Mrs. Foxe's secretary, whose face on greeting

Charles is so cheerful that it seems to be intense and anxious. These people create an atmosphere unknown and oppressive to Nick.

Peter and Nick are together at school the following term. Peter remarks that he enjoys the more common things and that Charles' home life must be filled with too many good things. This is almost Charles' view of his stepfather. Peter adds that even lunch must have been rather stuffy. The judgment surprises Nick, but is one subsequently made of Charles himself.

Nick stays with Templer's family before he goes to France. The household is quite different from Stringham's fashionable London home. Templer's father, a graceless widower, made his money in cement; he talks exclusively about the stock market. Here Nick meets Jean Templer and falls in love with her. The Templer home is described with fantasy in hyperbolic terms. This device creates an atmospheric heightening which is often employed before an emotional encounter between characters. The expansive villa is built on a cliff where clouds drift in the sky and the waves against the stones create a sense of being cryptic, a place of adventure. Immediately, Nick sees Jean and feels a conflict swell in him, a desire and a fear of being close to her.

After this visit Nick travels to France, where he meets Widmerpool again and falls fleetingly in love with a girl whom he regards as the French counterpart to Jean. From France, Nick goes up to Oxford. Section four of *A Question of Upbringing* covers his first term there. At Oxford Nick is again with Stringham, who detests university life and is increasingly afflicted with melancholy and drunkenness.

Powell treats Oxford in terms of personality, introducing Nick's life there through Sillery, an elderly don and *éminence grise* figure. Characters who play a large part in subsequent novels are gathered at Sillery's tea parties: Truscott, a graduate of promise; Quiggin, uncouth, belligerent, and provincial; and Mark Members, bohemian, precious, a poet, rumored to come from the same Northern town as Quiggin.

By the end of *A Question of Upbringing* the main themes are stated and the world of *A Dance to the Music of Time* has been created. The next novels enlarge variously on the arts and politics of the period and on social mores, aspects of life of which the narrator, Nick, has as yet so little intimation.

The first part of *A Buyer's Market* is a good example of the conjunction of disparate elements from which Powell's social comedy is structured. Nick sees four paintings by Edgar Deacon for auction with a conglomeration of other objects that reminds him of Deacon's own shop and home at the time when he knew him well. Deacon is an old acquaintance of Nick's parents. Nick meets him at the Louvre on the day he has tea with the Walpole-Wilsons. Sir Gavin Walpole-Wilson is working at the Peace Conference with Nick's father. Years later Nick sees his first Deacon painting in the Walpole-Wilson house. The importance to Nick of the Walpole-Wilson's "Deacon" is not the quality of the painting but that seeing it always implies the proximity of their niece, Barbara Goring. The auction recalls those years to Nick and also the debutantes' dinner and ball at which he and the socially determined Widmerpool both renounced Barbara.

At the ball, Widmerpool, in an accident of the kind that has dogged him throughout life, is covered in sugar by Barbara. Under the stress of this incident he tells Nick as they walk through London streets that he too was in love with her.

While walking, Nick and Widmerpool meet Deacon at Hyde Park. Deacon, now an old man, is with an attractive but scruffy girl, Gypsy Jones. Gypsy is aggressive, egotistical, and politically extremely left wing. These ill-assorted four go to a coffee stall. There they encounter Stringham, whom neither Widmerpool nor Nick has seen for several years.

The cumulative impact of Powell's work is strengthened by this technique of scattering and reuniting his characters. Their circumstances change, their spheres of influence enlarging or declining as they bring with them on remeeting a new friend or associate who shifts the focus of the narrative.

Stringham takes the other four to Milly Andriadis' party. The party is held in a house rented from Jean Templer's husband, and the guests include Sillery, Prince Theoderic of the Balkans, Sir Magnus Donners, and Bill Truscott, who works for him. Milly herself, once the mistress of a person of the court, is now Stringham's mistress.

After this strangely fascinating party there is an elegiac description of Nick's walk home which culminates in another unexpected meeting when he runs into Uncle Giles. Before Nick goes to sleep he wonders if he should take his uncle seriously. If he could solve this problem, then possibly other answers in life might be made clear.

Section three of *A Buyer's Market* starts with an assessment of Nick's maturer philosophy of life. He realizes that life is not divided into compartments, but that individual worlds eventually find that they have something common to all. Feeling himself socially isolated for the moment, Nick tries to look up Deacon. Instead, he meets the painter Barnby, whose studio is in Deacon's house. Barnby informs Nick of Widmerpool's involvement with Gypsy Jones and asks if Nick is also an admirer. Barnby himself is engaged on a mural for the Donners-Brebner building and painting a portrait of Baby Wentworth. Thus he finds himself in the delicate situation of courting his patron's mistress.

Subsequently Nick stays at Hinton, the country house of the Walpole-Wilsons. The house party guests visit Stourwater, Sir Magnus Donners' country home, a too perfectly reconstructed medieval castle. Jean Duport is there as a friend of Baby Wentworth and Nick finds himself attracted to her once more. Stringham is engaged. He, Truscott, and Widmerpool are all working for Sir Magnus.

Widmerpool, power-oriented and egotistical, is evidently successful in business but seems doomed to failure with women. He confesses to Nick that Gypsy had been pregnant when he met her and that he had illegally procured her abortion. Attempting to leave Stourwater after a conference with Sir Magnus, Widmerpool has another of his ludicrous accidents, reversing his car into an ornamental urn and toppling it onto the lawn. Nick concludes that Widmerpool habitually rises, like the phoenix, from the ashes of humiliation.

At the opening of the last section of *A Buyer's Market,* Nick remains an onlooker, an autumn walk impressing on him only a sense of experience endured. Depressed by String ham's wedding, where the strife it had caused was unsuccessfully concealed, Nick learned the same day of Deacon's death, caused by a fall after a party he had given the week before.

Although Deacon's party was a complete outward contrast to Milly's, inelegant, bohemian, and literary, the same elements of social and sexual strife, ambition, and the reunion of acquaintanceships distinguish it. Mark Members, now an established writer, is brought by an artist's model, Mona. Quiggin had become a friend of Deacon and is much admired by Gypsy for his journalism and left-wing politics. These two are seen to be bound, through their careers, by the bonds of a love-hate relationship.

On the day of Deacon's funeral, Nick finds Gypsy alone. Feeling that they have been projected out of their unrelated selves, he makes love to her. Only then does he realize how like to Barbara Goring Gypsy is. That same evening Nick dines with Widmerpool and his mother, when they both learn of Barbara's totally unexpected engagement.

When he leaves Widmerpool and his mother, Nick suddenly connects in his mind Mrs. Foxe, her secretary, and Milly Andriadis. Such insights into the similarity of people variously connected validifies Powell's constant use of chance coincidence. Given Stringham's relationship to these three women, their similarities are psychologically sound.

After this traumatic day Nick's life appears to have meaning. Hardly conscious of what has happened, he begins the trip down the road of life.

Volume Three, *The Acceptance World,* is set in the 1930's, by which time the narrator is deeply involved in work and aware of politics. The change in mood from the 1920's is reflected in supper parties at the Ritz and a rather scruffy weekend at Maidenhead which contrast with pre-ball dinners and country house visits. Nick's friends have altered and hardened in their molds. New anxieties harass them, some predictable, some surprising. The older characters naturally change less.

Nick has tea with his Uncle Giles at his private hotel. His uncle's life was aimless, embattled, and shifty. He constantly enlists Nick in a fruitless attempt to extract more money from the family trust. The country's abandonment of the gold standard and the formation of the National Government annoys Uncle Giles considerably.

This oblique reference to events vital to England not only illustrates Uncle Giles's character but also gives the exact flavor of a historical period without disrupting the atmosphere of a comedy of manners.

After the hotel tea with Uncle Giles, Nick waits for Mark Members at the Ritz. This hotel is described in a passage of soaring fantasy and imagination, the glory of which is subtly modified by Peter Templer's entry.

Templer had married the model Mona, and Nick senses it is not a good marriage. They discuss Stringham's early divorce and his schoolboy imitations of

Widmerpool, who, Templer says, is joining the Acceptance World of credit finance. Nick is fascinated by Templer's acceptance of Widmerpool as a normal city acquaintance no longer regarded as a dislikable oddity.

Before Mona and Jean Duport, now separated from her husband, join Peter, Quiggin arrives to see Nick instead of Mark Members. Nick is professionally an art publisher's editor who is trying to obtain an introduction to the painter Isbister's work from St. John Clarke, the novelist for whom Members and Quiggin successively act as secretary. Nick, however, refuses to discuss the introduction with Quiggin that evening.

He dines with the Templers and Jean and spends the weekend with them, at last beginning the inevitable love affair with Jean. Mona is so bored with her life with Peter that she invites Quiggin to Sunday lunch. He accepts, despite worries about leaving St. John Clarke, and is patently irritated by the other guests, Peter's ex-brother-in-law and Mrs. Erdleigh, who appears in some way to be looking after Stripling.

In Chapter Three of *The Acceptance World* Nick's love affair with Jean continues. After the Isbister Memorial exhibition he has a long talk with Members, whose feelings are lacerated by the loss of his post with St. John Clarke. They walk in Hyde Park, where there is a rally for the Hunger Marchers, the unemployed of the 1930's from the North. The march has, for Nick and Members, some preposterous elements. Quiggin is pushing the ailing St. John Clarke in a wheel chair and helping him is Mona.

Powell's treatment of the interest in left-wing politics by intellectuals of the 1930's and of the depressed economy is expanded in a meeting between Nick and Jean with Umfraville, a friend of Stringham's father in Kenya. Umfraville bewails the lack of social life in London; everyone he knows seems to have grown serious. Nick says that the economic slump is the cause. Umfraville takes Nick and his friends to visit Milly Andriadis. Now living in a flat, Milly's changed circumstances—she is keeping a young man who is a German Trotskyite—completes the picture of social decline and political reversals. Nick's second meeting with Milly has the added Powell nuance that it was in Jean's house that he first met her and learned that Jean was married.

In the last section of the book, Nick re-examine's Widmerpool's Acceptance World in the light of his own experience. The main part of this section describes an old boys' reunion dinner. Templer is distressed by his loss of Mona to Quiggin. Stringham is distressingly drunk. Widmerpool is self-important and absorbed in his business success. Nick meets Tolland, who as a member of the large Warminster family plays a part in the subsequent novels.

Powell's stated theme at the beginning of *A Question of Upbringing* is this: people traveling closely together take meaning or lose their meaning, sometimes separating and getting together again to return to the picture of life.

Outlining the variations on this theme can give only a slight impression of the vitality and variety of the original. Powell's satirical approach to the period gives his novels objectivity, and his appreciation of social nuances and informed vision of human personality give his numerous characters and complex plots richness and clarity. This social and human perceptiveness, combined with a sensitive ear for dialogue and talent for descriptive prose, makes Powell's comic survey of England since World War I the most trenchant and accomplished yet attempted.

A DANCE TO THE MUSIC OF TIME: SECOND MOVEMENT

Type of work: A trilogy of novels
Author: Anthony Powell (1905-   )
Time: 1914-1939
Locale: London and the country
First published: At Lady Molly's, 1957; Casanova's Chinese Restaurant, 1960; The Kindly Ones, 1962

Principal characters:

NICHOLAS JENKINS, the narrator, a novelist
CHIPS LOVELL, a friend of Nick and nephew of Lord Sleaford
LADY MOLLY JEAVONS, the former Lady Sleaford, an indiscriminate hostess
TED JEAVONS, her husband
GENERAL AYLMER CONYERS, a retired hero of the Boer War
ALFRED LORD WARMINSTER, called "Erridge," an eccentric, left-wing peer
ISOBEL TOLLAND, Erridge's sister, Nick's wife
PRISCILLA TOLLAND, another sister, Chips Lovell's wife
MILDRED BLAIDES HAYCOCK, Lady Jeavons' raffish sister
KENNETH WIDMERPOOL, a school acquaintance of Nick, a financier
J. G. QUIGGIN, a left-wing critic
MARK MEMBERS, Quiggin's friend and rival, a literary critic
HUGH MORELAND, a composer, Nick's friend
MATILDA WILSON, Moreland's wife, an actress
MACKLINTICK, a music critic, the friend and admirer of Moreland
CAROLO, a violinist, Matilda's first husband
PETER TEMPLER, a school friend of Nick
CHARLES STRINGHAM, another friend
MISS TUFFY WEEDON, the former secretary to Stringham's mother, Mrs. Foxe, and guardian of Stringham during his dipsomania
GILES JENKINS, Nick Jenkins' radical and disreputable uncle
BOB DUPORT, the ex-husband of Jean Templer, Nick's former mistress
SIR MAGNUS DONNERS, a great industrialist

At Lady Molly's, Casanova's Chinese Restaurant, and *The Kindly Ones,* the three novels that form the second movement of Powell's novel series, treat mainly the years from 1934 to 1939. The first long section of *The Kindly Ones* is set in 1914 at the outbreak of World War I. The first volume, *At Lady Molly's,* is a novel of personalities based on the complex, interrelated, and exceptionally large Sleaford and Tolland families. Nick Jenkins' school and university friends of the first trilogy are mainly minor characters here. *Casanova's Chinese Restaurant* subordinates the Tolland-Sleaford theme and enlarges on love and marriage and the careers of Nick's friends. The new characters here, notably Moreland and his musical associates,

were initially introduced to Nick by Barnby, the painter who was a major character in *A Buyer's Market.* The *Kindly Ones* enlarges the themes of the first two volumes, reconsiders some of Nick's early experiences, and details more specifically the sexual aspects of various relationships. This volume is, however, dominated by the start of the two world wars. This vital political theme is prepared for, in *At Lady Molly's,* by Widmerpool's direct reference to Hitler and in *Casanova's Chinese Restaurant* by the involvement sympathetically and actively of several characters in the Spanish Civil War.

The first chapter of *At Lady Molly's* can be read as a self-parody of the structure of Powell's novels where the same

1293

characters meet again and again at different times, often after an interval of several years and, outwardly at least, in much changed circumstances. If it is parody it is also a superb justification of Powell's method. The key lines in this reading occur when Lady Molly asks Alfred Tolland if he and Nick are related. She continues by saying that she believes he has more relatives than she, and she has a grandfather who had ninety-seven first cousins and a grandmother with ninety-four.

Thus, the vast network of blood relationships caused by the intermarrying of the Tolland and Sleaford families, although their actual contacts are infrequent, is demonstrably more complex even than the ties of love, work, and friendship among the other characters and is no more involved than the relationship of many old families in England today.

The second important function of Lady Molly Jeavons' party at the start of the second trilogy is that it establishes the decline of society and illustrates exactly how it has declined. The guests are poorer, less smart, less at ease together, even less courteous. They are, in fact, a mixed bunch in which Lady Molly herself symbolizes the whole process of disintegration. Her first marriage was to Lord Sleaford, whereby she was mistress of a fabled country house, Dogdene. Her second marriage was to the ex-soldier Jeavons, a fascinating and important character who, nevertheless, has been incapable of earning a living after the Armistice.

Nick's introduction into Lady Molly's world comes through Chips Lovell, her nephew. Nick, by 1934, had left art publishing and is a film script writer. He he has also published two novels. Nick meets Mrs. Conyers at Molly's party; she and General Conyers are old friends of Nick's parents. In between the long talks on family by Molly and Tolland, Mrs. Conyers tells Nick that her raffish, twice-married sister, Mrs. Blaides, is to marry again. Her fiancé is the ubiquitous, power-dominated Widmerpool with whom Nick was at school.

Widmerpool lunches Nick at his club and worriedly asks Nick's advice on sleeping with Mildred Blaides before their marriage. That afternoon Nick has tea with General Conyers and his wife. Conyers is equally worried about his own performance on the cello and Widmerpool's ability to "handle" Mildred Blaides. Mrs. Conyer's friend, the widowed Frederica Budd, takes Nick to visit one of her sisters, Norah Tolland, who lives in a reputedly lesbian ménage with Eleanor Walpole-Wilson, the cousin of Nick's, and Widmerpool's, first love. The same evening Nick meets Quiggin, who has eloped with Peter Templer's wife Mona. He is invited for a weekend at their house in the country.

At Quiggin's house Nick meets the head of the Tolland family, Alfred Warminster, known as Erridge, a young left-wing peer regarded as hopelessly eccentric and irresponsible. He is currently Quiggin's landlord and patron. At dinner with Quiggin and Mona at Thrubworth, the Warminster family home, Nick meets two of Erridge's sisters, Isobel, whom he knows instantly he will marry, and Susan, whose engagement they came to announce.

At Lady Molly's house Nick again meets Miss Tuffy Weedon and learns that his school friend Stringham is practically an alcoholic and being looked after by Tuffy. He meets Jeavons in a pub and joins him in one of Jeavons' periodic wild nights. At a night club run by a Kenya acquaintance of Stringham, Dicky Umfraville, Nick and Jeavons join Widmerpool and Milfred and their host Peter Templer with his new girl friend Betty. Nick learns that Erridge has gone to China, taking Mona with him. Widmerpool's engagement to Mildred is broken after a weekend with her sister, Lady Sleaford, at Dogdene. Lady Molly holds an engagement party for Nick and Isobel. There Nick meets Members, Quiggin's rival in the literary world. He also has a discussion with General Conyers, who is studying psychology, concerning Widmerpool's sexual incompetence; the general accurately classifies Widmerpool as an intuitive extrovert.

In *Casanova's Chinese Restaurant*, the dowager Lady Warminster, stepmother to the nine Tollands, replaces her sister Molly Jeavons as a dominant character from an earlier era. The main character in this novel is the musician Moreland. Standing outside a blitzed pub, the Mortimer, Nick remembers meeting Moreland and his friends there with Deacon, the antique dealer of *A Buyer's Market*. Moreland asks Nick which *three* wives he would choose from their girl friends. Nick, still in love with Templer's sister, Jean Duport, answers at random. Moreland refuses names but says he intends to marry. Nick, Barnby, Moreland, two music critics, Gossage and Macklintick, and the violinist Carolo, dine at Casanova's and discuss women. Moreland invites Nick to a performance of *The Duchess of Malfi*. In this play Matilda Wilson plays the Cardinal's mistress. She had herself been the mistress of Sir Magnus Donners, who at one time employed Stringham and Widmerpool. Backstage, Nick meets Matilda and Norman Chandler, a homosexual dancer and actor for whom Mrs. Foxe, Stringham's mother, has developed an intense affection. Matilda marries Moreland. A year later Nick marries Isobel.

At Lady Warminster's the elderly novelist, St. John Clarke, is the only non-family lunch guest. Isobel is in a hospital following a miscarriage. Erridge has gone to Spain, leaving St. John Clarke to deal with his political affairs in England. Tuffy and Stringham are living in a flat in Lady Molly's house. Norman continues to influence Mrs. Foxe. When Nick visits Isobel in the hospital, he meets Moreland, whose wife is having a baby, Widmerpool, who is having treatment for boils, and Brandreth, the physician who is treating them all. Moreland

takes Nick to visit the Macklinticks. Their relationship is bitter and abusive, the atmosphere exacerbated by the presence of Carolo as lodger. Nick takes Widmerpool to lunch at his club. Widmerpool, who favors appeasement with Germany, is excited by his new acquaintance with preabdication royal society.

Because Isobel and Matilda have become close friends, the Morelands and the Jenkinses are together a great deal. Matilda's baby died at birth. Moreland finishes a new symphony. Mrs. Foxe arranges a party to celebrate the first performance of the symphony. At the party the Macklinticks have an appalling quarrel and Nick is embarrassed when Matilda intimates that Moreland is in love with Priscilla, Isobel's sister. Stringham, escaped from Miss Weedon's care, arrives at his mother's house in the middle of the party. He is fairly sober, evidently because he is kept without money. Tuffy arrives and gently maneuvers him home. Chips Lovell reports to Nick Widmerpool's distress at the abdication.

St. John Clarke dies and both Quiggin and Members write obituaries. Nick and Isobel see less of the Morelands because of Priscilla. Erridge returns from Spain. Nick and Moreland visit Macklintick, who is deeply depressed; he has lost his job and his wife has left him with Carolo. Two days after their visit he commits suicide. This shock leads Moreland to give up Priscilla. Erridge inherits St. John Clarke's estate. Priscilla and Chips Lovell become engaged.

Casanova's Chinese Restaurant contains hints of the approaching holocaust. *The Kindly Ones* begins just before World War I bursts on an almost wholly unaware Britain.

Nick's family lives at Stonehurst near his father's army post. He is about seven years old and fascinated when he learns that Stonehurst is supposed to be haunted. He gossips with Albert, the handyman-cook, Bracey, his father's army servant, and the neurotic parlor maid Billson. One Sunday there he remembers forever. General and Mrs. Conyers are expected to lunch. Before church, Albert gives notice. Nick's father receives a telegram notifying him of Uncle Giles' arrival in the afternoon, news which infuriates him. After lunch Billson, distracted by the ghosts and the fact that Albert is leaving to marry, arrives in the drawing room, naked, to give notice. General Conyers leads her away wrapped in a shawl snatched from the grand piano. As they start to drive home, the Conyers are stopped by Dr. Trelawney and his followers. Trelawney, who has a sinister reputation, is the leader of a strange religious group; General Conyers has known him for years. While they talk, Giles arrives and announces that Archduke Franz Ferdinand has been assassinated. Only General Conyers realizes war is now imminent.

In the late 1930's everyone is obsessed by the probability of war while continuing, until 1939, to lead their usual lives. Matilda has returned to acting, but, believing she is inadequate, retires again. The Morelands move to a country cottage near Stourwater. Just after "Munich," Isobel and Matilda meet. The Jenkinses go to the Morelands' cottage for the weekend. While there, they are invited to Stourwater for dinner. Peter Templer collects them in his car. Peter is now married to Betty, who is in a state of mental collapse. Anne Umfraville is Sir Magnus' new mistress. After dinner the guests act the Seven Deadly Sins, which Sir Magnus photographs. Widmerpool, in uniform, arrives to discuss a job for Bob Duport with Sir Magnus. Templer accepts the fact that he is now Widmerpool's inferior in the city. Stringham is said to be acting as the agent at Glimber, his mother's country home, with Tuffy Weedon.

A few weeks later Uncle Giles dies in a seaside hotel run by Albert. Nick goes to attend to his funeral. Bob Duport and Dr. Trelawney are staying in the same hotel. During an evening of drinking Duport discusses his ex-wife Jean's infidelities with Nick, who discovers that while she was in love with him she was also having an affair with Jimmy Brent. Duport says he loathes Widmerpool, who had ruined the job he was doing in Turkey for Sir Magnus. Dr. Trelawney is attended by Mrs. Erdleigh, the spiritualist friend of Uncle Giles, whose money she inherits.

When Nick returns from Uncle Giles' funeral, he arranges for Isobel, who is pregnant, to live with Frederica in the country during the early months of the war. Anxious to get into the army as an officer, he applies to General Conyers for help. He can do nothing for Nick but announces his own engagement, his wife having died a short time before, to Tuffy Weedon. She tells Nick that Stringham is now cured of his dipsomania. Nick asks Widmerpool to help him get into the war. Widmerpool says that this is impossible, but he requests Nick to visit Lady Molly's with him and his mother. At Lady Molly's, Nick encounters Jeavons' brother Stanley, an army officer who promises to find Nick's paper and obtain his commission. Moreland is staying at Lady Molly's. Moreland is in a state of collapse because Matilda has left him. At dinner they meet Quiggin, Members, and Anne Umfraville. Nick reflects that another stage of life has now passed as on the memorable day at Stonehurst.

In *The Kindly Ones*, Nick observes that understatement and overstatement sometimes hit upon truth better than a flat declaration of fact. This, of course, is exactly Powell's method of creating truth by understatement or overstatement, both in description of events and in characterization. Powell's many paired characters contrast so vividly that taken as a whole they form a succinct cross section of humanity. General Conyers and Mr. Jeavons provide an excellent example. Both spent the early years of their maturity in the army. Both married women younger than themselves. The general, however, is specifically a man of action. Seemingly born to command, he has a superb knack of handling people and situations. His knowledge and awareness grow with the years. He studies psychoanalysis intelligently, reads modern fiction, and plays the cello with fervor; one of the oldest characters in the novels, he is thoroughly modern. Jeavons, on the other hand, has never advanced since 1918. Unemployable, he appears to live in a vague mist, permanently missing the point of whatever is happening. Subject to the occasional binge, he plays a more usual role by being prodded into pouring drinks at his wife's parties.

Nick Jenkins and Widmerpool are another pair who meet constantly and unexpectedly. Each is suspicious of everything the other most values. Widmerpool, gauche and unattractive, is determined to live by the will, snobbish, ambitious, impervious to any aesthetic pleasure or values. His pursuit of power is so singleminded that he soon outstrips his seemingly more talented and charming contemporaries. To Nick, the arts and personal relationships are the most important aspects of life, yet he recognizes Widmerpool's drive toward success and even ceases to be surprised by it. Widmerpool, however, remains amazed at Nick's drifting and lack of seriousness. General Conyers describes Widmerpool's objective orientation as a need to be always on the move after some definite thing. But it could be doing harm to a person in ordinary life when it affects what his personal objectives may be. The general, of course, is right; Widmerpool's relationships with women, except with his adored mother, are always disastrous. The subjective, emotionally analytic Nick, on the other hand, makes a successful marriage before he is thirty.

Love and marriage in Powell's novels are also treated with either exaggeration or understatement. There is an extraordinarily high incidence of marital and sexual failure among Nick's friends. Templer, Stringham, Moreland, Macklintick, and Quiggin have all been divorced or separated by the end of *The Kindly Ones.* The successful relationships are

only obliquely treated. Nick's courtship and marriage to Isobel are implied to be worthwhile. The Jeavonses and General Conyers and his wife are said to be happily married. But Nick's relationship with Jean, felt at the time to be wonderful and treated in depth, is later shown to have been a travesty of love. Although this development follows Tolstoy's dictum that happy marriages are all alike and only the unhappy ones are interesting, the overall effect of this treatment is to make love and marriage appear insubstantial and precarious.

This attitude toward love is in accord with Powell's whole philosophy of the total uncertainty of existence, its kaleidoscopic quality, and the necessity of constant revaluation if any meaning is to be extracted from the patterns in life. For if life and its significance are uncertain they are for Powell certainly patterned, and only by studying the pattern can any meaning be extracted. "Time" is of course the key word of the series, and Powell often uses a work of art as a touchstone for reflections of time. The same work of art, Bernini's *Truth Unveiled by Time,* is mentioned twice in *Casanova's Chinese Restaurant* when the same people are together, once in a seedy pub, and once at Mrs. Foxe's party for Moreland. On the first occasion Deacon refers to the figure; on the second he examines a cast of the work with Nick at a party. These contrasting scenes, separated by several years, built around the same object, characterize the whole of Powell's work. The same characters in contrasting environments, the one object eliciting totally different responses, the preoccupation with time and with values: these are constant aspects of every novel. The two methods, direct speech and the narrator's observations, mingling sadness and satire, illustrate Powell's style at its resonant best.

The importance of *A Dance to the Music of Time* increases with every new volume because of the superb balance Anthony Powell maintains in his complex literary structure. Each volume adds significance to the preceding ones and propels the reader eagerly forward to the novels which will follow. Still incomplete, the series has already established a place in the English tradition of great comic novels.

DANGEROUS ACQUAINTANCES

Type of work: Novel
Author: Pierre Choderlos de Laclos (1741-1803)
Type of plot: Psychological realism
Time of plot: Mid-eighteenth century
Locale: Paris and environs
First published: 1782

Principal characters:

CÉCILE DE VOLANGES, a young girl of good family
MADAME DE VOLANGES, her mother
THE COMTE DE GERCOURT, betrothed to Cécile
THE CHEVALIER DANCENY, Cécile's admirer
THE MARQUISE DE MERTEUIL, a fashionable matron, Gercourt's former
mistress
THE VICOMTE DE VALMONT, a libertine
MADAME DE TOURVEL, the wife of a judge
SOPHIE CARNAY, Cécile's confidante
MADAME DE ROSEMONDE, Valmont's aunt

Critique:

Dangerous Acquaintances (*Les Liaisons Dangereuses*) is the only novel of a French artillery officer turned writer. It is a slow-paced but fascinating story in which Laclos proved himself a master of the epistolary form popularized by Samuel Richardson and other novelists of the eighteenth century. The letters are so skillfully interplayed and the characterizations so scrupulously presented that the reader willingly accepts the letters as real and the characters as people rather than as tools for telling a story. The illusion is furthered by Laclos' use of frequent footnotes explaining details in the letters. On its publication the novel achieved a *succès de scandale* which has caused the book to be stigmatized as a pornographic work. In actuality, the writer employed a theme of sexual intrigue in order to dissect the decadent society of his age and to lay bare its underlying tensions and antagonisms, so that it stands in sharp contrast to contemporary erotic romances which threw an atmosphere of glamor about a subject Laclos revealed in all its starkness. Interestingly, examples of the Freudian concepts of sex appear throughout the novel.

The Story:

When Cécile de Volanges was fifteen years old, her mother removed her from a convent in preparation for the girl's marriage to the Comte de Gercourt, a match already arranged by Madame de Volanges but without her daughter's knowledge. Shortly after her departure from the convent Cécile began an exchange of letters with Sophie Carnay, her close friend. Except for trips to shops for the purchase of an elaborate wardrobe, Cécile had few contacts with her fashionable mother. The little she knew about the plans for her future she learned from her maid.

Knowing of the match, the Marquise de Merteuil, an unscrupulous woman, saw in the proposed marriage an opportunity to be revenged on Gercourt, who some time before had deserted her for a woman of greater virtue. In her wounded vanity she schemed to have the Vicomte de Valmont, a libertine as unscrupulous as she, effect a liaison between Cécile and the Chevalier Danceny. Such an affair, circulated by court gossip after Cécile and Gercourt were married, would make the husband a laughing stock of the fashionable world. To complete her plan for revenge, the marquise also wanted Valmont to seduce Madame de Tourvel, the wife of a judge. Madame de Tourvel was the woman for whom Gercourt had abandoned the Marquise de Merteuil. As a reward for carrying out these malicious designs she promised to reinstate Valmont as her own lover.

Valmont was able to arrange a meeting between Cécile and Danceny. Although she was attracted to the young man, Cécile hesitated at first to reply to his letters. Her final consent to write to him, even to speak of love, was concealed from Madame de Volanges.

Valmont, meanwhile, had turned his attention to Madame de Tourvel. A woman of virtue, she tried to reject the vicomte's suit because she was aware of his sinister reputation. In spite of her decision she nevertheless found herself attracted to him, and in time she agreed to write to him but not to see him. She stipulated also that Valmont was not to mention the subject of love or to suggest intimacy. Eventually Valmont and Madame de Tourvel became friends. Aware of her indiscretion even in friendship, she finally told Valmont that he must go away, and he accepted her decision.

In the meantime, although she wrote him letters in which she passionately declared her love, Cécile was steadfast in her refusal to see Danceny. With love Cécile had grown more mature. She still wrote to Sophie Carnay, but not as frankly as before. Instead, she turned to the Marquise de Merteuil, whom she saw as a more experienced woman, for advice. In turn the marquise, impatient with the slow progress of the affair between Cécile and Danceny, informed Madame de Volanges of the matter, with the result that the mother, in an angry interview with her daughter, demanded that Cécile forfeit Danceny's letters. The marquise' plan produced the effect she had anticipated; Cécile and Danceny declared themselves more in love than ever.

Hoping to end her daughter's attachment to Danceny, Madame de Volanges took Cécile to the country to visit Madame de Rosemonde, Valmont's ailing aunt. Valmont soon followed, on the Marquise de Merteuil's instructions, to keep alive the affair between Cécile and the young chevalier and to arrange for Danceny's secret arrival. Then Valmont, bored with rustic life, decided to take Cécile for himself. Under the pretext of making it safer for him to deliver Danceny's letters, he persuaded her to give him the key to her room. At the first opportunity that arose Valmont seduced her. At first the girl was angered and shocked by his passion, but before long she was surrendering herself to him willingly. At the same time Valmont was still continuing his attentions to Madame de Tourvel. Deciding that persistence accomplished nothing, he began to ignore her. Madame de Tourvel then wrote offering her friendship.

Cécile, deep in her affair with Valmont, wrote asking the Marquise de Merteuil's advice on how to treat Danceny. Madame de Volanges, not knowing the true situation, also wrote the marquise and said that she had considered breaking off the match with Gercourt; her daughter's happiness, she declared, was perhaps worth more than an advantageous marriage. In reply, the marquise earnestly cautioned Madame de Volanges on a mother's duty to guide a daughter and to provide for her future.

Madame de Tourvel, also a guest of Valmont's aunt, gave that gallant the opportunity to seduce her. Although tempted, he took greater pleasure in seeing her virtue humbled. After his refusal and Madame de Tourvel's own moral scruples had forced her to flee in shame, she wrote Madame de Rosemonde a letter in which she apologized for her abrupt departure and explained fully her her emotional straits. Madame de Rosemonde's reply was filled with noble sentiments and encouragement for her friend.

Valmont was surprised to find himself deflated by Madame de Tourvel's departure. His ego suffered another blow when Cécile locked him out of her room.

The marquise, more impatient than ever with Valmont's slow progress, decided to work her revenge through Danceny. Her first step was to captivate the young chevalier. An easy prey, he nevertheless continued to write impassioned letters to Cécile.

Valmont then decided to possess Madame de Tourvel. Her initial hesitation, surrender, and complete abandon he described in a triumphant letter to the Marquise de Merteuil. His account closed with the announcement that he was coming at once to claim the reward she had promised him. But the marquise managed to put off his importunate claim by reproving him about his handling of his affair with Madame de Tourvel. The difference between this and his other affairs, she said, was that he had become emotionally involved; his previous conquests had been smoothly and successfully accomplished because he had regarded them only as arrangements of convenience, not relationships of feeling. The irony of her attitude was that she was still in love with Valmont and had not counted on losing him, even for a short time. She had lost control of the strings by which she had dangled Valmont to satisfy her desire for vengeance.

Valmont, meanwhile, was trying to free himself of emotional involvements with Cécile and Danceny. Cécile had miscarried his child; Danceny's devotion no longer amused him. Although he made every effort to win the favor of the marquise, she held herself aloof, and after a quarrel she capriciously turned from him to Danceny and made that young man a slave to her charms and will.

Both Valmont and the marquise were eventually defeated in this duel of egotistic and sexual rivalry. Danceny, having learned of Valmont's dealings with Cécile, challenged the vicomte to a duel and mortally wounded him. As he was dying, Valmont gave the chevalier his entire correspondence with the marquise. Her malice exposed, she faced social ruin. After an attack of smallpox which left her disfigured for life, she fled to Holland. Madame de Tourvel, already mentally upset because of the treatment she had received from Valmont, died of grief at his death. Cécile entered a convent. Danceny gave the incriminating letters to Madame de Rosemonde and, vowing celibacy, entered the order of the Knights of Malta. Madame de Rosemonde sealed the letters which had brought disaster or death to all who had been involved with so dangerous an acquaintance as the Marquise de Merteuil.

Further Critical Evaluation of the Work:

Frequently, in the history of Western literature, certain works have been initially castigated as indecent, immoral, or blasphemous, only to be acknowledged later not only as artistic triumphs, but also as powerful moral analyses and statements. Such was the case with Choderlos de Laclos' *Dangerous Acquaintances*. Enormously popular, yet roundly condemned, the novel was seen as an openly scandalous book. The real hostility toward the book, however, may have stemmed, not from its immorality, but from Laclos' ruthless honesty in portraying the social, intellectual, and erotic climate of mid-eighteenth century French society, unmitigated by stylistic indirection or sentimental distortion.

But even today there is a chilling quality to the manner in which Valmont and Mme. de Merteuil manipulate and destroy the lives of others as players would move pieces around a chessboard. Although called an "erotic" novel, there is, in fact, little sexual passion and no emotional involvement in these intrigues. It is almost an entirely intellectual activity—which is Laclos' primary moral point. Valmont and Mme. de Merteuil represent the final product of eighteenth century rationalism; they have reasoned their feelings out of existence.

A closer look at the "game," however, suggests deeper and more complex motivations than the simple pleasures of manipulation and petty spite. Although Valmont and Mme. de Merteuil for the most part maintain a tone of light, elegant bantering between themselves, comparing notes as friendly rivals, their competition is in deadly earnest and their opponents are not the various victims, but each other. Cécile de Volanges, Chevalier Danceny, and Mme. de Tourvel are merely surrogates that Valmont and Mme. de Merteuil use to get at each other. *Dangerous Acquaintances* is, finally, one of the most brilliant, elegant, and brutal "battle-of-the-sexes" works ever written.

Valmont and Mme. de Merteuil are both products and victims of their society. They have absorbed and accepted its rationalistic basis. They have subjugated their emotional impulses to it, and they are both suppressed by its social norms and rituals. Valmont is simply a soldier without a war. Predisposed by training to military command, social position, and inclination, Valmont is bored, restless, and agitated by the stagnant, aimless, ritualized society in which he finds himself, so he uses amatory combat as a weak substitute for the real thing.

Mme. de Merteuil's situation and psychology are much more complicated. As an aristocratic woman her freedom of action is severely circumscribed. Potentially passionate, she is forced into an arranged marriage with a dull old man; brilliant and resourceful, she faces a lifetime of meaningless social activity that will stultify her capacities; free spirited and experimental, she is bound by behavioral norms and a rigid double standard that threatens to ostracize her for the slightest dereliction. Mme. de Merteuil has, however, refused to accept these limitations—or, rather, she has determined to *use* them to her own advantage. "Ought you not to have concluded," she writes Valmont, "that, since I was born to avenge my sex and to dominate yours, I must have created methods unknown to anybody but myself?" Thus, although Mme. de Merteuil impresses the modern reader as a "moral monster," one has to wonder what made her that way? Given a society in which she could develop and realize her extraordinary gifts, might she not become a constructive, "moral" person? In many ways she seems to be an earlier version of Henrik Ibsen's Hedda Gabler, whose frustrated passions and abilities also turned to viciousness and eventually to self-destruction.

In a real sense Mme. de Merteuil also destroys herself. Her suppressed passion for Valmont is too strong and her need to dominate him is too great to allow the conflict to remain permanently stalemated. For his part, Valmont, too, feels he must dominate and when he puts his ultimatum to Mme. de Merteuil—"from this day on I shall be either your lover or your enemy"— she responds in kind: *"Very well—War!"*

Thus, rationalistic erotic intrigue becomes mutual self-destruction because the suppressed emotions must burst to the surface, rational self-control giving way to vindictive impulse, and love being replaced by self-defeating hate. One can hardly call a book "corrupt" in which the transgressors are so thoroughly punished for their machinations. Indeed, to the modern reader the ending seems too easy and perhaps melodramatic. Valmont's death-bed conversion is almost sentimental and Mme. de Merteuil's smallpox seems gratuitously moralistic.

DANIEL DERONDA

Type of work: Novel
Author: George Eliot (Mary Ann Evans, 1819-1880)
Type of plot: Social realism
Time of plot: Mid-nineteenth century
Locale: Rural England, London, the Continent
First published: 1876

Principal characters:
DANIEL DERONDA
MIRAH LAPIDOTH, a girl he saves from drowning
SIR HUGO MALLINGER, Daniel's guardian
LADY MALLINGER, his wife
GWENDOLEN HARLETH, a beautiful young lady
MRS. DAVILOW, her mother
MRS. GASCOIGNE, Mrs. Davilow's sister
MR. GASCOIGNE, her husband
REX GASCOIGNE, their son
ANNA GASCOIGNE, their daughter
MALLINGER GRANDCOURT, Gwendolen's husband, Sir Hugo's heir
LUSH, his follower
HERR KLESMER, a musician
CATHERINE ARROWPOINT, his wife, an heiress
HANS MEYRICK, one of Deronda's friends
MRS. MEYRICK, his mother
EZRA COHEN, a shopkeeper in the East End
MORDECAI, a boarder with the Cohens, Mirah's brother
MRS. LYDIA GLASHER, Grandcourt's former mistress

Critique:

Daniel Deronda shifts from a novel depicting the difficulties and romances of a group of people in English society to a treatment of anti-Semitism in Victorian England. The character Daniel Deronda, the ward of Sir Hugo Mallinger, provides a bridge between the two portions of the book. With all its heavy evidence against the evil of anti-Semitism, the novel does not become an essay, for throughout the work George Eliot maintains sharp observation of the follies and delusions of Victorian life, as well as a keen sense of moral discrimination between her characters. Like *Middlemarch*, this novel is distinguished by realistic appraisals of people in all levels of society from the august and benevolent Sir Hugo Mallinger to Ezra Cohen, the crafty yet generous shopkeeper in the East End. If the novel does not show the consistency of theme or careful construction of George Eliot at her best, it still propagandizes skillfully for worthy causes and creates a vivid, clear, and varied scheme of life.

The Story:

Gwendolen Harleth, a strikingly beautiful young woman, was gambling at Leubronn. Playing with a cold, emotionless style, she had been winning consistently. Her attention was suddenly caught by the stare of a dark, handsome gentleman whom she did not know and who seemed to be reproving her. When her luck changed, and she lost all her money, she returned to her room to find a letter from her mother requesting her immediate return to England. Before she left, Gwendolen decided that she would have one more fling at the gaming tables. She sold her turquoise necklace for the money to play roulette, but before she could get to the tables the necklace was repurchased and returned to her with an anonymous note. Certain that the unknown man was her benefactor, she felt that she could not very well return to the roulette

1304

table. She went back to England as soon as she could. Her mother had recalled her because the family had lost all their money through unwise business speculations.

Gwendolen a high-spirited, willful, accomplished, and intelligent girl, was Mrs. Davilow's only child by her first marriage, and her favorite. By her second marriage —Mr. Davilow was also dead—she had four colorless, spiritless daughters. About a year before, she had moved to Offendene to be near her sister and brother-in-law, the prosperous, socially acceptable Gascoignes and to see what she could do about arranging a profitable marriage for her oldest daughter. Gwendolen's beauty and manner had impressed all the surrounding gentry, but her first victim was her cousin, affable Rex Gascoigne. Although he had been willing to give up his career at Oxford for Gwendolen, his family refused to countenance so unwise a move. Rex, broken in spirit, was sent away temporarily, but Gwendolen remained unmoved by the whole affair.

Soon afterward the county became excited over the visit of Mallinger Grandcourt, the somewhat aloof, unmarried heir to Diplow and several other large properties owned by Sir Hugo Mallinger. All the young ladies were eager to get Grandcourt to notice them, but it was Gwendolen, apparently indifferent and coy in conversation with the well-mannered but monosyllabic Grandcourt, who had most success. For several weeks, Grandcourt courted Gwendolen, yet neither forced to any crisis the issue of possible marriage. Gwendolen's mother, uncle, and aunt urged her to try to capture Grandcourt. Just when it seemed that Grandcourt would propose and Gwendolen would accept, Mrs. Lydia Glasher appeared, brought to the scene by the scheming of Grandcourt's companion, Lush, to tell Gwendolen that she was the mother of four of Grandcourt's illegitimate children and that she had left her husband to live with Grandcourt. She begged Gwendolen not to accept Grandcourt so that she might have the chance to secure him as

the rightful father of her children. Gwendolen, promising not to stand in Mrs. Glasher's way, had gone immediately to join friends at Leubronn.

Before he came to Leubronn, Daniel Deronda, the man whom Gwendolen had encountered in the gambling casino, had been Sir Hugo Mallinger's ward. He did not know his parents, but Sir Hugo had always treated him well. Sir Hugo, who had married late in life, had only daughters. Although he lavished a great deal of expense and affection on Deronda, his property was to go to his nephew, Mallinger Grandcourt. At Cambridge, Deronda had been extremely popular. There, too, he had earned the undying gratitude of a poor student named Hans Meyrick, whom Deronda helped to win a scholarship at the expense of his own studies. One day, after leaving Cambridge, while in a boat on the river, Deronda saved a pale and frightened young woman, Mirah Lapidoth, from committing suicide. She told him that she was a Jewess, returned after years of wandering with a brutal and blasphemous father, to look for her lost and fondly remembered mother and brother in London. Deronda took her to Mrs. Meyrick's home. There Mrs. Meyrick and her daughters nursed the penniless Mirah back to health.

When Gwendolen returned to Offendene, she learned that her family would be forced to move to a small cottage and that she would have to become a governess. The idea oppressed her so strongly that when she saw Grandcourt, who had been pursuing her on the Continent, she agreed at once to marry him, in spite of her promise to Mrs. Glasher. Her mother, aunt, and uncle knew nothing of Mrs. Glasher; Grandcourt knew only that she had spoken to Gwendolen, knowledge that he kept to himself.

After their marriage, Grandcourt soon turned out to be a mean, domineering, demanding man. He had set out to break Gwendolen's spirit, and he did. In the meantime, at several house parties, Gwendolen had met Daniel Deronda and found herself much attracted to him. At a New

Year's party at Sir Hugo Mallinger's, Gwendolen, despite her husband's disapproval and biting reprisals, had spoken to Deronda frequently. When she told Deronda her whole story and confessed her guilt in breaking her promise to Mrs. Glasher, Deronda suggested that she show her repentance by living a less selfish life, caring for and helping others less fortunate than she. Gwendolen, realizing the folly of her marriage to Grandcourt, and wishing to find some measure of happiness and peace, decided to follow the course Deronda had proposed.

Meanwhile, Deronda was attempting to secure Mirah's future and, if possible, to find her family. Mirah had been an actress and had some talent for singing. Deronda arranged an interview for her with Herr Klesmer, a German-Jewish musician with many connections, who could get Mirah started on a career. Herr Klesmer was very much impressed with Mirah's singing. He had known Gwendolen at Offendene and, in his honesty, had refused to help her when she also asked for singing engagements; he had thought her without sufficient talent and had

given her ego its first blow. Herr Klesmer had also married Miss Arrowpoint, the most talented and attractive girl, save Gwendolen, in the vicinity of Offendene.

Still trying to find Mirah's family, Deronda went wandering in the London East End. There he became friendly with the family of Ezra Cohen, a shopkeeper of craft and generosity. For a time, on the basis of some slight evidence, Deronda believed that the man might be Mirah's brother. There also, through Ezra's family, he met Mordecai, a feeble and learned man who immediately felt a great kinship with Deronda. Mordecai took Deronda to a meeting of his club, a group of men who discussed scholarly, political, and theological topics far removed from the commercial interests of Ezra.

Deronda was delighted when he finally learned that Mordecai was really Mirah's brother. This discovery helped Deronda himself to acknowledge and accept his own spiritual and literal kinship with the Jews. The boy of unknown origin, able to move successfully in the high society of England, had found his real home in London's East End.

Further Critical Evaluation of the Work:

Daniel Deronda, George Eliot's last novel, is not her greatest, but it is still a powerful and in some ways inspired work. It is as fascinating in its defects as in its successess, since both reflect not only the author's established strengths as a novelist, but her inventiveness and willingness to explore new areas and strive for greater depth and breadth in her fiction. Thus *Daniel Deronda* shares with its predecessors a penetrating insight into human relationships, a sensitive portrayal of individual moral and emotional growth, an astute and critical analysis of Victorian values, and a unifying moral vision of life. At the same time, many of the novel's shortcomings result from Eliot's ambitious experimentation with new methods, issues, and emphases; *Daniel Deronda* contains several new departures. A love story like the earlier works, this novel presents a love story with entirely new angles: Gwendolen marries for power, only to be later attracted to a man (Daniel) whose loyalties are divided between her and another woman; the sexual aspect of love relationships is explored with uncommon openness; certain feelings and emotions are treated which were almost universally ignored by Eliot's contemporaries; and the typical happy ending is denied the heroine, who instead grows in emotional and moral maturity as a result of her sufferings.

The two major weaknesses in the novel lie in the presentation of the Jewish problem and in the characterization of Daniel Deronda. Eliot tends to paint too consistently glowing a picture of the Jewish characters. Mirah's father, Lapidoth, whose portrayal is splendid, is the exception, but in general, Mirah, Mordecai, Daniel and the others suffer from idealization and from their language, which is often sentimental, stylized, or over-simplified. The author's almost uniform approval of the Jewish characters is further accentuated by contrast to her portrayal of the English figures, who are without exception (although to varying degrees) treated critically or satirically. The Wessex gentry are exposed for their shallowness, hypocrisy, and greed; Grandcourt represents a particular type of English gentleman in his cruelty, oppressiveness, contemptuous superiority, and narrow-mindedness; and the numerous minor characters serve as indictments of such Victorian faults as snobbishness, dullness, pretentiousness, and complacency. The second quite noticeable flaw in the novel is in the delineation of Daniel's character. Eliot endowed him with all the qualities requisite to make an interesting and complex personality —his excessive altruism, his ambivalence toward lower-class Jews, his jealousy of Hans Meyrick—and yet he comes across as a static, somewhat wooden, and rather unengaging figure; his actions are all predictable, his personality transparent. The main reason for this problem is Eliot's failure to develop Daniel's complexity, as she does all the other characters, through varied and shifting point of view.

In spite of its weaknesses, however, *Daniel Deronda* exhibits Eliot's novelistic genius in numerous ways. The portrayal of Gwendolen Harleth is splendid; Eliot's masterful use of flashback and retrospection in the first half is highly effective; and the novel's conclusion is of rare force and realism. If Eliot's performance in *Daniel Deronda* falls short of her demanding and ambitious intent, the "experiment in life" that she has left us is nevertheless a great work of literature.

DANTE

Type of work: Critical essay
Author: T. S. Eliot (1888-1965)
First published: 1929

In his poetry T. S. Eliot experimented with a number of techniques, one of the best known of these being the persistent use of direct and indirect allusions to other poets and poetry. These allusions are from an impressively wide range of sources, but one of the most important sources is the poetry of Dante.

The epigraph of Eliot's first volume of poetry, *Prufrock and Other Observations,* is from the *Purgatorio,* while the epigraph to the poem, "The Love Song of J. Alfred Prufrock," is from the *Inferno.* There are a number of allusions to these sections of *The Divine Comedy* in *The Waste Land,* and Eliot himself identifies them in his "Notes on 'The Waste Land.'" One of the central images of "The Hollow Men" is the "Multifoliate rose," which had been for Dante a symbol of Paradise, and which for Eliot represents the only hope of the hollow man. There are allusions to Dante's poetry scattered throughout Eliot's work. In "Little Gidding," the final section of Eliot's last great work of poetry, *Four Quartets,* the long concluding passage of Section II is, as Eliot himself said, intended to be as close an equivalent as possible to a canto of the *Inferno* or the *Purgatorio.*

The point need hardly be stressed: there is value in this study of Dante, not only for the student of Dante, but for the student of Eliot as well. In the preface to *Dante,* Eliot writes that this work is an account of his own acquaintance with the Italian poet's writings. Eliot himself acknowledges that the acquaintance has been, for him, a fruitful one because he had found no other poet to whom he could refer so frequently and for so many purposes in his own work. His essay is in no way, he emphasizes, to be considered as a definitive statement on Dante; he did not regard himself as a scholar. Instead, his intention is to deal with Dante's im-portance as a master poet and as a figure of interest to anyone concerned with modern poetry.

The first point Eliot makes about Dante is that he is, even for non-Italians, surprisingly easy to read because of his universality, even in the modern languages. But that is not to say that he is the greatest poet, or the poet who has dealt with more that is common to all men. Dante's universality, in the sense that Eliot is using the term, is a result of his particular time and place, and of the language and poetic traditions afforded him by that time and place.

The Italian language of Dante's day was the product of the universal language, Latin. Medieval Latin was universal in that in it men of various lands and languages found a common means of communication. And in the Italian vernacular that Dante used such universality is also evident. Other languages are more localized: the associations of words belong more to a particular culture or race. But Dante's culture is not so much Italian as it is European, and his language is equally universal (meaning European). The language of Shakespeare was more localized; he had no way to express himself other than in a local fashion.

Europe, in Dante's time, was intellectually more closely joined than we realize, and its unity was not simply a matter of a universal language. Dante's method and thought were commonly known and generally understood throughout Europe because of the common culture of medieval times. That method, that poetic tradition, was allegory, and allegory makes for simplicity and lucidity of style.

Because allegory, as Dante used it in *The Divine Comedy,* is in itself one great metaphor, Dante employed few metaphorical images within the work itself: his effort was chiefly to make us see.

What few metaphors he employs, therefore, enable us to visualize a given scene; they are explanatory and intensive. Shakespeare's metaphors, by way of contrast, are expansive and even decorative; they add to what we see rather than making us see more clearly.

So far Eliot bases his statements on his understanding of the *Inferno,* and the point he draws from his reading of that work is that great poetry may be written with strict economy of words, figures of speech, and elegance of style. The point he wishes to make about the *Purgatorio* is that great poetry can also be made from direct philosophical statement.

The *Purgatorio* is, says Eliot, the most difficult of the three parts of *The Divine Comedy,* and there are several reasons for this. Not only is it true that damnation is more dramatic than purgation; it is also true that the allegory in the *Inferno* is more visual, more rooted in the concrete, than is that of the *Purgatorio.* The *Inferno* can be enjoyed by itself; the *Purgatorio* cannot. It can only be fully understood and appreciated as a part of the whole work.

The greatest difficulty with the *Purgatorio,* for the modern mind, is accepting the terms of Dante's philosophical and theological beliefs. But we must accept them if we are to understand and accept the whole of Dante's vision. We can no more ignore the philosophy and theology than we can the allegory. But Eliot distinguishes between philosophical *belief* and poetic *assent,* and it is the latter that we need. He says that what is needed in appreciation of the *Purgatorio* is not belief, but willing suspension of belief. One must enter, in effect, the world of thirteenth century religious faith, and we cannot enter that world, we cannot appreciate the poem, unless we accept as *given* the philosophy and theology which are essential to it—literally, of its essence.

The point Eliot wishes to make about the *Paradiso* is that the state of beatitude, though rarefied, can also be the substance for great poetry. Our age finds it difficult to appreciate the *Paradiso* because of the prevailing prejudice against beatitude as material for poetry. For Dante, the difficulty in treating this sort of subject matter was the necessity of allowing us to apprehend it sensuously. That, from Eliot's point of view, Dante succeeded in overcoming this difficulty is obvious. The secret of Dante's power and success lies in his ability to express the almost inapprehensible in concrete, visual images.

In this study Eliot continually measures Dante's stature as poet against the usual standard, Shakespeare. His comparison of the two poets results in the conclusion that Shakespeare shows breadth in the variety of human life and passion he presents, but that Dante achieves greater depths and heights of degradation and exaltation. *The Divine Comedy* gives us the complete range of human emotion.

The last section of *Dante* is on the *Vita Nuova,* which Eliot describes as a series of poems connected by a "vision-literature" prose. This youthful work is important to Eliot chiefly because it aids in an understanding of *The Divine Comedy.* Paradoxically, however, it is *The Divine Comedy* that we should read first because it introduces us to the world of medieval imagery, thought, and dogma. The *Vita Nuova,* on the other hand, introduces us to the medieval sensibility. It is constructed of materials which are generally acknowledged to be based, in some degree, on Dante's own experience, but these materials are transformed by being placed in a larger perspective than the merely personal one. On reflection, the attraction of the poet toward Beatrice is seen as a manifestation of something greater; the attraction toward God. From an understanding of Dante's method in the *Vita Nuova* we can come to a clearer understanding of Dante's method, on a far greater scale, in *The Divine Comedy.*

DAPHNIS AND CHLOË

Type of work: Tale
Author: Attributed to Longus (third century)
Type of plot: Pastoral romance
Time of plot: Indefinite
Locale: Island of Lesbos
First transcribed: Third century manuscript

Principal characters:
  DAPHNIS, a young shepherd
  CHLOË, a shepherdess

Critique:

A product of decadent Greek literature, *Daphnis and Chloë* is one of the most popular of the early predecessors of the modern novel. Highly romantic in both characterization and incident, it centers about the innocent though passionate love of two children of natrue amid idyllic scenes of natural beauty. We forgive the many extravagant improbabilities of the story because of the charming portrayal of the refreshing, often amusing, naïveté of two children unspoiled by contact with city manners.

The Story:

On the Greek island of Lesbos a goatherd named Lamo one day found a richly dressed infant boy being suckled by one of his goats. Lamo and his wife, Myrtale, hid the purple cloak and ivory dagger the boy had worn and pretended he was their own son. They named him Daphnis. Two years later a shepherd named Dryas discovered in a cave of the Nymphs an infant girl being nursed by one of his sheep. This child also was richly dressed. Dryas and his wife Nape kept the girl as their own, giving her the name Chloë.

When the two children were fifteen and thirteen respectively, they were given flocks to tend. Daphnis and Chloë played happily together, amusing themselves in many ways. One day, while chasing a goat, Daphnis fell into a wolf-pit, from which he was rescued unharmed by Chloë and a herdsman she had summoned to help her. Daphnis began to experience delightful but disturbing feelings about Chloë. Dorco, a herdsman,

asked permission to marry Chloë but was refused by Dryas. Disguising himself in a wolfskin, Dorco shortly afterward attempted to seize Chloë. Attacked by the flock dogs, he was rescued by Daphnis and Chloë, who innocently thought he had merely been playing a prank. Love, little understood by either, grew between Daphnis and Chloë.

In the autumn some Tyrian pirates wounded Dorco, stole some of his oxen and cows, and took Daphnis away with them. Chloë, who heard Daphnis calling to her from the pirate ship, ran to aid the mortally wounded Dorco. Dorco gave her his herdsman's pipe, telling her to blow upon it. When she blew, the cattle jumped into the sea and overturned the ship. The pirates drowned, but Daphnis, catching on to the horns of two swimming cows, came safely to shore.

After the celebration of the autumn vintage Daphnis and Chloë returned to their flocks. They attempted in their innocence to practice the art of love, but they were not successful. Some young men of Methymne came to the fields of Mitylene to hunt. When a goat gnawed in two a withe used as a cable to hold their small ship, the Methymneans blamed Daphnis and set upon him. In a trial over the affair Daphnis was judged innocent. The angry Methymneans later carried away Chloë. The god Pan warned the Methymnean captain in a dream that he should bring back Chloë, and she was returned. Daphnis and Chloë joyfully celebrated holidays in honor of Pan.

The two lovers were sad at being

parted by winter weather, which kept the flocks in their folds. In the spring the lovers happily drove their flocks again to the fields. When a woman named Lycaenium became enamored of the boy, Daphnis finally learned how to ease the pains he had felt for Chloë; but Lycaenium warned him that Chloë would be hurt the first time she experienced the ecstasy of love. Through fear of doing physical harm to his sweetheart the tender Daphnis would not deflower his Chloë. Meanwhile many suitors, Lampis among them, asked for the hand of Chloë, and Dryas came near consenting. Daphnis bewailed his inability to compete successfully with the suitors because of his poverty. Then with the aid of the Nymphs he found a purse of silver, which he gave Dryas in order to become contracted to Chloë. In return Dryas asked Lamo to consent to the marriage of his son, but Lamo answered that first he must consult his master, Dionysophanes.

Lamo, Daphnis, and Chloë prepared to entertain Dionysophanes; but Lampis ravaged the garden they had prepared because he had been denied Chloë's hand. Fearing the wrath of his master, Lamo lamented his ill fortune. Eudromus, a page, helped to explain the trouble to Lamo's young master Astylus, who promised to intercede with his father and blame the wanton destruction on some horses in the neighborhood. Astylus' parasite, Gnatho, fell in love with Daphnis but was repulsed. Finally the depraved Gnatho received Astylus' permission to take Daphnis with him to the city. Just in time Lamo revealed the story of the finding of Daphnis, who was discovered to be Dionysophanes' son. Meanwhile Lampis stole Chloë, who was later rescued by Gnatho. After Dryas told how Chloë had been found as a child, it was learned that she was the daughter of Megacles of Mitylene. Thus the supposed son and daughter of Lamo and Dryas were revealed as the children of wealthy parents who were happy to consent to their marriage. The wedding was celebrated amid the rural scenes dear to both bride and groom. Daphnis became Philopoemen and Chloë was named Agéle. On her wedding night Chloë at last learned from Daphnis how might be obtained the delights of love.

Further Critical Evaluation of the Work:

The romance is the least "classical" of ancient literary genres. The name itself derives many centuries later, since the ancients apparently did not know what to call this prose that was not history, this adventure that was not epic, this love story that was neither tragedy nor comedy, this pastoral that was not bound by the verse forms of Theocritus and Vergil. Romance finds its origins perhaps in late Hellenistic times, having developed from erotic and exotic approaches to literature in Euripides, Menander, and Apollonius Rhodius, but it did not reach full bloom until the age of the Second Sophistic in the second century A.D., when rhetoricians encouraged their students to create improbable human situations rife with problems on which they might conduct debate.

Daphnis and Chloë is such an improbable theme, but the resolution of its incredible complications amid such faraway un-Roman places casts a unique charm deepened by the idealized devotion of the young lovers. The story provides an escape to a primeval state for a reader jaded by the violence and sophistication of the Roman Empire. Daphnis and Chloë personify innocent, ignorant love. They are taught by hard experience and the cruel selfishness of the real, urbane world, but they manage to survive and return to their idyllic, simple remove.

An intelligible structure is canonical in classical composition, and appropriately this work is divided into four "books" which define movements from spring to autumn, to winter and a second spring and summer, and finally to a second autumn. The blooming love of Daphnis and Chloë must be tested by the seasons, both of nature and of human life, before the matured lovers can reap the harvest. Longus uses the imagery of Philetas' and Lamon's gardens to convey the natural morality of the children's love shaped and cultivated by experience. So, too, he entrusts them to the care of Pan and Dionysus, gods of natural sexuality, and to Eros, god of irresistible love. This is further enforced by the motif of milk and wine, symbolizing innocence and passion.

THE DARK JOURNEY

Type of work: Novel
Author: Julian Green (1900-   )
Type of plot: Psychological realism
Time of plot: Early twentieth century
Locale: France
First published: 1929

Principal characters:
PAUL GUÉRET, a neurotic tutor
ANGÈLE, a young laundress
MADAME LONDE, a restaurant proprietress
MONSIEUR GROSGEORGE, Guéret's employer
MADAME GROSGEORGE, his wife
FERNANDE, a young girl

Critique:

Like all of Julian Green's work, *The Dark Journey* is a bleak and somber book, impressive both in its realistic evocation of French provincial life and in its metaphysical overtones of human destiny. Shadows of disaster and doom brood over his pages; his characters, as in the case of Paul Guéret and Madame Grosgeorge, have premonitions of their fates, but they are powerless to help themselves. This novel, published in France under the title *Léviathan*, deals with the twin themes of violence and lust. Nothing is trivial, however, and little is vulgar. Instead, with impersonal detachment and classic gravity of style, the writer tells a story of disturbing but compelling vigor, in which violence and melodrama are only incidental to his vastly greater effects of cumulative passion and tragic finality.

The Story:

Paul Guéret was an incompetent, prematurely-aged tutor hired to instruct the sickly, backward son of a prosperous provincial family named Grosgeorge. Knowing himself a failure and tired of the wife whom he no longer loved, he had hoped that life would be better in Chanteilles; but within a month he was just as wretched there as he had been in Paris, where his feelings of self-pity and frustration had often driven him into sordid love affairs. In Chanteilles, bored by his dreary surroundings, he soon found himself infatuated with Angèle, a young girl who worked in a laundry. Hoping to become her lover, he began to write letters asking her to meet him. Sometimes he followed her at a distance when she delivered washing to her customers.

One night he accosted her at a footbridge on the outskirts of the town. Hating himself for his shabby clothes and stammering speech, he offered her a cheap ring stolen from his wife. Although she accepted the ring, the girl did not encourage his attentions. His abrupt yet furtive ardor both attracted and repelled her.

That same night Guéret went by chance to the Restaurant Londe in nearby Lorges. There Madame Londe, the proprietress, presided majestically behind her cashier's desk. A sly woman whose days were given over to spying and gossip, she delighted in alternately cajoling and bullying her patrons, who seemed to hold her resentfully in awe. When Guéret entered, she was disturbed because he was a stranger and she knew nothing about him. Refusing to let him pay for his dinner, she had him write his name in her account book. Her desire was to add him to her regular clientele.

Madame Londe's hold over her patrons was a sinister one, maintained through her niece, Angèle. Because the girl was in-

THE DARK JOURNEY by Julian Green. By permission of the publishers, Harper & Brothers. Copyright, 1929, by Harper & Brothers.

debted to her for food and a room, she forced Angèle to sell her favors to the habitués of the restaurant. With knowledge thus gained of the guilt and secret vices of her patrons, she was able to dictate to them as she pleased. Her own position as a procuress gave her no worry; her only concern was her lust for power over others.

Upset by his desire for Angèle, Guéret paid little attention to his duties as a tutor. André Grosgeorge was a poor student, but his mother shrewdly blamed Guéret for her son's slow progress. Madame Grosgeorge was a woman in whom the starved passions of her girlhood had turned to a tortured kind of love which found its outlet in cruelty and treachery. Because the husband whom she despised ignored her nagging tirades, she took special pleasure in beating her son and in humiliating Guéret.

Monsieur Grosgeorge felt sorry for the browbeaten tutor. Having guessed that Guéret was unhappily married, he bluntly advised him to find a mistress before he wasted his years in moping dullness. That, said Grosgeorge, was the course he himself had followed. One day he boastingly produced a note in which the writer asked Grosgeorge to meet her the next night. Guéret, staring at the letter, shook with suppressed rage. He recognized the scrawl as Angèle's handwriting.

Angèle, after several meetings with Guéret, became more independent in her attitude toward Madame Londe. Because his conduct was quite different from that of other men who sought her favors, she no longer wished to sell herself in order to act as her aunt's informant. During a quarrel Angèle, who refused to keep an assignation the old woman had arranged, threatened to run away. Madame Londe was worried. Afraid that she would lose her hold over her patrons, she began to train Fernande, a twelve-year-old girl, to take Angèle's place.

Guéret returned to the Restaurant Londe. During the meal he learned from the talk of the other diners that Angèle was Madame Londe's niece and that she

had given herself to most of the men there. That night, driven to desperation by his knowledge, he broke into her bedroom. It was empty. When Madame Londe, aroused by his entry, screamed for help, he ran away and hid in a wood. On his way back to Chanteilles he met Angèle. In sudden, brutal fury he picked up a branch and struck at her until blood covered her face and head.

All that day he skulked beside the river. While he was sneaking back into town after dark, he met a feeble old man. Fearing capture, he seized the old man's stick and beat him to death. Filled with blind terror, he fled across the yards of unknown houses and through back streets of the town.

The neighborhood was shocked by the brutality of Guéret's crime, and for weeks the townspeople refused to venture into the streets at night. Angèle, disfigured for life, refused to give the name of her assailant and remained shut up in her room above the restaurant. Only Madame Grosgeorge scoffed at those who bolted their doors at dusk. Indeed, she seemed to relish the fact that the shabby, blundering tutor had scarred the face of her husband's mistress and violently disrupted the monotony of her own existence.

At last the hue and cry died down. Guéret, unable to stay away from Angèle, returned to the district. Madame Grosgeorge, out walking, saw him near the footbridge and called after him that she would meet him there the next evening. Guéret did not appear, although she waited impatiently for more than an hour. Later he came to her villa, and she, unknown to her husband, hid the fugitive in her private sitting-room. She promised that she would give him money and some of her husband's clothing before she sent him away in the morning.

But his presence in the house gave her such strange satisfaction that she refused to let him go as she had promised. The next morning she went to her sitting-room and tried to talk to him about his crimes. When his answers showed only that he was still in love with Angèle, Madame Grosgeorge felt cheated. She had admired him for his violence; now she despised him for his foolish passion. Again she locked him in the room while she tried to decide what to do. Little Fernande came to deliver some laundry. On impulse Madame Grosgeorge wrote a note telling Angèle that Guéret was in her house and asking that the police be called.

Madame Londe, always on the alert, intercepted the message and hurried to give the alarm. Angèle, learning what had happened, sent Fernande to warn the fugitive that he must escape at once.

Madame Grosgeorge, meanwhile, had returned to Guéret. When he insisted that she let him go, she locked the door and threw the key out of the window. Then she told him that Angèle knew his whereabouts and that if he were betrayed the laundress would be to blame. Taking a revolver from her desk, she put it in her belt and calmly prepared to write a letter. Fernande ran into the garden. Guéret, leaning out of the window, asked her to pick up the key and unlock the door. A report sounded behind him. Madame Grosgeorge had shot herself.

Further Critical Evaluation of the Work:

The reader might be repelled by the content of this novel, but he cannot help being drawn into its strange dark world. The stark and intense style, the depth and sureness of the author's insight, and the inevitability of the narrative all unite to give *The Dark Journey* a unique beauty. One is reminded of the trapped, tormented souls in Hawthorne's New England and Sherwood Anderson's Midwest. Although Julian Green has a rare sense of detail, the detail does not impede his action. There is at all times a fine harmony of character and action with the background. The picture of the damned is so powerfully drawn that even the prosaic landscape seems transformed into a dream Inferno.

A bland self-centeredness seems to dominate the individuals in the story. Madame Londe is a frustrated petty tyrant, incapable of being happy, although she relishes obtaining power over other people—especially men. A deep and fundamental anger drives her to irrational acts. Desperately, she wants *to be in control*; so do all of the characters, but none of them are or can be. Paul Guéret is defined by his relations with the women in his life: his boring wife; Madame Londe, who wants only to dominate him; Madame Grosgeorge who would love him, but settles for domination; and Angèle, whom he desires so much that he destroys her. Together, these women destroy him. Only the sixty-year-old M. Grosgeorge is at all satisfied with his life; he exudes a vitality which the other characters lack. He is not profound, and his advice to Guéret can only cause the tutor more misery. Guéret's desperate craving for happiness opposes his wife's stolid acceptance of a life without joy. Life appears to Angèle as a kind of lottery, good or bad according to one's luck, but irrevocable. Green deliberately draws in the limitations of his characters, as a more romantic author might sketch in the qualities which make his characters exceptional.

The irony of the girl's name, Angèle, heightens the sense of a game master toying with these desperate lives in the drab provincial village. Angèle comes to believe that life does not give one a second chance. One should grasp what one can with eager hands. Later, she realizes that fate's treachery is prepared long in advance and only bears the appearance of chance because its workings are invisible. The message of the book is bleak, but the artistry is extraordinary and the impact strong. The image of the murderer unable to retrace his footsteps, condemned to go forward carrying the plague of his crimes, into new avenues of nightmare, is haunting and profound.

DARK LAUGHTER

Type of work: Novel
Author: Sherwood Anderson (1876-1941)
Type of plot: Psychological realism
Time of plot: 1920's
Locale: Old Harbor, Indiana
First published: 1925

Principal characters:
BRUCE DUDLEY, formerly John Stockton, a Chicago reporter
SPONGE MARTIN, a workman close to the grass roots
FRED GREY, owner of an automobile wheel factory
ALINE, his wife

Critique:

Dark Laughter, Sherwood Anderson's most popular novel, is a book of moods rather than of plot. Its simple story is that of two individuals in revolt against the restrictions of modern life and seeking happiness together. Anderson seems to say that Bruce Dudley and Aline Grey were unhappy because they were repressed; they gave themselves over to the secret desires within them and therefore they became happy. One may question whether Bruce and Aline were not merely restless and somewhat adolescent emotionally, rather than strong and brave in their attempt to live by amoral standards.

The Story:

Bruce Dudley's name was not Bruce Dudley at all. It was John Stockton. But he had grown tired of being John Stockton, reporter on a Chicago paper, married to Bernice who worked on the same paper and who wrote magazine stories on the side. She thought him flighty and he admitted it. He wanted adventure. He wanted to go down the Mississippi as Huckleberry Finn had done. He wanted to go back to Old Harbor, the river town in Indiana where he had spent his childhood. And so, with less than three hundred dollars, he left Chicago, Bernice, and his job on the paper. He picked up the name Bruce Dudley from two store signs in an Illinois town. After his trip to New Orleans he went to Old Harbor and got a job varnishing automobile wheels in the Grey Wheel Company.

Sponge Martin worked in the same room with Bruce. Sponge, a wiry old fellow with a black mustache, lived a simple, elemental life. That was the reason, perhaps, why Bruce liked him so much. Sometimes when the nights were fair and the fish were biting, Sponge and his wife took sandwiches and some moonshine whiskey and went down to the river. They fished for a while and got drunk, and then Sponge's wife made him feel like a young man again. Bruce wished he could be as happy and carefree as Sponge.

When Bruce was making his way down the Mississippi and when he stayed for five months in an old house in New Orleans—that was before he came to Old Harbor—he watched the Negroes and listened to their songs and laughter. It seemed to him that they lived as simply as children and were happy, laughing their dark laughter.

Aline, the wife of Fred Grey, who owned the Grey Wheel Company, saw Bruce Dudley walking out the factory door one evening as she sat in her car waiting for Fred. Who he was she did not know, but she remembered another man to whom she had felt attracted in the same way. It happened in Paris after the war. She had seen the man at Rose Frank's apartment and she had wanted him. Then she had married Fred, who was recovering from the shock of the war. He was not what she wished for, but, somehow, she had married him.

One evening Bruce Dudley passed by the Grey home as Aline stood in the yard. He stopped and looked first at the house and then at Aline. Neither spoke but something passed between them. They had found each other.

Aline, who had advertised for a gardener, hired Bruce after turning down several applicants. Bruce had quit his job at the factory shortly before he saw her advertisement. When Bruce began to work for her, the two maintained some reserve, but each was determined to have the other. Bruce and Aline carried on many imaginary conversations. Fred apparently resented Bruce's presence about the grounds, but he said nothing to the man. When he questioned his wife, he learned that she knew nothing of Bruce except that he was a good worker.

As Aline watched her husband leave for the factory each morning she wondered how much he knew. She thought a great deal about her own life and about life in general. Her husband was no lover. Few women nowadays had true lovers. Modern civilization told one what he could not have. One belittled what he could not possess. Because one did not have love, one made fun of it, was skeptical of it, and besmirched it. The little play of the two men and the woman went on silently. Two Negro women who worked in Aline's house watched the proceedings. From time to time they laughed, and their dark laughter seemed mocking. White folks were queer. They made life so involved. Negroes took what they wanted—simply, openly, happily.

One day in June, after Fred had gone to march in a veterans' parade and the Negro servants had gone to watch the parade, Aline and Bruce were left alone. She sat and watched him working in the garden. Finally he looked at her, and he followed her into the house through a door she purposely left open. Before Fred returned, Bruce had left the house. He disappeared from Old Harbor. Two months later Aline told Fred she was going to have a child.

As Fred came home one evening in the early fall, he saw his wife and Bruce together in the garden. Aline calmly called to him and announced that the child she was expecting was not his. She and Bruce had waited, she went on, so that she might let him know they were leaving. Fred pleaded with her to stay, knowing she was hurting herself, but they walked away, Bruce carrying two heavy bags.

Fred told himself, as he stood with his revolver in his hand a few minutes later, that he could not dispassionately let another man walk away with his wife. His mind was filled with confused anger. For a moment he thought of killing himself. Then he followed the pair along the river road. He was determined to kill Bruce. But he lost them in the darkness. In a blind fury he shot at the river. On the way back to his house he stopped to sit on a log. The revolver fell to the ground and he sat crying like a child for a long time.

After Fred had returned to his home and gone to bed, he tried to laugh at what had happened. He could not. But outside in the road he heard a sudden burst of laughter. It was the younger of the two Negresses who worked in the Grey home. She cried out loudly that she had known it all the time, and again there came a burst of laughter—dark laughter.

Further Critical Evaluation of the Work:

Dark Laughter is an interesting, serious novel that emerged from the aftermath of World War I. Anderson's novel reflects the literary and stylistic devices pioneered in the era following that war.

World War I meant, for writers, artists, and thinkers, the end of intellectual, scientific, political, moral, and psychological certainties. Before the outbreak of war, intellectuals considered Western culture the finest flowering, the highest expression of human civilization. But the outbreak of the war, and its barbarism, and the duration and intensity of its savagery, unprecedented in human history, shattered that belief. Scientific discoveries shook hitherto unquestioned assumptions about the Newtonian universe. Marx's theories and the Russian Revolution undermined confidence in social classes and political systems. Freud, by elaborating a theory of an active unconscious, and an unconscious life, destroyed the idea that man was a given, known quantity.

All these developments form the context for "literary modernism," a movement in literature in which accepted patterns of characterization, sequence, and symbols were altered radically. It is in this context that Anderson's *Dark Laughter* can be understood best. *Dark Laughter* is a novel that tries both to formulate a criticism of the old values (made disreputable by the war), and at the same time to set forth new values by which men can live.

Given this disillusionment *and* hope, it is appropriate that Anderson establishes two dramatic poles in the novel: one embodies a natural, honest, sincere relationship to life; the other (embodying the old, prewar values) represents an artificial, mechanical, and dishonest approach.

Fred Grey and Bernice Stockton are characters leading superficial and distant lives. Grey, who imagines himself sensitive, cultured, and generous is actually a morally coarse, suspicious, and tight-fisted factory owner. He is, above all, separated from the realities of life by his economic position and his inner sterility.

Bernice Stockton, the wife that Bruce Dudley fled, is a variation of the same type. Her "specialty" is literature, but from hints of the story she is writing—a precious, unreal thing—her characters and plot only reflect her own superficial romanticism, not the actual conditions of life. She is a member of an "in group" of writers and intellectuals, and Anderson indicates that this membership is more important to her than infusing her art with truth.

Standing in opposition to these characters are Bruce Dudley, Sponge Martin and, to an extent, Aline Grey. For Anderson, these people represent the new, hopeful values which have come to life after the trauma of war. Sponge Martin (and his wife), for example, have a genuine connection to real life. Their sexual life is natural and unaffected; they have few pretensions; they are generous and simple. Dudley himself, the central character in the novel, is a writer more interested in the truth than in "word slinging." Leaving Bernice was a rejection of her literary pretensions. Falling in love with Aline, and fathering her child, meant answering the deeper, underlying currents in life.

For Aline, who vacillated between these poles, the marriage to Grey represented a confused surrender to the conventional life. Running away with

Dudley meant coming to terms with life as it is—not as it exists in the decadent literary circles of postwar France, in the romantic fantasies of her adolescence, or in the expected routines of upper middle class life in the United States.

It is also clear that, just as Anderson is criticizing an outworn and mechanical value system, he is also criticizing an earlier literary tradition. Does literature come to terms with the natural, primitive side of life? Does it seek out the unconscious and explore it? Does it portray the uncertainties and difficulties of life? If the answer to these questions is yes, then Anderson approves; but if literary tradition only discusses the superficial and agreeable aspects of life, then Anderson heartily disapproves. Thus, as literature, Anderson hopes *Dark Laughter* both supports and represents a new literary tradition that corresponds to the new postwar values.

Anderson himself said the literary quality of *Dark Laughter* was influenced by James Joyce, and it is true that Anderson uses a number of modernist techniques: sections of narrative broken into fragments; parts of poems scattered through the text; subjective, semi-stream-of-consciousness narration; switches in point of view. But Anderson does not have Joyce's verbal facility, depth of allusion, grammatical mastery, or density of detail.

The techniques of *Dark Laughter* probably reflect the more general literary climate of the 1920's rather than Joyce's specific influence. In a period of intellectual uncertainty, when old beliefs were brought into question, prose style itself assumed a fragmented, subjective, and somewhat disjointed character.

At the same time, *Dark Laughter* also displays certain negative features of the American literary climate of the 1920's. One of these negative qualities, perhaps the most visible, is the racist aspect of many of Anderson's passages. For example, the title of the novel, *Dark Laughter,* refers to the natural, honest pole that Anderson supports. But associated with this naturalness is the "primitive," "uncivilized," and "amoral" qualities that Anderson links to black people. In fact, *Dark Laughter* refers to the laughter of black maids in the Grey household when they learn of Aline's adultery.

Such prejudices, commonplace in the era in which *Dark Laughter* was written, need not overshadow the major intent of the book. *Dark Laughter* expresses an important opposition of ideas in modernist literary terms; the reader is asked to choose between real life and superficial life; and, in that sense, Anderson has presented the reader with a profound moral choice.

Howard Lee Hertz

DARKNESS AT NOON

Type of work: Novel
Author: Arthur Koestler (1905-   )
Type of plot: Social criticism
Time of plot: 1930's
Locale: Russia
First published: 1941

                    Principal characters:
                NICHOLAS RUBASHOV, a political prisoner
                IVANOV, a prison official
                GLETKIN, another official
                MICHAEL BOGROV, another prisoner
                KIEFFER (HARE-LIP), an informer

Critique:

This remarkable modern novel by Arthur Koestler is a highly analytical piece of writing which transports the reader into a Russian prison and into the very consciousness of a political prisoner, accused of crimes he never committed. *Darkness at Noon* represents an ironic and scathing criticism of the Moscow trials. At the same time, it presents a careful analysis of the Soviet principles. Reference to Russia is made only in the foreword, however, and the party leader is known only as No. 1 in this powerful but highly restrained social document.

The Story:

Nicholas Rubashov, ex-Commissar of the People and once a power in the party, was in prison. Arrested at his lodgings in the middle of the night, he had been taken secretly to cell 404, which bore his name on a card just above the spy-hole. He knew that he was located in an isolation cell for condemned political suspects.

At seven o'clock in the morning Rubashov was awakened by a bugle, but he did not get up. Soon he heard sounds in the corridor. He imagined that someone was to be tortured, and he dreaded hearing the first screams of pain from the victim. When the footsteps reached his own section, he saw through the judas-eye that guards were serving breakfast. Rubashov did not receive any breakfast because he had reported himself ill. He began to pace up and down the cell, six and a half steps to the window, six and a half steps back.

Soon he heard a quiet knocking from the wall of adjoining cell 402. In communicating with each other prisoners used the "quadratic alphabet," a square of twenty-five letters, five horizontal rows of five letters each. The first series of taps represented the number of the row; the second series the number of the letter in the row. From the tappings Rubashov pictured his neighbor as a military man, one not in sympathy with the methods of the great leader or with the views of Rubashov himself. From his window he saw prisoners walking in the courtyard for exercise. One of these, a man with a hare-lip, looked repeatedly up at Rubashov's window. From his neighbor in cell 402, Rubashov learned that Hare-lip was a political prisoner who had been tortured by a steam bath the day before. A little later Hare-lip, in cell 400, sent Rubashov his greetings, through the inmate of 402, but he would not give his name.

Three days later Rubashov was brought up for his first examination. The examiner was Ivanov, Rubashov's old college friend and former battalion commander. During the interview the prisoner learned that he was accused of belonging to the opposition to the party and that he was suspected of an attempt on the party leader's life. Ivanov promised a twenty-year prison term instead of the death penalty if Rubashov confessed. The prisoner was given a fortnight to arrive at a decision.

After the hearing Rubashov was allowed to have paper, pencil, soap, towels, and tobacco. He started writing in his journal and recasting his ideas about the party and the movement. He recalled a young man named Richard arrested in Germany while Rubashov was at the head of the party Intelligence and Control Department. He could not forget an incident which had happened in Belgium two years later. There Rubashov had been tortured and beaten. In Belgium he expelled from the party a hunchbacked, eager worker who later hanged himself in his room. Rubashov also thought constantly of Arlova who had been his mistress and who had met her death because of him.

The night before the time set by Ivanov had expired, Rubashov felt a tenseness in the atmosphere. His friend in 402 communicated to him that one of the prisoners was to be shot. This prisoner was Michael Bogrov, who had always been Rubashov's close friend. As the condemned man was brought through the corridors, the prisoners tapped his progress from one cell to another and drummed on the doors of their cells as he passed. The beaten, whimpering figure of Bograv came by Rubashov's cell. Rubashov believed that his friend shouted to him as he was dragged down the stairs.

Rubashov's second hearing took place late at night. Ivanov came to Rubashov's cell with a bottle of brandy and convinced him that to keep faith with the living was better than betrayal of the dead. Accordingly, Rubashov wrote a letter to the Public Prosecutor renouncing his own oppositional attitude and acknowledging his errors. The third night after delivering the letter to the warder, Rubashov was awakened and taken to the office of Gletkin, another official of the prison. Under blinding lights in Gletkin's office, he was questioned day and night for an interminable period of time. Ivanov, he learned, had been liquidated for conducting Rubashov's case negligently. Gletkin called in Hare-lip as a witness against Rubashov. It was only with great difficulty that Rubashov recognized in that broken, cringing man the son of his former friend and associate, Keiffer. The bright spotlight, the lack of sleep, the constant questionings—these factors combined to make Rubashov sign a trumped-up charge that he had plotted to take the life of the party leader.

Rubashov had committed none of these crimes. He was merely the victim of a change in party policy. One night he heard the sound of drumming along the corridor. The guards were taking Hare-lip to be executed. When the drumming started again, Rubashov knew that his time had come. He was led into the cellar. An officer struck him twice on the head with a revolver. Another party incident was closed.

Further Critical Evaluation of the Work:

Based on Koestler's own experience as a European Communist and his imprisonment in France and Spain, *Darkness at Noon* signaled his rejection of his political beliefs. Yet the novel is more profitably examined as an analysis of the totalitarian mentality that permitted such dictators as Hitler, Stalin, and Franco to control the whole of Europe at the time of the novel's publication. Koestler reveals with profound and cogent insight that the totalitarian mind, such as he dramatizes in Rubashov, is not to be understood as a manifestation of Machiavellian ethics. That is old style politics and hardly explains such historical incidents as the Moscow trials or the imprisonment of a party leader like Rubashov.

Rubashov's arrest, trial, and execution, like Ivanov's or Kieffer's, does not make good political sense seen from a pragmatic point of view. Since they are all good party men, it would seem that No. 1 would be undermining his own position by liquidating them. But No. 1 is not really interested in solidifying his political power in a conventional way, but rather in creating a mystique, more nearly a religion, which cannot be tested on rational or logical grounds. His *realpolitik,* his agents seem to suggest, is an irrational mystery that even his most faithful adherents can betray unconsciously.

A forerunner of George Orwell's Winston Smith in *Nineteen Eighty-Four,* Rubashov goes to his death actually believing he has betrayed No. 1 and yet never really understanding the nature of his treachery. With only a glimpse of the truth, he dies a good and faithful servant. As Koestler points out, such a death is only possible because Rubashov, like his comrades, agreed from the beginning to permit No. 1 to establish all truth. Having given up the freedom of their own minds, they are mere automatons in the irrational scheme of the State.

DAVID COPPERFIELD

Type of work: Novel
Author: Charles Dickens (1812-1870)
Type of plot: Sentimental romance
Time of plot: Early nineteenth century
Locale: England
First published: 1849-1850

Principal characters:
DAVID COPPERFIELD, the narrator
CLARA COPPERFIELD, his mother
MISS BETSEY TROTWOOD, David's great-aunt
CLARA PEGGOTTY, a nurse
MR. DANIEL PEGGOTTY, her brother
LITTLE EM'LY, his orphan niece
HAM, his orphan nephew
MR. MURDSTONE, David's stepfather
MISS JANE MURDSTONE, his sister
MR. CREAKLE, master of Salem House
JAMES STEERFORTH, David's schoolmate
TOMMY TRADDLES, a student at Salem House
MR. WILKINS MICAWBER, a man of pecuniary difficulties
MR. WICKFIELD, Miss Trotwood's solicitor
AGNES WICKFIELD, his daughter
URIAH HEEP, a clerk
MR. SPENLOW, under whom David studied law
DORA SPENLOW, his daughter, later David's wife
MR. DICK, Miss Betsey's protégé

Critique:

One of the many qualities that distinguish *David Copperfield* from more modern and more sophisticated novels is its eternal freshness. It is, in short, a work of art which can be read and re-read, chiefly for the gallery of characters Dickens has immortalized. The novel has its flaws. These faults seem insignificant, however, when the virtues of the novel as a whole are considered. The first-person point of view adds much to realistic effects and sympathetic treatment of character and helps to explain, in part, why *David Copperfield* is the most loved piece of fiction in the English language.

The Story:

David Copperfield was born at Blunderstone, in Suffolk, six months after his father's death. Miss Betsey Trotwood, an eccentric great-aunt was present on the night of his birth, but she left the house abruptly and indignantly when she learned that the child was a boy who could never bear her name. David spent his early years with his pretty young mother, Clara Copperfield, and a devoted servant named Peggotty. Peggotty was plain and plump; when she bustled about the house her buttons popped off her dress.

The youthful widow was soon courted by Mr. Murdstone, who proved, after marriage, to be stingy and cruel. When his mother married a second time, David was packed off with Peggotty to visit her relatives at Yarmouth. There her brother had converted an old boat into a seaside cottage, where he lived with his niece, Little Em'ly, and his sturdy young nephew, Ham. Little Em'ly and Ham were David's first real playmates, and his visit to Yarmouth remained a happy memory of his lonely and unhappy childhood. After Miss Jane Murdstone arrived to take charge of her brother's household, David and his mother were never to feel free again from the dark atmosphere of suspicion and gloom the Murdstones brought with them.

One day in a fit of childish terror David bit his stepfather on the hand. He was immediately sent off to Salem

House, a wretched school near London. There his life was more miserable than ever under a brutal headmaster named Creakle. But in spite of the harsh system of the school and the bullyings of Mr. Creakle, his life was endurable because of his friendship with two boys whom he was to meet again under much different circumstances in later life— lovable Tommy Traddles and handsome, lordly James Steerforth.

His school days ended suddenly with the death of his mother and her infant child. When he returned home, he discovered that Mr. Murdstone had dismissed Peggotty. Barkis, the stage driver, whose courtship had been meager but earnest, had taken Peggotty away to become Mrs. Barkis and David was left friendless in the home of his cruel stepfather.

David was put to work in an export warehouse in which Murdstone had an interest. As a ten-year-old worker in the dilapidated establishment of Murdstone and Grinby, wine merchants, David was overworked and half-starved. He loathed his job and associates such as young Mick Walker and Mealy Potatoes. The youngster, however, met still another person with whom he was to associate in later life. That was Wilkins Micawber, a pompous ne'er-do-well in whose house David lodged. The impecunious Mr. Micawber found himself in debtor's prison shortly afterward. On his release he decided to move with his brood to Plymouth. Having lost these good friends, David decided to run away from the environment he detested.

When David decided to leave Murdstone and Grinby, he knew he could not return to his stepfather. The only other relative he could think of was his father's aunt, Miss Betsey Trotwood, who had flounced indignantly out of the house on the night of David's birth. Hopefully he set out for Dover, where Miss Betsey lived, but not before he had been robbed of all his possessions. Consequently, he arrived at Miss Betsey's home physically and mentally wretched.

David's reception was at first not cordial. Miss Betsey had never forgotten the injustice done her when David was born instead of a girl. However, upon the advice of Mr. Dick, a feeble-minded distant kinsman who was staying with her, she decided to take David in, at least until he had been washed thoroughly. While she was deliberating further about what to do with her bedraggled nephew, she wrote to Mr. Murdstone, who came with his sister to Dover to claim his stepson. Miss Betsey decided she disliked both Murdstones intensely. Mr. Dick solved her problem by suggesting that she keep David.

Much to David's joy and satisfaction, Miss Betsey planned to let the boy continue his education, and almost immediately sent him to a school in Canterbury, run by a Mr. Strong, a headmaster quite different from Mr. Creakle. During his stay at school David lodged with Miss Betsey's lawyer, Mr. Wickfield, who had a daughter, Agnes. David became very fond of her. At Wickfield's he also met Uriah Heep, Mr. Wickfield's cringing clerk, whose hypocritical humility and clammy handclasp filled David with disgust.

David finished school when he was seventeen. Miss Betsey suggested he travel for a time before deciding on a profession. On his way to visit his old nurse, Peggotty, David met James Steerforth and went home with his former schoolmate. There he met Steerforth's mother and Rosa Dartle, a girl passionately in love with Steerforth. Years before, the quick-tempered Steerforth had struck Rosa, who carried a scar as a reminder of Steerforth's brutality.

After a brief visit, David persuaded Steerforth to go with him to see Peggotty and her family. At Yarmouth, Steerforth met Little Em'ly. In spite of the fact that she was engaged to Ham, she and Steerforth were immediately attracted to each other.

At length David told his aunt he wished to study law. Accordingly, he was articled to the law firm of Spenlow and Jorkins. At this time David saw Agnes Wickfield, who told him she feared Steerforth and asked David to stay away from him. Agnes also expressed a fear of Uriah Heep, who was on the point of entering into partnership with her senile father. Shortly after these revelations, by Agnes, David encountered Uriah himself, who confessed he wanted to marry Agnes. David was properly disgusted.

On a visit to the Spenlow home, David met Dora Spenlow, his employer's pretty but childish daughter, with whom he fell instantly in love. Soon they became secretly engaged. Before this happy event, however, David heard some startling news—Steerforth had run away with Little Em'ly.

Nor was this elopement the only blow to David's happiness. Shortly after his engagement to Dora, David learned from his aunt that she had lost all her money, and from Agnes that Uriah Heep had become Mr. Wickfield's partner. David tried unsuccessfully to be released from his contract with Spenlow and Jorkins. Determined to show his aunt he could repay her, even in a small way, for her past sacrifices, he took a part-time job as secretary to Mr. Strong, his former headmaster.

But the job with Mr. Strong paid very little; therefore David undertook to study for a position as a reporter of parliamentary debates. Even poor simple Mr. Dick came to Miss Betsy's rescue, for Traddles, now a lawyer, gave him a job as a clerk.

The sudden death of Mr. Spenlow dissolved the partnership of Spenlow and Jorkins, and David learned to his dismay that his former employer had died almost penniless. With much study on his part, David became a reporter. At twenty-one he married Dora, who, however, never seemed capable of growing up. During these events, David had kept in touch with Mr. Micawber, now Uriah Heep's confidential secretary. Though something had finally turned up for Mr. Micawber, his relations with David, and

even with his own family, were mysteriously strange, as though he were hiding something.

David soon learned what the trouble was, for Mr. Micawber's conscience got the better of him. At a meeting arranged by him at Mr. Wickfield's, he revealed in Uriah's presence and to an assembled company, including Agnes, Miss Betsy, David, and Traddles, the criminal perfidy of Uriah Heep, who for years had robbed and cheated Mr. Wickfield. Miss Betsey discovered that Uriah was also responsible for her own financial losses. With the exposure of the villainous Uriah, partial restitution both for her and for Mr. Wickfield was not long in coming.

His conscience cleared by his exposure of Uriah Heep's villainy, Mr. Micawber proposed to take his family to Australia. There, he was sure something would again turn up. To Australia, too, went Mr. Peggotty and Little Em'ly; she had turned to her uncle in sorrow and shame after Steerforth had deserted her. David watched as their ship put out to sea. It seemed to him the sunset was a bright promise for them as they sailed away to a new life in the new land. The darkness fell about him as he watched.

The great cloud now in David's life was his wife's delicate health. Day after day she failed, and in spite of his tenderest care he was forced to see her grow more feeble and wan. Agnes Wickfield, like the true friend she had always been, was with him on the night of Dora's death. As in his earlier troubles, he turned to Agnes in the days that followed and found comfort in her sympathy and understanding.

Upon her advice he decided to go abroad for a while. But first he went to Yarmouth to put into Ham's hands a last letter from Little Em'ly. There he witnessed the final act of her betrayal. During a storm the heavy seas battered a ship in distress off the coast. Ham went to his death in a stout-hearted attempt to rescue a survivor clinging to a broken mast. The bodies washed ashore by the rolling waves were those of loyal Ham and the false Steerforth.

David lived in Europe for three years. On his return he discovered again his need for Agnes Wickfield's quiet friendship. One day Miss Betsey Trotwood slyly suggested that Agnes might soon be married. Heavy in heart, David went off to offer her his good wishes. When she burst into tears, he realized that what he had hoped was true—her heart was already his. They were married, to matchmaking Miss Betsey's great delight, and David settled down to begin his career as a successful novelist.

Further Critical Evaluation of the Work:

"But, like many fond parents, I have in my heart of hearts a favorite child. And his name is David Copperfield."

This is Charles Dickens' final, affectionate judgment of the work which stands exactly in the middle of his novelistic career, with seven novels before and seven after (excluding the unfinished *The Mystery of Edwin Drood*). When he began the novel, he was in his mid-thirties, secure in continuing success that had begun with *Sketches by Boz* (1836), and *Pickwick Papers* (1836-1837). It was a good time to take stock of his life, to make use of the autobiographical manuscript he had put by earlier. Nor did he try to conceal the personal element from his public, which eagerly awaited each of the nineteen numbers of *David Copperfield*. The novel was issued serially from May, 1849, through November, 1850. Charles Dickens, writer, is readily identified with David Copperfield, writer, viewing his life through the "long Copperfieldian perspective," as Dickens called it.

Although much in the life of the first-person narrator corresponds to Dickens' own life, details are significantly altered. Unlike David, Dickens was not a genteel orphan but the eldest son of living and improvident parents; his own father served as the model for Micawber. Dickens' childhood stint in a shoeblacking factory seems to have been somewhat shorter than David's drudgery in the warehouse of Murdstone and Grinby, wine distributors, but the shame and suffering were identical. Young Charles Dickens failed in his romance with a pretty young girl, but the author Dickens permits David to win his Dora. However, Dickens inflicts upon Dora as Mrs. Copperfield the faults of his own Kate, who, unlike Dora, lived on as his wife until their separation in 1858.

However fascinating the autobiographical details, *David Copperfield* stands primarily on its merits as a novel endowed with the bustling life of Dickens' earlier works but controlled by his maturing sense of design. The novel in its entirety answers affirmatively the question posed by David himself in the opening sentence: "Whether I shall turn out to be the hero of my own life. . . . "

In addition to the compelling characterization of the protagonist, the novel abounds with memorable portrayals. The square face and black beard of Mr. Murdstone, always viewed in conjunction with that "metallic lady" Miss Murdstone, evoke the horror of dehumanized humanity. Uriah Heep's writhing body, clammy skin, and peculiarly lidless eyes suggest a subhuman form more terrifying than the revolting nature of his "umbleness." Above all the figures that crowd the lonely world of the orphan rises the bald head of Wilkins Micawber, flourishing the English language and his quizzing glass with equal impressiveness, confidently prepared in case some opportunity turns up.

Nevertheless, David Copperfield is very definitely the hero of his own story. This is a novel of initiation, organized around the two major cycles of the hero's development, first in childhood, then in early manhood. It focuses steadily upon the testing which will qualify him for full manhood. He makes his own choices, but each important stage of his moral progress is marked by the intervention of Aunt Betsey Trotwood.

To begin with, David is weak simply because he is a child, the hapless victim of adult exploitation. But he is also heir to the moral weakness of his childish mother and his dead father, who was an inept, impractical man. David's birth is, portentously, the occasion of a conflict between his mother's Copperfieldian softness and Aunt Betsey's firmness, displayed in her rigidity of figure and countenance.

From a state of childish freedom, David falls into the Murdstone world. The clanking chains of Miss Murdstone's steel purse symbolize the metaphorical prison which replaces his innocently happy home. Indeed, for David, the world becomes a prison. After his five days of solitary confinement at Blunderstone, he enters the jail-like Salem House School. After his mother's death, he is placed in the grim warehouse, apparently for life. Nor is his involvement with the Micawbers any real escape, for he is burdened with their problems and retains his place in the family even after their incarceration in the King's Bench Prison.

Although David repudiates the tyrannical firmness of which he is a victim, he does not actively rebel, except for the one occasion when he bites Mr. Murdstone. Instead, like his mother, he indulges his weakness; he submits, fearfully to the Murdstones and Creakle, worshipfully to the arrogant Steerforth. In addition, he escapes into the illusory freedom of fantasy—through books and stories and through the lives of others, which he invests with an enchantment that conceals from him whatever is potentially tragic or sordid.

Nevertheless, David's pliant nature shares something of the resolute spirit of Aunt Betsey, despite her disappearance on the night of his birth. Looking back upon his wretched boyhood, David recalls that he kept his own counsel, and did his work. From having suffered in secret, he moves to the decision to escape by his own act. The heroic flight is rewarded when Aunt Betsey relents and takes him in. Appropriately, she trusses up the small boy in adult clothes and announces her own goal of making him a "fine fellow, with a will of your own," with a "strength of character that is not to be influenced, except on good reason, by anybody, or by anything." The first cycle of testing is complete.

The conventionally happy years in Dover and Canterbury mark an interlude before the second major cycle of the novel, which commences with David's reentry into the world as a young man. Significantly, he at first resumes the docile patterns of childhood. Reunited with Steerforth, he once again takes pride in his friend's overbearing attitude. He allows himself to be bullied by various inferiors. He evades the obligation to choose his own career by entering into a profession which affects him like an opiate. In Dora's childlike charms he recaptures the girlish image of his mother. However, at this point, the firm Aunt Betsey, having cut short his childhood trials, deliberately sets into motion his adult testing with her apparent bankruptcy.

In response to his new challenges, David is forced back upon his childhood resources. At first, he unconsciously imitates Murdstone in trying to mold Dora; but he again rejects tyranny, choosing instead resignation, understanding that she can be no more than his "child-wife." He responds with full sympathy to the tragedy of Little Em'ly's affair with Steerforth, but he is finally disenchanted with the splendid willfulness which had captivated his boyish heart. Most important, he recovers the saving virtue of his childhood, his ability to suffer in secrecy, to keep his own counsel, and to do his work. As his trials pile up—poverty, overwork, disappointment in marriage, his wife's death, and the tribulations of the friends to whom his tender heart is wholly committed—he conquers his own undisciplined heart.

The mature man who emerges from his trials profits from his experiences and heritage. His capacity for secret suffering is, for him as for Aunt Betsey, a source of strength; but his, unlike hers, is joined to the tenderheartedness inherited from his parents. Her distrust of mankind has made her an eccentric. His trusting disposition, though rendering him vulnerable, binds him to mankind.

Although Aunt Betsey sets a goal of maturity before David, Agnes Wickfield is the symbol of the hard-won self-discipline which he finally achieves. She is from the beginning his "better angel." Like him, she is tenderhearted and compliant. Yet, though a passive character, she is not submissive; and she is always in control of herself in even the most difficult human relationships. Moreover, her firmness of character is never distorted by fundamental distrust of mankind. Thus hers is the only influence which David should accept, "on good reason," in his pursuit of the moral goal which Aunt Betsey sets before him.

By the time David has recognized his love for Agnes, he has also attained a strength of character like hers. The appropriate conclusion to his quest for maturity is his union with Agnes—who is from the beginning a model of the self-disciplined person in whom gentleness and strength are perfectly balanced. Furthermore, the home he builds with her is the proper journey's end for the orphaned child who has grasped at many versions of father, mother, family, and home: "Long miles of road then opened out before my mind, and toiling on, I saw a ragged way-worn boy forsaken and neglected, who should come to call even the heart now beating against him, his own." He has outgrown the child-mother, the child-wife, the childhood idols, even the childhood terrors, and he is a mature man ready to accept love "founded on a rock."

In the context of a successful completed quest, the novel ends with a glimpse of the complete man, who writes far into the night to erase the shadows of his past, but whose control of the realities is sufficient in the presence of the woman who is always, symbolically, "near me, pointing upward!"

Catherine E. Moore

DAVID HARUM

Type of work: Novel
Author: Edward Noyes Westcott (1846-1898)
Type of plot: Regional romance
Time of plot: Late nineteenth century
Locale: Upstate New York
First published: 1898

Principal characters:
DAVID HARUM, a banker and horse trader
JOHN LENOX, Harum's assistant
MARY BLAKE, John's sweetheart
POLLY BIXBEE, Harum's widowed sister

Critique:

Westcott, who himself had been a banker in upper New York State, wrote *David Harum* to give the country at large a picture of his region and its people. The greatness of the book lies in the characterization of David Harum, that original and delightfully humorous horse trader who has fascinated two generations of readers. Harum was a dry, quaint, semi-literate countryman with a shrewd knowledge of human nature. Unfortunately, the horse-trading banker does not dominate the story completely. The novel is threaded together by a love story involving Harum's banking assistant and a young heiress. The best chapters, by far, are those in which David Harum tells stories in dialect, swaps horses, or indulges in reminiscences of other days.

The Story:

John Lenox was the son of a well-to-do businessman in New York. After college he lived for several years in Europe at his father's expense. He was twenty-six years old when he returned to America, without having done anything which fitted him to earn a living.

John returned to find that his father's business was failing rapidly and that he would soon have to make a living for himself. His father found a place for him with a New York law firm, but reading law proved uncongenial. When his father died, John left the firm. Then, through an old friend of his father's,

John became assistant to the owner of a small bank in Homeville, New York.

David Harum, the owner of the bank, was a crusty old man who enjoyed his reputation as a skinflint. What most of the townspeople did not know was that he was quite a philanthropist in his own way, but preferred to cover up his charity and good deeds with gruff words. Harum's one vice was horse trading. His sister, who kept house for him, firmly believed that he would rather trade horses than eat or sleep. Moreover, he usually came out ahead in any swapping deal.

David Harum was well pleased with the appearance of his new assistant, John Lenox. And when John took hold of his duties better than any other clerk in the bank had ever done, David Harum began to think seriously of looking after the young man's future. Harum felt that John should have an opportunity to better himself, but he wanted first to be certain that he was not mistaken in judging the young man's character. He set out to discover what he wanted to know in a peculiar way. He let John live uncomfortably in a broken-down hotel for several months to ascertain his fortitude. He also gave John several chances to be dishonest by practices which a sharp trader like Harum might be expected to approve. John's straightforward dealings won Harum's respect and approval. He casually gave John five ten-dollar gold pieces and asked him to move into a room in Harum's own large house with him and his sister, Polly.

John had begun to discover that Harum was not the selfish and crusty old man he appeared. He knew that Harum had called in a widow whose mortgage was overdue and had torn up the paper because the woman's husband had at one time taken Harum to the circus when the banker was a little boy without a cent to his name. Even Harum's horse trading was different when one came to know him. As John Lenox discovered, Harum only let people cheat themselves. If someone professed to know all about horses, Harum used the trade to teach him a lesson, but if a tyro professed his ignorance of the animals Harum was sure to give him a fair exchange. He was a living example of the proverb which propounds shrewdly that it is impossible to cheat an honest man, and the corollary, that it is almost impossible not to cheat a dishonest one.

John Lenox's life in Homeville was restricted, and he was thrown much on his own resources. He secured a piano for himself and played in the evenings or read from a small collection of books which he had saved from his father's library. His only real friends were David Harum and Harum's sister, Polly, both old enough to be John's parents. He spent many pleasant hours in Harum's company. They would often take Harum's horses out for a drive, during which the loquacious banker would regale the young man with stories of horse trading, of the foibles of the people in the community, or of Harum's early life when he had run away from home to work along the Erie Canal. On one of these rides Harum learned that John was in love with an heiress he had met in Europe. John felt that he could not ask her to marry him until he had proved himself a success.

Soon afterward Harum gave John an opportunity to make a large amount of money. Harum had a tip on a corner in pork on the Chicago market. Harum and John bought several thousand barrels of pork and sold them at a considerable profit. This deal was the first step Harum took to make John financially independent.

John's second year in Homeville was more eventful. By that time he had been accepted as a member of the community and had made friends both in the town and among the wealthy people who came to Homeville during the summer months. Meanwhile Harum revealed to his sister his plan to retire from active work in the bank and to make John his partner. He also revealed to her that John had a tract of land in Pennsylvania which everyone had considered worthless, but which was likely to produce oil. Harum, in his younger days, had spent some time in the Pennsylvania oil fields, and like most small-town bankers of the time, he knew something about a great many financial activities. What he did not reveal to his sister was that he also planned to leave his estate to John, for, excepting Polly, he had no relatives.

By the end of his third year in Harum's bank, John had made enough money through market operations to make himself independent, and he could have left the bank and the town for New York City if he had cared to do so. When the banker broached the subject to him, John admitted that two years before the prospect of returning to the city would have been welcome. Now he had come to like Homeville and had no desire to leave the home of David Harum and his sister. That was exactly what Harum wanted to hear. He told John that he was to become a partner in the bank. Harum also told him that a company wanted to lease his Pennsylvania land for the purpose of drilling for oil.

Then John fell ill, and his doctor sent him on a Mediterranean cruise. While aboard ship, John met Mary Blake, the young heiress with whom he had fallen in love several years before. At first John thought, because of an error in the ship's passenger list, that Mary Blake was already married. One moonlight night, on a mountain overlooking the bay at Naples, Mary informed John of his mistake and promised to marry him, and a few days later Harum was overjoyed to receive a cable announcing John's marriage. Harum wired back the good news that drilling had begun on the property in Pennsylvania.

When John and Mary Lenox returned to the United States several months later, they settled in Homeville and John took over the bank. Then David Harum was free to spend the rest of his days driving about the countryside and swapping horses.

Further Critical Evaluation of the Work:

David Harum grew directly from Westcott's experiences both with the people and the customs of upstate New York, and with a type of small-town American banker. *David Harum* is so convincingly rooted in northeastern rural America that it stands as a good example of American "local color" fiction, fiction that developed and flourished in the United States during the last half of the nineteenth century. Although local color as a literary movement contains diverse and often contradictory elements, the main energies of its writers were devoted to sketching regional geography, customs, and dialects; it developed partly as a counter to the "American novel," or attempts to capture the whole "American" experience in one work.

What is especially interesting in *David Harum* is Harum himself. Westcott has succeeded in uncovering, with generous detail, the moral and psychological forces, and the central impulses as well as the crotchets, of a small town banker in upstate New York. Harum's incessant horse trading, his Yankee sense, and above all his pragmatism form the central interest of the novel. On the one hand, Harum looks out for himself and so embodies that shrewd, self-interested outlook so characteristic of his type; on the other hand, Westcott has been careful to modify this selfishness with Harum's quiet charity and rough-hewn sense of economic justice. Thus David Harum stands as both a regional type and as an example of a certain economic morality. He is a banker, but he is also a good man.

The weakness in the novel is the plot concerning Lenox and his sweetheart. This plot, which takes the story too far from its central interest, both geographically and morally, seems both sentimental and contrived. Actually, the difficulty Westcott experienced in sustaining a purely regional narrative, as well as his sentimentality, are weaknesses common among the local colorists.

DE PROFUNDIS

Type of work: An apologia in the form of a letter
Author: Oscar Wilde (1856-1900)
First published: 1905, 1908

The eighty-page manuscript of this letter rests in the British Museum. It was written in Reading Gaol on prison paper during the last months, from January to March, of Wilde's two-year sentence for "unnatural practices." It was addressed to Lord Alfred Douglas, but when Wilde was not allowed to send it from prison he handed it to his friend Robert Ross the day after he was released on May 19, 1897, with instructions to type a copy and send the original to Lord Alfred, who always claimed he never received it. Part of the work was first published under Ross's title, *De Profundis,* in 1905, and again in 1908. A typescript was given by Ross to Vyvyn Holland, Wilde's younger son, who published it in 1949. Rupert Hart-Davis has shown in *The Letters of Oscar Wilde* that this first complete edition contained hundreds of errors, and he has now published the manuscript after it was released by the British Museum from the fifty-year restriction Ross placed on it when he deposited the manuscript in 1909. As a letter it becomes the center of the definitive edition of Wilde's letters; in the shorter form edited by Ross it is both an *apologia pro vita sua* and a literary essay. Nevertheless, in its entirety it has a unity and a unique value as Wilde's testament to his life as an artist which should encourage its publication for the first time as an independent work of art under the title which is customarily given it.

Since it is cast in the form of an epistle, the work needs for full understanding some contextual reference to Wilde's life and works before and after his imprisonment and the composition of the letter. The prison sentence marked the end of his marriage, his income, and his life in England; thereafter he lived in exile as Sebastian Melmoth. One link with the past, however, was not broken,

the association with Lord Alfred Douglas. Wilde's return to the young man, the cause of his imprisonment, divorce, and bankruptcy, and to the kind of associates whose evidence had convicted him, seems to invalidate the promise to lead a new life with which *De Profundis* closes. Wilde claimed, however, that on the one hand the conditions of exile, disgrace, and penury drove him to those acquaintances, and on the other they were the creations of his art and not the conditions of his life. Wilde's one conviction was that he was an artist and he doggedly transposed the terms of life and art. His term for the new life was the *Vita Nuova* of Dante; similarly *The Portrait of Dorian Gray* was to be the parable of his life and more true to life (because more artistic) than his biography. The strain of maintaining this paradox ended his life three years after his release and finished his writing career shortly after the composition of *De Profundis.* The resolution of the paradox is the intention of the long letter.

This epistle is therefore connected both with Wilde's biography (in which sense it is autobiography) and with his literary canon. In the letter he suggests that his sentence and fate are "prefigured" in works like *The Portrait of Dorian Gray;* the immediate artistic fruits of the "new life" are the two letters to the *Morning Chronicle* and *The Ballad of Reading Gaol,* his only writing after *De Profundis;* parts of the last amount to a prose poem somewhere between the prose of the two letters and poetry of the ballad, Wilde's longest and most effective poem. The two letters are included in Ross's 1908 edition and show plainly the real conditions under which *De Profundis* was written; Wilde sums them up as constant hunger, diarrhea from the rotten food, and insomnia from the diarrhea and the plank bed in his cell. His description of prison life is vivid and awful; out of his experience, immediately after his release, he showed courage in writing letters to defend a discharged warder and to plead for decent treatment of child prisoners. Perhaps he could have played a prominent role in prison reform had not exile intervened; yet it is difficult to see Wilde in that role unless he really meant what he said in *De Profundis*. As it was, events showed that this epistle belonged to the realm of art and not to life.

Wilde's request to have the letter copied by Ross showed that he thought of it as art, his "letter to the world"; the covering letter to Ross described his three intentions: he would explain, not defend, his past; describe his spiritual and mental crisis in prison; and outline his future plans. The aptness of Ross's title from Psalm 130 is obvious, but the work is not so much the salvation of a lost soul as Wilde's artistic equivalent, the groping toward an artistic resolution of a paradox: the pursuit of beauty leads to the ugliness of Reading Gaol. The past is disposed of mostly in the longer first half of the letter, in reproaches to Lord Alfred Douglas which were at least half merited but relevant only if Wilde recognized Lord Alfred as the alter ego of that past and not of the future. This failure to interpret his past life as a work of art indicates the failure of the remaining portion of the letter, printed in Ross's edition of 1908.

This general section of *De Profundis* is in two related parts. The first states Wilde's reliance on the paradox that art is life, life art; his problem is to see the art in his present situation, which he sums up in the word "sorrow." If he really feels sorrow, then sorrow must be artistic or of artistic value; he decides that his art (that is, life) lacked the dimension of shadow (that is, sorrow), and his present sorrow must have been intended for the purpose of improving his art. If Wilde can transpose his prison sentence into an aspect of art, then his paradox holds good. We have evidence in the letters of his friends that he did just this

soon after his release, when he wittily described Reading Gaol as an enchanted castle, complete with ogres, dungeons, and devices of torture.

The second part of this section then plays with an artistic creation or symbol of sorrow: The Man of Sorrows, by which Wilde intended himself, Christ, and all men to the limited extent that he could be interested in anyone but himself. He pursues the Christian analogy daringly (even blasphemously) to argue not that he is Christ but that Christ (like Wilde) was the supreme artist of life: He had the imagination to feel the sufferings of a leper without being that leper, while at the same time He preserved His individuality. Similarly, His sympathetic imagination and artistry compelled Him to turn Himself into an artistic symbol of the truth about life: The Man of Sorrows. Wilde is thus not serving a prison sentence; as an artist he is creating an artistic (that is, symbolic) statement about life. In this way he is able to absorb the most "sorrowful" experience of his life, the half-hour he stood on the center platform at Clapham Junction on his way to Reading Gaol and endured the mockery of the populace.

Having accomplished this artistic stroke (and advised Lord Alfred as a fellow poet to do likewise), Wilde proposes the two subjects on which he would like now to write. The first, the presentation of Christ as the forerunner of the Romantic movement in life, was largely covered in his outrageous analogy above; its extension here leads him to the proposition that the sinner is as near perfect Man as we can know because in repenting he can actually alter his past; thus he is the artist of the present and the past.

The second subject, the life of art considered in relation to conduct of life, is much more the nub of Wilde's attitude to his past and his future. As he admits, everybody will simply point to Reading Gaol as the logical conclusion of the artistic life as Wilde practiced it. He dodges the logic by three lofty assertions. He is now so much the repentant sinner that he can even pity those who mocked him at Clapham Junction; that it was reliance on the Philistines (that is, the original legal action he instituted against Queensbury) that brought him to Reading Gaol; that the supreme concern of the artist is what he says of himself, not what others say. His own statements, Wilde asserted, must be the truth because what he says will be an artistic creation.

Thus Wilde's perverse reading of the obvious analogies in the Christian story made him miss its whole point of sacrifice (though he considers he was sacrificed for Lord Alfred) and confirms his original paradox, absolves him from all blame, and nullifies the whole meaning of Reading Gaol. The artist had triumphed over his real situation but only at the cost of life itself. Wilde's enormous egotism prevented him from seeing the pain he had caused others. All he could appreciate was an artistically crucified Wilde.

DE RERUM NATURA

Type of work: Didactic epic
Author: Lucretius (Titus Lucretius Carus, c. 98 B.C.-55 B.C.)
First transcribed: First century B.C.

The *De rerum natura* (*On the Nature of Things*) is justly renowned as the greatest poetic monument of Epicurean philosophy. It is outstanding both as a scientific explanation of the poet's atomic theory and as a fine poem. Vergil himself was much influenced by Lucretius' dactylic hexameter verse, and echoes passages of the *De rerum natura* in the *Georgics*, a didactic epic modeled on Lucretius' poem, and in the *Aeneid*.

Lucretius, following his master Epicurus' doctrine, believed that fear of the gods and fear of death were the greatest obstacles to peace of mind, the object of Epicurean philosophy. He felt that he could dispel these unfounded terrors by explaining the workings of the universe and showing that phenomena interpreted as signs from the deities were simply natural happenings. His scientific speculations were based on Democritus' atomic theory and Epicurus' interpretation of it. Lucretius outlined the fundamental laws of this system in the first book of his poem.

According to Lucretius, everything is composed of small "first bodies," tiny particles made up of a few "minima" or "least parts" which cannot be separated. These "first bodies," atoms, are solid, indestructible, and of infinite number. They are mixed with void to make objects of greater hardness or softness, strength or weakness.

Lucretius "proves" these assertions by calling upon the reader's reason and his observation of nature, pointing out absurdities that might come about if his point were not true. For example, he substantiates his statement that nothing can be created from nothing by saying, "For if things came to being from nothing, every kind might be born from all things, nought would need a seed. First men might arise from the sea, and from the land the race of scaly creatures, and birds burst forth from the sky." These proofs, which may fill fifty or one hundred lines of poetry, are often unconvincing, but they reveal the author's knowledge of nature and his imaginative gifts.

The universe is infinite in the Epicurean system. Lucretius would ask a man who believed it finite, "If one were to run on to the end . . . and throw a flying dart, would you have it that that dart . . . goes on whither it is sped and flies afar, or do you think that something can check and bar its way?" He ridicules the Stoic theory that all things press toward a center, for the universe, being infinite, can have no center. Lucretius is, of course, denying the law of gravity. He often contradicts what science has since proved true, but he is remarkably accurate for his time.

Book II opens with a poetic description of the pleasure of standing apart from the confusion and conflicts of life: "Nothing is more gladdening than to dwell in the calm high places, firmly embattled on the heights by the teaching of the wise, whence you can look down on others, and see them wandering hither and thither." Lucretius is providing this teaching by continuing his discussion of atoms, which he says move continuously downward like dust particles in a sunbeam. They have a form of free will and can swerve to unite with each other to form objects. Lucretius adds that if the atoms could not will motion for themselves, there would be no explanation for the ability of animals to move voluntarily.

The poet outlines other properties of atoms in the latter part of the second book: they are colorless, insensible, and of a variety of shapes which determine properties of the objects the atoms compose. Sweet honey contains round, smooth particles; bitter wormwood, hooked atoms.

While Lucretius scorns superstitious fear of the gods, he worships the creative force of nature, personified as Venus in the invocation to Book I. Nature controls the unending cycle of creation and destruction. There are gods, but they dwell in their tranquil homes in space, unconcerned for the fate of men.

A passage in praise of Epicurus precedes Book III, the book of the soul. Lucretius says that fear of death arises from superstitions about the soul's afterlife in Hades. This fear is foolish, for the soul is, like the body, mortal. The poet describes the soul as the life force in the body, composed of very fine particles which disperse into the air when the body dies. Since man will neither know nor feel anything when his soul has dissolved, fear of death is unnecessary.

A man should not regret leaving life, even if it has been full and rich. He should die as "a guest sated with the banquet of life and with calm mind embrace . . . a rest that knows no care." If existence has been painful, then an end to it should be welcome.

The introductory lines of Book IV express Lucretius' desire to make philosophy more palatable to his readers by presenting it in poetry. His task is a new one: "I traverse the distant haunts of the Pierides (the Muses), never trodden before by the foot of man."

The poet begins this book on sensation with an explanation of idols, the films of atoms which float from the surfaces of objects and make sense perception possible. Men see because idols touch their eyes, taste the bitter salt air because idols of hooked atoms reach their tongues. Idols become blunted when they travel a long distance, causing men to see far-off square towers as round.

Lucretius blames the misconceptions arising from visual phenomena like refraction and perspective on men's reason, not their senses, for accuracy of sense perception is an important part of his theory: "Unless they are true, all reason, too, becomes false."

A second eulogy of Epicurus introduces the fifth book, for some readers the most interesting of all. In it Lucretius discusses the creation of the world and the development of human civilization. Earth was created by a chance conjunction of atoms, which squeezed out sun, moon, and stars as they gathered together to form land. The world, which is constantly disintegrating and being rebuilt, is still young, for human history does not go back beyond the Theban and Trojan wars.

The poet gives several explanations for the motion of stars, the causes of night, and eclipses. Since proof can come only from the senses, any theory which does not contradict perception is possible.

Lucretius presents the curious idea that the first animals were born from wombs rooted in the earth. Monsters were created, but only strong animals and those useful to man could survive. A delightful picture of primitive man, a hardy creature living on nuts and berries and living in caves, follows. Lucretius describes the process of civilization as men united for protection, learned to talk, use metals, weave, and wage war. Problems arose for them with the discovery of wealth and property, breeding envy and discord. It was at this point that Epicurus taught men the highest good, to free them from their cares.

The sixth book continues the explanation of natural phenomena which inspired men to fear the gods: thunder, lightning, clouds, rain, earthquakes. Lucretius rambles over a great many subjects, giving several explanations for many of them. He concludes the poem with a vivid description of the plague of Athens, modeled on Thucydides' account.

DEAD FIRES

Type of work: Novel
Author: José Lins do Rêgo (1901-1957)
Time: 1848-1900
Locale: Paraíba, Brazil
First published: 1943

Principal characters:
 José Amaro, a crippled, embittered saddlemaker
 Sinha, his wife
 Colonel José Paulino, owner of Santa Clara plantation
 Colonel Lula, owner of Santa Fe plantation
 Captain Victorino Carneiro da Cunha, a humane lawyer
 Lieutenant Mauricio, of the army
 Silvino, a bandit

Dead Fires (Fogo morto), the tenth novel by Lins do Rêgo, marks his return to the themes of his original Sugar Cane Cycle, after four weak experiments in other fields. The author, descendant of an aristocratic planter family settled for years in Northeast Brazil, was educated for the law, but friendship with Brazil's great sociologist, Gilberto Freyre, showed him the rich literary inspiration in Brazil's *ingenhos,* or sugar centers, and turned him to fiction writing. Beginning with the novel *Plantation Lad,* Lins do Rêgo went on with *Daffy Boy, Black Boy Richard, Old Plantation,* and *The Sugar Refinery,* all dealing with the same characters. In 1943, after four lesser novels based on other themes, came *Dead Fires,* his masterpiece, in which some of the characters from the earlier novels reappear. The novel is marked by improved technique, a greater use of dialogue, less morbidity and better character portrayal.

Some critics see in Victorino, the penniless, abused lawyer, a Brazilian Don Quixote, sure of what is right, hating bandits, cruel soldiers, and haughty plantation owners alike, and fighting all injustice, regardless of the cost to him. Like the Spanish don, Victorino was an aristocrat, related by blood to many of the important families of the region, but censuring their use of power because of his feeling for the common man. There is also a parallel with Don Quixote in the way Victorino was first ridiculed and then admired.

The main character, the crippled and ugly saddlemaker José Amaro, was a failure who tried to hide his sense of inferiority and cowardice behind a biting tongue and a scornful attitude toward everybody. He insisted that nobody owned him, or, as he expressed it more vividly, that nobody could scream at him. His only friends were the kindly Negro hunter Leandro, who occasionally left part of his bag at José's door, and white Victorino, sunk so low that even the *moleques,* the black boys, mocked him in the streets, calling after him "Papa Rabo."

José's attitude toward the bandit, Captain António Silvino, arose from the admiration of a coward for a man daring enough to brave the power of the plantation owners. The imagination of the saddlemaker built Silvino into a kind of Robin Hood, siding with the poor against the grasping landlords, especially at the moment when the bandit attacked the town of Pilar and sacked the strongbox of the prefect, Quinca Napoleon. Afterward he invited the villagers to pillage the house. José was grateful because the bandit came to his defense when he was ordered evicted from the house his father and he had occupied for half a century. However, Silvino's threats of interference stiffened the determination of José's landlord.

Not until the end was José disillusioned and the bandit's self-interest revealed. Attracted by rumors that Colonel

Lula still possessed the gold inherited from his father-in-law, Silvino came after it, threatening torture unless the hiding place was revealed. In reality, the wealth was not at the plantation. Lula, vanquished by circumstances and about to abandon his estate for the big city, had sent the money ahead. An attack of convulsions momentarily saved the landowner from torture; the protests of Victorino brought him further respite; but it was the arrival of Colonel Paulino that drove off the bandit. Until he realized Silvino's cruelty, José Amaro made sandals for him and his men, spied on his pursuers for him, and even got food and provisions to him when Lieutenant Mauricio and his soldiers were on his trail.

José's feelings toward the wealthy plantation owners were determined by their attitude toward him. The novelist introduces two of them as representative of the landed gentry of the nineteenth century in Northeastern Brazil, men who derived their titles from their social and political positions.

With Colonel José Paulino, whose family had long owned the Santa Clara plantation, José Amaro was continually at odds because, as the wealthy man rode past the saddlemaker's house in his family carriage, he would only nod condescendingly. At the beginning of the novel, when Laurentino, the house painter, paused to talk on a May afternoon, while on his way to help the colonel beautify his manor house for the wedding of his daughter, José from his doorway said angrily that he would never work for a man he hated as much as he hated Colonel Paulino.

His attitude toward the other big sugar planter, Colonel Lula César de Holanda Chacón, supposedly modeled on a cousin of the author's grandfather, was less bitter. He finally agreed to go to the Santa Fe plantation to repair the family carriage, whose history is related in the second part of the novel.

During the Revolution of 1848, Captain Tomás Cabral de Malo arrived with his cattle, his slaves, and his family in Parahyba (or Paraíba). He took possession of the Santa Fe plantation, adjoining Santa Clara, bought additional land from the Indians, and planted cotton. About then a penniless cousin, Lula, turned up and began courting the plantation owner's daughter.

Having won the captain's permission, Lula took her away on a honeymoon from which they returned with a pretentious carriage, practically useless in that roadless region. The rest of Lula's progress, as told in *Dead Fires*, makes him anything but admirable. At Captain Tomás' death, he fought the widow for control until her death. Then, in complete possession of the plantation and sugar refinery, he revealed his avaricious and cruel nature. José overlooked the past of his landlord, however, because Lula occasionally exchanged a word with him.

José's family is introduced early in the story. When Laurentino stopped to talk, the saddlemaker invited him for supper with his wife and their thirty-year-old daughter. The girl had never married because she insisted that she did not want to, but she nearly drove the old man frantic because she spent her days weeping. Eventually, in his exasperation, he beat her until he dropped unconscious; from that time on his wife thought only of ways to get herself and her daughter safely away. José had no other children. Lacking a son to carry on at his death, he had no incentive to enlarge his leather business or attract new customers.

Lins do Rêgo is continually making thrifty use of minor episodes, not only to carry forward the story, but to reveal character. For example, while working at Colonel Lula's plantation, José revealed his trait of showing contempt for those he tries to impress; and by his actions he so roused the enmity of the Negro Floripes, the Santa Fe overseer, that from then on he worked against José and hastened his tragedy. It was Floripes' lie, the report that José had promised aid to Victorino's candidate against the politician backed by Lula, that persuaded the land-owner that his tenant was ungrateful, and so José was ordered to leave the cabin occupied by his family for many years.

The kindness of the hunter in leaving a rabbit at José's door revealed the old man's nausea at the sight of blood, while the blood started a rumor that José was a werewolf. This rumor was crystallized into belief when he was found uncon-scious beside the river, where, in reality, he had collapsed trying to warn the ban-dits of the coming of soldiers.

In telling the story, Lins do Rêgo di-vides his narrative into three parts, with the second one, "The Santa Fe Planta-tion," a flashback of half a century, cov-ering the rise to power of Lula.

When Isabel, daughter of Emperor Pedro, freed Brazil's last slaves in 1888, Lula was left without anyone to run the plantation or the refinery, for his Negroes were quick to get away from a master who used to beat them until he fell down in convulsions. In contrast, Colonel Paul-ino's field hands, who had been treated kindly, stayed on even after the libera-tion, and so he was able to lend his cousin by marriage enough laborers to help with the work. But still the hearth fires of Santa Fe burned lower and the planta-tion was doomed. Neighbors brought suits against Lula that were settled only be-cause Colonel Paulino intervened. And Lula could find no one willing to marry his daughter.

José's fortunes also declined. Disillu-sioned about the outlaws, he found the soldiers of Lieutenant Mauricio even more cruel. Coming to protect the vil-lagers, Lieutenant Mauricio beat blind Torcuato as a spy, arrested José, and mis-treated Victorino, who had won the ad-miration of his fellow citizens by facing the domineering officer with a writ of habeas corpus in order to free the saddle-maker.

Freedom was meaningless now to old José. His family had left him, and he had no friends. He committed suicide in his empty house, where his Negro friend, Pajarito, found his body. Two cycles had ended. When Pajarito looked out the window, smoke was billowing from the chimneys of the Santa Clara sugar re-finery, but he saw no activity at Santa Fe —where the fires were dead.

DEAD SOULS

Type of work: Novel
Author: Nikolai V. Gogol (1809-1852)
Type of plot: Social satire
Time of plot: Early nineteenth century
Locale: Russia
First published: 1842

Principal characters:
PAVEL IVANOVITCH TCHITCHIKOFF, an adventurer
MANILOFF, from whom he bought souls
TENTETNIKOFF, whom he tried to marry off
PLATON PLATONOFF, with whom he later traveled
KLOBUEFF, whose estate he bought
SKUDRONZHOGLO, who lent him money
ALEXEI IVANOVITCH LYENITZEN, who threw him into jail

Critique:

This novel is written in high good humor. Its portraits of various Russian types—peasant, landholder, prince—are delightful. The plot itself is not complex. The length of the novel is accounted for by the author's numerous digressions, which add up to a rich picture of provincial Russian life in the early nineteenth century. The satire ranks with the best the world has produced.

The Story:

Pavel Ivanovitch Tchitchikoff had arrived in the town accompanied by his coachman, Selifan, and his valet, Petrushka. He had been entertained gloriously and had met many interesting people, who insisted on his visiting them in their own homes. Nothing could have suited Tchitchikoff better. After several days of celebration in the town, he took his coachman and began a round of visits to the various estates in the surrounding country.

His first host was Maniloff, a genial man who wined him and dined him in a manner fit for a prince. When the time was ripe, Tchitchikoff began to question his host about his estate and learned, to his satisfaction, that many of Maniloff's souls, as the serfs were called, had died since the last census and that Maniloff was still paying taxes on them and would continue to do so until the next census. Tchitchikoff offered to

buy these dead souls from Maniloff and so relieve him of his extra tax burden. The contract signed, Tchitchikoff set out for the next estate.

Selifan got lost and in the middle of the night drew up to a house which belonged to Madame Korobotchkina, from whom Tchitchikoff also bought dead souls. When he left his hostess, he found his way to an inn in the neighborhood. There he met Nozdreff, a notorious gambler and liar. Nozdreff had recently lost a great deal of money at gambling, and Tchitchikoff thought he would be a likely seller of dead souls. But when he broached the subject, Nozdreff asked him the reason for his interest in dead souls. For every reason Tchitchikoff gave, Nozdreff called him a liar. Then Nozdreff wanted to play at cards for the souls, but Tchitchikoff refused. They were arguing when a police captain came in and arrested Nozdreff for assault on a man while drunk. Tchitchikoff thought himself well rid of the annoying Nozdreff.

His next host was Sobakevitch, who at first demanded the unreasonable sum of one hundred roubles for each name of a dead soul. Tchitchikoff finally argued him into accepting two and a half roubles apiece, a higher price than he had planned to pay.

Pliushkin, with whom he negotiated next, was a miser. He bought one hundred and twenty dead souls and seventy-eight fugitives after considerable haggling. Pliushkin gave him a letter to Ivan Grigorievitch, the town president.

Back in town, Tchitchikoff persuaded the town president to make his recent purchases legal. Since the law required that souls when purchased be transferred to another estate, Tchitchikoff told the officials that he had land in the Kherson province. He had no trouble in making himself sound plausible. Some bribes to minor officials helped.

Tchitchikoff proved to be such a delightful guest that the people of the town insisted that he stay on and on. He was the center of attraction at many social functions, including a ball at which he was especially interested in the governor's daughter. Soon, however, rumors spread that Tchitchikoff was using the dead souls as a screen, that he was really planning to elope with the governor's daughter. The men, in consultation at the police master's house, speculated variously. Some said he was a forger; others thought he might be an officer in the governor-general's office; one man put forth the fantastic suggestion that he was really the legendary Captain Kopeykin in disguise. They questioned Nozdreff, who had been the first to report the story of the purchase of dead souls. At their interrogation Nozdreff confirmed their opinions that Tchitchikoff was a spy and a forger who was trying to elope with the governor's daughter.

Meanwhile Tchitchikoff had caught a cold and was confined to his bed. When at last he had recovered sufficiently to go out, he found himself no longer welcome at the houses of his former friends. He was, in fact, turned away by servants at the door. Tchitchikoff realized it would be best for him to leave town.

The truth of the matter was that Tchitchikoff had begun his career as a humble clerk. His father had died leaving no legacy for his son, who served in various capacities, passing from customs officer to smuggler to pauper to legal

agent. When he learned that the Trustee Committee would mortgage souls, he hit upon the scheme of acquiring funds by mortgaging dead souls that were still on the census lists. It was this purpose which had sent him on his current tour.

He turned up next on the estate of Andrei Ivanovitch Tentetnikoff, a thirty-three-year-old bachelor who had retired from public life to vegetate in the country. Learning that Tentetnikoff was in love with the daughter of his neighbor, General Betrishtcheff, Tchitchikoff went to see the general and won his consent to Tentetnikoff's suit. He brought the conversation around to a point where he could offer to buy dead souls from the general. He gave as his reason the story that his old uncle would not leave him an estate unless he himself already owned some property. The scheme so delighted the general that he gladly made the transaction.

Tchitchikoff's next stop was with Pyetukh, a generous glutton whose table Tchitchikoff enjoyed. There he met a young man named Platonoff, whom Tchitchikoff persuaded to travel with him and see Russia. The two stopped to see Platonoff's sister and brother-in-law, Konstantin Skudronzhoglo, a prosperous landholder. Tchitchikoff so impressed his host that Kostanzhoglo agreed to lend him ten thousand roubles to buy the estate of a neighboring spendthrift named Klobueff. Klobueff said he had a rich old aunt who would give great gifts to churches and monasteries but would not help her destitute relatives. Tchitchikoff proceeded to the town where the old woman resided and forged a will to his own advantage. But he forgot to insert a clause canceling all previous wills. On her death he went to interview His Excellency, Alexei Ivanovitch Lyenitzen, who told him that two wills had been discovered, each contradicting the other. Tchitchikoff was accused of forging the second will and was thrown into prison. In the interpretation of this mix-up, Tchitchikoff learned a valuable lesson in deception from the crafty lawyer he consulted. The lawyer managed to confuse the affair with every public and private scandal in the province, so that the officials were soon willing to drop the whole matter if Tchitchikoff would leave town immediately. The ruined adventurer was only too glad to comply.

Further Critical Evaluation of the Work:

Dead Souls, one of Russia's finest works of fiction, is also one of the most unique novels in any literature. It begins in comic realism and satire, and moves through fantasy into prophecy. Like Dostoevski's *The Idiot,* its purpose was no less than the salvation of Russian society. The early chapters present us with satirical portraits of typical Russian landowners: the canny old Korobotchkina; the energetic, violent, half-crazed Nozdreff; the "bear" Sobakevitch; the miser Pliushkin, a maltreater of serfs. All these in their puzzlement and greed are willing to sell the souls of their dead serfs to Tchitchikoff, who in turn will use these dead souls in his own special confidence racket. We are presented at once with a Russia which operates crookedly. The deadest souls are the ones who perform such acts, and Tchitchikoff is chief among them; he is the most typical and nondescript—a Russian everyman. Part I of the novel details the various petty cheats of Tchitchikoff and his kind. The mood is wonderfully comic and fantastic; Gogol's moral purpose is partially obscured.

In Part II this purpose becomes clear. The character of Tentetnikoff shows us another of Russia's problems, for he has great plans for reforming his estates but paltry execution. He is cheated by his peasants and reacts harshly. Naturally, Tchitchikoff fastens to him for all he is worth. Finally, in the character of Kostanzhoglo, Tchitchikoff encounters a man who presents us with a solution to Russia's problems—a solution which makes us wonder at Gogol. This landlord is a man of action rather than theory and loose words, as with Tentetnikoff and the others of Part I. His religion of simple agriculture has more than an edge of anti-intellectualism and puritanism (he won't produce tobacco or sugar!). But his reactionary stand fails fully to convert the ceaselessly mediocre Tchitchikoff. When Tchitchikoff, having contemplated cheating Kostanzhoglo, says at the end that many are more dishonest than he, he is voicing Gogol's indictment of Russian society. Still, the finest elements of *Dead Souls* have little to do with Gogol's moralizing. The comic and fantastic elements are the novel's chief rewards.

DEAR BRUTUS

Type of work: Drama
Author: James M. Barrie (1860-1937)
Type of plot: Romantic fantasy
Time of plot: Midsummer Eve
Locale: England
First presented: 1917

Principal characters:
LOB, the ancient Puck
MATEY, his butler
GUESTS AT LOB'S HOUSE PARTY

Critique:

Barrie's thesis—that the exigencies of human life are the fault of the individual, not of so-called Fate—is fancifully developed in *Dear Brutus* by means of a folk superstition concerning Midsummer Eve. The play is fantastic and realistic at the same time, fantastic in that its characters are transported into the realm of the unreal, realistic in the perfectly candid way in which the various relationships among the characters are set forth.

The Story:

Dinner was over, and the ladies of Lob's house party returned to the drawing-room after leaving the gentlemen to their cigars and wine. Matey, the butler, had stolen jewelry from one of the guests. The women called him in to tell him they knew he was the thief. When Matey returned the jewelry, the women stated that they would not report him if he told them why they were guests at the house. Matey either could not or would not give them a direct answer. In the course of the conversation it was learned that their host was mysteriously ageless and that Lob was another name for the legendary Puck. Matey admitted that Lob always asked a different party of guests to his house for Midsummer Week. He warned the women not to venture outside the garden on this Midsummer Eve. When he left them with the warning not to go into the wood, the women were puzzled because there was no wood within miles of the house.

Host Lob entered thoughtfully. He was followed by old Mr. Coade, who was collecting notes for a projected work on the Feudal System, and Mr. Purdie, an intellectual young barrister. Coade and Purdie suggested that the group take a walk to discover a mysterious wood. Lob said slyly that the villagers believed that a wood appeared in a different part of the neighborhood each Midsummer Eve. He pretended skepticism to sharpen the curiosity of his guests, who went to prepare for the adventure.

Among Lob's guests was Lady Caroline Laney, unmarried and of disdainful poise, and Joanna Trout, single and in love with love. Joanna and Mr. Purdie were caught kissing in the living room by Mabel Purdie, who saw them from the garden. She came in. Joanna, surprised, asked Mabel what she was doing in the garden. Mabel answered that she was looking for her lost love. Her calm candor caught Jack Purdie and Joanna completely off guard. Jack admitted his love for Joanna. Mabel left the lovers grieving that fate had not brought them together earlier. Alice Dearth entered. Cattishly, Joanna revealed that Mrs. Dearth had at one time been an artist's model. Dearth, an artist now broken by drink, entered. Alice Dearth had grown to despise him for his sottishness. Dearth regretted not having a child; Alice Dearth regretted not having married a former suitor.

DEAR BRUTUS by James M. Barrie, from THE PLAYS OF JAMES M. BARRIE. By permission of the publishers, Charles Scribner's Sons. Copyright, 1914, by Charles Scribner's Sons, 1918, 1928, by J. M. Barrie.

When the party reassembled, Lob revealed that to go into the forest gave one another chance, something nearly everyone in the group was seeking. Dearth drew aside the curtain to reveal a forest in the place of the garden. He entered the wood and disappeared. Mabel Purdie followed him. Next went Jack Purdie and Joanna, followed by Alice Dearth, Lady Caroline, and old Mr. Coade. Lob enticed Matey to the edge of the wood and pushed him into it.

In the moonlight of Midsummer Eve, in the fanciful realm of the second chance, Matey and Lady Caroline discovered that they were vulgar husband and wife. Joanna was in search of her husband. When Mr. Coade, now a woodlander, appeared dancing and blowing a whistle, Joanna said that she was Mrs. Purdie; she suspected her husband of being in the forest with another woman. They saw Purdie in the company of Mabel, whom he chased among the trees. In the forest, Mabel and Joanna had changed places. Purdie and Mabel mourned that they had met too late.

In another part of the forest, Will Dearth and his young daughter Margaret raced to the spot where the artist's easel was set up, for Dearth was painting a moonlit landscape. Margaret was worried over her excess of happiness; she expressed her fear that her father would be taken from her. The pair agreed that artists, especially, needed daughters and that fame was not everything.

Alice, a vagrant searching for scraps to eat, passed the happy pair. She told them that she was the Honorable Mrs. Finch-Fallowe, the wife of the suitor that she had recalled in Lob's house, and that she had seen good times. Dearth approached a nearby house to get food for the vagrant woman. Margaret, somehow afraid, tried to restrain him.

Back in the house, Lob was waiting for the return of his guests. There was a tapping on the window and Jack Purdie and Mabel, still charmed, entered. They noticed but did not recognize the sleeping Lob. Still under the influence of Midsummer magic, Purdie spoke words of love to Mabel. He was interrupted by the entrance of Joanna, his Midsummer Eve wife. Lob seemed to leer in his sleep. Suddenly the enchantment disappeared; the trio recognized the room and Lob. After the complete return to reality, Purdie realized that fate was not to blame for human destiny. Ashamed but honest, he admitted that he was a philanderer and asked Mabel to forgive him.

Matey returned, still the vulgarian in speech and dress. He stated, to the surprise of those present, that his wife was with him and he introduced Lady Caroline Matey. The charm was broken, to the horror of the fastidious Caroline Laney and to the embarrassment of Matey.

Still piping on his whistle, Mr. Coade returned. Although he did not recognize Mrs. Coade, he expressed his admiration for her lovable face. The old man returned to reality after making his wife proud that he had chosen her again in the world of the second chance.

Alice Dearth, hungry, entered and looked ravenously at the refreshments. Between mouthfuls of cake she bragged of her former affluence as Mrs. Finch-Fallowe; she mystified the other guests with talk of a painter and his daughter in the forest. Dearth, the happy painter of the forest, came in. In their disenchantment, Alice knew that she would have been unhappy with the former suitor, and that Will Dearth would have been happier without her. Dearth was momentarily crushed by the loss of Margaret, but he recovered to thank Lob for providing that night's experience.

Lob, who had been curled up in a chair in a trance-like sleep during the adventures, and who had leered and smiled in his sleep as his guests came back to the actual world, returned to the care of his beloved flowers. Midsummer Eve was past; the world of might-have-been had ended.

Further Critical Evaluation of the Work:

"Men at some time are masters of their fate," Cassius tells his co-conspirator in Shakespeare's *Julius Caesar* (II, ii), "the fault, dear Brutus, is not in our stars, but in ourselves that we are underlings." Beginning with this quote as a premise, James Barrie tests Cassius' notion in his play *Dear Brutus* by taking an oddly assorted group of characters and giving them that "second chance." But if the play's idea comes from *Julius Caesar,* its shape and mood are closer to that of another Shakespearean play, *A Midsummer Night's Dream*: the time of the second chance is Midsummer's Eve, the locale is an enchanted wood, and the manipulator of the action is Lob, a modernized Puck, a child-man of ancient, but indefinite age.

Matey, the butler, caught in the act of stealing the ladies' jewelry, sets up the action when he states ". . . it all depends on your taking the right or the wrong turn. . . . I would give the world to be able to begin over again." He gets his wish and proves himself to be, once again, a thief—albeit a rich one. His aristocratic antagonist Lady Caroline Laney, however, becomes his wife and thereby demonstrates that, beneath her haughty surface, she is actually servile. Jack Purdie sees himself as an exceptionally sensitive soul, trapped with an unresponsive wife, who wants only a woman who can "plumb the well of my emotions." After exchanging women and fantasies in the enchanted wood, he realizes that he is "not a deeply passionate chap at all. . . . I am just . . . a philanderer!" And it is Purdie who sums up the play's thesis:

> It's not fate, Joanna. Fate is something outside us. What really plays the dickens with us is something in ourselves. Something that makes us go on doing the same sort of things, however many chances we get.

Charming old Mr. Coade learns that he is not a potentially great scholar spoiled into amiable laziness by inherited money; he is simply a carefree, likeable man without ambitions. And Alice Dearth learns that her bad marriage could have been even worse, for she might always choose the wrong man—for her.

The one exception is Will Dearth, a mediocre, alcoholic, cynical artist who meets Margaret, his "might-have-been" daughter in the woods. The Will Dearth of Act II, "ablaze in happiness and health," is quite different from the "chop-fallen, gone-to-seed sort of person" we saw in Act I and the charming, happy-sad scene between father and daughter is one of the most touching in modern theater; few curtain lines are as memorable as Margaret's fearful lament, from the darkened stage, as she fades into nothingness: "Daddy, come back; I don't want to be a 'might-have-been.' "

The question Barrie leaves us with in the final act is whether or not the magical experiences of having seen themselves fail at "second turnings" will not enable the party guests to effect real changes in their personalities. When Joanna asks Matey about this, he replies that it only happens once in a while.

The audience is left with the feeling that at least the characters now understand their own mediocrity, even if they can do little about it. And, to Barrie, even such a modest shedding of illusions is a good thing. It is also hinted that for the best of them, Will and Alice Dearth, there is some possibility of a real change and revitalization of the "rather wild love" which, Barrie states in an early stage direction, they had for each other before it went "whistling down the wind."

DEATH COMES FOR THE ARCHBISHOP

Type of work: Novel
Author: Willa Cather (1873-1947)
Type of plot: Historical chronicle
Time of plot: Last half of the nineteenth century
Locale: New Mexico and Arizona
First published: 1927

<blockquote>

Principal characters:

FATHER JEAN MARIE LATOUR, Vicar Apostalic of New Mexico
FATHER JOSEPH VAILLANT, his friend, a missionary priest
KIT CARSON, frontier scout
JACINTO, an Indian guide

</blockquote>

Critique:

Death Comes for the Archbishop is a novel reaffirming the greatness of the American past. This chronicle of the Catholic Southwest is a story, beautifully told, which re-creates in the lives of Bishop Latour and Father Vaillant, his vicar, the historical careers of Bishop Lamy and Father Macheboeuf, two devout and noble missionary priests in the Vicarate of New Mexico during the second half of the nineteenth century. Bishop Latour is scholarly and urbane; Father Vaillant, energetic and passionately the man of feeling. A novel of these dedicated lives, the book presents also a picture of a region and a culture. There are many strands of interest here —the bleak desert country of sand and gaunt red mountains, colorful adobe towns and Mexican customs, conflicts with a stubborn and sometimes corrupt native clergy, missionary journeys in all weathers, the rituals and legends of the Indian pueblos, frontier heroes like Kit Carson and deperadoes like Buck Scales, relics of the conquistadores who brought the sword and the Cross into the New World. The novel lives in its bright glimpses of the past, stories that cut backward into time so that the action is not always upon the same level. Tales and legends that go beyond the period of American occupation into three centuries of Spanish colonial history and back to the primitive tribal life of the Hopi, the Navajo, and the vanished cliff-dwellers break this chronicle at many points and give the effect of density and variety to a work which recaptures so completely the spirit and movement of the pioneer West.

The Story:

In 1851 Father Jean Marie Latour reached Santa Fé, where he was to become Vicar Apostolic of New Mexico. His journey from the shores of Lake Ontario had been long and arduous. He had lost his belongings in a shipwreck at Galveston and had suffered painful injury in a wagon accident at San Antonio.

Upon Father Latour's arrival, in company with his good friend, Father Joseph Vaillant, the Mexican priests refused to recognize his authority. He had no choice but to ride three thousand miles into Mexico to secure the necessary papers from the Bishop of Durango.

On the road he lost his way in an arid landscape of red hills and gaunt junipers. His thirst became a vertigo of mind and senses, and he could blot out his own agony only by repeating the cry of the Saviour on the Cross. As he was about to give up all hope, he saw a tree growing in the shape of a cross. A short time later he arrived in the Mexican settlement called *Agua Secreta*, Hidden Water. Stopping at the home of Benito, Bishop Latour first performed the marriage ceremonies and then baptized all the children.

DEATH COMES FOR THE ARCHBISHOP by Willa Cather. By permission of the publishers, Alfred A. Knopf, Inc. Copyright, 1926, 1927, by Willa Cather.

At Durango he received the necessary documents and started the long trip back to Santa Fé. Manwhile Father Vaillant had won over the inhabitants from enmity to amity and had set up the Episcopal residence in an old adobe house. On the first morning after his return to Santa Fé the bishop heard the unexpected sound of a bell ringing the Angelus. Father Vaillant told him that he had found the bell, bearing the date 1356, in the basement of old San Miguel Church.

On a missionary journey to Albuquerque in March, Father Vaillant acquired as a gift a handsome cream-colored mule and another just like it for his bishop. These mules, Contento and Angelica, served the men in good stead for many years.

On another such trip the two priests were riding together on their mules. Caught in a sleet storm, they stopped at the rude shack of an American, Buck Scales. His Mexican wife warned the travelers by gestures that their lives were in danger, and they rode on to Mora without spending the night. The next morning the Mexican woman appeared in town. She told them that her husband had already murdered and robbed four travelers, and that he had killed her three babies. The result was that Scales was brought to justice, and his wife, Magdalena, was sent to the home of Kit Carson, the famous frontier scout. From that time of Kit Carson was a valuable friend of the bishop and his vicar. Magdalena later became the housekeeeper and manager for the kitchens of the Sisters of Loretto.

During his first year at Santa Fé, the bishop was called to a meeting of the Plenary Council at Baltimore. On the return journey he brought back with him five nuns sent to establish the school of Our Lady of Light. Next, Bishop Latour, attended by the Indian Jacinto as his guide, spent some time visiting his own vicarate. Padre Gallegos, whom he visited at Albuquerque, acted more like a professional gambler than a priest, but because he was very popular with the natives Bishop Latour did not remove him at that time. At last he arrived at his destination, the top of the mesa at Acoma, the end of his long journey. On that trip he heard the legend of Fray Baltazar, killed during an uprising of the Acoma Indians.

A month after the bishop's visit, he suspended Padre Gallegos and put Father Vaillant in charge of the parish at Albuquerque. On a trip to the Pecos Mountains the vicar fell ill with an attack of the black measles. The bishop, hearing of his illness, set out to nurse his friend. Jacinto again served as guide on the cold, snowy trip. When Bishop Latour reached his friend's bedside, he found that Kit Carson had arrived before him. As soon as the sick man could sit in the saddle, Carson and the bishop took him back to Santa Fé.

Bishop Latour decided to investigate the parish of Taos, where the powerful old priest, Antonio José Martinez, was the ruler of both spiritual and temporal matters. The following year the bishop was called to Rome. When he returned, he brought with him four young priests from the Seminary of Montferrand and a Spanish priest to replace Padre Martinez at Taos.

Bishop Latour had one great ambition; he wanted to build a cathedral in Santa Fé. In that project he was assisted by the rich Mexican *rancheros,* but to the greatest extent by his good friend, Don Antonio Olivares. When Don Antonio died, his will stated that his estate was left to his wife and daughter during their lives, and after their decease to the Church. Don Antonio's brothers contested the will on the grounds that the daughter, Señorita Inez, was too old to be Doña Isabella's daughter, and the bishop and his vicar had to persuade the vain, coquettish widow to swear to her true age of fifty-three, rather than the forty-two years she claimed. Thus the money was saved for Don Antonio's family and, eventually, the Church.

Father Vaillant was sent to Tucson, but after several years Bishop Latour decided to recall him to Santa Fé. When he arrived, the bishop showed him the stone for building the cathedral. About that time Bishop Latour received a letter from the Bishop of Leavenworth. Because of the discovery of gold near Pike's Peak, he asked to have a priest sent there from Father Latour's diocese. Father Vaillant was the obvious choice.

Father Vaillant spent the rest of his life doing good works in Colorado, though he did return to Santa Fé with the Papal Emissary when Bishop Latour was made an archbishop. Father Vaillant became the first Bishop of Colorado. He died there after years of service, and Archbishop Latour attended his impressive funeral services.

After the death of his friend, Father Latour retired to a modest country estate near Santa Fé. He had dreamed during all his missionary years of the time when he could retire to his own fertile green Auvergne in France, but in the end he decided that he could not leave the land of his labors for his faith. Memories of the journeys he and Father Vaillant had made over thousands of miles of desert country became the meaning of his later years. Bernard Ducrot, a young Seminarian from France, became like a son to him.

When Father Latour knew that his time had come to die, he asked to be taken into town to spend his last days near the cathedral. On the last day of his life the church was filled with people who came to pray for him, as word that he was dying spread through the town. He died in the still twilight, and the cathedral bell, tolling in the early darkness, carried to the waiting countryside the news that at last death had come for Father Latour.

Further Critical Evaluation of the Work:

When writing of her great predecessor and teacher, Sarah Orne Jewett, Willa Cather expressed her own belief that the quality that gives a work of literature greatness is the "voice" of the author, the sincere, unadorned, and unique vision of a writer coming to grips with his material. If any one characteristic can be said to dominate the writings of Willa Cather, it is a true and moving sincerity. She never tried to twist her subject matter to suit a preconceived purpose, and she resisted the temptation to dress up her homely material. She gave herself absolutely to her chosen material, and the result was a series of books both truthful and rich with intimations of the destiny of the American continent. By digging into the roots of her material, she found the greater meanings and expressed them with a deceptive simplicity. Her vision and craftsmanship were seldom more successful than in *Death Comes for the Archbishop*. So completely did Willa Cather merge her "voice" with her material, that some critics have felt that the book is almost too polished, without the sense of struggle necessary in a truly great novel. But this, in fact, indicates the magnitude of the author's achievement and the brilliance of her technical skill. *Death Comes for the Archbishop* resonates with the unspoken beliefs of the author and the resolved conflicts that went into its construction. On the surface, it is cleanly wrought and simple, but it is a more complicated and profound book than it appears at first reading. Cather learned well from her early inspiration, Sarah Orne Jewett, the secret of artless art, of craftsmanship that disarms by its very simplicity, but which is based in a highly sophisticated intelligence.

It is true that this novel is an epic and a regional history, but, much more than either, it is a tale of personal isolation, of one man's life reduced to the painful weariness of his own sensitivities. Father Latour is a hero in the most profound sense of the word, at times almost a romantic hero, with his virtues of courage and determination, but he is also a very modern protagonist, with his doubts and inner conflicts and his philosophical nature. His personality is held up in startling contrast to that of his friend and vicar, Father Vaillant, a more simple, although no less good, individual. Cather's austere style perfectly captures the scholarly asperity and urbane religious devotion that compose Father Latour's character. And always in this book, the reader is aware of a sense of the dignity of human life, as exemplified in the person of this individual. Cather was not afraid to draw a good man, a man who could stand above others because of his deeds and because of his innate quality. The novel must stand or fall on this character, and it stands superbly.

Although this book is based on a true sequence of events, it is not a novel of plot. It is a chronicle and a character study, and perhaps, more specifically, an interplay of environment and character. Throughout the book, the reader is aware of the reaction of men to the land, and of one man to the land he has chosen. Subtly and deeply, the author suggests that the soul of man is profoundly altered by the soul of the land, and Cather never doubts for a moment that the land does possess a soul or that this soul can transform a human being in complex and important ways. Willa Cather was fascinated by the way the rough landscape of the Southwest, when reduced to its essences, seemed to take human beings and reduce them to their essences. She abandoned traditional realism in this book, turning toward the directness of symbolism. With stark pictures and vivid styles, she created an imaginary world rooted in realism, but transcending realism. The rigid economy with which the book is written forces it to stand with a unique power in the reader's mind long after his reading. And the personality of Bishop Latour stands as the greatest symbol, like a wind-swept crag or precipice in the vast New Mexico landscape, suggesting the nobility of the human spirit, despite the inner conflicts against which it must struggle.

The descriptions of place set the emotional tone of the novel. The quality of life is intimately related to the landscape, and the accounts of the journeys and the efforts to survive despite the unfriendliness of the barren land, all help to create an odd warmth and almost surreal passion in the narrative. The personalities of Bishop Latour and Father Vaillant establish a definite emotional relationship with the country, and if the other characters in the book are less vividly realized as individuals, perhaps it is because they do not seem to have this relationship with the land. Some of them have become part of the land, worn down by the elements like the rocks and riverbeds, and others have no relationship to it at all; but none of them is involved in the intense love-hate relationship with the land with which the two main characters struggle for so many years.

Although the chronology of the book encompasses many years, the novel is essentially static, a series of rich images and thoughtful moments highlighted and captured as by a camera. This quality of the narrative is not a fault; it is a fact of Cather's style. The frozen moments of contemplation, the glimpses into Father Latour's inner world and spiritual loneliness, are the moments that give the book its greatness. Despite the presence of Kit Carson, the novel is not an adventure story any more than it is merely the account of a pair of churchmen attempting to establish their church in a difficult new terrain. The cathedral becomes the most important symbol in the final part of the book, representing the earthly successes of a man dedicated to nonworldly ambitions. This conflict between the earthly and the spiritual is at the heart of Bishop Latour's personality and at the heart of the book. But the reader understands, at the end, when the bell tolls for Father Latour, that the temptations were never very deep and the good man's victory was greater than he ever knew. The author does not spell out her meaning, but the emotional impact of her narrative brings it home to the reader.

Bruce D. Reeves

A DEATH IN THE FAMILY

Type of work: Novel
Author: James Agee (1909-1955)
Time: 1915
Locale: Knoxville, Tennessee
First published: 1957

Principal characters:
RUFUS FOLLET, a six-year-old boy
MARY FOLLET, his mother
JAY FOLLET, his father
CATHERINE, his small sister
JOEL LYNCH, Mary Follet's father
CATHERINE LYNCH, his wife
AMELIA and
ANDREW LYNCH, Mary's sister and brother
HANNAH LYNCH, Joel's spinster sister
RALPH FOLLET, Jay's brother

Perhaps the most significant aspect of *A Death in the Family* is the fact that it restored a world of feeling and moral value to American fiction. A Pulitzer Prize winner for 1957, it is a novel about love that is neither adult lust nor adolescent groping, about death as an inescapable part of the human condition, universal and therefore to be borne. In a very real but almost old-fashioned sense the book is a celebration of these two great mysteries of experience. At a time when most writers choose to treat of love as a process of glandular secretions and death as a meaningless commonplace of violence, nothing in this novel reveals the originality and power of James Agee more than this ability to suggest the atmosphere of wonder and awe which once surrounded man's awareness of his being and his mortality.

The essential difference found between James Agee and our leading specialists in primitivism and violence goes even deeper. *A Death in the Family* is a novel of compassion almost overwhelming in its sensitivity, a circumstance not entirely accounted for by its autobiographical theme and the writer's obvious attempt to get at the meaning of the central experience in his own life, the death of his father forty-odd years before. He is not dealing with that form of compassion which has left its mark on much recent fiction, the subverted sentimentality of a

growing concern for the alcoholic, the inarticulate brute, the lonely spinster, the inadequate male, the lost child, the homosexual, the bum—all the misfits and outcasts of our society. His compassion is for simple, decent people of ordinary lives—the very "ordinariness" of his material is one of the notable features of the novel—in a time of loss and grief. These are matters that he presents with a feeling of shared sorrow and sympathy for what is most personal and yet most general in the human situation.

Agee's sense of experience shared presupposes a universe of social continuity and moral order, not a world in which the values of the moment must be salvaged from the spectacle of fragmented, isolated lives within a disordered society, but one in which the human effort, in spite of its accumulation of grief, hunger, and waste, becomes meaningful and worthwhile when judged by community values and the idea of man's moral responsibility as man. As a serious writer Agee was interested in the nature of good and evil; in his novel death, the complement of life, is the chink in the armor that gives a small boy his first awareness of evil and threatens with the shock of loss a family in which the ties of kinship have been fulfilled by love. That he was able to shape on a purely domestic level a fable of compelling tenderness and compassionate insight, or to achieve within this framework his effects of lyricism, meditative speculation, and drama, is proof that James Agee's death lost to American letters one of the resourceful and authentic talents of his generation.

Behind this novel, however, lay years of preparation and apprentice work in a variety of media within the fairly short span of his writing career. He was born in Knoxville, the setting of *A Death in the Family*, in 1909, and he died of a heart attack in a New York taxicab in 1955. After schooling at Exeter and Harvard he had joined the staff of *Fortune* in 1932. His first book was *Permit Me Voyage*, a collection of poems published in the Yale Younger Poets Series in 1934. This verse was rather conventional in form, romantic in its display of strong personal feeling. As poetry written in a period of technical experiment and at a time when writers were expected to carry banners in the picket lines of the class war, the book, like *A Death in the Family*, seemed strangely old-fashioned. (Archibald MacLeish's somewhat ambiguous comment was that Agee had not assumed a "Position.") Later, out of an assignment to write a documentary report on the sharecropping system in the South, he produced one of the most original but least *read* books of its decade, *Let Us Now Praise Famous Men*, a curious blend of narrative, social history, satire, and philosophy. It is in many ways a youthful book but an impressive one in its praise of the American earth and its rage against the exploiters of the land and its workers. As a social document the book is still eloquent and moving, even though the first impression is likely to be one of tremendous power of language under poor control. Still later he wrote about motion pictures for *The Nation*, critiques which have become the classics of their kind, and reviewed books for *Time*. In 1948 he gave up journalism to devote himself to *A Death in the Family*, but he was constantly being diverted to other tasks: articles for *Life*, scenarios for *The*

Quiet One, The African Queen, Face to Face, The Bride Comes to Yellow Sky, The Night of the Hunter, a documentary on the life of Lincoln for television, and the novella, *The Morning Watch*, published in 1950.

Although Agee came late to fiction, his admirers saw in *The Morning Watch*, a moving study of adolescent confusion against the background of a boys' school, promise of the major work of which he was capable. *A Death in the Family* almost fulfills that promise. When Agee died in 1955 his novel was virtually complete except for the tying in of loose ends and the final polishing. In preparing the manuscript for publication the editors have inserted as thematic interludes several episodes not directly related to the time-scheme of the novel and have added as a prologue the sketch titled "Knoxville: Summer 1915," which had been written some years before. It is safe to say that if Agee had lived he would have given his book greater structural unity and might have recast in more dramatic form several sections which remain static in effect. It is doubtful, however, if he could have improved upon the rich contrasts of texture conveyed in characterization, mood, and scene, or refined to greater precision the beautiful clarity of his style.

As an introductory piece, "Knoxville: Summer 1915" creates the mood of affectionate reminiscence within which the novel is embodied. It is a twilight study of a summer evening when children play around the corner lampposts and men in shirt sleeves sprinkle their lawns after supper. Later crickets chirp in the early dark that seems filled with stars as a small boy lies with his father, mother, uncle, and aunt on quilts that have been spread on the grass in the back yard. This is the enchanted world of childhood as it appeared to young Rufus Follet: safe, warm, secure, a world of protection and understanding and love.

Rufus and his younger sister Catherine are asleep when the telephone rings summoning his father to the country, where his Grandfather Follet has been taken suddenly ill. The ties of family relationships, intimate, trivial, amusing, tender, are evoked as Jay Follet prepares to start out before daybreak and his wife Mary gets up to cook his breakfast. Because he expects to be back in time for supper he leaves without waking the children. They are asleep the next night when the telephone rings again and a stranger's voice tells Mary that her husband has been in an accident; on the way back from the country the steering mechanism of his car had broken and Jay, thrown clear when the car left the road, had been killed instantly. This, in outline, is the story of *A Death in the Family*, but not its whole substance. More important is the effect of death on the people involved. To Mary it brings the realization that death happens to many people and is very common. In her distress she turns to her faith for consolation. To Rufus his father's death is not the maturing experience it will eventually become, but only another baffling circumstance among the mysteries of his young life, like his nightmares, his mother's command that he must never mention the color of a Negro nursemaid's skin, the memory of a visit made a short time before to see his withered old great-great-grandmother in the country, or the reason why older boys ask him his name and then break into laughter and run away. Yet he knows that the event gives him some importance that he had never known before: slowly, to himself, he repeats the fact that his father is dead. Catherine is too young to understand her loss or her mother's sorrow. And beyond these is the widening circle of family: Grandfather Lynch, the agnostic; deaf Grandmother Lynch; Great-aunt Hannah, a tower of strength; An-

drew, the sharp-tongued artist uncle, and his sister Amelia; weak, drunken Uncle Ralph Follet, the undertaker, who asks to prepare his own brother's body for burial. These people give the novel its texture, establishing the world in which adults and children confront the fact of death while trying to understand its meaning in terms of grief and love.

The novel contains memorable passages in which deep feeling is combined with power and precision of language, as in the account of the relationship between father and son unfolded as Jay and Rufus walk slowly home after seeing a Charlie Chaplin movie, in the scene in which Great-aunt Hannah and Rufus go shopping and he wears down an adult's reasonable firmness with his small boy's persistence over the purchase of a loud-checked cap, in the moment when the mourning family seems to sense the dead man's presence in the house, and in the scene in which young Rufus, eager to display his new cap, runs to his parents' bedroom and sees that his father is not there. Instead, he finds his mother propped up on two pillows, looking as if she were sick or tired.

James Agee began as a poet and he never lost a poet's eye for the telling detail or the poet's ear. *A Death in the Family* contains passages which, even out of context, show the true quality of a writer to whom literature was a total job of action and feeling, of sights and sounds, of image and meaning, of language and mood. The book is not a perfect novel, perhaps not even a major work, but in the universality of its theme and the compassion which it invokes it uncovers a world of feeling in which all may share. This is more than the truth-telling for which the realist strives; it is truth itself.

DEATH IN VENICE

Type of work: Novelette
Author: Thomas Mann (1875–1955)
Type of plot: Symbolic realism
Time of plot: Early twentieth century
Locale: Italy
First published: 1912

> Principal characters:
> GUSTAVE VON ASCHENBACH, a middle-aged German writer
> TADZIO, a young Polish boy

Critique:

Death in Venice is a short novel of great psychological intensity and tragic power. To read it simply as the story of a middle-aged artist whose character deteriorates because of his hopeless passion for a young Polish boy and whose death is the final irony of his emotional upheaval is to miss almost all of the writer's intention in this fable. Here Mann brings together most of the conflicting themes which have occupied him in his longer works of fiction: being and death, youth and age, sickness and health, beauty and decay, love and suffering, art and life, the German North and the classic lands of the Mediterranean. The symbols are complex and numerous. One effective device is the reappearance of the same character on different crucial occasions in the narrative. As the stranger in the cemetery, for example, he is a summoner sent to lure Aschenbach from the discipline and devotion which are the standards of the writer's craft, but later, as the mysterious gondolier, he is Charon ferrying a lost soul on his last journey. In this work Mann examines understandingly and critically the solitary position of the artist in modern society, and he uses the theme of Aschenbach's infatuation to dramatize in symbolic fashion the narcissism which can be one of the fatal qualities of art.

The Story:

Gustave von Aschenbach was a distinguished German writer whose work had brought him world fame and a patent of nobility from a grateful government. His career had been honorable and dignified. A man of ambitious nature, unmarried, he had lived a life of personal discipline and dedication to his art, and in his portrayal of heroes who combined the forcefulness of a Frederick the Great with the selfless striving of a Saint Sebastian he believed that he had spoken for his race as well as for the deathless spirit of man. At the same time his devotion to the ideals of duty and achievement had brought him close to physical collapse.

One day, after a morning spent at his desk, he left his house in Munich and went for a walk. His stroll took him as far as a cemetery on the outskirts of the city. While he waited for a streetcar which would carry him back to town, he suddenly became aware of a man who stood watching him from the doorway of the mortuary chapel. The stranger, who had a rucksack on his back and a walking staff in his hand, was evidently a traveler. Although no word passed between the watcher and the watched, Aschenbach felt a sudden desire to take a trip, to leave the cold, wet German spring for the warmer climate of the Mediterranean lands. His impulse was strengthened by a problem of technique which he had been unable to solve in his writing. At last, reluctantly, he decided to take a holiday and leave his work for a time in order to find relaxation for mind

DEATH IN VENICE by Thomas Mann, from STORIES OF THREE DECADES by Thomas Mann. Translated by H. T. Lowe-Porter. By permission of the publishers, Alfred A. Knopf, Inc. Copyright, 1930, 1931, 1934, 1935, 1936, by Alfred A. Knopf, Inc.

and body in Italy.

He went first to an island resort in the Adriatic, but before long he became bored with his surroundings and booked passage for Venice. On the ship he encountered a party of lively young clerks from Pola. With them was an old man whose dyed hair and rouged cheeks made him a ridiculous but sinister caricature of youth. In his disgust Aschenbach failed to notice that the raddled old man bore a vague resemblance to the traveler he had seen at the cemetery in Munich.

Aschenbach's destination was the Lido. At the dock in Venice he transferred to a gondola which took him by the water route to his Lido hotel. The gondolier spoke and acted so strangely that Aschenbach became disturbed, and because of his agitation he never noticed that the man looked something like the drunk old scarecrow on the ship and the silent stranger at the cemetery. After taking his passenger to the landing stage, the gondolier, without waiting for his money, hastily rowed away. Other boatmen suggested that he might have been afraid of the law because he had no license.

Aschenbach stayed at the Hotel des Bains. That night, shortly before dinner, his attention was drawn to a Polish family, a beautiful mother, three daughters, and a handsome boy of about fourteen. Aschenbach was unaccountably attracted to the youngster, so much so that he continued to watch the family all through his meal. The next morning he saw the boy playing with some companions on the beach. His name, as Aschenbach learned while watching their games, was Tadzio.

Disturbed by the appeal the boy had for him, the writer announced his intention of returning home, but on his arrival at the railroad station in Venice he discovered that his trunks had been misdirected to Como. Since there was nothing for him to do but to wait for his missing luggage to turn up, he went back to the hotel. Even though he despised himself for his vacillation, he real-ized that his true desire was to be near Tadzio. For Aschenbach there began a period of happiness and anguish, happiness in watching the boy, anguish in that they must remain strangers. One day he almost summoned up enough courage to speak to the youngster. A moment later he became panic-stricken lest Tadzio be alarmed by the older man's interest. The time Aschenbach had set for his holiday passed, but the writer had almost forgotten his home and his work. One evening Tadzio smiled at him as they passed one another. Aschenbach trembled with pleasure.

Guests began to leave the hotel; there were rumors that a plague had broken out in nearby cities. Aschenbach, going one day to loiter on the Piazza, detected the sweetish odor of disinfectant in the air, for the authorities were beginning to take precautions against an outbreak of the plague in Venice. Aschenbach stubbornly decided to stay on in spite of the dangers of infection.

A band of entertainers came to the hotel to serenade the guests. In the troupe was an impudent, disreputable-looking street singer whose antics and ballads were insulting and obscene. As he passed among the guests to collect money for the performance, Aschenbach detected on his clothing the almost overpowering smell of disinfectant, an odor suggesting the sweetly corruptive taints of lust and death. The ribald comedian also had a strange similarity to the gondolier, the rouged old rake, and the silent traveler whose disturbing presence had given Aschenbach the idea for his holiday. Aschenbach was torn between fear and desire. The next day he went to a tourist agency where a young clerk told him that people were dying of the plague in Venice. Even that confirmation of his fears failed to speed Aschenbach's departure from the city. That night he dreamed that in a fetid jungle, surrounded by naked orgiasts, he was taking part in horrible, Priapean rites.

By that time his deterioration was almost complete. At last he allowed a barber to dye his hair and tint his cheeks, but he still refused to see the likeness between himself and the raddled old fop whose appearance had disgusted him on shipboard. His behavior became more reckless. One afternoon he followed the Polish family into Venice and trailed them through the city streets. Hungry and thirsty after his exercise, he bought some overripe strawberries at an open stall and ate them. The odor of disinfectant was strong on the sultry breeze.

Several days later Aschenbach went down to the beach where Tadzio was playing with three or four other boys. They began to fight and one of the boys threw Tadzio to the ground and pressed his face into the sand. As Aschenbach was about to interfere, the other boy released his victim. Humiliated and hurt, Tadzio walked down to the water. He stood facing seaward for a time, as remote and isolated as a young Saint Sebastian, and then he turned and looked with somber, secret gaze at Aschenbach, who was watching from his beach chair. To the writer it seemed as though the boy were summoning him. He started to rise but became so giddy that he fell back into his chair. Attendants carried him to his room. That night the world learned that the great Gustave von Aschenbach had died suddenly of the plague in Venice.

Further Critical Evaluation of the Work:

Thomas Mann is ranked with James Joyce and Marcel Proust as one of the greatest writers of the early twentieth century. Mann was born into a wealthy German family. He was awarded the Nobel Prize for literature in 1919. In 1933 he left Germany because of his opposition to Hitler and the Nazi Party. He later came to the United States, where he taught and lectured. A scholar as well as an artist, his works show the influence of such diverse thinkers as Friedrich Nietzsche, Arthur Schopenhauer, Richard Wagner, and Sigmund Freud. The problem of the artist's role in a decadent, industrialized society is a recurring theme in many of his works such as *Buddenbrooks* (1901), *Tonio Kröger* (1903), *Death in Venice* (1912), and *The Magic Mountain* (1924).

Death in Venice, Mann's best-known novella, is a complex, beautifully wrought tale dealing with the eternal conflict of the forces of death and decay with man's attempts to achieve permanence through art. Mann portrays the final triumph of death and decay, but not before the hero, Aschenbach, has experienced an escape into the eternal beauty created by the imagination of the artist. The escape of the famous writer, Aschenbach, is accomplished, however, not by his own writings, but by the art of his creator, Thomas Mann. Form and order do finally impose themselves on the chaos of his life; corruption and death are transformed into the purity of artistic beauty. To accomplish this, Mann utilizes an elaborate technical skill in structure, characterization, and symbolism which establishes Mann among the great writers of Western literature.

The characterization of Aschenbach, the literary hero of his age, is subtle and complex. Author of prose epics, philosophical novels, novels of moral resolution, and aesthetics, Aschenbach has created the hero for his generation. He is aware that his success and talent rely on a basis of physical stamina as well as moral and mental discipline; his key word is *durchhalten* (endure). His work is a product of strain, endurance, intellectual tenacity, and spasms of will. However, he recognizes that his writing has been to some degree a "pursuit of fame" at the expense of turning his back on a full search for truth. As the novella opens, Aschenbach, exhausted, finding no more joy in his craft, and aware of approaching old age and death, is faced with the fear of not having time to finish all the works he desired to write. Restlessly walking in the naturalistic beauty of the English Garden of Munich, Aschenbach is inspired to leave his relatively rootless life on a pilgrimage for artistic renewal in Venice, the perfect symbol of man's art imposed on nature's chaos. This journey motif begins with his glimpse of a stranger, a foreigner with a skull-like face and a certain animal ruthlessness, in a cemetery.

Arriving at the port of Venice, he discovers he is being taken out to sea, rather than into the city, by his gondolier, a figure whose physical description ominously echoes that of the stranger of the cemetery. The gondola itself is specifically compared to a black coffin. The trip, then, becomes the archetypal journey of life to death and of man into the depths of himself. Aschenbach discovers Venice, the symbol of perfect art in his memory, to be dirty, infected, corrupt, permeated by the odor of the human disease and pollution spread in the natural swamp on which the artifice is built. Aschenbach's own transformation to a "foreigner," one who belongs in Venice, is accomplished at an increasingly mad tempo after the moment when, turning his back on the possibility of escaping from Venice by train, he collapses at a fountain in the heart of the city. His death becomes almost self-willed; he dies not because of the plague, not because of his love of Tadzio, but because his will to live and to create atrophy.

The exterior events of the story, which are minimal, can be properly explained only in terms of the inner conflict of the artist. To produce art, Aschenbach believes he must practice absolute self-denial, affirming the dignity and moral capacity of man in the face of a world of self-indulgence that leads to personal abasement. Yet the artist is also a man, and, as such, has drives that connect him to the chaos of the formless elements of nature. This inner conflict is objectified in the person of the boy, Tadzio, who embodies all that Aschenbach has rejected in fifty long years of dedication to Apollonian art. As his desire for Tadzio becomes obsessive, driving him to neglect the care of his body and stricture of dignity, disintegration sets in and death becomes irrevocable. Subconsciously, Aschenbach is choosing to pursue the basic sensual, Dionysian side of himself that he has always denied.

Mann utilizes dream visions to underline and clarify the subconscious conflicts of Aschenbach. Aschenbach's first hallucination of the crouching beast in the jungle is evoked by the glimpse of the stranger at the Byzantine chapel in Munich. This vision literally foreshadows the trip to Venice and metaphorically foreshadows the inner journey where Aschenbach discovers the jungle and beast within himself. The second vision on the beach in Venice, cast in the form of a Platonic dialog, explores the inter-relatedness of art, love, and beauty with the beastial in man. In a third major dream hallucination, Aschenbach is initiated into the worship of the Dionysian rite and finally glimpses "the stranger god" of sensual experience, of formless, chaotic joy, and excesses of emotion. The most striking vision occurs at the end of the novella, when Aschenbach, viewing he amoral beauty of perfection of form in Tadzio silhouetted against the amoral, formless beauty of the sea, accepts the promise inherent in the sea's chaos as the equivalent of the beauty produced by order and moral discipline. The reader assumes the vision to be objective reality until he is brought sharply and suddenly into the present reality of Aschenbach's dead body. Hemingway utilized this same technique later in his own novella-length study of death and art, "The Snows of Kilimanjaro."

Mann's use of natural, geographical symbols also underlines the central conflicts of the novella. Aschenbach identifies the discipline of his art with Munich, a city of northern Europe, and with the snowy mountains. These places are associated with health, energy, reason, will, and Apollonian creative power. Against them, Mann juxtaposes the tropical marshes, the jungle animal and plant life, the Indian plague, the sun and the sea, which are associated with Dionysian excesses of emotion and ecstasy in art. The beast, the jungle, the plague, the chaos lie within the nature of man and art just as clearly as do the mountain, self-denial, will and reason, qualities which enable man to construct artifice upon the chaos of nature. Great art, Nietzsche says in *The Birth of Tragedy,* is a product of the fusion rather than the separation of the calm, ordered, contemplative spirit of Apollo and the savage, sensual ecstasy of Dionysius. This is what both Aschenbach and the reader discover in Mann's great work, *Death in Venice.*

Ann E. Reynolds

DEATH OF A HERO

Type of work: Novel
Author: Richard Aldington (1892-1962)
Type of plot: Social criticism
Time of plot: World War I
Locale: England
First published: 1929

> *Principal characters:*
> GEORGE WINTERBOURNE, killed in the war
> MR. GEORGE WINTERBOURNE, his father
> MRS. GEORGE WINTERBOURNE, his mother
> ELIZABETH, his wife
> FANNY WELFORD, his mistress

Critique:

With cynicism that is almost morbid in its brutality, Richard Aldington here tells the story of a soldier killed in World War I. It was the author's belief that the hero had deliberately allowed himself to be killed, so confused and miserable was the life which he had attempted to divide between his wife and mistress. The author, attempting to show that the shabby childhood through which the hero lived was responsible for his troubles, purports to tell only the truth. But the truth as he sees it is so bitter that in the telling Aldington condemns not only a generation but a whole society.

The Story:

When word was received that George Winterbourne had been killed in the war, his friend tried to reconstruct the life of the dead man in order to see what forces had caused his death. The friend had served with George at various times during the war, and it was his belief that George had deliberately exposed himself to German fire because he no longer wanted to live.

George Winterbourne's father had been a sentimental fool and his mother a depraved wanton. The elder Winterbourne had married primarily to spite his dominating mother, and his bride had married him under the mistaken notion that he was rich. They gave themselves up to mutual hatred, the mother showering her thwarted love on young George. She imagined herself young and desirable and was proud of her twenty-two lovers. Her husband conveniently went to a hotel when she was entertaining, but he prayed for her soul. All in all, they were the most depressing parents to whom a child could be exposed and undoubtedly they caused young George to hate them both. Soon after receiving word of their son's death, the elder Winterbourne was killed in an accident. Mrs. Winterbourne married her twenty-second lover and moved to Australia, but not before she had thoroughly enjoyed being a bereft mother and widow.

When he reached young manhood, George mingled with all sorts of queer people. He dabbled in writing and painting—the modern variety. Sexual freedom was his goal, even though he had experienced little of it. At an affair given by his pseudo-intellectual friends he first met Elizabeth. They were immediately compatible; both hated their parents and both sought freedom. At first Elizabeth was shocked by George's attacks on Christianity, morals, the class system, and all other established institutions, but she soon recognized him as a truly "free" man. In fact, it was not long before she adopted his ideas and went him one better. Free love was the only thing she could talk or think about. Thinking themselves extremely sensible, they saw no reason to marry in order to experience love as long as they were careful not to have a baby. Babies complicated matters, for the ignorant middle classes still frowned on such children. Unknowingly, George and Elizabeth were about as middle class as it was possible to be.

The two lovers planned carefully to have no sordidness cloud their affair. They did not talk of love, only sex. They were to take all the other lovers they pleased. That was freedom in an intelligent way. Elizabeth was even more insistent than George upon such freedom.

Finally, Elizabeth mistakenly thought that she was pregnant. Gone were the new freedoms, the enlightened woman; George must marry her at once, for female honor was at stake. All the old clichés were dragged out for poor old George. They were married, much to the horror of their families. When the mistake was discovered, supplemented by the doctor's statement that Elizabeth could not possibly have a child without an operation, back came freedom, stronger than ever. She became an evangelist, even though she detested the word, for sex. Marriage made no difference in their lives. They continued to live separately, meeting as lovers.

When Elizabeth had to make a trip home, George became the lover of her best friend, Fanny Welford, another enlightened woman. He was sure that Elizabeth would not mind, for she had become the mistress of Fanny's lover. Thus he was quite stunned when Elizabeth kicked up a row about Fanny. However, the girls remained surface friends, each one too free to admit horror at the other's duplicity.

War had been approaching fast while these friends had been practicing their enlightened living. George was drafted and sent quickly to France. The war poisoned George. Killing horrified him, and he began to imagine his own death. He was brave, but not from any desire to be a hero; it was just that the monotony of his existence seemed to demand that he keep going even though he was ready to drop from fatigue. The knowledge of the ill-concealed dislike between Fanny and Elizabeth began to prey on his mind. There seemed to be only two solutions: to drift along and accept whatever happened or to get himself killed in the war. It seemed to make little difference to him or anyone else which course he chose. His letters to his two women depressed each of them. Had he known their feelings he could have been spared his worry about them. Each took other lovers and gave little thought to George.

His own depression increased. He felt that he was degenerating mentally as well as physically, that he was wasting what should have been his best years. He knew that he would be terribly handicapped if he did live through the war, that those not serving would have passed him by.

George was made an officer and sent back to England for training. There he lived again with Elizabeth, but she left him frequently to go out with other men. Fanny, too, seemed to care little whether she saw him or not. Talk of the war and his experiences obviously bored them, and they made only a small pretense of being interested. He spent his last night in England with Fanny, Elizabeth being off with someone else. Fanny did not bother to get up with him the morning he left. In fact, she awoke lazily, then went to sleep again before he even left the flat.

Back at the front, George found that he was ill-suited to command a company. Although he did his best, he was constantly censured by his colonel, who blamed George for all the faults of his untrained and cowardly troops. George himself could think of little but death. During a particularly heavy German shelling he simply stood upright and let the bullets smash into his chest. Who knows whether his death was an act of heroism or one of complete and utter futility?

Further Critical Evaluation of the Work:

Richard Aldington records the incredible innocence and disillusionment of the first generation of the modern world—if we take that world to have begun in 1914. Like Ford Madox Ford's *Parade's End,* Robert Graves's memoir *Goodbye to All That,* and the poetry of Rupert Brooke, Charles Sorley and Siegfried Sasson, *Death of a Hero* dramatizes the impact of the "Great War" upon the children of the late Victorians. Raised in the twilight of that age to believe that their culture rested on granite, they discovered that it, as well as their own lives, had no more foundation than a bed of quick sand.

The accomplishment of Aldington's novel consists in his perception that the seeds of war lay not only in the greed and stupidity of the politicians, but also—and more importantly—in the anarchy of personal relationships. The first generation of the twentieth century was unprepared for war as well as unfit to carry on their own love lives. The repression and hypocrisy of their Victorian parents destroyed any chance that young George Winterbourne, Elizabeth and Fanny, for example, have of forming adult relationships. Their sexual lives are those of children let out of school who are unable to handle their new-found freedom; ignorance combined with license must always end in violence.

The title of the novel is of course ironic. The traditional idea of the hero —especially the military one—is of the great man who sacrifices himself for the good of society. George Winterbourne's end comes with a whimper, not a bang; his death is at last an admission that he no longer has the will to continue. Insofar as he represents his generation, his suicide suggests its inability to understand and unwillingness to deal with a world that it has not made.

DEATH OF A SALESMAN

Type of work: Drama
Author: Arthur Miller (1915-   )
Type of plot: Social criticism
Time of plot: Mid-twentieth century
Locale: New York
First presented: 1949

Principal characters:
  WILLY LOMAN, a salesman
  LINDA, his wife
  BIFF, and
  HAPPY, his sons
  CHARLEY, his friend
  BERNARD, Charley's son
  UNCLE BEN, Willy's brother
  THE WOMAN

Critique:

Death of a Salesman represents a successful attempt to blend the themes of social and personal tragedy within the same dramatic framework. For the story of Willy Loman is also the story of false values sustained by almost every agency of publicity and advertisement in our national life. Willy Loman accepts at face value the over-publicized ideals of material success and blatant optimism, and therein lies his tragedy. His downfall and final defeat illustrate not only the failure of a man but also the failure of a way of life. The playwright's ability to project the story of his tragic, lower middle-class hero into the common experience of so many Americans who sustain themselves with illusions and ignore realities makes this play one of the most significant in the American theater in recent years.

The Story:

When Willy Loman came home on the same day he had left on a trip through his New England territory, his wife Linda knew that he was near the breaking point. Lately he had begun to talk to himself about things out of the past. That day he had run off the road two or three times without knowing what he was doing, and he had come home in fear. Willy, sixty-three, had given all his life to the company. He told himself they would just have to make a place for him in the New York home office. Traveling all week and driving futile miles had become too much for him.

Willy had had such hopes before Biff came home from his last job. Biff had always been the favorite, though Happy was the more settled and successful son. Biff was thirty-four now and still had to find himself, but Willy knew he would settle down when the time came. The boy had been the greatest football player his school had ever known. In a game at Ebbets Field he had been a hero. Three colleges offered him scholarships. Biff had not gone to college, had not done anything but bum around the West, never making more than twenty-eight dollars a week. It was hard to understand him.

During the next two days, Willy's whole life unrolled before him, today's reality intermingled with yesterday's half-forgotten episodes. Broken as it was, the pictures told the story of Willy Loman, salesman.

Perhaps the first mistake was in not following his brother Ben to Alaska—or was it Africa? Ben had wanted Willy to join him, but Willy was a salesman.

DEATH OF A SALESMAN by Arthur Miller. By permission of the publishers, The Viking Press, Inc. Copyright, 1949, by Arthur Miller.

Some weeks he averaged two hundred dollars. No, that was not quite true; it was nearer seventy. But he would make the grade, he told Ben, and so he stayed in New York. Ben went into the jungle a pauper; four years later he came back from the diamond mines a rich man.

Willy's boys were both well liked; that was important. Bernard, Charley's son, was liked, but not well liked. Bernard had begged to carry Biff's shoulder pads that day at Ebbets Field. Sometimes Willy had worried a little about the boys. Biff stole a football from school, and a whole case of them from the sporting goods store where he worked. He did not mean any harm, Willy knew. Willy even laughed when the boys stole a little lumber from a construction job nearby; no one would miss it. Willy and the boys used it to make the front stoop.

But that day at Ebbets Field seemed to be the last great day in Biff's life. Willy had left for Boston after the game, but surely that little Boston affair had not made the difference in the boy. Willy was with a woman when Biff burst in on him. Biff had failed math and could not take one of the scholarships unless Willy talked to the teacher and got him to change the grade. Willy was ready to leave for New York at once, but when Biff saw the woman in Willy's room, he left. Things were never the same afterward.

There was also Happy, who used to stand in Biff's shadow. Happy was a magnificent specimen, just like Biff, and there was not a woman in the world he could not have. An assistant merchandising manager, he would be manager someday, a big man. So would Biff. Biff needed only to find himself.

On the day Willy Loman turned back home he dreamed his biggest dreams. Biff would go back to that sporting goods store and get a loan from the owner to set himself and Happy up in business. That man had always loved Biff. And Willy would go to young Howard Wagner, his boss's son, and demand to be given a place in the New York office. They would celebrate that night at dinner. Biff and Happy would give Willy a night on the town to celebrate their mutual success.

But Biff failed to get the loan. That man who had loved Biff did not even recognize him. To get even, Biff stole a fountain pen and ran down eleven flights with it. And when Howard heard Willy's story, he told him to turn in his samples and take a rest. Willy realized he was through. He went to Charley for more money, for he had been borrowing from Charley since he had been put on straight commission months ago. Bernard was in Charley's office. He was on his way to plead a case before the Supreme Court. Willy could not understand it. Charley had never given his life for his boy as Willy had for his. Charley offered Willy a job, but Willy said he was a salesman. They loved him in New England; he would show them yet.

Willy stumbled in to the dinner they had planned, a failure himself but hoping for good news about Biff. Hearing of Biff's failure, he was completely broken. Happy picked up two girls, and he and Biff left Willy alone.

When Biff and Happy finally came home, Linda ordered them out of the house by morning. She was afraid because Willy had tried to kill himself once before. Giving vent to his anger and sense of defeat, Biff cursed Willy for a fool and a dreamer. He forced himself and Willy to acknowledge that Biff had been only a clerk in that store, not a salesman; that Biff had been jailed in Kansas City for stealing; that Happy was not an assistant manager but a clerk and a philandering, woman-chasing bum; and that Willy had never been a success and never would be. When Biff began to weep, Willy realized for the first time that his son loved him.

Willy, left alone after the others went upstairs, began to see Ben again, to tell him his plan. Willy had twenty thousand in insurance. Biff would be magnificent with twenty thousand. Willy ran out to his car and drove crazily away.

At the funeral, attended only by Linda and the boys and Charley, Charley tried to tell Biff about his father. He said that a salesman had to dream, that with-out dreams he was nothing. When the dreams were gone, a salesman was finished. Sobbing quietly, Linda stooped and put flowers on the grave of Willy Loman, salesman.

Further Critical Evaluation of the Work:

Born in New York, the city that is the setting for *Death of a Salesman,* Arthur Miller in his earlier plays reacts to the social pressures and fervors of the 1930's (depression) and 1940's (World War II). But *Death of a Salesman,* Miller's most famous and most effective play, is also his most complex, and is far more than a social document. It is, of course, a very clear attack on at least one aspect of the American success myth or dream, as that dream is defined by Willy Loman. To Willy, success, respect, affection, and authority come to those who are "well liked." Greetings given gladly, doors opened eagerly, sales made readily—these represent the good life to Willy Loman. But the dream scarcely suits everyone. It does not suit Willy, despite his great dreams and restless longings. Since, despite constant failure, Willy keeps trying, he ultimately loses sight of his own identity. Biff laments at the end that his father never learned to know himself.

The dream, to Miller, is not only destructive; it is amoral. As a boy, Biff is told that, since he is "well liked," he can get away with anything. Disillusioned with his father, Biff, after running away, discovers that he has no direction, no skill, no vocation. The dream proves just as destructive to Happy, who is a weak caricature of his father. Nevertheless, the dream's enormous power is shown again and again, particularly at the conclusion of Act I, when Willy, Happy, and Biff grow wildly enthusiastic over the prospect of Biff asking for a business loan from a former employer, an employer whom Biff scarcely knew. When all else fails, Willy can call up the image of his brother, Ben, who represents an earlier get-rich-quick version of the success myth.

The Ben fantasies also suggest another level of the play. They help define a man whose world is crumbling. His weariness, his suicide efforts, his grumbling as he thinks of the little he has made of his life, his grandiose posturing—all these are the exterior cracks in a man who is also breaking up inside, as visions and memories out of the past cross and recross the present. The final crack-up is inevitable.

The play was at the center of an interesting controversy: can a common man be a suitable subject for tragedy? Miller, of course, insisted that he could. Interesting, too, is the fact that as his own interests changed, Miller himself announced that Willy was too pathetic for genuine tragic stature.

Miller's later plays—*After the Fall* and *The Price*—probe the nature not of society, but of man, asserting the individual's own responsibility for himself and his life.

THE DEATH OF ARTEMIO CRUZ

Type of work: Novel
Author: Carlos Fuentes (1929-   )
Time: 1889-1959
Locale: Mexico
First published: 1962

Principal characters:

ARTEMIO CRUZ, a dying tycoon
CATALINA, his wife
LORENZO, his son, killed in the Spanish Civil War
TERESA, his daughter
GLORIA, his granddaughter
GERARDO, his son-in-law
DON GAMALIEL BERNAL, his father-in-law
GONZAO BERNAL, a young lawyer executed by Villistas
FATHER PÁEZ, a priest
REGINA, a dead woman Artemio had loved
LILIA and
LAURA, Artemio's mistresses
PADILLA, Artemio's secretary
LUNERO, a mulatto peon

To the thinking Mexican, the Revolution of 1910 is the great and inescapable fact in his country's destiny and his own personal identity. A second conquest of the land and the past, it was the climax of four centuries of turbulent history and the adumbration of all that has happened since. For the revolution did more than topple the paternal dictatorship of Porfirio Díaz; it tore a nation apart by fratricidal strife and then put it together again in a strange new way that continues to disturb and puzzle its citizens. It swept away lingering remnants of colonialism, brought into being a revolutionary oligarchy still in power, created a new middle class, moved Mexico ahead into the twentieth century, helped to shape a literature both ancestral and prophetic in its pictures of a sad and violent land. And its force is still unspent.

In some ways this situation is comparable to the aftermath of the Civil War in the United States, where Americans are still trying to see their own fraternal conflict in perspectives of cause and consequence. Among Southerners, especially, we find a sense of the uniqueness of the regional experience, a response to events viewed imaginatively as a national tragedy. A somewhat similar spirit prevails in certain areas of Mexican life, but on a greater scale, complicated by a growing belief that the revolution has failed and that the real revolution is still to come. In fact, the Mexican intellectual today is often self-conscious in much the same manner that Faulkner and writers of his generation were self-conscious: obsessed by feeling for place, burdened by the past, uneasy in the new society, seeking to reclaim in their stories and poems old values lost in the processes of change. Feeling that history has isolated him in his own particular moment in time, the parochialism of the revolution, the Mexican writer often turns inward to create a literature that veers between moods of fury and outrage and the poetry of nocturnal silence. He lives, to borrow a phrase from the poet Octavio Paz, in a "labyrinth of solitude." It was José Luis Cuevas, the *avant-garde* painter, who first used the term "Cactus Curtain" in protest against the isolation of the Mexican artist. In an earlier novel, *Where the Air Is Clear,* Carlos Fuentes said that it is impossible to explain Mexico. Instead, the artist believes in it with anger and a feeling of outrage, with passion, and with a sense of alienation.

This statement carries the reader a long way toward an understanding of Carlos Fuentes' fiction. It is clear that he has rejected Mexican life as it is constituted today, but at the same time he uses it in his novels to test his sensuous powers and dramatic vigor. The country he writes about is not the land that tourists see or a land of tradition; it is the country of art, a place and people transformed by compelling imagination into something rich and strange and meaningful. This is one reason for his restless experiments with technique, the broken narrative structures, the shifting points of view, his lovely, solemn hymns to landscapes and time, the interior monologues by which he tries to probe the national conscience as well as the consciousness of his people. If he has not yet assimilated in his own writing the influences he has absorbed from such varied figures as Proust, Joyce, Faulkner, Dos Passos, and Wolfe, he has nevertheless put his borrowings to brilliant use in catching the tempo of Mexican life in its present stage of uncertainty and indirection.

Although his methods may vary in his discontinuity of form and the labyrinthine turnings of his style, his theme remains constant, for his novels are studies in the responsibility which power, knowingly or unknowingly, brings and the corruption which almost necessarily accompanies power. He began with *Where the Air Is Clear,* a novel set against the background of Mexico City. There the extremes of poverty and wealth allowed a study in breadth of what has happened on all levels of society after the revolution failed to fulfill its promises. Central to Señor Fuentes' theme is Federico Robles, once an ardent revolutionary but now a driving power in the country's political and financial life. His rise in the world, through treachery, bribery, ruthless exploitation, and the corruption of better men, has made him many enemies. The novel tells the story of his fall. But more than one man's ruin is involved in the

panoramic picture presented. Behind the events of the story the failed revolution throws long shadows into the present, the realization of wasted effort, of lives lost to no purpose, of high aims given over to meaningless deeds of sensuality, folly, and outrage. Robles is what he is, as we see at the end, because others in their selfishness and pride have assisted in his rise. Now they hate him because they see in him an enlarged image of themselves. *Where the Air Is Clear* is saved from becoming an ideological polemic by its roots that reach downward toward much that is flawed and gross in the human condition.

Fuentes tells much the same story in *The Good Conscience,* although here his concern is with a family, grandfather, father, and son, rather than a single individual. The setting is Guanajuato, where the oldest of the Ceballos, a dry-goods merchant, laid the foundation of a family fortune. Representative of the new middle class, the materialistic, ambitious Ceballos men marry for position, play a cynical political game for security, carry on their shady business deals for gain. Society accepts them; the State protects them; the Church sustains them. The writer's picture of chicanery and corruption is magnificent up to a point. But the book breaks abruptly in the middle to present in Jaime Ceballo, the youngest of the family, a study of adolescent confusion and rebellion. Torn between the self-seeking practices of his family and the teachings of the Church, he attempts to follow the example of Christ, fails, and falls back on radicalism as the only alternative to the greed, lust for power, and hypocrisy of his class. The ending is unconvincing after the ironical, somber overtones orchestrated through the earlier sections of the novel. The reader feels that the writer's own Marxist beliefs rather than the logic of character and experience dictated an ending that seems more contrived than real.

The Death of Artemio Cruz is the most limited presentation of this theme that Fuentes has attempted to date. True, the book is flawed by his bewildering cross-chronology, the points of view constantly shifting and intermingling, and his varied stylistic effects. In the end, however, the novel rises above its faults in its compelling picture of one man's life and the relation of that life to all the years of disorder and change that have conditioned the course of Mexican history from the beginning of the century to the present day. Again this central figure is a force in the land, a millionaire who has climbed to his position of wealth and power by violence, blackmail, bribery, brutal exploitation of the workers. Like Federico Robles, he is a former revolutionist who stands for the Mexican past as well as its present. (The robber bands who represented the extreme of the revolutionary effort, Fuentes seems to say, have now been replaced by the robber barons of modern finance and politics.) On the wall of his office a map shows the extent of his holdings: a newspaper, mines, timber, hotels, foreign stocks and bonds, and, not shown, money on deposit in English, Swiss, and United States banks.

Artemio Cruz is on his deathbed when the novel opens. Stricken by a gastric attack after his return from a business trip to Hermosillo on April 9, 1959, he lies in his mansion in a fashionable section of Mexico City, the moral corruption of his life as much a stench in his nostrils as the processes of decay already at work in his body. An officious priest tries to administer the last sacrament in spite of his protests; Cruz had abandoned the Church years before. Doctors subject him to the indignity of their instruments as they examine his body. In the background are his estranged wife and the daughter who despises him. Although they pretend concern for the dying man, their greatest anxiety is the whereabouts of his will, and he refuses to tell them. His only hold on reality is a tape recording, an account of business deals and proposed transactions, played by his secretary, Padilla. While these people jostle about his bed,

Artemio Cruz drifts between past and present, not in any coherent order but in a series of flashbacks tracing the course that has brought him to his present state.

Thus we see him in 1919, an ambitious young veteran of the revolution arriving at the home of the Bernal family in Perales, ostensibly to bring to a bereaved father and sister an account of Gonzalo Bernal's death before a Villista firing squad, in reality to insinuate himself into the confidence of the old *hacendado*, marry his daughter, and get possession of the Bernal estates. But his wife Catalina never fully realizes that Artemio had really fallen in love with her; influenced by Father Páez, the family priest, she believes that her marriage bought her father's security and her own at the cost of her soul, and she hates herself for the passion to which Artemio moves her at night. In the end the two despise each other, and she blames him when their son, whom he has removed from her control, is killed while fighting in the Spanish Civil War. Before Catalina there was Regina, the camp follower he also loved, taken hostage by Villa's troops and hanged. After her death there were other women: Lilia, the young mistress he took on a holiday in Acapulco and who betrayed him there, and Laura, who later married someone else. But Artemio's adventures are not all with women. We see him ruining his neighbors at Perales and getting possession of their lands, using bribery and blackmail to buy his first election as a deputy, giving his lavish parties where the guests who mocked him behind his back were not supposed to bore him with their conversation, negotiating big deals, ruining competitors, and all the while preparing himself for the loneliness and desolation he feels when his time comes to die. Close to the end of the novel Fuentes presents two episodes that throw light on the later years of Artemio's career. One is the story of his capture by a Villista troop. Sentenced to death, he decides to give information to the enemy. Although he later kills the officer to whom he had promised betrayal, he had at least been guilty by intent. Some justification for his deed is given in the words of Gonzalo Bernal, the disillusioned idealist who nevertheless goes bravely to his death. Bernal declares that once a revolution has been corrupted by those who act only to live well, to rise in the world, the battles may still be fought and won, but the revolution without compromise has been lost to the ambitious and the mediocre. The last episode tells how it all began. Artemio Cruz was born on the *petate*, the mat symbolic of the peon's condition, the son of a decayed landowner and a half-caste girl. His only friend during his early years is Lunero, a mulatto who serves the needs of Artemio's half-crazed old grandmother and his lazy, drunken uncle. After the boy accidentally shoots his uncle he runs away to Veracruz. There, as we learn indirectly, a schoolmaster tutors Artemio and prepares him for the part he is to play in the revolution before he loses his ideals and makes the choice of betrayal and rejection that leads him to the corrupting use of power in other men's lives and his own.

Fuentes' meaning in this final episode seems clear. The revolution, in the end, was betrayed by the common people who had made it.

The character of Artemio Cruz is handled with a considerable degree of subtlety and skill. Fuentes does not gloss over his cynicism, opportunism, or brutal ruthlessness. But he is saved from becoming a monster of pure abstraction and calculation by his relationships with the three people who mean most in his life: Lunero, the devoted mulatto for whose sake he committed a murder; Regina, the girl killed by Villistas, and his son Lorenzo. Through the novel, like a refrain, runs a reference to the time just before

Lorenzo went off to fight in the Spanish war when father and son took a morning ride toward the sea. By the end of the novel Artemio's story fulfills all that it promised to a young boy, one man's journey with no real beginning or end in time, promises of love, solitude, violence, power, friendship, disillusionment, corruption, forgetfulness, innocence, and delight. There is also the realization of how at the end a man's death is joined to his beginning.

To get his story told, Fuentes employs three voices. The first is the obvious third person, used to present in dramatic form the events of Artemio's life as they are pieced together in past time. The second is the "I" of the present as the old man lies dying, shrinks from the decay of his body, and takes fitful account of what is going on around him. The third is a vatic presence never identified—conscience? consciousness?—addressing Artemio as "you." This, we judge, is the unrealized Artemio, the man he might have been. He is a lover of the land that the real Artemio Cruz robbed and raped, the product of history, perhaps the re-created moral conscience of the revolution. He speaks in metaphors, poetry, and prophecy about history and time, places and people, because they belong to the beautiful but sad and tragic land of his birth.

The Death of Artemio Cruz is a divided book, terse yet chaotic, passionate, ironic. Too much has been made, undoubtedly, of Carlos Fuentes as one of Mexico's angry young men. In spite of his Marxist beliefs, he is essentially a romantic. He is also the possessor of an exuberant, powerful, very contemporary talent which has not yet found itself but which, aside from his surface effects of undisciplined but compelling style, comes through in clear, unhackneyed fashion, even in translation.

THE DEATH OF IVAN ILYICH

Type of work: Novella
Author: Count Leo Tolstoy (1828-1910)
Type of plot: Psychological realism
Time of plot: 1880's
Locale: St. Petersburg and nearby provinces
First published: 1884

Principal characters:
IVAN ILYICH GOLOVIN, a prominent Russian judge
PRASKOVYA FEDOROVNA GOLOVINA, his wife
PETER IVANOVITCH, his colleague
GERASIM, his servant boy

Critique:

The Death of Ivan Ilyich, a masterpiece of Tolstoy's later period, was written after he had published his most famous novels. Its theme is related to his own struggle against an obsessive fear of death and the conclusion that he had wasted his life, a struggle which culminated for him in a spiritual rebirth. The story itself is a supreme imaginative creation, however deep its roots in the author's own experience. Tolstoy presents, with frankness, simplicity, and kindness, an ordinary man confronted by the irrevocable fact of death. Here is one of the finest examples in literature of the portrayal of the particular—in this case the life and death of Ivan Ilyich—with such realistic understanding that it acquires universal significance.

The Story:

During a break in a hearing, a group of lawyers gathered informally. One, Peter Ivanovitch, interrupted the good-natured arguing of the others with the news that Ivan Ilyich, a colleague they greatly respected, was dead. Unwittingly, each thought first of what this death meant to his own chances of promotion, and each could not help feeling relief that Ivan Ilyich and not himself had died.

That afternoon Peter Ivanovitch visited the dead man's home, where the funeral was to be held. Although he met a playful colleague, Schwartz, he attempted to behave as correctly as possible under such sorrowful circumstances, as if observing the proper protocol would enable him to have the proper feelings. He respectfully looked at the corpse; he talked with Ivan's widow, Praskovya Fedorovna. But he was continually distracted during his talk by an unruly spring in the hassock on which he sat. As he struggled to keep his decorum, Praskovya spoke only of her own exhaustion and suffering. Peter, suddenly terrified by their mutual hypocrisy, longed to leave, and the widow, having gathered from him information about her pension, was glad to end the conversation. At the funeral Peter also saw Ivan's daughter and her fiancé, who were angrily glum, and Ivan's little son, who was tear-stained but naughty. Only the servant boy, Gerasim, spoke cheerfully, for only he could accept death as natural. Leaving, Peter hurried to his nightly card game.

Ivan Ilyich had been the second and most successful of the three sons of a superfluous bureaucrat. An intelligent and popular boy, he seemed able to mold his life into a perfect pattern. As secretary to a provincial governor after completing law school, and later as an examining magistrate, he was the very model of conscientiousness mingled with good humor. He managed the decorum of his official position as well as the ease of his social one. Only marriage, although socially correct, did not conform to his ideas of decorum; his wife, not content to fulfill the role he had chosen for her, became demanding and quarrelsome. As a result, he increasingly shut himself off from his family (for he now had two children), finding the order and peace he needed in his judiciary affairs.

In 1880, however, he was shattered by the loss of two promotions. In desperation he went to St. Petersburg, where a chance meeting led to his obtaining a miraculously good appointment. In the city he found precisely the house he had always wanted and he worked to furnish it just to his taste. Even a fall and a resulting bruise on his side did not dampen his enthusiasm. He and his wife were delighted with their new home, which they felt to be aristocratic, although it looked like all homes of those who wished to appear well-bred. To Ivan, life was at last as it should be: smooth, pleasant, and ordered according to an unwavering routine. His life was properly divided into the official and the personal, and the two halves were always kept dextrously apart.

Then Ivan began to notice an increasing discomfort in his left side. At last he consulted a specialist, but the examination left him frightened and helpless, for although he understood the doctor's objective attitude as akin to his own official one, he felt that it had given his pain an awesome significance. For a time he fancied he grew better from following prescriptions and learning all he could about his illness, but renewed attacks terrified him. Gradually Ivan found all his life colored by the pain. Card games became trivial; friends seemed only to speculate on how long he would live. When Ivan's brother-in-law came for a visit, his shocked look told Ivan how much illness had changed him, and he suddenly realized that he faced not illness but death itself. Through deepening terror and despair, Ivan shrank from this truth. Other men died, not he. Desperately he erected screens against the pain and the knowledge of death it brought, but it lurked behind court duties or quarrels with his family. The knowledge that it had begun with the bruise on his side only made his condition harder to bear. As Ivan grew steadily worse, drugs failed to help him. But the clean strength and honesty of a peasant boy, Gerasim, nourished him, for he felt that his family were hypocrites who chose to pretend that he was not dying. Death to them was not part of that same decorum he too had once revered and was therefore hidden as unpleasant and shameful. Only Gerasim could understand his pain because only he admitted that death was real and natural.

Ivan retreated increasingly into his private anguish. He hated his knowing doctors, his plump, chiding wife, his daughter and her new fiancé. Lamenting, he longed to have his old, happy life again. But only memories of childhood revealed true happiness. Unwillingly he returned again and again to this knowledge as he continued questioning the reasons for his torment. If he had always lived correctly, why was this happening to him? What if he had been wrong? Suddenly he knew that the faint urges he had consciously stilled in order to do as people thought proper had been the true urges. And since he had not known the truth about life, he also had not known the truth about death. His anguish increased as he thought of the irrevocable choice he had made.

His wife brought the priest, whose sacrament eased him until her presence reminded him of the deception his life had been. He screamed to her to leave him, and he continued screaming as he struggled against death, unable to relinquish the illusion that his life had been good. Then the struggle ceased, and he knew that although his life had not been right, it no longer mattered. Opening his eyes, he saw his wife and son weeping by his bedside. Aware of them for the first time, he felt sorry for them. As he tried to ask their forgiveness, everything became clear to him. He must not hurt them; he must set them free and free himself from his sufferings. The pain and fear of death were no longer there. Instead there was only light and joy.

Further Critical Evaluation of the Work:

Written in 1886, this story is only about sixty pages long, but it is one of the greatest pieces of fiction in any language. In it Tolstoy examines the hollowness of bourgeois existence. Ivan Ilyich is a successful member of the state bureaucracy. All his life he has carefully adjusted his conduct so as to please his superiors and to arrange a life which runs smoothly and without complication. He is the perfect example of the conforming, "other-directed" man. Only at his death does he discover the horror which lies behind his seemingly successful life.

The story opens in an unusual but significant way. Rather than tell us of Ivan's early years, Tolstoy presents us with the dead Ivan stretched out at home, attended by his wife and closest friend Peter Ivanovitch. The behavior of the mourners tells us more about Ivan's life than any chronicle could. Rather than grieve over his death, they are worried about their own affairs. His wife asks Peter Ivanovitch about her pension, hoping to persuade him to help her arrange for an increase, while he frets about missing the bridge game he had planned. To make matters worse, they both pretend to feelings of grief that they do not feel. At this point the reader may well ask what in Ivan's life could bring about so little concern about his death. The rest of the story answers this question in the most powerful terms; it dramatizes the statement which opens the second section: "Ivan Ilyich's life had been most simple and most ordinary and therefore most terrible."

Ivan's progress from law school to the position of examining magistrate is marked by careful obedience to authority both in legal matters and in matters of taste and style of life. His early pangs of conscience at youthful actions are overcome when he sees people of good position doing the same thing without qualms. Still, he never becomes a rake or hell-raiser; he is, rather, anxiously correct and proper. He makes a proper marriage—one that serves to advance him—and then gradually proceeds to alienate his wife and children by avoiding domestic complications in the name of his job. In this separation between his private life, with its potential for affection, and his public duties he furthers the process of fragmentation within himself. He becomes punctilious at home as well as at work. All of his life takes on an official and artificial character from which only the natural process of death can release him as it educates him. In the opening scene we are told that "his face was handsomer and above all more dignified than when he was alive." His death is a form of rescue.

His job is a game which he plays with great seriousness—like the bridge games he hurries to after work. He never abuses his power as a magistrate but instead conducts himself "by the book." Most of all, he is careful never to become personally involved in the carrying out of justice. He is a perfect arm of the state, a perfect product of its bureaucratic machinery. Naturally, he never questions the system of justice he is paid to administer. It is significant that he rises no higher than the middle rank of officialdom. Those above him have perceived that he is essentially mediocre.

Nevertheless, his life seems to flow along easily, pleasantly, and correctly. He decorates his new home, supervising much of the work closely. He imagines that the result is very special, but Tolstoy tells us that Ivan's home, characteristicaly, looks exactly like the homes of other people of his class and station. Underneath the smooth surface of this life there is something wrong which refuses to stay concealed. It manifests itself in the form of an illness, probably cancer, which gradually consumes Ivan's vitality. When he goes to the doctor he feels guilty and desperately uncertain. For the first time he learns what it is like to be the recipient of the games those in authority play —like a criminal dragged to the bar. The doctor cannot or will not tell him what is wrong (he probably doesn't know). Gradually Ivan declines until he is bedridden. His disintegrating flesh begins to give off a strange and unpleasant odor. He becomes hateful to himself and to his wife, who up to now has pursued a life of idle and superficial pleasures. Even more than physical pain, Ivan suffers from spiritual torment. His prior habits of life have given him no resources with which to face death. Moreover, he is perpetually troubled by the question of why he is suffering when he took such pains to lead a correct life. What if he has been wrong all along? In the grip of despair he searches for hope at any hand but no hope presents itself until he finds it possible to accept the kind attentions of his servant Gerasim.

Gerasim is the opposite of Ivan. A healthy, simple peasant, he has never known the artificial life of a bureaucrat and social climber. He does not fear death, and thus does not mind being in the presence of the dying Ivan. He is in tune with the natural. Ivan is able to accept him because he feels that there is no deception in Gerasim's attitude toward him, whereas he sees nothing but deception in the kind and cheerful attitudes of his wife and friends (a reaction in part, to the falseness of his former life). When Gerasim sits for hours with his master's legs propped up on his shoulders, Ivan feels unaccountable relief. Still, Gerasim's presence only modifies Ivan's agony somewhat.. Essentially he must go through the process of dying by himself. Perhaps Gerasim's naturalness does bring Ivan to the conviction of the worthlessness of his former life, but death is Ivan's best educator. It gradually and painfully strips away the artificial and the vain. It reduces Ivan to the elemental position of an organism dependent upon the natural processes of life. Interestingly, Ivan thinks most of all of his early youth at this time. He recalls when he was still an innocent, uncorrupted by the false system he slavishly aspired to enter. In a sense, he is yearning to recapture the natural instincts represented by Gerasim. Death offers him the chance. In the final hours of his interminable decline, Ivan grows still. He has a vision of light and freedom. Death becomes for him a door to a larger and purer existence.

Benjamin Nyce

THE DEATH OF THE GODS

Type of work: Novel
Author: Dmitri Merejkowski (1865-1941)
Type of plot: Historical romance
Time of plot: Fourth century
Locale: Ancient Rome
First published: 1896

Principal characters:
CAESAR CONSTANTIUS, the Roman Emperor
JULIAN FLAVIUS, Caesar's cousin
GALLUS FLAVIUS, Julian's brother
ARSINOË, Julian's beloved

Critique:

Merejkowski, one of the most successful of modern Russian novelists of the old régime, saw European civilization as a result of the meeting of Hellenism and Christianity. In this novel he attempted to show how that meeting was carried on in the reign of Julian the Apostate, a Roman emperor of the fourth century. The novelist's success in re-creating what is distant, both in point of time and place, is almost unparalleled in any national literature. Little street urchins of Constantinople, common soldiers in the Roman legions, innkeepers of Asia Minor, and fawning courtiers of Caesar's court, all take on flesh and life as they pass through the story, all of them reflecting in greater or lesser degree the struggle between the two great philosophies, paganism and Christianity.

The Story:

The Roman Emperor Constantius had risen to power by a series of assassinations. Two of his cousins, Julian and Gallus, were still alive, prisoners in Cappadocia. No one knew why they were permitted to live, for they were the last people who could challenge the right of the emperor to his position. Julian was the greater of the two, a young man steeped in the teachings of the philosophers. His brother was younger and more girlish in his habits. Both knew that they could expect death momentarily.

When Julian was twenty years old, Constantius gave him permission to travel in Asia Minor, where the lad affected the dress of a monk and passed as a Christian. His younger brother, Gallus, was given high honors as co-regent with Constantius and named Caesar. The affection which Constantius seemed to bestow on Gallus was shortlived, however, for soon the young man was recalled to Milan and on his journey homeward he was beheaded by order of the emperor. When word of his brother's death reached Julian, he wondered how much longer he himself had to live.

While Julian wandered about Asia Minor, he met many philosophers, and was initiated into the mysteries of Mithra, the sun god. Julian felt more power in the religion of the pagans than he did in the Christ which his grandfather had declared the official religion of the Roman Empire. Knowing the danger of his beliefs, Julian kept them secret.

One day, Publius Porphyrius took Julian to an ancient wrestling arena where they watched a young woman playing at the ancient Grecian games. She was Arsinoë, who, like Julian, found more joy in paganism than in Christianity. One night she told him that he must believe in himself rather than in any gods, and he replied to her that such was his aim.

Before long Julian had an opportunity to strike at Constantius. Raised to a position of honor at court and given the purple robe of a Caesar, he was trained as a warrior and sent to Gaul to tame the barbarians. Contrary to Constantius' hopes that the young man would be killed, he was highly successful in Gaul. When Constantius sent an emissary to recall several of Julian's legions, the soldiers revolted and hailed Julian as the emperor and made him accept the crown. Meanwhile Julian's anger against all Christians had risen; his wife refused to share his bed because she had decided to become a nun. He felt no pity when she fell ill and died. He thought her actions had disgraced him.

With his loyal legions Julian began a march of conquest through the empire. While he was crossing Macedonia, he received word that Constantius had died in Constantinople.

As soon as word spread among Julian's legions that he was now the rightful emperor, he gathered his men together for a ceremony at which he denied Christianity and affixed the statue of Apollo in place of the Cross on his standards. That act was only the beginning of changes in the empire. On his arrival in Constantinople he reinstated the pagan gods and returned to their temples the treasure which had been taken from them by the Christian monks.

The Christians were outraged at his practices, and his popularity waned. Few visited the reopened pagan temples. Soon Julian began to wonder if he would be successful in restoring a golden age of Hellenism to his empire. He discovered that even his beloved Arsinoë had become a Christian nun in his absence. When he went to visit her, she agreed to see him; but she refused to marry him and become the empress. Julian began to wonder to what end he was headed.

At the end of the first year of his reign as emperor of the Eastern Roman Empire, Julian found that he had become the laughing-stock of his people, despite his power as a ruler. His appearance and his scholarly activities

earned him the disrespect of all his subjects, who were accustomed to a Caesar of martial power. When the Christians began to ridicule him and openly defy his edicts, Julian decided to adopt a different course. He hit upon the idea of a campaign against Persia. He hoped that after he had conquered that country and returned as a victor, his people would respect both him and his anti-Christian views.

Julian's army assembled at Antioch, but before it was ready to march Julian had a demonstration of the feeling he had evoked by championing the Olympian deities against Christianity. When he ordered a Christian chapel removed from the temple of Apollo at Antioch, the Christians burned the temple and destroyed the idol in the presence of the emperor and his legions.

In the spring Julian and his armies left Antioch and started toward the Persian frontier. They marched along the Euphrates until they came to the canal which the Persians had built to connect that river with the Tigris. The Persians had flooded the area to halt the invaders, and Julian's army marched in water up to their knees until they were far down the Tigris. After days of marching under a burning sun, they reached Perizibar, a Persian fortress. The fort was gallantly defended, but the Romans finally battered down the walls.

After resting his army for two days, Julian pushed on to Maogamalki. By brilliant strategy and some luck, he carried the second of the Persian defense posts and then pushed onward to Ctesiphon, the Persian capital.

Arriving at a point across the river from the city, Julian consulted his pagan priests. When they failed to foretell a successful attack on the city, Julian became as enraged at Apollo and the other pagan gods as he had been at Christianity. In a frenzy he overturned the altars, said that he trusted no god but himself, and added that he meant to attack the city immediately.

By a ruse, Julian and his army crossed

the Tigris in boats at night. The next morning a single Persian came to their camp and persuaded Julian to burn his boats so that his men would not lose heart and retreat from the assault. He promised also to lead the Romans into the city by a secret way. Too late, his boats destroyed, Julian realized he had been tricked. Unable to take the city, he ordered a retreat. After the Romans had been weakened by forced marches under burning desert suns, the Persians attacked.

In the battle, the Romans won a victory against heavy odds; but it was a victory for the Romans, not for their emperor. In the battle Julian, dressed in his purple robes, refused to wear any armor. He was mortally wounded by a javelin while giving chase to a band of Persians. When he was carried to his tent, Arsinoë, who was still a nun, came to him and attempted to make him see that Christ was a god of beauty and mercy. Julian would not listen to her. As he died, he lifted himself up and cried out to his attendants that the Galilean had defeated him.

Further Critical Evaluation of the Work:

Like many authors of his generation, Dmitri Merejkowski attempted in his writings to search for solutions to the problems that plagued Tzarist Russia in the turbulent quarter of a century preceding the Bolshevik revolution. Merejkowski, one of the Russian symbolists as well as founder of the Religious and Philosophical Society of St. Petersburg, was intensely interested in identifying the philosophical underpinnings of Western civilization. This he tried to do in fictional form in his trilogy *Christ and Antichrist,* comprising *The Death of the Gods, The Gods Reborn* (1902), and *Peter and Alexis* (1905).

In *The Death of the Gods,* Merejkowski sets up the thematic structure of opposing concepts upon which the entire trilogy is built. On a general level, this structure reflects the author's perception of the dualistic nature of man, within whom the forces of flesh and spirit are constantly struggling, and his belief that all of human history has been shaped by this struggle. More specifically, he sets up two sets of values which cluster around Hellenistic and pagan beliefs on the one hand, and Christian values on the other, and counterposes them dramatically throughout the work. The author's purpose in doing this is to illustrate his theory that Western civilization grew out of and took its direction from the clash between paganism and Christianity.

The historical novel genre proved a perfect vehicle for a writer with Merejkowski's gift for recreating the past, and in *The Death of the Gods* this talent is at its best. The setting ranges from all the places visited by the young Julian during his travels in Asia Minor, to the capital of Constantinople, to the military posts along the Persian frontier which are stormed by the Roman legions. Each of these settings comes alive in the author's hands; his use of colorful and specific details infuses both time and place with uniqueness and vividness. The reader feels that he is very close to the real experience of life in the Roman empire of the fourth century.

When Herbert Trench, a fellow at All Soul's College, translated *The Death of the Gods* into English, he felt the novel to be one of the most significant works of the new generation of Russian authors and saw Merejkowski as the successor of Dostoevski. Although time has seen Trench's enthusiasm replaced by a more moderate critical appraisal, Merejkowski's novel nevertheless remains an excellent example of historical fiction inspired with crucial philosophical concerns.

THE DEATH OF THE HEART

Type of work: Novel
Author: Elizabeth Bowen (1899-1973)
Type of plot: Psychological realism
Time of plot: After World War I
Locale: London and Seale, England
First published: 1938

Principal characters:

THOMAS QUAYNE, of Quayne and Merrett, an advertising agency
ANNA QUAYNE, his wife
PORTIA QUAYNE, his sixteen-year-old half-sister
ST. QUENTIN MILLER, an author and a friend of the Quaynes
EDDIE, an employee of Quayne and Merrett
MAJOR BRUTT, a retired officer
MRS. HECCOMB, Anna's ex-governess

Critique:

The travail of adolescence and its painful emergence into maturity are recorded with keenness and sympathy in Elizabeth Bowen's *The Death of the Heart.* Maturity's gain in awareness, she implies, is offset by childhood's loss in idealism and simplicity; adulthood involves compromises with one's heart and thoughts which the young find intolerable, at least at first. And so the arrival of Portia, with her innocent longings and candid curiosity, provides a kind of catalyst for an upper middle-class English household where compromise and boredom have long held sway. Portia's loneliness and her search for love and understanding are characteristic of her age, sex, and particular situation; but Miss Bowen never allows the individual to be submerged in the typical. Although the ending of the story is no more conclusive than life itself, it crystallizes some truths that are often elusive.

The Story:

Anna Quayne's pique demanded an outlet—she could no longer contain it all within herself. Therefore, while St. Quentin Miller shivered with cold, she marched him around the frozen park, delivering herself of her discontent. The trouble, of course, had started with Portia, for the Quayne household had not been the same since the arrival of Tom's sixteen-year-old half-sister. Not that Portia was all to blame; the business had begun with a deathbed wish. Who could expect dying old Mr. Quayne to ask Tom to take a stepsister he hardly knew, keep her for at least a year, and give her a graceful start in life? Anna herself, she went on to St. Quentin, hardly knew how to cope with the arrangement, though she had tried to accept it with outward tranquillity. Now she had stumbled across the girl's diary, glimpsed her own name, and been tempted to read. It was obvious that Portia was rather less than happy, that she was scanning the atmosphere of her brother's house with an unflattering eye.

While Anna was thus unburdening herself, the subject of her discussion returned home quietly from Miss Paullie's lessons. She was vaguely disturbed to learn from Matchett, the housekeeper, that Anna had commented upon the clutter in Portia's bedroom. Later she shared tea with Anna and St. Quentin when they came in tingling with cold; but the atmosphere seemed a bit stiff, and Portia readily acquiesced in Anna's suggestion that she join her brother in his study. Portia felt more at ease with Tom, even though he obviously found conversation with her awkward.

Portia knew, by now, that there was no one in whom she could readily confide. At 2 Windsor Terrace, Matchett offered a certain possessive friendship; at school, only the inquisitive Lilian took notice of her. Major Brutt was better than either of these; his eyes, in her presence, showed a fatherly gleam, and she liked the picture puzzle he had sent. Anna tolerated the major—he was her only link with an old friend, Pidgeon—but Major Brutt seldom ventured to call, and Portia saw him mostly in the company of others.

Another of Anna's friends whom Portia sometimes saw was Eddie. But Eddie was Anna's property and seemingly beyond the range of Portia's clumsy probing for companionship. Too, he was twenty-three and brightly self-assured. Anna found it amusing to have him around, though she often rebuked his conceit and presumption; she went so far as to find him a job with Quayne and Merrett. One day Portia handed Eddie his hat as he took leave of Anna; the next day he wrote to her. Before long they were meeting regularly and secretly.

Eddie, having no wish to alienate Anna, cautioned Portia not to mention him in her diary. But he reveled in Portia's uncritical adoration. They went to the zoo, to tea, ultimately to his apartment. Matchett, who found Eddie's letter under Portia's pillow, soon became coldly jealous of his influence. Even Anna and Tom became slightly restive, as they began to realize the situation. Meanwhile Portia was falling deeper and deeper in love. When Eddie lightly declared that it was a pity they were too young to marry, Portia innocently took his remarks as a tentative proposal. Though he carefully refrained from real love making, Portia felt sure he returned her love.

With the approach of spring, Anna and Tom revealed their intention of spending a few weeks in Capri. Since Matchett would houseclean while they were gone, they decided to send Portia to Mrs. Heccomb, Anna's old governess,

who lived in a seaside house at Seale. Portia, dismayed by the prospect of separation from Eddie, was only partially consoled by his promise to write.

Eddie did write, promptly; so did Major Brutt, with the promise of another picture puzzle. And Seale, happily, turned out better than expected. Having none of Anna's remoteness, Mrs. Heccomb deluged her guest with carefree chatter. Her two grown-up stepchildren reacted somewhat more cautiously, since they were prepared to find Portia a highbrow. Finding her only shy, they quickly relaxed; the radio blared while they vigorously shouted over it about roller-skating, hockey games, and Saturday night parties. Portia gradually withdrew from her shell of loneliness. Within a few days she felt enough at home to ask Daphne Heccomb if Eddie might spend a weekend at Seale. Daphne consented to relay the request to her mother, whereupon Mrs. Heccomb affably approved.

Eddie's visit was not a success. His efforts to be the life of the party soon had Mrs. Heccomb wondering about the wisdom of her invitation. At the cinema his good fellowship extended to holding hands enthusiastically with Daphne. When Portia, distressed, uttered mild reproaches, he intimated that she was a naïve child. Walking together in the woods, on their final afternoon, Portia learned that Eddie had no use for her love unless it could remain uncritical and undemanding. Her vision of an idyllic reunion shattered into bits as she began to see his instability. Two weeks later her stay at Seale ended. Back in London, Matchett triumphantly informed her that Eddie had left word that he would be out of town a few days.

Walking home from school not long afterward, Portia encountered St. Quentin, who inadvertently revealed Anna's perusal of the diary. Upset, she sought comfort from Eddie once more. No longer gratified by her devotion, he made her feel even more unwanted; and the sight of a letter from Anna, lying on Eddie's table, convinced her that they were allied against her. As she left his apartment it seemed unthinkable that she could ever return to Windsor Terrace; her only possible refuge now was Major Brutt. To the Karachi Hotel, therefore, she went, surprising the worthy major as he finished his dinner. Surprise changed to alarm as she pleaded her case: would he take her away, would he marry her? She could relieve his loneliness, she could care for him, she could polish his shoes. Polishing shoes, the major affirmed, with as much serenity as he could muster, was a job women had little success with; with a little time and patience, her position would soon appear less desperate. He wished very much to call the Quaynes, for it was getting late and they would be worried. Portia felt that she had been defeated, but she could still choose ground on which to make a final stand. Very well, she finally agreed, he might call them, but he was not to tell them she was coming. That would depend, she finished enigmatically but firmly, on whether they chose to do the right thing.

The major had been right; the Quaynes were worried. After the telephone rang, their momentary relief was succeeded by real confusion. What, after all, would Portia consider the right thing for them to do? It would have to be simple, without fuss or feathers. With help from St. Quentin, they finally decided, and Matchett was sent in a taxi to fetch her.

Further Critical Evaluation of the Work:

Sixteen-year-old Portia Quayne may seem to be the protagonist of *The Death of the Heart,* but in fact her role is to point up the shallowness of the world of Thomas and Anna. Portia's progressive disillusionment with the "real" world of adult life is detailed in the three sections of the novel—"The World," "The Flesh," and "The Devil." Her disenchantment, sensitively portrayed by a sympathetic narrator, is in every case contrasted to Anna's passionless existence. Life at 2 Windsor Terrace, so idealized by Portia's dead father, is "the world" of the first stage of disillusionment. Eddie—with his fickle attention and passes at Daphne—constitutes the temptation and disillusionment of "the flesh." "The devil" is the novelist St. Quentin Miller, who with "no loyalty" reveals to Portia that Anna has been reading her diary and laughing with others about it. The structure of the novel is carefully worked out, so that Anna's opening revelation to St. Quentin of having read Portia's diary becomes the catalyst for the crisis of the end. The body of the novel gives the details of the contrast between Portia's romantic illusions and the Quaynes' disillusioning boredom. Significantly, the section titles of the novel refer to the baptismal rite in the Book of Common Prayer.

In the end, Portia's demand for "the right thing" forces Anna and Thomas to understand the sterility of their lives and of the "preposterous world," devoid of value. Anna finally empathizes with Portia as she muses that Portia must have a "frantic desire to be handled with feeling" as well as a wish "to be let alone." Matchett, the only adult interested in tradition or value, ends the novel with her interior monologue in the taxi. As she enters the hotel to meet Portia, the strident sounds of a piano come together in a harmonious chord. This resolution suggests, at least, a new beginning for Portia and Anna, each having learned from the other—Portia that the heart dies a little, and Anna that the heart does not completely die.

Bowen's greatest talent lies in detailing the inner life of a young person and the subtleties of the tensions between generations.

THE DEATH OF VIRGIL

Type of work: Novel
Author: Hermann Broch (1886-1951)
Type of plot: Poetic mysticism
Time of plot: 19 B.C.
Locale: Brundisium (Brindisi, Italy)
First published: 1945

Principal characters:
> PUBLIUS VIRGILIUS MARO, chief poet of Rome
> AUGUSTUS CAESAR, Emperor of Rome
> PLOTIA HIERIA, a woman Virgil had once loved
> LYSANIAS, a young boy
> A SLAVE

Critique:

In some respects this difficult yet extraordinarily beautiful novel may better be called a poem, for although it is written mostly in prose, its means of presentation and its effect are wholly poetic. There are three different levels of interest: the vivid imagery and uncanny presentation of both the real world and the fever-ridden, hallucinated, yet visionary world of the dying Virgil; the beauty of language and of the rhythmic sentences; the depth of the writer's attempts to explore metaphysical truth. Using a simple plot as a basis, Broch presents a symphony in four movements. Although the mood of the whole is meditative and elegiac, the style of each movement establishes its tempo, from the pages-long sentences of the second movement to the antiphonal bursts of conversation in the third. In each movement, symbols, incidents, and phrases are reëchoed and transformed, so that the meaning of the novel becomes clear to the reader only as the mystic knowledge which approaching death brings becomes clear to the poet.

The Story:

The imperial fleet returned from Greece to Brundisium, bearing with it the Emperor Augustus and his poet, Virgil, who lay dying. Augustus had sought Virgil and brought him back from the peace and calm philosophy in Athens to the shouting Roman throngs — to the

mob with its frightening latent capacity for brutality, its fickle adoration of its leaders. Yet these were the Romans whom Virgil had glorified; the nobles he had seen on shipboard greedily eating and gaming were their leaders; dapper, sham-majestic Augustus was their emperor.

Fever-ridden, the poet heard a boy's song as the ship entered the harbor. Later, as he was carried from the ship, a beautiful boy appeared from nowhere to lead his litter away from the tumult surrounding the emperor, through narrow streets crowded with garbage ripening into decay, streets full of the miseries of the flesh where women jeered at him for being rich and weak. The women's insults made him aware of his own sham-divinity and of the futility of his life. Dying, he at last saw clearly what hypocrisy his life had been, like the shining, hollow emperor whom he served.

At the palace he was taken to his chambers. The boy, Lysanias, remained with him as night fell. In the depths of a violent attack Virgil recognized his own lack of love. As he lay, conscious of his dying body and the infested night, he knew that, like the Augustus-worshiping masses, he had followed the wrong gods; that in his devotion to poetry he had from the beginning given up the service of life for that of death; that it was too late for him to be fulfilled, for even the *Aeneid* lay unperfected. Some recurrence of vigor drove him to the window. Look-

THE DEATH OF VIRGIL by Hermann Broch. Translated by Jean Starr Untermeyer. By permission of the publishers, Pantheon Books, Inc. Copyright, 1945, by Pantheon Books, Inc.

ing into the night, he knew that not his poem alone remained to be fulfilled; some knowledge still lay ahead for him to achieve. For the necessity of the soul is to discover itself, since through self-discovery it finds the universe: the landscape of the soul is that of all creation. One must learn, not through the stars, but through man.

Interrupting his thoughts, two men and a woman came through the streets quarreling and shouting good-natured obscenities, guffawing their bawdiness with that male laughter whose matter-of-factness annihilates rather than derides. This laughter, juxtaposed against the beautiful night, revealed something of the nature of beauty itself. Beauty is the opponent of knowledge; because it is remote, infinite, and therefore seemingly eternal, it is pursued wrongly for its own sake. The same nonhuman laughter is hidden in it. The artist who pursues beauty plunges into loneliness and self-idolatry; because he chooses beauty rather than life, his work becomes adornment rather than revelation. This path Virgil had chosen: beauty's cold egotism instead of love's warm life which is true creativity. Thus he had died long before, even before his renunciation of the lovely Plotia, whom he now remembered.

The need for contrition because of his refusal of love, a refusal of the pledge given to each man with his life, overwhelmed him. The fever rose within him, bringing strangely prophetic visions of Rome in ruins with wolves howling, of giant birds droning. As reality returned, he knew that for his own salvation he had to do one thing: burn the *Aeneid*.

Lysanias read to him as he drifted into a calm dream, shining with a knowledge of all past earthly happenings and a vision of something to come. Not yet, but soon would come one in whom creation, love, immortality would be united; one who would bear salvation like a single star, whose voice he seemed to hear bidding him open his eyes to love, for he was called to enter the Creation. As the

fever left him and dawn broke, he momentarily doubted the voice. Then came the vision of an angel and, at last, undisturbed sleep.

Virgil awoke to find two old friends come to cheer him. Their bluff reassurances changed to incredulity when they heard he planned to burn the *Aeneid*. Their arguments against his own conviction that his book lacked reality because he himself lacked love were blurred by his fevered perception. Lysanias, whose existence seemed questionable to his friends, appeared with a Near Eastern slave to reaffirm that Virgil was the guide, although not the savior. Plotia came and called him on to an exchange of mutual love and the destruction of his work, the renunciation of beauty for love. Suddenly he and Plotia were exposed and power thundered around him.

Augustus had come to ask Virgil not to burn the *Aeneid*. In the ensuing interview, Virgil's rising delirium made him not only supernaturally aware of truth but also confused as to reality: the invisible Plotia guarded the manuscript; the invisible Lysanias lurked nearby; the room sometimes became a landscape. Augustus insisted that the poem was the property of the Romans, for whom it had been written. Virgil tried to explain that poetry is the knowledge of death, for only through death can one understand life; that unlike Aeschylus, whose knowledge had forced him to poetry, he, Virgil, had sought knowledge through writing poetry and had therefore found nothing.

Then Augustus and the slave seemed to be talking, and Augustus was the symbol of the state he had created, which was order and sobriety and humanity's supreme eternal reality. The slave, awaiting the birth of the supreme ancestor's son, was steadfastness and the freedom of community. The truth of the state must be united to the metaphysical by an individual act of truth, must be made human to realize perfection. Such a savior will come, whose sacrificial death will be the supreme symbol of humility and charity. Still Virgil insisted that he must sacrifice his work because he had not sacrificed his life, that destroying a thing which lacked perception redeemed both himself and the Romans.

Augustus, growing angry, accused Virgil of envy, and in a moment of love Virgil gave him the poem, agreeing not to destroy it. He asked, however, that his slaves might go free after his death. As he talked of his will to his friends, renewed attacks of fever brought him more and more strange hallucinations. He called for help and found he could at last say the word for his own salvation.

After he had finished dictating his will, it seemed to him that he was once more on a boat, one smaller than that which had brought him into the harbor the day before, rowed by his friend Plotius and guided by Lysanias. About him were many people he knew. Gradually all disappeared as he floated into the night; the boy became first a seraph whose ring glowed like a star, then Plotia, who led him into the day again. Reaching shore, they entered a garden where, somehow, he knew that she had become the boy and the slave and that he had become all of them; then he was also the animals and plants, then the mountains, and finally the universe, contained in a small white core of unity—and nothing. Then he was commanded to turn around, and the nothing became everything again, created by the word in the circle of time. Finally he was received into the word itself.

Further Critical Evaluation of the Work:

The Death of Virgil, which has been called a five-hundred-page lyric poem, began as an eighteen-page story, written for reading on an Austrian radio series. Broch selected the subject of Virgil's last day and his desire to burn his work as a vehicle for the discussion of a theme then intensely important to him—the role of literature at the end of a cultural epoch. He saw considerable parallels between the first century B.C. and his own time, 1936. The theme became even more personally relevant to Broch in 1938, when he was arrested by the Nazis and for a time faced his own death. The composition was finished in the years following Broch's escape to the United States, and was published simultaneously in German and English.

The term "composition" is quite accurate: Broch wished to create a new genre, and his work has a conscious relationship to symphonic form and to the lyric poem. Each of the four movements presents a new step in Virgil's development: his confrontation with the ugliness of life forms the theme of the first street scenes; his awareness that he has falsified the fullness of experience by devoting himself to the beautiful to the exclusion of the ugly leads to a decision to burn his works in the second section. In the third section, in the confrontation with Augustus, Virgil, in an abrupt change of mind, passes beyond his own selfish will and gives the manuscript to the Emperor, an act of that love which he believes necessary for healing the world. He asks, finally, that his slaves be freed. The last section depicts the return to unity as Virgil dies, passing from the conflict of opposites which opened the book to an awareness of life as a whole, and of life and death as one; the unity is symbolized by his sea voyage, and constitutes one of the most remarkable passages in modern literature.

THE DEATH SHIP

Type of work: Novel
Author: B. Traven (1900-1969)
Time: The 1920's
Locale: Belgium, Holland, France, Spain, the Mediterranean Sea
First published: 1926

      Principal characters:
          GERARD "PIPPIP" GALES, a young American sailor
          STANISLAV, a Polish sailor, Gerard's friend

Based on the author's own experiences, written when he was about twenty-four, *The Death Ship* is unique, apparently free of direct influences, just as B. Traven is in some ways unlike any other writer. The book may be classified as a proletarian novel, written in the style of tough-guy fiction. But its thesis is not as doctrinaire, as deliberately worked out as that of a proletarian novel, nor is its style as conscious as that of a tough-guy novel.

For Gerard Gales, the young American narrator, stranded in Antwerp when his ship returns to New Orleans without him, the passport has displaced the sun as the center of the universe. Unable to prove his citizenship, he is a man without a country, and his physical presence is no official proof of his birth. Like Kafka's K. in *The Trial,* he moves through a labyrinth of bureaucracy; officials empowered to dispense passports, certificates, sailors-books, receipts, affidavits, seals, and licenses conduct the inquisition of the modern age. The war for liberty and democracy has produced a Europe in which to be hungry is human, to lack a passport is inhuman—unless you are rich.

A victim of nationalism, moving among fading echoes of speeches on international brotherhood, Gerard is an individualist. Immigration officials conspire to smuggle him from Belgium into Holland, then back into Belgium, then into France, where he is jailed for riding a train without a ticket and later sentenced to be shot as a suspected spy. Ironically, when he senses the universal animosity toward Americans and pretends to be a German, he is treated royally. In Spain he is left entirely alone. A people politi-cally oppressed, the Spanish seem freer than other men and Gerard loves them. But the peasants are so good to him that he feels useless and hates himself; he senses the error in a Communist state where the individual is denied the privilege of taking his own risks. Because he is a sailor without a ship, and because he wants to return to his girl, Gerard signs aboard *The Yorikke.*

If he once thought that the world consisted of deckhands and men who made paint, he descends now into a sailor's hell as drag man in a stokehold. Its name obscured on the bow, *The Yorikke,* too, appears to lack a proper birth certificate; but though she seems ashamed of her name, Gerard exhibits a kind of nationalism himself when he withholds his true name and country and signs on as an Egyptian; no American would sail on such a ship, and he realizes that, despite its many faults, he loves his country and is wretchedly homesick. *The Yorikke* resembles no ship he has ever seen; she appears to be insane. A model death ship, she has no life jackets. A death ship is so called because her owners have decided to scuttle her for the insurance. The crew, desperate men called "deads," at the end of their tether when they come aboard, do not know when the ship will go down. The sea, Gerard imagines, will probably eructate the diseased ship for fear of infection. No supplies—spoons, coffee cups, blankets—are provided; the men repeatedly steal a single bar of soap from one another until it has been through every filthy hand; conditions are worse than in a concentration camp. The only thing in ample supply is work, and if a man tries to collect overtime on a ship pathologically committed to profits he may find himself in a black hold with rats that would terrify a cat. Traven conveys a vivid sense of what "she" means as pronoun for a ship; Gerard constantly describes *The Yorikke* in very intimate and telling female terms.

Gerard admires his mysterious captain whose intelligence sets him apart from the old style pirate. He takes care of his men, and they would rather sink with the ship than inform the authorities that she is carrying contraband for the Riffs. *The Yorikke* crew is the filthiest Gerard has ever seen; the men wear bizarre rigs and rags. Some appear to have been shanghaied off the gallows. In the towns, other sailors shun them; men, women, and children fear them; and the police, afraid they may leave the town in ashes, follow them.

The filthiest member of the black gang is the drag man, who must perform extra and loathsome chores. Work is at the center of this novel—the struggle to get it, and, under extreme conditions, the horror and ultimate beauty of it. Delight in conveying an inside view is a characteristic of tough-guy literature. Gerard gives all the details of various work routines. One of the most horrific passages in literature is Traven's description of putting back fallen grate bars while the boiler is white hot. After his first bout at what becomes a daily task, Gerard declares that he is free, unbound, above the gods; he can do what he wishes and curse the gods, because no hell could be greater torture.

Gerard resurrects the freshness of the cliché that men become like machines. He feels like a gladiator for Caesar's fight-to-the-death spectacles. Bravery on the battlefield is nothing when compared to the bravery of men who do certain work to keep civilization afloat. No flag drapes the bodies of casualties; they go like garbage over the fantail. On a death ship no laws keep a man in line; each worker is crucially necessary and work is a common

bond. With no sense of heroics, Gerard helps save two men and is himself saved. His true countrymen, he discovers, are those workers who are scalded and scorched at the same furnace with him; he does not desert because his friend Stanislav would then have to work alone. Though Traven appears to show how men grow accustomed to misery and filth, he insists that nobody really gets used to them; one simply loses the capacity to feel and becomes hard-boiled. Few fictive descriptions of the life, the hopes, the illusions and attitudes of the doomed sailor, his qualities of ingenuity, improvisation, and audacity are as complete as Traven's.

Ironically, just as Gerard, despite his misery, learns to live and laugh on the ship, he senses *The Yorikke's* imminent doom. A further irony comes when Gerard and Stanislav are shanghaied from *The Yorikke* to serve on the new but disastrously slow *Empress of Madagascar,* which is to be scuttled in a few days. But the *Empress* kills her plotting captain and stands like a tower between the rocks before she sinks. Stanislav eats like a shipowner before he drowns. He and Gerard are safely tied to a piece of wreckage, but Stanislav has a hallucination in which he sees *The Yorikke* leaving the dock. Wanting to go with her, he detaches himself and slips into the sea. Not yet rescued, Gerard pays his respects to his comrade in the last lines of the novel.

The style of the story—rough, garrulous, full of completely justified profanity—sounds translated, but it is consistent with Gerard's semi-literate immigrant background. Though these qualities become wearisome in three hundred pages, the sheer energy of the telling achieves a special eloquence. Traven is overly fascinated by the way words come about; Gerard indulges in figurative rhetoric; many of his wisecracks seem lame, probably because his slang is dated. Humor, wit, and comedy are interwoven quite naturally among the darks of Traven's narrative. The style provides an amplification of theme through the play of language. Although Traven does not set up satirical situations, his diction and metaphorical pretenses create a satirical distortion in the telling of such episodes as those involving bureaucracy.

No plot, no story line as such holds the novel together; narratively, it seems split in half, but the handling of theme, the picaresque looseness, and the personality of the narrator create an appropriate effect to the material. The static quality is relieved by sudden transitions and by the frequent use of tales and anecdotes, as in *The Treasure of the Sierra Madre*. Gerard is a storyteller who never tires of retelling a tale. The consulate scenes are repetitious; we get variations on the same routine, though speeded up and foreshortened sometimes; and toward the end, Stanislav tells Gerard a story about himself that closely resembles Gerard's earlier experiences. Gerard is especially fond of ridiculing popular fiction and movie versions of the seafaring life; the difference between living and listening to an experience is discussed in the beginning and at the end. Gerard tells his general story the way a sailor would, commenting with joking metaphors and reflecting constantly on the meaning of events. The reader is visualized as a captive audience for a man who has at last found a way to speak without interruption on various social, political, and economic conditions. The novel has some poignant moments, too, but, as is typical of the tough-guy novel, sentimentality occasionally intrudes.

Gerard and Stanislav are not to be associated with the victims of recent literature. They are more victims of the nature of things than of conditions that can be reformed. Gerard may gripe with every breath he takes, but he does not whine. He proudly insists that he can do work any man can do, anywhere. He contemptuously refuses to bow to circumstance. He refuses to blame the shipowners; having failed to take his fate in his own hands by jumping ship, he has no

right to refuse to be a slave. But he can hope that he will be resurrected from the "deads" by his own will and fortitude. He knows that for the courageous man who survives the ordeal of *The Yorikke* anything is possible. By going to the bottom of agony in his daily task of replacing grate bars, Gerard comes out with a kind of peace, aware of his place in a universe that now has meaning in the slightest thing. This earned romanticism enables him to see beauty in the conventionally ugly.

Although Gerard covers, directly to the reader and in dialogue, almost every grievance of the laborer of the first twenty-five years of this century, he is not interested in easy working conditions and fringe benefits. Repeatedly, he preaches the gospel of hard work, not because work is good for the soul, which seems less involved than muscle, but because it is good for man the animal. Unlike proletarian writers, Traven achieves a kind of mystique about work. One thinks of Albert Camus' Sisyphus: for his disobedience of the officials, Sisyphus was condemned to the futile task of rolling a huge rock to the top of a mountain, after which it rolled back down to the plain. Camus likened this labor to that of the proletariat. Unintentionally, perhaps, Traven has translated Sisyphus' mythic task into existential reality. The intentions of the novel are uncertain; but at moments it appears to be an allegory about the laboring class. Working unseen at sea, deep in the black hole of an ash pit, these men, who were never born, in a sense, who are without a country, go to their deaths on a ship that does not exist officially. Gerard constantly speaks of the ship metaphorically as being over five thousand years old. The flag is so dirty it could represent any country, and thus represents all. Many nationalities are represented among the crew; each nameless person is called, ironically, by the name of the country he claims, but which has denied his existence.

DEATH'S DUELL

Type of work: Sermon
Author: John Donne (1572-1631)
First published: 1632

About a year prior to his death John Donne preached his last sermon before the king at Whitehall on February 12, 1630. His publisher, Richard Redmer, who printed the first edition in 1632 of "Death's Duell, or, A Consolation to the Soule, Against the Dying Life, and Living Death of the Body," said that it was called "The Doctors Owne Funerall Sermon." The text is from Psalm 68, the twentieth verse: *And unto God the Lord belong the issues from death.*

The language of the sermon is as imaginative, musical, and perverse as that of Donne's poetry in which he suggests, "Go and catch a falling star," or observes with interest that in the body of a flea his blood mingles with that of his beloved. Like the poetry, the sermon stretches the mind that would follow its eloquent, shocking, and neatly ordered expression. The Trinity probably inspires the division into three parts. Donne begins with the image of a building with a firm foundation, buttresses, and an unarchitectural "knitting" of the materials. These three particulars he compares to the actions of the Persons of the Trinity. God the Father lays the foundation for man's life: he leads us from death into life. The Holy Ghost, like the buttresses which hold up the building, supports us at the hour of death when we shall enter eternal life. The God of Mercy, the Son, like the knitting together of the building, took upon himself flesh, knitting the divine and the human natures into one and delivering us by his death. The images are startling: the winding sheet which we bring with us into the world, the dust with which our mouths are filled after death, the worm that incestuously unites son, mother, and sister in its body. The figure of Christ on the cross "rebaptized in his owne teares and sweat, and enbalmed in his own blood alive" is almost as uncomfortably vivid as the last sentence of the sermon. In the concluding portion of "Death's Duell," Donne, with revival preacher fervor, calls his hearers to repentance, prayer, and dependence upon Christ.

The significance of the title seems to lie in the double aspect in the subtitle, the dying life and the living death. For Donne, the phrase "the issues of death" has three interpretations: deliverance from death by God; the manner and disposition of death by the Holy Ghost; and the deliverance from this life by death which Jesus Christ experienced because he had taken on human flesh and could have no other exit. The sermon is built around these three points.

In the first section, Donne says that throughout life we pass from one death to another. These transitions are deliverances from death. In the womb, we are in a kind of death from which we are delivered into life, the manifold deaths of the world. We come in a winding sheet to seek a grave. Birth dies in infancy, infancy in youth, youth and the rest in age. Age also dies and "determines all." We progress in evil. Youth is worse than infancy; age laments that it cannot pursue the sins of youth. So many calamities accompany each age that death itself would be "an ease" in comparison. After death, the body progresses to corruption, putrefaction, and dispersion. Christ, however, did not suffer the corruption of the grave; and those who are alive at His second coming shall not see it. All else shall suffer dispersion; but at the resurrection God will recompact bodies and souls.

In the second section of the sermon, Donne says that "it belongs to God, and not to man to passe a judgement upon us at our death." Man is incapable of judging the state of the soul at its passing. When men think that a man dies peacefully like a lamb, God only knows if he is really stupified and unaware of dying or actually dying without reluctance. Even Christ suffered agony at the prospect of death; so reluctance to accept death is not to be condemned. The mercies of God are instantaneous and imperceptible to bystanders. Men should not judge in the violent deaths of criminals, for Christ died a shameful death and many honestly felt that he was a malefactor. God governs not by examples but by rules. Therefore, no man can judge another by his attitude at death. God judges his whole life; so if a man dies without faith apparently, none should make evil conclusions about him. God does not promise a quiet death, but "live well here and thou shalt live well for ever."

The third section of the sermon deals with Christ's incarnation and resultant death. In this "issue of death" men are delivered by the death of another, by the death of Christ. "That God, this Lord, the Lord of life could die, is a strange contemplation." That God would die is "an exaltation" of this. That God "shold die, must die," and had no issue but by death is a "superexaltation" of this aspect of God and death. Since God is the God of revenges, he would not pass over the sin of man unpunished. Christ, therefore, was bound to suffer. God would not spare himself. "There was nothing more free, more voluntary, more spontaneous than the death of Christ." The decree that Christ was to suffer was eternal; so is Infinite love, eternal love. His Father calls this death only a bruising of his heel. Christ calls it a baptism. He accepts the cup without detestation. The cup is now salvation, a health to all the world. "As God breathed a soule into the first Adam, so this second Adam breathed his soule into God, in the hands of God. There wee leave you in that blessed dependancy, to hang upon him that hangs on the Crosse, there bath[e] in his teares, there suck at his woundes, and lie downe in peace in his grave, till hee vouchsafe you a resurrection, and an ascension into that Kingdome, which hee hath purchas'd for you with the inestimable price of his incorruptible blood."

Commonly in Donne's time sermons were first delivered and then written from notes and memory. The words as Donne records them may not be exactly the ones which he spoke.

DEBIT AND CREDIT

Type of work: Novel
Author: Gustav Freytag (1816-1895)
Type of plot: Social realism
Time of plot: Early nineteenth century
Locale: Eastern Germany and Poland
First published: 1855

Principal characters:
ANTON WOHLFART, an intelligent, industrious middle-class German
T. O. SCHRÖTER, Anton Wohlfart's employer
SABINE SCHRÖTER, T. O. Schröter's young sister
FRITZ VON FINK, an Americanized German, Wohlfart's friend
EUGEN VON ROTHSATTEL, a German nobleman
LENORE VON ROTHSATTEL, the baron's beautiful daughter
HIRSCH EHRENTHAL, a Jewish usurer
VEITEL ITZIG, a rascally former schoolmate of Anton Wohlfart

Critique:

While Gustav Freytag's novels exhibit certain aspects of romanticism, they also contain a greater, more influential element of realism. The combination has sometimes been compared to the work of Freytag's distinguished British contemporary, Charles Dickens. Freytag, a great champion of the German middle class, believed that Germans as a whole were better, more honorable, more stable people than other Europeans and that in the sober, industrious middle class lay the future greatness of his country. With the nobility Freytag had little patience, portraying them, as he did in *Debit and Credit*, as a group with little talent, little common sense, and an empty sense of honor. Of all Freytag's work, both in drama and fiction, *Debit and Credit* has received the highest praise as an example of the combination of the romance and the realistic social novel.

The Story:

Upon the death of his father, an accountant, Anton Wohlfart, a very young man, traveled to the capital of his province in eastern Germany. In the city he found employment in the mercantile establishment of T. O. Schröter, an industrious and honorable German businessman. During his journey, Wohlfart encountered two people who were later to play an important part in his life. He wandered accidentally onto the estate of

Baron von Rothsattel, whose beautiful daughter Lenore made a lasting impression on the boy. He also met Veitel Itzig, a young Jew who had been a former schoolmate, making his way to the city to seek his fortune.

Being an industrious and intelligent young man, as well as personable, Anton Wohlfart soon made a place for himself among his fellow workers and in the esteem of his employer. Among the other clerks in the firm was Fritz von Fink, a young Americanized German whose sense of industry and honor had been warped by a stay in New York City. Von Fink became a close friend of Wohlfart's despite the differences in their social standing and the escapades into which von Fink led Wohlfart, sometimes to the latter's embarrassment and chagrin.

In the meantime Baron von Rothsattel, who had little talent for managing his estates or business, was led to accept the advice of Hirsch Ehrenthal, an unscrupulous Jewish usurer and businessman who plotted the baron's financial ruin so that he might buy up his estates at a fraction of their value. Ehrenthal, who had persuaded the baron to mortgage his estates in order to purchase lands in Poland and to build a factory to extract sugar from beets, depended on the baron's lack of business acumen to ruin him, with a little help from Ehrenthal on the way. Ehrenthal did not realize at the time that Itzig, whom he had taken into his employ, was also plotting to acquire the baron's estates by a dishonest manipulation of documents and the knowledge he had of Ehrenthal's affairs. Itzig was coached in his scheme by a drunken lawyer who also hoped to make some profit from the nobleman's ruin.

Fritz von Fink finally decided to return to America to take over the affairs of a wealthy uncle who had recently died. Before he left, he proposed marriage to Sabine Schröter, Wohlfart's employer's sister, but the young woman refused the nobleman's offer. Shortly after his departure, revolt broke out in the nearby provinces of Poland. In order to prevent business losses and reëstablish his affairs there, Schröter bravely entered Poland, accompanied by Wohlfart. During their stay Wohlfart saved his employer's life, winning his and his sister's gratitude. Because of his employer's trust, Wohlfart was left in Poland for many months as the firm's agent, to reorganize the business of the company. He returned to Germany to be honored by his employer and given a position of considerable responsibility. During his stay in Poland he had met Eugen von Rothsattel, the baron's son, who proved to be a gallant but impractical young man. Because of his admiration for the young nobleman and his romantic regard for Lenore von Rothsattel, Wohlfart had lent a large sum of money to Eugen.

As time passed the financial affairs of Baron von Rothsattel became worse and worse; falling deeper into debt, the nobleman gave personal notes and mortgages to Ehrenthal and the other usurers who were his accomplices. When the baron thought himself on the edge of ruin, a ray of hope appeared in the person of Ehrenthal's son, an upright and noblehearted young man who tried to persuade his father to give up dishonest gains and let the baron keep his family estates. The young man was ill, however, and he died before he was able to influence his father's actions. On the night of his death a casket filled with important documents was stolen from Ehrenthal's office by Itzig's accomplice.

The baron, desperate, attempted suicide. He failed in this, but the blast of the pistol blinded him. In desperation, Lenore von Rothsattel appealed to Wohlfart to become her father's agent. After much soul-searching, the young man agreed, although his departure from Schröter's firm made his employer angry and opened a breach between the two men. Schröter felt that the nobility, who constantly proved their inability to manage their affairs, should be allowed to ruin themselves and so lose their place of influence in German culture.

Wohlfart journeyed again to Poland, this time to try to salvage the estate which the baron had acquired in that country. He found the estate in run-down condition and the Poles decidedly incompetent and unfriendly. With the help of loyal German settlers in the area, Wohlfart managed to bring some order to the farms of the estate, to which the baron, his wife, and his daughter moved, knowing that the family estates in Germany were lost. After many months Wohlfart managed to put the baron's affairs in order; however, his efforts were lost on the baron, who had a misplaced sense of rank. Only Wohlfart's regard for Lenore kept him in the position of responsibility after he had been repeatedly insulted.

When the revolutions of 1848 broke out, the troubles spread to the Polish provinces in which the von Rothsattel estate was located. Fortunately, Fritz von Fink appeared and under his leadership the estate was defended from the rebel depredations until help from a military force arrived on the scene. During this period von Fink and Lenore discovered their love for each other. When danger was past, the baron's resentment against Wohlfart exploded, and the young man was dismissed. The baroness, who realized what the young man had sacrificed for her family, spoke to him of her gratitude and asked him to try to straighten out their affairs with the usurers.

Returning to his home city, Wohlfart

found a cordial welcome from his former employer's sister, but a rather cool one from Schröter himself. Schröter feared that living with the nobility had spoiled the young man, and he still resented the fact that Wohlfart had left his firm. Through his own efforts and those of a detective, Wohlfart began to trace down the plots which had ruined Baron von Rothsattel. He was informed that Ehrenthal was not the real villain, and soon it appeared that Itzig had been the true culprit in the affair. When the broken-down lawyer who had been Itzig's mentor learned of the investigations, he went to Itzig for money and a chance to leave Germany; he was the one who had stolen the baron's documents and he feared arrest. Itzig, driven by panic, drowned his accomplice. Just at the hour he was to marry Ehrenthal's daughter, a beautiful woman and the usurer's only heir, Itzig was told that the authorities were ready to arrest him. In his attempt to escape, Itzig himself was drowned at the place where he had murdered his accomplice. The documents were recovered, however, and the fortune and honor of Baron von Rothsattel were redeemed.

Having recovered the fortune of the baron's family and overcome his sentimental regard for Lenore, Wohlfart decided to leave the city, for he believed that he had no future in the firm of T. O. Schröter. Before he left, however, he went to see Sabine Schröter, his employer's sister, and the two young people confessed to each other that they were in love. The girl took the young man to her brother, who amazed Wohlfart by his warmth. Sabine revealed to Wohlfart that he was to marry her and become a partner in the firm, if that was his wish.

Further Critical Evaluation of the Work:

Gustav Freytag's *Debit and Credit* was one of the most popular German novels of the nineteenth century, enjoying high sales among that class whose virtues it glorifies, the solid German bourgeoisie. Perhaps the very absence of deeper artistic qualities which have led to its later neglect was responsible for its enthusiastic reception by the audience for which it was written. It presents an idealized view of German history and society, eschewing the flights of fancy typical of Romantic literature but by no means wholly realistic in its view of German culture, which was far more complex and tension-filled than one might guess from the novel.

Anton Wohlfart is the very model of the industrious businessman, and the middle class is regarded as the representative of all that is best in German life. Freytag had been involved in the revolutionary movement of 1848, and was firmly committed to the cause of German unity under Prussian leadership, and to the exclusion of the various non-German groups which had become part of the German cultural sphere through incorporation into the Austrian Empire. This feeling of German superiority is clearly developed in the novel; Jews, Poles, and even Americans are regarded negatively, though not condemned as groups. It would be wrong to see the figure of Veitel Itzig as demonstrating anti-Semitism on Freytag's part. The slight tendency toward caricature, derived from Dickens' character portraits, reflects rather Freytag's desire to simplify and clarify the structure of his novel, especially through strong contrast.

Freytag began as a dramatist, and his novels all share something of the tight organization of a drama. His style strives for objectivity, excluding the realm of fantasy and illusion. Indeed, what he criticizes in the nobility, in the Poles, and in Itzig, is precisely the tendency toward egocentricity, illusory values, and romantic longings. Wohlfart succeeds because of his objective concentration and dispassion. He does not strive beyond his class, but steadfastly maintains his moderate and diligent way of life, representing for generations the ideal fulfillment of bourgeois values.

THE DECAMERON
(SELECTIONS)

Type of work: Tales
Author: Giovanni Boccaccio (1313-1375)
Types of plots: Romantic tragedy, farce, folk tradition
Times of plots: Graeco-Roman times and the Middle Ages
Locale: Italy
First transcribed: 1353

> Principal characters:
> THE THREE TEDALDO SONS, gentlemen of Florence
> ALESSANDRO, their nephew
> THE DAUGHTER OF THE KING OF ENGLAND
> TANCRED, Prince of Salerno
> GHISMONDA, his daughter
> GUISCARDO, her lover
> ISABETTA, of Messina
> LORENZO, her lover
> HER THREE BROTHERS
> GALESO, of Cyprus, known as Cimon
> EFIGENIA, his love
> LISIMACO, of Rhodes
> FEDERIGO DEGLI ALBERIGHI, of Florence
> MONNA GIOVANNA, his love
> PERONELLA, a wool carder of Naples
> HER HUSBAND
> STRIGNARIO, her lover
> NATHAN, a rich man of Cathay
> MITRIDANES, envious of Nathan
> SALADIN, Sultan of Babylon
> MESSER TORELLO, of Pavia
> GUALTIERI, son of the Marquess of Saluzzo
> GRISELDA, his wife

Critique:

Boccaccio, Dante, and Petrarch were the leading lights in a century that is considered the beginning of the Italian Renaissance. Dante died while Boccaccio was a child, but Petrarch was the friend of his middle and later life. Dante's work was essentially of the spirit; Petrarch's was that of the literary man; Boccaccio's broke free of all tradition and created a living literature about ordinary people. His *Decameron* is his most famous work. This collection of one hundred tales is set in a framework much like that in the *Arabian Nights' Tales*, or in Chaucer's *Canterbury Tales*, written later in the same century. A terrible plague was ravaging Florence. To flee from it, a group of seven girls and three young men, who had met by chance in a church, decided to go to a villa out of town. There they set up a working arrangement whereby each would be king or queen for a day. During the ten days they stayed in the country, each told a story following certain stipulations laid down by the daily ruler. The stories range from romance to farce, from comedy to tragedy. They are all told with a wit that carries them above the range of the licentious, a term sometimes used unjustly about the tales. It may be true that none of the plots was original with Boccaccio, but he wrote one hundred excellent stories, and many are the authors since his day who have borrowed from him.

The Stories:

PAMPINEA'S TALE ABOUT THE THREE
TEDALDO YOUNG MEN

When Messer Tedaldo died, he left all

1397

his goods and chattels to his three sons. With no thought for the future, they lived so extravagantly that they soon had little left. The oldest son suggested that they sell what they could, leave Florence, and go to London, where they were unknown.

In London they lent money at a high rate of interest, and in a few years they had a small fortune. Then they returned to Florence. There they married and began to live extravagantly again, while depending on the monies still coming to them from England.

A nephew named Alessandro took care of their business in England. At that time there were such differences between the king and a son that Alessandro's business was ruined. He stayed in England, however, in hopes that peace would come and his business would recover. Finally he returned to Italy with a group of monks who were taking their young abbot to the pope to get a dispensation for him and a confirmation of the youthful cleric's election.

On the way Alessandro discovered that the abbot was a girl, and he married her in the sight of God. In Rome the girl had an audience with the pope. Her father, the King of England, wished the pope's blessing on her marriage to the old King of Scotland, but she asked the pope's blessing on her marriage to Alessandro instead.

After the wedding Alessandro and his bride went to Florence, where she paid his uncles' debts. Two knights preceded the couple to England and urged the king to forgive his daughter. After the king had knighted Alessandro, the new knight reconciled the king and his rebellious son.

FIAMMETTA'S TALE OF TANCRED AND THE GOLDEN CUP

Tancred, Prince of Salerno, loved his daughter Ghismonda so much that when she was widowed soon after her marriage he did not think to provide her with a second husband, and she was too modest to ask him to do so. Being a lively girl, however, she decided to have as her lover

the most valiant man in her father's court. His name was Guiscardo. His only fault was that he was of humble birth.

Ghismonda noticed that Guiscardo returned her interest and they met secretly in a cave, one entrance to which was through a door in the young widow's bedroom. Soon she was taking her lover into her bedroom, where they enjoyed each other frequently.

Tancred was in the habit of visiting his daughter's room at odd times. One day, when he went to visit, she was not there and so he sat down to wait in a place where he was by accident hidden by the bed curtains from his daughter and her lover, who soon came in to use the bed.

Tancred remained hidden, but that night he had Guiscardo arrested. When he berated his daughter for picking so humble a lover, she defied him for letting so brave a man remain poor in his court. She begged nothing from Tancred except that he kill her and her lover with the same stroke.

The prince did not believe Ghismonda would be as resolute as she sounded. When her lover was killed, Tancred had his heart cut from his body and sent to her in a golden cup. Ghismonda thanked her father for his noble gift. After repeatedly kissing the heart, she poured poison into the cup and drank it. Then she lay down upon her bed with Guiscardo's heart upon her own. Tancred's own heart was touched when he saw her cold in death, and he obeyed her last request that she and Guiscardo be buried together.

FILOMENO'S TALE OF THE POT OF BASIL

Isabetta lived in Messina with her three merchant brothers and a young man named Lorenzo, who looked after all their business. Isabetta and Lorenzo fell in love. One night, as she went to Lorenzo's room, her oldest brother saw her. He said nothing until the next morning, when the three brothers conferred to see how they could settle the matter so that no shame should fall upon them or upon

Isabetta.

Not long afterward the three brothers, setting out with Lorenzo, said that they were going part way with him on a journey. Secretly they killed and buried the young man.

After their return home the brothers answered none of Isabetta's questions about Lorenzo. She wept and refused to be consoled in her grief. One night Lorenzo came to her in a dream and told her what had happened and where he was buried. Without telling her brothers, she went to the spot indicated in her dream and there found her lover's body. She cut off his head and wrapped it in a cloth to take home. She buried the head in dirt in a large flower pot and planted basil over it. The basil flourished, watered by her tears.

She wept so much over the plant that her brothers took away the pot of basil and hid it. Because she asked about it often, the brothers grew curious. At last they investigated and found Lorenzo's head. Abashed, they left the city. Isabetta died of a broken heart.

PAMFILO'S TALE OF CIMONE, WHO BE-
CAME CIVILIZED THROUGH LOVE

Galeso was the tallest and handsomest of Aristippo's children, but he was so stupid that the people of Cyprus called him Cimone, which means Brute. Cimone's stupidity embarrassed his father until the old man sent the boy to the country to live. There Cimone was contented until one day he came upon a sleeping girl, Efigenia, whose beauty completely changed him.

He told his father he intended to live in town. The news worried his father for a while, but Cimone bought fine clothes and associated only with worthy young men. In four years he was the most accomplished and virtuous young man on the island.

Although he knew she was promised to Pasimunda of Rhodes, Cimone asked Efigenia's father for her hand in marriage. He was refused. When Pasimunda sent for his bride, Cimone and his friends pursued the ship and took Efigenia off the vessel, after which they let the ship's crew go free to return to Rhodes. In the night a storm arose and blew Cimone's ship to the very harbor in Rhodes where Efigenia was supposed to go. Cimone and his men were arrested.

Pasimunda had a brother who had been promised a wife, but this girl was loved by Lisimaco, a youth of Rhodes, as Efigenia was loved by Cimone. The brothers planned a double wedding.

Lisimaco made plans with Cimone. At the double wedding feast, Lisimaco and Cimone with many of their friends snatched the brides away from their prospective husbands. The young men carried their loved ones to Crete, where they lived happily in exile for a time until their fathers interceded for them. Then Cimone took Efigenia home to Cyprus, and Lisimaco took his wife back to Rhodes.

FIAMMETTA'S TALE OF FEDERIGO
AND HIS FALCON

Federigo degli Alberighi was famed in Florence for his courtesy and his prowess in arms. He fell in love with Monna Giovanna, a woman who cared nothing for him, though he spent his fortune trying to please her. Finally he was so poor that he went to the country to live on his farm. There he entertained himself only by flying his falcon, which was considered the best in the world.

Monna's husband died, leaving her to enjoy his vast estates with one young son. The son struck up an acquaintance with Federigo and particularly admired the falcon. When the boy became sick, he thought he might get well if he could own Federigo's bird.

Monna, as a last resort, swallowed her pride and called upon Federigo. She told him she would stay for supper, but Federigo, desperately poor as he was, had nothing to serve his love except the falcon, which he promptly killed and roasted for her.

After the meal, with many apologies, Monna told her host that her son, thinking he would get well if he had the falcon, desired Federigo's bird. Federigo wept to think that Monna had asked for the one thing he could not give her.

The boy died soon after and Monna was bereft. When her brothers urged her to remarry, she finally agreed to do so. But she would marry no one but the generous Federigo, who had killed his pet falcon to do her honor. So Federigo married into great riches.

FILOSTRATO'S TALE OF PERONELLA, WHO HID HER LOVER IN A BUTT

Peronella was a Neapolitan woolcomber married to a poor bricklayer. Together they made enough to live comfortably. Peronella had a lover named Strignario, who came to the house each day after the husband went to work.

One day, when the husband returned unexpectedly, Peronella hid Strignario in a butt. Her husband had brought home a man to buy the butt for five florins. Thinking quickly, Peronella told her husband that she already had a buyer who had offered seven florins for the butt, and that he was at that moment inside the butt inspecting it.

Strignario came out, complaining that the butt was dirty. The husband offered to clean it. While the husband was inside scraping, Strignario cuckolded him again, paid for the butt, and went away.

FILOSTRATO'S TALE OF NATHAN'S GENEROSITY

There was once in Cathay a very rich and generous old man named Nathan. He had a splendid palace and many servants, and he entertained lavishly anyone who came his way.

In a country nearby lived Mitridanes who was not nearly so old as Nathan but just as rich. Since he was jealous of Nathan's fame, he built a palace and entertained handsomely everyone who came by. One day a woman came thirteen times asking alms. Furious when Mitridanes called her to task, she told him that she had once asked alms of Nathan forty-two times in one day without reproof. Mitridanes decided that he would have to kill Nathan before his own fame would grow.

Riding near Nathan's palace, Mitridanes came upon Nathan walking alone. When he asked to be directed secretly to Nathan's palace, Nathan cheerfully took him there and established him in a fine apartment. Still not realizing who Nathan was, Mitridanes revealed his plan to kill his rival. Nathan arranged matters so that Mitridanes came upon him alone in the woods.

Mitridanes, curious to see Nathan, caught hold of him before piercing him with a sword. When he discovered that Nathan was the old man who had first directed him to the palace, made him comfortable, and then arranged the meeting in the woods, Mitridanes realized that he could never match Nathan's generosity, and he was greatly ashamed.

Nathan offered to go to Mitridanes' home and become known as Mitridanes, while Mitridanes would remain to be known as Nathan. But by that time Mitridanes thought his own actions would tarnish Nathan's fame. He went home humbled.

PAMFILO'S TALE OF SALADIN AND MESSER TORELLO

In the time of Emperor Frederick the First, all Christendom united in a crusade for the recovery of the Holy Land. To see how the Christians were preparing themselves and to learn to protect himself against them, Saladin, the Sultan of Babylon, took two of his best knights and made a tour through Italy to Paris. The travelers were disguised as merchants.

Outside the little town of Pavia they came upon Messer Torello, who was on his way to his country estate. When they asked him how far they were from Pavia, he told them quickly that the town was too far to be reached that night and sent his servants with them to an inn. Having sensed that the three men were foreign gentlemen and wanting to honor them, he had the servants take them by a roundabout way to his own estate. Meanwhile he rode directly home. The travelers were surprised when they saw him in his own place, but, realizing that he meant only to honor them, they graciously consented to spend the night.

The next day Messer Torello sent word to his wife in town to prepare a banquet. The preparations being made, both Torellos honored the merchants that day. Before they left, the wife gave them handsome suits of clothes like those her husband wore.

When Messer Torello became one of the crusaders, he asked his wife to wait a year and a month before remarrying if she heard nothing from him. She gave him a ring to remember her by. Soon afterward a great plague broke out among the Christians at Acre and killed many men. Most of the survivors were imprisoned by the sultan. Messer Torello was taken to Alexandria, where he trained hawks for Saladin and was called Saladin's Christian. Neither man recognized the other for a long time, until at last Saladin recognized a facial gesture in Torello and made himself known as one of the traveling merchants. Freed, Torello lived happily as Saladin's guest and expected daily to hear from his wife, to whom he had sent word of his adventures. His messenger had been shipwrecked, however, and the day closely approached when his wife would be free to remarry.

At last Torello told Saladin of the arrangement he and his wife had made. The sultan, taking pity on him, had Torello put to sleep on a couch heaped with jewels and gold. Then the couch, whisked off to Italy by magic, was set down in the church of which his uncle was abbot. Torello and the abbot went to the marriage feast prepared for Torello's wife and her new husband. No one recognized Torello because of his strange beard and oriental raiment until he displayed the ring his wife had given him. Then with great rejoicing they were reunited, a reward for their early generosity.

DINEO'S TALE OF THE PATIENT GRISELDA

Gualtieri, eldest son of the Marquess of Saluzzo, was a bachelor whose subjects begged him to marry. Though he was not anxious to take a wife, he decided to wed poor Griselda, who lived in a nearby hamlet. When he went with his friends to bring Griselda home, he asked her if she would always be obedient and try to please him and never be angry. Upon her word that she would do so, Gualtieri had her stripped of her poor gown and dressed in finery becoming her new station.

With her new clothes Griselda changed so much in appearance that she seemed to be a true noblewoman, and Gualtieri's subjects were pleased. She bore him a daughter and a son, both of whom Gualtieri took from her. In order to test her devotion, he pretended to have the children put to death, but Griselda sent them off cheerfully since that was her husband's wish.

When their daughter was in her early teens, Gualtieri sent Griselda home, clad only in a shift, after telling her that he intended to take a new wife. His subjects were sad, but Griselda herself remained composed. A short time later he called Griselda back to his house and ordered her to prepare it for his wedding, saying that no one else knew so well how to arrange it. In her ragged dress she prepared everything for the wedding feast. Welcoming the guests, she was particularly thoughtful of the new bride.

By that time Gualtieri thought he had tested Griselda in every possible way. He introduced the supposed bride as her daughter and the little boy who had accompanied the girl as her son. Then he had Griselda dressed in her best clothes and everyone rejoiced.

Further Critical Evaluation of the Work:

Since its composition readers and critics have made much of *The Decameron's* hundred entertaining and worldly tales, comic and tragic, bawdy and courteous, satiric and serious, that compose this work. Unfortunately, much early criticism was moralistic, and Boccaccio was faulted for devoting his mature artistic skill to a collection of "immoral" stories. *The Decameron* has fared better in the latter half of this century, with more solid critical inquiries into the work's literary significance and style. Boccaccio's collection has been considered representative of the Middle Ages; it has also been viewed as a product of the Renaissance. The work is both. *The Decameron* not only encompasses literary legacies of the medieval world; it also goes far beyond Boccaccio's own time, transcending in tone and style artistic works of previous as well as later periods.

The structure with its frame characters has many analogues in medieval literature; the frame story (a group of tales within an enclosing narrative) was a device known previously, even in the Orient. Two twelfth century collections were *The Seven Sages* and the *Disciplina Clericalis*. The material for many of Boccaccio's stories was gleaned from Indian, Arabic, Byzantine, French, Hebrew, and Spanish tales.

Although *The Decameron* is not escapist literature, the idea and nature of the framework have much in common with medieval romance. There is the idealistic, pastoral quality of withdrawal into the "pleasant place" or garden, away from the ugly, harsh reality of the surrounding world. The ten young people who leave Florence—a dying, corrupt city which Boccaccio describes plainly in all its horrors—find only momentary respite from the charnel house of reality; but their existence for ten days is that of the enchanted medieval dreamworld: a paradise of flowers, ever-flowing fountains, shade trees, soft breezes, where all luxuries of food and drink abound. Furthermore, virtue reigns along with medieval *gentilesse* in its finest sense. There is no cynicism or lust in the various garden settings where the pastimes are strolling, weaving garlands, or playing chess. Even Dioneo, who tells the most salacious stories, is as chaste in his conduct as Pampinea, Filomena, Filostrato, and the others. One critic has even seen in these frame characters a progression of virtues, and their stories actually groups of *exempla* praising such qualities as wisdom, prudence, or generosity.

Against this refined and idealized medieval framework are the stories themselves, the majority marked by intense realism in a world where dreams and enchanted gardens have little place. The locale of the novella is usually that of actual geography; the Italian cities of Pisa, Siena, and especially Florence figure largely as settings. The entire Mediterranean is represented with its islands of Sicily, Corfu, Rhodes, Cyprus, Ischia. France, England, and Spain also serve as backgrounds. In one oriental story, the Seventh Tale on the Second Day, beautiful Altiel, the Sultan of Babylon's daughter, after being kidnaped, travels in the space of four years over most of the Mediterranean, the islands, Greece, Turkey, and Alexandria. Boccaccio is also concerned with restricted spatial reality, and he sketches in close detail internal settings of abbeys, bedrooms, churches, marketplaces, castles, and inns. Different social classes have their own language and clothing. Many characters like Ciappelletto, living in profanation of the world; Rinaldo abandoned in nakedness and cold by his fellow men; Peronella, the deceitful Neapolitan woolcomber cuckolding her husband; the whole convent of nuns eagerly lying with the youth Masetto—these Boccaccio describes in believable human conflicts.

Although he draws upon the entire arsenal of medieval rhetoric, the author of these one hundred novella goes beyond figures of speech and linguistic tools in his modern paradoxical style and cynical tone. Although his satire often bites deep, his comic mood generally embraces evil and holiness alike with sympathy and tolerance. His treatment of themes, situation, and character is never didactic. Like Chaucer, he is indulgent, exposing moral and social corruption but leaving guilty characters to condemn themselves.

A novella like the comic tale of Chichibio, told on the Sixth Day, is pure comic farce, moving rapidly by question and answer, playfully rollicking to a surprise ending brought about by this impusive, foolish cook. The story of Rossiglione and Guardastagno, Ninth Tale of the Fourth Day, has a tragic plot. But the narrators draw no moral in either case. The interaction of character, scene, and plot brings into relief forces that motivate the world of humanity and allow the reader to judge if he must. Again and again characters in the tales are relieved from moral responsibility by the control of Fortune.

Throughout *The Decameron* Boccaccio concerns himself primarily with presenting a very human world as he observed and understood it. In this presentation there is no pedantry or reticence; he paints men and women in all their rascality, faithlessness, nobility, and suffering, changing his Italian prose to suit the exigency of purpose, whether that results in a serious or comic, refined or coarse, descriptive or analytical style. Boccaccio has command of many styles; in fact, his "Commedia Umana" comprehends most, and its author changes easily from one to another.

It is true that in utilizing fables and anecdotes from many medieval sources, in employing figurative and rhythmical devices from books on medieval rhetoric, in structuring his framework according to the chivalric world of valor and courtesy, his work is a product of the Middle Ages. But in its frank, open-minded treatment of flesh as flesh, its use of paradox, cynicism, and realistic handling of character, *The Decameron* transcends the medieval period and, going beyond the Renaissance, takes its place as universal art.

Muriel B. Ingham

DECLINE AND FALL

Type of work: Novel
Author: Evelyn Waugh (1903-1966)
Type of plot: Social satire
Time of plot: Twentieth century
Locale: England and Wales
First published: 1928

Principal characters:

PAUL PENNYFEATHER, a serious-minded young Oxonian
SIR ALASTAIR DIGBY-VAINE-TRUMPINGTON, a young aristocrat
ARTHUR POTTS, a noble-minded young man
DR. AUGUSTUS FAGAN, head of Llanabba Castle School
FLOSSIE, and
DIANA, his daughters
MR. PRENDERGAST, an ex-clergyman
CAPTAIN GRIMES, a public-school man
PETER BESTE-CHETWYNDE, one of Paul's pupils
MARGOT BESTE-CHETWYNDE, his mother
SOLOMON PHILBRICK, a confidence man
SIR HUMPHREY MALTRAVERS, later Lord Metroland, a British politician

Critique:

Decline and Fall mingles farce with grim tragedy. Episodic in form, with many of its scenes no more than a page or so in length, it is a penetrating yet hilarious study of disordered English society in the period between wars. Mr. Waugh insists that his books are not intended as satires, since the satirical spirit presupposes a stable and homogeneous society against which to project its critical exposure of folly and vice. For all that, the writer demonstrates in this novel, his first, a tremendous talent for comic satire. Paul Pennyfeather's misadventures reflect one phase of the contemporary mood of disillusionment. On the other hand, Grimes, a bounder and a cad, is timeless, a figure who would have been as much at home in the days of the Caesars as he was in the reign of King George V. Waugh's distortions and exaggerations have also the quality of fantasy, for in his pages the impossible and the believable exist on the same plane at the same time.

The Story:

At Scone College, Oxford, the annual dinner of the Bollinger Club ended with the breaking of glass. Reeling out of Sir Alastair Digby-Vaine-Trumpington's rooms, the drunken aristocrats ran to earth Paul Pennyfeather, an inoffensive divinity student, and forcibly left him trouserless before they went roaring off into the night.

Bollinger members could be fined, but the college authorities felt that Paul deserved severer punishment for running across the quadrangle in his shorts, and he was sent down for indecent behavior. His unsympathetic guardian, after informing him that under his father's will his legacy could be withheld for unsatisfactory behavior, virtuously announced his intention to cut off Paul's allowance.

Through a shoddy firm of scholastic agents Paul became a junior assistant master at Llanabba Castle, Wales. Llanabba was not a good school. Its head was Dr. Augustus Fagan, whose lectures on service were intended to cover up the inadequacies of his institution. He had two daughters, Flossie, a vulgar young woman of matrimonial ambitions, and Diana, who economized on sugar and soap. One of the masters was Mr. Prendergast, a former clergyman who suffered from doubts. The other was Captain Grimes, who wore a false leg and was, as he frankly admitted, periodically in the soup. A bounder and a scoundrel, he put his faith in the public-school system, which may kick a man out but never lets him down. Grimes thought he had been put on his feet more often than any public-school man alive. His reluctant engagement to Flossie was his protection against the next time he found himself in trouble.

Paul was in charge of the fifth form. When he met his class for the first time, most of the boys claimed that their name was Tangent. An uproar arising between would-be Tangents and a few non-Tangents, Paul announced that the writer of the longest essay would receive half a crown. Mr. Prendergast wondered why Paul's classes were always so quiet. His own students behaved outrageously and made fun of his wig. Paul found young Peter Beste-Chetwynde the most interesting of his pupils.

Arthur Potts, one of the few men Paul had known at Scone, wrote that Alastair Trumpington, regretting Paul's dismissal, wanted to send him twenty pounds. Grimes, hearing of the offer, wired for the money in Paul's name.

Some parents planned to visit Llanabba Castle. Dr. Fagan decided to honor their visit with the annual field sports meet. Philbrick, the butler, objected to his extra duties. To Paul he confided that he was a crook who had taken the post in order to kidnap little Lord Tangent, but that he had reformed after falling in love with Diana. He told Mr. Prendergast that he was really Sir Solomon Philbrick, a millionaire shipowner, and he left Grimes under the impression that he was a novelist collecting material for a book.

The sports meet was not a gala occasion. Lady Circumference, Lord Tangent's mother, was rude to everyone in distributing the prizes. The Llanabba Silver Band played. Margot Beste-Chetwynde created a social flurry when she arrived with a Negro. Mr. Prendergast, the starter, accidentally shot Lord Tangent in the heel. Later he became abusively drunk. But Paul, without intending to, fell in love at first sight with Peter Beste-Chetwynde's beautiful widowed mother.

The term dragged to a close. Lord Tangent's foot became infected and he died. Grimes, landing in the soup once more, announced his engagement to Flossie, but the marriage turned out as badly as he had expected. Detectives arrived to arrest Philbrick on charges of false pretense, but their man had already flown. A few days later Grimes' clothing and a suicide note were discovered on the beach.

Paul, engaged to tutor Peter during the vacation, went to Margot's country house, King's Thursday. When she bought the place from her impoverished bachelor brother-in-law, Lord Pastmaster, it had been the finest example of Tudor domestic architecture in England. Bored with it, however, she had commissioned Otto Silenus, an eccentric designer, to build a modernistic house in its place. Silenus built a structure of concrete, glass, and aluminum, a house for dynamos, not people, but people went there anyway for endless house parties.

When Paul finally found enough courage to propose to Margot, she accepted him because Peter thought the young Oxonian would make a better stepfather than a rival suitor, Sir Humphrey Maltravers, Minister of Transport. During preparations for the wedding Paul learned that Margot still carried on her father's business, a syndicate vaguely connected with amusement enterprises in South America. Grimes turned up mysteriously in her employ. Potts, now working for the League of Nations, also took an unexplained interest in Margot's business affairs.

A few days before the wedding Margot asked Paul to fly to Marseilles and arrange for the passage of several cabaret entertainers to Rio de Janeiro. He did so without realizing that he was bribing the officials he interviewed. On his wedding morning Paul was having a final drink with Alastair Trumpington when a Scotland Yard inspector appeared and arrested him on charges of engaging in an international white-slave traffic.

Margot fled to her villa at Corfu and did not appear at the trial. Potts, a special investigator for the League of Nations, was the chief witness for the prosecution. Convicted of Margot's crimes, Paul was sentenced to seven years' penal servitude. The first part of his sentence he served at Blackstone Gaol, where he found Philbrick a trusty and Mr. Prendergast the chaplain. Shortly after Prendergast was killed by a crazed inmate, Paul was removed to Egdon Heath Penal Settlement. Grimes was one of his fellow prisoners, but not for long. One day, while serving on a work gang, he walked off into the fog. Everyone supposed that he perished later in a swamp, but Paul believed otherwise. Grimes, whose roguery was timeless, could never die. Margot came to visit Paul. She announced her intention to marry Maltravers, now Lord Metroland and the Home Secretary.

Paul's escape from Egdon Heath was carefully contrived. On orders from the Home Secretary he was removed for an appendicitis operation in a nursing home owned by Dr. Fagan, who had forsaken education for medicine. After a drunken doctor had signed a death certificate stating that Paul had died under the anesthetic, Alastair Trumpington, who had become Margot's young man, put him on a yacht which carried him to Margot's villa at Corfu. Officially dead, Paul enjoyed the rest he thought he deserved. Some months later, wearing a heavy mustache, he returned to Scone to continue his reading for the church. When the chaplain mentioned another Pennyfeather, a wild undergraduate sent down for misconduct, Paul said that the young man was a distant cousin.

At Scone the annual dinner of the Bollinger Club ended with the breaking of glass. Paul was reading in his room when Peter Beste-Chetwynde, Lord Pastmaster since his uncle's death, came in, very drunk. Paul's great mistake, Peter said, was that he had ever become involved with people like Margot and himself. After his departure Paul settled down to read another chapter in a book on early church heresies.

Further Critical Evaluation of the Work:

Decline and Fall is the first and possibly the best work of Evelyn Waugh, a luminary of the brave company of English satirists. The novel is notable for its economy of time and space. The action extends over a year, and the protagonist's circumstances at the beginning and end are virtually identical, lending a neat roundness to the story. Another feature is the spareness of the prose, and the unlabored epigrams, as, for example, Paul Pennyfeather's quip that the English public school is a perfect conditioner for life in prison. Waugh lays low individuals and whole classes of society with a flick of a proper name: Digby-Vaine-Trumpington for a vain, trumpeting young aristocrat; Maltravers for a Secretary of Transportation; Prendergast for a clergyman aghast at his apprehension of divine indifference; Grimes for an earthy rascal; Pennyfeather for an impecunious, half-fledged scholar.

The tone is persistently cheerful. No amazement is expressed, even by the innocent and beleaguered protagonist, at anything that befalls him. Tragedies occur offstage. The death of Prendergast, for instance, is revealed in a hymn. Lord Tangent's demise is recorded as follows: in chapter eight, he is shown crying because he has been wounded in the foot by a bullet from the starter's pistol; in chapter twelve, Beste-Chetwynde reports, in an aside, that Tangent's foot is gangrened; in chapter thirteen comes the news that the foot is being amputated; and finally in chapter nineteen, it is reported in an offhand way that he has died. The list of groups and institutions which excite the author's scorn is extensive; his opprobrium falls on the aristocracy, the newly rich, the universities, the public schools, old-school penology, newfangled penology, the House of Lords, the House of Commons, the Church of England, historical landmarks, modern architecture, and the League of Nations, to name a few. But though the novel manages to be hilarious at the expense of practically everybody, it has a serious side, or rather a serious center; namely, the schoolboy virtue of Pennyfeather contrasted with the cheery rascality of Grimes.

That Paul Pennyfeather is a right thinker and a square shooter is evident from the start. He owes his educational opportunities as much to his own industry, intelligence, and moderation as to the legacy left by his parents. He is earnest, diffident, and idealistic; in short, he is the very model of a middle-class English divinity student. The incredible things that happen to him seem at first reading to represent repeated assaults of a corrupt society on a genuinely decent character. Captain Grimes, on the other hand, shows up as a bounder of the very worst kind, a poseur who relies on public-school connections to rescue him from his frequent immersions in "the soup." He milks the fellowship of honor and duty for all it is worth and does not hesitate to abandon ship at the first sign of bad weather—women, children, and gentlemanly behavior notwithstanding.

But for all his roguery, Grimes is not a villain. He is instead the most sympathetic character in the novel. The chief element of his personality is common sense; it is he, and not Pennyfeather, who is the author's *persona,* who embodies the impulses of sanity as opposed to the precepts of class and culture. During the war, for example, when faced with court-martial or honorable suicide, he relies on drink and old school ties to see him through alive, and they do. Trapped into marriage, he simply bolts, once into the public schools, once into the sea. Imprisoned, he makes his escape by sinking into a quicksand from which, Paul and the reader are confident, he will rise to drink his pint in new guise but with the old elemental verve. He is self-indulgent, brave, resourceful, and not to be humbugged.

Contrarily Paul, though self-disciplined, is meek, credulous, and fundamentally passive. Everything that happens to him, good or bad, simply *happens.* His rather mild passion for Margot Beste-Chetwynde strikes him like lightning; his actual proposal of marriage is all Margot's doing. He acquiesces alike to expulsion from college and rescue from prison with the same spongy plasticity cloaked in a sort of ethical good-sportism. In fact, it may be argued that believers in this schoolboy code of ethics suffer from a profound moral laziness and invite the outrages perpetrated on them in its name by those who do not believe in it. Paul's explanation of why he does not outface Potts and take money from Trumpington is illustrative. He defines a gentleman as someone who declines to accept benefits that are not his by right, or to profit from windfall advantage. Implicit in this stance are (a) a kind of flabby ethical neutrality disguised as self-respect, and (b) a certain pride in taking no action. Grimes' judgment is sounder, and more vigorous, for he recognizes Potts as a stinker in prosecuting Paul for a crime he committed inadvertently.

The author remarks at one stage that Paul has not the makings of a hero. No more has he the makings of a villain, for villainy requires a certain enterprise, as exemplified by Margot. It is not Paul's decline and fall which are recorded here, but the degeneration of a society in which custom and privilege combine to nurture all manner of waste and wickedness. Paul is merely part of the problem. Grimes, the voice of blackguardism and good sense, is part of the solution. Paul toasts the stability of ideals, Grimes the passing moment.

Despite Grimes, however, *Decline and Fall* ends on a rather grim note, with Peter Beste-Chetwynde a wastrel and Paul embracing a pinched orthodoxy. The underlying sense is of honorable old forms giving way to a new and nastier regime, a theme which Waugh pursued in later works. Indeed, he espoused it in his own life to the extent of rejecting the new order altogether, and as a result he was virtually a hermit at the time of his death.

Jan Kennedy Foster

DEEPHAVEN

Type of work: Tales
Author: Sarah Orne Jewett (1849-1909)
Type of plot: Regional romance
Time of plot: Nineteenth century
Locale: Maine seacoast
First published: 1877

Principal characters:
HELEN DENIS, the narrator
KATE LANCASTER, her friend
THE CAREWS, and
THE LORIMERS, Deephaven's society
MRS. KEW, wife of the lighthouse keeper
CAPTAIN LANT,
CAPTAIN SANDS, and
DANNY, Maine seamen
MRS. BONNY, an elderly eccentric
MISS CHAUNCEY, an elegant woman

Critique:

Deephaven, Miss Jewett's first collection of tales and sketches, contains those characteristics of nature study and character drawing which the author used throughout her later work. This book, although unified in background and theme, is too diffuse in its effects to be called a novel; it is a series of sketches describing an idyllic summer in an almost forgotten town on the New England coast. It illustrates also Miss Jewett's belief that a writer must know the village well before he can know the world. Willa Cather, in her reminiscences of Sarah Orne Jewett, revealed that the older woman set her on the path to literary achievement by telling her to write about people and places that she knew best. When Miss Cather followed Miss Jewett's advice, books like O Pioneers! and My Antonia were the result. While Miss Jewett may not have reached Willa Cather's heights as a writer, she wrote pleasantly and nostalgically of familiar things; and Miss Cather never failed to pay her literary debt to her preceptor.

The Story:

Kate Lancaster's great-aunt, Katherine Brandon, had died, leaving to Kate's mother a charming old house and the family estate, including wharf rights, at Deephaven, a quaint sea town that had known better days. Since Kate's family was scattering for the summer, she asked Helen Denis, a friend, to spend the season with her in the old house on the Maine coast. They took with them two maids who came from that part of New England, and they left Boston without regret.

Riding with them in the stagecoach from the railway station was a large, weather-beaten, but good-natured woman who turned out to be Mrs. Kew, the wife of the lighthouse keeper. She was a keenly observant person but so warmhearted that the girls knew that she meant her invitation to visit the Light, and by the end of the summer they knew that wherever she was there was always a home and a heart for them.

Great-aunt Brandon's house was a sedate and imposing one full of furnishings brought home by generations of seagoing ancestors. Its closets were filled with china and its walls were covered by family portraits. The girls rummaged the place from cellar to attic until they felt that they knew Katherine Brandon as well as if she were still alive. Then they started to learn their way around the shore, out to the lighthouse, through the town, and out into the country.

People who had known Katherine Brandon and Kate's mother felt themselves the girls' friends by inheritance and the girls were never lonely. Those people had held Katherine Brandon in great respect but with fond admiration. The girls tried to do nothing to hurt the Brandon name. Through Widow Jim Patton they realized that Kate's aunt had been a thoughtful, generous soul who remembered in her will her less fortunate neighbors.

To the girls it seemed as though the clocks had stopped long ago in Deephaven and that the people went on repeating whatever they had been doing at that time in the past. Even their faces looked like those of colonial times. The people attached a great deal of importance to the tone of their society, handed down from the fabulous times of Governor Chantrey, a rich shipowner and an East India merchant. Now there were few descendants of the old families left; these were treated almost with reverence by the others. Even the simple fishermen felt an unreasoning pride in living in Deephaven. There were no foreigners, and there were no industries to draw people from out of town.

The Carews and the Lorimers, old friends of Katherine Brandon, became friends of Kate and Helen. Mr. Dick Carew had been an East India merchant. Mr. Lorimer was the minister. The ladies were of the old order, inordinately proud of their mementos of the old days and always happy to tell reminiscences of earlier times.

Naturally, in a seacoast town, there were also old sailors, all of whom were called captain by the time they reached a certain age. When attacks of rheumatism did not keep them home, they gathered on the wharves. Huddled close together, for many had grown deaf, they told over and over again the tales of their distant voyages. The girls noticed that silence fell when anyone approached the group, but on one occasion they hid close by to hear the yarns the old men told.

Singly the old mariners were pleased to have a new audience, and before long Kate and Helen were friendly with many of the old men. While some of them told stories of marine superstitions and adventures, others told supernatural tales they swore were true. Captain Lent related the story of Peletiah Daw, to whom he had been bound out in his youth. Old Peletiah put more store by his wild nephew Ben than he did by his own sons. One night, when Peletiah was old and feeble, he cried out and begged his sons to cut down Ben, whom he had seen hanging from a yardarm. The sons thought their father was delirious, but a short time later a sailor came to tell them that Ben had died of a fever. Peletiah called the man a liar, but the sailor held to his story before the women. Outside, he told the sons that Ben had been hanged from the yardarm, just as the old man had said, and on the day Peletiah had cried out.

Kate and Helen came to know Danny, a silent, weather-beaten fisherman who spent most of his time cleaning fish but who told them shyly about a pet cat he owned. Another good friend was Captain Sands, who kept in a warehouse all the souvenirs of his sea voyages that his wife refused to have cluttering her house.

When they took Mrs. Kew with them to a circus in nearby Denby, they all had a hilarious time, although the circus turned out to be a droopy and dispirited performance. Their high spirits were dampened for a while when Mrs. Kew recognized the fat lady as a girl who had once been her neighbor in Vermont.

The girls learned to know people all over the countryside as far as their horses would carry them. The person they liked best was Mrs. Bonny, who they thought looked so wild and unconventional that they always felt they were talking to a good-natured Indian.

One family along the coast was so forlorn that the thought of them preyed on the girls' minds all summer. Neither the father nor the mother had health, and there were several little children with whom they had made friends. Early in the fall Kate and Helen went back along the coast to see them. Receiving no answer, they were standing undecided at the door when some neighbors came up to say that the mother had died a short time before. The father, after drinking heavily, was now lying dead, and the children had been parceled out as best they could be. Not daring to go to the funeral, the girls watched it from a distance. They felt that their everyday world was very close to the boundary of death.

Still closer to that boundary was Miss Chauncey of East Parish, a town even smaller and more forgotten than Deephaven. She was a splendid-looking, aristocratic old lady who had been mildly insane but harmless for years. Hers had been a rich and happy childhood until her father lost his fortune during the embargo early in the century. It was said that a sailor to whom he had broken a promise cursed her father and his family. One brother killed himself; another died

insane. Miss Chauncey herself had been so ill that her guardian sold all her household goods to pay her hospital bills. Suddenly she became well, her mind unclouded. No one had told her that her house furnishings had been sold. Her shock at seeing the bare house unbalanced her mind again, but she remained harmless. She refused to leave the house and she never seemed to realize that it was bleak and empty. She was still an elegant woman, possessed of unusual worldly advantages; she lived, however, without seeing the poverty of her surroundings. Although she had no idea of time, she always knew when Sunday came. She read the Bible beautifully. Faith sustained her.

By fall Kate and Helen had become so attached to their friends in Deephaven that they postponed their return to Boston as long as possible. Helen thought that, though they might never return, they would always remember their completely happy summer in that old-fashioned village.

Further Critical Evaluation of the Work:

The provincial characters in *Deephaven* do not yet possess the universality that they would acquire in Sarah Orne Jewett's latest stories and novels. But the author acutely observes this small fishing village, clearly defining its social gradations and representative types. Equally well detailed are the varieties of "fashion" adopted by the inhabitants of Deephaven. But it is the people themselves—their faces, their speech, and their lives—that the reader best remembers.

Life in Deephaven moves slowly, so that even the details of common existence assume importance and become leisurely and pleasant activities. The narrator details with obvious relish the housekeeping routine, and the quiet day-to-day village life. Always, a gentle humor pervades the book.

Memories constitute much of *Deephaven's* narrative. The old sailors, their widows, village spinsters, old bachelors, everyone, seems to live at least half of his or her life recollecting the past. And the "ancient mariners" of the village are the heroes, if the book has any. Sometimes, they romanticize the past, sometimes they view it clearly, but always it is present before them, as real as the ever-changing bay and the tides. The ships remembered by the old skippers assume vivid personalities. The rich history of bygone days is preserved by the people who lived it. Sarah Orne Jewett saw history as basically the story of human beings and the events of their lives. This vision dominates and shapes *Deephaven*.

The whalers and seafaring men and their families have had more contact with the world than most villagers and are not as narrow-minded as many small-town people. They possess more than folk wisdom; along with trinkets from foreign ports, they have picked up an awareness of the larger issues that face humanity. Sarah Orne Jewett especially loved and respected these people.

THE DEERSLAYER

Type of work: Novel
Author: James Fenimore Cooper (1789-1851)
Type of plot: Historical romance
Time of plot: 1740
Locale: Northern New York State
First published: 1841

> *Principal characters:*
> NATTY BUMPPO, called Deerslayer by the Delawares
> HURRY HARRY, a frontier scout
> CHINGACHGOOK, Deerslayer's Indian friend
> THOMAS HUTTER, owner of the lake
> JUDITH HUTTER, a girl Thomas Hutter claims as his daughter
> HETTY HUTTER, Judith's sister
> WAH-TA!-WAH, Chingachgook's beloved

Critique:

There is no question that the savages and the woodsman, Natty Bumppo, come off best in this first of the Leatherstocking Tales. Deerslayer and the Indians, good and bad, are depicted as having codes of honor and morality. Tom Hutter and Hurry Harry are motivated by greed and viciousness in their efforts to obtain Iroquois scalps and in their murder of an innocent Indian girl. The simpleminded Hetty Hutter and Judith, her vain sister, are but two-dimensional characters, however, in this novel of atmosphere and exciting action.

The Story:

Natty Bumppo, a young woodsman known as Deerslayer, and Hurry Harry traveled to the shores of Lake Glimmerglass together. It was a dangerous journey, for the French and their Iroquois allies were on the warpath. Deerslayer was planning to meet his friend Chingachgook, the young Delaware chief, so that they might go against the Iroquois. Hurry Harry was on his way to the lake to warn Thomas Hutter and his daughters that hostile Indians were raiding along the frontier. Harry was accustomed to hunt and trap with Hutter during the summer, and he was an admirer of Hutter's elder daughter, the spirited Judith.

Hutter and his daughters lived in a cabin built on piles in the middle of the lake. Hutter had also built a great, scow-like vessel, known among frontiersmen as the ark, on which he traveled from one shore of the lake to the other on his hunting and trapping expeditions. On their arrival at the lake the two found a hidden canoe. Having paddled out to the cabin and found it deserted, they proceeded down the lake and came upon the ark anchored in a secluded outlet. Hutter had already learned of the Indian raiders. The party decided to take refuge in the cabin, where they could be attacked only over the water. The men managed to maneuver the ark out of the narrow outlet and sail it to the cabin. They had one narrow escape. As the ark was clearing the outlet, six Indians tried to board the boat by dropping from the overhanging limbs of a tree. Each missed and fell into the water.

Under cover of darkness, Hutter, Deerslayer, and Hurry Harry took the canoe and paddled to shore to get Hutter's two remaining canoes hidden there. They found the canoes and, on their way back to the ark, sighted a party of Indians camped under some trees. While Deerslayer waited in a canoe offshore, the other two men attacked the Iroquois camp in an attempt to obtain scalps, for which they could obtain bounties. They were captured. Deerslayer, knowing that he was powerless to help them, lay down to sleep in the canoe until morning.

When Deerslayer awoke, he saw that one of the canoes had drifted close to shore. To rescue it, he was forced to shoot an Indian, the first man he had ever killed.

Returning to the fort with his prizes, Deerslayer told the girls of their father's fate. It was agreed that they should delay any attempt at rescue until the arrival of Chingachgook, whom Deerslayer was to meet that night.

Under cover of darkness, the party went in the ark and met Chingachgook at the spot where the river joined the lake. Back in the cabin, Deerslayer explained that the Delaware had come to the lake to rescue his sweetheart, Wah-ta!-Wah, who had been stolen by the Iroquois. Suddenly they discovered that Hetty Hutter had disappeared. The girl, who was somewhat feeble-minded, had cast off in one of the canoes with the intention of going to the Indian camp to rescue her father and Hurry Harry.

The next morning Wah-ta!-Wah came upon Hetty wandering in the forest. She took the white girl to the Iroquois camp. Because the Indians believed deranged persons were protected by the Great Spirit, she suffered no harm.

It was Deerslayer's idea to ransom the prisoners with some rich brocades and carved ivory he and Judith found in Tom Hutter's chest. Its contents had been known only to Hutter and the simple-minded Hetty, but in this emergency, Judith did not hesitate to open the coffer. Meanwhile a young Iroquois had rowed Hetty back to the cabin on a raft. Deerslayer told him that the party in the cabin would give two ivory chessmen for the release of the captives. He was unable to drive quite the bargain he had planned. In the end, four chessmen were exchanged for the men, who were returned that night.

Hetty brought a message from Wah-ta!-Wah. Chingachgook was to meet the Indian girl at a particular place on the shore when the evening star rose above the hemlocks that night. Hurry Harry and Tom Hutter were still determined to obtain scalps, and when night closed in they and Chingachgook reconnoitered the camp. To their disappointment, they found it deserted and the Indians camped on the beach, at the spot where Wah-ta!-Wah was to wait for Chingachgook.

While Hutter and Harry slept, the Delaware and Deerslayer attempted to keep the rendezvous. Unfortunately, the girl was under such close watch that it was impossible for her to leave the camp. The two men entered the camp and boldly rescued her from her captors. Deerslayer, who remained at their rear to cover their escape, was taken prisoner.

When Judith heard from Chingachgook of Deerslayer's capture, she rowed Hetty ashore to learn what had become of the woodsman. Once more Hetty walked unharmed among the superstitious savages. Deerslayer assured her there was nothing she could do to help, that he must await the Iroquois' pleasure. She left to return to Judith.

As the girls paddled about, trying to find the ark in the darkness, they heard the report of a gun. Torches on shore showed them that an Indian girl had been mortally wounded by a shot from the ark. Soon the lights went out. Paddling to the center of the lake, they tried to get what rest they might before morning came.

When daylight returned, Hutter headed the ark toward the cabin once more. Missing his daughters, he had concluded the cabin would be the most likely meeting place. Hutter and Harry were the first to leave the ark to go into the cabin. There the Iroquois, who had come aboard in rafts under cover of darkness, were waiting in ambush. Harry managed to escape into the water, where he was saved by Chingachgook. Judith and Hetty came to the ark in their canoe. After the savages had gone ashore, those on the ark went to the cabin. They found Hutter lying dead. That evening he was buried in the lake. Hurry Harry took advantage of the occasion to propose to Judith, but she refused him.

Shortly afterward they were surprised to see Deerslayer paddling toward the ark. He had been given temporary liberty in order to bargain with the fugitives.

The Iroquois sent word that Chingachgook would be allowed to return to his own people if Wah-ta!-Wah and Judith became brides of Iroquois warriors. Hetty, they promised, would go unharmed because of her mental condition. Although Deerslayer's life was to be the penalty for refusal, these terms were declined.

Deerslayer did not have to return to his captors until the next day, and that evening he and Judith examined carefully the contents of her father's chest. To the girl's wonder, she found letters indicating that Hutter had not been her real father, but a former buccaneer whom her mother had married when her first husband deserted her. Saddened by this knowledge, Judith no longer wished to live at the lake. She intimated slyly to Deerslayer that she loved him, only to find he considered her above him in education and intelligence.

When Deerslayer returned to the Iroquois the next day, he was put to torture with hatchets. Hetty, Judith, and Wah-ta!-Wah came to the camp and attempted to intercede for him, but to no avail. Suddenly Chingachgook bounded in, and cut his friend's bonds. Deerslayer's release was the signal for the regiment from the nearest fort to attack, for Hurry Harry had gone to summon help during the night.

The Iroquois were routed. Hetty was mortally wounded during the battle. The next day she was buried in the lake beside her parents. Judith joined the soldiers returning to the fort. Deerslayer departed for the Delaware camp with Chingachgook and his bride.

Fifteen years later, Deerslayer, Chingachgook, and the latter's young son, Uncas, revisited the lake. Wah-ta!-Wah was long since dead, and, though the hunter inquired at the fort about Judith Hutter, he could find no one who knew her. Rumor was that a former member of the garrison, then living in England on his paternal estates, was influenced by a woman of rare beauty who was not his wife. The ark and the cabin in the lake were falling into decay.

Further Critical Evaluation of the Work:

The Deerslayer is the fifth and last published of the Leatherstocking Tales; when the entire series was republished in 1850 it became the first. Having written two books about Leatherstocking in middle age and two picturing him in his declining years, Cooper turned back to young Natty Bumppo before he had gained fame among the Indians as Hawkeye or Long Rifle. In *The Deerslayer* Natty is the idealized "natural man."

Deerslayer is initiated into warfare when he first kills a fellow man—in self-defense—and then comforts his dying foe, who confers upon him the new name, Hawkeye, which honors him as a fighter. He also learns of some of the evil in the world through his acquaintance with Thomas Hutter and Hurry Harry who kill Indians—including women and children—for profit only. Cooper's idealization of Indian character is brought out partly through what he himself writes about Indians and partly through what Natty says of them.

The common theme which ties the Leatherstocking Tales together is the protagonist. Although he is known by different names in the various novels, he is identified throughout the series by his qualities as a brave and honorable hero. As a character, he is developed from youth to old age. He is a loner and an individualist and has moral and ethical concerns about the environment. He commands a strong integrity in dealing with other human beings, treating both friends and enemies with courtesy and respect. Ultimately, he follows his own simple moral scheme and demonstrates unwavering dedication to the principle of self-reliance. *The Deerslayer* is one of two Leatherstocking Tales (the other was *The Pathfinder*) which Mark Twain chose to mock amusingly but rather unjustly in his "Fenimore Cooper's Literary Offenses." The defects of plot, characterization, and style are easily seen by modern readers, but the romance is a far better book than Twain's comments would lead one to believe. Some critics have seen it as perhaps the best of the five tales. Cooper in his 1850 Preface said *The Pathfinder* and *The Deerslayer* were "probably the two most worthy an enlightened and cultivated reader's notice."

THE DEFENCE OF GUENEVERE AND OTHER POEMS

Type of work: Poetry
Author: William Morris (1834-1896)
First published: 1858

The Defence of Guenevere and Other Poems, the first collection of poems published by William Morris, is one of the three or four principal expressions of Pre-Raphaelitism in poetry. Although Morris had just turned twenty-four when the volume appeared, it epitomizes his qualities and foreshadows his artistic attainment. Swinburne, his contemporary, wrote concerning it: "Such things as are in this book are taught and learned in no school but that of instinct." It was Swinburne's opinion that no other literary work had ever shown more distinctly the mark of native character and that the poetry was entirely original. He saw Morris as "not yet a master," but "assuredly no longer a pupil." Not unmindful of certain technical faults and an occasional hint of confusion, Swinburne nevertheless went on to say that Morris' volume was incomparable in its time for "perception and experience of tragic truth" and that no other contemporary poet had a "touch of passion at once so broad and so sure."

Swinburne may have overstated the case for the originality of the poems; Morris shows strong influences of Malory and Froissart, though more in regard to selection of subject matter than in its interpretation. His Arthurian poems reveal a genuine passion and exceptional beauty, especially in passages such as the vibrant, breath-taking narrative description which opens the title poem. Yet, despite their freshness and strong feeling, these poems are in what may be designated the tapestry tradition, whereas those poems derived more clearly from Froissart than from Malory—among them "Sir Peter Harpdon's End," "Concerning Geoffrey Teste Noir," and the grim "Haystack in the Floods"—attest to Morris' realization that, even in the Middle Ages, the tourney was not the only aspect of war.

Although Morris had a lifelong passion for beauty, a passion kept by his vigorous nature from any Victorian effeminacy, he had a need for certain harsh or stark elements which are already present in these poems but which he did not fully employ until, after discovering the Icelandic sagas, he wrote some of his greatest poetry in *Sigurd the Volsung.* The touches of this later power evident in this first volume of his poems are the stark descriptions such as these lines from "Concerning Geoffrey Teste Noire":

> I think 'twas Geoffrey smote him on
> the brow
> With some spiked axe; and while he
> totter'd, dim
>
> About the eyes, the spear of Alleyne
> Roux
> Slipped through his camaille and his
> throat; well, well!

And when Sir Peter Harpdon's wife Alice, upon hearing of her husband's death, cries:

> I am much too young to live,
> Fair God, so let me die,

we recognize in the cry a kind of Shakespearean poignancy. Among the many other qualities of this first book of poems is the apparent simplicity of a lyric like "Golden Wings," which attains deep sincerity as it smoothly reflects early memories in a manner distinctly Morris' own. There is also the plain perfection of the little poem, "Summer Dawn," in which, departing momentarily from the dreams and histories of long-past lives and battles, Morris speaks simply in his own voice of his desire for communion in nature.

Morris, while studying medieval romances and admiring them for their curious intrinsic beauty, became convinced that if we could move backward through time to the age of the sea kings, we should find the essential characteristics of the race to be exactly like those of today. Admittedly, he found the Middle Ages much more ignorant, cruel, and savage than the ages preceding or following; nevertheless, he concluded that people of those times must have thought about particular things and issues just as modern men and women do. Why then, he asked, should we not study all possible facets of this terrible society?

Morris gives us some brief, sudden, and flashing pictures of that far-off time. The title poem presents a queen about to be burned at the stake; then, at the sound of a horse's hoofs, she knows that her lover is coming to her rescue. One of the most powerful of these pictures is presented in "The Haystack in the Floods." Not revealing either how the tragedy began or how it ended, the poem opens with the haunting questions:

Had she come all the way for this
To part at last without a kiss?
Yea, had she borne the dirt and rain
That her own eyes might see him slain
Beside the haystack in the floods?

We are at first told just enough about the woman Jehane to make us wonder about her character and to know that as she rides along she is miserable. Her lover Robert, who rides some distance ahead of her with a few armed men, is confronted by his adversary Godmar and numerous armed men. At first she fears for her own safety rather than Robert's:

My God! my God! I have to tread
The long way back without you; then
The court at Paris; those six men;
The gratings of the Chatelet;
The swift Seine on some rainy day
Like this, and people standing by,
And laughing, while my weak hands try
To recollect how strong men swim.

In her despair she contemplates accepting Godmar, the man whom she hates. Robert, whose men refuse to fight against the heavy odds, charges the enemy and is captured, disarmed, and bound. When after long hesitation Jehane refuses to come willingly to his castle, Godmar and his men brutally murder Robert before her eyes. The poem ends with an uncertainty about her fate. Does she go mad? Will she be taken back and burned at the castle from which she has escaped? The reader may even suspect that she is feigning madness and that before the castle is reached she will selfishly yield to Godmar, who may then retain her until he tires of her. Having given us this glimpse of medieval passion, selfishness, suffering, and cruelty, Morris ends the poem, after Godmar's men had beaten Robert's brains out, on this note:

Then Godmar turned again and said:
So, Jehane, the first fitte is read!
Take note, my lady, that your way
Lies backward to the Chatelet!
She shook her head and gazed awhile
At her cold hands with a rueful smile,
As though this thing had made her
    mad.
This was the parting that they had
Beside the haystack in the floods.

Another grim, moving poem, a Browningesque monologue called "The Judgement of God," supplies a second example of the same device.

Other noteworthy poems in the book are "The Little Tower," "The Wind," "The Eve of Crecy," "In Prison," and "The Blue Closet." All extremely original, they display a wide range in idea and theme. In their ability to make us understand the feelings of pain, terror, or heroic effort at particular moments in the lives of people, they all have a high psychological quality. For example, Guenevere's natural and horrible soliloquy, revealing that she has wondered how the fire would quiver yards above her head, in its startlingly true psychology improves upon the narrative of the original story. Especially in his use of monologue and dialogue, Morris successfully demonstrates that the poet can best revive the past not by detailed description of things but by faithful expression of the feelings of persons who lived long ago.

Without exaggeration, William Morris's *Defence of Guenevere* may be called an outstanding first volume of poetry. However, not unlike the early volumes of most poets, it did not make any particular impact upon the reading public when it appeared in 1858. This lack of widespread acclaim for the volume may have been a factor in Morris' withdrawing for some time from the writing of poetry.

Another factor, of course, was his feeling that writing poetry was neither particularly notable nor difficult and that it had no precedence over the new and exciting experiments in tapestry-weaving and dyeing in which he was already engaged. Morris was content with the appreciation accorded the volume by a few of his friends, among them Burne-Jones and Dante Gabriel Rossetti—to the latter of whom it was dedicated.

DEFENCE OF POESIE

Type of work: Literary criticism
Author: Sir Philip Sidney (1554-1586)
First published: 1595

Sir Philip Sidney's *Defence of Poesie* is an attempt to raise poetry above the criticism that had been directed at it by contemporary critics and to establish it as the highest of the arts, best fitted both to please men and to instruct them, the two aims stated by Horace in his *Ars Poetica.* The first part of *Defence of Poesie* is primarily theoretical; Sidney weighs the respective merits of philosophy, history, and poetry as teachers of virtue. In the final section, he surveys the state of English literature soon after 1580.

Sidney's first argument for the supremacy of poetry, and by poetry he means all imaginative writing in both verse and prose, is that it was the "first light-giver to ignorance"; the first great works of science, philosophy, history, and even law were poems. Both the Italian and the English languages were polished and perfected by their poets, Dante, Boccaccio, and Petrarch on the one hand, Chaucer and Gower on the other. Even Plato illuminated his philosophy with myths and dramatic scenes.

Both the Hebrews and the Romans gave high distinction to poets, considering them prophets, messengers of God or the gods. The Greeks called their writers "makers," creators, who alone could rise above this world to make a "golden" one. Sidney writes of the poet: "So as he goeth hand in hand with Nature, not enclosed within the narrow warrant of her gifts, but freely ranging only within the zodiac of his own wit."

The aim of poetry, of all earthly knowledge, is "to lead and draw us to as high a perfection as our degenerate souls, made worse by their clayey lodgings, can be capable of." The moral philosopher feels himself the best teacher, for he can define and discuss virtue and vice and their causes; the historian argues that his examples from the past are far more

effective instructors than the abstractions of the philosopher. Sidney finds the virtues of both combined in the poet, who can give both precept and example. He cites Homer's demonstration of wisdom personified in Ulysses; of valor, in Achilles; of anger, in Ajax. The poet is free to portray the ideal, while the historian must be faithful to his subjects, and they, being human, mingle faults with their virtues. The poet may show evil punished and good rewarded; the historian must record the vagaries of fortune, which allows the innocent to suffer and the vicious to prosper.

The poet has other advantages over the philosopher; however true his statements may be, they are hard to follow. The poet "doth not only show the way, but giveth so sweet prospect into the way as will entice any man to enter into it." Men will willingly listen to stories of Aeneas or Achilles, unaware of the lessons they are learning.

Having established the superiority of poetry to his own satisfaction, Sidney analyzes both the pleasing and the instructive aspects of the various literary genres, trying to determine what faults can have brought poetry into disrepute. The pastoral can arouse sympathy for the wretchedness of the poor or illustrate civil wrongs in fables about sheep and wolves; satire makes man laugh at folly, and reform. Comedy, which has been disgraced by "naughty play-makers and stage-keepers," is valuable for the ridicule it casts upon our faults, making us scorn them as we laugh. Tragedy, stirring up feelings of wonder and pity, "teacheth the uncertainty of this world, and upon how weak foundations gilden roofs are builded."

Sidney finds nothing to criticize in the work of the lyric poet, who lauds virtuous acts, gives moral precepts, and sometimes praises God, and he defends epic poetry as the greatest of all the genres: "For, as the image of each action stirreth and instructeth the mind, so the lofty image of such worthies most inflameth the mind with desire to be worthy, and informs with counsel how to be worthy."

Concluding his defense, Sidney takes up the most frequently repeated criticisms of poetry, that it is merely rhyming and versifying, that there are other kinds of knowledge which are more worthy of men's time, that poetry is "the mother of lies," that it inspires evil lusts in men, and, finally, that Plato banished it from his commonwealth. Against the first objection Sidney reiterates his statement that poetry is not exclusively that which is written in verse, though he defends the use of verse on the grounds that it is a great aid to the memory and that it is "the only fit speech for music."

The second argument has already been answered; if poetry be the greatest of teachers and inspirations to virtue, it must be worthy of the greatest share of man's attention. To the contention that poets are liars, Sidney replies that since they never affirm their subjects to be literally true or "real," they cannot lie. They do not, indeed, reproduce details of life from specific incidents, but neither do they attempt to prove the false true. They rather call upon men's imagination for the "willing suspension of disbelief" and tell, not "what is or is not, but what should or should not be."

Sidney confesses that there is some justice in the condemnation of poetry for its scurrility, but he imputes the fault to bad poets who abuse their art, rather than to poetry itself. He suggests that Plato, in banishing poets from his Republic, was barring those bad writers who corrupted youth with false pictures of the gods, not the art of poetry itself.

Satisfied with these answers, Sidney then turns to the specific problems of literature in England in his own day. He sees no reason for poetry to flourish in Italy, France, Scotland, and not in his own nation, except the laziness of the poets themselves. They will neither study to acquire ideas nor practice to perfect a style for conveying these ideas. A few English writers and works are, however, worthy of a place in world literature. Sidney praises Chaucer's *Troilus and Criseyde*, the "beautiful parts" of the *Mirror for Magistrates*, and the lyrics of the Earl of Surrey, and he finds that the *Shepheardes Calendar* "hath much poetry in his eclogues," though he objects to Spenser's use of "rustic language," on the grounds that neither Theocritus nor Virgil, the most famous classical writers of pastoral, employed it. For the rest of English poetry Sidney has only scorn, for it seemed to him meaningless: "One verse did but beget another, without ordering at the first what should be at the last; which becomes a confused mass of words, with a tinkling sound of rime, barely accompanied with reason."

The public criticism of drama seems to him justified, with a very few exceptions. He commends *Gorboduc*, a melodramatic Seneca-type tragedy, for its "stately speeches," "well-sounding phrases," and "notable morality," but he is disturbed by the authors' failure to observe the unities of time and place. The rest of the tragedies of the age seem absurd in their broad leaps in space and time, spanning continents and decades in two hours. A true Aristotelian in his views on drama, Sidney is convinced that stage action should be confined to one episode; other events may be reported in the dialogue to provide necessary background for the central events. He objects, too, to the presence of scurrilous comic scenes, chiefly designed to evoke loud laughter from the audience, in the tragedies.

Sidney's last target is the affected artificial diction of lyric poetry, especially of love poetry. He believes that the wildly imaginative conceits of the Euphuists are tedious, and he praises, in contrast, the sense of decorum, of fitting diction and imagery, of the great classical orators.

After a few comments on the relative

merits of qualitative and quantitative verse and on types of rhyme, Sidney addresses his readers, promising fame and blessings to those who will appreciate the values of poetry and laying this curse on those who will not: "While you live you live in love, and never get favor, for lacking skill of a sonnet; and when you die, your memory die from the earth, for want of an epitaph."

The *Defence of Poesie* presents principles generally accepted by the critics throughout the Renaissance: the author leans heavily upon the dicta of the most noted classical critics, Aristotle, Plato, and Horace, and his standards are echoed by the major English critics of the seventeenth and eighteenth centuries, Dryden, Pope, and Johnson. Sidney's essay is one of the most polished and interesting pieces of Elizabethan prose, and his comments on the writing of his own time have been borne out by the judgment of the centuries. Although this work is the first major piece of English literary criticism, it has seldom been surpassed in the centuries since Sidney's death.

A DEFENCE OF POETRY

Type of work: Literary essay
Author: Percy Bysshe Shelley (1782-1822)
First published: 1840

In this essay Shelley is defending poetry—"my mistress, *Urania"*—against the attack by Thomas Love Peacock in "The Four Ages Of Poetry," published in the first and only number of the *Literary Miscellany* in 1820. The polemical exchange came to nothing for *A Defence of Poetry* remained unpublished until 1840. In his essay Peacock elaborated the familiar figure of the Golden and Silver Ages of classical poetry into four (Iron, Gold, Silver, and Brass), skipped over "the dark ages" and repeated the succession in English poetry. Peacock's point was that poetry never amounts to much in civilized society; Shelley's defense is that poetry is the essential man. Their views were antithetical and neither made contact with the other: Peacock's attack is a boisterous satire, Shelley's defense is an elevated prose poem.

Nevertheless, Peacock's article is still a necessary preface to Shelley's arguments, not because one prompted the other or because Shelley adopted Peacock's historical method in the middle section of his essay, but because as a pair they show clearly the opposing preferences of the older public for eighteenth century wit and of the younger for enthusiasm. Peacock's "Four Ages" has also the merit of amusing; Shelley is never amusing. Peacock's argument is that poetry belongs properly to primitive societies, that as they become civilized they become rational and nonpoetical; hence it was not until the late seventeenth century that England equaled in the work of Shakespeare and Milton the Golden Age of Homeric Greece. Early nineteenth century England seemed to him to have reached the Age of Brass in poetry but a kind of Golden Age in science; therefore, he argued, leave poetry to the primitive societies where it belongs. He is most amusing in his picture of the first Age of Iron, in which the bard of the tribal chief "is always ready to celebrate the strength of his arm, being first duly inspired by that of his liquor." Apart from Homer, Peacock respects no poet, not even Shakespeare who mixed his unities and thought nothing of "deposing a Roman Emperor by an Italian Count, and sending him off in the disguise of a French pilgrim to be shot with a blunderbuss by an English archer." Peacock's jest turns sour as he tires of his figure, and his strictures on contemporary poetry become a diatribe of which the gist is that "a poet of our times is a semi-barbarian in a civilized community." Shelley, to whom Peacock sent a copy of his essay, was stirred to write his only prose statement on his craft. In it he came to the memorable conclusion that "Poets are the unacknowledged legislators of the world."

A Defence of Poetry falls into three parts. First, Shelley presents an argument that all men are poets in some degree, for poetry is an innate faculty of Man; hence it is seen in all societies at all times and to eternity. In the second part he attempts the historical proof, which he abandons in the third to make a subjective and poetic affirmation of the perpetual presence and ennobling virtue of poetry. In presenting his beliefs, Shelley used the ideas that inspire his poems and attempted to codify them from the base Peacock had given him. But Peacock could begin at once with his first age; Shelley found it necessary to define at the outset his notion of poetry. Two major ideas run through this first section and are reflected in the rest of the essay: The Platonic idea of mimesis, in which the imagination responds to the eternal verities it glimpses behind the material form, and the eighteenth century idea of the "sympathetic imagination" which of its own initiative extends itself and assumes an empathy with external objects and beings. The first idea leads Shelley to assert the superiority of the poet as the most active in using the glimpses of truth and conveying them to lesser beings for their uplifting; for this reason the poet is the most powerful influence on mankind, a "legislator." The second idea gives the poet an insight into the ills of mankind which, once understood, can be corrected; here is the second meaning of "legislator."

The first part presented is in two sections, dealing first with the mimetic, then with the expressive powers of poetry, which powers are part of the definition of poetry; the other two parts of the definition are contained in four paragraphs on the form of poetry, especially on its use of language, the medium which makes it superior to other art media and which is called "measured" in contradistinction to "unmeasured" language or prose. But the whole essay is prefaced by four paragraphs which define poetry in the largest or organic sense, not by its mechanics. These paragraphs go to the heart of the difference between Peacock and Shelley.

Shelley begins with a distinction between reason and imagination, leaving to the former the work of numbering, analyzing, and relating objects; the imagination perceives the similitude of objects in their innate values, not in their appearance, and synthesizes these values, presumably, into a valid and Platonic One or Truth. The synthetic principle of the imagination is poetry; Man is compared to "an Aeolian lyre," subject to impressions external and internal but possessing an inner principle (poetry) which produces not simply melody but harmony, not merely the sound of poetry but the potential of the poetic product to harmonize Man or bring him closer to the poetry of being. Poetry is thus both the name of a form of language (measured) and of the power of producing it and benefiting from the poem. Here Shelley announces that poets are "the institutors of laws, and the founders of civil society" because

they discover the laws of harmony and become "legislators" by giving these laws the form of a poem. The poetic product or poem may be an act of mimesis, but the act proceeds from the poetic faculty highly developed in the poet and contained in all men: "A poem is the very image of life expressed in its eternal truth."

The argument in the second section of the first part, devoted to the effects of poetry on society, has been anticipated in the foregoing analysis. *A Defence of Poetry*, as an "apologia," could well end at that point but Shelley wanted to convince Peacock that his theory has external evidence. This he offers in the second part of the essay.

The historical method had already been touched on in Shelley's example of the propensity of the savage or child to imitate the impressions it receives, like a "lyre" producing melody only. Shelley's reading of history is as willful as Peacock's in his assertion that the morality of an age corresponds to the goodness or badness of its poetry; he adduces Greek classical drama as an evidence of a healthy society and Hellenic bucolic poetry as a sign of decay when the poets ceased to be the acknowledged legislators of the Alexandrian Hellenes. In order to cope with the same progression of health and decay in the literature of Rome, which would seem to prove Peacock's scheme, Shelley shifts the whole cycle into "episodes of that cyclic poem written by time upon the memories of men." He encounters further difficulty in coping with Christianity, for by Shelley's theory Jesus must be a great poet: "The scattered fragments preserved to us by the biographers of this extraordinary person, are all instinct with the most vivid poetry." But something went wrong in the Dark Ages: ". . . the extinction of the poetic principle . . . from causes too intricate to be here discussed." Shelley feels safer with Dante and Milton: "But let us not be betrayed from a defence into a critical history of poetry. . . ."

After abandoning the historical method which, had he followed Peacock step by step, would have brought him up to his contemporaries, Shelley returns to his defence by attacking "the promoters of utility" and, by implication, Peacock. To the utilitarian objection that poetry simply produces pleasure and that pleasure is profitless, Shelley asserts that the pleasure of poetry lies not in its superficial melody but in its innate harmony, alone capable of checking "the calculating faculty" which has already produced "more scientific and economical knowledge than can be accomodated to the just distribution of the produce which it multiplies." Shelley follows this with a paragraph which summarizes the duality of the "poetic faculty"; by synthesis it "creates new materials of knowledge and power and pleasure," and by its expressive powers it reproduces those materials "according to a certain rhythm and order which may be called the beautiful and the good."

Shelley's peroration, his personal and poetic justification for poetry, opens with three paragraphs beginning: "Poetry is indeed something divine." "Poetry is the record of the best and happiest moments of the happiest and best minds." Poetry turns all things to loveliness. . . ." This is the moving genius of *Adonais*. Searching for the best proof to defend poetry from the rationalizations of Peacock, Shelley followed the prompting of his own "poetic principle" in concluding *A Defence of Poetry* with a sustained lyric in prose that Peacock could never match. The power of this essay is still inspiring. It constitutes Shelley's best claim outside his verse to be a "legislator" to the world.

A DEFENSE OF THE CONSTITUTIONS OF GOVERNMENT OF THE UNITED STATES OF AMERICA

Type of work: Political treatise
Author: John Adams (1735-1826)
First published: 1787-1788

This sprawling work consists of John Adams' selections from writings on republican governments ranging from ancient Greece to America of the 1780's, material interspersed with his own maxims and observations on historical characters and events. He excused his faulty arrangement and style on the grounds of "hasty," fourteen-month compilation, prompted by news of Shays' Rebellion in Massachusetts and moves toward revising the constitution of the American union. Some regard the work as possibly the most complete examination into the philosophy and institutions of republicanism by any American.

Adams' purposes were several: to rebut the French *philosophe* Turgot's charge that Americans showed themselves slavish followers of England in their state constitutions, most of which, like that of Adams for Massachusetts, provided for constitutional checks and balances; to show such governments superior to "simple" ones which centralized authority in an omnipotent, unicameral legislature, like those advocated by Turgot and instituted in Pennsylvania by Benjamin Franklin; and to prove by comparing historic forms of republics that their ruin proceeded from improper division of power.

Adams was convinced that, regardless of all differences, governments "move by unalterable rules." He declared his repugnance for absolutism, whether monarchial or egalitarian, basing his argument on the practical grounds that neither gave "full scope to all the faculties of man," enlisted the talents of all citizens, or checked administrative abuses. Instead, he saw absolutisms sowing furtive suspicion which pitted against one another family and family, rich and poor, educated and ignorant, the gifted and the dull. He espoused a "mixture" of the advantages of democracy, aristocracy, and monarchy. Although his statement of the favorable aspects of aristocracies and monarchies was turned against him by political rivals later on, the *Defense* contains as many strictures against these two forms of government as against democracy. Alleging that "there can be no free government without a democratical branch in the constitution," Adams even said America would be better off to risk civil war arising from improper balance of power in a democratic republic than to establish an absolute monarchy.

Sure that sovereignty was derived from a majority of the mass of people and that a representative branch of the legislature should be organized on democratic principles, Adams feared to trust without restraint all power to the masses. As a check on the representative house, he advocated a senate in terms which have seldom been duplicated. It would be not only a forum where property interests might be defended against leveling tendencies of the representatives, but also an honorable place whither demagogues might be banished by election to render their ambition safe to and their abilities conserved for an empire of liberty. Adams' advocacy of coördinate but independent executive, judicial, and legislative branches of government causes no surprise. He advocated a single executive in order for it to be censorable for administrative abuse. By these forms, he contended, America would realize a practical government of laws and not of men.

Less hopeful of mankind and distrustful of a supposed passion for democracy, Adams denied Turgot's assertion that "a love of democracy is the love of equality," saying that "every man hates to have a superior . . . [and] no man is willing to have an equal," that "democracy signifies nothing more or less than a nation of people without any government at all, and before any constitution is instituted." Adams deemed "reason, conscience, a regard for justice, and a sense of duty and moral obligation" the only defenses against "desire for fame, and the applause, gratitude, and rewards of the public" as well as "the real friends of equality." He was so confident of the beneficent effects of a republic of mixed characteristics that he averred it would make honest men of knaves from having one rogue to watch another.

Believing that "God and nature" ordained inequalities of wealth, birth, and ability among men, Adams declared there was a natural aristocracy. Not dangerous in itself, he believed it would transform an omnipotent unicameral legislature into an oligarchy or monarchy, destroying *"all equality and liberty, with the consent and acclamation of the people themselves."* Believing man more selfish than public-spirited, he would no more trust all of an omnipotent, unicameral legislature than any one man's ambition for gold or power or acclaim. Unless "the rich and the proud" and the representatives of the masses were thrown into separate, coequal assemblies, each could do mischief and neither check the other or an executive.

He declared that "conviction," not "habit," caused Americans to retain their English inheritance of preserving governmental equilibrium by division of powers between executives, two-house legislatures, and a separate judiciary. Only in such institutions did he find hope for avoiding the hypocrisy, superstition, flattery, and corruption which had overturned earlier republics. Advancing from the individual states to the federal government, Adams dismissed the continental congresses under the Articles of Confederation as "only a diplomatic assembly," necessitating that the states themselves have balanced governments to check the aristocratical traits of the congressmen. "Mixing the authority of the one, the few, and the many confusedly into one assembly," said he, created a train of events which would proceed from aristocratical wrangling over offices to "division, faction, sedition, and rebellion." He observed political parties in every country, controlled only by monarchial armies or by "a balance in the constitution." Thinking virtue "too precarious a foundation for liberty," he declared that governments needed power to compel "all orders, ranks, and parties" to "prefer the public good before their own," but that power was surest if based on "reverence and obedience to the laws."

With enthusiasm for the proposed federal constitution, Adams hailed the old confederation as inadequate and the new frame of government, so similar to Adams' own views, to be the "greatest single effort of national deliberation that the world has ever seen."

DEIRDRE

Type of work: Novel
Author: James Stephens (1882-1950)
Type of plot: Legendary romance
Time of plot: The Heroic Age
Locale: Ireland
First published: 1923

> *Principal characters:*
> CONACHÚR MAC NESSA, King of Ulster
> CLOTHRU, his first wife
> MAEVE, his second wife
> CATHFA, his father, a magician
> LAVARCHAM, his conversation-woman
> FERGUS MAC ROY, his stepfather
> NESSA, his mother
> FELIMID MAC DALL, his story-teller
> DEIRDRE, Felimid's daughter, ward of Conachúr
> UISNEAC, Conachúr's brother-in-law
> NAOISE,
> AINNLE, and
> ARDAN, Uisneac's sons

Critique:

James Stephens was a brilliant Irish writer of poetry and prose, whose best work was grounded in the early literature of his own country. Just as he attempted to bring Irish folklore to life in *The Crock of Gold,* so he tried to revitalize ancient Gaelic legend in *Deirdre.* In this novel he wrote of the beautiful and mystical Deirdre, of brave and handsome Naoise, and of strong and willful Conachúr, who was loved by all his people and who was almost great. But it is not only the people in the story that are remembered afterward; there are also memorable scenes, like the one of Maeve taking her goods and chattels back to her father's kingdom, or the fight in the Red Branch fortress, or the picture of Deirdre falling dead over Naoise's body just as Conachúr is ready to claim her. *Deirdre* is a novel of legend and fantasy, but there is also a core of realism at its center.

The Story:

The King of Ulster had a daughter who was called Assa, the Gentle. She loved knowledge and had many tutors. One day, returning from a visit to her father and finding her tutors killed, she buckled on her armor and set out to find the murderer. Henceforth her name was Nessa, the Ungentle. While she was bathing in the forest, Cathfa, the magician, saw and loved her. He offered to spare her life only if she would marry him. Their son was Conachúr mac Nessa. After a while Nessa left Cathfa, taking her son with her.

When Conachúr was sixteen, Nessa was still the most beautiful woman in the land. Fergus mac Roy, the new King of Ulster, was only eighteen, but he fell in love with Nessa as soon as he saw her. She promised to marry him only if Conachúr could be king for a year while she and Fergus lived away from court. Fergus agreed, but after the year was up Conachúr kept the throne and Fergus became one of his most trusted followers.

Nessa arranged a marriage between Conachúr and Clothru, daughter of the High King of Connacht. On a visit to her father, Clothru was killed by her sister Maeve. Conachúr's first son was born just before she died.

Bent on vengeance, Conachúr went to Connacht. There he saw Maeve and, changing his mind, married her against

DEIRDRE by James Stephens. By permission of the publishers, The Macmillan Co. Copyright, 1923, by The Macmillan Co. Renewed, 1931, by Cynthia Stephens.

her wishes. When she went to Ulster with him, she took along great riches and also a guard of one thousand men.

During one of his journeys at a time when Maeve had refused to accompany him, he stopped at the house of Felimid mac Dall, his story-teller. That night Conachúr sent a servant to say that Felimid's wife should sleep with him. The servant returned to say that Felimid's wife could not accommodate him as she was then in childbed. Soon the men heard the wail of the newborn infant. Conachúr asked Cathfa, his father, to interpret the wail and other evil omens that men had seen recently. Cathfa prophesied that the child then born, a girl, would be called The Troubler and that she would bring evil and destruction in Ulster. When one of his followers suggested that Conachúr have the child killed immediately, he sent for the infant. But he decided it was not becoming a prince to evade fate, and he let the child live. Deirdre was her name.

Conachúr had Deirdre brought up at Emania by Lavarcham, his conversation-woman, who let the girl see no one but women servants and a guard of the oldest and ugliest swordsmen in Ulster. Lavarcham could adapt herself to any situation or group of people and, while acting as a spy for Conachúr, she also learned everything that had to be taught to Deirdre to prepare her for the place Lavarcham had decided she should have in the kingdom.

Lavarcham reported regularly to Conachúr so that, while he never saw Deirdre, the king knew how she progressed month by month. He refused to believe Lavarcham's glowing reports; besides, at that time, he was well satisfied with Maeve. On the other hand, Lavarcham reported at length to Deirdre about Conachúr until the child knew all his whims, his boldness, and his majesty.

Maeve, who had never forgiven Conachúr for marrying her against her will, finally decided to leave him. She was so unforgiving that she refused to leave behind one thread of her clothes or one bit of her riches. Since some of those riches included great herds of cattle, flocks of sheep, heaps of silver and jewelry, and pieces of furniture, she had to make careful plans to get everything away when Conachúr was not looking. She trusted no one entirely, but she had a spy, mac Roth, who was even more diligent than Conachúr's Lavarcham. He discovered that Conachúr was to take a trip to Leinster; he even followed Conachúr's company for two full days until he felt the group was far enough away to be unable to get back in time; then he returned to help Maeve in her flight. Only Lavarcham guessed that something might happen, but her messengers did not reach Conachúr before Maeve had fled.

Conachúr grieved for Maeve, but he was unable to bring her back to Ulster. In the meantime Lavarcham began to brood about the matter. The whole kingdom wanted the king to remarry, and Deirdre was sixteen. Lavarcham persuaded the king to come to see Deirdre.

Although Lavarcham had taught Deirdre all that she needed to know about Conachúr, she did not realize that the child thought of the king as an ancient and feared him a little. Nor did Lavarcham know that Deirdre, longing for people of her own age, had learned how to escape the guards around Emania.

Deirdre was first tempted to go beyond the walls to investigate a campfire. Around it she saw three boys: Naoise, who was nineteen; Ainnle, who was seventeen: and Ardan, who was fourteen. They were the sons of Uisneac, who had married Conachúr's sister. Deirdre startled them when she first appeared in the light of the fire, but they all laughed and told so many good stories that she knew she would have to go back again. The younger boys insisted that Naoise would soon be the champion of Ulster, and Deirdre did not doubt it.

When Conachúr went to see Deirdre, he found her the most beautiful girl in Ulster, and he intended to marry her immediately. Lavarcham made him wait a week, after which he would have a three-month feast. Deirdre, in love with Naoise. was horrified at the idea of marrying one so old and huge, but several nights passed before she could make her way to the campfire again. At her pleading, the brothers took her out of the country.

Six years later Conachúr decided that Deirdre and the sons of Uisneac should be brought back from Scotland, where they had found refuge, but the boys would not return except under the protection of one of Conachúr's trusted men. Fergus and his sons were sent to Scotland with assurances of safety. Deirdre had a dream and begged Naoise not to leave. but he declared that Fergus was honorable.

When the travelers reached the coast of Ulster, Fergus was detained by one of Conachúr's men, and Fergus' sons took Deirdre and the sons of Uisneac under their protection. Arriving at Conachúr's court at night, they were lodged in the fortress called the Red Branch. Then Deirdre knew there would be trouble because Conachúr had not received them under his own roof.

Conachúr sent his men to batter down the doors and to bring Deirdre to him. The sons of Uisneac and Fergus made quick sallies, dashing out one door and in another, and killed so many of Conachúr's warriors that at last the king ordered the fortress set afire. As Deirdre and the boys fled, Conachúr asked Cathfa to stop them. Cathfa cast a spell which made the boys drop their arms, and they were captured. Conachúr had Fergus' and Uisneac's sons killed. When Deirdre knelt over Naoise's dead body, she sipped his blood and fell lifeless.

Further Critical Evaluation of the Work:

One of the primary features of the Irish Literary Renaissance was the discovery, regeneration, and translation of ancient Irish myths into modern forms. Among the great Celtic legends, perhaps the most popular was the tragic love story of Deirdre, The Troubler, and her lover, Naoise. Probably the greatest artistic representations of this fable of fate, love, betrayal, and death are the dramatic versions by William Butler Yeats (*Deirdre,* 1907) and John Millington Synge (*Deirdre of the Sorrows,* 1910). However, although James Stephens' prose interpretation of the myth may lack the austere poetic grandeur of Yeats's play or the tragic intensity of Synge's, it has a psychological penetration and lively narrative thrust that makes it not unworthy of mention alongside those great predecessors.

In many ways Stephens' is the most modern version of the Deirdre legend. Although very different from each other, both Yeats and Synge sought to capture the atmosphere of the romantic Irish past of legend and folklore in their plays. Stephens, however, is more interested in a modern psychological analysis of the characters and their actions. At the same time he did not ignore the flavor of archaic Celtic myth; in developing his story he took great pains to present the medieval culture and background as authentically and thoroughly as he could. Thus, *Deirdre* contains that mixture of the lyrical and the realistic, the ancient and the modern, and the solemn and the irreverent that characterizes Stephens' best work in all genres.

It has been claimed—with some justice—that Stephens' emphasis on detailed psychological analysis and explanation slows down the action in the first book, and that he fails in the crucial scene—the flight of the lovers—by having it reported secondhand. But if the first book is uneven, the second is delightful and occasionally powerful. Their personalities and motivations having been carefully delineated in the first book, the characters, and their decisions and actions, are thoroughly believable in the second one. All of Book Two is excellent, and several moments—such as the suppressed tragedy evident in the gaiety of Naoise's younger brothers, Deirdre's realization of Conachúr's treachery, and especially the finale, when Deirdre dies on the body of her freshly killed lover—approach greatness.

It was not Stephens' purpose to idolize the old Irish myths, but to make them alive and familiar for his own times. In spite of a setting eight centuries in the past, readers of *Deirdre* have little difficulty in believing in, and relating to, a gallery of vivid, passionate characters: the gentle, aristocratic King Fergus, too casual and perhaps lazy to avert tragedy; Conachúr, brave, yet insecure, whose sense of honor and duty cannot overcome his passionate nature; the sons of Uisneac, united, yet individualized, apparently carefree, yet serious and heroic; and finally, Deirdre herself, intense, intuitive, innocent yet wise, who passionately and courageously strives for a happiness that she knows from the beginning will never be granted to her.

DEIRDRE OF THE SORROWS

Type of work: Drama
Author: John Millington Synge (1871-1909)
Type of plot: Romantic tragedy
Time of plot: The legendary past
Locale: Ireland
First presented: 1910

Principal characters:
DEIRDRE, a heroine of Gaelic legend
NAISI, Deirdre's lover
CONCHUBOR, High King of Ulster
FERGUS, Conchubor's friend
LAVARCHAM, Deirdre's nurse
AINNLE, and
ARDAN, Naisi's brothers
OWEN, Conchubor's attendant and spy

Critique:

Deirdre of the Sorrows, Synge's last play, was never performed until after his death. The play deals with the Irish legendary past, dramatizing an account of the beautiful Irish heroine who preferred death along with her lover to life as the wife of the king. The play is full of this romantic dedication, fully developed in Synge's rich Irish idiom. The language of the Irish peasant is given both power and dignity as it is shaped into the tragic movement of the play. And the play is not without touches of humane characterization. The king is not simply the cruel ruler; he is also a sad and lonely man who deeply regrets the deaths he has caused. Naisi is not simply the martyred hero, but also the husband who rants that his wife has caused him to be a softer man and allowed him to desert the ways of his brothers and his companions in arms. The play contains both the rich warmth of Synge's local and distinctively Irish characterizations and the romantic quality of the legendary.

The Story:

King Conchubor had been keeping Deirdre, the beautiful young girl whom he had resolved to make his bride, at the home of Lavarcham, the old nurse, on Slieve Fuadh. One rainy evening, Conchubor and his friend Fergus arrived to find that Deirdre, to the king's displeasure, was still out gathering nuts and sticks in the woods. Lavarcham warned the king that Deirdre would not be anxious to see him, and she repeated the old prophecy that Deirdre had been born to bring destruction into the world. When Deirdre came in, the king presented her with rings and jewels and remonstrated with her for staying out in the woods. Deirdre defended her behavior and said that she had no desire to go to Emain to become queen.

Conchubor pleaded with her, talking of his loneliness, his love for her, the rooms he had prepared for her in his castle at Emain, but Deirdre insisted that in spite of the fact that she was pledged to Conchubor she would prefer to remain in the simple cottage with Lavarcham as long as possible. Conchubor, growing impatient, insisted that she be ready to go to Emain and become his queen within a few days.

After he left, Lavarcham urged Deirdre to be sensible and bend to Conchubor's wishes, but Deirdre kept talking about other defiant legendary heroines and about the hero, Naisi, and his broth-

DEIRDRE OF THE SORROWS by John Millington Synge, from THE COMPLETE WORKS OF JOHN M. SYNGE. By permission of the publishers, Random House, Inc. Copyright, 1935, by Random House, Inc.

ers, the bravest men in the woods. Deirdre went to dress elegantly for the last night or so of her freedom.

In the meantime Naisi and his brothers arrived at the cottage to take refuge from the storm. Lavarcham was not eager to let them in, but they claimed that a beautiful lady whom they had met in the woods had promised them refuge from the storm. They entered, but Lavarcham, sensing trouble, tried unsuccessfully to get rid of them. They were still in the room when Deirdre returned. Deirdre provided food for Ainnle and Ardan. When they left the cottage she asked Lavarcham to leave also. Alone with Naisi, she told him of Conchubor's imminent suit. Deeply in love by this time, they decided to marry and run away in spite of their knowledge of the troubles foretold. They asked Ainnle, who had returned to the cottage, to marry them before they fled into the night.

Seven years passed during which Deirdre and Naisi, with Ainnle and Ardan, lived happily beside the sea in Alban. One day Lavarcham arrived to announce that Fergus was on his way with peace offerings from King Conchubor and to plead with Deirdre to accept the king's offer. Deirdre insisted on her loyalty to Naisi. Owen, Conchubor's trusted man, arrived with word that Naisi and Fergus were already talking on the path below; he rudely advised Deirdre to leave Naisi and return to the king, for Owen thought that seven years of love were more than enough and that Deirdre would one day be old and yearn for the comfort of the royal palace. The messenger also revealed that he was jealous of Naisi and hated him because he had killed Owen's father some time before.

Fergus, on his arrival, said that Conchubor in his peace offering had invited both Naisi and Deirdre back to Emain in peace. Naisi and Deirdre wondered if they should accept the offer. They talked of age, the possible death of love, and the happiness of their seven years, despite some difficult times, at Alban. Because they had experienced such per-

fect years, they decided to accept Conchubor's offer and return to Emain, for they felt they would never know such complete happiness at Alban again. Owen returned, screaming that it was all a plot, and then ran out and split his head against a stone. Believing Owen mad, Naisi and Deirdre accepted Fergus' promise that no trick was involved, and they set out for Emain to meet Conchubor again.

Lavarcham, arriving first to speak with Conchubor, found him a lonely old man. After assuring the king that he could never gain Deirdre's love, she reported that Owen, despairing of ever gaining Deirdre, had run mad and destroyed himself. Conchubor's warriors arrived and reported that they had separated Naisi and Deirdre from Naisi's brothers. When Naisi and Deirdre arrived, they found themselves in a tent. A freshly-dug grave was concealed by curtains next to the tent. They spoke mournfully, for they strongly suspected a plot against them. Conchubor returned, welcomed them, and seemed, in spite of the evidence of the tent, the grave, and warriors lurking nearby, to mean his offer of peace seriously. Then, as he and Naisi were about to clasp hands of friendship, Naisi heard his brothers cry for help. Naisi started to leave, although Deirdre pleaded with him to stay. Naisi cursed the softness of women and ran out. The king's warriors killed Naisi, as they killed his brothers.

Conchubor urged Deirdre to end her mourning for Naisi and become his queen. But Deirdre continued to lament and would have nothing to do with Conchubor. Fergus appeared and announced that he had burned Emain because the king had gone back on his pledge not to harm Naisi. Fergus, who had acted in good faith, tried to protect Deirdre, but Deirdre used Naisi's knife to commit suicide and join him in another world without defiling their love. After Deirdre's death, all mourned. Conchubor, old and broken, was led away by Lavarcham.

Further Critical Evaluation of the Work:

In spite of his relatively small output, four full length plays and two one-acters, John M. Synge is justly considered one of the finest dramatists of the modern stage and the Abbey Theatre's most important playwright prior to Sean O'Casey. Completed shortly before his death, but never revised to the author's complete satisfaction, *Deirdre of the Sorrows* can be seen as Synge's final statement on the joys of life, the possibilities, both good and bad, of love, and the inscrutability of human destiny.

The real strength of the play, and the thing that probably sets it apart from the many other dramatic versions of this famous Irish myth, comes from the way Synge combines an austere mood of classic, almost Grecian tragedy with characterizations that are immediate, human, and sympathetic. Deirdre first impresses us as a flighty girl who chases in the woods gathering twigs and nuts with little concern for her future queenly role. Her initial reaction to King Conchubor's demand for immediate marriage is to simply beg, like a petulant child, for more time. But almost immediately her inner strength asserts itself. Faced with Conchubor's implacability, she grows into maturity almost instantly: "From this day," she tells her old nurse Lavarcham, "I will turn the men of Ireland like a wind blowing on the heath." She then dons her royal regalia, assuming the status of a queen, and, by giving herself without hesitation to Naisi, unflinchingly accepts the doom foretold for her. And yet, for all of her tragic grandeur, the "little girl" element in her character remains evident throughout.

Likewise, the other principle characters contain aspects of both the tragic and the mundane. Naisi is heroic and passionate, willing to risk exile and death for the love of Deirdre. But he is also irritable, impulsive, and occasionally inconsistent. Towards the end of the play he admits to Fergus that: "I've had dreams of getting old and weary, and losing my delight in Deirdre."

Conchubor is also pictured as a mixture of the grand and the petty. On the one hand he establishes himself as a ferocious king, given to extremes of heroism and violence. His desire for Deirdre is intense, and his plans for her are grandiose. The strength of his feelings are evidenced by the lengths to which he is willing to go to secure her, including the destruction of his own kingdom, and by the vengeful rage that is aroused against those who stand in his way, especially Naisi and his brothers. But at the same time he is a pitiful old man desperately denying the effects of time and clinging to an image of himself as virile by taking a young and beautiful wife. "There's one sorrow has no end surely," he tells Deirdre, "that's being old and lonesome."

This powerful merging of the heroic and the human reaches its dramatic peak in the scene where the lovers separate forever. Deirdre believes that the only way they can escape inevitable disillusionment and acrimony in their passion is to give themselves up to Conchubor's vengeance, thereby avoiding the slower, but more painful ravages of time. Naisi agrees because he, too, sees that their passion has spent itself, their youth is fading, and the price of their destiny must be paid. "It should be a poor thing to see great lovers and they sleepy and old." But at the moment of parting, they have a bitter, petty squabble. Thus, their deaths represent not a victory of passion over fate, but a concession to human imperfection, even in the most noble of characters.

Deirdre of the Sorrows represented a change in direction for Synge. He had previously avoided Irish myth on purpose, feeling it to be unrealistic and irrelevant to modern man. What further directions he would have taken had he lived, can only be left to conjecture. That John Synge died so young is one of the tragedies of modern theater; that he lived to write the fine plays he did is one of its glories.

DELPHINE

Type of work: Novel
Author: Madame de Staël (Baronne de Staël-Holstein, 1766-1817)
Type of plot: Romantic tragedy
Time of plot: Late eighteenth century
Locale: France
First published: 1802

Principal characters:
DELPHINE D'ALBEMAR, a rich, talented young widow
MATILDA DE VERNON, her kinswoman, daughter of Madame de Vernon
MADAME DE VERNON, Delphine's close friend and confidante
LÉONCE MONDEVILLE, affianced to Matilda de Vernon
MADAME D'ERVIN, a friend of Delphine
MONSIEUR DE SERBELLANE, Madame d'Ervin's lover
MONSIEUR DE VALORBE, in love with Delphine

Critique:

In terms of world literature, this novel is an anachronism. It appears in the form of letters, the epistolary form which, although prevalent seventy years before, was almost outmoded by the time of Madame de Staël. In addition, the tone of the novel is in the sentimental vein of many French and British novels of the first rank in the first half of the eighteenth century. The origin of the sentiment was undoubtedly Rousseau, for whom Madame de Staël had a very high regard. In *Delphine* there is constant reflection of the ideas of Rousseau and other advanced political thinkers and philosophers of the late eighteenth century, for such doctrines as the education of women, political equality, freedom of religious conscience, anti-clericism, and devotion to reason appear constantly in the letters written by Delphine to the other characters in the novel. The novel is, therefore, an index to the temper of Madame de Staël's circle at the time.

The Story:

Delphine d'Albemar was a rich young widow who had been married to her guardian after her father's death. Her husband, who had been her tutor in childhood, had instilled in her the best of sentiments and virtues. As a result of her education, however, she did not wish to submit to the dogmas of society or church. Although she was a member of the French nobility, she was a believer in revolutionary doctrine, a dangerous way of thinking in France during the years immediately preceding the French Revolution. In addition, she, unlike most women of her time and position, refused to let men do her thinking for her. After her husband's death, which occurred in her twentieth year, Delphine was emotionally, intellectually, and financially independent.

Shortly after her husband's death, Delphine proposed giving away a large part of her fortune to Matilda, a relative of her husband and the daughter of Delphine's close friend, Madame de Vernon. Despite the warnings of Mademoiselle d'Albemar, Delphine's sister-in-law, that Madame de Vernon was a very treacherous person, the gift was made so that Matilda could marry Léonce Mondeville, a Spanish nobleman. No one had met Léonce Mondeville, for the marriage had been arranged by Matilda's mother, a long-time friend of the proposed bridegroom's mother.

When Mondeville arrived in Paris, he met his future wife and Delphine. Much to Delphine's dismay, she fell in love with him and he with her. To Delphine, who had bestowed on Matilda the fortune which was making the marriage possible, it seemed that fate had played its worst trick of irony. For a time it seemed as if the two lovers might find a way out of the difficulty. As her confidante in the problem, Delphine took

Matilda's own mother, Madame de Vernon. Matilda's mother had no intention of allowing so advantageous a match to slip through her and her daughter's fingers, and she plotted to turn Mondeville against Delphine.

Delphine, meanwhile, had been aiding Madame d'Ervin in a love affair with Monsieur de Serbellane. Because de Serbellane was seen going into Delphine's house late at night, scandal linked her name with his, although he had actually gone there to see Madame d'Ervin. A short time later Madame d'Ervin's husband surprised the two lovers in Delphine's home. When de Serbellane killed the husband in a duel, scandal named Delphine as the woman in the case. Delphine, desiring to keep her friend's honor, did not relate the true cause of the quarrel which had precipitated the duel. Anxious to clear herself with Mondeville, however, Delphine asked Madame de Vernon to act as her friend. Instead of telling what really happened, the older woman told him that Delphine and de Serbellane were lovers and that Delphine was about to leave France to join de Serbellane in Italy.

Mondeville prepared to marry Matilda, although he did not love her. Although Delphine realized that someone had misrepresented her to her lover, she could find no way to prevent the marriage. Only after the marriage had taken place did Delphine learn that Madame de Vernon's duplicity had caused the rift between herself and Mondeville. At that time, anxious not to hurt Matilda, Delphine promised herself not to see Mondeville and to try to forget her passion for him. Unfortunately, they continued to love one another greatly. A few months later Madame de Vernon, on her deathbed, confessed her guilt.

Feeling themselves cheated, the lovers decided to continue seeing each other, even though their course was dangerous to their honor and unfair to Matilda. Society was soon whispering that Delphine and Mondeville were lovers. Actually, there was nothing immoral in their affair, but society assumed the worst.

De Valorbe, a friend of Delphine's late husband, learned of the state of affairs and resolved to marry her in order to remove her from a compromising situation. His intention aroused Mondeville's jealousy, even though Delphine protested that she did not love de Valorbe and would never marry him. One night de Valorbe went to Delphine's house in the hope that she would hide him from the police. Mondeville saw him there and challenged him to a duel. De Valorbe, hoping to escape from the country before he was imprisoned on political charges, refused to fight. A witness set scandal going once again. Soon everyone believed that the two men had accidentally met while both going to assignations with Delphine, and so her name was publicly dishonored. In addition, de Valorbe's refusal to meet Mondeville placed him in disgrace.

Learning at last that her husband and Delphine were in love, Matilda went to Delphine and revealed that she was to have a child. Delphine, moved by Matilda's pleas, decided to leave France. She went to Switzerland and became a pensionary at a convent which was under the direction of Mondeville's aunt. De Valorbe followed her there and caused her name to become common gossip. When he offered to clear her name by marriage, Delphine refused his proposal and decided to remain in the convent. De Valorbe, moved to distraction, caused his own death, but before he died he cleared Delphine's reputation with Mondeville.

Word came to Mondeville's aunt that Matilda was dying. She, in league with Mondeville's mother, persuaded Delphine to become a nun. They were able to have the pope waive the required year's novitiate. By the time Mondeville went to the convent to claim Delphine, she had already taken her vows.

Meanwhile the republican government had taken over in France and had disallowed the vows of religious orders.

Friends persuaded Delphine that she should renounce the vows and return to France to marry her lover. She left the convent, only to discover that public opinion condemned her action. Rather than make her lover live a life of misery, she refused to marry him.

Mondeville went to join the royalist forces fighting against the republican French government, but before he could join them he was captured and sentenced to death as a traitor. Delphine tried unsuccessfully to secure his pardon. When she failed, she took poison and then joined him when he went to the execution ground. She died on the spot where he was to be executed. At first the soldiers refused to shoot Mondeville. Having no desire to live, he taunted them until they picked up their muskets and killed him. Friends took the bodies of Delphine and her lover and buried them side by side, so that they, kept apart in life, might be close in death.

Further Critical Evaluation of the Work:

Delphine is a difficult novel in many ways. The manner in which it is written, the characterizations, the plot, and Madame de Staël's ideas, all make reading the novel somewhat of an ordeal. At the same time, however, beneath the narrative complexities and emotional excesses, there is a fundamental honesty and sincerity of purpose.

The use of letters offers Madame de Staël some advantages. She is able to provide a continuing psychological analysis of her characters, in some depth, and sustain a rather complicated plot. Still, letters as a narrative medium can be severely limiting, and even confining. There are logistical problems to solve—who will write to whom?—but there are also matters of tone. One problem in *Delphine* is that the letters, though differing in content and in intellectual point of view, sound rather as if they have all been written in the same voice. This difficulty tends to blur character and motives. A second problem has to do with Madame de Staël's idealization of her main characters. Though the Vernons, Madame d'Ervin, and her lover appear lifelike enough, Delphine herself and Léonce are not as believable; passions, in the worst romantic tradition, appear stronger than characters, and motives are purer than real life generally allows.

Delphine is more important, perhaps, as a document in literary and intellectual history than as a work of fiction. Madame de Staël used *Delphine* especially to explore the role of women in society and in the cultural, religious, political, and intellectual life of the nation. Although the subtitle of the novel is "A man must be able to brave opinion, a woman to submit to it," Madame de Staël does not advocate the submission of women; on the contrary, taking an advanced position for her day, she argues that women have been placed in an especially precarious social role, and that they must be strong enough in their own feelings to be independent of the narrow and limiting prescriptions of social convention.

The idea that people must be free to follow their deepest passions echoes the sentiments of the most important romantic novels of the nineteenth century. It is in that tradition, as well as in the tradition of the novel of ideas, that *Delphine* should be placed.

DELTA WEDDING

Type of work: Novel
Author: Eudora Welty (1909-   )
Type of plot: Regional realism
Time of plot: Early 1920's
Locale: Mississippi
First published: 1946

Principal characters:
    LAURA McRAVEN, cousin to the Fairchilds
    DABNEY FAIRCHILD, a bride-to-be
    ELLEN, her mother
    BATTLE, her father
    SHELLEY, her sister
    GEORGE FAIRCHILD, her uncle
    ROBBIE, George's wife
    TROY FLAVIN, a plantation manager

Critique:

Delta Wedding is the chronicle of a remarkable family living in Mississippi in the early 1920's. The Fairchilds seemed to draw excitement to them just by doing nothing. Although the plot centers around the preparations for the wedding of one of the Fairchild daughters to a man considered in all ways her inferior, the main theme of the story is in reality the portrayal of this unusual family and a regional way of life. Through the eyes of a child we see the cousins and aunts and great-aunts, all criticizing the others but uniting against any outsider. Life on the Delta is a thing apart from that in other sections of the country, and Eudora Welty has shown in her novel a superb picture of this segment of America.

The Story:

Nine-year-old Laura McRaven made her first journey alone from Jackson to the Delta, to visit her dead mother's people, the Fairchilds. One of her cousins, Dabney Fairchild, was to be married, and Laura's chief regret was that she could not be in the wedding party because of her mother's recent death. She remembered Shellmound, the Fairchild plantation, and knew that she would have a wonderful time with her exciting cousins and aunts. The Fairchilds were people to whom things happened, exciting, unforgettable things.

At Shellmound, Laura found most of the family assembled for the wedding. Although children her age were her companions, she was aware also of the doings of the grownups. It was obvious that the family was not happy about Dabney's marriage. Her husband-to-be was Troy Flavin, the manager of the plantation, whose inferior social position was the main thing against him. Uncle Battle, Dabney's father, was most of all reluctant to let one of his family go from him, but he could not bring himself to say anything to Dabney, not even that he would miss her. In fact, that seemed to Laura to be a strange thing about her cousins. They seldom talked as a united family, but they always acted as one.

There were so many members of the family that it was hard for Laura to keep them straight. Uncle Battle's wife was Aunt Ellen, and their oldest daughter was Shelley, who was going to be a nun. Again the whole family disapproved of her plan, but there was hardly ever any attempt to get her to change her mind. The obvious favorite was Uncle George, Battle's brother. Uncle George had also married beneath himself. He and his

DELTA WEDDING by Eudora Welty. By permission of the publishers, Harcourt, Brace & Co., Inc. Copyright, 1945, 1946, by Eudora Welty.

wife Robbie lived in Memphis, where everyone knew poor Uncle George could never be happy.

When George arrived for the wedding festivities, he was alone and miserable. Robbie had left him, and he had come down alone to see his family. Not wanting to make Dabney unhappy, they did not tell her of Robbie's desertion. The children and the aunts and great-aunts were not told either, although one by one they began to suspect that something was wrong. Ellen could have killed Robbie for making George unhappy, but she kept her feelings to herself except when she was alone with Battle, her husband.

Robbie's anger at her husband began on the afternoon of a family outing. George had risked his life to save one of the cousins, a feeble-minded child caught in the path of a train as they crossed a railroad trestle. After that incident Robbie was never the same with George. She seemed to want him to prove that he loved her more than he loved his family.

Probably Shelley understood the family best. She knew that they had built a wall against the outside world. But she suspected that they were more lonely than self-sufficient. Most people took the family as a group, loving or hating them all together. Only Uncle George seemed to take them one by one, loving and understanding each as an individual. Shelley thought that this was why they all loved Uncle George so much.

Dabney herself seemed to wish for more than she had in her love for Troy. Sometimes she felt left out, as if she were trying to find a lighted window but found only darkness. She loved Troy, but she wanted to feel even more a part of him. She wished also that her family would try to keep her with them, wanted to make certain of their love.

Preparations for the wedding created a flurry. The dresses had been ordered from Memphis, and when some of the gowns failed to arrive there was the usual hubbub among the women, a concern that the men could not appreciate. One of the children fell sick at the last minute, so that Laura was made one of the wedding party after all. Troy's mother sent some beautiful handmade quilts from her mountain shack. Troy felt proud, but the Fairchilds were even more self-consciously and unwillingly ashamed of his background.

After their wedding Dabney and Troy would live at Marmion, an estate owned by the family. Dabney rode over to see the house. Looking at the stately buildings and the beautiful old trees, she knew that best of all she would love being inside it looking out on the rest of the world. That was what she wanted the most, to be inside where she was a part of the light and warmth. That was what marriage must give her.

All the time, unknown to any of the family but Shelley, Robbie was not far away. She had come after George in hopes that he was looking for her. What had almost defeated Robbie was the fear that she had not married George but the whole Fairchild family. It was that fear which had made her angry at the affair on the railroad trestle. Wanting desperately to come first with George, she knew instinctively that he could never set her apart from or above the family. Contrite and humble, she went to Shellmound. The fact that George was not even there at the moment hurt her even more, for she wanted very much for him to be miserable without her. He was, of course, but it was not the Fairchild way to let anyone see his true feelings.

Robbie probably hit the secret of the family when she said that the Fairchilds loved each other because in so doing they were really loving themselves. But of George that fact was not quite true. He was the different one. Because of his gentleness and his ability to love people as individuals, he let Robbie see his love for her without ever saying the words she had longed to hear.

The wedding was almost an anticlimax, a calm scene following gusty storms of feeling. Troy and Dabney took only a short trip, for Troy was needed to superintend the plantation. While they were gone Battle worked the hands hard to get Marmion ready for them. Dabney was anxious to move in, but the move was not so necessary after her marriage as it had seemed before; she no longer felt left out of Troy's life. She thought her life before had been like seeing a beautiful river between high banks, with no way to get down. Now she had found the way and she was at peace. Indeed, the whole family seemed to have righted itself.

When Aunt Ellen asked Laura to live with them at Shellmound, her being wanted by the Fairchilds seemed too wonderful for her belief. Laura knew that she would go back to her father, but still feeling that she really belonged to the Fairchilds seemed like a beautiful dream. She clung briefly to Aunt Ellen, as if to hold close that wonderful moment of belonging.

Further Critical Evaluation of the Work:

Eudora Welty has created in Shellmound, the home of the Fairchild family in *Delta Wedding,* a world set apart from the rest of Southern plantation society of the 1920's. Shellmound is a haven, isolated from the mainstream of Southern life and unaffected by extremes of grief and suffering: there is no racial tension; no poverty; no war or natural catastrophe; none of the sense of alienation and instability generated by contact with modern urban society; and none of the severe moral deficiencies in the characters that would preclude natural human happiness. The Fairchild estate is thus the perfect stage upon which to play out a drama about the growth of every type of love, from romantic to filial to platonic.

The main focus of the book, therefore, is on the nature of the numerous members of the Fairchild clan and on their relationships; Welty shows how the men are different from the women, how the "insiders" are different from those who have married into the family, how each person relates to the others, and how each person grows individually and privately. In order to explore these various aspects, the author utilizes different narrative voices, thus enabling the reader to view the characters from different perspectives. Aunt Tempe, for example, provides the older generation's point of view; she believes that Delta women have inherited traits that cannot be learned by outsiders, traits which enable them subtly to control their men and the plantations. At the young end of the spectrum is nine-year-old Laura, who comes to live at Shellmound temporarily after her mother's death; she provides the child's viewpoint of events during the hectic wedding preparations. The most objective, wise, and clearsighted outlook, however, is provided by Aunt Ellen. As an "outsider" (she married Battle Fairchild), she not only sees more accurately than her more involved and subjective relatives, but brings to her judgment insights from the world beyond the plantation.

What distinguishes the Fairchilds most of all is their simultaneous independence from and reliance upon one another; each person is at once intensely caught up in family concerns and fiercely private and separate. The only member who transcends the insular closeness of the circle to achieve a more universal outlook on life is Uncle George; able to feel and see beyond the limitations of life at Shellmound, he is nevertheless tied to the Fairchilds in his heart. Through the family's constant attempts to study and understand George, and through George's emotional involvement in events at the estate, Welty reveals a group of people at once selfishly exclusive and warmly affectionate, tender, loving, and devoted.

DEMOCRACY IN AMERICA

Type of work: Essays in political science
Author: Alexis de Tocqueville (1805-1859)
First published: Volume I, 1835; Volume II, 1840

Alexis de Tocqueville lived in a time of enormous political change, when every conceivable variety of political theory flourished. He was born shortly after the French Revolution had turned itself into the Empire, and in his lifetime occurred those further changes which transformed France, at least nominally, into a Republic. His object in writing *Democracy in America* was twofold: to write about the new nation that he so much admired and to establish a. new way of examining ideas of politics. Instead of proceeding from ideas of right and responsibility, de Tocqueville preferred to begin by analyzing social institutions as they functioned in reality. Instead of working, as Rousseau had worked, from an arbitrary picture of the beginnings of humanity in a "natural" condition, de Tocqueville preferred to work from what was statistically observable. Thus, *Democracy in America* begins with a picture of the geography of the new continent, its weather, its indigenous tribes, its economy, and its natural resources. In this respect *Democracy in America* is the forerunner of the scientific spirit in the investigation of social structures.

Much of *Democracy in America* is concerned with institutions, and the first of these described by its author is that of the partition of property. He points out that it is customary in the nations of Europe to divide property by the laws of primogeniture. The result is that property remains fixed in extent and in possession; the family, no matter how changed in each generation, is linked to the wealth and political power of landed property. The family represents the estate, the estate the family, and naturally a strong inequality is carried from one generation to another. The foundations of American culture are to be found, de Tocqueville points out, in the equal partition of land

and fortune. Land is continually broken up into parcels, sold, developed, and transformed. The accompanying wealth and power is much more fluid than in societies in which descent really dominates fortune. The subsidiary effect of equal partition is the access of careers to men who might in another system be blocked from advancement.

De Tocqueville was fascinated by the practice of equality, a phenomenon rarely encountered in France during his lifetime. His next series of chapters concerns political equality; he is one of the first great commentators on the democracy of the township and corporation in early nineteenth century America. He emphasizes that it is fundamental to understand the nature of the township, particularly in its New England tradition. The key to the nature of the American nation, he finds, is the wide and responsible nature of freedom at the level of municipal government. This gives the citizen direct voice in his government and trains him for the representative democracy of the Federal government. De Tocqueville points out that under this form of government power is actually concentrated in the hands of the voter; the legislative and executive branches have no power of their own, but merely represent those who appoint them. To us this fact is commonplace, but it was a new idea for the citizens of Europe.

Although much of this work is in praise of American democracy, de Tocqueville makes some important qualifications. His first principle is that abuse in government occurs when one special interest is served to the exclusion of all others. This kind of abuse, he remarks, formerly occurred when the upper classes imposed their will on the lower, when the military, or feudal, or financial, or even religious values operate to the exclusion of all others. His great qualification of democracy is that in this form of government a kind of tyranny is also possible, that of the majority. He states that it is conceivable that the free institutions of America may be destroyed by forcing all minorities to give up their freedoms for what is supposedly the good of the majority. In that case, he concludes, democracy will give way first to despotism and then to anarchy. Above all things de Tocqueville is taken with equality, and that principle, regardless of the greatest good for the greatest number, is what animates his opinion.

Democracy in America is of course principally about its great subject, but there are in it many reminders of a larger view that its author has. One constant theme of the book is that the Old World must learn from the New; in fact, the book functions not so much as an independent study of a unique phenomenon as a study of comparative political science. We will not succeed in France, the author remarks, if we do not succeed in introducing democratic institutions. There will be independence for none, he adds, unless, like the American republic, we grant independence for all. With uncommon clarity he predicts the totalitarian potentialities of the twentieth century, where unlimited power restricts itself not to a class, but first to a party, and then to a single man. The famous ending of the first volume carries this insight to a more elaborate and specific culmination. There are two nations, de Tocqueville says, which will probably dominate the next century, the United States and Russia. One, he says, is driven by the desire for power and war, the other by the desire to increase domestic prosperity. He predicts that there will be no peace until the aggressiveness of Russia is checked by the peacefulness of the United States: in his own words, he looks to a future in which the principle of "servitude" will encounter that of "freedom."

The second volume of *Democracy in America* was published after a lapse of five years. The first volume had established its author as one of the best political thinkers in Europe. It won for him not only the esteem of the best minds of the Continent, but rewards financial and even political, so that from the time of its publication de Tocqueville was to take an active part as a member of the French government. The second volume is concerned not with the basic economic and social characteristics of America, but with subsidiary questions about the nature of American culture. He asks, for example, how Americans cultivate the arts and whether or not eloquence is to be encountered in the rhetoric of Congress. He covers the progress of science as well as that of poetry, the position of religious minorities, even the meaning of public monuments in a democracy. His general conclusion on the arts in America is that they do not flourish as they do in other political climates, for the arts require an atmosphere of privilege and an amount of money that a tax-conscious public is quite unlikely to spend. The "useful," he says, is much preferred in a democracy to the "beautiful." The artist becomes an artisan and, the author remarks with some delicacy, he tends to produce "imperfect commodities" rather than lasting works of art.

If these qualifications are admitted they are also weighted; de Tocqueville believes that a lowering of some standards is amply compensated by a heightening of others. Particularly in the matter of foreign policy does he admire the republican sense as well as form of government. Toward the end of *Democracy in America* he spends much thought on the inclinations toward war and peace of different forms of government. The democratic form, he judges, is predisposed to peace because of various influences: the rapid growth of personal wealth; the stake in property; the less material but equally important "gentleness of heart" which allows the citizens of a democracy a more humane view of life. Yet, when the democratic government is involved in war, the same application of ambition and energy that is so marked in commercial life results often in military success as well. De Tocqueville's last thoughts about the democracy and its army deal with the danger to any society from its own standing army, and he covers substantially the same ground on this matter as do the authors of the *Federalist* papers.

Democracy in America ends with the restatement that despotism may be encountered even in republics. While democracies can, the author admits, on occasion be violent and unjust, he believes these occasions are exceptional. They will be more and more frequent, however, in the proportion that equality is allowed to lapse. Among the last of de Tocqueville's animated descriptions is that of the "flock of timid and industrious animals" who have given up their individuality to a strong central government. He urges a balance between central and decentralized power, the constant consciousness of equality for all members of the polity.

DEMOCRATIC VISTAS

Type of work: Social and literary criticism
Author: Walt Whitman (1819-1892)
First published: 1871

Written when Whitman was in his early fifties, *Democratic Vistas* demonstrates the author's discouragement at what he saw in America. The sobering effects of the Civil War, the death of Lincoln, and the overwhelming change resulting from the industrial revolution are quite evident as Whitman attempts to introduce a plan for the development of a golden age in the New World.

Like Whitman's poetry, the work has no substantial organization. It is usually repetitious and rambling. Nevertheless, in its portrait of Whitman's philosophy, and in its analysis of the potentiality of the American society, *Democratic Vistas* is extremely significant. Its criticism of American politics, culture, and values in general was partly the result of the disillusionment that existed after the Civil War, but the considerations are still quite applicable to American society.

Simply stated, the thesis of *Democratic Vistas* is that while America is surpassing all other nations industrially and has the material facilities to continue its advancement, it lacks a distinct culture or spiritual identity. According to Whitman, such an identity could only come about through works of literature written in new literary styles by new artists. In effect, he is stating that America has the human resources, the material resources, and the sound political structure to make itself the most ideal society which has ever existed. As Whitman views the American scene, however, he sees no unique values, no real expression of these new concepts, but only a materialistic society relying on old ideas and traditional expression. Thus, the overall result of the work is a plea for great literary works which would serve as a foundation for a new society.

Though the work has no organization other than the repetition of this same theme, Whitman's approach follows four general divisions: a portrait of the American society and its values; a statement of the basic principles and ideals which represent the goals of the "mass, or lump character" of America; the principle of the individual as the focal point for the ideal society; and great literature as the force which will bring about this society.

Whitman begins by stating his central theme—that America will never be great unless it is able to separate itself from the Old World tradition:

> I say that democracy can never prove itself beyond cavil, until it founds and luxuriantly grows its own forms of art, poems, schools, theology, displacing all that exists, or that has been produced anywhere in the past, under opposite influences.

Whitman further states that America is a new experiment founded on new principles and cannot rely on old ideas. While some might argue that the "republic is, in performance, really enacting today the grandest arts, poems, etc., by beating up the wilderness into fertile farms, and in her railroads, ships, machinery, etc.," Whitman responds that "society, in these States, is canker'd, crude, superstitious and rotten":

> The official services of America, national, state, and municipal, in all their branches and departments, except the judiciary, are saturated in corruption, bribery, falsehood, maladministration; and the judiciary is tainted.

After dwelling on the "lamentable conditions" which exist in America, Whitman states that the answer to such a problem is a "new-founded literature" which would be "consistent with science, handling the elements and forces with competent power, teaching and training men."

Having thus established the tone of his essay, Whitman proceeds to the first main consideration, an analysis of the present American society. His portrait of the "lump character" shows that the artist has, in the past, had to struggle against the masses. He also shows that the reverse has been true, for literature "has never recognized the People." It is Whitman's belief that America is experiencing the birth of a new sort of mass personality which is courageous, all-inclusive, and potentially great. To deny cultural identity to this mass would be to destroy this potentiality.

> We believe the ulterior object of political and all other government, (having, of course, provided for the police, the safety of life, property, and for the basic statute and common law, and their administration, always first in order), to be among the rest, not merely to rule, to repress disorder, etc., but to develop, to open up to cultivation, to encourage the possibilities of all beneficent and manly outcroppage, and of that aspiration for independence, and the pride and self-respect latent in all characters.

In other words, Whitman believed that physical freedom is only part of America's goal. The society as a whole can progress only when it possesses a cultural freedom and a set of ideals which will enable the people to attain a transcendent spirituality. Still, the law and the political form are important to Whitman, for it is only in this governmental structure that men of all races and backgrounds can be brought together. Whitman even sees in the future a greater prosperity of the masses and a tremendous physical growth: "The true gravitation-hold of liberalism in the United States will be a more universal ownership of property, general homesteads, general comfort—a vast, intertwining reticulation of wealth."

According to Whitman, this wealth, plus a genuine solidarity of mass spirit and integrity, will make this system survive. Two examples which he gives to prove this point are that "the land which could raise such as the late rebellion, could also put it down," and that the fervor of the Americans is also evident in the interest which they show in the election of their leaders: "I know nothing grander, better exercise, better digestion, more positive proof of the past, the triumphant result of faith in human kind, than a well-contested American national election."

Having discussed the quality of America's political system and the character of its people, Whitman then turns to the individual, for "rich, luxuriant, varied personalism," argues Whitman, is the key to civilization. All else, such as literature or government, is important only insofar as it assists in the "production of perfect characters among the people." It was Whitman's belief that this principle is the basis for America's future.

Whitman defines individuality as creativity, that independent thought by which each person is able to transcend the mass, and he states that it is precisely this quality that Americans lack. He attributes this failure to an attachment to "Culture," or traditional learning. The scholar, for example, is taught what to believe, and consequently believes in nothing. Rather than serving to motivate creativity, this type of culture only systematizes and stagnates individuality.

It is not that Whitman objected to culture. But he believed that instead of being limited to the "parlors or lecture rooms," it should be distributed among all people of all classes. In short, the masses should be given the opportunity to achieve identity. We have indeed developed people who are physically strong and educated, says Whitman, but the "gloomiest consequences" will result if people are left with an "unsophisticated Conscience."

The third and final section of the essay is devoted to the power which would enable the development of this "primary moral element," a great American literature:

A boundless field to fill! A new creation, with needed orbic works launch'd forth, to revolve in free and lawful circuits— to move, self-poised, through the ether, and shine like heaven's own suns! With such, and nothing less, we suggest that New World Literature, fit to rise upon, cohere, and finalize in time, these States.

By "New World Literature" Whitman does not mean quantity; we have, he states, more publications than any other country. Rather, he is referring to literary forms which would represent America as the Bible, the works of Homer, Plato, and Aeschylus represent their respective civilizations. Nor should we resort to the achievements of the past, for these works were written for remote times and problems.

Ye powerful and resplendent ones! ye were, in your atmospheres, grown not for America, but rather for her foes, the feudal and the old—while our genius is democratic and modern.

Whitman summarizes what has thus far been accomplished by describing the stages of development in American writing. He states that America has gone through two stages in preparation for a third and final stage, without which the first two become useless: "The First stage was the planning and putting on record the political foundation rights of immense masses of people. . . . The Second stage relates to material prosperity, wealth, produce. . . ."

The third and final stage will be "a native expression-spirit," "a sublime and serious Religious Democracy sternly taking command." This spirit of impetus can come from no other land, because the foundations for this literature exist only in America.

The artist who will produce this literature will be a student of nature. "Part of the test of a great literatus," says Whitman, "shall be the absence in him of the idea of the covert, the lurid, the maleficent, the devil, . . . hell, natural depravity, and the like." More important, however, will be his faith, his simplicity of statement, and his "adherence to natural standards."

Whitman is no less explicit in his description of the themes of these great works. He says that "Nature, true Nature, and the true idea of Nature, long absent, must, above all, become fully restored, enlarged, and must furnish the pervading atmosphere to poems, and the test of all high literary and aesthetic compositions."

Here Whitman is not referring to the "posyes and nightingales of the English poets," but to the spiritual significance, symbolic and implicit, in the unity of all created matter. By means of this expression all men will be able to understand the essential harmony in the universe and thus regain their faith which has been "scared away by science."

Exactly how the artist will go about this process is not really made clear; but Whitman does say that a whole new idea of composition must be the means. In any case, he assures us that we cannot rest on what has already been accomplished; our hope is in the future.

The final tone of Whitman's essay is one which pervades the whole work; he is desperate and is trying to convince the reader that he should also be concerned. Earlier in his career Whitman had thought that great American literature was on the verge of being created. At the writing of *Democratic Vistas* he saw that what he dreamed of had not occurred, and he attempted to motivate the potential philosopher-artists through this essay. The result is that when he has not obscured his message with too many words, he has given an excellent critique of American society which is as significant now as it was in Whitman's day.

THE DEMON: AN EASTERN TALE

Type of work: Poem
Author: Mikhail Yurievich Lermontov (1814-1841)
First published: 1841

The biographical approach to literature explains the work of a writer by relating the events of his life to a study of his art and style. The problem thus created is that often such an approach assumes a principle of determinism which obscures the less superficial and more significant aspects of the work. The biographer finds in the early life of the artist the beginnings of an inevitable development and the causes of all his preoccupations, and he becomes a sort of prophet after the event. In the case of Mikhail Lermontov, however, there exists a curious and solid relationship between biography and work that calls for close inspection.

Lermontov is considered to be the outstanding representative of Russian romanticism. From 1826 to 1834 he admittedly imitated Byron, but at the same time this imitation was more than a pose for him. In a poem of 1832 he wrote: "No I am not like Byron, like him I am a persecuted wanderer, but mine is a Russian soul. . . . I began earlier, and earlier I shall end. . . . Who will communicate my thoughts to the world? Either myself, or God, or nobody." Lermontov was admittedly egoistic, but he himself saw his narcissism as a misfortune and as a self-destructive element in his personality. He felt that the poet is made for suffering in a world where angelic and demonic principles constantly war with each other. Lermontov's long verse-narrative, *The Demon,* illustrates his feeling of the always-present contradiction of good and evil. Unlike Byron, he often described "glimpses of perfection" or "a state of bliss," and in *The Demon* he gave full rein to his ambivalent nature, to his preoccupation with evil along with a sincere though ineffectual craving for what is good. The reasons behind this juxtaposition of seemingly contradictory ideas reveal the poem to be one of Lermontov's most personal creations.

Lermontov wrote the first draft of *The Demon* when he was only fifteen. He reworked the theme in 1830 and 1833, and again in 1838 after being exiled to the Caucasus for his eulogistic poem to Pushkin. *The Demon* was finally completed, after work on several more drafts, shortly before his death in 1841. The constant revisions show that Lermontov was intensely preoccupied with the ideas of the poem and desired to express them with precision. The poem was extensively reworked at least eight times, but the final variant still retained some of the original lines of 1829.

While Lermontov was working on the first draft, he also wrote a short lyric called "My Demon." It has been said that he wrote this poem in imitation of a verse by Pushkin with the same title. Whether this claim is true or not, Lermontov did express an attitude entirely his own. Instead of denouncing the spirit of negation as Pushkin had done, Lermontov was attracted to "the sinister collection of evils." His demon was at first a fierce being: "He scorns pure love; he rejects all prayers; he beholds blood indifferently." Two years later he is less forbidding and violent. He has become more intimately bound to life, and in a sense he is a more direct representation of Lermontov himself. "The proud demon will not depart, as long as I live, from me." The dark side of the poet's personality taunts him with images of bliss and purity, but they are wholly unattainable.

The 1838 variant of *The Demon* replaces the previous indefinite locale with an exotic Caucasian setting. In his childhood Lermontov had twice been to the Caucasus, and doubtless the mountains and the strange customs and folklore of the region made a strong impression on him. The critic Janko Lavrin has said that Lermontov's poetic gift began to develop early and was fostered by two circumstances, one of which was his visits to the Caucasus. Lermontov was indeed impressed by the mountains, as is evidenced by his repeated descriptions of them in his verse.

The heroine of the early versions had been an anonymous nun, but in the 1838 version she is a passionate Georgian princess named Tamara. It is believed that Lermontov used as the basis for this element an Ossetian folktale about a mountain demon in love with a beautiful mortal maiden. Perhaps he was also influenced by Byron's *Cain* and *Heaven and Earth,* Thomas Moore's *Love of the Angels,* or Alfred de Vigny's *Eloa.* In any case, the final variant of *The Demon* is Lermontov's alone. He took a theme which other writers had used and related it to himself. In the dedication to the second draft Lermontov personalized his idea; "Like my cold and cruel Demon, I enjoyed doing evil in this world; deceit was not new to me, and my heart was full of poison. But now, like that gloomy Genius, I have been reborn through your presence for innocent delights, for hope and freedom."

Lermontov's Demon is, characteristically enough, a former angel who has rebelled against God. Despite his pride in his independence, he still remembers his former bliss. After he sees the beautiful Tamara, he begins to think his love for her might reconcile him to life and to God, "In Paradise again I'd shine, like a new angel in new splendor." Tamara cannot resist his impassioned words, but as soon as they kiss, she dies and her soul is taken by God. The Demon is left alone, doomed to dwell in the same void until the end of time. Whereas Tamara redeemed her sin by death, the Demon is incapable of sacrifice. Lermontov's personal Demon is more human than a Satan or a Mephistopheles. He is ruled by appetite, passion, and cold self-absorption.

Although Lermontov expressed in this poem his own isolation and deracination, the poem remains artificial when judged by modern standards. The theme is vague and contrived; the critic D. S. Mirsky finds significance in the fact that it became the libretto for a theatrical opera by Anton Rubenstein. *The Demon* was censored during the reign of Nicholas I for being "anti-religious." It was, however, circulated privately and by the second half of the nineteenth century was one of the most popular poems in Russia. The lyrical, musical quality of the poem made it especially popular. Many poets, among them Blok, Gorky, and Pasternak, have recognized it as a source of inspiration.

Perhaps it is difficult to take the theme of *The Demon* seriously. But even if we do not, the poem remains a powerful psychological document. It speaks of man as an exile who, after rejecting human society, still longs to be a part of it. The critic R. Poggioli has said that *The Demon* is simply a monologue which the poet utters through the undramatic protagonists. Accordingly, the instrument Lermontov uses in *The Demon* is the confession device employed simply and directly, revealing a true image of himself and his life, mirroring his guilt and shame, and becoming the source of repentance as well as hope. In other words, *The Demon* attempted to reconcile the angelic and demonic elements which were aspects of the poet's view of himself. Undeniably, *The Demon* was a very personal poem. Yet it speaks of emotion and attitude on an unrealistic level. It was not until Lermontov wrote his most outstanding work, the novel titled *A Hero of Our Time,* that he was able to transfer his personal complexity and contradiction to a romantic but realistically conceived tale. The protagonist of his great work of fiction is no longer a demon but a very earthy soldier. He is bitter and cynical toward life, and he, like Pushkin's Eugene Onegin, is an example of the superfluous man. The place Lermontov's Demon had as a forerunner of this idea is obvious. Despite the tendency to discount *The Demon* as a significant work today, it is essential to an understanding of Lermontov and perhaps even more to an understanding of the evolution of his art.

DESCENT INTO HELL

Type of work: Novel
Author: Charles Williams (1886-1945)
Time: June and July, in the 1930's
Locale: Battle Hill, a residential area near London
First published: 1937

Principal characters:
PAULINE ANSTRUTHER, an orphaned girl in her twenties
MARGARET ANSTRUTHER, her grandmother
PETER STANHOPE, an eminent poet
LAWRENCE WENTWORTH, a military historian
ADELA HUNT, an aspiring actress
HUGH PRESCOTT, her suitor
MRS. LILY SAMMILE, a neighbor
MRS. PARRY, a civic leader engaged in directing a play

The events of this novel are on two planes which intersect at so many points that the ordinary barriers between the natural and supernatural worlds disappear. On the realistic plane of activities in the suburb of Battle Hill, the narrative concerns the production of a verse drama written by Peter Stanhope, an eminent poet and inhabitant of the Manor House, which had belonged to his family before the housing estate was built. A group of his neighbors, under the leadership of the capable Mrs. Parry, have the privilege of performing his new play in his garden, but only one of them, Pauline Anstruther, even remotely grasps the spiritual significance of his pastoral fantasy. Pauline's sensibility is so quickened by the nuances of his verse that she confides to him the terror which has haunted her for years: the recurrent appearance of her *doppelgänger*.

Peter Stanhope explains to her the principle of substitution which was fundamental in Charles Williams's thought: one person through love can take over and bear the burden of another so that the sufferer is relieved. When Pauline is willing to accept his offer to bear her burden, she discovers that she is no longer tortured by her own problem; instead, she is given the opportunity to bear someone else's burden of fear. Her growth in grace is the principal subject of the novel.

As the rehearsals for the play proceed, Pauline's role as leader of the chorus is

paralleled by her role in the supernatural drama which takes place concurrently in Battle Hill. The spiritual energy released through the play sets in motion a series of events which transcend ordinary time, affecting a number of other inhabitants of the suburb. The housing estate built in the 1920's had taken its name from the hill, which had been a scene of battle from the time of the ancient Britons to the period of the Tudors. While the estate was being built, the timeless "magnetism of death," still alive on the Hill, as the suburb was usually called, had touched a despairing unskilled laborer, who had hanged himself on the scaffolding of an unfinished house. His unresting spirit still inhabits the area, unrecognized by the occupier of the finished house, Lawrence Wentworth, a noted military historian and adviser to the producer of the play. As a middle-aged bachelor Wentworth has developed a secret passion for pretty, conceited Adela Hunt, who is both the heroine in the play and the girl friend in ordinary life of the leading man, Hugh Prescott. Wentworth's jealousy is so consuming that he is destroying himself as surely as the suicide did. Also dying is Pauline's grandmother, Margaret Anstruther, but her death is the natural fulfillment of a well-spent life. Shortly before she dies, she is visited by an unpleasantly ingratiating and vaguely sinister neighbor, Mrs. Lily Sammile, who appears unexpectedly at several crises in the novel. Each of these characters is involved in the action of which Pauline is the protagonist.

The plot is comprehensible only in terms of the theme: the triumph of love over death. Pauline's love for her grandmother has been dutiful but detached during the years since her parents' death when she has lived in Mrs. Anstruther's house as dependent and companion. It is not until Stanhope has relieved her of her fear that Pauline can talk to her grandmother about it and appreciate the depth of the old woman's love. Mrs. Anstruther initiates Pauline further into the doctrine of substituted love by explaining that she may be called upon to bear the pain of their ancestor, John Struther, whose martyrdom by fire is well-known as family history.

As the dying woman approaches the limits of mortality, she can see the face of the suicide as he looks into her window during his ceaseless wandering, and soon she tells Pauline that the girl must go out in the middle of the night because someone needs her near Mr. Wentworth's. The nurse thinks the patient's mind is wandering, but Pauline knows that she must go. She discovers she no longer fears the dark, and she sees the dead man in ordinary mortal form. He asks the way to London, gently refuses her offer to pay his fare, and sets off to walk to the city. As she watches him, his form is transmuted into the agonized body of her ancestor, and she is given the opportunity of bearing his burden by enduring the fire in a mystical experience of very real pain. All this happens during the night between the dress rehearsal and the performance of the play. Mrs. Anstruther dies five minutes after Pauline gets home, but the death does not keep her from acting in the play as the producer had feared: Love has given Pauline a new perspective on time and mortality.

As a counterpoint to Pauline's experience throughout the novel, Lawrence Wentworth's love operates negatively because it is focused on himself. His passion is for his idea of Adela Hunt rather than for the real person, and his jealousy of Hugh Prescott is so powerful that it creates a tangible image of the girl who, he imagines, visits him with increasing frequency and becomes his mistress. In the bedroom where the suicide hanged himself, Wentworth's reason is destroyed by his fantasies of false love. The crisis of his descent into hell is reached on the day of the dress rehearsal, when Mrs. Parry consults him as a military historian on a detail in the costumes of the guards. Wentworth knows that they are wrong and that he could arrange for them to be altered; but he is so preoccupied with his erotic experience that he cannot be bothered and tells a lie instead of the truth. This sacrifice of the historian's integrity confirms the loss of his soul. The next day his seat at the play is empty.

On the afternoon of the performance there is an unnatural stillness in the atmosphere, like the calm before a storm. Some of the cast complain of the heat, but the play proceeds successfully and the only disturbance is Mrs. Sammile's fainting at the end. After that a number of residents of the Hill feel unwell, but life proceeds normally. Margaret Anstruther is buried. Pauline makes plans to move into London and take a job.

A few days after the funeral Adela and Hugh are walking and carrying on a mild argument which reveals the difference between them: Hugh's love for Adela is consistent with his habit of seeing life clearly, while Adela's love for him is an aspect of her desire to manipulate others. As their walk takes them near the cemetery they meet Mrs. Sammile. While they are talking to her, they become transfixed by the sight of the graves opening. Mrs Sammile shrieks and disappears into a small shed at the edge of the cemetery. Adela screams and starts running, pursued by Hugh shouting that the illusion was caused by the wind blowing up loose earth on the graves. His mind clears rapidly, and just as quickly his love fades, so that he gives up the pursuit.

Adela's wild flight leads her instinctively to the house of the man who she knows idolizes her, but when she looks through the window she too sees the image of herself which his diseased imagination has created, and she collapses in terror. Found by a policeman and taken home, she awakens delirious with the impression that she has forgotten her part in the play, a key passage about perception and love. When Pauline calls to see her, Adela insists that Pauline must find Mrs. Sammile in the shed by the cemetery, to give her Adela's part, and thus make her well. Pauline, sensing that Lily Sammile is in fact Lilith, the image of false love, tries to offer Adela her own help in recovering her part, but she finds that only by promising to look for the old woman can she ease the tortured spirit.

The climax of love's triumph over death in the novel comes when Pauline goes, as she went out into the night at the request of her dying grandmother, to confront Lily Sammile in the cemetery shed. Recognizing her as the illusion rather than the reality of love, Pauline rejects her promises of rewards with a laugh of such pure contented joy that Lilith and her murky retreat dissolve into the dust and rubble of an old unused shed that has collapsed from her strong push on the door. In attempting to bear Adela's burden, Pauline has thus found the completion of her own part in the drama of Battle Hill and is ready to leave for London. Seen off on the train by Stanhope, who says his own role is to comfort the many people in the community who are ill, she looks forward with joy to her new life in the city. Lawrence Wentworth travels on the same train but refuses her company and goes in a daze to a historian's dinner at which his lifelong historical rival is honored and he himself sinks into complete insensibility.

The surrealistic effect of supernatural events taking place in a natural setting is the keynote of Charles Williams' narrative treatment of spiritual experience.

Ordinary life is revealed as an image of a deeper reality. The play in which all the characters are involved becomes an image of life itself in which each person must perfect his own role in harmony with others. The setting of Battle Hill suggests the hill of Golgotha, and Lily Sammile's lair is revealed to Pauline as an aspect of Gomorrah. For Wentworth the journey into the city becomes the way to Gomorrah; but Pauline's destination is the eternal City. She tells Stanhope that it seems funny to be discussing the times of trains to the new Jerusalem, but for the poet the interdependence of the temporal and the eternal is fully assimilated fact.

The characterization, like the plot, is determined by the theme. Only Pauline Anstruther and Lawrence Wentworth, who experience salvation and damnation respectively, are fully delineated. The other characters are sketched in with just enough detail to give them substance as examples of different aspects of love. Stanhope and Mrs. Anstruther are seen only in relation to Pauline, Adela Hunt primarily in contrast to Pauline, and Hugh Prescott in contrast to Wentworth. Williams never falls into the error often attributed to Milton and others of making his diabolical characters more attractive than the good ones. Mrs. Sammile is described with a few telling details which make her seem real, slightly pathetic, and obscurely repulsive. Peter Stanhope, in contrast, expresses his sanctity through an easy kindliness and sense of humor. The essence of goodness is seen as a quality of joy which permeates the lives of those who accept it in love. This joy is reflected not only in the characters but in the style, taking the form of wry humor in the descriptions of the play rehearsals and almost poetic rhapsody in the passages of mystical experience. The great variety in style and mood emphasizes Williams's conviction, exemplified in the plot, that reality in human life exists in multiple planes of time and space.

THE DESCENT OF MAN, AND
SELECTION IN RELATION TO SEX

Type of work: Biological study
Author: Charles Darwin (1809-1882)
First published: 1871

Although *The Descent of Man, and Selection in Relation to Sex* has been condemned by intelligent men as little more than sophisticated drivel, most of Darwin's critics consider it to stand second only to *On the Origin of Species.* Problems beset Darwin when he turned from his brilliant biological study of 1859 to the more particular analysis of the relation of man to the natural world. These problems are immediately seen in the organization of this long argument: well over two-thirds of the book is a digression, exhaustive and often exhausting, on sexual selection. The book lacks the inspiration of *On the Origin of Species,* but in its summary and evaluation of the anthropological thought after the publication of that earlier masterpiece *The Descent of Man* is one of the most important books of the nineteenth century.

In his introduction Darwin says that he plans to consider three things: whether man descended from some pre-existing form, how he developed if indeed he did descend, and what value the differences between races have to such a development. He draws evidence of the descent of man from his vast knowledge of medicine and biology. That man shares bodily structure, embryonic development, and rudimentary organs with other mammals seems to him to be evidence enough for asserting a common ancestry. Since anthropologists and paleontologists had not at that time discovered significant relics of prehistoric man, Darwin's affirmation of the descent of man was based on logic alone; thus he amasses an almost overwhelming number of analogies to strengthen his case. These analogies enable him to trace the development of man from lower animals, but in order to do so he must assume a definition of man. Darwin maintains that man's

uniqueness is not due to any one characteristic but to a combination of many: upright position, acquisition of language and tools, a delicate and free hand, and superior mental powers. In the possession of these traits man is different only in degree. In fact, Darwin musters evidence to show that animals have curiosity, imagination, attention, and reason, attributes that earlier philosophers thought set man apart from the rest of the animal world.

Writing as a biologist, not a moral philosopher or a theologian, Darwin does not try to consider all the implications of his theory. The single attribute that separates man from the rest of the animal world, Darwin thinks, is moral sense. But moral sense, the offspring of conscience, was the result of an evolutionary process; conscience came to early man from a struggle between duty (sympathy and the social instincts) and desire (the urge for complete freedom). The belief in God also evolved, originating in dreams and developing through "spiritual agencies" into gods. It was this application, a logical outcome of Darwin's theories, that horrified both conservative Christians and idealistic philosophers, for the theory completely eliminated the validity of revelation or of supramundane enlightenment.

Darwin, well aware of the implications of his theory, concentrates on the rise of civilization from savagery. Natural selection and the struggle for survival advanced the intellectual powers so that the history of human institutions is the history of the evolution of the intelligence of man. As tribes grew stronger, the members learned to perceive the consequences of their actions, thereby developing moral sense. Then, as man became more and more aware of his moral sense, advanced civilizations with sophisticated religions and technologies were able to develop.

This discussion of the rise of civilization brings Darwin to the differences between races. Because individual members of different races can be mated so as to form fertile offspring and because the similarities between races far outnumber the differences, Darwin assumes that races are "sub-breeds" of the species. Furthermore, Darwin discards the hypotheses that each race descended from a primal pair, that the racial differences were caused by the conditions of life, and that the races evolved independently. The only theory that can explain the differences between races is sexual selection. The question of sexual selection, necessary to prove his assumption about race, leads Darwin into the digression that fills two-thirds of his book.

In *On the Origin of Species*, Darwin had based his theory of evolution primarily on natural selection or the struggle for survival. In other words, a slight modification in an animal's structure might allow it to survive whereas another animal that lacked this modification would die. Existence, then, is a continual warfare in which the animal with the slight advantage always wins. In *The Descent of Man* Darwin considerably modifies his view of nature by analyzing sexual selection, a different kind of biological warfare. When animals have their sexes separated, the male and female organs of reproduction differ; these are primary sexual characters. But there are other differences not directly connected with the act of reproduction, and these are secondary sexual characters. Usually the males have the most pronounced secondary sexual characters (for example, the brilliant plumage of many male birds); the males acquired these characters not from being better fitted for existence (natural selection) but from having gained advantage over other males and having transmitted their advantages to male offspring. There are usually more males than females, so that there is a struggle between males for the possession of the female; hence the female has the opportunity of selecting one out of several males. The strongest females would have first choice among the males; therefore, the secondary sexual characters that pass through the strongest male and female would have the most chance of outnumbering those characters that pass through weaker partners. In this way, the dominant characters are also the strongest. The more active the rivalry between the males, the more pronounced will be the variations between male and female, the female having remained unmodified because she does not enter into the competition.

Basing his analysis of the animal world upon these principles, Darwin begins with the lower classes of the animal kingdom. In the lowest classes these characters are absent because most often the sexes are joined in the same individual, but in the sub-kingdom of the Arthropoda undoubtable examples of secondary sexual characters appear. Darwin presents his most convincing case, however, in his long discussions on insects and birds. In both of these sub-kingdoms the characters are so clearly noticeable that Darwin can accumulate material until he overwhelms the reader in a *tour de force;* the reader is presented with so much detailed information that he is willing to accept the evidence submitted before Darwin applies his principles to man.

The secondary sexual characters of man are more complex than those of birds or insects because man is more complex, but this is a difference only in degree. The adult male, for example, has a beard and hairiness of the body (although there is wide variation between tribes or races); he loves to fight and hence has greater endurance and strength than the female. Because of his love of battle, the male has a delight in competition and develops his intellect more than woman, who is consequently more tender and less selfish. Having noted a few of these characters, Darwin asks how they came to be. Because men vied with one another for the woman, the choice of the woman led to certain secondary sexual characters. For example, racial differences are the result of ancient concepts of beauty; the remote ancestors of the Negro race preferred women who were dark-skinned and flat-nosed. Thus, Darwin is able to describe the differences between races without violating his basic theory of the descent of man from lower forms of life.

Darwin anxiously waited for the publication of *The Descent of Man* and was surprised when he discovered that people were interested but not shocked. In fact, the book was anticlimactical. The disturbance caused by *On the Origin of Species* had calmed and was not again stirred up, and *The Descent of Man* became, as it should have, a book primarily for biologists.

DESIRE UNDER THE ELMS

Type of work: Drama
Author: Eugene O'Neill (1888-1953)
Type of plot: Romantic tragedy
Time of plot: 1850
Locale: The Cabot farmhouse in New England
First presented: 1924

Principal characters:
EPHRAIM CABOT, a farmer
SIMEON,
PETER, and
EBEN, his sons
ABBIE, his third wife

Critique:

Desire Under the Elms was the last of O'Neill's naturalistic plays and one of his most effective. The structural set, showing the entire farmhouse with one wall removed, was an innovation in its day. In this play O'Neill's daring reduction of human motives to the simple impulses of love, hate, lust, and greed gives an impression of human nature as convincing and complete as the more complex studies of his later, longer plays.

The Story:

When the news of gold discoveries in California reached New England, Simeon and Peter Cabot, who had spent their lives piling up stones to fence their father's farm, became restless. In the summer of 1850 they were ready to tear down the fences which seemed to hem them in, to rebel against their close-fisted old father, and for once in their lives to be free. One day Ephraim Cabot hitched up his rig and drove off, leaving the farm in charge of his three sons, Sim, Peter, and their younger half-brother, Eben. All three sons cordially hated their father because they saw him for what he was, a greedy, self-righteous old hypocrite. The older brothers hated old Ephraim for what he had done to them, but Eben had a further grievance. He hated his father because he had stolen the land which had belonged to his mother, and had then worked her to death on the farm. Eben felt the farm belonged to him, and he meant to have it. He had inherited some of old Ephraim's stony implacability, as well as his sensuality, and he gave expression to the latter on his trips down the road to visit Minnie, the local prostitute who had belonged to his father before him.

Realizing that Sim and Peter wanted to go to California, yet had no money to take them there, Eben thought up a plan to get rid of them once and for all. During old Ephraim's absence he offered them three hundred dollars apiece in gold if they would sign a paper renouncing all claims to the farm. The money had belonged to Eben's mother, and Eben had found it buried beneath the floorboards of the kitchen. The brothers accepted Eben's offer and set off for California.

Shortly afterward old Ephraim drove home with his third wife. He was seventy-six, she was thirty-five. But Abbie Putnam had decided that she wanted a home of her own. When old Ephraim offered to marry her she accepted him at once, and when she moved into the Cabot homestead she was already determined that whatever happened the farm would be hers someday. She tried unsuccessfully to make friends with Eben. But the thought of another woman's coming to take his mother's place and the farm which rightfully belonged to him made him hate Abbie at first.

After a time Eben began to notice that life on the farm was easier since his stepmother had arrived. But the realization that Abbie could influence his father as she desired only strengthened Eben's determination to resist her attempts to conciliate him. Finally some of his taunts became so pointed that Abbie complained to Ephraim. When she falsely hinted that Eben had been making advances toward her, the old man threatened to kill his son. Realizing that she had gone too far, and that she must make a different approach, Abbie subtly built up in Ephraim's mind the idea that a son and heir who would inherit the farm upon his death would be a better way of getting back at Eben than to kill him outright. The thought that at the age of seventy-six he might have a son flattered the old man, and he agreed to let Eben alone.

One night, after Ephraim had gone out to sleep in the barn, Abbie saw her opportunity to make her hold on the farm secure. She managed to lure Eben into his mother's parlor, a room which had not been opened since her death, and there she seduced him, breaking down his scruples with the suggestion that by cuckolding his father he could get revenge for Ephraim's treatment of his mother.

The result of this move on Abbie's part was the son whom Ephraim wanted as an heir. To celebrate the child's birth, Ephraim invited all the neighbors to a dance in the kitchen of the farmhouse. Many of the guests suspected the true circumstances and said so as openly as they dared. Ephraim paid no attention to the insinuations and outdanced them all until even the fiddler dropped from sheer exhaustion.

While the revelry still was going on the old man stepped outside to cool off. There he and Eben, who had been sulking outside, quarreled over the possession of the farm. Spitefully Ephraim taunted his son with a revelation of how Abbie had tricked him out of his inheritance. Furious, Eben turned on Abbie, threatening to kill her, and telling her he hated her and the child he had fathered when she tricked him with her scheme. But by this time Abbie was genuinely in love with Eben, and, thinking the child was the obstacle which was keeping them apart, she smothered it in an effort to prove to her lover that it was he and not the child she wanted. When he discovered what had happened, Eben was both enraged and shocked, and he set off to get the sheriff for Abbie's arrest.

When Ephraim discovered that Abbie had killed the child that was not his, he too was shocked, but his heart filled with contempt at his son's cowardice in giving Abbie over to the law.

On his way to the farm Eben began to realize how much he loved Abbie, and the great love she had shown for him in taking the child's life. When the sheriff came to take Abbie away, he confessed that he was an accomplice in the crime. The two were taken off together, both destined for punishment, but happy in their love. Ephraim Cabot was left alone with his farm, the best farm in the county. It was, the sheriff told him, a place anybody would want to own.

Further Critical Evaluation of the Work:

One of O'Neill's most admired and frequently performed plays, *Desire Under the Elms* provoked enormous controversy during its first stagings. Some audiences were scandalized by what one critic called "distresses" which "range from unholy lust to infanticide, and include drinking, cursing, vengeance, and something approaching incest." In Los Angeles, the cast was arrested for having presented a lewd, obscene, and immoral play. A bizarre trial followed—at one point the entire court witnessed a special private performance. The jury was finally dismissed, having deadlocked with eight members voting for conviction and four for acquittal. However, it gradually became apparent that O'Neill was aiming at something more than a shocking revelation of unconscious drives and primordial fears. These elements were clearly subordinated to his larger purpose of reintroducing authentic tragic vision to American theater. And O'Neill's supporters could point out that the Greek and Biblical sources which inspired the play are replete with the very "immoralities" he depicted.

Euripides' *Hippolytus* and Racine's *Phèdre* served as O'Neill's principal models. These works both draw on the archetypal plot in which a father returns from a journey with a wife who falls in love with her new stepson. This attachment, at first resisted or concealed, results in a struggle between father and son. The father achieves a Pyrrhic victory which costs him both son and spouse. The situation is tragic in that all participants are forced to make conscious choices of evil for the sake of a higher good. It is Fate which so structures events as to necessitate the downfall of these essentially noble characters. O'Neill complicates the classic plot by introducing Old Testament motifs: the "hardness" and vengeance of God; the superiority of justice over mercy; and the battle among sons for birthrights and fatherly favor. He also relies on Freudian psychology in treating all sexual relationships.

Does O'Neill finally succeed in giving true tragic stature to his characters? There can be no doubt that the drama possesses genuinely tragic aspects; this much has been confirmed by two generations of criticism. But that the whole deserves the term "tragedy" is doubtful. Three considerations sustain this judgment. First, Eben's basic motivation remains unclear throughout the play as does the central matter of whether he is the rightful heir to the farm. Second, both Abbie and Eben are far too preoccupied with struggles for possession and revenge; they lack that nobility of purpose which we associate with tragic characters like Oedipus, Antigone, or Hippolytus. Third, Eben is made to seem so totally a victim of psychological drives that his choices are not freely arrived at. Especially this latter element makes *pathos,* not tragedy, the dominant quality in *Desire Under the Elms.*

Edgar F. Racey, Jr., has persuasively argued that O'Neill designed his play around a single moral fact: Ephraim Cabot ruined the life of Eben's mother —"murdered her with his hardness," as Eben says—and this sin now cries out for retribution. O'Neill's opening stage directions indicate his intention. The two enormous elms which bend over the farm house are to be expressionistically rendered; they should suggest suffering women and dominate the entire scene with "a sinister maternity." From the beginning, Eben proclaims his monomaniacal desire to take "her vengeance on him—so's she kin rest quiet in her grave." When Abbie enters the parlor, her scheming and erotic tendencies are momentarily subdued by the felt presence of the dead woman's spirit. Eben does not allow himself to be seduced until he is assured that he is doing his mother's will.

The structure of the action reinforces this central theme. In Part One, Eben solidifies his claim to the farm by inducing his half brothers to leave. He uses his mother's money in the process, thus depriving Ephraim of both the fortune and the assistance of his older sons. In Part Two, Eben takes Ephraim's wife from him, begets a son, and sets in motion the process whereby Ephraim is humiliated in the eyes of the community. In Part Three, Abbie's killing of the child prevents Ephraim from naming a new heir. Further, the departure of Abbie and Eben dooms Ephraim to that condition of isolation which he has always feared above all. He becomes in effect an exile, living on a farm which now is a curse to him. The pattern of crime and justified punishment has been completed.

Tragic in outline, *Desire Under the Elms* is, however, less than tragic in substance. Quite inexplicably, O'Neill lets the basic issue of Ephraim's persecution of Eben's mother become clouded. Since we learn of her suffering only from Eben himself, some skepticism about his truthfulness is engendered. This skepticism grows when two additional factors come into view: Eben's overwhelming Oedipus complex and his deep desire to inherit the farm. That Eben stands to benefit economically by his revenge-taking tends to tarnish his character and further undermine his credibility. O'Neill intensifies this economic theme both by showing how deeply Peter and Simeon covet the farm, and by casting doubt on Eben's claim that he has a clear legal right of ownership. Ephraim discounts this claim completely, and we are inclined to believe that his long work of reclamation gives him at least some moral right to the property.

More importantly, O'Neill does not seem to realize that the addition of certain Freudian motifs is not compatible with his purpose. For Freud, fathers and sons are natural rivals; despite the outward show of paternal and filial love, they both unconsciously desire to monopolize the love and sexual favor of "their" woman. This tendency operates even if the father treats the mother with perfect love and respect. This Ephraim most certainly did not do. But how much of Eben's motive is Oedipal and how much is filial devotion? The very fact that such a question can arise demonstrates O'Neill's failure to produce a convincingly tragic work. Had Eben's duty to avenge his mother's suffering run directly counter to his psychological and economic needs, he might have assumed tragic stature. In this respect the case for *Mourning Becomes Electra* as tragedy is much stronger.

Ironically, the fact that *Desire Under the Elms* is not fully realized tragedy probably accounts partially for its appeal, as does O'Neill's choice of a pastoral, precivilized setting which helps convey the workings of unconscious forces with astonishing power.

Despite the fact that the outraged protests responsible for such odd and sensational events as the Los Angeles court case came from irate middle-class viewers, such viewers were only a small minority; actually it was the literate American middle class which formed O'Neill's most avid audience. O'Neill was an iconoclast whose attacks, likened in one of his early poems to torpedoes fired from the submarine of his soul, were directed against middle-class complacency. Much to its credit, however, the audience whose values were under fire responded to plays such as *Desire Under the Elms* with that respect and enthusiasm which springs from recognition of the truth, however disconcerting or uncomfortable that truth may be.

Leslie E. Gerber

DESTINY BAY

Type of work: Short stories
Author: Donn Byrne (Brian Oswald Donn-Byrne, 1889-1928)
Type of plot: Regional romance
Time of plot: Early twentieth century
Locale: Ireland
First published: 1928

Principal characters:
SIR VALENTINE MACFARLANE, lord of Destiny Bay
JENEPHER, his blind sister
KERRY, his nephew and heir
JAMES CARABINE, his valet and friend
JENICO HAMILTON, Kerry's cousin
ANN-DOLLY, Jenico's wife
PATRICK HERNE, Jenepher's husband
COSIMO, Sir Valentine's brother
ANSELO LOVERIDGE, Cosimo's friend

Critique:

Reading Donn Byrne's short stories is like being lifted up out of a flat country and being set down in a wonderfully clean, colorful, and powerful land. There the characters are courtly, their stories full of courage, humor, and skill. *Destiny Bay* is a series of nine of these stories, differing greatly in length, told by Kerry MacFarlane, heir to Destiny Bay, a house and a district in the north of Ireland. This place is a region of high hills, wild ocean, sun, and heather; the characters are equally bold, wild, warm, and beautiful.

The Story:

Kerry's uncle, Sir Valentine MacFarlane, lord of Destiny Bay, with his great fan-shaped red beard that came to his waist, was the courtliest and most hospitable of men. In twenty minutes he had persuaded the old Duke of la Mentera and his grandson that he could not allow Spanish royalty to stay at the Widow McGinty's village hotel when there was room and plenty at Destiny Bay. With the simplicity which comes with great age, the duke said that his life had been full of many turnings; now he was on the last path and he had come hoping to find a treasure chest, said to have been lost when one of his ancestors was killed off the Irish coast after Drake's defeat of the Armada. His grandson must be provided for; he had nowhere else to turn.

Aunt Jenepher, beautiful, blind, but seeming to see people better than anyone, said the duke and Don Anthony, his grandson, were noble and good, and she treated them with that kindness of hers which went straight to the heart.

A short time later the duke died, leaving his girlish-looking grandson to the MacFarlanes' several cares—the courtliness of Uncle Valentine, the trust of his valet, James Carabine, the kindness of Aunt Jenepher, and Kerry's companionship. That friendship was not always pleasing to Don Anthony, since he could not bear to see their prize fights or cock fights, though he was beside himself with joy at their horse races. But it was Jenico for whom the boy conceived a hero worship.

Jenico was not a large man like Uncle Valentine, but he had that look of burnished strength which made women try to get his attention, and he was innately courteous, though his mind might be a thousand miles away. His home was near Destiny Bay and nearer Spanish Men's

Rest, that spot where the Spaniards were buried after their ships had been wrecked. For a long time the bees and birds had shunned the place, and it was a chill on the heart to go there. But when Jenico and Kerry took Don Anthony to Spanish Men's Rest, they heard the bees and birds again and the place seemed sunnier.

Jenico, trying to get the boy's mind off the settlement of the grandfather's estate, finally asked him to take off with him on a trip to the Atlas Mountains. The boy was flattered and obviously wanted to go, but begged off. Shortly after, as the three walked near the river, Jenico and Kerry decided to go swimming. Jenico went on ahead and Kerry could see his head like that of a sleek seal in the waves. When Kerry started to strip, Don Anthony begged him not to take off his clothes. Jenico laughed and told Kerry to strip the boy and throw him in. Kerry headed for the boy. Don Anthony flashed a knife, then ducked away. As Kerry turned to follow him, there was Uncle Valentine, roaring that there was once a time when a lady could be trusted amongst Irishmen.

With a change of clothes, Ann-Dolly, as she asked to be called, was one of the loveliest girls they had ever seen, and there was a new spirit in her. So that she would feel free to stay, they made her companion to Aunt Jenepher. At that time her relations with Jenico were strained, but whenever they were in a room together she would look at him when he was not looking, and then he would look at her when she had turned away.

Jenico tried a fool scheme of planting treasure for her to find, but he and Kerry had a fight about that and he never told her. Finally she had enough of the MacFarlanes and ran away in the night. Jenico and James Carabine and Kerry used horses, bicycles, and even bloodhounds to follow her. At last they found her huddled in an old ruin. She was

deathly white and scared, and nothing they did could make her move. James Carabine plucked Kerry's sleeve, suggesting that they return the horses, the bicycles, the dogs they had borrowed, but Kerry brushed him off. Finally Carabine picked Kerry up like a feather and forcibly carried him out, to leave Jenico and Ann-Dolly together.

After Ann-Dolly became mistress of Jenico's house, the birds always sang and the bees knew it was a fair and happy home.

One never knew what or whom Uncle Valentine might bring back from a trip. One of the kindest of men was Patrick Herne, a man who looked like a double for Digory Pascoe, who was to have married Aunt Jenepher after he made his fortune. Digory had died in a fight, but Uncle Valentine had kept him alive for twelve years by writing letters from him, until he found Patrick Herne and brought him home as Digory. Aunt Jenepher played along for a while until she had to ask who the man really was who thought just as she did. Theirs was a happy wedding.

One time Uncle Valentine went off to America to find James Carabine, who had once saved his life. James Carabine was the Irish champion in the prize ring when he had an urge to sail to America to take care of a drunken friend. Because the friend died at sea, he was lonesome in New York and married a hard-faced and, as it turned out, two-faced singer whose friends ran illegal fights in and around the city. When Uncle Valentine found him, he had taken to drink after losing a bad fight and his wife; but he regained his self-respect and rewon his title before Uncle Valentine took him home. There was no more devoted valet and friend in Ireland than Uncle Valentine's James Carabine.

It was not only Uncle Valentine who traveled distances to help a friend. Anselo Loveridge, the gipsy whom Uncle Valentine's brother Cosimo saved from the hangman's noose, worried about Uncle Cosimo's heavy drinking, brought on, Uncle Cosimo told him, because of a Chinese girl he called the Fair Maid of Wu, whom he had seen three times and never spoken to. Anselo disappeared for six years, and when he came back he brought the Chinese girl as a present to Uncle Cosimo. Having lost his heart in those hard years, he would not wait to see Uncle Cosimo, but continued his wanderings. Uncle Cosimo was happy, his pocket bulging with his big flask, when he went to see what Anselo had brought. After one look his head cleared and he turned on his heel and left the country. From that day he worked to reclaim drunks in the slums of London and became so straight-laced that he was made Bishop of Borneo.

Further Critical Evaluation of the Work:

In the preface to one of his works, Donn Byrne made the rather immodest claim that he was the last of the great Irish storytellers. Certainly the statement was an exaggeration, but it nevertheless accurately identified the author's two main appeals: his gift for engaging the reader's imagination through romantic and effectively-told tales; and his ability to capture in his prose the spirit of the Irish people and the beauty of the land where he grew up. All of Byrne's fiction, whether novels or short stories, reflects these two concerns, and reveals the author's preoccupation with Irish themes and love of his childhood home.

Destiny Bay was the first of a series of Byrne's works which were published posthumously. In form it is a collection of nine short stories which are unified by their common narrator, Kerry Macfarlane, who will inherit his uncle's estate in Destiny Bay. The point of view of Kerry—a thinly-disguised version of the author as a young man—gives consistency to the tales, as does Byrne's use of the same cast of characters throughout the book, with a different character coming into prominence in each new story. The characterizations in *Destiny Bay* are not deep, but they are colorful and memorable in their lovable eccentricities. Leading the cast is the protective, patriarchal figure of Uncle Valentine, with his red beard so huge that it covers his chest like a breastplate, and his blind sister Jenepher, who whistles bird calls and "sees," with her wisdom and kindliness, much more clearly than anyone around her. The minor characters are equally romantic and eccentric: Uncle Cosimo, driven to alcohol over love of a Chinese girl he has seen but never met; his faithful gipsy friend Anselo, who travels six years to find Cosimo a replacement for the "Fair Maid of Wu"; James Carabine the prizefighter, who is taken in by a scheming New York singer and left heartbroken; the Spanish duke's shy and elusive "grandson," who turns out to be Ann-Dolly; and her eventual husband, the courtly and sensitive dreamer Jenico.

The incidents which form the plots of Byrne's stories are as romantically improbable as his characters. Stories such as that of Ann-Dolly's disguise as Don Anthony, Cosimo's deliverance from drink and subsequent missionary work in London, and Uncle Valentine's twelve-year correspondence with Aunt Jenepher under the name of her dead lover Digory, abound in *Destiny*

Bay. But what ties such scattered events as these together is the ever-present Irish background. The nostalgic mood and vivid setting is established early in the first tale, and remains, as tangible a presence almost as the characters themselves, throughout the book. Although Destiny Bay is not on any map of Ireland, Byrne's stories make it a real place, with its thirty square miles of territory on the North Sea, unvisited by any trade save that of the gipsies; with its sometimes gentle, sometimes ruthless coast, and its brown bogland studded with flowers and inhabited only by snipes and moor hens; with its tall mountains purple with heather and its tiny, ten-house village of Ballyfale.

When Donn Byrne died in 1928 in an automobile accident, he was only thirty-nine years old. When one reads his lyrical descriptions, rich with Gaelic imagery and vivid scenes of natural beauty, one feels that if his talent falls far short of excellence, he nevertheless died with a great deal of his potential yet unrealized.

THE DEVIL'S ELIXIR

Type of work: Novel
Author: Ernst Theodor Amadeus Hoffmann (1776-1822)
Type of plot: Psychological fantasy
Time of plot: Eighteenth century
Locale: Germany and Italy
First published: 1815-1816

> *Principal characters:*
> MEDARDUS, a monk
> AURELIA, a young noblewoman
> FRANCESCO, a painter
> PRINCE VON ROSENTHURM
> COUNT VICTORIN, Medardus' brother
> LEONARDUS, a prior
> AN ABBESS
> PIETRO BELCAMPO, a hairdresser

Critique:

E.T.A. Hoffmann was a writer, musician, and artist whose stories will be remembered for their presentation of the bizarre as an ironic facet of the natural. Hoffmann took evident pleasure in creating odd situations and weaving out of them a confusing and fantastic web of associations, intimations, and recapitulations, all made grotesque, of what had gone before. For example, Medardus is an insane priest who finds himself in a devilish hall of distorted mirrors. As soon as a reasonable pattern begins to emerge from the course of events, a new mystery rises to destroy it. The story deals with an innocent who has sinned and who is then confronted by all the devices of the powers of darkness.

The Story:

Francis was born at the Convent of the Holy Lime-Tree in Prussia, at the very moment that his father lay dying. At Kreuzberg, the abbess of the Cistercian convent made him her pupil. When he was sixteen he became a monk at the Capuchin convent in Königswald and took the name of Medardus.

Medardus was put in charge of the relics of the convent. Among them was a strange elixir. Legend said that all who drank of the potion would belong to the devil, and that if two persons drank of it, they would share the same thoughts and desires but secretly wish to destroy each other.

On St. Anthony's Day Medardus preached a sermon about the elixir. While he was talking he saw in the audience a painter whom he had once seen at the Convent of the Holy Lime-Tree. The sight disturbed him so much that he began to rave like a madman. Later, in an attempt to regain his full senses, he drank some of the elixir.

One day, during the confessional a beautiful woman, in appearance exactly like a painting of St. Rosalia, told Medardus that she loved him, and then left. Medardus determined to run away to find her. Before he could escape from the convent, however, Prior Leonardus sent him on an errand to Rome.

On the way to Rome Medardus saw an officer leaning over a precipice. When Medardus tried to save him, the officer fell over the ledge. Just then a page appeared and told Medardus that his disguise was very good. Medardus, hardly knowing what he did, went to the nearby castle, where he met an old man, Reinhold, who seemed to be expecting him. Reinhold told him that Baron von F——, the owner of the castle, had a son, Hermogen, and a daughter, Aurelia, by an Italian wife who later died. The baron had then married Euphemia, a sinister woman who was carrying on an affair with Count Victorin, an ex-suitor. The count was in the habit of disguising himself in order to gain entrance to the castle.

Medardus became convinced that he was Victorin. When he saw that Aurelia was the mysterious lady who looked like St. Rosalia, he felt that fate was guiding him. He tried to approach Aurelia, but she ran away. Because Hermogen had witnessed the incident, Medardus killed him. As Medardus fled from the castle, he heard that Euphemia was dying of a poison she had intended for him. Taking refuge in the woods, Medardus cut off his beard and changed into clothes that Victorin's page had brought him.

When Medardus arrived in Frankenburg, he recognized the painter who had disturbed his sermon on St. Anthony's Day. After he had tried to kill the man with a stiletto, Medardus was rescued from an angry mob by Pietro Belcampo, an odd hairdresser.

At the forest house of the Prince von Rosenthal, Medardus met a monk who looked like him and who drank some of his elixir. Medardus later went to the castle, where the court physician showed him a picture of a person who again looked just like him. The man was Francesco, who, together with a strange painter, had been brought to the court by the prince's brother, the Duke of Neuenburg. The duke had become engaged to an Italian countess and married her, but on their wedding night the duke had been found murdered by a stiletto wound. The bride claimed, however, that the groom had come to the bridal chamber without a light, consummated the marriage, and left. The painter, accused of the murder, escaped, and the countess went to live in a distant castle.

Francesco was engaged to the sister of the princess. During the marriage ceremony the painter reappeared. Francesco, trying to kill the painter with a stiletto, fainted. The next day he left, still unwed. It was later learned that the Italian countess had given birth to a son named Victorin. Francesco's intended bride left

to become the abbess at Kreuzberg.

Hearing these tales, Medardus realized that Francesco must be his father. At a party that night Medardus was astonished to see that the princess was accompanied by Aurelia. When Aurelia recognized him, he was charged with the murder of Hermogen and imprisoned. Later he was released because his double, a mad monk who greatly resembled him, had confessed to the crime. Medardus also learned that he and Victorin were stepbrothers.

Medardus became engaged to Aurelia. On the day that he was to marry her he saw the mad monk being taken to the scaffold. Suddenly Medardus began to rave. In his frenzy he stabbed Aurelia, rescued the monk from the cart, and escaped into the woods. When he regained consciousness he found himself, dressed as a monk, in an Italian madhouse. He had been taken there by Belcampo, the hairdresser, who said that he had found Medardus in the woods, naked, with a monk's robe lying beside him.

Medardus went next to a Capuchin convent near Rome. While there, he learned that Aurelia was alive. He also saw a strange book that a mysterious painter left at the convent. It contained sketches of paintings Medardus had seen at the Convent of the Holy Lime-Tree and the history of the artist. He was Francesco, a painter who had drunk of St. Anthony's elixir.

Among his works, according to the account, was a painting of the martyrdom of St. Rosalia. One day he had met a woman who looked just like the painting. They married, but his wife died soon after their son was born. Then Francesco, accused of sorcery, fled with his child, whom he nourished on the elixir. From Francesco's son the family branched out and included the Princess von Rosenthurm, the abbess, the first Baroness von F——, Euphemia, and Victorin.

Medardus, now repenting his past, punished himself so much that he became known to the Pope, who spoke of making the monk his confessor. Having incurred the antagonism of the papal confessor in this manner, Medardus, realizing that his life was in danger, left Rome.

He returned to the Cistercian monastery and saw Prior Leonardus, who said that Victorin had come there, claimed to be Medardus, and then disappeared. By piecing together the strange sequences of events, Medardus and Leonardus realized that Medardus and Victorin, two brothers who had drunk of the elixir, had tried to destroy each other.

Leonardus also told Medardus that Aurelia was to become a nun that day, taking the conventual name of Rosalia. This news so disturbed Medardus that while Aurelia was taking her vows he had an impulse to stab her, but after an inward struggle he conquered his demon and had peace in his soul. Suddenly there was a disturbance in the church. Medardus' double, dressed in rags, ran to the altar, shouted that Aurelia was his intended bride, stabbed her in the heart, and escaped. Medardus rushed to Aurelia's side. Close by he saw the mysterious painter, who said that Medardus' trials would soon end. Aurelia regained consciousness, told Medardus that he and she were destined to expiate the guilt of their family, and then died. The people in the church, having seen the painter emerge from a picture over the altar, believed that a miracle had occurred; they regarded Aurelia, now called Rosalia, as a saint.

Medardus, having fully recovered, could clearly tell truth from falsehood, and from Leonardus and the abbess he received forgiveness for his past deeds. Leonardus then asked him to commit his life story to writing. Having completed this task, he was awaiting the time when he would join Aurelia in Heaven.

Father Spiridion, the librarian of the Capuchin monastery at Königswald, appended a note to Medardus' manuscript. He wrote that one night, hearing strange sounds from Medardus' cell, he investigated and saw a tall man who said that the hour of fulfillment would come soon. Then Medardus died, one year to the minute from the time of Aurelia's death. Father Spiridion added that the painting of St. Rosalia, which the monastery had acquired, bore, on the day of Medardus' funeral, a wreath of roses. The wreath had been put there by Pietro Belcampo, who later joined the order and became Brother Peter.

Further Critical Evaluation of the Work:

From a plot summary, this novel seems like the purest madness, barely comprehensible, a series of nightmarish adventures woven into an incredible framework of family relationships. While it is true that Hoffmann's talent leaned more to the short story form, this work, his only completed novel, does reveal beneath all the fantastic elements, a coherent structure and a conscious plan. There is a polarity between the convent world, where the novel begins and ends, and the world of sin and chaos, represented in the central section of the work. The life of Medardus follows the traditional pattern of a redemption myth. One is reminded inevitably of Parzival, or of a saint's life. The elixir, in fact, is a relic of Saint Anthony, given to him as a temptation, which he resisted. Medardus, lacking the strength of that hero of asceticism, succumbs, falls from grace, and sinks into crime, sin, and guilt. This life of crime is also one of madness, from which he is released only as he comes to expiation and reconciliation with the world of faith. Many of the trappings of the fantastic adventures are simply borrowed from popular literary tastes of the day: the family curse, the hidden relationships, fatal dangers, and the like. But Hoffmann himself had a deep fascination with the dark side of the human psyche. He was acquainted with the director of an insane asylum, and he feared at times for his own sanity. The device of the *Doppelganger,* or Double, expresses this potential for madness hidden within every sane man. This madness seems rampant in the world of chaos Hoffmann depicts; here as in several works, the convent appears as a symbol for the refuge which he could never obtain, a world ordered by Christian faith, where the Divine still intervenes in human life.

THE DEVOTION OF THE CROSS

Type of work: Drama
Author: Pedro Calderón de la Barca (1600-1681)
Type of plot: Religious tragedy
Time of plot: Seventeenth century
Locale: Siena, Italy
First presented: c. 1633

Principal characters:
EUSEBIO, a foundling
JULIA, his sister
LISARDO, his brother
CURCIO, their father
GIL, a peasant
MENGA, a peasant woman
ALBERTO, a priest

Critique:

To understand a religious play like *The Devotion of the Cross,* one must always keep in mind that Spain was, and still is, a deeply religious nation, and that Calderón most truly expressed its feelings and ideas in the seventeenth century. The most popular of Spanish playwrights after the death of Lope de Vega in 1635, he wrote both secular and religious dramas until he took holy orders in 1651. From that time until his death he wrote only religious plays, including two Corpus Christi plays a year. *The Devotion of the Cross* is one of his early works. Since the characters and the setting are Italian, some critics assign it to the period when he was a soldier in Italy. Another version called *The Cross in the Sepulchre* has been found in a rare "suelta," or play printed separately, undated but signed "Ivan de Alarcón." Its discoverer believes that Calderón used it as a basis for his improved version. Valbuena Prat, on the other hand, wonders whether it may be a later version of Calderón's play, done by a less skilled dramatist. Another version of it, assigned—as was practically every other unclaimed play during the Golden Age—to Lope de Vega, can be found in a collection dated 1634. All that is definite is that Calderón claimed it under its present title in his *Primera Parte* of 1636. The plot is less complicated than is usual in Calderón's work.

The Story:

Two rustics, Gil and Menga, were looking for a lost donkey when they spied two men preparing to fight a duel. One was Lisardo, angry that anyone as low-born as Eusebio should aspire to marry his sister Julia.

Eusebio explained by telling a miraculous story. He had been one of two infants abandoned beneath a wayside cross. Taken home by a shepherd, the famished baby bit the breast of his foster mother, who threw the child into a well where his rescuers found him floating safely with arms crossed. Later the house in which he was living burned, but the fire broke out on the Day of the Cross, and once more he survived unharmed. More recently, in a shipwreck, he had floated to safety on a raft of two crossed planks. He explained that since he had obviously acquired nobility by devotion to the cross, he deserved the girl. Lisardo denied the claim and they fought. Again nothing could harm Eusebio. As Lisardo lay dying of his wound, he begged in the name of the cross for Eusebio to save him. The amazed peasants reported that they had seen Eusebio pick up his dying enemy and carry him to a convent.

Back in Siena, Julia was fearful of her father's discovery of letters she had received from Eusebio. When her lover appeared, wanting to take her away with him before she learned about her brother's death, her father's arrival forced him

1471

to hide and listen to Curcio as he voiced his long-held suspicions of his wife's infidelity. Curcio was interrupted by the arrival of four peasants carrying the body of Lisardo. Julia, grieving, ordered the killer out of her life forever.

Eusebio, broken-hearted, turned bandit and through his cruelty rose to command a troop of outlaws. Only captives mentioning the cross escaped death at his hands. One day a bullet-creased prisoner was brought in carrying a volume titled *Miracles of the Cross*. He was Father Alberto, and in gratitude for having his life spared the priest promised Eusebio that he would be on hand to hear the bandit's last confession.

News arrived that Lisardo's father, having put Julia into a convent, was pursuing Eusebio with soldiers. Scorning danger, Eusebio let his passion for Julia take him to the convent, where he found the girl in bed. Before he could take her, he saw on her breast the same sign

of the cross that was on his own skin. The mark told him that she had been the other child left beside the cross, his sister, and so he ran away. Julia, who had tried to fight him off in her cell, now pursued him in masculine attire; she did not know why he refused to love her.

When the soldiers overtook him, Curcio wounded Eusebio fatally. Then the cross on the young man's body revealed to Curcio that he had slain his own son, exposed with his twin sister because of the father's baseless suspicions of his wife's unfaithfulness.

With his dying breath, Eusebio called for Father Alberto. Four shepherds arrived to bury his body. The priest also appeared as he had promised. He explained that because of God's pleasure in Eusebio's devotion to the cross, his soul had been left in his body long enough for him to make his confession and be redeemed.

Further Critical Evaluation of the Work:

For Calderón's contemporaries, *The Devotion of the Cross* was little more than a religious thriller, a lesson in heavenly clemency steeped in blood and spiced with incest. Some modern readers, however, have been annoyed by the play's apparent hypocrisy, its religious propaganda, and its perverse morality, a code that pardons the devout, but is unsympathetic to the criminal. But only when the play is read allegorically does it become intelligible despite its strange morality.

To the allegorical, the world is a permanent battleground for the conflict between body and soul. Calderón's *The Devotion of the Cross* presents just such a struggle. The soul (Eusebio) and the body (Julia) seek to be reunited but are frustrated. Yet Calderón's allegory goes deeper. Through Eusebio, its chief character, the play represents the figurative fall and redemption of mankind. Eusebio gradually becomes transformed from the human agent of his crimes into a symbolic force voicing the redemptive hope of all mankind. In this manner, he defeats the exactions of earthly penalties, and also overcomes the harsh, tyrannical laws of honor represented by Curcio, the father who survives his wife and all his children.

As a figure for the fallen Adam, Eusebio is redeemed by the Cross ("tree divine") which bears him heavenward, thus fulfilling his "secret cause."

Julia, Eusebio's twin, may be said to be Eve and shares a common destiny with Eusebio, part of which is to be restored through grace by the cross, the tree of eternal life. The concept of incest in this play represents original sin and frustrates the reunion of body and soul in the figures of Eusebio and Julia.

Calderón, whose favorite theme of honor is eclipsed in the play by the incest situation, is not as comfortable in these surroundings as he is within the confines of the themes of his other plays. There is a blurring of dramatic action and an impression of structural imbalance which weakens the drama. Yet these weaknesses are somewhat overcome by the play's resonant tone of outrage and the depths of implication at its center.

LE DIABLE BOITEAUX

Type of work: Novel
Author: Alain René Le Sage (1668-1747)
Type of plot: Picaresque romance
Time of plot: Early eighteenth century
Locale: Madrid
First published: 1707

Principal characters:
DON CLEOPHAS LEANDRO PEREZ ZAMBULLO, a student
ASMODEUS, the demon in the bottle
DON PEDRO DE ESCOLANO, a Spanish nobleman
DONNA SERAPHINA, his daughter

Critique:

Le Sage is chiefly remembered today for his long picaresque novel, *Gil Blas* (1715-1735), but his early publication of *Le Diable boiteux (Asmodeus; or, The Devil on Two Sticks)*, with its extensive revision and enlargement in 1725, created far more excitement in his own day and is still an interesting example of the early realistic novel of manners. As he did in most of his prose fiction, Le Sage worked from a Spanish original in this work, borrowing his title and some of the early incidents from *El Diablo Cojuelo* (1641), by Luis Vélez de Guevara. Once started, however, Le Sage drew further and further away from his Spanish beginnings and thereby entertained his contemporaries by introducing a wealth of anecdotes and reminiscences, portraits and sketches of some of the most prominent of Parisian personages, under the guise of Spanish names. His satire is trenchant and ironical, though never gross or vulgar. Le Sage saw humanity with a sharp and critical eye, and he was particularly successful in his witty portrayals of authors, actors, lawyers, the social world, and "persons of quality." Like most picaresque fiction, the novel is loosely plotted; within a central narrative concerning the fortunes of Don Cleophas, a young Spanish cavalier, Le Sage introduced scores of other tales, ranging from brief summaries of a few sentences to short stories running for several pages or chapters. But the major plot remains in evidence throughout the book, and the author concludes his tale with a suitably romantic ending.

The Story:

On a dark October night in Madrid, Don Cleophas Leandro Perez Zambullo, a student of Alcala, was in dreadful trouble. While visiting Donna Thomasa, his inamorata, in her apartment, three or four hired bravos set upon him, and when he lost his sword in the ensuing struggle, he was forced to take flight over the rooftops of the neighboring houses. Spying a light in a garret, he entered through a window and discovered an empty room furnished with all manner of a magician's strange gear. As he was taking stock of the place, he heard a sigh. Soon he realized that he was being addressed by a demon in a bottle. To the student's questionings the spirit replied that he was neither Lucifer, Uriel, Beelzebub, Leviathan, Belphegor, nor Ashtaroth, but Asmodeus, the Devil on Two Sticks, who always befriended hapless lovers.

Welcoming the help of this creature, Cleophas broke the vial, and out tumbled a monstrous dwarf, with the legs of a goat, a stature of less than three feet, and a grotesque and grimacing face. Half concealed by extraordinary clothing and a curiously embroidered white satin cloak were the two crutches on which the dwarf hobbled about.

Since Cleophas was eager to escape his pursuers and Asmodeus wished to avoid his captor, the magician, the two did not linger in the attic. Cleophas grasped the edge of the demon's cloak, and off they flew into the sky over Madrid. For the remainder of their association together, Asmodeus entertained his companion with views of all that was happening in the city, explaining the circumstances and characteristics of those into whose houses they looked.

At first they peered into the houses immediately beneath them. Asmodeus showed Cleophas some ridiculous views of a coquette and her artifices, a nobleman, a poet, and an alchemist. At last they came to a mansion where cavaliers and their ladies were celebrating a wedding. The demon proceeded to tell the story of the Count de Belflor and Leonora de Cespedes.

The Count de Belflor, a gallant of the court, fell in love with Leonora de Cespedes and wished to make her his mistress. By guile, the gift of a well-filled purse, and the promise of another thousand pistoles when he had accomplished his design, he secured the aid of her duenna, Marcella, who at last prevailed on the girl to admit the young nobleman to her chamber at night. One morning, as the count was making a hasty departure, for the dawn was breaking, he slipped and fell while descending the silken ladder lowered from Leonora's bedchamber, and the noise awakened Don Luis de Cespedes, her father, who slept in the room above. Uncovering the truth and affronted by this stain upon his family honor, the old don confronted his daughter's lover. The count offered to provide for Don Pedro, the son of the insulted father, but refused to marry the daughter, giving as his false excuse a marriage which the king had already arranged for the young courtier.

Later, after reading a reproachful letter written by Leonora, the count was moved to repentance. About the same time Don Pedro played truant from his studies at Alcala to pay court to an unknown young beauty whom he was meeting in secret. In a street brawl his life was saved by the count, who happened to be passing by. The count asked the young man to go with him to act as a watchman and guard while Belflor had an interview with Leonora. The truth being revealed when Don Luis confronted his son, the count asked for the hand of Leonora and bestowed that of his sister, Donna Eugenia, on his new friend and brother. Don Pedro was overjoyed when he in turn discovered that his secret love was the sister of the Count de Belflor. The two couples were married, and Cleophas, guided by the demon, witnessed the festivities of their double wedding. Only Marcella, the treacherous duenna, had no part in the mirth; Don Luis sent her to a nunnery where she could spend her ill-gotten pistoles and prayers to win pardon for her wickedness.

Directing Cleophas' attention to other homes in the city, Asmodeus showed him the plight of an impoverished marquis, a plagiarizing author, a procurer of young men for rich widows, and a printer of anti-religious books. At Cleophas' request, the dwarf secured revenge for his mortal companion on the faithless Donna Thomasa. As she was entertaining the assassins she had hired to attack Cleophas, Asmodeus put the men into a jealous rage over her and set them to fighting. So great was the disturbance they caused that neighbors summoned the police, who on their arrival found two of the men slain. The assassins were thrown into the city dungeon and Donna Thomasa was eventually sentenced to be transported to the colonies. Thus proud Cleophas had his revenge.

Next, Asmodeus revealed the circumstances of the wretches in the nearby prison and madhouse. Poisoners, assassins, servants falsely accused and servants deserving imprisonment, a dishonest surgeon, and others were all displayed in their cells. At the madhouse, Cleophas saw political and religious fanatics, as well as those maddened by jealousy, grief, and the ingratitude of their relatives. Asmodeus also took the opportunity of showing Cleophas other people who should have been confined in an insane asylum, for their brains were addled by avarice, egotism, and the uncontrollable pangs of love.

Suddenly from their vantage point above the city, the two glimpsed a raging fire in a house beneath them. To everyone's horror, the beautiful Donna Seraphina, daughter of Don Pedro de Escolano, was trapped in an upstairs room. Asmodeus, at the entreaties of Cleophas, assumed the shape and appearance of the young student and brought the girl out of the burning building safely. After the rescue Asmodeus told Cleophas that he had suddenly decided upon a grand design: the young man was ultimately to marry the lovely Donna Seraphina, whose noble father already believed himself deeply indebted to the handsome young cavalier.

Asmodeus continued this strange tour of Madrid with portrayals of the unrevealed secrets of those buried in the tombs of a churchyard and with glimpses of bedside death scenes of true grief, avarice, jealousy, and self-seeking. For contrast, he then told Cleophas a long and circumstantial tale of true friendship and love.

Having slain his false wife's lover, Don Juan de Zarata, a gallant of Toledo, fled to Valencia. Near the outskirts of that city he stopped a duel between Don Alvaro Ponzo and Don Fabricio de Mendoza, rivals for the hand of the beautiful young widow, Donna Theodora de Cifuentes. On the advice of Don Juan, the lady was allowed to choose between her suitors; her choice was Don Fabricio. Through that meeting the young Toledan and Don Fabricio became inseparable companions. The latter, however, could not understand his friend's seeming indifference to the charms of Donna Theodora. What he did not suspect was that the Toledan had been greatly attracted to the lady and she to him, but that out of regard for friendship Don Juan made every effort to repress his passion. Unhappy in her own unrealized love for Don Juan, the lady finally decided to return to her estate at Villareal. When the Toledan confessed the truth to Don Fabricio, that gentleman was so moved by Don Juan's delicacy of feeling that he vowed no rivalry in love could ever part them.

Meanwhile, Donna Theodora had been kidnapped by Don Alvaro's ruffians and put on a vessel bound for Sardinia. Don Fabricio and Don Juan set out in pursuit, but the ship on which they sailed was overtaken by Tunisian pirates and the two were made prisoners. Separated in their captivity, they were in despair. Don Juan, sold to the Dey of Algiers, was made a gardener. At length the dey, impressed by the bearing and courtesy of his Christian slave, made him his confidant. The dey had in his harem a Spanish lady whose grief appeared inconsolable; he asked Don Juan to speak to her as a countryman and assure her of her master's tender regard. To Don Juan's surprise, the lady proved to be Donna Theodora, also taken captive when her abductors were killed by Algerian pirates.

From that time on Don Juan planned to deliver Donna Theodora from her captivity, and at last, aided by an unknown accomplice, they made their escape. Their unknown benefactor turned out to be Don Fabricio, who had been rescued aboard a French privateer. Mistaking Don Juan for the false Don Alvaro, Don Fabricio stabbed his friend and then, discovering his error, plunged his sword into his own breast. The condition of Don Fabricio grew worse and he died soon after the arrival of the fugitives in Spain. Torn between their mutual love and grief for their friend, Donna Theodora and Don Juan were at last free to marry. A short time later Don Juan was mortally injured in a fall from his horse. Half mad with grief, Donna Theodora would soon follow him to the grave.

At length the sleeping city awoke. Protesting that he was not weary, Cleophas urged the little demon to let him see more. Asmodeus directed his glance to the activities in the streets of beggars, artisans, a miser, a philosopher. Then they came upon the throngs of people gathering for the king's levee: faithless and forgetful noblemen, those seeking their own good fortune, gamblers, an honest magistrate, and others awaited their turn to appear before the king. But Cleophas could not be shown into the king's presence, since the royal cabinet, as Asmodeus carefully explained, was under the exclusive control of other devils.

For diversion, Asmodeus took Cleophas to see the arrival of ransomed slaves at the Monastery of Mercy. Each captive had his own fears and hopes to realize, and Asmodeus recounted the past and future of scores of these wretches. A few met with happy circumstances upon gaining their freedom, but most of them found grief, loneliness, and disappointment for their reward.

At that point Asmodeus became aware that his master, the magician, had missed him, and he departed swiftly after making the student promise that he would never reveal to mortal ears all that he had seen and overheard that night.

Returned to his own apartment, Cleophas sank into a deep slumber that lasted a day and a night. When he awoke, he went to call on Donna Seraphina, where he was welcomed by the grateful Don Pedro, her father. During a later visit in the house where he was now an honored guest, Cleophas confessed that it was not he who had rescued the girl from the flames. Although overcome by astonishment, Don Pedro waved the explanation aside. After all, it was at Cleophas' insistence that Donna Seraphina had been brought from the blazing house unharmed. A few weeks later the wedding of Donna Seraphina and Cleophas was celebrated with much magnificence, and the happy bridegroom never had occasion to regret the night of freedom he had provided for the devil on two sticks.

Further Critical Evaluation of the Work:

Although a satire on human nature, *Le Diable boiteux* is an amiable, almost light-hearted work; the author attacks his victims with wit and grace, his high spirits and good humor balancing the grotesqueness inherent in the story. Asmodeus, the lame devil, helps Don Cleophas to see through the false fronts, both physical and moral, assumed by most people. The devil and his young rescuer thereby provide a framework for the stories that compose most of the narrative; Asmodeus shows Don Cleophas a man or woman and then exposes the person, telling his or her story with merciless truth. If there is any consistent message in *Le Diable boiteux,* it is always to doubt first impressions and to seek to penetrate beneath the façades that individuals hold up to the world.

Asmodeus is a unique character, a grotesque vision comparable to Caliban or Milton's fallen angels. Without possessing the dark powers of the greater demons, he presides over the vices and follies of mankind, rather than the crimes. He is malicious, but not cruel, and likes to tease and ridicule humanity, rather than to torture it. He possesses so much wit and playful malice and is so vividly portrayed that he almost walks away with the book, making the reader forget that he is not intended to be anything more than a momentarily friendly fiend.

Don Cleophas, the fiery young Spaniard, is the perfect foil for Asmodeus. He is lacking enough in discretion to be glad of the opportunity to peek behind closed doors and barred windows and discover the shocking truths about apparently respectable people. The other characters, who come and go in the secondary tales, are described with precision and amazing dexterity;

few authors can summarize human nature, in its many shades and phases, in so few words. Le Sage's satire is never heavy-handed and his humor is never blunted by anticipation. In many respects, *Le Diable boiteux* is surer of touch and wittier than the author's more famous *Gil Blas;* certainly, the skill of the drawing of the scenes and the richness of the characterizations are reason enough for the book to be at least as well known. And, at times, the author reaches heights in this book that he never does in *Gil Blas,* such as in his personification of Death. Even here, his humor breaks through to add still another dimension to his vision, when, having described one of the terrific phantom's wings painted with war, pestilence, famine, and shipwreck, he adorns the other with the picture of young physicians taking their degrees. The narratives that make up the book are of differing lengths and of varying interest, but all of them are entertaining and executed with wit and style.

DIALOGUE DES HEROS DE ROMAN

Type of work: Literary criticism in the form of satiric dialogue
Author: Nicolas Boileau-Despréaux (1636-1711)
First published: 1713

Principal characters:
MINOS,
PLUTO,
RHADAMANTHUS,
DIOGENES, and
MERCURY, judges of the heroes
CYRUS,
TAMYRIS,
HORATIUS COCLES,
CLÉLIE,
BRUTUS,
SAPHO, and
FARAMOND, heroes and heroines of French romances

The French literary scene of the late seventeenth and early eighteenth centuries was blessed with the corrective vigorous activity of two writers endowed with unsurpassed wit and common sense—Molière and Boileau. It was an age that desperately needed the scourge of satire. Life and letters were thoroughly corrupt; the topmost level of society rode like a gaudy, grinning monkey on the back of the miserable, millipedic populace, and the amusements of the idle betrayed clearly their innocent or deliberate unawareness of reality and the bizarre lengths to which they were willing to go in their futile attempt to conquer an enormous boredom.

One of their most fantastic solitary diversions was the writing and reading of romantic novels that often ran to a dozen or more volumes. Beginning with Honoré d'Urfé's *Astrée* (1607-1627), this papier-mâché fantasy went through a tortuous evolution in de Gomberville's *La Carithée* (1621) and *Polexandre* (1629-1637), Jean Desmarets' *Ariane* (1623), La Calprenède's *Cassandre* (1642-1650), *Cléopâtre* (1647-1658), and *Faramond* (1661-1670), and, finally, reached an apogee in the four romances of Mademoiselle Madeleine de Scudéry, darling of the famous Hôtel de Rambouillet salon before establishing her own popular Saturday nights. These novels probably constitute the most valueless literature of all time. Mlle. de Scudéry insisted that the language of her characters (like that of the dramatists Racine and Corneille) reproduce exactly the language of society, a carefully cultivated, artificial speech striving for novelty and preciosity and inevitably tumbling into absurdity. It is precisely this affectation that Molière made such hilarious fun of in his farce, *Les Précieuses Ridicules* (1659), but apparently the institution was so well-established and so satisfying to its practitioners that not even the blows of the great Molière could strike it down. Boileau soon joined his friend in the attack, composing in 1664 his *Dialogue des héros de roman*, which he enjoyed reciting with great zest and elaborate mimicry to his friends. However, as he says in the preface to his first published version, he was unwilling to publish or even to circulate his satire in manuscript while Mlle. de Scudéry was still alive, "since she was after all a woman of considerable merit and honor even if her writing did not reflect those attributes." Even after her death, the satire would probably not have appeared in print with Boileau's blessing had not a pirated version been published anonymously in Prussia in 1687. Boileau's devoted young friend Brossette, who discovered and reported the piracy to him in 1704, urged him to add this to the nine satires which had already contributed to his fame. Although Madame de Lafayette had established a basis for a change to the modern novel of sentiment with *La Princesse de Clèves* in 1678, there was still a large target of fantasy-romance for Boileau's *Dialogue,* since romantic literary faddism had spread not only across France but in England as well. Addison recommended *Faramond* and *Cassandre* to the readers of the *Spectator Papers;* multi-volume translations found a fascinated public; imitations (such as Aphra Behn's *The Young King*) rolled off the presses, and stage adaptations like Dryden's *Almanzor and Almahide* (1670-1672) hastened the vogue of neo-classic tragedy.

It is impossible to present in a short space any satisfactory vision of the enormous tedium of the seventeenth-century French romances. Even Desmarets' *Ariane,* remarkable for its unusual brevity, runs to well over a thousand pages. Shepherds, guided by gods and goddesses, make fleshless love in stilted prose and verse; characters from Greek, Roman, and Celtic tradition roam across fairy wonderlands in pursuit of or in escape from monsters or powerful enemies in disguise. Elaborate allegorical dreams, involuted love letters, intensely polite conversations, portraits in enameled prose, and grandiose heraldry and tournaments pad out complex, disorganized plot lines that make Italian opera classically simple by comparison. Boileau declared himself unable to stomach "their precious affectation of language, frivolous and pointless conversations, flattering portraits at every turn, of obviously mediocre persons, endless verbiage about love leading nowhere." But the leading practitioner of that romantic nonsense, Mlle. de Scudéry, gained an astonishing international fame —gifts from the Queen of Sweden, membership in the Italian academy, homage from English writers, as well as pensions from Cardinal Mazarin and the King of France.

Witty and polished conversation in writing as well as in society was a favorite seventeenth-century art, witness Mlle. de Scudéry's own ten volumes of model *Conversations.* For this reason Boileau, like many another critic of his day, adopted the dialogue: "I have taken as a point of departure in this attack on the novel . . . the manner of Lucian" (the greatest of the second-century Sophists, who also used humor and buffoonery to attack manners and ideas of his time). Although Boileau says that this is "the least frivolous work to issue from my pen," the *Dialogue* is hilarious good fun. Like Lucian, he sets his scene in Hades. Minos comes running frantically to Pluto with a report that hell has suddenly become populated with idiots afflicted with a "fury to talk . . . a certain language they call gallantry":

"One even assured me that this pestilent gallantry had infected all the infernal countries and even the Elysian fields so that the heroes and, above all, the heroines who live there today are the most foolish people in the world, thanks to certain authors who have taught them that fine language and have made them bashful lovers."

As Pluto resolves to examine these strange people, Rhadamanthus arrives with the news that the fiercest criminals in Hades—Prometheus, Tantalus, Ixion, and Sisyphus—have revolted. While preparations are being made for war, Diogenes arrives to contribute his walking stick to the arsenal. He warns Pluto not to expect much help from the newly arrived heroes: "They are a troop of madmen . . . I've never seen anything so effeminate and gallant!" But Pluto, eager for heroic aid, summons them. He is delighted when the first hero turns out to be the great Cyrus, the Persian warrior-king who had conquered the Medes and ravaged more than half the world. But his delight quickly turns to dismay when he learns that Cyrus has adopted the [Scudérian] name of Artimin and is engaged in an eternal quest to find his kidnapped princess, though he fears that even if he finds her she will not return to him because he is so unworthy. "Chase away this rain-bucket, this great sobber!" cries Pluto as he turns to welcome Tamyris, savage queen of the Massagetes who had plunged the great Cyrus' head into a bucket of human blood. Tamyris, however, is now distraught because she has lost the madrigal which she had composed to woo Cyrus. Next comes Horatius Cocles, the Roman warrior who alone had held off an entire army at the bridge. He is now a shepherd troubadour singing a song he had made from an echo for Clélie. "The nut! the nut!" cries Pluto, dismissing him; "to amuse himself with such trifles he must have entirely lost his senses!"

The mad parade continues. Clélie, once the audacious hero of Titus Livius, is now completely absorbed with the map of Tendre-Land, tracing the path from Constant Love along Inclination River, through Billet Doux and Sincerity to New Amity. Lucretia, who once killed to defend her chastity, now babbles of love; and Brutus, savior of Rome against the Tarquins, also prattles of love. Diogenes tries unsuccessfully to explain to Pluto:

"Lucretia who is in love with and loved by Brutus says to him in transposed words: 'How sweet it would be to love, if one loved always! But alas, there are no eternal loves.' And Brutus answers: 'Permit me to love, marvel of our days. You will see that one can have eternal loves.' "

To which Pluto shouts, "By these bagatelles I recognize that they're possessed with infinite folly. Chase them away!" Then Mlle. de Scudéry herself arrives in the person of Sapho, once a famous Lesbian, now a poser of elaborate parlor-game questions on friendship: "Define for me what a tender heart is, what tenderness in friendship, tenderness in love, tenderness of inclination, and tenderness of passion." As indignant Pluto is about to send for the Fury Tisiphone, the "impertinent wench" subjects him to a ridiculous, flattering character sketch of that deadly harridan.

At last, after several more of these impossible heroes of the novel have passed in review, Mercury (one of the most frequently invoked gods of the romance) arrives to denounce them all as fakers. He has brought with him a Frenchman who identifies them as the common bourgeoisie of his quarter. Pluto wrathfully summons all the demons and furies of hell to skin alive these chimerical heroes. "The last act of the comedy is over!" he cries as the heroes call in vain upon the authors who created them.

Thus Boileau, whose epitaph rightly names him the "not unequal rival of Horace," redeemed the reputation of the French mind for common sense, clarity, and wit from one of the greatest threats in France's literary history.

THE DIALOGUES OF PLATO

Type of work: Philosophical dialogues
Author: Plato (427-347 B.C.)
Time: About 400 B.C.
Locale: Greece, principally Athens
First transcribed: c. 387-347 B.C.

Principal personages:
SOCRATES, the Athenian philosopher
GORGIAS, a Sophist
PROTAGORAS, a Sophist
CRITO, Socrates' contemporary, an aged friend
PHAEDRUS, a defender of rhetoric
ARISTOPHANES, a poet and playwright
THEAETETUS, hero of the battle of Corinth
PARMENIDES, the philosopher from Elea
PHILEBUS, a hedonist
TIMAEUS, a philosopher and statesman
PLATO, Socrates' pupil

The Platonic *Dialogues* rank with the extant works of Aristotle as the most important collection of philosophical works so far produced in the Western world. Although Plato's influence is partly due to the fact that his works have survived, unlike many writings of earlier Greek philosophers, and also to the fact that at various times in the history of the Christian church his ideas have been utilized in one form or another in the process of constructing a Christian theology—although Aristotle's influence in this respect has been greater—the principal cause of his past and present effect on human thought is the quality of his work.

The distinctive character of Platonic thought finds adequate expression in the dialogue form. Although Plato, like all philosophers, had his favored perspectives from which he interpreted and, consequently, saw the world, he realized better than most philosophers that philosophy is more an activity of the mind than the product of an investigation. This is not to say that philosophy does not, in some legitimate sense, illuminate the world; it means that in the process of making sense out of experience the philosopher is restless: no one way of clarifying an idea or a view is entirely satisfactory, and there is always much to be said for some alternative mode of ex-

planation. When distinctive Platonic conceptions finally become clear, they do so against a background of penetrating discussion by means of which alternative ideas are explored for their own values and made to complement the conception which Plato finally endorses. As an instrument for presenting the critical point counterpoint of ideas, the dialogue is ideal; and as a character in control of the general course and quality of the discussion, Socrates is unsurpassed.

Socrates was Plato's teacher, and it was probably out of respect for Socrates the man and philosopher that Plato first considered using him as the central disputant in his dialogues. Reflection must have enforced his decision, for Socrates was important more for his method than for his fixed ideas, more for his value as a philosophical irritant than as a source of enduring wisdom. The Socratic method is often described as a question-answer method designed to bring out the contradictions and omissions in the philosophical views of others; but it is better understood as a clever technique for so playing upon the ambiguities of claims as to lead others into changing their use of terms and, hence, into *apparent* inconsistency.

The question concerning the extent to which Plato uses the dialogues to record the ideas of Socrates and the extent to which he uses Socrates as a proponent of his own ideas will probably never be conclusively answered. The question is, of course, historical; philosophically speaking, it makes no difference whose ideas find their way into the dialogues. A fairly safe assumption is that Socrates emphasized the importance of philosophical problems of value, knowledge, and philosophy itself. He probably did argue that it is important to know oneself, that the admission of one's own ignorance is a kind of wisdom possessed by few men, and that virtue is knowledge.

Certainly Socrates must have had a devotion to his calling as philosopher and critic: no man who regarded philosophy as a game would have remained in Athens to face the charge that by philosophy he had corrupted the youth of Athens, nor would he have refused a chance to escape after having been condemned to death. The courage and integrity of Socrates are recorded with poignant power in the *Apology,* the dialogue in which Socrates defends himself and philosophy against the charges brought against him; the *Crito,* in which Socrates refuses to escape from prison; and the *Phaedo,* in which Socrates discusses the immortality of the soul before he drinks the hemlock poison and dies.

Of the ideas presented in the dialogues, perhaps none is more important than Plato's theory of Ideas or Forms. This idea is most clearly expressed in the *Republic* (q.v.), the dialogue in which the problem of discovering the nature of justice in man is resolved by considering the nature of justice in the state. Plato distinguished between particular things, the objects we experience in our daily living, and the characters that things have, or could have. Goodness, truth, beauty, and other universal characters—properties that can affect a number of individual objects—are eternal, changeless, beautiful, and the source of all knowledge. Although some critics have claimed that Plato was speaking metaphorically when he talked, through Socrates, about the reality of the Forms,

speaking as if they enjoyed a separate existence, the dialogues leave the impression that Plato considered the Forms (Ideas) to be actually existing, in some sense peculiar to themselves, as universals or prototypes which things may or may not exemplify.

If one reviews, however inadequately, the range of questions and tentative answers to be found in the dialogues, a bare inkling of Plato's power as a philosopher is then realized. But the dialogues must be read before the depth of Plato's speculative mind and the skill of his dialectic can be appreciated. Furthermore, only a reading of the dialogues can convey Plato's charm, wit, and range of sympathy. Whether the final result may be in good part attributed to Socrates as Plato's inspiring teacher is not important. Socrates as the subject and Plato as the writer (and philosopher—in all probability more creative than Socrates) combine to leave us with an unforgettable image of the Hellenistic mind.

Although many of the dialogues concern themselves with more than one question, and although definitive answers are infrequent so that discussions centering about a certain subject may crop up in a number of different dialogues, it may be helpful to indicate the central problems and conclusions of the dialogues:

Charmides centers about the question, "What is temperance?" After criticizing a number of answers, and without finally answering the question, Socrates emphasizes the point that temperance involves knowledge. *Lysis* and *Laches* consider, respectively, the questions, "What is friendship?" and "What is courage?" The former discussion brings out the difficulty of the question and of resolving conflicts of values: the latter distinguishes courage from a mere facing of danger and makes the point that courage, as one of the virtues, is a kind of knowledge involving willingness to act for the good. The *Ion* exhibits Socratic irony at work on a rhapsode who is proud of his skill in the recitation of poetry. Socrates argues that poetry is the result of inspiration, a kind of divine madness. In the *Protagoras* Socrates identifies virtue and knowledge, insisting that no one chooses evil except through ignorance. One of a number of attacks of the Sophistical art of fighting with words is contained in the *Euthydemus*.

In the *Meno* the philosopher Socrates and his companions wonder whether virtue can be taught. The doctrine that ideas are implanted in the soul before birth is demonstrated by leading a slave boy into making the correct answers to some problems in geometry. At first it seems that since virtue is a good and goodness is knowledge, virtue can be taught. But since there are no teachers of virtue, it cannot be taught; and, in any case, since virtue involves right opinion, it is not teachable.

"What is piety?" is the question of the *Euthyphro*. Euthyphro's idea that piety is whatever is pleasing to the gods is shown to be inadequate.

The *Apology* is the most effective portrait of Socrates in a practical situation. No moment in his life had graver consequences than the trial resulting from the charge that he had corrupted the youth of Athens by his teachings, yet Socrates continued to be himself, to argue dialectically, and to reaffirm his love of wisdom and virtue. He pictured himself as a gadfly, stinging the Athenians out of their intellectual arrogance. He argued that he would not corrupt anyone voluntarily, for to corrupt those about him would be to create evil that might harm him.

Socrates is shown as a respecter of the law in the *Crito;* he refuses to escape after having been pronounced guilty. In the *Phaedo* he argues that the philosopher seeks death because his whole aim in life is to separate the soul from the body. He argues for the immortality of the soul by saying that opposites are generated from opposites; therefore, life is generated from death. Also, the soul is by its very nature the principle of life; hence, it cannot itself die.

The dialogue *Greater Hippias* does not settle the question, "What is beauty?" but it does show, as Socrates points out, that "All that is beautiful is difficult."

The subject of love is considered from various philosophic perspectives in the *Symposium,* culminating in the conception of the highest love as the love of the good, the beautiful, and the true.

Gorgias begins with a discussion of the art of rhetoric, and proceeds to the development of the familiar Socratic ideas that it is better to suffer evil than to do it, and it is better to be punished for evil-doing than to escape punishment.

The *Parmenides* is a fascinating technical argument concerning various logical puzzles about the one and the many. It contains some criticism of Plato's theory of Ideas. Plato's increasing interest in problems of philosophic method is shown by the *Cratylus,* which contains a discussion of language beginning with the question whether there are true and false names. Socrates is not dogmatic about the implications of using names, but he does insist that any theory of language allow men to continue to speak of their knowledge of realities.

The *Phaedrus* is another discourse on love. It contains the famous myth of the soul conceived as a charioteer and winged steeds. In the *Theaetetus* Socrates examines the proposal by Theaetetus that knowledge is sense perception. He rejects this idea as well as the notion that knowledge is true opinion.

The *Sophist* is a careful study of sophistical method with emphasis on the problem of Being and Not-being. In the *Statesman* Plato continues the study of the state he initiated in the *Republic,* introducing the idea—later stressed by Aristotle—that virtue is a mean.

Socrates argues in the *Philebus* that neither pleasure nor wisdom is in itself the highest good, since pleasure that is not known is worthless and wisdom that is not pleasant is not worth having; only a combination is wholly satisfactory.

A rare excursion into physics and a philosophical consideration of the nature of the universe are found in the *Timaeus*. Here Plato writes of God, creation, the elements, the soul, gravitation, and many other matters.

The *Critias*, an unfinished dialogue, presents the story of an ancient and mythical war between Athens and Atlantis; and with the *Laws*, the longest of the dialogues, Plato ranges over most of the areas touched on in his other dialogues, but with an added religious content: Soul is the source of life, motion, and moral action; and there is an evil soul in the universe with which God must deal.

DIANA OF THE CROSSWAYS

Type of work: Novel
Author: George Meredith (1828-1909)
Type of plot: Psychological realism
Time of plot: Nineteenth century
Locale: England
First published: 1885

    Principal characters:
      DIANA MERION WARWICK, a woman of beauty and charm
      AUGUSTUS WARWICK, her husband
      LADY EMMA DUNSTANE, Diana's friend
      THOMAS REDWORTH, Diana's friend and admirer
      LORD DANNISBURGH, another friend
      SIR PERCY DACIER, a young politician in love with Diana

Critique:

Any novel by George Meredith requires attention not only to the book in question but also to the wider aspects of the technique of fiction, for Meredith, always an original, was a writer of deep concentration and mature force. His Diana is a character head and shoulders above most heroines in nineteenth-century English novels. She offers the charm of femininity, perplexed by convention and yet aware of its force. Her predicament is at once an error in judgment and a glory to her. Her career compels our belief that a life which will not let go its harvest of errors until they are thoroughly winnowed is a human drama of deepest interest, for that life extracts the wisdom experience can offer. Diana, beautiful, witty, skeptical of social convention and moral expediency, is the embodiment of Meredith's philosophy and art.

The Story:

All of fashionable London was amazed and shocked when Diana Warwick suddenly left her husband's house. Society should not have been surprised at her action, however; the marriage had been ill-fated from the start. For Augustus Warwick, a calculating, ambitious politician, his marriage to the beautiful and charming Diana Merion had been largely one of convenience. Diana, in her turn, accepted his proposal as a refuge from unwelcome attentions to which her own position as an orphan had exposed her.

Diana Merion had first appeared in society at a state ball in Dublin, where her unspoiled charm and beauty attracted many admirers. Lady Emma Dunstane introduced Diana to Thomas Redworth, a friend of her husband, Sir Lukin Dunstane, and Redworth's attentions so enraged Mr. Sullivan Smith, a hot-tempered Irishman, that he attempted to provoke the Englishman to a duel. Redworth pacified the Irishman, however, to avoid compromising Diana by a duel fought on her account.

Later, while visiting Lady Emma at Copsley, the Dunstane country home in England, Diana was forced to rebuff Sir Lukin when he attempted to make love to her. Leaving Copsley, she went to visit the Warwicks. Meanwhile, Thomas Redworth announced to Lady Emma that he loved Diana. His announcement came too late. Diana was already engaged to Augustus Warwick.

In London the Warwicks took a large house and entertained lavishly. Among their intimates was Lord Dannisburgh, an elderly peer who became Diana's friend and adviser. While Warwick was away on a government mission, the two were often seen together, and Diana was so indiscreet as to let Lord Dannisburgh accompany her when she went to visit Lady Emma. Gossip began to circulate. On his return Warwick, who was incapable of understanding his wife's innocence and charm, served Diana with a process in suit. Accusing her of infidelity, he named Lord Dannisburgh as corespondent. Diana disappeared from Warwick's house and from London. In a letter to Lady Emma she had said that she intended to leave England. Her friend, realizing that flight would be tantamount to confession, felt sure that Diana would go to Crossways, her father's old home, before she left the country. Determined that Diana should remain and boldly defend the suit, Lady Emma sent Redworth to Crossways with instructions to detain Diana and persuade her to go to stay with the Dunstanes at Copsley.

Lady Emma had guessed correctly; Diana was at Crossways with her maid. At first Diana was unwilling to see Lady Emma's point of view, for she thought of her flight as a disdainful stepping aside from Warwick's sordid accusations; but at last she gave in to Redworth's arguments and returned with him to Copsley.

Although the court returned a verdict of not guilty to the charge Warwick had brought against her, Diana felt that her honor had been ruined and that in the eyes of the world she was still guilty. For a time she was able to forget her own distress by nursing her friend, Lady Emma, who was seriously ill. Later she left England to go on a Mediterranean cruise. Before her departure she had written a book, *The Princess Egeria*.

In Egypt she met Redworth, now a brilliant member of Parliament. He was accompanied by Sir Percy Dacier, Lord Dannisburgh's nephew and a rising young politician. Falling in love with Diana, Sir Percy followed her to the continent. He was recalled to London by the illness of his uncle. Diana followed him a short time later, to learn on her arrival in London that Redworth had been active in making her book a literary triumph. He had stirred up interest among the critics because he knew that Diana was in need of money.

Lord Dannisburgh died, with Diana at his bedside during his last illness. He had been her friend, and she paid him

that last tribute of friendship and respect regardless of the storm of criticism it created. When Lord Dannisburgh's will was read, it was learned that he had left a sum of money to Diana.

In the meantime Diana had made an enemy of the socially ambitious Mrs. Wathin, who thought it her social duty to tear Diana's reputation to shreds. Part of her dislike was motivated by jealousy that Diana should be accepted by people who would not tolerate Mrs. Wathin. Some of her actions were inspired by Warwick, Mrs. Wathin's friend, who, having lost his suit against Diana, was trying to force his wife to return to him.

Sir Percy's attentions were also distressing to Diana. Half in love with him, she was not free to marry again. She faced a crisis in her affairs when Mrs. Wathin called to announce that Warwick, now ill, wanted Diana to return and to act as his nurse. Diana refused. Warwick then threatened to exercise his legal rights as her husband. Sir Percy, who informed her of Warwick's intention, asked her to elope with him to Paris. She agreed. She was saved from that folly by the appearance of Redworth, who arrived to tell her that Lady Emma was ill and about to undergo a serious operation at Copsley. Diana went with him to be at her friend's side.

Lady Emma nearly died, and the gravity of her condition restored Diana's own sense of responsibility. She ordered Sir Percy to forget her, but in spite of her protests he continued to follow her about. One day he confided a tremendous political secret to her—the prime minister was about to call upon Parliament to pass some revolutionary reform measures. Having told her his secret, he attempted to resume his former courtship. Diana refused to listen to his pleadings. After he had gone, she felt broken and cheated. If she would not have Sir Percy as a lover, she felt, she could not keep him as a friend. Diana was desperately in need of money. She had been forced to sell Crossways to pay her debts and her later novels had been failures. Feeling herself a complete adventuress, she went to the editor of a paper which opposed the government party and sold him the information Sir Percy had given her.

When the paper appeared with a full disclosure of the prime minister's plan, Sir Percy accused her of betraying him and broke with her. A short time later he proposed to a young lady of fortune. About the same time Warwick was struck down by a cab in the street and killed. Diana had her freedom at last, but she was downcast in spirit. She knew that she was in public disgrace. Although she had burned the check in payment for the information she had disclosed, it was common knowledge that she had betrayed Sir Percy and that he had retaliated by his marriage to Constance Asper, an heiress. When Sullivan Smith proposed for her hand, Diana refused him and sought refuge in the company of her old friend, Lady Emma. Her stay at Copsley freed her of her memories of Sir Percy, so much so that on her return to London she was able to greet him and his bride with dignity and charm. Her wit was as sharp as ever, and she took pleasure in revenging herself upon those who had attempted to destroy her reputation with their gossip and slander.

On another visit to Copsley she again encountered Redworth, now a railroad promoter and still a distinguished member of Parliament. When he invited her and Lady Emma to visit Crossways, Diana learned that it was Redworth who had bought her old home and furnished it with her own London possessions, which she had been forced to sell in order to pay her debts. He bluntly told Diana that he had bought the house and furnished it for her because he expected her to become his wife. Not wishing to involve him in the scandals which had circulated about her, she at first pretended indifference to his abrupt wooing. Lady Emma, on the other hand, urged her to marry Redworth, who had loved her for many years, so that he could protect her from social malice. At last, knowing that she brought no real disgrace to Redworth's name, she consented to become his wife.

Further Critical Evaluation of the Work:

Diana of the Crossways is the most emphatically "feminist" of Meredith's novels, but the woman too intelligent and spirited to accept willingly her "place," as defined by Victorian society, figures prominently in virtually all of his fiction. Some, such as Diana's friend Emma Dunstane or Lady Blandish of *The Ordeal of Richard Feverel,* manage to confine their protest to witty commentary while playing their assigned roles; others, like Diana, are forced by circumstances into active rebellion.

It is generally agreed that Meredith's chief model for his beautiful, brilliant, and hard-beset heroines was his own first wife. In the fine poem-sequence *Modern Love,* he traces in thin disguise the course of their marriage, from its happy and passionate beginnings, through the conflicts that led to his wife's running off with an artist, to her early death. Although bitter at first, Meredith learned much from the failure of his first love and came to accept major responsibility for it. His novels repeatedly depict a loving and loyal woman virtually driven into the arms of another man by the blind egotism of her husband or lover. Asked by Robert Louis Stevenson whether the protagonist of *The Egoist* was not a portrait of him, Meredith replied that his fatuous hero was drawn "from all of us but principally from myself."

Meredith saw his society as dominated by egotism, chiefly male, and both fearful and suspicious of the bright and beautiful because of the threat they posed to complacency. He shared the Victorian belief in progress, but he defined progress in terms of intelligence and sensibility. Choosing the comedy of wit as his preferred mode, he attacked the dull and smug, and called for "brain, more brain." He recognized the tragedy of life but ascribed it to human failure. As he wrote in *Modern Love,* "no villain need be. We are betrayed by what is false within." The falseness may spring from self-deception or from unquestioning acceptance of what "the world" proclaims. What can save us is the ability to be honest with ourselves and see the world as it is, and the courage to act on our perceptions even in defiance of social norms.

Many of Meredith's contemporaries shared his belief in a continuing evolution of man's spiritual and intellectual capacities, but few besides Browning were as ardent in affirming also "the value and significance of flesh." For Meredith, the goal of life was to realize one's full potentialities in a vital balance: "The spirit must brand the flesh that it may live."

Meredith's Diana fully exemplifies his philosophy of life. The central metaphor of the novel is the "dog-world" in hot pursuit of its quarry, a beautiful woman too intelligent and sensitive to play the roles society demands of her, either "parasite" or "chalice." Yet Diana is no spotless, perfect victim of malign persecutors. In precept and practice, Meredith scorned sentimental melodrama. Young and inexperienced, Diana brings much of her trouble on herself. She marries for protection and position, a prudent move by worldly standards, but disastrous in its consequences. Achieving a measure of independence, she soon endangers it by her extravagance, and she is finally almost destroyed by an impulsive act of desperation. Although elements of the "dog-world" are moved by envy and malice, most of Diana's adversaries act "honorably" in their own eyes; it is the conventions of honor, respectability, and—most importantly—of woman's place in Victorian society that nearly overpowers her.

The resolution of the plot would seem a compromise if the novel were the feminist tract it has been called: Diana does not finally triumph as a fully independent person, accepted by society on her own terms and admired for her wit and nerve. Only rescued from despair by her friend Emma, she does prove herself capable of standing alone but chooses instead to marry again. As Meredith presents her choice, however, it is not compromise but fulfillment. Her marriage to Redworth, who truly understands and values her, represents the ideal wedding of flesh and spirit, achieved not by good luck but by striving, blundering, learning from mistakes, and finally seeing and accepting life as it is.

Diana of the Crossways was an immediate success upon publication, probably because its theme had been taken from a recent scandal involving a brilliant and beautiful Irishwoman, Mrs. Caroline Norton, who had been accused (as it proved, falsely) of selling an important government secret. However, the novel has not maintained its popularity, despite its wit, its vitality, and its vivid characterizations. Critics generally rate it high among Meredith's works, often second only to his masterpiece *The Egoist,* and its themes are of perhaps even broader interest today than they were in 1885, yet it is apparently little read. The difficulty is probably with Meredith's famous style, the joy and the despair of his admirers.

From his first work of fiction, *The Shaving of Shagpat,* to his last, the prose of this admirable poet became progressively more poetic in its richness, its precision, its compactness, and its indirection. In the earlier novels, it is a beautiful addition to plot and characterization; in the later, it may detract from or even obscure them. Oscar Wilde may not have been entirely right in saying that as a novelist Meredith could do everything but tell a story; but in *Diana of the Crossways* and other later novels, he often seems fastidiously averse to saying anything directly. The texture of his prose places demands upon his readers that not all are willing to meet. The attentive reader is richly rewarded in beauty, wit, and subtlety of thought and expression. Let his attention waver, though, and he may find that he has missed a significant turn in the plot.

The very dazzle and density of Meredith's style, embodying as it does his vigorous and invigorating vision of life, will certainly continue to delight those willing to submit to it; among less strenuous readers, however, he may continue to be as he has been for decades, more honored than read.

Katharine Bail Hoskins

THE DIARIES OF KAFKA: 1910-1923

Type of work: Journals
Author: Franz Kafka (1883-1924)
First published: 1948-1949

Around the turn of the century and continuing until the years following World War I, a circle of German writers in Prague exerted great influence on German literature. Franz Werfel, Rainer Maria Rilke, and Max Brod were the most widely read authors of this group, but in the closing decades of the period Franz Kafka, sometimes called the author of anxiety, found an ever increasing audience. Biographers of Kafka complain that his short life does not offer anything dramatic to report: his existence could be termed provincial because the major part of his life, except for a short period of travel, was spent within a few city blocks in Prague. His father was a merchant and his mother the daughter of a brewery owner. The family, financially well-to-do, tried to maintain a nineteenth century upper-class living standard: French governess, humanistic education for the children, and efforts to preserve a bourgeois concept of German culture. The sensitive Kafka found no understanding at home; he had almost no communication with his family and the Jewish faith practiced by his parents offered him few consolations. Thus Kafka grew up in a withdrawn isolation, constantly groping for some kind of salvation which he could only find in his writings. He earned a doctor of law degree and worked for fourteen years with an insurance company.

Kafka's continuous anxiety of being directed by forces over which he had no control and about which he had no knowledge is superbly described in his best-known novel *The Trial;* however, it is in his diaries that he reveals most about his motivations and his innermost feelings. His friend and fellow writer, Max Brod, has published these diaries with the care of a loving friend, though admitting the omission of a few intimate entries. The diary was compiled out of thirteen notebooks. The first dated entry is May 17, 1910; last notes were written in the summer of 1923. There are also three travel diaries covering Kafka's travels in Germany, Switzerland, Italy, and France during the years 1911 and 1912. Since these entries are quite different from the usual character of the diary, the travel journals have been separated from the rest.

The diary was a necessity for Kafka, who said that the advantage in keeping one is that it gives awareness of change in thought and feeling. When he realizes that he has neglected his diary, he promises that he will continue to keep it because it is the only place where he can hold on to experience. His urge to write was the safety valve for the hypersensitive and withdrawn Kafka, a means of relieving his anxieties through writing down his deepest feelings so that later he could reverse the process. Literature is his only obsession because, he wrote, literature was the only thing that did not bore him. Whether this fact was only in his mind does not disturb him. He feels that he can only observe family life, not participate in it.

Contemporary historic events are without interest to him. His entry on August 2, 1914, when World War I started, notes that Germany has declared war on Russia and that he went swimming in the afternoon. He is conscious of the direction of his work and states that his fate as a writer will be to record his inner life of dreams; he feels that his life has dwindled and will continue to dwindle, but this record is the only kind of writing that will satisfy him.

The silent stroller along the streets and parks of Prague is a most inquisitive observer of people and events as he ponders on their work, their salaries, what they will be doing tomorrow, how life in their old age will be, their sleeping habits, if he could do their jobs, or how he would like doing another man's work. In spite of his talent, writing is to him an arduous task, as if he were drawing words out of empty air. Sometimes he worries about his emotional state and the struggle to find adequate words. He feels as though he is his own tombstone, that every word he puts down slaps against the next; he hears the consonants rub heavily against one another and the vowels accompany them as though they were minstrel-show Negroes.

Kafka is his own critic and seldom finds reason to be satisfied. He is sure that his preconceived ideas are dry, flat, and embarrassing to those around him. Worst of all, he feels that his ideas remain incomplete, even when he has put them down exactly as he has conceived them. He accuses himself frequently of failing and laments, while looking at a simple girl's dress, that he seldom succeeds in creating anything truly beautiful. Besides the lack of understanding shown toward his writing ambitions by his parents, his employment by an insurance firm conflicts with his literary work, and he longs to be freed of the confining office. Only when his illness becomes critical does he leave off seeing people. His earlier works were written in his parents' home. His constant struggle with noise is shown in a passage telling how he can hear every sound in the house: the front door, the oven door, singing, and housecleaning.

Kafka knew that he was not capable of married life, but he also hated the life of a bachelor. He feared becoming an old man fighting to retain his dignity while begging for an invitation when the need for companionship was felt, or the dreariness of carrying home his meals, not returning home to a calm spouse. He was three times engaged, twice to the same girl, yet all efforts to find a partner for life failed. His self-examination provides entries which indicate that he was striving to come to terms with his surroundings, to know the whole of the human and animal community, to reduce life to simplified forms and rules: to make his life conform to these rules as quickly as he could so that he could retain favor in the eyes of the whole world. However, his opinions on basic subjects are uncompromising. He said that education is part of an adult conspiracy in dealing with children.

The diaries contain many notations which demonstrate Kafka's fierce struggles with symptoms of fear, and he states that only devils could account for the misfortunes in men's lives. There are a great number of story ideas among the entries. Some are well known to Kafka readers. A great many more fragments leave the reader with the regretful realization that this life ended too soon to complete the outpouring of his unique imaginative power. In the words of Albert Camus, everything in Kafka's work is meaningful.

The travel diary reveals a lesser known side of his talent. Because he was absorbed in recording experiences outside himself, he was able to interject some humorous notes, as in his description of a linguistic encounter during a train ride in Italy. He states that the Italian language when spoken commands one's attention whether or not what is being said can be understood, even though one who is uncertain of his Italian cannot prevail against the fluent Italian speaker.

Kafka was not afraid of death. Several years before his illness he wrote that he would be content on his deathbed if the pain were not too great; he believed that the best of his writing revealed his serenity and contentment in the face of death. But a death without pain was not destined for Kafka. As his tuberculosis progressed, the entries of the diary reflect his anxiety of losing the strength to keep on writing. The entries become shorter. One of the last entries, written on June 12, 1923, states that his days and nights are filled with pain, almost without interruption.

Kafka died in a sanatorium near Vienna on June 3, 1924. In spite of the many volumes which now have been written about him, it still appears that he defies any clear definition in literary terms. A minority of critics feel that his mastery of the German language is limited because he lived in linguistic isolation and never was part of the contemporary stream of German writing. The German spoken in Prague did not encompass the *avant-garde* innovations which flourished shortly before and after World War I in Germany and Switzerland. But the strength of Kafka's style seems to derive from this lack of participation in literary fashions; it left him with simple word choices which expressed even more poignantly the complexities of his imaginary inner world. Whatever the criteria may be, it is undeniable that Kafka is today, in the words of a German critic, a "focal-point author." One of Kafka's few friends, Milena Jesenská, wrote that he stood beside mankind and looked at humanity in amazement, that he exposed himself to life like a naked man among the clothed. The nakedness of innocence, of wonder, of the mystery of creation in art, is clearly revealed in his diaries. The document is human because a man of deep sensibility is speaking.

DIARY

Type of work: Diary
Author: John Evelyn (1620-1706)
Time: 1620-1706
Locale: England and the Continent
First published: 1818-1819

Principal personages:
JOHN EVELYN
CHARLES I
CHARLES II
JAMES II
OLIVER CROMWELL
SAMUEL PEPYS
QUEEN MARY
WILLIAM OF ORANGE
QUEEN ANNE
JEREMY TAYLOR, English divine

An intimate of people in high places, John Evelyn was able to observe at first hand many of the significant events and developments of his time. To his observation, he brought a mind remarkable in a turbulent era for its calmness, balance, and acuity. His diary is a contribution of exceptional value to our understanding of seventeenth-century England.

Evelyn, the son of a large landowner, was a royalist and an Anglican. He served briefly in the army of Charles I, but, after the king's retreat in 1641, he resigned, believing that further service would mean financial ruin for himself and would little aid the royalist cause. Finding it difficult to maintain a neutral position, he left England in 1643 for the Continent, where he spent most of the next nine years traveling and studying European culture. After his return to England in 1652, he occupied himself with gardening and with improving his estate. He refused a position under Cromwell and maintained secret correspondence with Charles II. From the Restoration until his death in 1706, he enjoyed the favor of the crown and held several important minor positions in the government.

Evelyn lived in an era of unrest and calamity. Three times he saw the existing English government overthrown; he observed the Dutch war from the vantage point of an official position; he remained in London during the plague of 1665; he watched the progress of the Great Fire from its start to its engulfment of the city; he noted with disapproval the licentiousness of the court of Charles II; he attended the spectacular trials of the men accused of complicity in the Popish Plot. In religion, he witnessed the shifting fortunes of the various sects; in politics, he saw the rise and the fall of a multitude of favorites.

The diary, in addition to providing an inside view of these major events, reveals the ordinary conditions of existence in the seventeenth century. Life was filled with hazards. On voyages, pirates were frequently a threat, Evelyn himself barely escaping them on one occasion. For travel on the Continent, an armed escort was often necessary for protection against highwaymen. Within a brief period, Evelyn was robbed three times; and once, in England, he was robbed and bound, and narrowly missed being killed. Also in the seventeenth century, many barbarous practices were still sanctioned by law. Evelyn tells of beheadings that required several blows of the ax, of men put on the rack to elicit confessions, of the public display of bodies that had been hanged, then drawn, and quartered. The plague, smallpox, and other diseases constantly reminded men of their mortality. Evelyn made frequent references in his diary to death among his friends and his children, seven of whom never reached adulthood.

Amid the public tumult and private insecurity, Evelyn was throughout a truly civilized man. While many were dominated by the emotions that religious and political controversy aroused, he retained his sanity. Of a compassionate nature, he deplored acts of cruelty, and expressed his opposition to many accepted practices, such as the harsh treatment of criminals and the baiting of animals. During the Dutch war he served as commissioner for the care of the sick, wounded, and prisoners of war. He was not deterred from his duties by the plague or by the frustrating difficulties involved in securing funds.

At a time when apostasy was commonplace, Evelyn remained firm in his religious and political convictions. His life was guided, first, by his belief in the Church of England and, secondly, by his belief in the monarchy. A large part of the diary is concerned with church affairs, ranging from discussions of major issues to records of fasting days. A devoutly religious man, he based his conduct upon his conception of the Christian ideal, and accepted blessings and misfortunes alike as the will of God. Although he feared rival sects—the Jesuits, in particular—and believed that certain laws were necessary to protect the Church of England, he was a generally tolerant man and opposed punitive laws against Catholics and Nonconformists.

As a monarchist, he felt that the execution of Charles I was the blackest spot on English history. He regarded the Restoration as the greatest blessing God could bestow, and he continued to celebrate its anniversary even after King James II was deposed in 1688. Initially, he had misgivings about the Glorious Revolution, but, probably because of its preservation of the Church of England, he came to approve of it.

However unwavering he may have been in his royalist sympathies, he was no absolutist, nor did he hesitate to criticize the actions of royalty. When the king overstepped his traditional authority—as Charles II did. for example, in revoking the charter of London, and as James II did in dispensing with the Test Act—Evelyn was firm in his objections. He frequently protested against the profligacy of the court; and once, after having observed some disabled soldiers, he wrote: "What confusion and mischief do the avarice, anger, and ambition of Princes, cause in the world!"

Evelyn apparently could have aspired to higher positions than he attained, but he enjoyed his "private condition" and cared not for "the extreme slavery and subjection that courtiers live in." There was in him none of the sycophant. Generally he avoided offices that might beget a clash between his personal interests and his principles. In one position which did create such a conflict, he followed his principles. As a commissioner of the Privy Seal, he twice refused, against the wishes of James II, to license the illegal sale of Catholic literature.

His independent nature can also be seen in his loyalty to friends. When Samuel Pepys was placed in the Tower on suspicion of treason, Evelyn immediately went to see him. He was the last person to visit Clarendon before that deposed official fled England to escape the wrath of Parliament and king. Many others found in Evelyn a friend who was unmoved by the tergiversations of courtly favor.

Despite the heavy demands of private business and public service, Evelyn found time to acquire a vast amount of knowledge. His range of interests was prodigious, with the novel as well as the important attracting his attention. Amid more weighty topics, such subjects as fire-eating and knife swallowing are soberly discussed in the diary. Much of his intellectual curiosity, however, was directed toward practical matters. His concern with the depletion of forests in England led him to write *Sylva* (1664), a highly significant book on afforestation. His knowledge of gardening was considerable, and his gardens at Saves Court attracted thousands of visitors. The smoke nuisance in London was attacked by Evelyn as early as 1661. After the Great Fire he drew up plans for rebuilding the city. His publications include works on government, education, English customs, horticulture, science, chalcography, and architecture.

Evelyn was also active in promoting the work of others. He was closely associated with England's creative leaders, men such as Robert Boyle and Christopher Wren. A patron of the arts, he introduced Grinling Gibbons to the notice of Charles II, and he persuaded the Duke of Norfolk to present the Arundel marbles to Oxford University. His most productive efforts of this kind were those connected with the Royal Society, of which he was an original promoter and, for many years, an active member.

Unlike the other great diarist of the seventeenth century, Samuel Pepys, Evelyn had little talent for bringing warm, personal touches to his writing. In reading the objective, factual presentation of the earlier part of the diary—with its absence of feeling and with little, even, of personal opinion—one wishes that more of John Evelyn were in the work. In the later part of the diary there is greater freedom of expression. Never, however, is Evelyn able truly to share his emotional experiences with the reader. He was a man of reason, and his writing is formal, dignified, and cerebral.

DIARY

Type of work: Day-to-day journal
Author: Samuel Pepys (1633-1703)
Time: 1660-1669
Locale: London
First published: 1825; first complete edition, 1848-1849

Principal personages:
> SAMUEL PEPYS, Clerk of the Acts of the Navy Board, the diarist
> ELIZABETH ST. MICHEL PEPYS, his wife
> SIR EDWARD MONTAGUE, the First Earl of Sandwich, his patron
> CHARLES II, King of England
> THE DUKE OF YORK, his brother, later James II
> SIR WILLIAM PENN, a Commissioner of the Navy Board
> EVERY OTHER IMPORTANT STATESMAN, POLITICIAN, COURTIER, MUSICIAN, POET, PLAYWRIGHT, ENTERTAINER, SYCOPHANT, ROYAL MISTRESS, AND CHARLATAN THAT INHABITED THE LONDON OF 1660-1669

The *Diary* of Samuel Pepys is a unique document in the annals of English literature—perhaps of all literature. There are other fascinating day-to-day accounts of interesting and momentous times, and some of these were written by men of genius; but there is only one other autobiographical collection—the recently discovered journals of James Boswell—which combines fascinating subject matter and genius of composition with the intriguing detective-story discovery that is associated with the *Diary* of Pepys.

The author of the greatest of all biographies must bow to this lesser Samuel in one respect: Boswell, as his editors admit, was writing for posterity; Pepys was not. Pepys' *Diary* was written for himself only, apparently for the sole purpose of allowing its author to savor once more, at the end of each day, the experiences of the preceding twenty-four hours. There is no evidence of revision of any kind, and it was written in a shorthand which protected it from posterity for over a hundred years after its author's failing eyesight had forced him reluctantly to give it up.

Pepys' method of composition gives the *Diary* an immediacy that makes Boswell's *Journals* appear sedulously organized. And the protective coloration of the shorthand allows for admissions of personal animosities and revelations of scandalous behavior that otherwise would not be found in the confessions of a responsible public official. Also, the point that Pepys was a responsible public official is the last factor that contributes to the importance of his work. Boswell was the scion of an important Scottish family and a member of the Scottish bar, but (aside from his Corsican experience) the only history he was involved in was literary history. Pepys was involved with the history of a nation at a very important time.

The *Diary* is important in a number of ways. First, it is of great value as a document of the Restoration period. No writer of a historical novel based on the history of the time could possibly create a character familiar with as many important events as was that opportunistic busybody, Samuel Pepys. One of the most influential figures in bringing about the return of the Stuarts in 1660 was the former Cromwellian, Sir Edward Montague, who was assisted by his able cousin and protégé, Samuel Pepys. It was Sir Edward who commanded the fleet that sailed from Holland and returned triumphantly with the king. On board the flagship, kissing the king's hand, firing a cannon to salute the new monarch (and burning an eye in the process), commenting on the plainness of the queen, taking charge of the king's dog in the landing at Dover was, again, Samuel Pepys. Later, made Clerk of the Acts of the Navy Board because of his assistance to the

Stuarts (Sir Edward Montague was made Earl of Sandwich), he remained at his post in London and wrote down his observations of the terrible plague from which most members of his class fled in panic. It was Pepys, again, who did his best to keep the English Navy afloat during the Dutch Wars, and Pepys who defended the Navy in a brilliant speech before Parliament in the investigation that followed (1668). Earlier (September 2, 1666), when the great fire of London broke out, it was Pepys who rushed to the king to inform him of the catastrophe and to suggest the blowing up of houses to prevent the spread of the fire. Pepys, who had a part in all these events, tells of them in a straightforward, unself-conscious account unvarnished by fear of what his contemporaries would have thought or of what posterity would think.

Along with vivid pictures of the major events of Restoration history are day-to-day accounts of the less earthshaking but equally revealing activities in the life of the London that Pepys shared, accounts that make the *Diary* a document of social, cultural, and artistic history as well. Here Pepys' concern with—his actual delight in—detail brings a particular world of the past to life. We see the crowded, unsanitary, and often impassable London streets. At times, during trips to Pepys' father's house in Brampton or during excursions to the country, we catch glimpses of rural existence in the days of Charles II. We see life in the houses of the well-to-do and the noble and, occasionally, at court. On a more mundane scale, there is Pepys' concern with clothes (his father was a tailor and he reflects a professional knowledge) and his greater concern with managing his own household. Unfortunately for revelations on this score, Pepys had no children, but his problems in household management included his handling of the affairs of his rather shiftless parents, brothers, and sister, the maintenance of a staff of servants that grew as his own wealth increased, and

domestic supervision of his beautiful but erratic—sometimes docile, sometimes temperamental—young wife. In regard to the arts, there is a wealth of material on the theater and on music. Pepys was an inveterate playgoer. Though his frequent attendance bothered his basically Puritan conscience and though he made intermittent vows to refrain, it is seldom that many entries go by in which some play that he has seen is not commented on. So frequent are these comments, in fact, that the *Diary* is an invaluable source of information to the student of Restoration drama. It is equally valuable to the specialist in the history of music: Pepys was not only an accomplished musician but also a composer, and the delight in music which he expresses gives an insight into a particularly musical age.

Nor was artistic beauty the only kind that captivated the practical and mercenary Pepys. Since he was equally attracted to beauty in its carnal manifestations, his pursuit of beauty in feminine form and his diligent (but finally unsuccessful) attempts to hide these pursuits from his wife provide an insight into the mores of the Restoration period. These accounts of the diarist's philanderings—honest, but hidden by the elaborate code—are a part of the personal revelation that the work provides.

In spite of its importance as historical and social document, the *Diary* is, on its most intriguing level, the portrait of a man, a self-portrait drawn in strong and certain lines with no detail, however uncomplimentary, however compromising, omitted. That it is the portrait of a man active in the affairs of his day adds to its interest; but the main value comes from its unstinting wealth of circumstantial detail. Yet the detail and the man cannot be separated: the love of detail and the love of life that inspired the keeper of the *Diary* make up the essence of the man himself. The *Diary* is a celebration of the things of this world and a portrait of the man who praised them.

THE DIARY AND LETTERS OF MME. D'ARBLAY

Type of work: Epistolary journal
Author: Fanny Burney (Mme. d'Arblay, 1752-1840)
First published: 1842

Principal personages:

FANNY BURNEY, later MME. D'ARBLAY
ESTHER SLEEPE BURNEY, her mother
DR. CHARLES BURNEY, her father
CHARLES, her brother
SUSANNA ("SUZY") ELIZABETH and
CHARLOTTE ANN, her sisters
ELIZABETH BURNEY, her stepmother
SARAH HARRIET ("HETTY") and
SALLY, her half sisters
STEPHEN ALLEN, her step-brother
MARIA ALLEN and
ELIZABETH ALLEN, her step-sisters
GENERAL ALEXANDRE D'ARBLAY, her husband
MRS. HESTER THRALE PIOZZI
SIR JOSHUA REYNOLDS
DR. SAMUEL JOHNSON
JAMES BOSWELL
KING GEORGE III
QUEEN CHARLOTTE
CHARLES MAURICE DE TALLEYRAND-PÈRIGORD
MADAME DE STAËL
DAVID GARRICK
THOMAS BABINGTON MACAULAY

From the first entry in the diary of a sixteen-year-old girl to the last letter written by an old lady seventy-one years later, Fanny Burney's record of her experiences covers an enthralling range of personalities and events. As a daughter in the talented household of Dr. Charles Burney, the first music historian, a literary young woman in Dr. Johnson's London, a lady-in-waiting at the court of King George III, the wife of a French exile after the Revolution, a resident in Paris during the Empire, and finally a lonely widow in Jane Austen's Bath, Fanny Burney d'Arblay was a perceptive and witty observer behind the scenes that have become history. Her remarkable balance of passionate involvement and ironic detachment achieved a unique synthesis of autobiography and social history.

The diary begins with a young girl's self-dramatization in its statement of purpose: "To have some account of my thoughts, manners, acquaintance and ac-

tions, when the hour arrives in which time is more nimble than memory, is the reason whch induces me to keep a Journal. A Journal in which I must confess my *every* thought, must open my whole heart!" With innate literary discrimination, she realized that it would be more effective if addressed to an imaginary intimate; but the only confidante to whom she could reveal all her secrets was "Nobody."

To Nobody, then, will I write my Journal! since to Nobody can I be wholly unreserved—to Nobody can I reveal every thought, every wish of my heart, with the most unlimited confidence, the most unremitting sincerity to the end of my life!

Her embarrassment when her father found her journal; her excitement at every meeting with Mr. Garrick, a frequent visitor in the Burney household; her admiration for Miss Linley, the singer who eloped with Sheridan—all were increasingly tempered by her sense of humor, as in her account of a sailing excursion:

The waves foamed in little white mountains rising above the green surface of the sea; they dashed against the rocks off the coast of Brixham with monstrous fury; and really to own the truth, I felt no inclination to be boat wrecked, however pathetic and moving a Tale our adventure might have made.

Taking herself and her diary less seriously in her early twenties, she confessed that she had burned everything she had written up to her fifteenth year, "thinking I grew too old for scribbling nonsence, but as I am less young, I grow, I fear, less wise, for I cannot any longer resist what I find to be irresistible, the pleasure of popping down my thoughts from time to time on paper."

The purpose and technique of Fanny's early diary formed the basis of the novel which first brought her recognition: "I doubt not but this memorable affair [publication of *Evelina*] will, in future times, mark the period whence chronologers will date the zenith of the polite arts in this island!" This characteristic of poking fun at herself reveals the objectivity with which the character of Evelina was created. The sentimental heroine, pouring out her heart in a long series of voluminous letters to her guardian, expresses not the author's view of the world, but the author's view of how the world appears to a naïve girl of seventeen. Published first under a pseudonym, *Evelina* became an immediate hit, and some of the most delightful passages in the diary are the accounts of Fanny Burney's unaffected pride in its success and amusement at everyone's attempts to guess the identity of the author. She seemed to enjoy the mystery more than the praise heaped upon her when the secret became known, but that too was sweet when it came from Dr. Johnson: "I almost poked myself under the table. Never did I feel so delicious a confusion since I was born!"

From 1777, when she first met Dr. Johnson, until 1784, when she visited him regularly during his last illness, Fanny Burney filled her journal with conversations which she claimed to remember almost verbatim. Although Johnson was often violent or overbearing in his arguments with fellow critics, his manner to Fanny was always kindly and courteous. The scenes in Mrs. Thrale's drawing room, in Sir Joshua Reynolds' dining room, or in Dr. Johnson's own small parlor, where Fanny met the blue-stocking ladies of Mrs. Thrale's circle and the literary men of the doctor's circle, sparkle with wit and polished repartee; but Dr. Johnson is more genial when seen through Fanny's eyes than through Boswell's. Five years after the death of their revered friend, just before the publication of Boswell's *The Life of Samuel Johnson, LL.D.*, Fanny met Boswell at Windsor and was embarrassed by his request for some of Johnson's letters to herself, to show him in a new light as "gay Sam, agreeable Sam, pleasant Sam." She refused his request, but she has performed the same service for Dr. Johnson in her own recollections of his talk.

During the summer before Dr. Johnson's death, Fanny had lost another friend, Mrs. Hester Thrale, through opposition to her marriage to the Italian tenor, Gabriel Piozzi. With the literary circle thus broken, Fanny's scope became socially wider, though intellectually narrower. She was introduced to Queen Charlotte, whom she found charming, and who was so impressed with the novelist that she offered her a position at court as a Keeper of the Wardrobes. Fanny felt too honored to refuse the appointment, but she had grave doubts about sacrificing her independence for the rigid routine of court life. Her doubts proved amply justified during her five-year stint, but even when her hours on duty were from six o'clock in the morning until after midnight, she usually found time to record some of her experiences. Her devotion to the royal family, her dislike of her German superior, her conscientious attitude about her duty, and her sharply observant eye and mocking wit combine to give a vivid picture of life at the court of King George III. In a letter to a sister, Fanny explained the etiquette of deportment in the royal presence:

> In the third place, you must not, upon any account, stir either hand or foot. If, by chance, a black pin runs into your head, you must be sure to bear it without wincing; if it brings tears into your eyes, you must not wipe them off; if they give you a tingling by running down your cheeks, you must look as if nothing was the matter. . . . If, however, the agony is very great, you may, privately, bite the inside of your cheek, or of your lips, for a little relief: taking care, meanwhile, to do it so cautiously as to make no apparent dent outwardly. And, with that precaution, if you even gnaw a piece out, it will not be minded, only be sure either to swallow it, or commit it to a corner of the inside of your mouth till they are gone—for you must not spit.

This whimsical cynicism was dubious for a beginner in court duties, but Fanny's admiration for members of the royal family seemed unaffected by her impatience with formality. Her account of the assassination attempt in 1786 is typical. When she first heard the news she was "almost petrified with horror at the intelligence. If this King is not safe,—good, pious, beneficent as he is,—if his life is in danger, from his own subjects, what is to guard the Throne? and which way is a monarch to be secure?" She was particularly impressed by the fact that the king, on his return to his weeping family ". . . with the gayest good-humour, did his utmost to comfort them; and he gave a relation of the affair, with a calmness and unconcern that, had any one but himself been his hero, would have been regarded as totally unfeeling." In giving her family an accurate account to correct the rumors they had heard, Fanny stressed the way in which the king stopped the crowd from attacking his mad assailant and insisted that she should be taken care of.

This emphasis on the king's goodness was maintained throughout the record of the sad period of his own madness. After some months of illness he seemed greatly changed:

> I had a sort of conference with his Majesty, or rather I was the object to whom he spoke, with a manner so uncommon, that a high fever alone could account for it; a rapidity, a hoarseness of voice, a volubility, an earnestness—a vehemence, rather—it startled me inexpressibly; yet with a graciousness exceeding even all I ever met with before —it was almost kindness! Heaven— Heaven preserve him!"

Months later Fanny met him by accident in Kew gardens, tried to slip away, and was terrified when he ran after her. When both of them were stopped by his attendants, she was surprised to meet "all his wonted benignity of countenance, though something still of wildness in his eyes," and even more astonished when he kissed her on the cheek. Her observation on this action reveals as much of her own character as of his: ". . . it was but the joy of a heart unbridled, now, by the forms and proprieties of established custom and sober reason. To see any of his household thus by accident seemed such a near approach to liberty and recovery that who can wonder it should serve rather to elate than lessen what yet remains of his disorder!" Seeing George III through Fanny Burney's eyes alters more perspectives than does seeing Dr. Johnson in a different light.

One of Fanny's most interesting assignments was to attend the trial of Warren Hastings in order to give the queen an accurate account of the proceedings. The long passages in her diary reveal her relief at this occasional freedom from formality of the court and her delight in the opportunity to see her London friends. Her comments on who was there and with whom, who spoke to whom and to whom one could not speak, are reminiscent of dialogue in Restoration comedy, but her reaction to Hastings himself was in terms of tragedy: "What an awful moment for such a man!—a man fallen from such a height of power to a situation so humiliating." She also followed the main stages of the trial with alert intelligence, so that she was able to give the chancellor's opening speech from memory: "The newspapers have printed it far less accurately than I have retained it, though I am by no means exact or secure." Of the speech by Edmund Burke which she heard, she gave no particulars because she assumed it would be accurately printed, but she praised her friend's eloquence while disagreeing with his views. She revealed the influence of Johnson when she wrote: "When he narrated, he was easy, flowing, and natural; when he declaimed, energetic, warm, and brilliant."

Close though she was to the great affairs of her day, Fanny Burney was occupied for most of her five years at court with the domestic life of the royal family. Because of a demanding schedule, long hours, cold palace passages, and draughty carriages, her health declined. At last she resigned her post and went to live again with her father. But within a year, while staying with friends in the country, she was again drawn as by a magnet into an important circle, a group of French exiles which included Talleyrand and Madame de Staël. Engaged as their tutor in English, she soon married M. d'Arblay and thus began a new life when she was nearly forty. After 1800 her husband was able to go back to France, where they lived until 1815, when d'Arblay was appointed a commander of the king's bodyguard and sent Fanny with other refugees to Brussels. Her narrative of the events of the Hundred Days, and particularly of Brussels during the Battle of Waterloo, though written some years later, preserved the balance of emotional involvement and critical detachment that characterizes the entire journal. During her last twenty-three years of life as a widow settled in Bath, she was busy editing her father's paper, revising her own diaries, and sorting out her letters, in a spirit more critical than sentimental:

> For the rest of my life I shall take charge and save my own executor the discretionary labours that with myself are almost endless; for I now regularly destroy all letters that either may eventually do mischief, however clever, or that contain nothing of instruction or entertainment, however innocent. This, which I announce to all my correspondents who write confidentially, occasions my receiving letters that are real conversations.

Because Fanny Burney's own diaries and letters were always real conversations, they provide an atmosphere as well as a record of her times. Her style was sometimes colloquial, sometimes Johnsonian, depending on her subject. The death of her old friend, Mrs. Hester Thrale Piozzi, led to a comparison between her and Madame de Staël in the manner of the *Lives of the Poets:*

> Their conversation was equally luminous, from the sources of their own fertile minds, and from their splendid acquisitions from the works and acquirements of others. Both were zealous to serve, liberal to bestow, and graceful to oblige and praising whatever was admirable that came in their way.

In this passage, as throughout her journal, both in what she says and in the way she says it, Fanny Burney throws a light upon her times in which she herself stands clearly revealed.

THE DIARY OF A COUNTRY PRIEST

Type of work: Novel
Author: Georges Bernanos (1888-1948)
Type of plot: Psychological realism
Time of plot: The 1920's
Locale: France
First published: 1937

Principal characters:

A PARISH PRIEST, the diarist
THE CURÉ DE TORCY, a superior of the narrator
DR. MAXENCE DELBENDE, the narrator's friend
SERAPHITA DUMOUCHEL, a young parishioner
MONSIEUR DUFRETY, a former classmate of the narrator
THE COUNT, a wealthy resident of the parish
THE COUNTESS, his wife
MADEMOISELLE CHANTAL, their daughter
MADEMOISELLE LOUISE, governess at the chateau

Critique:

Meager of plot because Bernanos is interested more in showing a man's thoughts and basic principles than in picturing human behavior, *The Diary of a Country Priest* is fictional presentation of priestly attitudes, functions, and tribulations. Through this philosophical and realistic treatment of life in a small French parish, it is easy to see Bernanos' high regard for Joan of Arc as the symbol of France. In their simplicity the Maid's peasantry and saintliness are not unlike those phases of the diarist's life. Fittingly, compassion and tenderness characterize the writing, which, in translation, sustains the poetic charm and fluency of the original. Mankind's holiness is Bernanos' keynote.

The Story:

A young priest, thirty years old, in charge of the Ambricourt Parish in France, recorded in his diary his impressions and activities over a period of one year. His purpose in keeping the diary was to maintain frankness with himself in his relationships with his parishioners and in his service to God.

The priest was a man of marked humility, sympathy, simplicity, and great loneliness. Son of a poor family in which there had been much suffering and hardship, he planned to raise the scale of living in his parish. His plans for a village savings bank and for coöperative farming were discussed at his first monthly meeting with the curates, but his plans were disapproved because of their pretentious scope and his lack of personal influence in the parish. This saddening blow, which caused him to question whether God would use his services as He did the services of others, was intensified by the words of his superior and ideal, the Curé de Torcy, and of his friend, Dr. Maxence Delbende, who soon afterward committed suicide because of his disappointment at not receiving a legacy he expected.

These two men thwarted the young priest's ambition with their opinions that the poor were not to be raised from their low level because of religious and social reasons. God gave the poor a dignity, the Curé de Torcy said, which they do not wish to lose in His sight. According to the doctor, poverty served as a social bond and a mark of prestige among the poor. In the eyes of the Church, the curate believed, the rich are on the earth to protect the poor.

Undaunted and hopeful, the priest accepted an invitation to the chateau, where he hoped to get financial help from the Count for his parish projects. Thwarted in his attempt, he gave his physical energy, which was limited because of insomnia and a chronic stomach disorder, to the spiritual advancement of his parish. But his efforts in this direction were ill-spent. He questioned his success in teaching a catechism class, for the children did not respond as he had hoped, and he was tormented and plagued by the unsavory attentions of Seraphita Dumouchel, a young student in the class, who discomfited him by her suggestive questions and remarks to the other children and by her scribbled notes left about for the young priest to find.

Seraphita later befriended him, when on a parish visit he suffered a seizure and fell unconscious in the mud. A few days later Seraphita, bribed by sweets, offset her beneficence to the priest by telling Mademoiselle Chantal, the Count's strong-willed, jealous daughter, that the priest had fallen in drunkenness. The story was believed because it was known generally among the parishioners that the priest drank cheap wine, and because his physical condition was growing progressively worse.

The priest's spiritual strength was shown in his theological dealings with the Count's family. Mademoiselle Chantal had told, in conversation and in confession, that her father was having an affair with Mademoiselle Louise. The daughter, believing that she was to be sent to England to live with her mother's cousin, declared that she hated everyone in her household—her father and the governess for their conduct, and her mother for her blindness to the situation. After asserting that she would kill Mademoiselle Louise or herself and that the priest would have to explain away her conduct to God, she got his promise that he would discuss the girl's problems with her mother.

The priest went to the chateau to confer with the Countess regarding her daughter's spiritual state. There he found the mother in a more pronounced atheistic frame of mind than that of her daughter. Her spiritual depression resulted from the death of her baby son, twelve years before. During a prolonged philosophical discussion the Countess, after ridiculing the priest for his theological idealism and his lack of vanity and ambition, described with bitterness the hateful selfishness of her daughter, and related with indifference the Count's many infidelities.

Before he left the chateau, the priest sensed a spiritual change in his wealthy parishioner when she threw into the fire a medallion containing a lock of her son's hair. The priest, always humble, tried to retrieve the locket. In a letter delivered to him at the presbytery later in the day the Countess informed him that he had given her peace and escape from a horrible solitude with the memory of her dead child.

The Countess died that night. The priest's success in helping to redeem her soul left him with an uncertain feeling. He did not know whether he was happy or not.

If his reaction was happiness, it was short-lived. When the details of his session with the Countess became common knowledge, for Mademoiselle Chantal had eavesdropped during the interview, criticism and derision were heaped upon him. The canon reprimanded him because he had assumed the role of her confessor, and the Curé de Torcy ridiculed his approach in dealing with the Countess. Members of the family, unstable as they were in their relationships, accused him of subversive tactics to realize a childish ambition.

His social ineptness, his personal inadequacies, and his professional inaptitude—deficiencies repeatedly mentioned in his introspective moods—seemed to increase as his physical condition grew worse. His hemorrhages continuing, he decided to consult Dr. Lavigne in Lille.

His last major bungle was in connection with this medical aid. Because he forgot the name of the doctor recommended to him, in Lille he turned to the directory and mistakenly chose the name of Dr. Laville. The physician, a drug addict, bluntly diagnosed the priest's ailment as cancer of the stomach.

From the doctor's office, the priest went

to the address of his old schoolmate at the seminary, Monsieur Dufrety, who had long been urging his friend to visit him. There he died that night.

In a letter from Monsieur Dufrety to the Curé de Torcy, details of the priest's death were described. In great suffering and anguish, following a violent hemorrhage, the priest held his rosary to his breast. When he asked his old friend for absolution, his request was granted and the ritual performed in a manner, Monsieur Dufrety wrote, that could leave no one with any possible misgivings. The priest's last words affirmed his great faith in the whole scheme of things, because of God's existence.

Further Critical Evaluation of the Work:

A Catholic novelist in the manner of Julian Green and François Mauriac, Georges Bernanos was a visionary for whom the forces of good and evil were genuine presences. He shows a fierce integrity in his writing, although sometimes his views are oversimplified or inconsistent. His characters, while representing extremes of human behavior from saintliness to depravity, are battlegrounds for good and evil, and their souls the prize. These people are powerfully imagined and realistically drawn, particularly the priests and other individuals who devote their lives to God.

One of the themes of *The Diary of a Country Priest* is that of the conflict between individual religious ecstasy and the day to day "housekeeping" of the Church. The young priest's aspirations, at once naïve and noble, are very touching, but his failure to live up to them causes him increasing unhappiness. Above all, he wants to be of use to God and to his parishioners, but he feels thwarted at every step and is not sure why. The picture of the hard, narrow villagers, with their materialistic and shallow ways, their stubbornness and malice, is vivid and complete; the reader soon understands the pain of the youthful priest's frustration at his inability to elevate them spiritually.

Boredom, Bernanos suggests, is the beginning of evil, or at least the ground in which it grows. The young priest sees that life for his parishioners is nothing but boredom. The nature of injustice worries him as does the nature of true poverty. Everyone constantly gives him advice, warning him of intolerance, excessive dedication, or pride, but none of them can see into his heart and mind and understand what really troubles him. The naïve and unworldly qualities of the young priest give him an innocent charm, despite his almost frightening intensity.

Despite his inexperience, the priest knows that "each creature is alone in his distress." His growing wisdom is a growing realization of the loneliness of each individual. From the beginning, he is beset by ailments and becomes obsessed by them; soon, illness dominates his physical existence. But his spiritual life grows richer and more intense.

At the end, the priest has learned that true humility does not lie in self-hatred, but rather that the supreme grace is to "love oneself in all simplicity." His death is revealed in a moving letter from his friend to his superior, expressing his ultimate sense of peace.

DIARY OF A WRITER

Type of work: Periodical journalism
Author: Fyodor Mikhailovich Dostoevski (1821-1881)
First published: 1873, 1876-1878, 1880, 1881

Dostoevski began his series of articles in the Petersburg *Citizen* with the plan of talking in an informal way about any subject in current events that impressed or appealed to him. He did not intend the articles to be a specifically literary endeavor and they are not, although literary subjects appear frequently. Nor did he intend his writing to be predominantly political, although he expounds his political philosophy and his slavophilic ideas at intervals throughout. This was to be a personal and freely-ranging undertaking; hence he called it a diary. It combines characteristics found in current journalism, column, editorial, and feature story. The style is flowing, associative, digressive.

The author frequently and half humorously complains that he is having no success in keeping to his main subject because the things which were intended to take up but a few words have absorbed all the space. In fact, the announced subjects are often but launching points for what Dostoevski really has to say. At the end of the 1876 issues, he admits that his main object in writing the *Diary* is to explain the ideas of Russia's national spiritual independence, that is, the qualities of the human mind and heart as he observes them in his countrymen. Always fascinated by the consciousness and emotions of people all of kinds, Dostoevski makes many profound observations, and the pages of his *Diary* reveal keen observation and sensitivity to our essential humanity. This prime interest accounts for the rambling and discursive form of his writings. As he explains, he writes of the things he has seen, heard, read. But in life, these things do not fit together, do not form patterns. All is strange, all is "segregation." The lack of order and coherence in his writings mirrors the disorder and unrest in life, which are his true subject:

what life is like in Russia in the last quarter of the nineteenth century.

Dostoevski shows the quirks and quiddities of the Russian character by sketches, by narrated incidents, and by simple rumination. A visit he made to a mineral-water spa provides him with material for comments about railway traveling, social behavior, particularly the propensity of many Russians for speaking poor French rather than good Russian. Dostoevski analyzes this affectation and criticizes it. He is quick to see the faults of his countrymen: their simplicity, their lying, their dissipations. He observes that most men are not bad but wretched, a situation that may be attributed partly to the social confusion in the country after the liberation of the peasants in 1861, when many Russians could not be secure in their identities or their social positions. The writer observes that everybody wants to revenge himself on the world for his own nullity. Because people lack an outlet to express their identities, they feel neglected and faceless; they debauch, they drink, they write anonymous letters to newspapers. However, he insists, the Russian people should be judged not by their villainies but by the great and holy things they long for, even while they are committing wrongs. In the long run, he argues, Russia will be redeemed because her problems all arise from errors of the mind, not of the heart. Errors of the mind are easily remedied, by the very logic of events in life. But errors of the heart are a spiritual blindness that refuses to be cured, and would sooner destroy everything in the world.

Dostoevski feels that Russia needs a greater sense of solidarity, both personally and politically, for a sound cohesive sentiment is happiness in the life of a nation. He points toward the time, before Peter the Great, when Russia was isolationist and contrasts it with the present time, when Russians try to love Europeans, become Europeans. He talks of Germany's problems as it strove to become a single nation and sees there a parallel for Russia's problems, makes political predictions, returns to them later to comment upon their working out, discusses Russia's finances, makes plans, explains how he has formulated them and even how he is expressing them. There is no strict method in his political musings; he explores topics as they occur to him: Russia's struggles against the Turkish empire, its relations with Europe, general problems of religion—can it prevail?—the Pope, European politics, personalities, patriots and politicians. War, he decides, need not always be a scourge. Sometimes it can be a salvation, if the people need it and are ready for it. His conclusion is that the changes which are occurring around the world ought not to be feared but welcomed by Russia; because her mission is a true and lofty one, the country will endure anything and always emerge triumphant.

More appealing and important than politics for readers of the Diary are Dostoevski's discussions of minor immediate and everyday events. In these he demonstrates his real knowledge of the human heart. He returns often to the theme of alienation and the breaking of old ties. A visit to the village in which he grew up leads him to ruminate about his childhood, childhood in general, the nature of families and the changing values in the family situation. He finds a blurring of family identity, an increasing casualness toward the old ties, that he regrets. The education of children, and their peculiar charm, are related subjects he speaks on.

Current newspaper accounts involving children often come up for comment in the Diary: trials of parents for cruelty to children are discussed at great length, and also digressively. Dostoevski begins a discussion of the ethical considerations of lawyers apropos of a particular case, then says in effect that since he knows little

about law, he will talk about talent in general. And he proceeds to do so. But eventually, as always, he returns to his topic. His breadth of mind constantly suggests to him new ideas related by association to the starting ones, and his pen is given free rein.

News stories of the deaths of children attract him and lead him into a consideration of Tolstoy's Childhood and Youth. Suicides are another kind of news item that provokes a response from Dostoevski. He relates long histories of suicides, speculates upon the forces that drive a man to such an extreme, and the sort of character that can accomplish self-destruction. He devotes one issue of the Diary to a short story called "The Meek One," which consists of a man's monologue just after his wife has committed suicide.

Life reminds Dostoevski of literature as faithfully as literature embodies life. Despite his frequent remarks that he does not mean to deal directly with literature and criticism, he is often led into it because, as he explains, the Diary is meant as a record of his impressions and his strongest impressions are about literature. The death of George Sand in 1876 occasions a long discussion of her popularity as a novelist, her heroines, her religion. Besides "The Meek One," Dostoevski produces another short story called "The Dream of a Strange Man," and also gives a sketch of his plan for a satiric novel. He broods lovingly over Cervantes' Don Quixote and its knowledge of the heart. The single issue of the Diary for August, 1880, consists of the text of a famous address on Pushkin that Dostoevski made to a literary society earlier that year. The significance of Pushkin for Russia, he says, is that he was the first to recognize and portray in literature the negative type of man, who is restless, suffering, without faith or cooperation, refusing to be reconciled to his world. Pushkin's universal susceptibility allowed him truly to capture the artistic beauty of the Russian spirit. There is for Dostoevski the essence of the Russian personality in this type of man, and Pushkin himself is its perfection.

The *Diary* met with immense acclaim during the years it appeared, but the author's death in 1881 cut short the publication of what had been, and still is, a continuing document of a sensitive man's confrontation of his world and the meaning he found in it.

THE DIARY OF HENRY CRABB ROBINSON

Type of work: Diary, reminiscences, and correspondence
Author: Henry Crabb Robinson (1775-1867)
First published: 1870

Because of his passion for literature and metaphysics, and his special affinity for knowing those men of his time who were worth knowing, Henry Crabb Robinson managed to encompass in his person many of the significant intellectual trends of the first half of the nineteenth century. His *Diary* reveals him as a highly characteristic post-Enlightenment mind; his encounters with German, French, and particularly English literary figures have produced a mine of information about the special temper of exuberance during the period; yet there emerges from the work as well the picture of a modest and engaging man. While still a young man, having turned to the Law for a living, he realized he could never become great; but he never ceased to follow the lure of the controversial ideas and outstanding men of his age. His mild demeanor, his exquisite tact and generosity, made him the friend of writers as various as Goethe, Wordsworth, Blake, Lamb, Landor, and Coleridge.

Robinson's life as he recorded it in the *Diary* was outwardly uneventful, yet full of pleasurable transitions from introspection to social intercourse. He never married, but the range of his acquaintances and friendships was enormous, as was the extent of his correspondence. Yet we also have frequent glimpses of the solitary Robinson, alone in a room reading voluminously in the philosophy and literature of his contemporaries, cultivating his *Diary*, or traveling on the Continent to improve his mind.

Robinson was born on May 13, 1775, at Bury St. Edmunds. His childhood was a happy one; however, because the Robinsons were Dissenters he was excluded from education at a public school or a university, and at age fifteen he was articled as a law clerk to a Colchester attorney. During the next few years he went to see John Wesley preach, rejoiced at the outbreak of the French Revolution, became a Jacobin, and read Godwin's *Political Justice*. Then after an unsettled life in London during the closing years of the eighteenth century, a time when he began in earnest his reading and theater-going habits and developed a mature interest in politics, he went to Germany in 1800 with money from a legacy. The next five years of independent travel and study in Germany were the crucial period of his life. With no settled plans, he began to absorb the German language and culture. By the time he returned home, he had traveled widely in Germany, had read deeply in its literature and in the emerging transcendental philosophy, had known Weimar in its great days and talked with Goethe, Schiller, Brentano, Voss, and many others. With Coleridge and Carlyle, he became one of the first English Germanophiles, an extremely eloquent advocate, for example, of the strengths and beauties of Goethe in literature and of Kant in philosophy. If the formative influence of Germany on English thought during the period between 1810 and 1850 can hardly be overrated, Robinson himself deserves much of the credit.

At Frankfurt, his first major stop, Robinson became acquainted with the poet Clemens Brentano. In July, 1801, he moved on to Grimma where, with great difficulty, he began reading Kant in earnest. After meeting Goethe and Herder at Weimar, he remarked on Goethe's immense dignity and oppressive handsomeness. Finally he settled at Jena, enrolled in the University there, and began studies in Latin and Greek and in contemporary German writing. He heard Schelling's lectures on aesthetics and thought them obscure; his acute sympathetic insight and strength of mind won him an intimacy with von Knebel; while at the same time he indulged in some good-natured student clowning, got into trouble for parodying an inept professor named Eichstädt, and was friendly enough with his fellow students to learn a good deal about their secret dueling societies. In 1804 he met Mme. de Staël. Not knowing Parisian customs, he was puzzled to be shown into her bedroom to meet the great lady as she sat decorously in her bed. In return for her introductions to many of the literary giants of Weimar, Robinson gave her lucid explanations of current German philosophies. He was later to perform the same task of intermediary for English audiences.

After a stay in England, Robinson returned to Germany as a correspondent for *The Times* in 1807. Later he went to Spain, where he covered the revolution in 1808. He left *The Times* during the next year, lived a literary life in London for a time, all the while uncertain of his future, and then in January, 1812, entered the office of a barrister. He went to the bar, he said, to acquire a "gentlemanly independence" and "society with leisure." In spite of his own disclaimers, it is clear that he was an active lawyer on the Norfolk circuit, and an able one; at the end of every year he noted accurately in pounds the steady increase in his income. From this time on he agitated for the reform of legal process in England, and he became an active enemy of the slave trade.

The *Diary* itself begins in 1811, during his thirty-sixth year, at a time when he was solidifying friendships with Blake, Wordsworth, Lamb, and Coleridge. The months on the circuit alternated with summer tours to Wales or the Continent, and Robinson combined with his professional life an amazingly varied round of dinners, lectures, theater-going, reading, and social intercourse with people of all ranks and opinions.

Robinson was fifty-three when, in 1828, he gave up the practice of law to devote himself to self-improvement, talk,

and philanthropy. It was during this harvest of leisure that he increased his correspondence, became a mentor to many young writers, paid hundreds of social visits to the great and the insignificant alike, and watched his old friends die off one by one. In the year of his retirement he was one of the first to buy shares in the recently founded London University, afterwards University College. His long and honorable connection with University College as a member of the Managing Council extended to the time of his death. It was here too that he practiced the art of conversation, which even then was becoming a rare phenomenon and indistinguishable from argument. Henry Crabb Robinson was always an eminently clubbable man, someone who could listen as well as perform, whether he was dining at College or spending his annual Christmas vacation with the Wordsworths at Rydal Mount.

It was as a genial and social man that Robinson was remembered after his death in 1867. As the conversationalist and companion of several generations of Englishmen, he never made an enemy. In fact, this talent for conversation makes the *Diary* a work of continuing importance. Robinson the diarist is a mine of information on nineteenth century literary history. He was one of the first men to argue for the greatness of Goethe and Wordsworth. He saw immediately the significance of the *Lyrical Ballads,* and he was one of the initial supporters of Hazlitt and Keats. He transcribed the opinions, and catalogued the eccentricities, of both Coleridge and Blake; he was the friend of Charles Lamb and it is not insignificant to note that he recorded many of Lamb's best puns. He went to the theater for pleasure and recorded his responses to performances in Weimar and London from the days of Mrs. Siddons, at the turn of the century, to the 1865 performance of *Twelfth Night* with Miss Kate Terry in the title role. Again, over a period of years, he attended the lectures of Coleridge and Hazlitt, of Flaxman on the fine arts, and, later, of Emerson, Faraday, and Carlyle. In many cases his notes are all we possess of those lectures.

Robinson's *Diary* remains one of the most important single contemporary sources on the life and opinions of Wordsworth. He was Wordsworth's contemporary in time and temperament and shared with the poet an enthusiasm for the French Revolution and for Godwin in the 1790's. Both resided in Germany at the turn of the century; both gave their pity and friendship to the unfortunate Lambs; and both profited from the brilliant monologues of Coleridge. They were twice traveling companions on picturesque tours to the Continent. Robinson in the *Diary* evinced an affectionate but skeptical regard for the poet. Often forgetting or garbling his friend's remarks, or merely listening for the sake of pleasure and not transcription, he lacked —to use his own phrase—"the Boswell faculty." Instead, we see Wordsworth *en famille,* or walking around the lake at Grasmere, or wondering whether he ought to travel three hundred miles to London for the Queen's dance, or reacting stoically to the unexpected death of his daughter Dora. Robinson was the intermediary between Wordsworth and Coleridge during their misunderstanding; and his description of the motives and the frequent pettiness of the great men involved is our best record of this literary quarrel. There are accounts as well of Wordsworth on Byron, on Chatterton, on Milton, on the penny post, on politics, on the order in which his poems should be read, as well as some engaging discussion of Wordsworth's faults and virtues as a friend. This personal material is invaluable. In addition, it is worth noting that Robinson's comments on Wordsworth's poems are just and often demonstrate an acute knowledge of their texture, spirit, and relative importance. Almost all of Robinson's correspondence, particularly that with Wordsworth, exhibits an intense literary discussion of a sort unknown in our day in personal letters.

Often enough Robinson was a prosy and unselective diarist. One is obliged to use the index to find topics and names of importance. But he was alert to much of the best writing and talking of his age, and he himself evoked a portion of that intellectual activity. Obviously the thread of his own life as it is conveyed by his memoranda is for us not so important as the particulars of interesting men which the *Diary* preserves. Nevertheless his day to day jottings show him as a shrewd and generous man, possessed with a keen scent for literary and human greatness and a marvelous capacity for friendship.

DIGBY GRAND

Type of work: Novel
Author: George J. Whyte-Melville (1821-1878)
Type of plot: Picaresque romance
Time of plot: Early nineteenth century
Locale: England
First published: 1853

Principal characters:
    DIGBY GRAND, a spirited young Englishman, officer in the Guards
    SIR PEREGRINE GRAND, Digby's father
    SHADRACH, a money-lender
    TOM SPENCER, Digby's friend
    CAPTAIN LEVANTER, a fellow officer
    COLONEL CARTOUCH, Digby's commanding officer
    FLORA BELMONT, loved by Digby

Critique:

Because George J. Whyte-Melville's works have been catalogued as sporting fiction, they have never been given their rightful place in the history of English literature, and most scholars pass them by completely. It is true that Whyte-Melville wrote particularly for the sporting world, but his novels, especially *Digby Grand,* have interested wider audiences in their time. His writings have an air of liveliness, a note of authenticity, and an ineffable freshness. *Digby Grand* was Whyte-Melville's first novel, and it was truly termed by the novelist an autobiography, for the author's own early career as an officer in a Highland regiment and the Guards is mirrored in the novel. Digby Grand is, in fact, partly young Whyte-Melville. Considered in his time an authority on fox hunting, the author refers to the sport frequently in *Digby Grand,* as in his other novels.

The Story:

Digby Grand's father, Sir Peregrine Grand, of Haverley Hall, had one fond wish with respect to his son: he wanted Digby to be a man of fashion and to know his position in society. With that in mind, he decided that when Digby, then a youngster at Eton, should finish school he would be commissioned in the British Army. Digby, taken with the idea, wished to have his appointment made at once.

As luck had it, Digby met General Sir Benjamin Burgonet, who, pleased with the young man, made every effort to secure Digby's commission. Within a matter of weeks Digby received a letter announcing his commission in the army as an ensign in a regiment of infantry.

Digby Grand reported to his regiment's headquarters in Scotland, where he rapidly adjusted himself to military life. Being of an adventurous turn and liking sports and gambling, he quickly became a sought-out addition to any party. He soon discovered, however, that the slim allowance made him by his father and his small pay as an ensign did not cover his large expenditures, and so he fell into the habit of gambling on horses, cards, and billiards to augment his income. Most of his fellow officers existed in much the same fashion.

While in Scotland, Digby had a narrow escape from marriage when an officer's daughter, a woman in her thirties, induced Digby to become engaged. His friends saw through the woman's plot, however, and rescued him from his predicament. He had the satisfaction of seeing her become instead the wife of Dubbs, the regimental drum major.

Shortly after that incident Digby was sent to Canada for a tour of duty. Memorable events of that short tour were the slaughter of a huge bull moose and a love affair with a French-Canadian girl named Zoë. Colonel Cartouch, Digby's commanding officer, having taken a liking to the high-spirited young man, prevented him from marrying the girl because he felt that the teen-age ensign was not yet ready for marriage.

Upon his return to England, Digby found himself with a new commission in Her Majesty's service; his father had purchased a lieutenancy in the Life Guards for him during his absence in Canada. Digby was now in the most honored and most social brigade in the service, the Guards being the units which were stationed in London. Within a short time Digby had once again won for himself a place in fashionable London life. He was voted into several of the choicest gambling clubs, appeared in the best society, and was taken up by some well-known people. One of his friends was a youthful peer named St. Heliers; another was an officer named Levanter; a third was Mrs. Mantrap, a woman who basked in the attentions of young men.

To keep up his life of ease, including gambling for high stakes, maintaining good rooms, drinking only the best wines, and buying expensive horses, required all of Digby's resourcefulness. Because his resourcefulness was not enough at times, his friend Levanter introduced him to a money-lender named Shadrach, who was quite willing to lend Digby money at a high rate of interest, the principal to be repaid when Digby inherited the family estates. Not once but many times Digby borrowed from Shadrach.

One day, while in charge of a small group of military police at parade, Digby met Flora Belmont, who had attended the parade with her father, a retired colonel. Immediately Digby fell in love, in spite of the fact that the colonel had little or nothing to pass on to his daughter in the way of a fortune.

On his twenty-first birthday, spurred on by his own love and that which Flora Belmont had declared for him, Digby went home to Haverley Hall to request a definite income of size from his father so that he and Flora could be married. Sir Peregrine, instead of being happy, was furious that Digby would even think of

marrying anyone but an heiress, for the Grand estate was in poor financial condition and Sir Peregrine had been counting on a brilliant marriage by his son to recoup the family fortunes.

Downhearted, Digby returned to duty in London. To while away the time he continued his old life, living beyond his means and borrowing money to pay his expenses. He even borrowed from Shadrach when his boyhood chum, Tom Spencer, who was studying for holy orders at Oxford. had to sign the notes with him. For a time Digby had an affair with Coralie de Rivolte, a famous dancer, but that romance ended, though only after Digby had made an enemy of a scarfaced Spaniard who seemed to be the dancer's relative.

Eventually Digby got so deeply into debt that only a change of regiments could help him. As an officer in the Guards he had too many social responsibilities, and he exchanged commissions with an officer in a dragoon regiment stationed in Kent, at some distance from London. Within a few weeks he made still another move. Old General Sir Benjamin Burgonet, who had secured Digby's original commission, made him his aide, and Digby prepared to go with the general to India. He was somewhat aghast, however, to learn that the girl who had married the drum major was now Lady Burgonet.

In spite of his precautions, Digby was unable to leave England without falling into the hands of Shadrach and other creditors, who had him imprisoned for debt. To satisfy his creditors, Digby had to sell his commission and give up all he owned. At that black hour word came that Sir Peregrine had died, leaving Digby with the title and the estate. When the will was settled, however, it became apparent that the estate was too heavily in debt to be of any use to the new heir. To salvage himself, Digby had to sell the land; he inherited only the title.

He was saved by a meeting with Tom Spencer, who had been prevented from finishing his degree at Oxford by an arrest made for a note he had signed on Digby's behalf. Spencer, far from being downcast, had become a successful wine merchant. He took Digby into the business with him and the two built up a flourishing trade. Digby had, by that time, acquired a great deal more discretion and a few gray hairs.

After some years Digby ran across his old commanding officer, Colonel Cartouch. The colonel was engaged in prosecuting a man who had forged checks on his name, and the two discovered that the man was married to Coralie de Rivolte, Digby's old love. That surprise was not

the end, for the colonel discovered also that Coralie was his own daughter by a Spanish woman who had run away from him after killing her sister, whom she believed in love with Cartouch.

The appearance of Coralie reminded Digby of Flora Belmont, the girl whom his father had forbidden him to marry because she lacked a fortune. Digby found her in mourning for her father but still single. Through friends Digby learned that she had remained faithful to him. In a short time they had made plans for their approaching marriage. Digby Grand was ready to be tamed.

Further Critical Evaluation of the Work:

The values and traditions of Eton play a significant part in this rambling tale of "old boys." The horseman and huntsman (the two aspects of the "gentleman" considered most important, aside from perfect grooming and decorum) are the models that the motherless hero aspires to emulate. His interests are as narrow as those of the people around him; lacking intellectual drive, he is content with a physically active but superficial existence. The military is considered the only "acceptable" career for a gentleman or sportsman such as he early considers himself. Cigars, sherry, and horses are the main interests of the men in the book, except for brief encounters with a tepid form of romance.

The preparations for a career in the Guards are detailed with humor and enthusiasm, and the six-week voyage of the young soldier across the Atlantic is exhaustively presented. The author tends to overwhelm the reader with unselective details, but the enthusiasm of the telling carries the reader over the dull spots, and the unusual facts and novelty of some of the events are often interesting in themselves, although they contribute to no pattern or plot in the book. The novel, like a genuine "autobiography" (as the book is subtitled) simply recounts one event after another. The life of the Guards, on duty in Canada, is described with as much indefatigable detail as everything else in the narrative. The narrator-protagonist devotes much space to describing the scenery he encounters in his travels, from Niagara and Lake Erie to the northwoods sites of hunting parties to the fields and streams of England. In England, America, or wherever the hero is, horses, horseracing, and hunting play the major part in both his thoughts and actions.

The book is not subtle in either its humor or its efforts for effect. The names of most of the characters suggest caricatures rather than efforts to create fully-developed personalities: for example, the reader encounters Admiral Portfire, Mr. Stubble, Arabella Ramrod, Lawyer Sheepskin, and Mrs.

Mantrap. The heroines are all conventional, pale maidens, with little personality of their own; they are merely mannequins of ethereal beauty upon which the hero can shine his admiration and devotion.

The strengths of the novel lie in the density of the narrative and the variety and vividness of the boldly-sketched characterizations. Some of the characters are overdrawn, but others are humorous and colorful, and often entertaining. The accounts of the activities of the class portrayed (gambling, hunting, racing) are described with authenticity. As a record of the attitudes and occupations of these people and their age, the mid-Victorian period, the book presents an interesting, if limited, portrait. By the highest, most objective standards, the book is greatly flawed, but it has a place in literary history as an example of a type of popular novel and in social history as a document of a bygone era.

THE DINNER PARTY

Type of work: Novel
Author: Claude Mauriac (1914-   )
Time: The present
Locale: Paris
First published: 1959

Principal characters:

BERTRAND CARNÉJOUX, the host, an editor and novelist
MARTINE (PILOU) CARNÉJOUX, his wife
EUGÉNIE PRIEUR, an aging belle of Parisian society
GILLES BELLECROIX, a scenarist and aspiring novelist
LUCIENNE OSBORN, the egocentric wife of an American film producer
ROLAND SOULAIRES, a rich but frustrated bachelor
MARIE-ANGE (MARIETTA) VASGNE, an actress, mistress to Bertrand
JÉRÔME AYGULF, a childhood friend of Martine and a substitute guest

The Dinner Party is an experimental novel in the sense that it employs devices which would have amounted to experiment thirty or forty years ago: no narrator; no identification of speakers except by subject matter, leitmotif, or an occasional self-apostrophe; a fusion of conversation and soliloquy; the cross currents of two or three different subjects—stichomythic or protracted; and the illusion of simultaneity in the varied mental associations evoked by some passing remark. The difficulties of following such a presentation of multiple experience are only initial, being resolved in the development of character patterns which emerge despite the loss in translation of the uniqueness of language assigned to individual characters.

But if the experimental novel has become the sub-species of a traditional one, an example should not be dismissed as merely one more repetitive experiment but must be assessed as a work of art in an established medium. Claude Mauriac's performance in The Dinner Party is an impressive one. To treat at book length the incidental chatter and random musings of eight people during a dining period of perhaps two hours is the kind of *tour de force* liable to a reaction of boredom on a reader's part. But without telling a very significant story or symbolizing any extensive meaning, Mauriac sustains his kaleidoscope of sophicated sensibili-

ties with remarkable intensity. Not a single character in the book emerges as a great or memorable one; their relations to one another are rather trivial, in fact represent clichés of the *beau monde.*

There is no perceptibly dominant theme; all is dinner party experience observed and recorded by means of the dramatic method and the interior monologue. Yet the characters are thoroughly interesting people. Their talk—about history, about aristocratic geneology, about literature (Proust, Barrès, Anatole France, Graham Greene, and Gerard Manley Hopkins), about astrology, about travel, about God, and even about intellectual parlor games—is generally absorbing, occasionally informative, and often amusing. Their thoughts about one another, about themselves, and about the matters which happen to arise, are compounded of vanity, lust, boredom, jealousy, creative perceptivity, intelligence, insight, and hopeful intentions—all projected with a psychological subtlety and effectiveness which give the book its true unity. Other characters, in the persons of servants like the seductive Armande, or members of fashionable society who are talked about or recalled in memory, add to the dimensions of the emanating reality. Even details of the courses served, descriptions of spots on the table cloth or crumbs on a chair, and appraisals of the quality of the champagne being consumed are brilliantly integrated into the vibrant texture of the writing.

The situation which Claude Mauriac creates out of his assemblage of characters suggests Proust. The atmosphere they breathe is rarified. His people are elegant, aristocratic (or socially pretentious), artistic, and sensual. They are aware of social stratification, youth fading into age, their desire for one another, the interplay of their sensibilities, and the projection of their personae. Bergson hovers over the table: the diners indulge in flights of memory stimulated by simple words or sensations; they consider their future; but everything is focused upon the present moment of consciousness.

There is no head of the table as such, but the host sits as nearly opposite his wife as a round table seating four men and four women will allow. He is Bertrand Carnéjoux, the forty-six-year-old editor of the magazine *Ring* and author of a successful novel entitled *Sober Pleasures* (the original manuscript bore the more revealing title, *Metaphysics of Physical Passion*.) Preëminent in Carnéjoux's mind is the desire to write another novel of even greater artistic integrity, formulated in a new way which will bring into immediate juxtaposition the words and thoughts of his characters. More than once, as he notes his conversation at table, he regrets that he does not find it possible to achieve the same brilliance, the same eloquence when he is at work over a manuscript in his study. Meanwhile he presides over the party, secure in his knowledge of amorous success with every woman present except one. His conversation is mainly about literature, his thoughts divided between love affairs and plans for writing.

His wife Martine is twenty-six, intimately known as Pilou, and the wealthy and innocent daughter of Irene, one of Bertrand's former mistresses. Throughout the party her thoughts are mainly radiant expressions of love for her two children Rachel and Jean-Paul; but she is also tempted to respond to the attentions of Bellecroix.

Gilles Bellecroix, forty-nine, is a screen writer who is more famous than Bertrand but who is not satisfied inwardly with his achievement. He is obsessed with the idea that he must produce a good novel in order to realize himself. Meanwhile he observes the dinner guests with a cinematic eye, visualizing meaningful scenes in flickers of pose or behavior. Between him and Bertrand there is a latent rivalry which carries over into Gilles's flirtation with Martine, the motion of whose dancing on an earlier occasion is unforgettable to him. But Gilles finds his real center of being in his wife Bénédicte, knows that for him true happiness lies in love, fidelity, monogamy.

Eugénie Prieur, still, at sixty-seven, called "Gigi" by young blades of Paris, is the oldest guest (too old to have been one of Bertrand's conquests), full of rich nostalgic memories, the wisdom of long experience, and an intimate knowledge of social machinations. The perspective with which she endows her world is further documented by her conversations about historic family connections.

Roland Soulaires, forty-five, is temperamentally a Prufrock who hides his fears and insecurity behind his idle dreams and his clever talk with Eugénie about social identification. Extremely wealthy, but fat and bald, he fails to interest the beautiful guest at his left.

She is twenty-four-year-old Marie-Ange Vasgne, formerly named Marietta, a Canadian farm girl, but now a sultry blond model and aspiring actress. Marie-Ange is Bertrand's current mistress who dares near the end of the party to tease him by inquiring after Marie-Plum, another mistress whom Bertrand has never been able to forget. Everyone's knowledge of these affairs, admitted or not, is the measure of civilization for these people. Marie-Ange toys with the numbers one through six, as though seeking a pattern of sense in the world.

Lucienne Osborn, forty-two, is married to an American film producer, not present at the dinner. Her mind vapid, her body faded, she is preoccupied with thoughts of television sets, suntan, her dog Zig, and her lover, Léon-Pierre.

Jérôme Aygulf, who is twenty, finds himself out of his element. A childhood friend of Martine, he was invited only at the last moment after another guest had sent regrets. Jérôme, aspiring but naïve, is at the opposite end of the scale from Eugénie. He finds himself longing for the attention and patronage of Bertrand more than for anything else. Insecure and a little awkward in this society, he nonetheless attracts the attention of Marie-Ange.

The Dinner Party belongs in that class of novels, including also *The Sacred Fount* and *The Counterfeiters,* in which a novelist as a character thinks interchangeably about experience and the novel. The center of interest in Mauriac's book really lies in the thoughts and comments expressed by Bertrand and Gilles about the novel form. Referring to his novel, Bertrand speaks of a new kind of fiction, one in which on some common occasion, such as the present dinner party, time and space would be suspended. And contemplating his next one, which will fuse thought and speech, Bertrand responds to Claudel's definition of the simplicity of truth along the line of Diderot's Proustian statement that "Everything we have ever known . . . exists within us without our knowing it." The book is studded with criticism of novelists and theories of the novel, ideas which reveal character but also illuminate the practice of Claude Mauriac in this particular novel. In one way or another *The Dinner Party* raises a host of interesting questions about modern fiction.

THE DISCIPLE

Type of work: Novel
Author: Paul Bourget (1852-1935)
Type of plot: Psychological realism
Time of plot: Late nineteenth century
Locale: Paris and Riom
First published: 1889

> *Principal characters:*
> ADRIEN SIXTE, a philosopher
> ROBERT GRESLOU, his disciple
> M. DE JUSSAT, a hypochondriac nobleman
> CHARLOTTE, his daughter
> LUCIEN, her younger brother
> ANDRÉ, her older brother

Critique:

Bourget represents in some ways the transition in French letters from naturalistic materialism to the more traditional religious and moral disciplines, and *The Disciple* is the mid-point in the work of this distinguished critic, novelist, and academician. This novel is a psychological study of the moral bases in abstract learning. Bourget has written an impeccable novel which combines solid psychological analysis with a sensational murder story.

The Story:

Adrien Sixte grew up in a peculiar way. His hardworking father wanted him to study for one of the professions, but despite the boy's early promise in school he never went to a university. His indulgent parents allowed him to spend ten lonely years in study. In 1868, at the age of twenty-nine, Adrien Sixte published a five-hundred-page study of *The Psychology of God*. By the outbreak of the Franco-Prussian War, Adrien had become the most discussed philosopher in the country. He followed his first study with two books even more provocative, *The Anatomy of the Will* and *The Theory of the Passions*.

Soon after the death of his parents, Adrien settled down to a well-regulated life in Paris. So regular was he that the inhabitants of the quarter could set their watches by his comings and goings. He spent eight hours of the twenty-four in work, took two walks each day, received callers, chiefly students, one afternoc . a week, and on another afternoon made calls on other scholars. By patient labor and brilliant insight he developed to his complete satisfaction his deterministic theory that each effect comes from a cause, and that if all causes are known, results can be predicted accurately. He applied his theory to all forms of human activity, to vices as well as virtues.

One day the neighbors were startled to see Adrien leave his apartment hurriedly at an unusual hour. He had received, to his great consternation, a notice to appear before a magistrate in the affair of Robert Greslou, one of his students, and he had also a letter from Robert's mother saying that she would visit him that very day at four on an urgent matter.

The sophisticated judge was incredulous when he learned that Adrien never read the papers. The celebrated savant had not heard of Greslou's imprisonment after being charged with the murder of Charlotte de Jussat. Adrien soon learned that the suspect had been arrested on purely circumstantial evidence, that the proof of his guilt or innocence might well be only psychological. Hence Adrien, the master, must testify as to his

THE DISCIPLE by Paul Bourget. By permission of the publishers, Charles Scribner's Sons.

disciple's ideas on multiplied psychological experience. Adrien explained that if a chemist can analyze water into hydrogen and oxygen, he can synthesize hydrogen and oxygen into water. Similarly, if a psychological result can be analyzed into its causes, the result can be reproduced by those same causes; that is, by scientific method one can predict human behavior. The judge was much interested and inquired if his theory applied to vices. Adrien said that it did, for psychologically vices are forms of behavior as interesting and valid as social virtues.

When he returned home, Adrien found Robert's mother waiting for him. She protested her son's innocence and begged Adrien to save her boy. Adrien remembered Robert as a precocious student of philosophy, but he really knew little of him as a person. The mother begged Adrien to help and gave him a manuscript written by Robert while in jail. On the outside of the manuscript was a note. If Adrien read the document, he must agree not to try to save Robert; if the condition were unacceptable, he must burn the manuscript immediately. With many misgivings Adrien took the document and read it. It was a minute and detailed account of Robert's upbringing, his studies, and his experiences in the de Jussat home.

Robert was always brilliant. He did outstanding work in school and early in his studies showed a pronounced talent in psychology. Most of his time was devoted to study, but a developing sensuality showed itself sporadically. Since he grew up at Clermont, he lacked some of the polish imparted at Paris; in consequence he failed an examination. While waiting another opportunity to enter the university, Robert accepted a year's appointment as tutor to Lucien de Jussat. At the de Jussat country home Robert found an interesting household. Lucien, his pupil, was a fat, simple boy of thirteen. André, the older brother, was an army officer fond of hunting and riding. The father was a hypochondriac and a

boor. But Charlotte, the daughter of the family, was a beautiful girl of nineteen.

Robert soon began the studied seduction of Charlotte. He had three reasons for such a step. First, he wanted to have some sort of revenge against the wealthy family. In the second place, his developed sexuality made the project attractive. Also, and probably more important, he wanted to test his theory that if he could determine the causes leading to love and sexual desire, he could produce desire by providing the causes. Robert kept careful notes on procedures and results.

He knew that pity is close to love. Consequently he aroused the pity of Charlotte by mysterious allusions to his painful past. Then, by carefully selecting a list of novels for her to read, he set about inflaming her desire for passionate, romantic love. But Robert was too hasty. He made an impassioned avowal to Charlotte and frightened her into leaving for Paris. Just as Robert began to despair of ever accomplishing his purpose, the illness of Lucien recalled Charlotte. Robert wrote her a note telling her he would commit suicide if she did not come to his room by midnight. He prepared two vials of strychnine and waited. When Charlotte came, he showed her the poison and proposed a suicide pact. Charlotte accepted, provided she could be the first to die. They spent the night together. Robert had triumphed.

Robert repudiated the pact, prompted in part by a real love for Charlotte. The next day she threatened to call her brother if Robert attempted to stop her own attempt at suicide, for she had read Robert's notes and knew she was simply the object of an experiment. After writing to her brother André a letter telling him of her intended suicide, she drank the strychnine. Robert was arrested soon afterward on suspicion of murder.

When Adrien Sixte came to the end of the manuscript, he began to feel a moral responsibility for his disciple's act. Disregarding the pledge implicit in his reading, he sent a note to André asking him if he intended to let Robert be convicted of murder by concealing Charlotte's letter. André resolved to tell the truth, and in a painful courtroom scene Robert was acquitted.

Immediately after the trial, André went to look for Robert. Scarcely able to resist, since he had been ready to die with Charlotte's secret safe, Robert went with André willingly. On the street, André pulled out a gun and shot Robert in the head. Robert's mother and Adrien mourned beside the coffin, Adrien because he accepted moral responsibility for the teachings that had prompted his disciple's deed.

Further Critical Evaluation of the Work:

Paul Bourget defines the moralist as a writer who not only portrays life exactly as it is, but deals with its profound lessons of secret atonement. In the Preface of *The Disciple,* he proclaims that it is a writer's duty to point out the cure for the evils of his time. With an almost Jansenistic rigor, Bourget in this novel, denounces perversities and disorders of human nature and attempts to find the remedy for them. Inspired by the environmental theory, he attacks belief in the power of science and certain types of progress that stem from scientific systems. *The Disciple* caused Bourget to be widely acclaimed as the founder of the Catholic psychological novel, due in part to his proposed solutions to social problems. His ideas in *The Disciple* are reactions against the positivism and skepticism that dominated the novels of some of his contemporaries in the French literary world, notably Anatole France.

Although Bourget vigorously criticizes society in *The Disciple,* he was able to see a solution to its problems. He found it not in socialism as did Zola and France, for example, but in a return to Christianity. This marked a change in the author's point of view from detached psychologist to a convinced moralist. Further, it marked the arrival of a new epoch in the French novel. The book caused a sensation, and certain intellectual battles raged over it. Anatole France, as might be expected, expressed a strong negative reaction to it, but others, notably the critic Ferdinand Brunstiere, himself a moralist, hotly defended it. It was admitted by all factions, however, that *The Disciple* marked an important date in the intellectual and moral history of France. Modern critics have found Bourget's moralistic attitude and Roman Catholic sympathies disproportionately evident in this book and the ones following it, but the novel is still widely read for its superb psychological studies and for its influence on the modern psycho-sociological novel.

DISCOURSE ON THE ORIGIN OF INEQUALITY

Type of work: Political and philosophical essay
Author: Jean Jacques Rousseau (1712-1778)
First published: 1754

The *Discourse on the Origin of Inequality* is one of the early works in which Rousseau examines and expounds his rebellion against the social order as it exists, a revolt that the writer was to continue throughout his life. Rousseau believed that the evils which plague mankind have their origins not in sin but in man's departure from the natural state, in which man was happy and good. This is the typical Romantic view of the Noble Savage.

In his inquiry into the origins of inequality, Rousseau begins with man, the core and motivation of his study. He states that there are two kinds of inequality among men. One is "natural or physical" because it is created by nature and consists of the obvious physical differences. The second is what he calls "moral or political inequality," which grows out of convention and flowers because of the "consent of men." The inquiry accepts the beliefs of religion that God took man out of a state of nature by His will, but it considers also what might have become of man had he been left to develop by himself.

The first part of the inquiry concerns itself with man in his natural state, the state of nature, the "embryo of his species." In this animal state, he was the most promising of all other animals, and was therefore the most felicitously situated. He was free from artificial worries and not given to reflection. Rousseau asserts the extreme position that man thinking is a depraved animal. Nature is benign and treats all her creatures well. It is only as man departs from the cradle of nature that he begins to degenerate both physically and morally, for he is physically and morally superior in the state of nature. Metaphysically, he is superior because he is motivated solely by instinct to desire and to fear. He cannot, therefore, be either good or bad, vicious or virtuous.

Rousseau attacks directly the political philosophy of Thomas Hobbes's *Leviathan* and its insistence that man is fundamentally vicious and must be controlled. Rousseau urges that Hobbes should have concluded that the state of nature affords man the greatest opportunity for self-preservation without doing injury to others and therefore should be the state in which man is least vicious, wicked, and injurious to his fellow man. Hobbes failed signally in making two key observations: one, that savages are not bad merely because they cannot know good, but rather because their passions are peaceful; two, that man is by nature compassionate because of an innate repugnance to see fellow creatures suffer, and this compassion moderates the violence of egotism.

The second part of the essay concerns itself with proving that man became wicked as he became a social animal. Society began when the first man staked out property and claimed it as his own. One of Rousseau's most powerful sentences condemns this false claim and the long string of crimes, murders, misfortunes, and general horrors that sprang from it. A savior of mankind would have been the man who declared in ringing terms: "Be sure not to this imposter; you are lost, if you forget that the fruits of the earth belong to us all, and the earth itself to nobody." Rousseau quotes with approval John Locke's famous statement that "There can be no injury, where there is no property."

As men congregated into groups, each person began to think about the others and to consider public esteem. Each man who excelled in some particular thing—singing best, dancing best, hunting best, or the like—began to assert his excellence, and nobody could deny the rating. As superiority grew, so did another complication, morality. In savage minds morality had been simple. In more advanced societies punishments for offenses by one person against another became more numerous and severe. Increasingly, Rousseau asserts, it became clear to all men that there were advantages to appearing to be what one actually was not. From the difference between seeming and being sprang pomp and trickery, as well as all the lesser vices that go in their train.

From this situation it was not a long step to another vice, the establishment of law. Clever, powerful men, Rousseau says, seeing the advantage of joining their strength to exploit the weak, seduced the powerless into allowing themselves to be protected by the strong, when they had nothing to be protected against, for the sake of harmony among them all. Rousseau drives home his point with one of the most ringing statements in the book, anticipating in its power and direction the powerful statement which begins *Du Contrat Social,* stating that man is born free but is everywhere enslaved: "All offered their necks to the yoke in hopes of securing their liberty. . . ." The result of this flight into slavery was the eternal fixing of the laws of property and inequality. "Clever usurpation" had been converted into "unalterable right," and for the benefit of a few ambitious individuals all mankind had been reduced to perpetual labor, slavery and misery.

Political distinctions always breed civil distinctions, and the nature of man in society being what it is, men gladly submit to slavery if they are filled with the hope that they can themselves enslave others. From the great inequalities among men rise numerous evils, one of the greatest being despotism, which is bound to result in the overthrow of the despot through revolution.

Rousseau ends his discourse with a ringing declaration of the superiority of man in the state of nature over man in a state of society. The former is diametrically opposed to the latter. Man in nature is peaceful and free, wanting only to live and be free from work. Man in society is always toiling and sweating, moving, even rushing into death in order to live. Rousseau's conclusion is that all inequalities that now weigh man down result from the development of man's faculties and working of his mind. Further, it is clear that moral inequality opposes natural right.

The essay is in general a passionate explanation of the author's belief in the ideal state of man. It purports to be, and usually is to a certain extent, an unbiased and learned examination. Rousseau slights certain areas and telescopes others, passing over them with a brief word of what he could prove had he the time or inclination to present evidence; however, these passages do not invalidate or even weaken the argument in general.

Stylistically, the essay is often weak because the arguments are not tightly organized and presented. Though impassioned, it does not have the power of Rousseau's later works, especially *Du Contrat Social* or the *Confessions.*

DISCOURSES

Type of work: Dialogues
Author: Pietro Aretino (1492-1556)
Time: Sixteenth century
Locale: Rome
First published: Part I, 1534; Part II, 1536

Principal characters:
NANNA, a courtesan
ANTONIA, her friend
PIPPA, Nanna's daughter

Pietro Aretino won his reputation as "the Scourge of Princes" with his sharp, scurrilous attacks on the important men of his time; he is best known as a writer for his vigorous, witty, often obscene plays and dialogues that show him as a realist and something of an ironist. He was deeply conscious of the moral corruption of his age, but he was for the most part content to portray it vividly without endeavoring to reform it.

The *Discourses* (*Ragionamenti*) is based on an underlying premise that sex is the overriding concern of all human beings. Aretino treats the subject with great humor and gusto. He is a gifted storyteller and an acute observer of the mores of society, skillful at painting every detail of a lavish banquet or a lady's costume.

In this work Aretino has linked together a succession of tales, beast fables, and anecdotes with a narrative framework, using a pattern successfully employed by Chaucer in *The Canterbury Tales* and Boccaccio in *The Decameron;* the tone of his work is close to that of Chaucer's *fabliaux,* the tales of the miller, the reeve, the friar, and others of the bawdier pilgrims. Each of the two parts of Aretino's *Discourses* consists of three days' conversation. In Part I, Nanna takes up successively the life of the nun, the wife, and the courtesan. Part II deals with rules for the successful prostitute, the "Betrayals of Men," and the "art" of the procuress.

On the first day Nanna, a witty, experienced courtesan, tells her friend Antonia about her entrance into a con-

vent. Leaving grieving lovers behind, she went with fear and trembling toward what she feared was to be a grim, ascetic existence. She describes, ironically in the light of what follows, the solemn ceremony in which they divested her of her worldliness, then goes on to recount the sights that greeted her when she entered the nunnery. Pretty young nuns and handsome, merry priests feasted together in the greatest luxury, eating and drinking their fill while laughing and talking throughout the meal that was theoretically governed by the rule of silence. The banquet concluded with what can only be described as an orgy, while Nanna and a companion went strolling down the hall, entertaining themselves by spying through cracks in the wall on the grotesque amours of the older nuns. Aretino spares no details to make the scene as corrupt and disgusting as possible.

To enlighten Antonia about the deceptions commonly practiced by wives, Nanna tells several tales, all calculated to reveal the cleverness of women. In the first a doctor's wife, renowned throughout her village for her ostentatious piety, pays frequent visits to a hermit, who "stole time for his devotions" from tending his elaborate garden. The "holy couple" was discovered in bed by a villager, who promptly summoned his friends and the parish priest to see the sight. The hermit, awakened by the commotion, was unperturbed. Everyone knows, he explained, that holy men sin only when they are possessed by demons; he could not be blamed for his actions. Taking her cue from him, the doctor's wife immediately feigned madness, recovering her senses only after she had three times touched the holiest relics in the church, the two knuckle bones of the holy innocents.

Heavy irony pervades Nanna's second tale of unfaithful wives. The "heroine" is described in lyric terms. She seems to float in the air when she walks, and she genuflects with such grace that "it seemed it must be the way they did it in paradise." This paragon of virtue is desperately anxious to escape the close surveillance of her elderly husband, "called the Count from some worthless old castle or other with two chimneys and a crumbling moat." She pretends to walk in her sleep, sure that her husband will follow her, and causes him to fall and break his leg. Bedridden, he hires ten stalwart young men to guard his wife for him, and she, having accomplished what she wanted, "sleepwalks" nightly with these guards.

Nanna's description of the courtesan's life is filled with similar stories. She tells Antonia how she deceived her various lovers and filled her purse in the process. Each of her stories indicates that avarice and not lust is the dominating force in this kind of life.

At the end of the third day Antonia, considering all that Nanna has told her, advises her to make her daughter Pippa a prostitute, for it seems the most honest life of the three. Both the nun and the wife betray sacred vows, while the whore, like the soldier, "is paid for doing wrong, and doing it, she is not to be held for so doing, because that is what her shop has to sell." Her life is a luxurious one, and a little penitence at the end will clear her of her sins.

The second part of the *Discourses* is briefer and more disconnected than the first; it seems to have been written to capitalize on the popularity of its predecessor. The first day's discussion begins as Pippa pouts and begs her mother to make her a courtesan, as her godmother Antonia has advised. Nanna agrees and gives her daughter a few basic rules of the profession. In dealing with Spaniards, who carry on their courtships with flowery language and much hand kissing, return bow for bow and kiss for kiss, but get rid of them as quickly as possible. A Frenchman, on the other hand, should be welcomed at once, for in making love to him, one can steal the shirt from his back. Nanna reserves her greatest praise for the men of Venice, where Aretino made his home for the latter part of his life; they are generous and kind—ideal lovers, in fact.

Nanna recounts several anecdotes in the same vein as the stories told on the third day of the first group of dialogues: accounts of elaborate schemes for fleecing unsuspecting customers. She deceived one violent-tempered suitor with an elaborate plot, provoking him to strike her, then hiring a friend to paint a hideous scar on her face. Hoping to avoid arrest for assaulting her, her lover sent lavish gifts, money, and doctors to attend her. He made a settlement of five hundred ducats and paid more to have the scar "healed" by another swindler. Nanna finally restored him to her favors in return for the promise of a new dress.

Perhaps the most famous passage in the *Discourses* is the description of the sack of Rome by the Germans, described by Nanna as an example of the "Betrayals of Men." Aretino displays great scorn for the Romans who, hearing of the invaders, decked themselves in their finest uniforms, then fled in panic. There is a vivid description of the horrors of the night when no church, no home, no hospital offered sanctuary from the enemy. "The pity was to hear husbands, red with the blood which streamed from their wounds, calling for their lost wives in a voice that would have made the solid block of the Coliseum weep."

A stark description of the rape of a young prostitute by thirty-one stablemen reinforces Nanna's comments on men. A lighter tale, the account of the deception of a silly young wife by a poet she had been pursuing, concludes the second day's conversation.

Nanna and Pippa listen to a godmother and a nurse as they comment upon the superiority of the procuress to the prostitute, the subject of the final dialogue. The godmother tells them how she once lured strangers to the homes of young courtesans, where they were robbed of their cloaks as well as of their cash. She also boasts of her part in the elopement of a young wife, whose elderly husband was duped into admitting her lover into their home to cure his toothache.

Although Aretino's *Discourses* is not great literature, it is entertaining in much the same way that the Elizabethan comedies about clever rogues are. The author, giving a lively picture of the seamier side of life in his time, writes in a style that, applied to more significant topics, might have given him a much higher place among Renaissance men of letters than he now holds.

THE DIVAN

Type of work: Poetry
Author: Hāfiz (Shams ud-din Mohammed, c.1320-c.1388)
First transcribed: c.1350

The *Divan* of Hāfiz is one of the glories of Persian literature in its Golden Age and a classic of Eastern literature. Hāfiz was the pen name of Shams ud-din Mohammed, a Persian who early in life turned to the serious study of philosophy, poetry, and theology. The pen name he adopted means "a man who remembers," a title normally bestowed upon persons who have committed the Koran to memory. In Hāfiz' case the title was not unwarranted, for he was a dervish who taught the Koran in an academy founded by his patron, the Vizier Haji Kiwam-ud-din.

The *Divan* is the best known of Hāfiz' works. In addition, he wrote in various other patterns common to Persian poetry. The *Divan* itself is a collection of short poems, lyric in quality, in the form known as *ghazals*. In the original Persian these poems consist of from five to sixteen couplets (called *baits*), and the particular poetical form has been compared to the ode and the sonnet in English-language poetry because of the lyric qualities, the length, and the subject matter. One curious feature of Hāfiz' *ghazals* is that the last two lines normally contain the poet's name. The first line of each *ghazal* introduces the rhyme, which is repeated in every other succeeding line within the poem.

Although relatively little known in the Western world, Hāfiz' *Divan* has remained the most popular poetry ever written in his native land. It has even been considered oracular, and Persians sometimes consult the book by opening the book and placing a finger on a chance passage, hoping to have an answer thereby to whatever question has arisen. Such a procedure, or a variation of it, was supposedly done at the death of the poet.

Because of exception taken to some of his poems, his corpse was at first denied the usual burial rites. To settle the question, some of his *ghazals* were written on slips of paper and placed in an urn, one to be drawn out by a child. According to legend, the verse drawn by chance from the urn said that Hāfiz should be given appropriate funeral rites, as he would enter Paradise; thus the question was settled.

Through the centuries there has been debate over whether his poetry should be taken literally or symbolically, with those who want to see in the *Divan* a serious work by a great Persian philosopher and student of the Koran taking one side of the question, those who wish to see in the work a fine expression of a warmly alive human being taking the other. Western readers who cannot see anything religious in these superficially hedonistic poems should call to mind the religious expression, veiled in imagery though it is, of such poetry as that of John Donne and Richard Crashaw in England and Edward Taylor in America.

Whether one may wish to take it literally or on a symbolic level, the imagery of Hāfiz' poetry is warm, human, even passionate. There is no escaping, even in translation, the sincerity of the poet. Like most Eastern poetry, the imagery may even seem lush to Western readers, as in the following example:

The east wind at the dawn of day brought a perfume from the tresses of my beloved, which immediately cast my foolish heart into fresh agitation.
I imagined that I had uprooted that flower from the garden of my heart, for every blossom which sprang up from its suffering bore only the fruits of pain.

THE DIVAN by Hafiz. Translated by Henry Bertram Lister. Published by La Boheme Club, San Francisco, Calif. Excerpts reprinted by permission of the Executors of the Estate of Henry B. Lister. Copyright, 1950, by Henry B. Lister.

From fear of the attacks of her love, I
set my heart free with bloody strife;
my heart dropped gouts of blood
which marked my footsteps.
I beheld from her terrace how the glory
of the moon veiled itself in confusion, before the face of that dazzling
sun.

In his poems Hāfiz praises love between man and woman, and he praises
also the beauty of women, their eyes,
their lips, their hair, their features, their
forms. He also sings of wine and men,
as in these lines:

O Cupbearer! bring the joy of youth;
bring cup after cup of red wine.
Bring medicine for the disease of love;
bring wine, which is the balm of old
and young.
Do not grieve for the revolution of
time, that it wheeled thus and not
thus. Touch the lute in peace.
Wisdom is very wearisome; bring for its
neck the noose of wine.
When the rose goes, say, "Go gladly,"
and drink wine, red like the rose.
If the moan of the turtle does no remain, what matter? Bring music in
the jug of wine.

Whether one can interpret this praise of
wine as symbolic of spiritual substance is
open to question. That there is passion,
grace, and charm in the lines is, however,
undeniable. The same is true of the
following, also typical of Hāfiz:

O interpreter of dreams! give good tid-
ings because last night the sun
seemed to be my ally in the joy of
the morning sleep.
At the hour when Hāfiz was writing
this troubled verse, the bird of his
heart had fallen into the snare of
love.

An interesting legend about one of Hāfiz' poems in the *Divan* has come down
through the ages. In the poem he offered
willingly to exchange both the rich cities
of Bokhara and Samarkand for the mole
on the cheek of his beloved. When the
great conqueror Tamerlane learned of the
poem and had an opportunity, he sent
for the poet and rebuked him, saying
that Hāfiz should not have offered to
give away what did not lay in his power
to bestow. Not entirely subdued, even in
the presence of the great Tamerlane,
Hāfiz is supposed to have replied that it
was through such generosity that he came
to the attention of the mighty conqueror.
Over and over again in the *Divan* another city is mentioned, his own native
city of Shiraz, which he loved greatly.
("Hail, Shiraz! incomparable site! O
Lord, preserve it from every disaster!")
From the fame of Hāfiz and his poems,
Shiraz came to be a symbol of poetic
inspiration among poets who followed
him.

The reader of the *Divan* will find himself making comparisons between Hāfiz'
lyrics and those of Omar Khayyám, an
earlier Persian poet and one whose work
is more widely known among English-
speaking readers through the adaptation
by Edward FitzGerald. The works of the
two poets have much in common. The
apparent hedonism, the similar imagery,
and the same flowing mellifluousness are
found in the work of both men. The
obvious difference is the superficial one
of form, Omar Khayyám having written
in quatrains, as the word "Rubáiyát" indicates, Hāfiz in the form of the *ghazal*.
But a more important difference lies in
the attitudes expressed in the poems. Hāfiz is the more serious of the two, despite
an apparent hedonism. There is a greater
inclination on the part of Hāfiz to be
religious, to place his faith in Allah and
his wisdom, inscrutable as the poet may
find it. One result is that it is easier to
think of Hāfiz growing old gracefully
than of Omar Khayyám facing inevitable
old age with equanimity.

THE DIVINE COMEDY

Type of work: Poem
Author: Dante Alighieri (1265-1321)
Type of plot: Christian allegory
Time of plot: The Friday before Easter, 1300
Locale: Hell, Purgatory, Paradise
First transcribed: c.1320

Principal characters:
DANTE
VIRGIL, his guide
BEATRICE, the soul of Dante's beloved

Critique:

No words can describe the greatness of this work, a greatness both of theme and poetry. As a poet, Dante takes his place in the ranks of the foremost artists the world has ever known. The theme which he treats is universal; it involves the greatest concepts which man has ever attained. Only a master could find the loftiness of tone and the splendor and variety of images and scenes which are presented in *The Divine Comedy*.

The Story:

Dante found himself lost in a dark and frightening wood, and as he was trying to regain his path, he came to a mountain which he decided to climb in order to get his bearings. Strange beasts blocked his way, however, and he was forced back to the plain. As he was bemoaning his fate, the poet Virgil approached Dante and offered to conduct him through Hell, Purgatory, and blissful Paradise.

When they arrived at the gates of Hell, Virgil explained that here were confined those who had lived their lives without regard for good or evil. At the River Acheron, where they found Charon, the ferryman, Dante was seized with terror and fell into a trance. Aroused by a loud clap of thunder, he followed his guide through Limbo, the first circle of Hell. The spirits confined there, he learned, were those who, although they had lived a virtuous life, had not been baptized.

At the entrance to the second circle of Hell, Dante met Minos, the Infernal Judge, who warned him to take heed how he entered the lower regions. Dante was overcome by pity as he witnessed the terrible punishment which the spirits were undergoing. They had been guilty of carnal sin, and for punishment they were whirled around without cessation in the air. The third circle housed those who had been guilty of the sin of gluttony. They were forced to lie deep in the mud, under a constant fall of snow and hail and stagnant water. Above them stood Cerberus, a cruel monster, barking at the helpless creatures and tearing at their flesh. In the next circle, Dante witnessed the punishment of the prodigal and the avaricious, and realized the vanity of fortune.

He and Virgil continued on their journey until they reached the Stygian Lake, in which the wrathful and gloomy were suffering. At Virgil's signal, a ferryman transported them across the lake to the city of Dis. They were denied admittance, however, and the gates were closed against them by the fallen angels who guard the city. Dante and Virgil gained admittance into the city only after an angel had interceded for them. There Dante discovered that tombs burning with a blistering heat housed the souls of heretics. Dante spoke to two of these tormented spirits and learned that all the souls in Hell, who knew nothing of the present, can remember the past, dimly foresee the Future.

The entrance to the seventh circle was guarded by the Minotaur, and only after Virgil had pacified him could the two travelers pass down the steep crags to the base of the mountain. There they discerned a river of blood in which those who had committed violence in their lifetimes were confined. On the other side of the river they learned that those who had committed suicide were doomed to inhabit the trunks of trees. Beyond the river they came to a desert in which were confined those who had sinned against God, or Art, or Nature. A stream flowed near the desert and the two poets followed it until the water plunged into an abyss. In order that they might descend to the eighth circle, Virgil summoned Geryon, a frightful monster, who conducted them below. There they saw the tortured souls of seducers, flatterers, diviners, and barterers. Continuing along their way, they witnessed the punishment accorded hypocrites and robbers. In the ninth gulf were confined scandalmongers and spreaders of false doctrine. Among the writhing figures they saw Mahomet. Still farther along, the two discovered the horrible disease-ridden bodies of forgerers, counterfeiters, alchemists, and all those who deceived under false pretenses.

They were summoned to the next circle by the sound of a trumpet. In it were confined all traitors. A ring of giants surrounded the circle, one of whom lifted both Dante and Virgil and deposited them in the bottom of the circle. There Dante conversed with many of the spirits and learned the nature of their particular crimes.

After this visit to the lowest depths of Hell, Dante and Virgil emerged from the foul air to the pure atmosphere which surrounded the island of Purgatory. In a little while, they saw a boat conducted by an angel, in which were souls being brought to Purgatory. Dante recognized that of a friend among them. The two poets reached the foot of a mountain, where passing spirits showed them the easiest path to climb its slope. On their way up the path they encountered many spirits who explained that they were kept in Ante-Purgatory because they had delayed their repentance too long. They pleaded with Dante to ask their families to pray for their souls when he once

again returned to earth. Soon Dante and Virgil came to the gate of Purgatory, which was guarded by an angel. The two poets ascended a winding path and saw men, bent under the weight of heavy stones, who were expiating the sin of pride. They examined the heavily carved cornices which they passed, and found them covered with inscriptions urging humility and righteousness. At the second cornice were the souls of those who had been guilty of envy. They wore sackcloth and their eyelids were sewed with iron thread. Around them were the voices of angels singing of great examples of humility and the futility of envy. An angel invited the poets to visit the third cornice, where those who had been guilty of anger underwent repentance. Dante was astonished at the examples of patience which he witnessed there. At the fourth cornice he witnessed the purging of the sin of indifference or gloominess. He discussed with Virgil the nature of love. The Latin poet stated that there were two kinds of love, natural love, which was always right, and love of the soul, which might be misdirected. At the fifth cornice, avarice was purged. On their way to the next cornice, the two were overtaken by Statius, whose spirit had been cleansed and who was on his way to Paradise. He accompanied them to the next place of purging, where the sin of gluttony was repented, while voices sang of the glory of temperance. The last cornice was the place for purging by fire of the sin of incontinence. Here the sinners were heard to recite innumerable examples of praiseworthy chastity.

An angel now directed the two poets and Statius to a path which would lead them to Paradise. Virgil told Dante that he might wander through Paradise at his will until he found his love, Beatrice. As he was strolling through a forest, Dante came to a stream, on the other side of which stood a beautiful woman. She explained to him that the stream was called Lethe, and helped him to cross it. Then Beatrice descended from heaven and reproached him for his unfaithfulness to her during her life, but the virgins in the heavenly fields interceded with her on his behalf. Convinced of his sincere repentance and remorse, she agreed to accompany him through the heavens.

On the moon Dante found those who had made vows of chastity and determined to follow the religious life, but who were forced to break their vows. Beatrice led him to the planet Mercury, the second heaven, and from there to Venus, the third heaven, where Dante conversed with many spirits and learned of their virtues. On the sun, the fourth heaven, they were surrounded by a group of spirits, among them Thomas Aquinas. He named each of the spirits in turn and discussed their individual virtues. A second circle of blessed spirits surrounded the first, and Dante learned from each how he had achieved blessedness.

Then Beatrice and Dante came to Mars, the fifth heaven, where were cherished the souls of those who had been martyred. Dante recognized many renowned warriors and crusaders among them.

On Jupiter, the sixth heaven, Dante saw the souls of those who had administered justice faithfully in the world. The seventh heaven was on Saturn, where Dante found the souls of those who had spent their lives in meditation and religious retirement. From there Beatrice and her lover passed to the eighth heaven, the region of the fixed stars. Dante looked back over all the distance which

extended between the earth and this apex of Paradise and was dazzled and awed by what he saw. As they stood there, they saw the triumphal hosts approaching, with Christ leading, followed by Mary.

Dante was questioned by the saints. Saint Peter examined his opinions concerning faith; Saint James, concerning hope, and Saint John, concerning charity. Adam then approached and told the poet of the first man's creation, of his life in Paradise, and of his fall and what had caused it. Saint Peter bitterly lamented the avarice which his apostolic successors displayed, and all the sainted host agreed with him.

Beatrice then conducted Dante to the ninth heaven, where he was permitted to view the divine essence and to listen to the chorus of angels. She then led him to the Empyrean, from the heights of which, and with the aid of her vision, he was able to witness the triumphs of the angels and of the souls of the blessed. So dazzled and overcome was he by this vision that it was some time before he realized Beatrice had left him. At his side stood an old man whom he recognized as Saint Bernard, who told him Beatrice had returned to her throne. He then told Dante that if he wished to discover still more of the heavenly vision, he must join with him in a prayer to Mary. Dante received the grace to contemplate the glory of God, and to glimpse, for a moment, the greatest of mysteries, the Trinity and man's union with the divine.

Further Critical Evaluation of the Work:

Dante was born into an aristocratic Florentine family. Unusually well educated even for his time and place, he was knowledgeable in science and philosophy and was an active man of letters as well as an artist. He lived in politically tumultuous times and was active in politics and government. All of his knowledge, his experience, and his skill were brought to bear in his writings. During an absence from Florence in 1302, he was sentenced to exile for opposing the government then in power. For a time, he engaged in revolutionary activities, but even later he was never allowed to return to his beloved Florence upon pain of being burned. In exile, Dante wrote *The Divine*

Comedy. He died in Ravenna.

This masterpiece was originally written in Italian, but Dante also wrote in Latin, the language of scholarship at that time. His Latin treatise *De Vulgari Eloquentia* (On the Vulgar Tongue)—a compelling defense of the use of the written vernacular, instead of Latin—argued in conventional Latin the superiority of unconventional written Italian as a medium of expression. His other major Latin treatise was *De Monarchia* (About Monarchy), a political essay. He also used Latin for some very important letters and for a few poems. But Dante's choice was his native Italian. His earliest major work—*La Vita Nuova* (The New Life), a mystical-spiritual autobiography, combining prose and poetry—was written in Italian. So, too, was *Il Convivio* (The Banquet), a scholarly and philosophical treatise. And he wrote a number of lyric poems in Italian, as well. But standing above all as a tribute to the eloquence of written Italian is *The Divine Comedy.*

La Commedia—as it was first titled; *Divina* was added later—is an incredibly complex work. It is divided into three sections, or canticles, the *Inferno* (Hell), the *Purgatorio* (Purgatory), and the *Paradiso* (Heaven). The entire work is composed of 100 cantos, apportioned into segments of 34 *(Inferno)*, 33 *(Purgatorio)*, and 33 *(Paradiso)*. The rhyme scheme is called *terza rima*—aba bab cbc dcd—resulting in each rhyme occurring three times to create an interlocking scheme which produces a very closely knit poem. This structure is neither arbitrary nor a mere intellectual exercise.

Number symbolism plays an important part in *The Divine Comedy.* As an essentially Christian poem, it relies heavily on mystical associations with numbers. Inasmuch as the poem deals with Christian religious concepts, it is not difficult to discern the relationship between one poem in three canticles and one God in Three Persons. So, too, *terza rima* becomes significant. But then more complex intricacies come into play. The unity or oneness of God is diffused on a metric basis: one is divided into one hundred cantos, for example. And two becomes the duality of nature: corporeal and spiritual, active and contemplative, Church and State, Old Testament and New, and so on. Three signifies Father, Son, Holy Ghost; Power, Wisdom, Love; Faith, Hope, Charity; and other combinations. Four—as in seasons, elements, humors, directions, cardinal virtues—combines with three to make a mystical seven: days of creation, days of the week (length of Dante's journey), seven virtues and seven vices (cf. seven levels of Purgatory), planets and many more. Moreover, multiples of three—three times three equals nine—create further permutations: choirs of angels, circles of Hell, and the like. And adding the mystical unity of one to the product nine makes ten, the metric permutation of one discussed above.

These complex relationships of number symbolism were deliberately contrived by Dante and other medieval writers. Dante himself explained, in *Il Convivio,* his view of the four levels of interpretation of a literary work and by doing so legitimized such explanations of number symbolism. He proposed that a text be read (1) literally, (2) allegorically, (3) morally, and (4) anagogically. The literal reading was, of course, the story itself. The allegorical reading uncovered hidden meanings in the story. The moral reading related to matters of human behavior. And the anagogical reading, accessible to only the most sophisticated, pertained to the absolute and universal truths contained in a work. Hence, *The Divine Comedy* has something of each of these four levels of interpretation.

As a literal story, it has the fascination of autobiographical elements as well as the features of high adventure. The protagonist Dante, led by Vergil, undertakes a journey to learn about himself, the world, and the relations between the two. In the course of his journey, he explores other worlds in order to place his own world in proper perspective. As his journey progresses, he learns.

As an allegorical story, *The Divine Comedy* traces the spiritual enlightenment of Dante's soul. It also delineates social, political, cultural, and scientific parables. By integrating all of these aspects into an intricately interwoven pattern, the poem becomes an allegory for the real and spiritual world order.

As a moral story, the work has perhaps its greatest impact as a cautionary tale to warn the reader about the consequences of various categories of behavior. In the process, it helps the reader to understand sin (Hell), penance (Purgatory), and salvation (Heaven). Thus, *The Divine Comedy* becomes a vehicle for teaching moral behavior.

As an anagogical story, the poem offers a mystical vision of God's grand design for the entire universe. The complex interdependency of all things—including the web of interrelationships stemming from number symbolism—is, in this view, all part of the Divine Plan, which humankind can grasp only partially and dimly. For God remains ineffable to the finite capacities of human beings, and His will can never be fully apprehended by humans, whose vision has been impaired by sin. The anagogical aspects of *The Divine Comedy* are thus but aids for the most spiritually enlightened to approach Eternal Truth.

To be sure, no brief explanation can do justice to the majesty of this monumental achievement in the history of Western poetry. The very encyclopedic nature of its scope makes *The Divine Comedy* a key to the study of medieval civilization. As such, it cannot be easily or properly fragmented into neat categories for discussion, and the reader must advance on tiptoe, as it were. Background in history and theology are strongly recommended. But, above all, the reader must recognize that no sweeping generalization will adequately account for the complexity of ideas or the intricacy of structure in *The Divine Comedy*.

Joanne G. Kashdan

THE DIVINE FIRE

Type of work: Novel
Author: May Sinclair (1870?-1946)
Type of plot: Psychological romance
Time of plot: The 1890's
Locale: England
First published: 1904

Principal characters:
SAVAGE KEITH RICKMAN, the genius
HORACE JEWDWINE, a literary editor
LUCIA HARDEN, loved by Rickman
FLOSSIE WALKER, betrothed to Rickman
MR. PILKINGTON, a financier

Critique:

Written by a popular English author of the early twentieth century, *The Divine Fire* is the chronicle of a gifted but unknown poet. His story was one of conflict between the genius and the man. First one, then the other was supreme, and he fought unsuccessfully to reconcile the two. It was only through the help of a good and inspiring woman that he was at last able to find himself.

The Story:

Horace Jewdwine, a literary editor, had a problem. He thought he had discovered a genius in Savage Keith Rickman, a young and unknown poet who earned his living by making catalogs for his father, a bookseller. But Jewdwine was afraid to say openly that Rickman was a genius, afraid for his reputation if he called Rickman a genius publicly and then the young man proved otherwise. He encouraged Rickman privately but failed to give him the public recognition that would have meant so much to the young writer.

Rickman himself cared little for fame or money. He knew too that he was a genius. That is, part of him was a genius. He was also a student, a young man about town, a journalist, a seeker after simple home life, and sometimes a drunk. It was hard to have so many facets to one's nature. One part warred constantly with the others. But no matter in what form he found himself, honor never left him. Even when drunk he continued to be honorable.

Rickman's intelligence and his ability to judge books were the foundations upon which the elder Rickman had built his financial success as a book dealer. The father and son could never understand each other. Money was the father's god; the muse was Rickman's. The father was backed by and supported by Mr. Pilkington, a financier of questionable ethics but great success. When Pilkington informed him that the Harden library might soon be on the market, the old man sent his son to evaluate it. At the same time Miss Lucia Harden, daughter of the owner of the library, asked for someone to catalog it for her. Rickman was sent because his knowledge of old books was infallible.

Rickman was awed by Lucia. She was the daughter of a baronet, so far above him that he could never hope to have her return his affection, but from the first he knew that she was destined to be his inspiration. Lucia was Jewdwine's cousin, and he was unhappy when he learned of her association with Rickman. He knew Rickman was beneath her, but he knew too that his cousin was moved by poetry. In addition, Jewdwine himself thought he would one day marry Lucia and inherit the library and the country estate. However, he could not bring himself to ask for her hand; decisions were almost impossible for Jewdwine.

Rickman soon learned, as he worked for Lucia, that his father and Pilkington were planning to pay a ridiculously low price for the Harden library. In order to help the girl, he wrote to Jewdwine and asked him to buy the library at a fair figure. Jewdwine failed to answer the letter. When Lucia's father died suddenly, leaving her indebted to Pilkington, Rickman went to his father and tried to persuade him to change the offer. The old man refused, and Rickman left the bookshop forever, refusing to compromise his honor in return for the partnership his father offered him if he would stay. Not wanting to hurt Lucia, he told her little of what had happened. He even tried to excuse Jewdwine's failure to buy the library and so salvage some of her father's estate.

Pilkington took the Harden house and furniture and Rickman's father the library. After Rickman left him the old man's business began to fail, and he had to mortgage the library to Pilkington. The books were stored, pending redemption. Rickman left Lucia and returned to his rooming-house, not to see her again for five years.

Back in London, Rickman continued to write for various journals. Jewdwine gave him a junior editorship on the journal which he edited, and the job allowed Rickman to live fairly comfortably. His serious writing he had put away in a drawer. The product of his genius, it would bring no money. Meanwhile he was trapped into a proposal by little Flossie Walker, a fellow boarder. Flossie was a girl who could never understand the ways of genius; her proper world was a house in the suburbs, decorated with hideous furniture. Rickman found himself with the house bought and the wedding date set.

Chance was to save him. Lucia, after five years, visited a friend in Rickman's boarding-house and the two met again. No word of love was spoken, for Lucia, even without her fortune, was still above

him. And Rickman had no desire to hurt Flossie, who had waited two years for him to make enough money for their marriage. But he and Lucia found inspiration and comfort in renewed acquaintance. The real blow to Flossie's dreams came when Rickman's father died, leaving him a small inheritance. With it, Rickman could possibly redeem from Pilkington the mortgaged Harden library and return it to Lucia. To do so would mean a wait of at least two more years for Flossie. This she could not understand. A legal debt was one thing, a debt of honor another. With great relief Rickman learned that she refused to wait. She quickly married another boarder and found her house in the suburbs, complete with nursery.

Rickman lived through years of the most killing labor he would ever know. He worked all night, starved himself, lived in an unheated attic in order to redeem the complete library. He got extensions from Pilkington, who enjoyed the sight of genius chasing an impossible goal. His friends lost track of him. He lost his job with Jewdwine because he would not compromise his honor even in his desperate need to help Lucia. At last he seemed doomed to fail, for his lack of food and his feverish work made him desperately ill. Friends found him and took him, unconscious, to a hospital. Later, going through his things, they found the work of his genius. When it was published, Rickman's fame was assured. Poor Jewdwine! How he wished now that he had had the courage to claim Rickman in time. But Jewdwine had by that time sacrificed his own principles, and success was beyond hope for him.

Recovered, Rickman went to Lucia. He found her ill, unable to walk. When she learned that his illness had been caused by work for her, the gift was almost more than she could bear. With his aid she arose from her bed. Cured of the malady which she knew now was only heartbreak, she saw Rickman whole, the genius and the man fused at last.

Further Critical Evaluation of the Work:

The Divine Fire, one of May Sinclair's numerous and varied novels, deals with the frustrations of a young poet of exceptional talent whose valuable energies are wasted in the struggle to make a living and to fulfill an enormous self-imposed financial obligation. Despite the wide variety in her work, Sinclair uses techniques in *The Divine Fire* which are characteristic of her general style; the novel also contains many of the same attitudes and psychological concerns frequently found in her fiction.

Stylistically, May Sinclair is somewhat of a naturalist. Although *The Divine Fire* is relatively long and leisurely-paced compared to her other works, it shares with them an acute attention to detail and an objectivity of observation. Through her skillful and unobtrusive selection of which details are to be presented, Sinclair creates a powerful impression of realism that carries its own meaning without need of comment by the author. Thematically, this novel—like her others—reveals a strain of naturalism. Influenced by H. G. Wells, Sinclair was interested in exposing the mediocrity of middle-class values and their deadening effect on the spirit, and in dramatizing how an individual life—whether an unusual one like Keith Rickman's or a quite ordinary one such as Harriet Frean's—is molded by external forces. Thus, Keith Rickman's career illustrates to some extent the dictum found in an earlier novel, *Audrey Craven* (1897): "In our modern mythology, Custom, Circumstance, and Heredity are the three Fates that weave the web of human life." Nevertheless, Sinclair does not approach the pessimisim of Hardy or Dreiser, and she is often unwilling to accept the naturalist solution; Rickman, after all his suffering, is finally recognized as a genius and united with Lucia.

Although May Sinclair was not a Freudian, she was certainly aware of the important psychological assumptions beginning to be made in her generation, and of their implications. We find in all of her work that same sensitivity and insight into emotions and motivations that inspires *The Divine Fire.* She is particularly aware of the various kinds of oppression that produce frustration; one type that appears frequently—and reminds us of Sinclair's similarities to Henry James—is the oppressiveness of parents toward their children. Also reminiscent of James are her portraits of seemingly nice people who are in reality self-serving and unscrupulous—portraits which reflect not only her interest in the discrepancy between appearances and reality, but her desire to expose hypocrisy and false values.

DIVINE LOVE AND WISDOM

Type of work: Theosophical treatise
Author: Emanuel Swedenborg (1688-1772)
First published: 1763

During the earlier part of his life Emanuel Swedenborg established for himself a lasting reputation as a man of science, doing research in many scientific fields, including physics, astronomy, mathematics, engineering, and human anatomy. His research in several of these fields culminated in important publications which showed him well in advance of his time. His work in anatomy, for example, anticipated some of the theories of modern physiology, including those involving the functions of the ductless glands.

With respect to his later writings in religion and theosophy Swedenborg's reputation is a mixed one. Between 1743 and 1745 he suffered a mental and religious crisis which changed his life and his work. During the crisis, according to his own report, he underwent mystical experiences during which he was given access to the spiritual world, enjoying visions of that world, hearing and taking part in celestial conversations, and receiving divine instruction. In 1745, during a third great spiritual experience, reported Swedenborg, he witnessed the second advent of Christ and was instructed to establish a "New Church." From his visions and the instructions he purportedly received grew Swedenborg's theosophical writings, written in Latin. Although he wrote voluminously on his doctrines, Swedenborg did not himself found a sect, for he believed that members of any church could follow his doctrines. Later his followers did constitute the Church of the New Jerusalem, or New Church.

Like all theosophical writings, those of Swedenborg depend for their importance on how seriously one is willing to take the author's reports of divine inspiration and revelation. If acceptance is granted by the reader, then the writings assume tremendous, even cosmic, significance, for

Swedenborg did not attempt to disguise or conceal the supernatural source of his doctrines. He stated as actual fact that his doctrines were the results of visions granted to him by God, and he calmly and routinely noted certain facts and points either overheard in conversations among the angels or witnessed during the times he was transported spiritually to heaven. He regarded his mission seriously, sincerely believing that he had been commanded to interpret the spiritual world and explicate the Bible's true spiritual intent to mankind.

Swedenborg's most important theosophical work is the *Divine Love and Wisdom,* in which he stated his system most comprehensively and succinctly. The premises of his doctrine are that God is Man (or God-Man) and that God is Love. He reported that the conception of God as Man is held in all the heavens, the reason he vouchsafed being that heaven as a whole and in every part resembles the human form, and the Divine itself, together with the angels (who are also human in form) constitutes heaven. Swedenborg added that all angels and other heavenly spirits are men in perfect form. The essence or being of God, according to Swedenborgian doctrine, is love, an infinite love which mankind knows only as existing and not through an acquaintance with its nature, inasmuch as mankind is, without God, held to the natural world.

For Swedenborg, the manifestation of God and His infinite love is a sun, in the spiritual world a living sun. That spiritual sun corresponds in heaven to the "dead" sun of the natural world, and is the source of spiritual life. The sun of the natural world, according to Swedenborg, is the source of life in nature, which is but a receptacle of life, not a source. Just as the spiritual sun and the natural sun are distinct but analogous in part and whole, so are heaven and earth distinct but analogous. Swedenborg warned, however, that space and time are concepts only of the natural world and are not to be found in the structure of the infinite and perfect realm of heaven. In heaven, according to the cosmology expounded in *Divine Love and Wisdom*, are three uncreated, distinct, and eternal degrees, corresponding to which in the natural world there are three finite degrees. Swedenborg did not describe in *Divine Love and Wisdom* how these degrees exist, but only stated that they are love, wisdom, and use, or to put it another way, end, cause, and effect. The three degrees exist, said Swedenborg, in every man at birth, although as a creature of the natural world the human being is unaware of them. As the degrees are opened successively to the individual, so is God in man and man in God, according to the doctrine. Light from the spiritual sun flows into man as he shuns evil, meaning that he can gain in wisdom; but the "heat" of the spiritual sun, or love, man cannot receive. The natural mind of the lowest degree, said Swedenborg, is a hell in itself, while the mind which is spiritualized becomes a heaven. In other words, by love and the opening of each of the successive degrees man can rise toward God. According to *Divine Love and Wisdom*, the end of creation, both spiritual and natural, is to become perfectly the image of God-Man.

Swedenborg undertook to answer the question of creation that has bothered countless numbers of theologically-minded persons in every generation: Did God create the universe out of nothing, or did He form a cosmos from the stuff of chaos? He wrote:

> Every one of enlightened judgment sees that the universe was not created out of nothing, because it is impossible to make anything out of nothing; for nothing is nothing, and to suppose anything to be made out of nothing is absurd and therefore contrary to the light of truth, which comes from the divine Wisdom; and whatever is inconsistent with the divine Wisdom is also inconsistent with the divine Omnipotence. Everyone of enlightened judgment also sees that all beings were created out of self-existent substance, the very BEING out of which all things that exist come forth: and as God is the only self-existent Substance, and thus is essential BEING, it is plain that this is the source of all things that exist. Many have seen this because it is consistent with reason; but they have not dared to confirm it, fearing to be led to suppose that the created universe is God, because it exists from Him, or that nature is self-existent, and thus that what is called God is only nature in her utmost recesses.

Swedenborg suggests that there are pairs in all parts of the body in order that every man may achieve the love and wisdom of divinity. He notes that the eyes, ears, nostrils, hands, loins, and feet exist in pairs, that the heart, brain, and lungs are divided into two parts. The right-hand parts, according to his views, have a relation to love and the left-hand parts a relation to wisdom.

The doctrine propounded in *Divine Love and Wisdom* grants to all human beings the means of achieving the spiritual heaven, for in the Swedenborgian view it is a false doctrine that the Lord admits or excludes members of the human race arbitrarily from salvation.

DOCTOR FAUSTUS

Type of work: Novel
Author: Thomas Mann (1875–1955)
Type of plot: Philosophical chronicle
Time of plot: 1885-1945
Locale: Germany
First published: 1947

Principal characters:

ADRIAN LEVERKÜHN, an arrogant, sickly musical genius
SERENUS ZEITBLOM, his lifelong friend, the narrator
WENDELL KRETSCHMAR, Adrian's music teacher
EHRENFRIED KUMPF, and
EBERHARD SCHLEPPFUSS, teachers of theology
RÜDIGER SCHILDKNAPP, a poet, Adrian's friend
RUDOLF SCHWERDTFEGER, a violinist befriended by Adrian
INEZ INSTITORIS, in love with Schwerdtfeger
CLARISSA RODDE, her sister
MARIE GODEAU, loved by Adrian
NEPOMUK SCHNEIDEWEIN, Adrian's young nephew

Critique:

Doctor Faustus: The Life of the German Composer Adrian Leverkühn as Told by a Friend offers several approaches to an understanding of Mann's purpose and narrative pattern. On one level, it may be taken simply as the biographical story of a strange and fascinating genius, written in simple, honest prose by his lifelong friend and admirer, Serenus Zeitblom, a retired professor of philology. Again, it may be regarded as an excursion into a field which present-day fiction has neglected, a story of the destruction of a human soul in that demon-haunted world of the imagination which modern science has almost destroyed. Or it may be read as a study of the problem of the artist in contemporary society, of the conflict between his love of beauty and his moral responsibility to the kind of world in which he lives today. Beneath and beyond these levels of meaning, however, the novel is a political and philosophical allegory deeply charged with suggestion and purpose. Leverkühn, who gave his soul to the devil for twenty years of creative genius, symbolizes the German break-through to world power, the tortured nationalism of the Nazi state.

As the narrator digresses to comment on the progress of the war the reader perceives that the rise and collapse of the Nazi dream runs side by side with Leverkühn's tragic story, like musical counterpoint creating a mood of increasing shame and community guilt, and a realization of inescapable doom. The novel is intricately constructed, profoundly serious, and beautifully written, with meanings which extend beyond the purely national and the temporal.

The Story:

At the outset Serenus Zeitblom doubted his ability to make understandable the life story of his friend Adrian Leverkühn, a musical genius whose strange, doomed career had much in common with the fated course of German history in the twentieth century. A former professor of philology, living in retirement and out of sympathy with the Hitler regime, greatly concerned for the future of his country, Zeitblom hesitantly began his task in May, 1943.

Adrian Leverkühn was born in 1885 on a farm near Kaiseraschern, in Thuringia. His family was of superior yeo-

DOCTOR FAUSTUS by Thomas Mann. Translated by H. T. Lowe-Porter. By permission of the publishers, Alfred A. Knopf, Inc. Copyright, 1947, by Thomas Mann. Copyright, 1948, by Alfred A. Knopf, Inc.

man stock, and his father, a man interested in curious natural phenomena, did everything in his power to stimulate his son's intellectual curiosity. Adrian's boyhood friend was Serenus Zeitblom, a frequent visitor in the Leverkühn household. Years later Zeitblom could remember his friend's absorbing interest in a book filled with pictures of exotic lepidoptera. One in particular, *Heræra Esmeralda*, fascinated the boy because of its unusual beauty and protective coloring. Adrian had his introduction to music from a hired girl who taught him old folk songs.

A boy of brilliant mind and arrogant disposition, Adrian was educated to become the scholar of the family, since the farm was intended for an older brother. When he was ten he entered the gymnasium in Kaiseraschern. Living in the house of his uncle, a dealer in musical instruments, he had the run of the shop and began to play chords on an old harmonium. His uncle, overhearing his efforts, decided that the boy ought to have piano lessons. Adrian began to study under Wendell Kretschmar, the organist at the cathedral. His chief interest at that time, however, was theology, and he entered the University of Halle with the intention of preparing himself for the clergy. Zeitblom, certain that his friend's choice was dictated by the arrogance of purity, went with Adrian to his theological lectures. One of the teachers was Ehrenfried Kumpf, a forthright theologian who enlivened his classes by insulting the devil with epithets that Martin Luther might have used. Another instructor was Eberhard Schleppfuss, whose lectures were filled with anecdotes and sly undertones of demonism and witchcraft.

Because of the variety of his talents Adrian was soon ready for a career in scholarship, theology, or music. At last, unable to reconcile his interest in philosophy and science with theological precepts, he turned to music and began, still under Kretschmar's training, experiments in theory and technique which were to determine the highly original nature of his art. Before long the pupil had surpassed the instructor. Then Zeitblom was called up for a year of military duty, service from which Adrian was exempt because of his frail constitution, and the two friends separated for a time.

Adrian went to Leipzig for further study. With Kretschmar's encouragement he began to compose music of his own. A new friend was Rüdiger Schildknapp, an Anglophile poet whose enthusiasm for Shakespeare led to Adrian's decision to plan an opera based on *Love's Labor's Lost*. One night a sinister guide, somewhat like Schleppfuss in appearance, lured Adrian to a brothel. When a girl in the house—an Esmeralda, he called her—approached him, he ran from the place. Later he tried to see the girl again, but she had gone to Pressburg. Adrian followed her and there voluntarily contracted the venereal infection which was to account for the strange flowering of his genius and the eventual wreckage of his life. Several years afterward, during a holiday in Italy, he imagined a medievalistic, hallucinated encounter with the devil, who in return for his soul promised him twenty-four years in which to fulfill his powers as an artist.

Before his Italian journey Adrian had lived for a time in Munich. There his friends were artists and young intellectuals, including Rüdiger Schildknapp, the poet; Jeanette Scheurl, a novelist; Rudolf Schwerdtfeger, a young violinist; several actors, and the daughters of his landlady, Inez and Clarissa Rodde. Through Adrian, Zeitblom met these people and became interested in them. In 1912 Zeitblom married. A short time later, on his return from Italy, Adrian retired to a Bavarian farm presided over by motherly Frau Else Schweigestill. In his retreat, during the next twenty years, he composed the music that established his fame. Zeitblom went to teach at Freising, not far away, and from that time on the friends saw each other frequently. Zeitblom wrote the libretto for

Love's Labour's Lost.

In 1914 Zeitblom went into the army and served until invalided home with typhus. Adrian, in retirement, wrote *Marvels of the Universe* and a composition based on the *Gesta Romanorum.* During the war Inez Rodde married Dr. Helmut Institoris. Secretly in love with Rudolf Schwerdtfeger, however, she kept up an adulterous relationship with the violinist for years. Adrian's health began to improve after the war. His great work of that period was an oratorio, *Apocalypse.* As his fame grew he acquired a patroness, Madame de Tolna, a wealthy Hungarian widow whom Zeitblom never met. Schwerdtfeger, in the meantime, had broken off his love affair with Inez. Their first meeting after their separation was at the funeral of Clarissa Rodde, an actress driven to suicide by a blackmailing lover.

Adrian yielded at last to Schwerdtfeger's urging and composed for the musician a violin concerto. About that time Adrian met attractive Marie Godeau. Hoping to marry her, he sent Schwerdtfeger to act as his emissary in his courtship, but the violinist fell in love with the girl and wooed her for himself. Shortly after the engagement had been announced Inez Institoris boarded a streetcar in which Schwerdtfeger was riding and shot her former lover. Adrian blamed himself for his friend's death.

Fate had one more blow in store for the composer. Adrian had a nephew, Nepomuk Schneidewein, of whom he was paternally fond. While convalescing from an illness, little Echo, as his uncle called him, went to stay with Adrian at the Schweigestill farm. Taken suddenly ill with cerebrospinal meningitis, the child died. It seemed to Adrian that he had lost the child he himself might have had. He was never to recover completely from his grief.

Meanwhile he was at work on his masterpiece, a symphonic cantata called *The Lamentation of Doctor Faustus.* In the early summer of 1930 he invited a number of his friends and some critics to hear excerpts from the work, but his explanation of his composition was so disordered and blasphemous that many of the guests left before he sat down to begin playing the score. As he struck the first chords he fell senseless to the floor.

Adrian Leverkühn lived in madness for the next ten years, and he died, tenderly cared for by his aged mother, at his Thuringian birthplace in 1940. Serenus Zeitblom was among the few old friends present at the funeral. It seemed to him then, and the certainty grew upon him while he was writing the story of Adrian's life, that his friend had somehow reflected the destiny of the German nation, a land arrogant, isolated, dehumanized, and at last reeling to that destruction which was the price of its power as the old philologist penned his final pages in April, 1945.

Further Critical Evaluation of the Work:

This immensely complex work, written in America during the years of Mann's emigration, is both a continuation of his investigation of the relationship between the artist and society begun in his first novel, *Buddenbrooks* (1901), and a symbolic representation of the fate of Germany in this century, intertwining three levels of time in a fabric that is in itself akin to the highly structured, mathematical compositions of the protagonist, Adrian Leverkühn, who may be seen as a projection of Mann, as well as of Germany as a whole. The Faust figure is a creation of the German sixteenth century, a troubled time of religious and political unrest leading up to the catastrophic Thirty Years' War, a time when it seemed to many that the Devil was literally loose upon the earth. The identification of Faust with the German soul is more due to Goethe's *Faust,* however, and the precarious mingling of the demonic with the controlled creativity of art was the subject of Mann's previous novel, *Lotte in Weimar.*

With the historical time level constantly in mind, the actual life of Leverkühn is recounted by his friend, Serenus Zeitblom, who works during the rise and fall of the Nazi regime. If Leverkühn, who, like Faustus, obtains to the highest levels of human knowledge and abstract intellect, falls prey to an inner demon which fructifies his art but at the cost of his capacity to love, so Germany, the "land of poets and philosophers," gives birth to an inner demon who brings about the destruction of the whole society. Nazism is likened to an infection, which is at the same time a pact with the Devil.

Mann constantly shifts from the subject of the novel, Leverkühn, to develop the character of the narrator, Zeitblom, and in the counterpoint between the ironic, isolated, infected artist and the unextraordinary, sometimes bewildered, indeed slightly philistine recorder, Mann creates a texture of interrelationships that demands the utmost concentration from the reader, but which repays him with one of the most profound meditations upon the malaise of our century.

DOCTOR FAUSTUS

Type of work: Drama
Author: Christopher Marlowe (1564-1593)
Type of plot: Romantic tragedy
Time of plot: Sixteenth century
Locale: Germany
First presented: c. 1588

Principal characters:
FAUSTUS, master of all knowledge
WAGNER, his servant
LUCIFER, the fallen angel
MEPHOSTOPILIS, a devil
GOOD ANGEL
EVIL ANGEL

Critique:

This drama should be regarded as a skeletal structure of the play written by Marlowe, for the surviving manuscripts are so interspersed with comic scenes and the lines themselves so often revised according to whims of the actors that the original writing must be culled out of the surviving version. Even so, *The Tragical History of Doctor Faustus* is worth reading and study because of the many remaining examples of the poet's skill it contains. In addition to the adulterated poetry in this play there is also the problem of the tainted characterization and symbolism; for while the personality of Mephostopilis is often caricaturized and while the exploits of Faustus are frequently rendered pure low comedy, still the Marlowe version of the two principal characters is evident in the sober and more consistent moments of the play. As an added contribution to existing Faustian literature, Marlowe's *Doctor Faustus* is an artistic effort, although not comparable in depth or scope to the treatment given this theme in Goethe's *Faust.*

The Story:

Faustus had been born of base stock in Rhodes, Germany. In his maturity, while living with some relatives in Wittenberg, he studied theology and was called a doctor. However, Faustus was so swollen with conceit that, Daedalus-like, he strove too far, became glutted with learning, conspired with the devil, and finally fell, accursed.

At the outset of his downward path Doctor Faustus found himself complete master of the fields of knowledge which men at that time studied. As a medical doctor he had already achieved huge success and great renown. But after obtaining good health for men no challenge remained in medicine except immortality. Law, Faustus concluded, was nothing but an elaborate moneymaking scheme. Only divinity remained, but theology led to a blind alley. Since the reward of sin was death and since no man could say he was without sin, then all men must sin and consequently die.

Necromancy greatly attracted Faustus. Universal power would be within his reach, the whole world at his command, and emperors at his feet, were he to become a magician. Summoning his servant Wagner, Faustus ordered him to summon Valdes and Cornelius, who could teach him their arts.

The Good Angel and the Evil Angel each tried to persuade Faustus, but Faustus was in no mood to listen to the Good Angel. He exulted over the prospects of his forthcoming adventures. He would get gold from India, pearls from the oceans, tasty delicacies from faraway places; he would read strange philosophies, cull from foreign kings their secrets, control Germany with his power, reform the public schools, and perform many other fabulous deeds. Eager to acquire knowledge of the black arts, he went away to study with Valdes and Cornelius.

Before long the scholars of Wittenberg began to notice the doctor's prolonged absence. Learning from Wagner of his master's unhallowed pursuits, the scholars lamented the fate of the famous doctor.

Faustus' first act of magic was to summon Mephostopilis. At sight of the ugly devil, he ordered Mephostopilis to assume the shape of a Franciscan friar. The docile obedience of Mephostopilis elated the magician, but Mephostopilis explained that magic had limits in the devil's kingdom. Mephostopilis claimed that he had not actually appeared at Faustus' behest but had come, as he would have to any other person, because Faustus had cursed Christ and abjured the Scriptures. Whenever a man is on the verge of being doomed, the devil will appear.

Interested in the nature of Lucifer, Faustus questioned Mephostopilis about his master, the fallen angel, and about hell, Lucifer's domain. Mephostopilis was wary. He claimed that the fallen spirits, having been deprived of the glories of heaven, found the whole world hell. Mephostopilis urged Faustus to give up his scheme, but Faustus scorned the warning, saying that he would surrender his soul to Lucifer if the fallen angel would give to Faustus twenty-four years of voluptuous ease, with Mephostopilis to attend him.

While Faustus indulged in a mental argument concerning the relative merits of God and the devil, the Good Angel and the Evil Angel, symbolic of his inner conflict, appeared once again, each attempting to persuade him. The result was that Faustus was more determined than ever to continue his course.

Mephostopilis returned to assure Faustus that Lucifer was agreeable to the bargain, which must be sealed in Faustus' blood. When Faustus tried to write, however, his blood congealed and Mephostopilis had to warm the liquid with fire.

Significantly the words, "Fly, man," appeared in Latin on Faustus' arm. When Faustus questioned Mephostopilis about the nature of hell, the devil claimed that hell had no limits for the damned. Intoxicated by his new estate, Faustus disclaimed any belief in an afterlife. Thus he assured himself that his contract with Lucifer would never be fulfilled, in spite of the devil's warning that he, Mephostopilis, was living proof of hell's existence.

Faustus, eager to consume the fruits of the devil's offering, demanded books that would contain varied information about the devil's regime. When the Good Angel and the Evil Angel came to him again, he realized that he was beyond repentence. Again the opposing Angels insinuated themselves into his mind, until he called on Christ to save him. As he spoke, wrathful Lucifer descended upon his prospective victim to admonish him never to call to God. As an appeasing gesture Lucifer conjured up a vision of the Seven Deadly Sins.

Faustus traveled extensively throughout the world, and Wagner marveled at his master's rapid progress. In Rome, at the palace of the Pope, Faustus, made invisible by his magic arts, astounded the Pope by snatching things from the holy man's hands. Like a gleeful child Faustus asked Mephostopilis to create more mischief. When Faustus returned home the scholars questioned him eagerly about many things unknown to them. As his fame spread, the emperor invited him to the palace and asked him to conjure up the spirit of Alexander the Great. Because a doubtful knight scoffed at such a preposterous idea, Faustus, after fulfilling the emperor's request, spitefully placed horns on the head of the skeptical nobleman.

Foreseeing that his time of merriment was drawing to a close, Faustus returned to Wittenberg. Wagner sensed that his master was about to die when Faustus gave his faithful servant all his wordly goods.

As death drew near, Faustus spoke with

his conscience, which, assuming the form of an Old Man, begged him to repent before he died. When Faustus declared that he would repent, Mephostopilis cautioned him not to offend Lucifer. Faustus asked Mephostopilis to bring him Helen of Troy as a lover to amuse him during the final days of his life.

In his declining hours Faustus conversed with scholars who had loved him, and the fallen theologian revealed to them his bargain with Lucifer. Alone, he uttered a final despairing plea that he be saved from impending misery, but in the end he was borne off by a company of devils.

Further Critical Evaluation of the Work:

Marlowe's *Doctor Faustus* is a problematic play, and scholars are strongly divided as to its interpretation. Its dating is uncertain, and its text highly controversial. Yet it is regarded by many as Marlowe's masterpiece, and many scholars argue that even the comic scenes are part of an overall artistic intention, and contribute to, rather than detract from, the serious aspects of the play.

The work is based upon the *Doctor Faustus* published in Germany by Johann Spiess in 1587, in which the characters and almost all the episodes of Marlowe's version appear. But Marlowe concentrated the plot, arranged the episodes in a significant way, and developed the characters of Faustus and Mephostopilis. In Marlowe's hands, Faustus becomes a representative of Renaissance man, intoxicated with the rapid expansion of knowledge, and filled with pride in the power of the human mind. This humanistic pride, however, is countered by the doctrines of the Christian faith, in which man's knowledge is regarded as irrelevant in comparison to God's, and grace, rather than knowledge, is the supreme good.

Faustus in his willful pride rejects God's grace for knowledge and power, though these are offered him by Mephostopilis, a fallen angel damned for his own pride in trying to usurp God's position. Marlowe stresses the irony of Faustus' blindness repeatedly, but Faustus, who is as much poet as scholar, loses himself in grandiose visions and ignores the reality of his situation. Faustus, in fact, gives his soul for trifles—a fact pointed up by the interspersed comic scenes where Faustus' servants imitate his conjuring, expressing their own petty desires. Faustus himself sinks to the level of petty tricks, and finally consoles himself by conjuring up Helen of Troy—who is really only another demon in disguise. At the end, his pride turns to despair, the unforgivable sin, and he wastes his time in irresolution. His life and death are a warning, but more, perhaps, the tragic expression of a man caught between two worlds: Renaissance will and Christian faith.

THE DOCTOR IN SPITE OF HIMSELF

Type of work: Drama
Author: Molière (Jean Baptiste Poquelin, 1622-1673)
Type of plot: Farce
Time of plot: Seventeenth century
Locale: Paris
First presented: 1666

Principal characters:
SGANARELLE, a woodcutter
MARTINE, his wife
GÉRONTE, a gentleman of means
LUCINDE, his daughter
VALÈRE, his attendant
LÉANDRE, Lucinde's lover

Critique:

This drama, ordinarily considered one of Molière's less important works, nevertheless demonstrates his ability to ridicule the fads of his day, in this case the vogue, not wholly extinct three centuries later, of showing obsequious deference to men of science no matter what their real qualifications may be. Exposing the fact that ignorance often hides behind a smattering of superficial learning, he levels his barbs against the doctors of his time. The comedy was an immediate success and has always been popular. Sixty-five years after its first presentation, Henry Fielding, English novelist and dramatist, adapted the basic plot in a play presented at the Drury Lane Theatre under the title of *The Mock Doctor; or, the Dumb Lady Cur'd.*

The Story:

Sganarelle, a faggot gatherer, was driven to extremes because Martine, his nagging wife, accused him of always being drunk instead of working, and finally he took a stick and beat her soundly. When their neighbor M. Robert sought to interfere, Martine boxed his ears and declared she liked to have her husband beat her. But as Sganarelle went off to the woods after promising to bring back a hundred faggots that day, Martine itched for wifely revenge.

Géronte's daughter Lucinde had feigned illness and loss of speech in order to escape marriage to a wealthy suitor her father had chosen for her; she herself was in love with Léandre, who returned her love. Her father had summoned many physicians to treat her, but all had failed to find a cure. At last Géronte sent his attendants, Valère and Lucas, in search of a specialist.

When they encountered the offended Martine and confided in her the reason for their journey, she saw in their search an opportunity to get even with her husband. She told them that he was a marvelous curer of any illness, a doctor who pretended to be a woodcutter who dressed absurdly and pretended complete ignorance of his art, so that it might actually be necessary to thrash him violently to gain from him admission of his real talents. Her boasts of the wonderful cures he had performed so impressed her listeners that they set off in immediate search of this medical prodigy. They found Sganarelle in the wood, relaxing with his bottle, and, being rebuffed by him after their first ceremonious introduction, they thrashed him severely and finally forced him to say he was a doctor and to follow them to see Lucinde.

The attendants persuaded Géronte that Sganarelle, though he loved a joke and seemed to be off his head, was really the greatest doctor in the world. When Sganarelle was introduced to Géronte, he inquired, as he himself had been asked, if the other man were a doctor.

Géronte replied that he was not, where-upon Sganarelle, following the pattern applied to him, gave him a sound thrashing. The attendants thereupon explained to the bewildered Géronte that this was merely an example of the great doctor's eccentricity, a sure sign of his greatness.

When Géronte brought in his daughter, she replied to Sganarelle's questions by signs, gestures, and grunts. From these noises Sganarelle diagnosed Lucinde as dumb, a malady caused by loss of speech because of an impediment in the action of her tongue, on which subject Aristotle said—thus and so. Using some learned-sounding Latin words which meant nothing at all, he prescribed that the patient be put to bed and given plenty of bread soaked in wine; his explanation was that in this manner parrots were induced to speak.

Géronte, overwhelmed by the brilliance of Sganarelle's diagnosis and vast medical knowledge, felt absolute confidence in the ability of this eccentric to cure his daughter of her strange action. What pleased Sganarelle most was the generous fee Géronte gave him.

Léandre came to the fake physician to ask his help in carrying out a plan by which the young man hoped to see Lucinde; but Sganarelle pretended to be beyond influence in such matters, until the lover offered him a handsome fee. Léandre then told him that Lucinde's illness was put on and that its cause was not the brain, the spleen, or intestines, but love. Sganarelle and the young man plotted to disguise Léandre as an apothecary's assistant so that he could speak with Lucinde. Sganarelle also confided that he was not really a doctor but had been forced to appear one in spite of himself, for a reason he did not know. Once the error had spread, however, everyone had taken him for a man of great reputation, and so he had made up his mind to stick to his new calling, for it paid very well.

As if to substantiate his story, Thibaut and his son Perrin, country fellows who had heard of Sganarelle's powers, asked him to prescribe for Thibaut's ailing wife; but Sganarelle gave no ear to their troubles until they gave him gold crowns. As a cure, he prescribed a piece of cheese, which, he said, was made of mixed gold, coral, pearls, and other precious things, and must be used as directed. He also warned them that if the patient died they should bury her as decently as possible.

Géronte reported to Sganarelle that his patient had grown worse since taking his remedy. When the nurse brought in Lucinde, Sganarelle asked his disguised assistant to feel her pulse, meanwhile keeping Géronte occupied in conversation in order to keep him from overhearing the lovers' plans. But Géronte caught a few words spoken by Lucinde and exclaimed in surprise and in praise of the doctor. Lucinde approached her father and acknowledged that she had now recovered her speech, but only to tell him that she would marry no one except Léandre and that nothing would shake her resolution.

Géronte stubbornly insisted that she must marry Horace, the man of his choice, that very evening. When Lucinde declared she would rather die, Sganarelle stepped in and assured the father that her actions were merely a sign of additional madness and that the apothecary was the man who could effect a cure. Summoning Léandre, and, sprinkling his instructions with Latin polysyllables to mislead the others, he urged the lover to fly with Lucinde immediately. Sganarelle engaged Géronte in conversation while Lucinde and Léandre made their escape. When their flight was reported to the irate father, he threatened Sganarelle with hanging for aiding in his daughter's elopement.

In the midst of this predicament Martine overtook her husband. On being told he was about to hang for helping his master's daughter elope, she bewailed the fact but added she would have been somewhat comforted if only he had finished chopping their wood. Sganarelle told her to leave, but she said she preferred to stay and see him hanged.

At that critical moment Lucinde and Léandre returned to confront Géronte with the news that Léandre's uncle had just died and named the young man heir to a considerable fortune. Géronte, overjoyed at the turn of events which would bring him a rich son-in-law, gave the couple his blessing. Martine insisted that since Sganarelle was not to be hanged he could thank her for having achieved the

honor of being a doctor; but Sganarelle pointed out that this distinction had gained him innumerable thwacks with a stick. He forgave the beatings, however, because of his new dignity as a doctor. But he took occasion to remind his shrewish wife that henceforth she must show greater respect for a man of his consequence, one whom the world now looked up to and honored—in spite of himself.

Further Critical Evaluation of the Work:

Molière was France's greatest writer of comic drama, and his forte was farce. *The Doctor in Spite of Himself (Le Médecin malgré lui)* is one of his best pure farces. In this play, he takes to task two issues with special contemporary relevance: medical venality and the medical mystique. It was as much a fact of life in Molière's time as it is now that doctors are more concerned about money than about the welfare of patients. Thus, when Sganarelle accedes to the role forced upon him, he does so out of greed, rather than for any other motive. Furthermore, he is able to pull off the charade because of the general cultural attitude toward physicians—a religious respect for the doctor's presumably arcane knowledge. Hence, Sganarelle can indulge his most outrageously eccentric fantasies in the course of deceiving—and bilking —Géronte while pretending (as an authentic doctor would) to cure Lucinde, all the while abetting the latter to elope with the mate of her choice.

In the course of these wildly hectic machinations, Molière manages to assail not only the medical profession but also its gullible clients, as well as social climbers, materialists, impractical lovers, faithless servants, and many other social types endemic to his times and persistent in ours. Such, after all, is the impetus and goal of satire, whether it be couched in Molière's farce, in irony, or in some other comedic form. The point of this kind of drama is to expose human folly and social foibles—a feat which Molière accomplishes with considerable finesse. He makes Sganarelle out to be as foolish as Géronte, and Léandre hardly lags far behind. Lucinde at first appears to have some reasoned craft behind her actions, but finally she is revealed to be as vulnerable, and as crafty, as the rest.

The Doctor in Spite of Himself is not usually included among Molière's masterpieces—*Tartuffe* (1664), *The Misanthrope* (1666), and *The Miser* (1668); however, *The Doctor in Spite of Himself* shares many of the qualities of the presumably greater works. It is superbly crafted as drama; it demonstrates keen insight into character; it portrays universal character types; and it maintains an unflagging sense of the comic. Although Molière wrote some of his plays—*Tartuffe,* for example—in verse, *The Doctor in Spite of Himself* is written in prose, but without detriment to the play or its pointed barbs. All in all, the play has retained its acerbic wit over the years remarkably well, and Molière's reputation is in no way diminished by its continuing popularity.

DR. JEKYLL AND MR. HYDE

Type of work: Novelette
Author: Robert Louis Stevenson (1850-1894)
Type of plot: Fantasy
Time of plot: Nineteenth century
Locale: London
First published: 1886

Principal characters:
DR. HENRY JEKYLL, a London physician
MR. UTTERSON, counselor for Dr. Jekyll
POOLE, Dr. Jekyll's manservant
DR. HASTIE LANYON, Dr. Jekyll's close friend

Critique:

The Strange Case of Dr. Jekyll and Mr. Hyde has steadily maintained the popularity which it had originally. The story is basically one of romantic adventure and fantasy, of the type currently found in paper pulps. Yet by merit of Stevenson's understanding of human nature and his mastery of English prose, the story holds subtle values as an illustration of man's dual nature. It is not necessary to believe the story in order to understand and believe the symbolism.

The Story:

Mr. Richard Enfield, and his cousin, Mr. Utterson, a lawyer, were strolling according to their usual Sunday custom when they came upon an empty building on a familiar street. Mr. Enfield told that some time previously he had seen an ill-tempered man trample down a small child at the doorway of the deserted building. He and other indignant bystanders had forced the stranger, who gave his name as Hyde, to pay over a sum of money for the child's welfare. Enfield remembered the man Hyde with deep loathing.

Utterson had reasons to be interested in Hyde. When he returned to his apartment he reread the strange will of Dr. Henry Jekyll. The will stipulated that in the event of Dr. Jekyll's death all of his wealth should go to a man named Edward Hyde.

Utterson sought out Hyde, the man whom Enfield had described, to discover if he were the same who had been named heir to Dr. Jekyll's fortune. Sus-

picious of Utterson's interest, Hyde became enraged and ran into his house. Questioned, Dr. Jekyll refused to discuss the matter, but insisted that in the event of his death the lawyer should see to it that Mr. Hyde was not cheated out of his fortune. The lawyer believed that Hyde was an extortioner who was getting possession of Dr. Jekyll's money and who would eventually murder the doctor.

About a year later Hyde was wanted for the wanton murder of a kindly old man, Sir Danvers Carew, but he escaped before he could be arrested. Dr. Jekyll presented the lawyer and the police with a letter signed by Hyde, in which the murderer declared his intention of making good his escape forever. He begged Dr. Jekyll's pardon for having ill-used his friendship.

About this time Dr. Lanyon, who had been for years a great friend of Dr. Jekyll, became ill and died. Among his papers was a letter addressed to Utterson. Opening it, Utterson discovered an inner envelope also sealed and bearing the notice that it was not to be opened until after Dr. Jekyll's death. Utterson felt that it was somehow associated with the evil Hyde, but he could in no way fathom the mystery.

One Sunday Enfield and Utterson were walking again in the street where Enfield had seen Hyde mistreating the child. They now realized that the strange deserted building was a side entrance to the house of Dr. Jekyll, an additional wing used as a laboratory.

Looking up at the window, they saw Dr. Jekyll sitting there. He looked disconsolate. Then his expression seemed to change, so that his face took on a grimace of horror or pain. Suddenly he closed the window. Utterson and Enfield walked on, too overcome by what they had seen to talk further.

Not long afterward Utterson was sitting by his fireside when Poole, Dr. Jekyll's manservant, sought entrance. He related that for a week something strange had been going on in Dr. Jekyll's laboratory. The doctor himself had not appeared. Instead, he had ordered his meals to be sent in and had written curious notes demanding that Poole go to all the chemical houses in London in search of a mysterious drug. Poole was convinced that his master had been slain and that the murderer, masquerading as Dr. Jekyll, was still hiding in the laboratory.

Utterson and Poole returned to Dr. Jekyll's house and broke into his laboratory with an ax. Entering, they discovered that the man in the laboratory had killed himself by draining a vial of poison just as they broke the lock. The man was Edward Hyde.

They searched in vain for the doctor's body, certain it was somewhere about after they discovered a note of that date addressed to Utterson. In the note Dr. Jekyll said he was planning to disappear, and he urged Utterson to read the note which Dr. Lanyon had left at the time of his death. An enclosure contained the confession of Henry Jekyll.

Utterson returned to his office to read the letters. The letter of Dr. Lanyon described how Dr. Jekyll had sent Poole to Dr. Lanyon with a request that Dr. Lanyon search for some drugs in Dr. Jekyll's laboratory. Hyde had appeared to claim the drugs. Then, in Dr. Lanyon's presence, Hyde had taken the drugs and had been transformed into Dr. Jekyll. The shock of this transformation had caused Dr. Lanyon's death.

Dr. Jekyll's own account of the horrible affair was more detailed. He had begun early in life to live a double life. Publicly he had been genteel and circumspect, but privately he had practiced strange vices without restraint. Becoming obsessed with the idea that people had two personalities, he reasoned that men were capable of having two physical beings as well. Finally, he had compounded a mixture which transformed his body into the physical representation of his evil self. He became Hyde. In his disguise he was free to haunt the lonely, narrow corners of London and to do the darkest acts without fear of recognition.

He tried in every way to protect Hyde. He cautioned his servants to let him in at any hour; he took an apartment for him, and he made out his will in Hyde's favor. His life proceeded safely enough until he awoke one morning in the shape of Edward Hyde and realized that his evil nature had gained the upper hand. Frightened, he determined to cast off the nature of Hyde. He sought out better companions and tried to occupy his mind with other things. However, he was not strong enough to change his true nature. He finally permitted himself to assume the shape of Hyde again, and on that occasion Hyde, full of an overpowering lust to do evil, murdered Sir Danvers Carew.

Dr. Jekyll renewed his effort to abandon the nature of Hyde. Walking in the park one day, he suddenly changed into Hyde. On that occasion he had sought out his friend Dr. Lanyon to go to his laboratory to obtain the drugs which would change him back to the personality of the doctor. Dr. Lanyon had watched the transformation with horror. Thereafter the nature of Hyde seemed to assert itself constantly. When his supply of chemicals had been exhausted and could not be replenished, Dr. Jekyll, as Hyde, shut himself up in his laboratory while he experimented with one drug after another. Finally, in despair, as Utterson now realized, he killed himself.

Further Critical Evaluation of the Work:

The Gothic Novel in England enjoyed its heyday in the eighteenth century. In this sense, Robert Louis Stevenson's *Dr. Jekyll and Mr. Hyde* is but a late appendage to a popular trend. In terms of content and style, however, it is in the mainstream of that highly popular genre. The novel has predilections for the far and remote, the marvelous and abnormal. It is an escape from reality, emphasizing intuition over reason and impulse over rationality. Like most romantic novels, it values impulsive, childlike, savage, or peasant behavior as uncorrupted by civilized ways. It is transcendental, grotesque, and bizarre while maintaining a sensitive approach to nature, beauty, and women. It is anti-intellectual and Rousseauistic in philosophy, but it is notable for being remote, simple, and democratic while focusing on the supernatural.

The central feature of *Dr. Jekyll and Mr. Hyde* is its theme of duality. Two personalities—opposite and antagonistic—mesh within one body, a psychological insight which, in its time, was remarkably prescient. Dr. Jekyll, an essentially good man, was fascinated by the idea of evil. As a research scientist, he pursued the idea to the point of developing a drug which would alter his conscious state from an intrinsically good person to a fundamentally bad one. Taking the drug, he developed a dual personality, combining the extremes of good and evil. The evil self emerged as the violent Mr. Hyde. This schizophrenia persisted until the "bad" Mr. Hyde overcame "good" Dr. Jekyll to become the dominant personality of the two—at which time it became apparent that Mr. Hyde would have to be annihilated—by then a solution both inevitable and desirable.

The process of transformation was alchemic, tainted with witchcraft. This touch of the occult—a distinct Gothic feature—rescued the novel from the banal, and elevated it to the realm of genuine Gothic horror. Alchemy, witchcraft, and the occult were to earlier ages what technology—especially the computer—is to the present day: a threat to the status quo and comfortable assumptions. The occult and technology are usually treated in like manner: with awe and apprehension. *Dr. Jekyll and Mr. Hyde* continues to fascinate readers—as well as motion picture audiences—for just those qualities of verisimilitude, fear, and hostility. The novel ultimately succeeds by terrifying us, for who among us does not contain the potential for developing that split-personality of good and evil which the protagonist so vividly portrays. It is Stevenson's almost mystical capacity in language and characterization to evoke reader identification with his protagonist which accounts for the powerful impact of his novel.

DOCTOR PASCAL

Type of work: Novel
Author: Emile Zola (1840-1902)
Type of plot: Naturalism
Time of plot: Late nineteenth century
Locale: The south of France
First published: 1893

Principal characters:
>DOCTOR PASCAL, a doctor interested in heredity
>CLOTILDE, his niece
>MARTINE. their devoted old servant
>FÉLICITÉ ROUGON, Dr. Pascal's mother
>DOCTOR RAMOND
>MAXIME, Clotilde's brother

Critique:

Doctor Pascal is the twentieth and last volume of the Rougon-Macquart series, in which Zola intended to apply the methods of the experimental sciences to the social novel. Dr. Pascal, himself a Rougon, is doing research on the problem of heredity. Using experimental methods, he has chosen his own family as his field of investigation. Thus the novel affords Zola a double opportunity: to conclude the whole series with flashbacks to the former volumes, and to expose his own conception of reality through Dr. Pascal's exposition of his theories. When Dr. Pascal remarks that his files on the family contain the materials for a fresco of life during the Second Empire, the parallel is obvious. What Dr. Pascal has meant to do on the subject of heredity, Zola intended to do on the subject of social life. As in the preceding volumes, a dominant characteristic of the book is its objectivity. Although Zola has often been accused of insensibility, Dr. Pascal seems to testify more to his great passion for truth, whether pleasant or not.

The Story:

The July afternoon was extremely hot, but the room was well protected from the heat by heavy wooden shutters. In front of a huge carved oak armoire, Dr. Pascal was patiently looking for a paper. The search was not easy. For some thirty years, the doctor had been amassing manuscripts related to his work on heredity.

A smile came over his face as he found the paper and handed it to his niece, asking her to copy it over for their friend, Dr. Ramond. Clotilde took it without interrupting her pastel drawing of some flowers intended to provide illustration plates for the doctor's work.

Martine, the housekeeper, came in to repair the tapestry on an armchair. She had been with the doctor for thirty years, ever since he had come to Plassans as a young doctor. Thirteen years later, Dr. Pascal's brother, following the death of his wife, had sent Clotilde, then seven years old, to live with him. Martine had cared for the child according to her own zealous religious conviction.

For his part, Dr. Pascal completed Clotilde's instruction by trying to give her clear and healthy ideas on everything. The three had lived in peaceful happiness, although a certain uneasiness was now beginning to grow out of their religious conflicts. Martine considered it a pity that such a kind man as her master refused to go to church; the two women had agreed that they would force him to attend services.

Toward the end of the afternoon old Madame Rougon came for a visit, but under a false pretext; she was actually there to inspect everything. Hearing her son in the next room, she appeared quite displeased that he was again doing what she called his "devilish cooking." She told

Clotilde of the unpleasant rumors going around about the doctor's new drug. If only he could try spectacular cures on the famous people of the town, she declared; but he was always treating the poor. She had always wanted him to be a success, like his two brothers or his nephew, Clotilde's brother. But Dr. Pascal was most unlike the rest of his family. He had practiced medicine for only twelve years; then he had invested his money with a private broker and was now living on its returns. Martine was getting the money every three months and using it to the best advantage. When his patients paid him, Dr. Pascal would throw the money in a drawer, taking it only as he needed it. When he visited a poor patient he often left money there instead of receiving payment. He was completely lost in his research work, his faith in life, and his fight against suffering.

Madame Rougon was upset most by the fact that the big oak armoire contained detailed information on each member of the family. Afraid that the doctor's papers might fall in the hands of a stranger, she asked Clotilde to give her the key. She opened the cupboard, but as she was reaching for the famous files, Dr. Pascal entered; she left demurely as if nothing had happened. It was Clotilde who received the explosion of the doctor's anger.

From that time on Dr. Pascal felt that he was being betrayed by the two human beings who were dearest to him, and to whom he was dearest. He kept all the drawers of his desk tightly locked.

One day Maxime came for a visit. He was still young, but worn out by a dissolute way of life. Seeing that his sister was not planning to get married, he asked her to come to Paris with him. Clotilde was frightened at the idea of leaving Dr. Pascal's home, but she promised to go to her brother if some day he really needed her.

After Maxime's visit the house returned to its state of subdued tension until a Capuchin came to Plassans to preach. Clotilde, deeply shaken by his preaching, asked Dr. Pascal to burn all his papers. He refused. He also had another fruitless discussion with his mother, who was constantly begging the young girl to destroy his files.

One night, after Clotilde had taken the key to the armoire, he found her trying to steal the papers. While she was helping him replace them, he made a last attempt to convince her of the value of his work. He showed her the files and explained the use he was making of them. Clotilde, almost convinced, asked for time to think about the matter.

One day the doctor returned in an upset state from a call he had made. A patient had died of a heart attack while he was giving the man an injection. After Dr. Pascal had refused Clotilde's attempted comfort, his mother hinted that he might be going insane, and he nearly believed the suggestion. He felt he might be suffering from the same insanity as his grandmother, who had never been well-balanced and who was still in a sanitarium at the age of one hundred and four. Anxious and helpless, Clotilde and Martine watched over him.

When Dr. Ramond came to ask Clotilde to marry him, she said that she needed time to consider his proposal but that she would answer him soon. In the meantime she wanted to learn from him what he thought about her uncle's condition. Dr. Pascal overheard the conversation, and from that time on his health became worse. Although he allowed Clotilde to take care of him, he would not let her come into his room when he was in bed. She finally persuaded him to try some of his own injections, as Dr. Ramond had suggested. As he began to show improvement she tried to restore his faith in his research. He was overjoyed when she found the key to the armoire and brought it to him.

At last Dr. Pascal declared that he felt greatly improved, and he told Clotilde that she should begin to think about a date for her marriage. Clotilde did not seem concerned. One day, as they were coming back from a walk, she asked him to help untie her hat. Suddenly, as he bent close to her, he realized how greatly he desired her. Disturbed by the strength of his feelings, he insisted that she give Dr. Ramond a definite date for the wedding. A short time later he bought her an extravagant present of lace, which he put on her bed. That night Clotilde came running to his door and told him that if her marriage was the occasion for the gift, she was not going to marry Dr. Ramond. He, Pascal, was the man she loved. That night she was his.

A period of extreme happiness for both followed. Martine, after disappearing for a full day to show her disapproval, continued her faithful service.

One day Martine returned with the news that the broker had embezzled the doctor's funds and fled. She performed miracles in preparing meals, using the money accumulated in the drawer, but at last their situation became really desperate. Dr. Pascal and Clotilde seemed quite unconcerned, however, and waited patiently for the matter to be settled in court.

Meanwhile, Madame Rougon kept busy. She produced a letter from Maxime, now disabled, in which he asked for his sister; she shamed Dr. Pascal for

keeping this young girl without even marrying her and for not being able to feed her properly. Dr. Pascal was happy when Clotilde refused to go to her brother. Then, feeling guilty, he tried working hard in order to keep his mind busy. Finally, pretending that he needed time to devote himself to his research, he insisted that she should go. Clotilde, deeply hurt, obeyed.

Dr. Pascal went on working, waiting, meanwhile, for the painful joy of Clotilde's letters. In poor health, he suffered two heart attacks. Dr. Ramond brought him the news that some of his money had been recovered. About the same time he received a letter from Clotilde saying that she was pregnant. He immediately wired her to return. She left at once, but two hours before she arrived he died. However, he had gathered enough strength at the end to complete his files concerning himself, Clotilde, and their unborn child.

While Clotilde was in Dr. Pascal's room, Madame Rougon, with the help of Martine, burned all his papers. Later on, Clotilde used the shelves to store her baby's clothes.

Further Critical Evaluation of the Work:

Doctor Pascal, the twentieth and final novel in Zola's Rougon-Macquart series, is significant both as a reflection of Zola's personal life and as the culmination of his vast, ambitious "history of the Second Empire." If *Doctor Pascal* does not possess the literary energy of some of the other novels in the Rougon-Macquart series, it does reveal many of Zola's characteristic interests and obsessions.

Doctor Pascal centers on the love between an older doctor and a young woman, his niece. This relationship mirrors Zola's love for Jeanne Rozerot, a seamstress that Zola's wife had hired. Jeanne was a beautiful, modest girl twenty years old. Zola made her his mistress in 1888 (he was near fifty at the time) and promptly went on two crash diets to lose weight. Apparently, he loved her very much and eventually had two children by her (although he had none by his wife, Alexandrine). He was not willing to divorce his wife, however, despite the fact that he scorned extramarital affairs. Alexandrine had stuck by him in very hard times, and no matter how much he loved Jeanne, he was not willing to walk away from his wife. Alexandrine was furious when she heard about the affair. But after Zola died, she acted most humanely, met the children, treated them kindly, and even made it legally possible for them to bear their father's name.

In any case, it is clear that *Doctor Pascal* is a very personal novel in terms of the life of the novelist. But it is also personal in the sense that Doctor Pascal, as much as any other character in Zola's fiction, directly reflects the intellectual interest and commitments of the author. Doctor Pascal the scientist is devoted to curing nervous disorders and to keeping a record of his family. First, Zola often viewed himself and his work as "scientific." In opposition to what he considered to be the unreality of the romantics, Zola was determined to place his work on a firm scientific basis; and, in fact, he often saw his own fiction as a form of "experimentation." Second, Doctor Pascal's record of the Rougon-Macquart family permits Zola to review the chronicle of the figures and incidents in this "history" and, at the same time, to express his views on the significance of heredity in the affairs of men and families. Doctor Pascal and, by inference, Zola take the genetic material of the Rougon-Macquarts with extreme seriousness. Although the laws of heredity may not be completely understood, and although Dr. Pascal's injections are not medically successful, Doctor Pascal's belief in the power and explanatory force of science remains unshaken.

In fact, Doctor Pascal's belief in science—and the opposition to that belief —form the chief intellectual concern of the novel. There are two objections to the doctor's scientific approach, religious and social. The former, though virulent, is ultimately less threatening to Zola than the latter. Doctor Pascal's treasured servant, Martine, is opposed to Pascal's "tampering" with God's plan. But she only takes action to help destroy the doctor's valued historical files when she is incited by Madame Rougon, Doctor Pascal's mother.

Madame Rougon's motives are entirely selfish. She does not want the honor of the family stained by an exposure of defects. Her only pride is her family, and she cannot tolerate the prospect of the family's being shamed in years to come when Pascal's files are opened. Taking advantage of Martine's simplicity, she finally succeeds in destroying all of Pascal's meticulously recorded chronicle. In a sense, this destruction of the family records is a logical conclusion of the degeneration of the Rougon-Macquarts. The family —a few branches still growing, others degenerated and collapsed—is self-destructive.

But an interesting question, if the parallel between Pascal and Zola holds, is whether Zola's literary work is also metaphorically destroyed as the Rougon-Macquart series comes to an end. Perhaps Zola believed that life would take its revenge on literature, that the truth he sought to express could not be borne. The forces of reaction, both social and religious, would stifle and burn his work.

That fate was not in store for Zola's literary work, though it was, in a sense, in store for Zola himself. Shortly after the publication of *Doctor Pascal,*

Zola intervened in the notorious Dreyfus affair. Dreyfus, a Jewish officer, was convicted of treason by the French authorities. The conviction was, incredibly, upheld despite the fact that another officer actually confessed to the crime and fled the country. Clearly, the issue was racism (anti-Semitism), not treason, and Zola could not resist attacking the authorities for their cover-ups, hypocrisy, lying, and racism. As a result, Zola was forced to go into temporary exile in England.

Zola's courageous action in behalf of Dreyfus, and his opposition to anti-Semitism, are especially important in evaluating Zola's naturalist theory, a theory that occupies such a central role in *Doctor Pascal*. Because of Zola's emphasis on genetic determinism, his work might be open to accusations of racialism. Because of the stress he places on forces that mold men's lives, over which they have no control, he also may be accused of fatalism. As a result, the critic Georg Lukacs, for example, refuses even to include Zola in the literary tradition of progressive realism. But the fact is that, in his literature as well as in his life, Zola affirmed his confidence in the forces of science, progress, and, above all, life. Despite the destruction of the doctor's files, the reader is left with the impression, at the end of the novel, that Doctor Pascal's work will continue after him. It is the love between the doctor and his niece which is responsible for this impression.

The emotional interest of the narrative, the center of gravity of the fiction, lies in the love of an older man for a young woman. Zola explores their feelings with extreme delicacy and insight; and the child resulting from their love is meant to signify the rebirth of hope and humanity. The child more than compensates for the destruction of the files. If that destruction is seen as revenge against scholarship, science, and art, then the birth of the child signals the victory of the positive forces of life over the forces of despair and negativism.

The literary qualities of the novel are, however, uneven. The style is sometimes lyrical and moving (as in physical descriptions of the countryside and of Clotilde's and Pascal's lovemaking), but at other times it is slow moving and even ponderous. Further, though Pascal, Martine, Madame Rougon, and Clotilde are well conceived and portrayed, there is an absence of those numerous, strong secondary characters which lend so much life to other novels in the Rougon-Macquart series.

Although there is significant intellectual content in the novel and although the novel is highly relevant to Zola's life and career, one feels a certain weariness in Zola's telling. But Zola had already written an enormous number of pages in his vast chronicle. Further, like Doctor Pascal, Zola was no longer a young man. If the narrative lacks the intensity of his earlier works, it nevertheless glows with compassion and loving faith; and these qualities, so rarely associated with the name of Zola or his works, certainly deserve to be recognized.

Howard Lee Hertz

DOCTOR THORNE

Type of work: Novel
Author: Anthony Trollope (1815-1882)
Type of plot: Domestic realism
Time of plot: Mid-nineteenth century
Locale: "Barsetshire," England
First published: 1858

Principal characters:
DOCTOR THORNE, a country doctor
MARY THORNE, his niece
SQUIRE GRESHAM, owner of Greshamsbury Park
LADY ARABELLA, his wife
FRANK GRESHAM, their son
ROGER SCATCHERD, a stonemason, later a baronet
LOUIS PHILIPPE, his son
MISS DUNSTABLE, an heiress

Critique:

The third in the series of Barchester Novels, *Doctor Thorne* continues the chronicling of clerical and county life begun in *The Warden* and *Barchester Towers.* The usual Trollopian theme of making money and a successful marriage is here portrayed against the background of an English country estate and the life connected with it. There is, as in other books of the series, a mixture of sentiment, humor, romance, and fidelity to human nature and experience. The chief value of these novels lies in their authentic depiction of middle-class country life in nineteenth-century England. The Barchester Novels do not contain the whole of Victorian society, but in them Trollope reflected, better than any other writer of his time, the manners and morals of the period.

The Story:

Greshamsbury Park, in the county of Barsetshire, dominated the life of the surrounding countryside. Unfortunately, Greshamsbury's lord, Squire Gresham, was rapidly spending himself into poverty.

Most of his financial troubles resulted from the desire of his wife, Lady Arabella De Courcy Gresham, to get him into politics. The squire had inherited his father's seat in Parliament. He had lost favor, however, because of his Whig leanings. Barsetshire, overwhelmingly Tory, did not approve of Gresham's Whig friends or the fact that his wife's aristocratic family, the De Courcys, were aggressively Whig in sentiment. Having lost his seat in the Parliamentary elections, Gresham twice tried to regain it. These attempts were stimulated by his wife, who fancied being the wife of a member of Parliament. But Gresham was not successful, and he lost a great deal of money in financing his campaigns.

Consequently, when his son Frank came of age, Squire Gresham had not much to offer him in the way of financial security. Lady Arabella saw as their only hope the possibility of Frank's marriage to a wealthy heiress. That he might do such a thing seemed rather doubtful, however, for, much to the distress of his mother and her family, young Frank was highly enamored of Mary Thorne, niece of the local doctor. Frank and Mary had known each other all their lives, and Mary had been educated along with the young Greshams at Greshamsbury Park. Hers was an interesting history.

She had been brought to live with her uncle, Doctor Thorne, when she was a mere infant. The real circumstances of her birth—that she was the illegitimate child of Doctor Thorne's brother and Mary Scatcherd, a village girl—were known only to the doctor. Even Mary Scatcherd's brother Roger, who had killed his sister's betrayer, did not know that Doctor Thorne had adopted the child. Roger

Scatcherd, a poor stonemason, had been sentenced to six months in prison for his crime. When his term was up, he was told that the child had died. Since the doctor stood in high favor with Squire Gresham and daily attended Lady Arabella, it was natural that his niece should visit the estate. Because she was an attractive child and near the age of the Gresham children, she soon took her lessons with them. By the time Frank was of age, Mary Thorne seemed part of the family. But Lady Arabella was determined that this was not to be the literal state of affairs; Mary had no money.

One of Squire Gresham's greatest misfortunes was the loss of a particularly choice part of his estate, land sold to pay off his numerous and most pressing debts. Doctor Thorne, acting as agent for the squire, found a buyer in Sir Roger Scatcherd, a wealthy baronet. Sir Roger was the former stonemason, who had prospered well after his jail term and was now the possessor of a title, a seat in Parliament, and a large fortune. Although he knew nothing of the existence of his sister's illegitimate child, Sir Roger was in close contact with Doctor Thorne. Sir Roger was a chronic alcoholic, and Doctor Thorne was often called on to attend him during his sprees.

To the Gresham family the loss of this piece of property was indeed a tragedy, for the sale greatly diminished the estate Frank would someday inherit. Nervously, Lady Arabella began to plan for the future of her family. Fortunately, one of the daughters was engaged to marry money, a politician who wanted the Gresham and De Courcy position and family connections. Another daughter would marry the local vicar and so would be assured of a respectable position, though one without much money. But Frank was his mother's real hope. If he could make a wealthy marriage, their troubles would be over. But Frank, in love with Mary Thorne, had no lofty matrimonial ambitions. Lady Arabella's family, to save him from an unfortunate romance, invited Frank to De Courcy Castle for a visit.

It was the Countess De Courcy's plan to make a match between Frank and Miss Dunstable, a family friend. Miss Dunstable was considered the wealthiest heiress in England, but she was wary and sharp-tongued. Mostly to humor his aunt, Frank pretended to woo the heiress, and to his surprise he found her rather good company. Miss Dunstable, ten years his senior and much more worldly-wise, soon uncovered his little plot. Thereafter they became the best of friends, and she acted as an adviser to Frank in his affair with Mary Thorne.

Meanwhile Sir Roger Scatcherd was in such poor health from excessive drinking that he decided to make his will, leaving everything to Louis Philippe, his equally alcoholic son. When Dr. Thorne learned the terms of the will, he told Sir Roger that Mary Scatcherd's child was still living. Sir Roger made her his second heir in the event of his son's death.

Otherwise matters were not going well for Mary. Lady Arabella, finding Frank's attachment for Mary unchanged, would not allow the girl to visit Greshamsbury. When Frank arrived home and became aware of the shabby treatment she had received, he was furious. But the family insisted that he had to marry wealth, particularly after his sister, who was to marry money, had been jilted.

Sir Roger was also in difficulties. Having discovered a fraud in his election, the committee unseated him, and the shock was too great for the old man. He went on one final drinking bout and died from the effects. Louis Philippe, having inherited the estate, also formed an attachment for Mary, but she remained true to Frank. Dr. Thorne's only hope for the happiness of Mary and Frank lay in the possible death of Louis Philippe. Meanwhile that young man was well on his way to fulfilling the doctor's half-wish. Having paid a visit to the squire for the purpose of foreclosing on some debts, Louis Philippe went on a drinking spree that rivaled any of his father's. Weak and very ill, he was finally sent home.

Soon afterward, in a stormy interview, Lady Arabella demanded that Mary end her engagement to Frank. Mary refused to break her promise, but she did ask the young man to release her because of the hopelessness of the situation in which they found themselves. Frank refused, insisting that they loved each other. Then it was that Louis Philippe died. Doctor Thorne jubilantly told Mary the news of her inheritance, news which opened the way for her marriage to Frank. With Mary now an heiress in her own right, not even the proud De Courcys could object to so excellent a match. For the first time in years an atmosphere of rejoicing hung over Greshamsbury Park.

Further Critical Evaluation of the Work:

The third novel in Trollope's Barsetshire series, *Doctor Thorne,* like its two predecessors, *The Warden* and *Barchester Towers,* describes with psychological insight the social realities of his mythical county. Unlike the first two works, which were concerned with the insular ecclesiastical world of a cathedral town, Trollope turns his attention in this novel to the landed wealth of Barsetshire. The gentry, represented by the Greshams, are in decline because of the political imprudence of the squire who early in his married life aligned himself with his wife's family, the De Courcys, notoriously aristocratic and notoriously Whig. Having lost his Tory constituency and his money, Squire Gresham attempts to retrench to save the estate for his son.

It is at this point that Doctor Thorne, one of Trollope's ideal gentlemen, enters the story. The squire's only confidant, he serves not only as the family physician, but also as its moral and spiritual counselor. Rigorous in his ethics, proud of his social station and in no way awed by the upper classes, Doctor Thorne joins the squire in an attempt to restore the estate to its former vigor. An enemy of the snobbish and pretentious aristocrats like the De Courcys, who have no loyalty to the life of the land, he seeks by advising various economies and by suggesting judicious loans to help his friend.

If the moral strength which saves Greshamsbury Park comes from the doctor, it is the money of Sir Roger Scatcherd, however, which enables Gresham to recoup and permits young Frank and Mary to wed. Scatcherd, part of the new industrial wealth, unwittingly saves the agriculture of the area from the moneylenders of London. It is in this alignment that Trollope reveals his political sympathies with the English upper-middle class and his antagonism to the aristocracy and their morality.

DOCTOR ZHIVAGO

Type of work: Novel
Author: Boris Pasternak (1890-1960)
Time: 1903-1943
Locale: Moscow, the Eastern Front, Siberia
First published: 1958

Principal characters:

YURII ANDREIEVICH ZHIVAGO, physician, poet, and a man of good will
EVGRAF ANDREIEVICH ZHIVAGO, his half brother
NIKOLAI NIKOLAIEVICH VEDENIAPIN (UNCLE KOLIA), his maternal uncle
ANTONINA ALEXANDROVNA GROMEKA (TONIA), his wife
LARISA FEODOROVNA GUISHAR (LARA), wife of Pavel Antipov
PAVEL PAVLOVICH ANTIPOV (PASHA), a Red commissar
INNOKENTII DUDOROV (NIKA), the son of a revolutionary terrorist
MISHA GORDON, the son of a Jewish lawyer and a friend of Yurii Zhivago
VICTOR IPPOLITOVICH KOMAROVSKY, a shady lawyer, seducer of Lara
LIBERIUS AVERKIEVICH MIKULITSYN, a Red partisan leader
TANIA, the daughter of Yurri Zhivago and Lara

It is unfortunate that the furor over *Doctor Zhivago* should have swept Boris Pasternak's novel so quickly into the realm of front-page news, an area of journalistic expediency in which the intense moral vision of experience functions awkwardly at best. For the true work of art never stands for this or that; it simply exists, separate and complete and self-contained, and it makes no compromises with the world of things as they are. This is one reason why the book, inevitably seized upon as a club with which to bludgeon the ideology and bureaucracy of the Kremlin, should have turned out to be a two-edged weapon, as much a reproach to certain attitudes of democratic complacency as it is an indictment of the totalitarian state. Understandably, Pasternak's literary position became embarrassing abroad as well as difficult at home, for the very simple reason that much of the acclaim which greeted his novel outside Russia was based on misunderstanding of his purpose. Pasternak was a poet-novelist, not a political pamphleteer. As a propaganda tool of the cold war, his sprawling, uneven novel lacks the single-minded concentration and drive of the inspired polemic. It is superb, however, as a statement of human dignity and of

man's capacity for integrity, faith, courage, and endurance; and it is as a work in the great moral tradition of Turgenev, Tolstoy, and Dostoevski that it must be judged.

The remarkable thing is that nothing in the external circumstances of Pasternak's career had prepared readers outside the Iron Curtain for the explosion his novel touched off. Son of Leonid Pasternak, the bourgeois painter who illustrated Tolstoy's novels, and Rosa Kaufman Pasternak, a concert pianist, he grew up in the cultured atmosphere of the pre-revolutionary Russian intelligentsia, studied music under Scriabin and philosophy in Germany, and published his first book of poems at twenty-three. With Esenin and Mayakovsky he emerged as one of the three leading poets of the early Soviet regime. To him, as to many of his generation, it may have seemed that the events of 1917 held the promise of the future. If so, the dream of freedom soon faded. Esenin and Mayakovsky died by their own hands during the decade of civil war, mass violence, and terror which followed. Pasternak survived the persecutions and purges by preserving a discreet public silence. Except for translations of some of his early poems and sketches, he was known to the Western world, if at all, as a poet who no longer wrote verse, a translator of Shakespeare and Goethe.

Perhaps Pasternak's years of silence were also a season of pondering and preparation. *Doctor Zhivago* contains a revealing passage in which Yurii Zhivago dreams of writing a prose work on a vast scale, a book of impressions of all he had seen and thought about; his poems are a preparation for this major task. He did not live to create his grand project, but this book is undoubtedly Pasternak's, a novel powerfully imagined, deeply concerned with the moral issues of human conduct, and set against the background of a world falling apart and, through loneliness and cruelty and fear, involving a whole society in the common destruction.

The opening chapters give an impression of complexity and spaciousness. In the leisurely fashion of the full-bodied nineteenth century novel, Pasternak sets his stage, introduces his people, and draws the threads of his story together. Ten-year-old Yurii Zhivago, the son of a wealthy profligate who has deserted his family, attends his mother's funeral in the company of his Uncle Kolia; they stay that night at a nearby monastery and to the boy, waking in the darkness, the snow-covered landscape beyond his window suggests an empty, alien world. Young Misha Gordon, traveling with his father, sees the older Zhivago kill himself in a leap from a moving train. Nika Dudorov, whose parents were a nihilistic terrorist and a Georgian princess, is being brought up in the household of Kilogrigov, a philanthropic industrialist. After his father, a revolutionary and a railway worker, has been exiled to Siberia, Pasha Antipov is taken in by the Tiverzin family, also revolutionaries. Amalia Guishar, the French widow of a Russian engineer, arrives in Moscow and opens a dressmaking establishment; her protector is Victor Komarovsky, an unscrupulous lawyer who eventually succeeds in seducing her daughter Lara.

Before long these lives begin to crisscross. During their schooldays Yurii Zhivago and Misha Gordon live in the home of Alexander Gromeko, a professor of chemistry; their companion is Tonia, daughter of Gromeko and his ailing wife, Anna Ivanovna. Pasha and Nika take part in student riots. One night, by chance, after Madame Guishar has attempted suicide, Yurii sees Lara looking at her betrayer and guesses their secret. Lara, following an unsuccessful attempt to shoot Komarovsky, becomes a governess in the Kilogrigov household; later she marries Pasha and goes to live with him in a hamlet beyond the Urals. Yurii discovers his vocation as a poet but instead chooses a career in medicine because he believes that art is not a vocation, any more than melancholy or cheerfulness is a profession. For him most choices are as simple as that. During his student years he reveals an almost Dostoevskian gift of innocence which he never loses and which makes him vulnerable, in the end, to forces beyond his power to order or control. This trait is part of the greater, enveloping *mystique* which in the novel throws over much that is brutal and sordid a radiance of goodness and truth, symbolized by the light seen briefly in a strange house as Yurii and Tonia drive by to a Christmas party. Later he writes a poem about that light in the window, and at the end he dies in the same house. He marries Tonia and their first child is born shortly before World War I.

The novel's early promise of Tolstoyan richness and profusion in character and scene is never fulfilled, for with the outbreak of the war the tempo of events quickens abruptly. Yurii Zhivago serves in a hospital unit at the front. Wounded, he is nursed by Lara Antipova, who is to become the great love of his life. So he finds himself married to a wife whom he sincerely respects and loves, but at the same time pulled toward Lara by a tide of passion which sweeps him along into the unsettled years ahead. The Moscow to which he returns after the October Revolution is a city ravaged by riots and disease, from which he flees with his family to an estate, the property of Tonia's grandfather, in the Urals. The account of this journey across Russia in winter is one of the great set pieces of the novel; all Russia is on the move, restless, threatening, violent. In the village where the Zhivagos settle Yurii meets Lara again and is once more drawn to her until he is seized by a band of Red partisans and forced into service as their doctor during a campaign of guerrilla warfare against the Whites in Siberia. After his escape he returns to find that his family has gone back to Moscow. He and Lara live together in an abandoned farmhouse for a brief period of perfect happiness. Then, about to be arrested because they have become politically suspect, he sends her to safety with Komarovsky, who has become an official of the new regime. Another great scene of the novel is that in which Zhivago encounters Pasha for the last time. Pasha, now called Strelnikov—"The Shooter"—has been a feared and hated commissar of the civil war, but he himself is in flight from Red authorities who have denounced him as he has denounced others. His suicide after a night of wild accusation and abject confession points eloquently to the revolutionary madness of the period.

Back in Moscow, Zhivago finds his life empty and meaningless. His family has found refuge in Paris. He marries a younger woman, the daughter of a former porter in the Gromeko house, practices medicine, and writes a few scientific papers. In the end he is befriended by his strange half brother Evgraf, an ambiguous figure whose relationship with Yurii Zhivago remains shadowy and symbolic. After the doctor dies of a heart attack, Evgraf arranges for the publication of a collection of Yurii's poems, some of which make up the last chapter of the novel. During World War II he also discovers Tania, the daughter of Yurii and Lara, and provides for her future.

The twenty-four poems printed at the end of the novel are not a mere appendage, as unwary readers have supposed, but an integral part of Pasternak's examination into the nature of life and death; they complete the pattern of meaning by a final statement on the themes of love, death, and resurrection. Pasternak's technique throughout reveals the working of a poet's imagination and a poet's strategy with imagery and symbol, rather than the logic of the novelist—one reason, perhaps, why the book conveys an effect of subtlety and richness. It is a novel filled with luminous, compelling images of the land itself in all weathers and seasons, so that the life of man remains rooted in the life of nature, not in systems or institutions. If this method results at times in awkwardness of structure, it gains nevertheless in perspective and insight. The mystery of personality is revealed but not explained away. And life, says Yurii Zhivago, is stronger than men's efforts to control it to their own ends. For him it is the principle of self-renewal.

Good as the novel is in its great sense of life and in tracing through the particular lives the special terror which is history's contribution to our century, it gains added vigor from its deep roots in the Christian tradition. The purity of Pasternak's religious feeling, uncomplicated by sect or dogma, is without the self-consciousness most Western writers display in dealing with matters of religion; the Crucifixion and the Resurrection are in his view part of an ever-renewing miracle. Early in the novel Uncle Kolia, who acts as one of his spokesmen, relates the condition of man to the march of history and the Passion of Christ. His argument is that history is the centuries-old record of man's attempt to explore the riddle of death and to overcome it. All scientific discoveries and creation in art, he says, are spiritual, based on the two ideas of modern man, the idea of freedom of spirit and the idea of sacrifice. This theme is magnificently restated in "Garden of Gethsemane," the closing poem of the novel, eloquent in its promise of a risen Christ and its imagery of the centuries coming like a caravan out of darkness for judgment.

Doctor Zhivago is a novel of honesty and passion, not a work of abstraction set within a frame of historical reference. At the same time it is not a fiction of profound psychological depth such as we have had from the great visionaries and the midnight-haunted writers of the past, nor a massive fable in the manner of Melville or Dostoevski. Its meaning and relevance are of a different order. Boris Pasternak has looked at the history of his own time with what Henry James called the "imagination of disaster." Out of poetic apprehension and the knowledge so gained he has spoken to the conscience of the world. And the world has listened to his testimony concerning the moral condition of modern man in the sweep of history. That is the important thing.

DODSWORTH

Type of work: Novel
Author: Sinclair Lewis (1885-1951)
Type of plot: Social criticism
Time of plot: The 1920's
Locale: United States and Europe
First published: 1929

Principal characters:
SAM DODSWORTH, an American manufacturer
FRAN DODSWORTH, his wife
KURT OBERSDORF, Fran's lover
EDITH CORTRIGHT, Sam's friend, later his fiancee
CLYDE LOCKERT, Fran's admirer
EMILY, the Dodsworths' daughter
BRENT, the Dodsworths' son

Critique:

Dodsworth is a successful novel in spite of its sprawling and sometimes rambling style. It describes convincingly the degeneration and unmasking of the shallow, snobbish Fran Dodsworth, and the disillusion and final rebellion of her idealistic husband. One of the last in the tradition of American novels on American materialism and European cultivation, the book contains brilliant insights into the relationships of the two cultures.

The Story:

In 1903, Sam Dodsworth married Fran Voelker whom he had met at the Canoe Club while he was assistant superintendent at the Zenith Locomotive works. Five years after their marriage Sam became vice-president and general manager of production for the Revelation Automobile Company. By 1925, the Dodsworths had two children, Emily, about to be married, and Brent, in school at Yale. When Sam sold his factory to the Unit Automotive Company, they decided to go to Europe for a leisurely vacation, a second honeymoon.

The first night out on the S.S. *Ultima*, Major Clyde Lockert seated himself at Sam's table in the smoking room. Lockert, who said he was growing cocoa in British Guiana, quickly became friends with Fran Dodsworth, and while Sam looked on like an indulgent parent, he squired her about, censuring and selecting the new friends she made. He continued to see the Dodsworths after they arrived in London.

Fran was snobbishly pleased when he took them to see his cousins, Lord and Lady Herndon. Between them Fran and Lockert made Sam feel almost like an outsider. He was a failure at the dinner party the Herndons gave, for he knew nothing about cricket or polo, and he had no opinions about the Russian situation.

One evening Hurd, manager of the London branch of the Revelation Motor Company, invited Sam to a get-together, along with about thirty representatives of American firms. Sam was surprised to learn that few of them wanted to go back to the United States except, perhaps, for a visit. They all preferred the leisureliness, the freedom from imposed moral restraint, which their adopted land afforded. These arguments made Sam see Europe in a different light.

When he returned to the hotel, he found Fran in tears. Lockert had taken her out that evening, and on their return had tried to make love to her. Fran, ashamed of the situation in which she had placed herself and sure that Lockert would be laughing at her, asked that they

DODSWORTH by Sinclair Lewis. By permission of the publishers, Harcourt, Brace & Co., Inc. Copyright, 1929, by Harcourt, Brace & Co., Inc.

leave for France as soon as possible. They started four days later.

France was a new experience for Sam Dodsworth. When Fran was willing to go sightseeing, he was able to see Paris and observe its people. When she chose to be fashionable and take tea at the Crillon with other American tourists, he was less fortunate. But the more he saw, the more convinced Sam became that he could not understand Frenchmen. In the back of his mind he was afraid that his inability to accept foreign ways, and Fran's willingness to adopt them, would finally drive them apart. He felt lonely for his old friend Tubby Pearson, president of the Zenith bank.

Before long Fran had many friends among expatriate Americans of the international set. With her constant visits to dressmakers and her portrait painter, her outings with the leisured young men who escorted her and her friends, she and Sam saw less and less of each other. When he went home for his college class reunion that summer, he left Fran to take a villa with one of her new friends. He was to join her again in the fall, so that they might go on to the Orient together.

Back in New York, Sam felt, at first, as if he had become a stranger to the life of noise and hurry which he had previously taken for granted. Nor was he interested in the newest model Revelation which had been, quite competently, developed without his aid. He discovered also that he and his son no longer had common ground. Brent was planning to sell bonds. The newly-married Emily, her father observed, was the very capable manager of her own home, and needed no assistance. Even Sam's best friend, Tubby Pearson, had gone on without him to new poker-playing and golfing companions.

At first his letters from Fran were lively and happy. Then she quarreled with the friend who shared her villa over one of their escorts, Arnold Israel, a Jew. Sam grew increasingly anxious as he realized that the man was trailing Fran from one resort to another and that their relationship was becoming increasingly more intimate. He made sailing reservations and cabled his wife to meet him in Paris.

Sam had no difficulty discovering that his wife had been unfaithful to him; she admitted as much during their stormy reunion in Paris. With the threat that he would divorce her for adultery if she did not agree to drop Israel, he forced her to leave for Spain with him the following day.

The Dodsworths wandered across Spain into Italy, and finally on to Germany and Berlin, and Sam had ample time to observe his wife. Increasingly he noted her self-centeredness, her pretentiousness, and his pity for her restlessness made him fonder of her.

At the home of the Biedners, Fran's cousins in Berlin, the Dodsworths met Kurt Obersdorf, a ruined Austrian nobleman. Kurt took them to places of interest in Berlin and became Fran's dancing companion.

When the news came that the Dodsworths were grandparents, for Emily now had a boy, they did not sail for home. In fact, they did not tell their friends of the baby's birth because Fran feared that as a grandmother she would seem old and faded to them. When Sam went to Paris to welcome Tubby Pearson and his wife, abroad for the first time, Fran remained in Berlin.

Sam and Tubby enjoyed themselves in Paris. Then Sam, driven by a longing to see his wife, flew back to Berlin. That night Fran announced that she and Kurt had decided to marry, and that she wanted a divorce. Sam agreed, on the condition that she wait a month before starting proceedings.

Sadly, Dodsworth left for Paris and later went on to Italy. While he was sitting on the piazza in Venice and reading one of Fran's letters, he saw Edith Cortright, a widow whom the Dodsworths had met during their earlier trip to Italy. Mrs.

Cortright invited Sam home to tea with her, and on his second visit he told her about his separation from Fran.

Sam spent most of the summer with Edith and her Italian friends. He began to gain a new self-confidence when he found that he was liked and respected by these new acquaintances, who admired him and were satisfied with him as he was. He grew to love Edith, and they decided to return to America together. Then Sam received a letter from Fran telling him that she had dropped divorce proceedings because Kurt's mother objected to his marriage with a divorced American.

Without saying goodbye to Edith, Sam rejoined Fran, homeward bound. He tried patiently to share her unhappiness and loneliness. But before long Fran became her old self, implying that Sam had been at fault for the failure of their marriage and flirting with a young polo player aboard ship. After breakfast, one morning, Sam sent a wireless to Edith, making arrangements to meet her in Venice. When the boat docked in New York, Sam left his wife forever. Three days later he sailed again to Italy and Edith Cortright.

Further Critical Evaluation of the Work:

Sinclair Lewis was born a member of the American middle class, and his novels suggest that he both loved and detested his own kind, a crucial fact in understanding the unevenness of his satirical portraits. Alfred Kazin (*On Native Grounds*) views Lewis with Sherwood Anderson as New Realists— post World War I reporters freed by the war into a struggle for "freedom of conduct" in middle America. Both writers, liberating forces in American literature of the 1920's, made "transcriptions of average experience," sometimes reproducing it and sometimes parodying it, but always participating in the native culture if primarily to reveal its shortcomings. Thus a typical Lewis novel, domestic satire, affords a mixture of scorn and compassion for its characters. To read his work in its own time was to see oneself or one's neighbor and to marvel at the likeness. He became immensely popular with such readers, an irony when one realizes that his ostensible intention was to expose the provincial, materialistic, bigoted, go-getters whom Mencken tagged the "booboisie."

Although Lewis published more than twenty novels, a play, short stories and sketches between 1914 and his death in 1951, his reputation as an artist now rests on four novels of the 1920's: *Main Street* (1920), *Babbitt* (1922), *Arrowsmith* (1925), and *Dodsworth* (1929). The protagonists of the "big four" continue to generate interest and empathy because Lewis' feeling for the characters as human beings overrode his abiding skepticism. These characters are memorable, living individuals whose natures and problems transcend Dickensian caricature and the topical.

Dodsworth, whose working title was *Exile*, was written in Europe, where Lewis had journeyed in the aftermath of his ruined marriage. There he found or imagined that he found a culture superior to that of America's half-educated, anti-intellectual boosters. Lewis' strong if troubled vision of middle-America appears to have come from a deep sense of his own inferiority (a chronic state documented in Vincent Sheean's *Dorothy and Red,* an account of the courtship and marriage of Lewis and Dorothy Thompson). Although he was the first American to receive the Nobel Prize for Literature, he later remarked that it ruined him; he could not "live up to it." This sense of native inferiority and resulting attempts to gain self-respect and love are duplicated in Sam Dodsworth's experiences in Europe. Lewis blends autobiography with fiction in a well-controlled third-person narrative technique in *Dodsworth,* focusing primarily on the protagonist, creating a fully realistic account of Sam's travels by simultaneously documenting the journeys and the reassertion of Dodsworth's value as a human being.

Lewis sees Dodsworth idealistically for the most part, but so skillfully that the romantic and nostalgic are veiled by the realistic surface of events. Sam is the Post-Victorian embodiment of American virtue. He is essentially honest, doggedly willing to remain open to new experience, boyish in his sincere if awed appreciation of femininity and womanliness but reluctant to be henpecked forever. His almost monkish physical courtship of Edith Cortright entails only kissing her hands. He is reserved, well-mannered, admirably dignified for an American even while clutching his Baedeker. By contrast, most other American male characters are inferior if not nefarious. Arnold Israel engages in questionable financial pursuits, is sensual, and is more European than the Europeans. Tub Pearson is the perennial adolescent whose idea of humor is to address French waiters as "Goosepeppy" and to ask for fricassee of birds' nests. Brent, the Dodsworths' son, decides to live by selling bonds, hoping to reach the "hundred and fifty thousand a year class."

Most significant in the characterization of Dodsworth, however, is his devotion to a work ethic of substance which proves to be his salvation. Sam slowly but persistently weighs his values against those of older cultures: England, France, Italy, Spain, and Germany. Europeans know wine, history, women, politics, and are not afraid of things theoretical, even socialism. Therefore, they can just "be"; that is, they can rest in the self-confidence inherent in their familial and cultural heritage. But Americans, Sam dimly realizes, are born apostles and practitioners of technology. They must "do." Forces beyond their knowledge and control harness their dreams and energies. Their destiny is to build more and better autos, plumbing, and electrical appliances. Sam and Edith decide to return to Zenith to work, but not on what Sam calls "kitchy banalities."

Lewis uses architecture as the symbol of Dodsworth's new life and work. In Europe, Sam, becoming absorbed in architecture, observes and sketches bridges, towers, doorways. He is impressed by their lines, their strength, their beauty, but he recognizes that they are European. So rather than return to Zenith to build a phony pastiche of villas and chalets in the San Souci development, Sam and Edith talk of building homes for Americans, native to the soil and spirit. Optimistically Edith cries that the American sky-scraper is the only new thing in architecture since the Gothic cathedral. Working together, their future promises a sharp contrast to that of the pitiful Fran, to whom all culture was interesting as "social adornment."

Occasionally Lewis abandons the detached third-person narrative technique to speak directly to the reader, to regale with satirical comments about travelers in general, or with a series of descriptions of American tourists complete with names in the comedy of humours tradition. Evident also are some forced metaphors, a few poorly integrated references to "morality hounds" in America or to the absurdities of Prohibition. Yet Lewis endows the novel with great power, basically by making Sam Dodsworth a sympathetic, authentic American whose life matters after all, to him and to the reader.

Mary H. Hayden

A DOLL'S HOUSE

Type of work: Drama
Author: Henrik Ibsen (1828-1906)
Type of plot: Social criticism
Time of plot: Nineteenth century
Locale: Norway
First presented: 1879

Principal characters:
> TORVALD HELMER, a bank manager
> NORA HELMER, his wife
> MRS. LINDE, Nora's old school friend
> KROGSTAD, a bank clerk
> DR. RANK, a friend of the Helmers

Critique:

A *Doll's House* is the best known and one of the most popular of Ibsen's works. A classic expression of the theme of woman's rights, the play shocked Ibsen's contemporaries, because in the end Nora leaves her husband and children. In the character of Dr. Rank there is a foreshadowing of the heredity theme later to be developed by Ibsen in *Ghosts*.

The Story:

On the day before Christmas, Nora Helmer was busying herself with last minute shopping, for this was the first Christmas since her marriage that she had not had to economize. Her husband, Torvald, had just been made manager of a bank and after the New Year their money troubles would be over. She bought a tree and plenty of toys for the children, and she even indulged herself in some macaroons, her favorite confection, but of which Torvald did not entirely approve. He loved his wife dearly, but he regarded her very much as her own father had seen her, as an amusing doll—a plaything.

It was true that she did behave like a child sometimes in her relations with her husband. She pouted, wheedled, and chattered because Torvald expected these things; he would not have loved his doll-wife without them. Actually, Nora was not a doll but a woman with a woman's loves, hopes, and fears. This was shown seven years before, just after her first child was born, when Torvald had been

ill, and the doctor said that unless he went abroad immediately he would die. Nora was desperate. She could not seek Torvald's advice because she knew he would rather die than borrow money. She could not go to her father, for he himself was a dying man. She did the only thing possible under the circumstances. She borrowed the requisite two hundred and fifty pounds from Krogstad, a moneylender, forging her father's name to the note, so that Torvald could have his holiday in Italy.

Krogstad was exacting, and she had to think up ways and means to meet the regular payments. When Torvald gave her money for new dresses and such things, she never spent more than half of it, and she found other ways to earn money. One winter she did copying, but she kept this work a secret from Torvald, for he believed that the money for their trip had come from her father.

Then Krogstad, who was in the employ of the bank of which Torvald was now manager, determined to use Torvald to advance his own fortunes. But Torvald hated Krogstad, and was just as determined to be rid of him. The opportunity came when Christina Linde, Nora's old school friend, applied to Torvald for a position in the bank. Torvald resolved to dismiss Krogstad and hire Mrs. Linde in his place.

When Krogstad discovered that he was to be fired, he called on Nora and informed her that if he were dismissed he would ruin her and her husband. He reminded her that the note supposedly signed by her father was dated three days after his death. Frightened at the turn matters had taken, Nora pleaded unsuccessfully with Torvald to reinstate Krogstad in the bank. Krogstad, receiving from Torvald an official notice of his dismissal, wrote in return a letter in which he revealed the full details of the forgery. He dropped the letter in the mailbox outside the Helmer home.

Torvald was in a holiday mood. The following evening they were to attend a fancy dress ball, and Nora was to go as a Neapolitan fisher girl and dance the tarantella. To divert her husband's attention from the mailbox outside, Nora practiced her dance before Torvald and Dr. Rank, an old friend. Nora was desperate, not knowing quite which way to turn. She had thought of Mrs. Linde, with whom Krogstad had at one time been in love. Mrs. Linde promised to do what she could to turn Krogstad from his avowed purpose. Nora thought also of Dr. Rank, but when she began to confide in him he made it so obvious that he was in love with her that she could not tell her secret. However, Torvald had promised her not to go near the mailbox until after the ball.

What bothered Nora was not her own fate, but Torvald's. She pictured herself as already dead, drowned in icy black water. She pictured the grief-stricken Torvald taking upon himself all the blame for what she had done and being disgraced for her sake. But the reality did not quite correspond with Nora's picture. Mrs. Linde, by promising to marry Krogstad and look after his children, succeeded in persuading him to withdraw all accusations against the Helmers, but she realized that Nora's affairs had come to a crisis and that sooner or later Nora and Torvald would have to come to an understanding.

This crisis came when Torvald read Krogstad's letter after their return from the ball. He accused Nora of being a hypocrite, a liar, and a criminal, of having no religion, no morality, no sense of duty. He declared that she was unfit to bring up her children. He informed her that she might remain in his household but she would no longer be a part of it.

Then another letter arrived from Krogstad, declaring that he intended to take no action against the Helmers. Torvald's whole attitude changed, and with a sigh of relief he boasted that he was saved. For the first time Nora saw her husband for what he was—a selfish, pretentious hypocrite with no regard for her position in the matter. She reminded him that no marriage could be built on inequality, and announced her intention of leaving his house forever. Torvald could not believe his ears and pleaded with her to remain. But she declared she was going to try to become a reasonable human being, to understand the world—in short, to become a woman, not a doll to flatter Torvald's selfish vanity. She went out and with irrevocable finality, slammed the door of her doll house behind her.

Further Critical Evaluation of the Work:

Although Henrik Ibsen was already a respected playwright in Scandinavia, it was *A Doll's House (Et Dukkehjem)* that catapulted him to international fame. This drama, the earliest of Ibsen's social-problem plays, must be read in its historical context in order to understand its impact not only on modern dramaturgy but also on society at large.

Most contemporary theater up to the time, including Ibsen's earlier work, fell into two general categories. One was the historical romance; the other was the so-called well-made (or "thesis") play, a contrived comedy of manners revolving around an intricate plot and subplots but ultimately suffocated by the trivia of its theme and dialogue as well as by its shallow characterization. An occasional poetic drama—such as Ibsen's own *Brand* and *Peer Gynt* —would also appear, but poetic form was often the only distinction between these plays and historical romances, since the content tended to be similar.

Into this dramaturgical milieu, *A Doll's House* injected natural dialogue and situations, abstinence from such artificial conventions as the soliloquy, the "aside," or observance of the "unities" of time and place, and insistence upon the strict logical necessity of the outcome without wrenching events into a happy ending. These theatrical innovations—now so familiar that twentieth century audiences hardly notice them—constitute Ibsen's fundamental contribution to the form of realistic drama.

Realism in the theater emphasizes believability; the guiding question is, "Could this event actually have happened in the lives of real people?" There is no attempt to achieve the comprehensiveness of, say, photographic reality; rather, realism is selective, striving for representative examples in recognizable human experience. And through selectivity, realism implicitly assumes a critical stance. Thus, the Helmers' domestic crisis had, and still has, a there-but-for-the-grace-of-God-go-I impact on theater audiences. Since *A Doll's House* was first produced, drama has not been the same. And it is for that reason that Ibsen is called the father of modern drama.

However, Ibsen's influence on modern drama was twofold, for he combined both technique and content in the realism of his *A Doll's House*. Specifically, Ibsen elevated playmaking to a level above mere entertainment by validating the respectability of plays about serious social issues. And one of the most volatile issues of his day was the position of women, for at that time women throughout virtually all of Western civilization were considered by law and by custom chattel of fathers and husbands. Women were denied participation in public life; their access to education was limited; their social lives were narrowly circumscribed; they could not legally transact business, own property, or inherit. In the mid-nineteenth century, chafing under such restrictions, women began to demand autonomy. They pushed for the right to vote and the opportunity for higher education and entry into the professions. By the last two decades of the nineteenth century, open defiance developed as women began engaging in such traditionally men's sports as bicycling, hunting, and golf. Their demands and their behavior predictably evoked cries of outrage from men.

Against this turbulent background, Ibsen presented *A Doll's House*. The response was electric. On the strength of the play, suffragists construed Ibsen as a partisan supporter, while their opposition accused the playwright of propagandizing and being an *agent provocateur*. Yet Ibsen was neither a feminist nor a social reformer in the more general sense. (Indeed, Ibsen personally deplored the kind of emancipation and self-development which brought women out of the domestic sphere into the larger world; he saw women's proper role as motherhood, and motherhood only.) His apparent feminist sympathies were but a facet of his realism. His own responsibility extended no further than describing the problems as he saw them; he did not attempt to solve them. Nevertheless, he had a sharp eye and many sharp words for injustice, and it was the injustice of Torvald's demeaning treatment of Nora— a deplorably common occurrence in real life, Ibsen conceded—that provided the impetus for the play.

In the raging debate over the morality of Nora's behavior, however, it is altogether too easy to neglect Torvald and his dramatic function in the play. For this smug lawyer-bank manager is meant to represent the social structure at large, the same social structure that decreed an inferior position for women. Torvald is, in effect, a symbol for society: male-dominated and authoritarian. Thus, he establishes "rules" for Nora—the petty prohibition against macaroons, for one; requires her to act like an imbecile; and insists upon the rightness, empirical as well as ethical, of his view in all matters. (In fact, Ibsen remarks in his "Notes" for the play that men make the laws and judge a woman's conduct from a man's point of view, "as though she were not a woman but a man.") His righteous refusal to borrow money is a particularly ironic example. And his contemptuous attitude toward Nora's intelligence and sense of responsibility—he calls her *his* "little lark," *his* "little squirrel," *his* "little feaherbrain," *his* "little spendthrift," and so on—-actually reflects the prevailing view of men toward women: that they are owned property, playthings, dolls to be housed in toy mansions and be indulged, but only sparingly.

In this Neanderthal context, it is difficult not to view Torvald as a thoroughgoing villain. But like society, Torvald is not completely devoid of redeeming grace—else why would Nora have married him to begin with; why would she commit forgery at great personal risk and use her utmost ingenuity to save his life and to protect him from shame; why would she continue to sacrifice for him, if he possessed not a shred of virtue to elicit from her a feeling of genuine love? For Nora is both sensible and sensitive, despite Torvald's disparaging insinuations, and her awareness of her own worth is gradually awakened as the play unfolds—and with it her sense of individual responsibility. When at last she insists on her right to individual self-development, the spoiled girl-doll becomes a full-fledged woman. She slams the door of the doll house in a gesture symbolic of a Biblical putting away of childish things and takes her rightful place in the adult world. Needless to say, that slam shook the very rafters of the social-domestic establishment, and the reverberations continue to the present time. So powerful an echo makes a powerful drama.

Joanne G. Kashdan

DOMBEY AND SON

Type of work: Novel
Author: Charles Dickens (1812-1870)
Type of plot: Sentimental romance
Time of plot: Early nineteenth century
Locale: England
First published: 1846-1848

Principal characters:
MR. DOMBEY, a rich London merchant
PAUL, his son
FLORENCE, his daughter
EDITH GRANGER, his second wife
MR. CARKER, his trusted agent
WALTER GAY, in love with Florence

Critique:

Dombey and Son, which appeared after Martin Chuzzlewit, was an effort by Dickens to regain popularity he had lost with the publication of his previous novel. Martin Chuzzlewit, which had heavily satirized America and Americans, had caused Dickens to lose a great deal of favor, a loss which greatly irritated Dickens, who was by that time in something of a competition for the public's attention with another great Victorian novelist, William Makepeace Thackeray. Dombey and Son is also a milestone in Dickens' work in that he placed the story at a higher social level that he had done in his previous novels. For the first time he indicated an interest and a sympathy in the upper middle classes and the aristocracy. The story is a very serious one, involving the downfall of a dignified and pompous merchant and his learning of the power of love as compared to the lesser power of money. In typical Dickensian style, however, there is a whole catalog of characters to provide a humorous background.

The Story:

Mr. Dombey was a stiff and dignified man who rarely showed emotion. But the birth of an infant son, who was named Paul, was cause for rejoicing, as Mr. Dombey had longed many years for a child who would fill the second part of the mercantile firm of Dombey and Son. Even the fact that Mrs. Dombey died shortly after the boy's birth did not particularly concern him; he was centered entirely on the little infant who he hoped would someday take over the business. Mr. Dombey also had a daughter, Florence, but she meant almost nothing to him, for she could not take a place in the firm.

Little Paul was first given over to a wet nurse, but the woman proved to be unreliable and was dismissed. After her dismissal little Paul was cared for by Mr. Dombey's sister and a friend of hers. Despite their vigilant care, however, little Paul's health was poor. He was listless and never cared to play. At last Mr. Dombey made arrangements to have him sent to a home, together with his sister, at Brighton, there to gain the benefits of the sea air.

Paul, in spite of his father's dislike for little Florence, loved his sister very much, and they were constant companions. Paul's love for Florence only made Mr. Dombey dislike the girl more, for the father felt that his daughter was coming between himself and his son.

One weekend, while Mr. Dombey was visiting at Brighton, Walter Gay, a young clerk in the firm, came to the inn where Mr. Dombey and his children were having dinner. Some time before the clerk had rescued Florence from an old female thief. Now his uncle was about to become a bankrupt, and Walter had come to ask for a loan to save his uncle's shop. Mr. Dombey let little Paul, who was then six years old, make the decision. Paul asked

1574

Florence what he should do; she told him to lend the money, and he did.

Shortly afterward, little Paul was placed in a private school at Brighton, where he was to be educated as quickly as possible. The pace of his studies proved too much for him, and before the year was out his health broke down. He never seemed to grow any better, even after his father took him home to London. Before many months had elapsed, little Paul died, mourned by his father and his sister, though for different reasons.

Mr. Dombey took his son's death as a personal blow of fate at his plans. His sister and her friend became so concerned about him that they planned to have him take a trip with Major Bagstock, a retired officer, to Leamington. While they were there, they met Edith Granger, a young widow whose mother the major had known. Mr. Dombey, seeing in Mrs. Granger a beautiful, well-bred young woman who would grace his household, immediately began to court her. Mrs. Granger, coaxed by an aged mother who was concerned for her daughter's welfare, finally accepted Mr. Dombey, although she was not in love with him.

Florence Dombey had seen young Walter Gay several times since their meeting at Brighton, and after her brother's death she came to look upon young Walter as a substitute brother, despite his lowly station. Then their friendship was broken temporarily when Mr. Dombey sent Walter on a mission to the West Indies. Weeks passed, but no word was heard of the ship on which he had sailed. Everyone believed that it had sunk and that Walter had been drowned.

After Mrs. Granger had accepted Mr. Dombey's suit, they began to make plans for the wedding and for reopening the Dombey house in London. It was at the house that Edith Granger first met Florence. The two immediately became fast friends, even though Mr. Dombey disliked his daughter and made it plain that he did not want his wife to become too fond of the girl.

Mr. Dombey's second marriage was unsuccessful from the start. Edith Granger was too proud to give in to Mr. Dombey's attempts to dictate to her and to his claim upon her as a piece of merchandise, and she resisted him in every way. Dombey, who was too dignified to argue with her, sent his business manager, Mr. Carker, to tell his wife that he was dissatisfied with her conduct. Carker warned Mrs. Dombey that, unless she obeyed Mr. Dombey, Florence would be the one to suffer. Edith Dombey then became outwardly cool to her stepdaughter, but still she resisted her husband. Mr. Carker was once more dispatched to tell her that Mr. Dombey meant to be obeyed in everything.

The wife then openly revolted. She felt that she could get complete revenge by running off with Carker, her husband's most trusted employee, who was also so far below Mr. Dombey socially that the blow would hurt even more. After she and the employee disappeared, Florence was only rebuffed in her attempts to comfort her father. When he struck her, she ran away from the house and went to the shop owned by Walter Gay's uncle, Sol Gills. There she found that Gills had disappeared and that an old ship's captain named Cuttle was in charge. Captain Cuttle recognized Florence and took her in.

Mr. Dombey at last learned the whereabouts of his wife and Carker from a young woman whom Carker had seduced and deserted. Mr. Dombey followed the pair to France but failed to locate them. Carker, meanwhile, returned to England. Mrs. Dombey had refused to have anything to do with him. She had her revenge, she said, in ruining him and her husband. Carker, trying to escape into the English countryside, met Mr. Dombey at a railway station. An accident occurred, and Carker was killed by a train.

Florence, staying with Captain Cuttle, hoped that Walter would return, even though everyone had given him up for dead. Her faith was at last rewarded. Walter had been picked up by a China-bound vessel and so had not had the opportunity to send back word of his safety. Shortly after his return he revealed to Florence that he no longer felt as a brother toward her, since she had become a woman during his absence. Realizing that she, too, had fallen in love with him, she accepted his proposal. Walter had found work as clerk on a ship, and after their marriage they sailed on a ship bound for the Orient.

The failure of his marriage had broken Mr. Dombey's spirit, and he took little interest in his firm from that time on. His lack of interest was unfortunate, for the firm had been placed in a difficult position by certain dealings of Carker's while he had been Dombey's trusted agent. As a result of Carker's mismanagement and Dombey's lack of interest, the firm went bankrupt. After the bankruptcy Mr. Dombey stayed alone in his house, saw no one, and gradually drifted into despair.

On the very day that Mr. Dombey had decided to commit suicide, Florence returned to London from the Orient with her year-old son, who was named Paul, after his dead uncle. Florence and the baby cheered up Mr. Dombey, and he began to take a new interest in life. Reconciled to his daughter, he realized that she had always loved him, even though he had been exceedingly cruel to her. Walter Gay succeeded in business, and all of them lived together happily, for his misfortunes had made a changed man of the almost indomitable Mr. Dombey.

Further Critical Evaluation of the Work:

In *Dombey and Son,* Dickens for the first time attempted to portray the full panorama of English society, from beggar to magnate, from baronet to housemaid. Although less successful than *Bleak House* in expressing the connection of each level of society to every other level, the novel is nonetheless prodigious in scope.

The theme of the work is the relationship between parents and children, chiefly Mr. Dombey's with Paul and Florence, and subordinately those of various parents and their offspring, ranging in social station from Mrs. Skewton and Edith down to Mrs. Brown and her Alice. Each family situation is thrown into relief by contrast with another, similar in social class yet utterly different in kind. Thus in opposition to Edith Granger, schooled almost from infancy to be "artful, designing, mercenary, laying snares for men," there is the son of Sir Barnet Skettles, whose parents willingly interrupt his studies at Dr. Blimber's academy in order to enjoy his company during their sojourn abroad. Mr. Dombey's crude attempt to mold his fragile son to a shape that does his father honor in the world's eyes contrasts with the honest and unpretentious course that Solomon Gills recommends to his nephew Walter: "Be diligent, try to like it, my dear boy, work for a steady independence, and be happy!" And the miserable devices of greed which Mrs. Brown urges on her daughter as the only recourse of the poor is given the lie by the love and warmth shown by Polly Toodle toward her erring son Rob.

The sad ends of Edith, little Paul, and Alice Marwood all result from two things, or perhaps two facets of one thing: the corruption of childhood by adult concerns, and that disregard of individuality in children which sees them as *things,* as counters in a game, or as a hedge against destitution or mortality. Mr. Dombey, for example, views Paul as an object, a little mirror of his own greatness. He expects his son to reflect himself, that is, to love him as he loves himself. When Paul in his stubborn individuality perceives the merit of Florence and turns to her, Mr. Dombey is amazed and outraged; because he sees Paul as an extension of himself, he cannot conceive of the little boy's having a private opinion. A mirror, after all, cannot have a point of view. Thus in Mr. Dombey's own mind, no blame accrues to himself; Florence, he decides, must be the cause of the "distortion" of Paul's feelings. In this way she too falls victim to her father's self-love, and becomes the object of his hatred, almost a scapegoat for his fiercely-repressed feelings of guilt about Paul's death; for in his view she had spoiled Paul as a tool for advancing his father's self-approbation, the function for which his elaborate education was to prepare him.

In the same way, Edith Granger was formed in her youth to fulfill her mother's nasty ambitions. And the shining ideal that both Mrs. Skewton and Mr. Dombey urge on their children is a glossy standing in the eyes of the world, a value which is essentially an adult concern. In contrast, Walter's mentor in his own invincible childishness (he rebukes himself for being "old-fashioned") guides his charge in the path of honesty, the natural behavior of childhood. Young Paul is the chief exemplar of this virtue in the novel, and his resistance to corruption is likewise referrable to that curious quality of being "old-fashioned." Paul was "born old"; he possesses that wisdom of extreme age which constitutes a return to the innocence of childhood. He is fey and resists classification. His obdurate honesty shows itself in his concern for first principles. For example, he inquires of his father what money can do, and when his father proudly replies that money can do anything, suggests two things that it cannot do: bring back his mother or give him health. Then he asks the question again, still more pointedly: "What's money, *afterall?*" as if to direct his father's attention to the extreme paltriness of those things which money *can do,* to that vain show which nurtures his father's pride. But his father takes no notice; it is not for him to be lessoned by a child. Florence, despised and neglected, not thought fit to prepare for any great purpose, has her brother's memory for a master, and educates herself to his truth rather than to her father's ambition.

Dombey and Son is unique among Dickens' novels in its profusion of strongly drawn female characters. Indeed, the author seems intent on ringing the changes on female nature from best to worst. For the most part these figures though vivid have but one dimension, but two evidence a greater depth of understanding than the author had heretofore achieved in his representation of women. One is the character of Florence, whose states of mind illustrate a classic psychological progression. Rejected by a loved parent, she reasons thus: "I am unloved, therefore unlovable." Her early conviction of unworthiness dictates not only her subsequent actions, but indeed shapes the main plot of the novel.

Dickens marks Florence with the token of ideal womanhood, a little display of housewifery in Solomon Gills's parlor; where she learned it though is a mystery. Still, she is truly good without being saccharine, a major advance in Dickens' treatment of women characters. Miss Tox is even more an unusual creation; for heretofore Dickens had not produced a female character at once such an object of satire and so generally sympathetic. She comes in for her share of ridicule for her delusions about Mr. Dombey's intentions and for her genteel pretentions in general, but the author allows her the virtue of her consistency: " . . . poor excommunicated Miss Tox, who, if she were a fawner and a toad-eater, was at least an honest and a constant one. . . ." She is as unlikely a vessel of kindness and simple wisdom as the dandy Toots, or Cousin Feenix the exhausted aristocrat; yet Dickens puts wisdom into their mouths, as if to show that though corruption might seem to reign supreme everywhere, truth remains, and though hidden, can flourish and even prevail.

Jan Kennedy Foster

DOMINIQUE

Type of work: Novel
Author: Eugène Fromentin (1820-1876)
Type of plot: Psychological romance
Time of plot: Nineteenth century
Locale: France
First published: 1862

Principal characters:
DOMINIQUE DE BRAY, a gentleman
MADELEINE DE NIÈVRES, his beloved
AUGUSTIN, his tutor
OLIVIER D'ORSEL, his friend

Critique:

Although Fromentin was primarily a painter, his writings quickly won the respect of the most distinguished of his contemporaries. In *Dominique* he drew from the experiences of his own youth; the powerful and permanent hold that the French countryside and the seacoast exerted upon his mind is evident throughout the book. The love theme is the old one of the moth being drawn to the flame, despite morality, orthodoxy, or common sense. The hero is also torn in a choice between the rigors of excellence and the pleasures of mediocrity. The psychology of personality is deftly explored in polished prose style.

The Story:

The narrator of the book first met Dominique de Bray at Villeneuve. Dominique lived at the large Château des Trembles with his wife and two children. The mayor of the commune, he was shy, unpretentious, and a friend to all in the community.

On St. Hubert's Day Dominique was visited by Olivier d'Orsel, a wealthy, solitary man with captivating manners and a passion for luxury, who had suddenly retired from social life. A few days after his visit Olivier tried to commit suicide. This event led Dominique to tell the narrator about himself.

Orphaned at an early age, Dominique grew up at Villeneuve. In his youth he became a lover of the outdoors. He was

cared for by Madame Ceyssac, his aunt, who provided him with a tutor named Augustin. The two differed greatly in temperament. Dominique was emotional and wild and loved nature; Augustin was well-read, exact, practical, and apparently oblivious to nature. When he was not tutoring Dominique, he would remain in his room, writing plays and letters. After four years the time came for Dominique to go away to school. Augustin went to Paris with high hopes of his own success.

Dominique went to live with Madame Ceyssac in her mansion at Ormesson. At school he befriended young Olivier d'Orsel, who also had an estate near Les Trembles. Dominique, who was a good student, helped Olivier with their schoolwork. Too shy to admit it, Dominique fell in love with Madeleine, Olivier's cousin. At night he would spend his time writing poetry. He also kept up a correspondence with Augustin, who warned him against confusing Olivier's love of pleasure with the true goals in life.

Dominique was surprised when Madeleine married M. de Nièvres, a well-established gentleman. After the ceremony Dominique was in despair because he realized that he loved a married woman.

After graduation, Dominique and Olivier went to Paris. There they saw Augustin, who grew to like Olivier but had no esteem for him. Olivier, in turn,

DOMINIQUE by Eugene Fromentin. Translated by Edward Marsh. By permission of the publishers, The Cresset Press. Copyright, 1948, by The Cresset Press.

esteemed Augustin without liking him.

Dominique, trying to forget his love for Madeleine, buried himself in his literary work. He went to libraries and lectures, and he read through the small hours of the night in the belief that the austere routine was good for him. After a few months, however, he burned his writings because he thought them stale and mediocre. Olivier, who saw what Dominique had done, told him to find other amusements and affections. Augustin, on the other hand, simply said that he would have to begin again. Augustin, who had experienced setbacks of his own, never complained. Having guessed Dominique's love problem, he told him to solve it by plunging into continuous work.

In spite of Augustin's advice and example, Dominique found it impossible to settle to his work. Through Olivier, he met a woman whom he saw steadily for two months. Then he learned that Nièvres and Madeleine were going to Ormesson, and he invited them to Les Trembles for the holidays. Although he never told Madeleine about his love for her, those were happy months for Dominique. That winter Nièvres and Madeleine decided to go to Paris.

Eventually Dominique wanted to make Madeleine admit that they loved each other, but the harder he tried to draw an admission from her the more she pretended to be quite unaware of his intention. One day, when he was determined to tell her of his love, he saw tears in her eyes; he understood then that there was nothing more to be said.

After that day their relationship became relaxed and natural, and Madeleine, wanting to encourage Dominique in his work, began to meet him at the risk of compromising her reputation. After a time Dominique realized that Madeleine was about to surrender herself to him. He then stopped seeing her, and she became gloomy and irritable. Her reactions made Dominique realize that he had deeply troubled her conscience.

Meanwhile, Augustin had married.

Visiting Augustin in his home, Dominique saw the near-poverty but great happiness in which his former tutor lived. At the same time Olivier, deeply involved with the women he had been seeing, began to hate the world and himself. It became evident that Julie, Madeleine's younger sister, loved Olivier. But Olivier, who claimed that happiness was a myth, refused to think of marrying her, and his attitude led to a loss of confidence between Dominique and Olivier.

One night, while Dominique and Madeleine were attending the opera, Dominique caught the glance of his former mistress. Madeleine saw the exchange and later told Dominique that he was torturing her and breaking her heart.

That night Dominique, determined to deal honestly with Madeleine, decided to claim her. For the next three weeks, however, she was not at home to him. Frustrated, Dominique moved to new quarters and, as a final effort, tried to escape the life of emotions and concentrate on the logical disciplines of the mind. He read much, saved his money, and published anonymously two volumes of his youthful poetry. He also wrote some political books which were immediately successful. When he evaluated his talents, however, he concluded that he was a distinguished mediocrity.

Several months later Olivier told Dominique that there was unhappiness at Nièvres, where Madeleine was staying. Julie was ill and Madeleine herself was not well. Dominique went to Nièvres at once and there found Julie recovering. No longer needed as her sister's nurse, Madeleine, with disregard for propriety, shared with Dominique three days of supreme happiness.

On impulse, after Madeleine had led him in a dangerous ride on horseback, Dominique decided to leave as he had come, without premeditation or calculation. When he was helping her to fold a large shawl that evening, Madeleine half-fainted into his arms, and they kissed. Dominique felt very sorry for her and let her go. After dinner Madeleine told him that, although she would always love him, she wanted him to go away, to get married, to take up a new life. That was the last Dominique saw of Madeleine. He returned to Les Trembles and settled down to quiet country life.

Dominique told the narrator that the years had brought forgiveness and understanding. Augustin, he said, had become a respected figure in Paris. Dominique himself had never repented his early retirement; he felt, in fact, that his life was merely beginning.

Further Critical Evaluation of the Work:

Dominique is part of the great romantic tradition of European literature that began with Rousseau and Goethe and swept into the nineteenth century with the fiction of George Sand. But the sentimental attitude of the Romantic school is almost overcome in this book by Fromentin's extraordinary sense of style and technical control. An evenness of tone and mood unusual for novels of the period is maintained throughout the book. An underlying realism gives the book a resonance that overcomes any excessiveness of sentimentality. The scene of the pressing of the grapes and the accompanying festivities near the beginning of the novel establish a tone of poetic realism which is carried through the work.

This novel explores the nature of friendship and the power of love. These themes, worked into an almost elegiac vision of time remembered, are treated in a surprisingly modern manner. The external plot is slight, and the incidents are used for the purpose of revelation of character; there is no melodrama in *Dominique* to attempt to maintain reader interest. Only four characters occupy the foreground of the novel: Dominique and Madeleine, the protagonists, with Olivier and the ill-fated Julie as foils. Their stories are bound up in a quest for happiness, and the reality that human beings must settle for, when the ultimate dream proves unattainable.

The unique vision of Fromentin lies in his approach to memory as the greatest reality. The significance of the present, in the novel, lies in the past. In *Dominique,* the beauty of the landscape is enhanced both by the experiences of childhood and the poignancy of the young love for which it was the background. The tranquil recollection of a life's joys and pains provides the subtle and fascinating center to this unusual novel. The prose is vivid and poetic, but restrained, and the descriptions of place are handled with the artistry and perceptive skill of a master painter. The framework of the narrator gradually discovering the truth about the past adds to the impression that the reader, during the course of the book, has had a glimpse into a bygone, pastoral age.

DON CARLOS

Type of work: Drama
Author: Johann Christoph Friedrich von Schiller (1759-1805)
Type of plot: Historical tragedy
Time of plot: Sixteenth century
Locale: Spain
First presented: 1787

> Principal characters:
> DON CARLOS, heir to the Spanish throne
> PHILIP II, King of Spain and Don Carlos' father
> ELIZABETH DE VALOIS, Queen of Spain, Don Carlos' stepmother
> MARQUIS DE POSA, Don Carlos' friend
> DOMINGO, confessor to the king
> DUKE OF ALVA, Philip II's trusted general and minister
> PRINCESS DE EBOLI, attendant to the queen

Critique:

This drama by Schiller was based chiefly on a historical novel of the same title published by the Abbe de Saint-Réal at Paris in 1672. The play, an exceedingly long one, was written in blank verse and represented a distinct advance over Schiller's earlier dramas, which had been written in prose. Within this play the reader finds Schiller's own ideas of humanity and liberty expressed in words spoken by Don Carlos and the Marquis de Posa. Although the title indicates that the hero was to be Don Carlos, heir to the Spanish throne, the marquis usurps the central position, as he did in Schiller's own mind while the play was being written. This was Schiller's last play before he turned to writing in the fields of aesthetics, ethics, and literary criticism.

The Story:

Philip II of Spain did not wish to trust his son, Don Carlos, with any of the crown's affairs, even though Don Carlos was twenty-three years old. Philip's ostensible reason was that Don Carlos was too hot-blooded. Probably the real reason was Philip's fear of his son, fear springing from the fact that Philip himself had forced his father, Charles V, from the throne. To aggravate the differences and the coldness between the king and his son, Philip was married to Elizabeth de Valois, with whom Don Carlos had been

in love. Indeed, both France and Spain had given permission for the courtship between the two, until Philip had decided to take Elizabeth for himself.

Don Carlos hid his love for his stepmother until the Marquis de Posa returned from Flanders, at which time Don Carlos revealed his secret to his friend. The marquis was horrified, but swore upon their boyhood friendship to help the prince, if the prince in turn would try to help the people of Flanders escape from the heavy and tyrannic policies forced upon them by Philip through his emissary, the Duke of Alva.

Stating that he could be more humane than the duke, Don Carlos went to his father and pleaded that he be made the king's agent in Flanders. Philip, refusing to listen, sent the duke over Don Carlos' protests. He did, however, ask the duke to be more friendly with the prince. When the duke went to speak to the prince, he found Don Carlos in the queen's antechamber. They had words and fought, until the queen intervened.

From one of the queen's pages Don Carlos received a mysterious note and a key to a room in the queen's apartments. Hoping against hope that the queen had sent it to him, he went to the room, an act for which his jealous father would have punished him severely. He found, instead of the queen, the Princess de Eboli. Having fallen in love with the prince, she had sent him the note. Loving Don Carlos, she asked his help in evading the importunities of the king, who sought her for his mistress. Don Carlos repelled the advances of the princess and thus incurred her anger. When he left, he took with him a letter which the king had sent to her. Hoping to use the letter as proof that the king was a tyrant and an evil man, he showed it to the Marquis de Posa. The marquis tore up the letter, saying that it was too dangerous a weapon and might hurt Don Carlos and the queen more than the king.

In the meantime the Princess de Eboli, infuriated at Don Carlos' refusal of her love, went to Domingo, the king's confessor and pander, and told him of her decision to become Philip's mistress. She also told about her meeting with the prince and his obvious hope that he was to meet the queen. That information pleased Domingo and the Duke of Alva, who wanted to rid the kingdom of both Don Carlos and the queen.

With the help of the princess, the duke and the confessor laid a trap for Don Carlos and the queen. Becoming suspicious of the conspirators' motives, Philip called in a man he thought would be completely honest in solving the problem. The man was, ironically, Don Carlos' friend, the Marquis de Posa. He quickly gained the king's confidence, even though some of his religious ideas were heretical, and he did his best to help Don Carlos. Having to work in secret, the marquis seemed to Don Carlos to be a traitor to his friend. Other courtiers reported to Don Carlos that a file of letters he had given to the marquis had been seen in the king's chamber. What Don Carlos heard was true, for the marquis had found it necessary to tell the truth about the letters to clear Don Carlos of the charge of illicit relations with the queen.

Don Carlos, not knowing the truth concerning the marquis' activities, went to the Princess de Eboli to seek her help. The Marquis de Posa, learning of Don Carlos' visit to the princess, entered immediately after the prince. Using the authority given him by the king to arrest Don Carlos, the marquis had him put incommunicado in prison, lest he talk to others who could do him harm. The easiest way to keep Don Carlos safe would have been to murder the Princess de Eboli, but the marquis did not have the heart to kill her, even when his dagger was at her breast.

Instead of assuming the guilt of murder, the marquis resolved to make himself the victim. The king had been convinced that Don Carlos and the queen had been involved in a treasonable plot against the crown in Flanders. To clear them, the marquis sent a letter he knew would be put into the king's hands. In it he stated that he, the marquis, was the real conspirator. Afterward the marquis had only enough time to go to the prison and reveal his true actions to Don Carlos. As he spoke, a shot was fired through the gratings by an assassin sent by Philip.

Popular wrath and the indignation of the grandees forced Philip to release his son, but Don Carlos refused to leave the prison until his father came in person to give him back his sword and his freedom. When Philip arrived, in the company of the grandees of the council, Don Carlos confronted him with the marquis' corpse and told him that he had caused the murder of an innocent man. Philip, seeing the truth of the accusation, and filled with remorse, became ill in the prison and was carried away by the grandees.

A friend reported to Don Carlos that the king and the Duke of Alva had been enraged by public reaction in favor of the imprisoned prince. Hoping to lift the yoke of tyranny his father and the Duke of Alva had placed upon that country and its people, Don Carlos decided to leave Spain immediately and go to Flanders. Before he left, he planned to see the queen once more and tell her of his plans. Donning a mask and the garb of a monk, he went through a secret passage to the wing of the castle in which the queen lived. There he went through open corridors to her rooms, able to do so because of a superstition that Charles V, garbed in like manner, haunted the castle. The superstitious soldiers let him pass.

The king, meanwhile, had sent for the Cardinal Inquisitor. Asked for his advice, the churchman rebuked Philip for his waywardness in letting the heretic marquis escape proper punishment for so long and then having him killed for political reasons. They discussed also the heresy of the young prince, and Philip resolved to turn his son over to the Inquisition for punishment. In person, Philip led the cardinal to the queen's apartments, for the king, having heard reports of the ghost, guessed who really was beneath the disguise. Don Carlos was found with the queen and handed over to the authorities of the Inquisition.

Further Critical Evaluation of the Work:

Don Carlos, though it was written over a period of only four years, shows strong signs of Schiller's change of conception. It was begun in prose and reworked in blank verse, printed first in individual installments through the third act, and then issued in a completed version of over six thousand lines, which was reduced later to about five thousand lines. During this process, Schiller's conception of the characters changed, as did the emphasis of the play, and most critics admit that the resultant complexities of motivation are sometimes baffling. Yet the play contains some of Schiller's greatest work, and many of its themes and speeches are among the classics of the German stage.

During the writing, Schiller's sympathy shifted from Carlos, the youthful, impetuous prince guided by pure emotion, to Posa, who himself begins as an idealist of noble sentiments, but who reveals the flaw in his nature by forgetting his love for individual men in his passion for humanity. In fact, the initially sentimental Carlos does gain in stature by his loyalty, even after the death of Posa. The truly tragic character of the drama is King Philip, initially conceived as a tyrant, the villain in the domestic tragedy of Carlos and Elizabeth. As the play progresses, Philip gains the sympathy of Schiller, and is revealed as a lonely man isolated by his kingship, unloved by his wife, hated by his son, needing a friend, and losing the hoped-for friendship of Posa. Ultimately, he is deprived even of the consolation of religion in the scene with the Grand Inquisitor, who represents the Church in a form that is authoritarian even above kings, and totally inhumane in its loyalty to a faith that has become an end in itself.

THE DON FLOWS HOME TO THE SEA

Type of work: Novel
Author: Mikhail Sholokhov (1905-   )
Type of plot: Historical chronicle
Time of plot: 1918-1920
Locale: Russia
First published: 1933, 1938

Principal characters:
GREGOR MELEKHOV, a soldier
PIOTRA, his brother
AKSINIA, his mistress
NATALIA, his wife
KOSHEVOI, a Communist

Critique:

The Don Flows Home to the Sea is a sequel to *And Quiet Flows the Don.* Here the fortunes of the Cossacks are lengthily and vividly portrayed after the peace with the Central Powers in 1917 up to the dominance of the Reds in 1920. Although *The Don Flows Home to the Sea,* published in two parts in 1933 and 1938, was written under the Soviet regime, the insurgent Cossacks are sympathetically portrayed. The beginnings of Soviet autocratic ruthlessness are seen as base and inhuman but probably inevitable. In scope the work is vast. It deserves to be ranked among the best Soviet productions.

The Story:

The Germans were still carrying off white flour, butter, and cattle. Every day their trucks rolled from the Don through the Ukraine. Various sections of Russia, however, were fighting each other. To the north of the Don Basin the White Army was driving back the Bolsheviks. Most of the Cossacks were in the White forces, although some were with the Reds.

Gregor and Piotra Melekhov were leaders in the White Army. Piotra, the elder brother, was decidedly anti-Red and waged battle viciously. Gregor was of two minds; perhaps the Reds would bring stable government. Gregor was opposed to pillaging civilians and killing prisoners. As best he could he kept his men in hand. When his father and his sister-in-law Daria visited him at the front, he was furious when they took home a wagon load of loot.

Back in Tatarsk the Whites were trying to win over the Cossacks to full support of the insurgent cause. In the spring of 1918 there had been a great defection of northern Cossacks to the Reds, and the southern Cossacks were only half-hearted in throwing back the Red tide. Koshevoi, a Red sympathizer, was caught when he returned to his home in Tatarsk. His companions were killed, but he was let off to join the drovers in the steppes.

Eugene Listnitsky, a rich Cossack from the district, spent a furlough with a brother officer. Eugene was attracted to Olga, the man's wife. After the officer was killed, Listnitsky married the widow. When he got home, invalided out with a missing arm, Aksinia, his former mistress, was still there, waiting for him. Eugene wanted nothing more to do with her after his marriage. He made love to her briefly under a currant bush and offered her money to go away. Aksinia was pained but stayed on in service. Her husband Stepan, miraculously alive after years in prison, tried in vain to get her to come home.

Gradually the Cossacks returned home; farmers, they had to till the land. The advancing Red Army passed through the village of Tatarsk. After them came the political men and the Red government

THE DON FLOWS HOME TO THE SEA by Mikhail Sholokhov. Translated by Stephen Garry. By permission of the publishers, Alfred A. Knopf, Inc. Copyright, 1940, by Alfred A. Knopf, Inc.

took charge. Gregor, glad to be home, had little longing now for Aksinia, who had been his mistress before she became Eugene's. After years of fighting Germans and Reds, he was content to be a little reconciled to Natalia, his wife.

Koshevoi was put in charge of the government of Tatarsk, and soon Stockman, a professional Red, came to help him. They began gradually, seizing a man here and there and spiriting him off to death or imprisonment. They wanted to arrest both Piotra and Gregor. A little afraid to take Piotra, who was friendly with Fomin, a Red commander, they did decide to take Gregor. Learning of their intentions in time, Gregor left Tatarsk and escaped.

As the political imprisonments and executions increased, the Cossacks revolted. Their wrongs were so great that in a comparatively short time the rebellion was succeeding. Piotra was made a commander immediately. He was a ferocious fighter and ruthless to the Reds. In a skirmish, however, he was captured by the enemy. Koshevoi, now a Communist, stepped out from a patrol and killed Piotra without compunction.

Gregor, after serving under Piotra, rose to command a division. He was cold with fury toward the Communists and had the reputation of never keeping live prisoners for long. Yet when the Cossacks began to imprison Red sympathizers from among the civilians, he dissented strongly. On one occasion he even forced open a prison and released old men and women who were suspected of helping the Reds.

Stockman and the others who had been the political rulers of Tatarsk were captured when a Red regiment deserted. Stockman was killed outright, and the others were returned to run a terrible gantlet at Tatarsk. Daria herself killed the man she thought responsible for the death of Piotra, her husband. Koshevoi was unsuspected at the time.

Daria recovered from Piotra's death rather speedily and soon was carrying on various affairs. When Gregor came home on furlough, she even made tentative love to him. But Gregor was tired from fighting and carousing, and he still had bitter memories of Aksinia. Natalia, who had heard of Gregor's conduct on his sprees, was cold to him. The day before he was to return to the army, Gregor met Aksinia at the Don. He thought of their former love and of her affair with Listnitsky. But the old love was not dead, and he took Aksinia again.

The Soviet government, realizing by May of 1919 that they had a formidable task on their hands, increased their forces and slowly pushed back the insurgent Cossacks. The rebels retreated toward the Don, taking with them crowds of refugees. At last the Cossacks crossed the river and held their positions.

The Reds came through Tatarsk as Natalia was recovering from typhus. Koshevoi was with them; he was indignant that Dunia, Gregor's young sister, was across the Don, for he had long been in love with her. Koshevoi's own family was missing and his father's house had been destroyed. He took pride in firing the houses of all the rich landowners in and near Tatarsk.

Gregor, busy as a division commander, took time to send for Aksinia and she came to live near him. Stepan returned, to her embarrassment, and although she did not take him back as her husband, they preserved appearances among the refugee families.

With the arrival of the White Army, the Reds were driven back. Now that the insurgents were incorporated into a regular army, Gregor was demoted to the rank of squadron commander, for he was an uneducated man. The Whites sent punitive patrols to punish those who had aided the Reds. To the horror of the Melekhovs, all of Koshevoi's relatives were executed. Daria caught syphilis and drowned herself. Natalia, learning of Gregor's return to Aksinia, refused to bear him another child. She had an unskillful abortion performed and bled to death.

With increasing Red pressure and desertion from the Cossack ranks, the White

Army was going down in defeat. Gregor and Aksinia fled south to try to board a ship. On the way Aksinia fell ill with typhus and had to be left behind. She later made her way back to Tatarsk. Gregor could not leave the country. With nothing better to do, he joined the Reds and fought valiantly against the Poles.

In spite of family protests Dunia married Koshevoi, now commissar of the village. When Gregor returned home, Koshevoi at once set in motion plans to arrest him. But Gregor again escaped, joining up with Fomin, a deserter from the Red Army. Fomin tried to rally the Cossacks to revolt against the Communists for levying heavy taxes and collecting grain. The revolt, however, was short-lived. The rebels were killed, and only Gregor came back to Tatarsk. This time, when Gregor fled, he took Aksinia with him, but she was killed by a pursuing Red patrol. Gregor threw his arms into the Don and came back to his house. Only his son was left to him now and he would fight no more.

Further Critical Evaluation of the Work:

Mikhail Sholokhov's work, *The Don Flows Home to the Sea,* is actually the last half of an immense historical work which follows a Don Cossack, Gregor Melekhov, from peacetime Czarist Russia through the German-Russian Civil War and Revolution. Although the focal point of the novel is war, the cultural life of Cossack Russia—its love for the land, and the roles of men and women in the agrarian family—is equally well portrayed. The length of the work enables a unique panorama of history to unfold.

Sholokhov intensely loves the Don, the steppe, and the cycles of the seasons and his poetic language beautifully captures the bond of the Cossacks with their land. Theirs is a peasant's life. They are in tune with the wind, the coming of rain, the swelling and cracking of the frozen Don. Numerous scenes begin with landscape paintings, subtle but insistent reminders that it is from the land that life comes. Death, undisguised, is omnipresent. Gory and detailed descriptions of the dying and of the dead become commonplace in the scourge of war, but the Don and the steppe survive all tragedies. Sholokhov evokes the sights, sounds, and smells of that earthy existence so vividly that the pain of Cossack uprootedness is totally convincing. Young soldiers who have fought valiantly near the Don are ineffectual, lifeless, on foreign soil; refugees wander meaninglessly when forced to flee their Don home.

The Melekhov family and the other townspeople of Tatarsk are typical of agrarian society and culture. Roles are assumed within family units unquestioningly, although not always obediently. The head of the Melekhov household, old Pantaleimon Prokoffivich, Gregor's father, is responsible for all who live under his roof: his wife, his sons and their wives and children, and his daughter until she marries. He is the patriarchal authority. Pantaleimon orders the marriage of Gregor and Natalia when he learns of Gregor's affair with Aksinia; Gregor complies. Old Pantaleimon becomes confused about his authority over his sons, however, when their military ranks surpass his.

Pantaleimon expects and demands to be served and respected by women who are his subordinates. In Cossack society, females are less valued than males and are treated as possessions by husbands. When Stepan Astakhov first learns of the affair between his wife, Aksinia, and Gregor, he returns home to beat, then stomp on Aksinia as if he were doing a Cossack dance. He is within his rights to thus punish her transgression.

The matriarch of the Melekhov family is Ilinichna, Pantaleimon's wife, who is not only the female head of the household (wife, mother, and grandmother), but also the mother to her sons' wives. The relationship between the mother-in-law and the daughters-in-law is an interesting one. Ilinichna gives orders to Daria, Pyotr's wife, and Natalia, as a mistress would to servants. The young married women have no rights except as granted by their husbands and mother-in-law.

Children are reared in an extended family and parental authority is often less than that of the grandparent. The middle generation—sons and daughters-in-law—are treated as overgrown children by the older generation. A major role for the young men (Cossacks) is to serve in the military. Service is seen as an honor, a duty that is fulfilled unquestioningly. The process of maturation for young men seems to occur in the military. When Gregor and his friends return home from war, the townspeople comment on how broad-shouldered they have become.

A strain of violence permeates Cossack life. Even during peacetime there is an air of exaggerated rivalry in which anger is expressed overtly. When old Pantaleimon proudly races through the village with his hero son, Gregor, he becomes infuriated with an old woman who scolds him for nearly running over her livestock. His anger could easily lead him to using his whip on her. Wartime violence is seen both on the battlefront and within the civilian population. There is an irony in the reverence a soldier holds for his own mother when he mistreats another's mother; an irony when he who has shared another soldier's wife returns home enraged to find that his wife has been similarly unfaithful.

The length of the novel gives the feeling of the flow of history, not in generalized sweeping trends or wartime strategies, but in a long series of specific circumstances that enables the reader to become involved with numerous major characters and to care about their lives and deaths as much as about the life of the one centralizing figure, Gregor Melekhov. A dead soldier by the side of the road becomes a vital loss, as the reader learns in retrospect from a small diary of the soldier's life and love. The relationship which grows between Podtielkov and Anna Pogodko is another mini-novel that is given life and death within the confines of Sholokhov's world. The deaths which affect Gregor most deeply are those of his and Aksinia's daughter, Piotra on the battlefield, Piotra's wife by suicide, Natalia by an unsuccessful abortion, Pantaleimon of typhus as a refugee, and, finally, Akinsia. The reader participates in Gregor's suffering because Sholokhov has fully developed all these characters.

This long-range focus on history through specific tragedies gives the indelible impression of the war-weariness, resignation, and readiness for death that Gregor feels when he finally returns home for the last time.

This work and the first part of the narrative, *And Quiet Flows the Don,* have been published together under the title of *The Silent Don.*

Mary Peace Finley

DON JUAN

Type of work: Poem
Author: George Gordon, Lord Byron (1788-1824)
Type of plot: Social satire
Time of plot: Late eighteenth century
Locale: Spain, Turkey, Russia, England
First published: By Cantos, 1819-1824

> *Principal characters:*
> DON JUAN, a young Spaniard
> DONNA INEZ, his mother
> DONNA JULIA, his first mistress
> HAIDÉE, his second love
> THE SULTANA, who coveted Juan
> CATHERINE, Empress of Russia
> LADY ADELINE AMUNDEVILLE, Juan's adviser
> DUCHESS OF FITZ-FULKE, who pursued Juan
> AURORA RABY, pursued by Juan

Critique:

Although Byron said that *Don Juan* was to be an epic, his story does not follow epic tradition but becomes a vehicle for digression on any and every subject and person that entered his mind as he wrote. The plot itself is almost a minor part of the poem, for much more interesting are Byron's bitter tirades on England, wealth, power, society, chastity, poets, and diplomats. For that reason, Juan's adventures being largely incidental, the poem holds a high place among literary satires, even though unfinished at Byron's death.

The Story:

When Don Juan was a small boy, his father died, leaving the boy in the care of his mother, Donna Inez. Donna Inez was a righteous woman who had made her husband's life miserable. She had her son tutored in the arts of fencing, riding, and shooting, and she herself attempted to rear him in a moral manner. But even though young Don Juan read widely in the sermons and lives of the saints, he did not seem to absorb from his studies the qualities his mother thought essential.

At sixteen, he was a handsome lad much admired by his mother's friends. Donna Julia, in particular, often looked pensively at the youth. Donna Julia was just twenty-three and married to a man of fifty. Although she loved her husband, or so she told herself, she thought often of young Don Juan. One day, finding herself alone with him, she gave herself to the young man.

The young lovers spent long hours together during the summer, and it was not until November that Don Alfonso, her husband, discovered their intrigue. When Don Alfonso found Don Juan in his wife's bedroom, he tried to throttle him. But Don Juan overcame Don Alfonso and fled, first to his mother's home for clothes and money. Then Donna Inez sent him to Cadiz, there to begin a tour of Europe. The good lady prayed that the trip would mend his morals.

Before his ship reached Leghorn a storm broke it apart. Don Juan spent many days in a lifeboat without food or water. At last the boat was washed ashore, and Don Juan fell exhausted on the beach and slept. When he awoke, he saw bending over him a beautiful girl who told him that she was called Haidée and that she was the daughter of the ruler of the island, one of the Cyclades. Her father, Lambro, was a pirate, dealing in jewels and slaves. Because she knew her father would sell Don Juan to the first trader who came by, Haidée hid Don Juan in a cave and sent her maids to wait on him.

When Lambro left on another expedition, Haidée took Don Juan from the cave and they roamed together over the island. Haidée heaped jewels and fine foods and wines on Don Juan, for he was the first man she had ever known except her father and her servants. Although Don Juan still tried to think of Donna Julia, he could not resist Haidée. A child of nature and passion, she gave herself to him with complete freedom. Again Don Juan lived an idyllic existence, until Haidée's father returned unexpectedly. Don Juan again fought gallantly, but at last he was overcome by the old man's servants and put aboard a slave ship bound for a distant market. He never saw Haidée again, and he never knew that she died giving birth to his child.

The slave ship took Don Juan to a Turkish market, where he and another prisoner were purchased by a Negro eunuch and taken to the palace of a sultan. There Don Juan was made to dress as a dancing maiden and present himself to the sultana, the fourth and favorite wife of the sultan. She had passed by the slave market and had seen Don Juan and wanted him for a lover. In order to conceal his sex from the sultan, she forced the disguise on Don Juan. But even at the threat of death, Don Juan would not become her lover, for he still yearned for Haidée. Perhaps his constancy might have wavered, if the sultana had not been an infidel, for she was young and beautiful.

Eventually Don Juan escaped from the palace and joined the army of Catherine of Russia. The Russians were at war with the sultan from whose palace Don Juan had fled. Don Juan was such a valiant soldier that he was sent to St. Petersburg, to carry the news of a Russian victory to Empress Catherine. Catherine also cast longing eyes on the handsome stranger, and her approval soon made Don Juan the toast of her capital.

In the midst of his luxury and good fortune, Don Juan grew ill. Hoping that a change of climate would help her favorite, Catherine resolved to send him on a mission to England. When he reached London he was well received, for he was a polished young man, well versed in fashionable etiquette. His mornings were spent in business, but his afternoons and evenings were devoted to lavish entertainment. He conducted himself with such decorum, however, that he was much sought after by proper young ladies and much advised by older ones. Lady Adeline Amundeville, made him her protégé, and advised him freely on affairs of the heart. Another, the Duchess of Fitz-Fulke, advised him too, but her suggestions were of a more personal nature and seemed to demand a secluded spot where there was no danger from intruders. Because of the Duchess of Fitz-Fulke's attentions to Don Juan, Lady Adeline began to talk to him about selecting a bride from the chaste and suitable young ladies attentive to him.

Don Juan thought of marriage, but his interest was stirred by a girl not on Lady Adeline's list. Aurora Raby was a plain young lady, prim, dull, and seemingly unaware of Don Juan's presence. Her lack of interest served to spur him on to greater efforts, but a smile was his only reward from the cold maiden.

His attention was diverted from Aurora Raby by the appearance of the ghost of the Black Friar, who had once lived in the house of Lady Adeline, where Don Juan was a guest. The ghost was a legendary figure reported to appear before births, deaths, or marriages. To Don Juan, the ghost was an evil omen, and he could not laugh off the tightness about his heart. Lady Adeline and her husband seemed to consider the ghost a great joke. Aurora Raby appeared to be a little sympathetic with Don Juan, but the Duchess of Fitz-Fulke merely laughed at his discomfiture.

The second time the ghost appeared, Don Juan followed it out of the house and into the garden. It seemed to float before him, always just out of his reach. Once he thought he had grasped it, but his fingers touched only a cold wall. Then he seized it firmly and found that the ghost had a sweet breath and full, red lips. When the monk's cowl fell back, the Duchess of Fitz-Fulke was revealed.

On the morning after, Don Juan appeared at breakfast, wan and tired.

Whether he had overcome more than the ghost, no one will ever know. The duchess, too, came down, seeming to have the air of one who had been rebuked. . . .

Further Critical Evaluation of the Work:

George Gordon Byron, who became the sixth Lord Byron by inheriting the title from his uncle, William, was born on January 22, 1788. Because his father, the notorious "Mad Jack" Byron, deserted the family, young Byron was brought up in his mother's native Scotland, where he was exposed to Presbyterian concepts of predestination which distorted his religious views throughout his life. In 1801 he entered Harrow, a public school near London; in 1808 he received the Master of Arts degree from Cambridge; in 1809 he took his seat in the House of Lords. From June 1809 to July 1811, Byron traveled in Europe in the company of his friend Hobhouse. In 1812 he met Lady Caroline Lamb, who later became his mistress; in 1813 he spent several months with his half-sister, Augusta Leigh, who later bore a daughter who may have been Byron's. Byron married Annabella Milbanke in 1815; she bore him a daughter, Ada, a year later and left him shortly thereafter. In 1816 Byron left England, never to return. That year found him in Switzerland with the Shelleys, where in 1817 Clare Clairmont bore his illegitimate daughter Allegra. After 1819 Countess Teresa Guicciola, who sacrificed her marriage and social position for Byron, became his lover and comforter. Byron died on April 19, 1824, in Missolonghi, where he had hoped to help Greece gain independence from Turkey. His most famous works are *Childe Harold's Pilgrimage, Manfred, Cain, The Vision of Judgment,* and *Don Juan,* his masterpiece.

Don Juan, an "epic" poem written in *ottava rima,* is permeated throughout with Byronic philosophy. Its episodic plot, narrated in first person by its author, tells the story of young Juan, who, victimized by a narrow-minded and hypocritical mother, an illogical educational system, and his own fallible humanity, loses his innocence and faith and becomes disillusioned with man and his institutions. The poem's rambling style allows for Byron's numerous digressions, in which he satirizes many aspects of English life: English government and its officials, religion and its confusions and hypocracies, society and its foibles, war and its irrationality, woman and her treachery, man and his inhumanity to his fellows. Even English poets feel the fire of Byron's wrath. Thus Byron has been accused of a completely negative view in *Don Juan*— anti-everything and pro-nothing. And though it is true that to Byron all is relative because there can be no absolutes in a world without reason, sanity, or justice and where the precepts of Christianity are so contradictory that they offer no panacea for life's problems, the philosophy of *Don Juan* is not wholly pessimistic. Admittedly, the undertone, especially in the digressions, is often sardonic; yet the overtone, created by a flippant refusal to take Juan's story (or life) too seriously and by extensive use of exaggerated feminine rhyme, such as "intellectual" and "hen-peck'd you all," is essentially comic. Thus the zest and the laughter in *Don Juan* belie the idea of total despair and lend an affirmation of life despite its ironies; the lapses into lyricism reveal a heart that sings despite the poet's attempt to stifle emotion with sophistication.

In *Don Juan,* Byron's philosophical confusion seems to be caused by his natural affinity for a Platonic, idealistic view, which has been crushed under the weight of a realism he is too honest and too perceptive to ignore. Though he denies that he discusses metaphysics, he comments that nothing is stable or permanent; all is mutable and subject to violent destruction. Yet Byron, in calling the world a "glorious blunder," is not totally blind to its temporary beauties. During the Juan-Haidée romance, the lovers live in an Edenic world of beautiful sunsets and warm, protective caves. Still, Juan's foreboding and Haidée's dream are reminders that nature's dangers always lurk behind its façade of beauty. And even Haidée, "Nature's bride," pursued pleasure and passion only to be reminded that "the wages of sin is death."

Byron's view of the nature of man is closely akin to his complex view of natural objects. Man has his moments of glory, integrity, and unselfishness. For example, Juan, the novice, does not flee from the horror of battle; he shuns cannibalism even though he is starving; he refuses to be forced to love the sultana; he risks his life to save young Leila. Often Byron emphasizes man's freedom of mind and spirit. Yet he believes that man's self-deceit is the chief factor in his decadence; his false ideas of glory lead to bloodshed. Ironically, Surrow lectures his soldiers on "the noble art of killing"; man kills because "it brings self-approbation." In fact, Byron suggests that man is more destructive than nature or God. Still, he does not condemn man; some taint at the heart of nature and of man turns "simple instinct and passion" to guilt; besides, society's corruption in turn corrupts man. Lord Henry as the elder sophisticate is perhaps the best example of man's inability to retain his innocence; caught in the trap of his own greed and hypocrisy and of society's political game, Lord Henry finds that he cannot turn back, even though "the fatigue was greater than the profit." Byron also strikes out against political corruption. He had strong hopes for England's budding liberalism: a "king in constitutional procession" had offered great promise in leading the world to political freedom and morality. Yet Byron boldly declares England's failure to fulfill this promise.

Byron does, however, offer positive values in *Don Juan*. He believes that momentary happiness and glory and love *are* worth living for. Although "A day of gold from out an age of iron/ Is all that life allows the luckiest sinner," it is better than nothing. Man must fight, though he knows that he can never redeem the world and that defeat and death are certain. Since hypocrisy is one of the worst sins, man should be sincere. To Byron, the creative act is especially important, for it is man's only chance to transcend his mortality.

Throughout *Don Juan,* then, one follows man through his hapless struggle with life. Born in a fallen state, educated to hypocrisy and impracticality, cast out into a world of false values and boredom, man follows the downward path to total disillusionment. He learns, however, to protect himself from pain by insulating himself with the charred shell of burned-out passion and crushed ideals. Blindly, he stumbles toward that unknown and unknowable end—death. Yet he goes not humbly but defiantly, not grimly but with gusto.

Therefore, Byron's philosophy, despite its harshness, is one which embraces life, seeking to intensify and electrify each fleeting, irrevocable moment. It is a philosophy of tangibles, though they are inadequate; of action, though it will not cure man's ills; of honesty, though it must recognize man in his fallen state. And, though death is inevitable and no afterlife is promised, Byron maintains his comic perspective: "Carpe diem, Juan, . . . play out the play."

Janet Wester

DON JUAN

Type of work: Drama
Author: Molière (Jean Baptiste Poquelin, 1622-1673)
Type of plot: Social satire
Time of plot: Seventeenth century
Locale: Sicily
First presented: 1665

Principal characters:
DON JUAN, a philanderer
SGANARELLE, his valet
ELVIRE, his betrayed wife
DON LOUIS, his father
DON CARLOS, and
DON ALONSE, Elvire's brothers
STATUE OF THE COMMANDER

Critique:

Don Juan is not really representative of Molière's work, but it holds lasting interest for the modern reader for two reasons. Written to fatten the lean exchequer of his company's theater because of the enforced closing of *Tartuffe,* as well as to please his fellow actors, it is an excellent example of the skill and speed with which Molière could turn out a play. It also departs from his usual technique in making use of the melodramatic and supernatural elements which characterized the original Spanish drama from which it was adapted. Here, as in his other dramas, Molière holds to his genius as a revealer of the hypocrisies and manners of his day, and the play brought down on itself the harsh criticism of those who had been shocked by the boldness of *Tartuffe.* By the spectacle-loving Parisians it was hailed with delight.

The Story:

Don Juan's philandering habits filled Sganarelle, his valet, with apprehension that such scandalous behavior could only bring on him the wrath of heaven and an evil end; but Don Juan blatantly affirmed that any love he had for one fair face could not withhold his heart from others, and as for heaven, he was not afraid of divine wrath. His valet knew him for the greatest scoundrel on earth, a man who was ready to woo a fine lady or country lass at any time but who tired of them in rapid succession. Through fear, however, he remained faithful to Don Juan and often applauded his master's acts, even though he really detested them.

In one of his many affairs Don Juan had killed a Commander. Though officially pardoned, he was believed not entirely free of guilt, and friends and relatives of the dead man sought revenge. They followed Don Juan on one of his philandering journeys to a town where he determined to separate a pair of lovers he had chanced upon and to gratify his passion for the lady. The happy pair had planned a sail on the sea, and he prepared to follow in another vessel manned by villains ready to do his bidding.

Meanwhile, Donna Elvire, whom Don Juan had seduced and carried off from a convent where her brothers, Don Carlos and Don Alonse, had placed her, had got wind of his escapade and followed him. She upbraided him for his desertion. Don Juan refused to admit that he was tired of her, but he wished her to believe that he repented his former madcap behavior in forcing her to marry him against her will. From this sin he would deliver her by allowing her to return to the convent and her former obligations. Elvire, seeing through this deception, threatened him with the anger of an injured woman and declared that heaven would punish him for the wrong he had done her.

Don Juan gave chase to the vessel which carried the object of his most recent infatuation. But his plans were upset when a sudden squall arose and both ships were wrecked. Don Juan was rescued by Pierrot, a country lad, and brought with his men to land. He made immediate love to Charlotte, Pierrot's sweetheart, and she, overwhelmed by his smooth talk and social bearing, promised to marry him. At that moment Mathurine, another country lass who had caught the philanderer's fancy, accosted Don Juan, but he cleverly led each girl to think she was his only love and the one he would marry.

When Don Juan heard that his pursuers were closing in on him, he changed clothes with his valet. Sganarelle devised a better disguise. Putting on the attire of a physician, he prescribed remedies at random for ailing country folk, not knowing whether his medicines would kill or cure.

In the wood through which they were traveling, Don Juan and Sganarelle sought to evade their pursuers. They discoursed on heaven, hell, the devil, and another life, Don Juan declaring himself a practical man who held no belief in such stupid and supernatural things. Deep in argument, they lost their way. Suddenly, through a clearing in the trees, they saw Don Carlos, Elvire's brother, being attacked by a band of robbers. Don Juan rushed to assist the stranger and succeeded in routing the attackers. Don Carlos, not knowing that his rescuer was his own sister's seducer, expressed his gratitude to Don Juan for saving his life. At this moment Alonse came upon them. Their friendly attitude horrified him, for he immediately recognized Don Juan and demanded of his brother that this betrayer of their sister be killed. Don Carlos pleaded for delay and won for Don Juan a day's respite, but he agreed that after this short delay justice would be done and vengeance satisfied.

As Don Juan and Sganarelle continued on their way, Don Juan gave voice again to the song that his heart belonged equally to all the fair sex and that his attraction to Elvire had entirely faded. Among the trees they came on a statue, part of the tomb which the Commander had been building when killed by Don Juan. On a sudden whim Don Juan insisted that the shocked Sganarelle approach the mausoleum and invite the Commander to dine with them. To their amazement the statue nodded its head in assent. Overwhelmed, they retreated hastily, although Don Juan boldly asserted that strong minds are not affected by a belief in anything supernatural.

Don Louis, father of Don Juan, threatened action to put an end to his son's irregularities, reproaching his son for his unworthy life and lack of virtue, from the consequences of which even a worthy name could not protect him. A tradesman and creditor, Monsieur Dimanche, also learned where Don Juan was hidden. Although he blandly acknowledged his indebtedness to the tradesman, Don Juan had no intention of meeting his obligations, and he put the honest man off with hypocritical words of solicitude and friendliness.

Elvire, veiled, let Don Juan know that her love for him was now wholly free from sensual attachment and that she would retire to the convent from which he had taken her. Fearing that he could not escape the wrath of heaven, she implored him to reform before he was utterly crushed.

Meanwhile, Sganarelle and Don Juan had forgotten their invitation asking the statue to dinner. When the meal was served, the statue knocked at the door and seated itself at their table. The statue challenged Don Juan to dine with it the next day.

These happenings led Don Juan to pretend conversion and penitence to his father, who was overjoyed. But his so-called reform was merely a sham to further another of his designs, for Don Juan still believed that hypocrisy was a fashionable and privileged vice. He would boldly don the clothes of hypocrisy, more relentlessly than ever continue to persecute his enemies, and, holding to a good opinion of himself alone, adapt himself to the vices of his age.

Don Carlos demanded that Don Juan recognize Elvire publicly as his wife, but Don Juan demurred, saying the matter was no longer in his hands as Elvire was resolved to go into retreat and he to reform. Sanctimoniously, he begged Don Carlos to leave everything to the will of heaven, but he also warned that if attacked he would fight.

Don Juan, in calling on heaven, had gone too far. A ghost in the form of a veiled woman warned him to repent of his sins immediately. Don Juan, thinking

he recognized the voice, challenged the figure and raised his sword to strike, but the shape changed to that of Time with a scythe before vanishing. Later the statue returned, adding its threat of a terrible death if Don Juan persisted in his wickedness. Scorched by an invisible flame, Don Juan cried out, but amid lightning flashes and thunderous sounds, the earth opened up and swallowed him. Thus he who neglected debts, seduced his victims, dishonored friends, and violated all laws finally offended heaven. The things which he held in scoffing disbelief brought about his doom.

Further Critical Evaluation of the Work:

Molière's *Don Juan* is one of the great examples of a work of literature or drama that was ahead of its time. The play scandalized and confused Molière's contemporaries, and only in modern times has it achieved a worthy appreciation. It was the complexity of Don Juan's behavior that made him a puzzle to the French and a fascinating figure to later audiences. The spectators of the classical age were bewildered by a play, really a tragi-comedy, in which the unities were neglected, and which contained magic, fantasy, and buffoonery. Yet today we are intrigued by the impossible task of analyzing the haughtiness and arrogance of Don Juan, of trying to understand the depths of his hypocrisy, villainy, and despair. Molière took the Spanish hero and made him not merely a heedless libertine and unbeliever, but, by strengthening the atheism suggested by his predecessors until it dominated the play, gave his hero the deep and bitter philosophy of the man who cannot help himself, who must deny even if it destroys him.

The play lays bare the hero's soul, yet the plot is surprisingly weak. It is structured in loose sequences of scenes, the main characters providing the only strong link; the great speeches, the rhetorical rhythm, are what carry the drama forward. Don Juan thought himself free from all obligations, believing neither in God nor hell nor doctors, nor in the sacredness of promises, yet as an aristocrat he assumed that others would keep their obligations to him. His servant, Sganarelle, was his opposite in every way, earthy where Don Juan was lofty, meek where the Don was scornful, superstitious where his master was skeptical. They were the perfect French counterpart to Don Quixote and Sancho.

Molière improved upon both the comic and retributive elements of the original story, and elected to make Don Juan's climactic act of self-damnation his decision to play the hypocrite, hypocrisy being the vice most loathesome to Molière. When Don Juan begins a speech by stating that he is entirely sincere, it is a sign to the audience that he is being quite the opposite. Don Juan combined in his personality the romantic qualities of the lover and the supreme egoism of the tragic hero. He gloried in his own exaggerated image of himself, even comparing himself to Alexander. Don Juan, like all tragic heroes, caused his own doom, by violating, through his hubris, the basic moral laws.

DON JUAN TENORIO

Type of work: Drama
Author: José Zorrilla y Moral (1817-1893)
Type of plot: Fantastic-religious comedy
Time of plot: c. 1545
Locale: Seville, Spain
First presented: 1844

Principal characters:
DON JUAN TENORIO, a nobleman of Seville
DON DIEGO TENORIO, his father
DON LUIS MEJIA, another Andalusian gentleman
DON GONZALO DE ULLOA, Comendador of Calatrava
INES DE ULLOA, his daughter
ANA DE PANTOJA, betrothed to Mejía
MARCOS CIUTTI, servant of Don Juan

Critique:

One of the best examples of Spain's romantic theater is this play in seven acts, four of which take place during a single night, the remaining three about five years later. The drama was written in twenty days for a theater owner threatened with bankruptcy. Though full of exaggeration and melodramatic improbabilities that even its author ridiculed, it has been popular in Spain since the time of its first presentation. Based on a well-loved Spanish legend, spiritedly written in excellent and varied poetry, traditionally it is produced all over the Spanish-speaking world for All Saint's Day, the first of November. Audiences see in it not only a play about a rollicking adventurer whom they would like to imitate, but also a story with a meaning deeper than that which appears on the surface. The implication of the drama seems to be that since God's love is infinite, a man can sin as much as he likes, provided at the end he wins the love of a pure woman. This combination of the romantic with the mystic has perennial appeal to the Latin temperament.

The Story:

It was the carnival season in Seville, and the Laurel Tavern was a strange place in which to find gallant young Don Juan Tenorio, when the streets outside were filled with masked merrymakers. But he was there with his servant, Marcos Ciutti, to keep a rendezvous with Don

Luis Mejía, another gallant. One year before each had wagered that he could do the most harm in the next twelve months. That night they were to decide the bet.

Don Gonzalo de Ulloa, father of the girl whom Don Juan hoped to marry, went masked to the inn, for he wanted to hear with his own ears an account of the wild and villainous deeds attributed to his prospective son-in-law. Don Diego, Juan's father, joined him, masked as well. Several officers, friends of Don Juan and Mejía, were also loitering in the tavern to learn the outcome of the wager, which had been talked about in the city for months. Mejía appeared promptly, just as the cathedral clock was striking eight.

With good-humored boasting the rivals compared lists of the men they had slain in duels and the women they had cruelly deceived during the year. Don Juan was easily the victor. Because his roster lacked only two types of women, a nun and the bride of a friend, he wagered that he could add both to his list within a week. Fearing that his rival had an eye on Ana de Pantoja, whom he was planning to marry, Mejía sent his servant to call the police. Angered by the evil deeds of which Don Juan had boasted, the comendador announced that he would never consent to the young scoundrel's marriage with his daughter Ines. Instead, the girl would be kept safe in a convent. Don Diego also disowned his son.

A patrol appeared to arrest Don Juan on Mejía's accusations. Other guards summoned by Ciutti took Mejía into custody at the same time.

Through the influence of powerful friends Mejía soon had himself freed. He hurried at once to the house of Ana de Pantoja, where he persuaded a servant to let him into the house at ten o'clock that night. His purpose was to keep Don Juan from attempting an entrance. When Ana appeared at the balcony, he told her his plan and got her acquiescence to it.

Don Juan, also released from custody, overheard their conversation, which gave him the idea of impersonating his rival in order to get into Ana's room. Ciutti had already bribed Ana's duenna to secure the key to the outer door. To make sure that Mejía was out of the way, Ciutti also hired several men to impersonate the police patrol. These bravos seized Mejía and bound him.

Don Juan next interviewed Brígida, the duenna of Ines, and bribed her to deliver a note to the girl in the convent. When the old woman reported that her charge was already in love with Don Juan, whom she had never seen, the gallant decided that he had time to go to the convent and abduct her before the hour for him to appear at Ana's house.

Meanwhile, at the convent, Ines listened abashed as the abbess praised the girl's godliness. Perhaps she had once been like that; now she no longer looked forward to taking holy orders. Half-frightened, half-eager, she kept thinking of Don Juan. The appearance of Brígida with the note upset her still more, so that when Don Juan himself appeared suddenly at the door of her cell she collapsed in a faint. In her unconscious state it was easy for him to carry her off. Don Gonzalo, worried by the young man's boasting and reports of conversations between him and Brígida, arrived at the convent too late to save his daughter.

Ines remained unconscious while Don Juan took her to his house beside the Guadalquiver River. When she came to, Brígida lied to her charge, saying that Don Juan had saved the girl's life when the convent caught on fire.

Later Don Juan returned, after he had successfully entered Ana's room. Mejía, seeking revenge, came in pursuit. Don Gonzalo, hoping to rescue his daughter, also appeared at the house. Enraged by their insults, Don Juan shot Don Gonzalo and stabbed Mejía. Then he jumped into the river to escape from police who were hammering at his front door. Abandoned by Don Juan, Ines returned to the convent and died of grief.

Five years later a sculptor was putting the finishing touches to the Tenorio pantheon. On Don Diego's orders the family mansion had been torn down and the grounds had been turned into a cemetery for his son's victims. Lifelike statues of the three chief ones, Mejía, Don Gonzalo, and Ines, gleamed in the moonlight. Patiently the sculptor explained his labors to a stranger who finally terrified the craftsman by revealing himself as Don Juan.

Repentant, Don Juan knelt before Ines' monument and begged her to intercede with God for mercy. When he looked up, her statue had disappeared from its pedestal and Ines herself stood beside him, sent reincarnate from Heaven either to bring him back with her to salvation or to be damned with him throughout eternity; he had until dawn to choose their fate. Don Juan, unable to believe that what was happening was real, thought it a trick of crafty priests.

When two officers who five years before had witnessed the outcome of his bet with Mejía came into the graveyard, he laughed at their fear of ghosts; fear had no entry to his heart. After inviting his old acquaintances to have supper with him and hear the story of his adventures, with rash bravado he also extended his invitation to the statue of Don Gonzalo. Only the comendador's presence at the table, Don Juan said, would convince him of a life beyond the grave. The statue kept its stony silence.

While the trio sat drinking at the table, they heard the sound of knocking, each time nearer, though all the doors were bolted. Then into the room stalked the statue of Don Gonzalo, to tell the skeptic about the life eternal that could be realized through God's mercy. The officers fainted, but Don Juan was so courteous a host that before the statue disappeared through the wall it invited him to a similar banquet in the cemetery.

Still unconvinced that one moment of repentance could wipe out thirty years of sin, Don Juan refused to be moved when Ines appeared to persuade him to make the right choice. Half believing that the whole affair was a joke concocted by the sleeping officers, he shook them back to consciousness and accused them of using him for their sport. They in turn charged him with drugging them. The argument ended in challenges to a duel.

In the half light of early morning the statues of Ines and Don Gonzalo were still missing from the pantheon of the Tenorio family when Don Juan, melancholy because he had killed his old friends in the duel, appeared to keep his appointment. His knock at the comendador's tomb transformed it into a banquet table that parodied his own bountiful spread of the night before. Snakes and ashes were the foods, illuminated by the purging fire of God, and ghostly guests crowded around the board. Although death was on his way, Don Juan still refused to repent as Don Gonzalo's statue once more told him about the redeeming power of Heaven.

As Don Juan's funeral procession approached, Don Gonzalo seized the sinner's arm and prepared to drag him off to Hell. At that moment Don Juan raised his free arm toward Heaven. Ines appeared and she and Don Juan, both saved, sank together into a bed of flowers scattered by angels. Flames, symbolizing their souls, mounted to Heaven.

Further Critical Evaluation of the Work:

José Zorilla fortunately missed the notorious years of repression under King Ferdinand VII that most Spanish Romanticists endured, but he was forced to flee his own authoritarian father and spend several years hiding in Bohemian poverty. One of Spain's few Romanticist poets destined to live a long life, Zorrilla was shy and evasive: his life resembled his escapist poetry, which shunned reality for the unreal. Zorrilla considered himself a troubadour. He loved to versify, and wrote poetry as easily as he conversed. At twenty, he became famous overnight by pushing forward suddenly at the funeral of the noted poet, José de Larra, and passionately reading poetry dedicated to the deceased.

Zorrilla is best remembered for *Don Juan Tenorio*, which became a Spanish national institution and still delights the average Spaniard today. Zorrilla scorned his own play and sold it for a trifling sum, since it was based on the original Don Juan created by Fray Tirso de Molina, a great Golden Century dramatist. Zorrilla's Don Juan is nevertheless a more human, flexible, and generous personality. He is also universal enough to belong to all cultures, not only displaying his romantic airs convincingly, but also using bewichment to attain his evil ends. The marrow of Don Juanism is the mysterious power of bewitchment through love; hence Zorrilla's Don Juan conquers through this element as well as through mere lying. Doña Ines dies of love for him, in a near-hypnotic state. Seduction is thus drawn by Zorrilla in its original sense of bewitchment, while Don Juan's dual hallucinatory-realism, along with his diabolic acumen, are exalted also. Don Juan was nonetheless perplexed before the hair-raising prospect of boiling in Hell's lake of fire, which floats in a fog before his rolling eyes. The play thus salutarily terrifies sinners, then soothes them with the theme of Don Juan's romantic redemption.

The First Act (*Libertinage and Scandal*) is almost architecturally exact. The stage represents a magnificent cemetery with Doña Ines' tomb in the foreground, while in the background are flowers and cypresses tapering upwards toward Heaven. Act IV (*The Devil at Heaven's Door*) is filled with love, vengeance, and the tension created by Don Juan's looming, last-minute intent of repentance. The latter element is the key to the action of *Don Juan Tenorio,* and helps compensate for its flaws and even the "improvising hastiness" with which Zorrilla claimed to have written it. Some critics see a superficial knowledge of theology in the work, but there is also an influence from Ferreira's Portuguese classic, *Inês de Castro,* which also has a theme of love beyond the grave. *Don Juan Tenorio* also has more original touches than even Zorrilla seems to have realized, along with vigor, freshness, color, and feeling that captivates audiences. Although several contemporaries of Zorrilla branded him as a hasty and wordy writer and a shallow thinker, Zorrilla was crowned poet laureate of Spain in his old age.

DON QUIXOTE DE LA MANCHA

Type of work: Novel
Author: Miguel de Cervantes Saavedra (1547-1616)
Type of plot: Picaresque romance
Time of plot: Late sixteenth century
Locale: Spain
First published: Part I, 1605; Part II, 1615

Principal characters:
DON QUIXOTE DE LA MANCHA, a knight-errant
SANCHO PANZA, his squire
DULCINEA DEL TOBOSO, a village wench
PEDRO PEREZ, a village curate
MASTER NICHOLAS, a barber
SAMSON CARRASCO, a young bachelor of arts

Critique:

Macauley said that *Don Quixote* is "the best novel in the world, beyond comparison." This belief was, is, and certainly will be shared by lovers of literary excellence everywhere. Cervantes' avowed purpose was to ridicule the books of chivalry which enjoyed popularity even in his day. But he soared beyond this satirical purpose in his wealth of fancy and in his irrepressible high spirit as he pokes fun at social and literary conventions of his day. The novel provides a cross-section of Spanish life, thought, and feeling at the end of the chivalric age.

The Story:

A retired and impoverished gentleman named Alonzo Quixano lived in the Spanish province of La Mancha. He had read so many romances of chivalry that his mind became stuffed with fantastic accounts of tournaments, knightly quests, damsels in distress, and strange enchantments, and he decided one day to imitate the heroes of the books he read and to revive the ancient custom of knight-errantry. Changing his name to Don Quixote de la Mancha, he had himself dubbed a knight by a rascally publican whose miserable inn he mistook for a turreted castle.

For armor he donned an old suit of mail which had belonged to his great-grandfather. Then upon a bony old nag he called Rosinante, he set out upon his first adventure. Not far from his village he fell into the company of some traveling merchants who thought the old man mad and beat him severely when he challenged them to a passage at arms.

Back home recovering from his cuts and bruises, he was closely watched by his good neighbor, Pedro Perez, the village priest, and Master Nicholas, the barber. Hoping to cure him of his fancies, the curate and the barber burned his library of chivalric romances. Don Quixote, however, believed that his books had been carried off by a wizard. Undaunted by his misfortunes, he determined to set out on the road again, with an uncouth rustic named Sancho Panza as his squire. As the mistress to whom he would dedicate his deeds of valor he chose a buxom peasant wench famous for her skill in salting pork. He called her Dulcinea del Toboso.

The knight and his squire had to sneak out of the village under cover of darkness, but in their own minds they presented a brave appearance: the lean old man on his bony horse and his squat, black-browed servant on a small ass, Dapple. The don carried his sword and lance, Sancho Panza a canvas wallet and a leather bottle. Sancho went with the don because in his shallow-brained way he hoped to become governor of an isle.

The don's first encounter was with a score of windmills on the plains of Montiel. Mistaking them for monstrous giants, he couched his lance, set spurs to Rosinante's thin flanks, and charged full tilt against them. One of the whirling vanes lifted him from his saddle and threw him into the air. When Sancho Panza ran to pick him up, he explained that sorcerers had changed the giants into windmills.

Shortly afterward he encountered two monks riding in company with a lady in a coach escorted by men on horseback Don Quixote imagined that the lady was a captive princess. Haughtily demanding her release, he unhorsed one of the friars in an attempted rescue. Sancho was beaten by the lady's lackeys. Don Quixote bested her Biscayan squire in a sword fight, sparing the man's life on condition that he go to Toboso and yield himself to the peerless Dulcinea. Sancho, having little taste for violence, wanted to get on to his isle as quickly as possible.

At an inn Quixote became involved in an assignation between a carrier and a servant girl. He was trounced by the carrier. The don, insulted by the innkeeper's demand for payment, rode away without paying. Sancho, to his terror, was tossed in a blanket as payment for his master's debt.

The pair came upon dust clouds stirred up by two large flocks of sheep. Don Quixote, sure that they were two medieval armies closing in combat, intervened, only to be pummeled with rocks by the indignant shepherds, whose sheep he had scattered.

At night the don thought a funeral procession was a parade of monsters. He attacked and routed the mourners and was called the Knight of the Sorry Aspect by Sancho. The two came upon a roaring noise in the night. Quixote, believing it to be made by giants, wanted to attack immediately, but Sancho judiciously hobbled Rosinante so he could not move. The next day they discovered the noise came from the pounding of a mill.

Quixote attacked an itinerant barber and seized the poor barber's bowl, which he declared to be the famous golden helmet of Mambrino, and his packsaddle, which he believed to be a richly-jeweled caparison.

Next, the pair came upon a chaingang being taken to the galleys. The don interviewed various prisoners and decided to succor the afflicted. He freed them, only to be insulted by their remarks concerning his lady, the fair Dulcinea. Sancho, afraid of what would ensue from their releasing of the galleyslaves, led Quixote into the mountains for safety. There they came upon a hermit, a nobleman, who told them a long story of unrequited love. Quixote and the hermit fought over the virtues of their inamoratas. Deciding to do penance and to fast for the love of Dulcinea, Quixote gave a letter to Sancho to deliver to the maiden. When Sancho returned to the village Don Quixote's friends learned from Sancho the old man's whereabouts. They returned with Sancho to the mountains, in hopes that they could trick Don Quixote into returning with them. The priest devised a scheme whereby a young peasant woman would pose as a distressed princess. Don Quixote, all but dead from hunger and exposure, was easily deceived, and the party started homeward.

They came to the inn where Sancho had been tossed in the blanket. The priest explained the don's vagaries to the alarmed innkeeper, who admitted that he, too, was addicted to the reading of romances of chivalry. At the inn Don Quixote fought in his sleep with ogres and ran his sword through two of the innkeeper's precious wine-skins. The itinerant barber stopped by and demanded the return of his basin and packsaddle. After the party had sport at the expense of the befuddled barber, restitution was made. An officer appeared with a warrant for the arrest of the don and Sancho for releasing the galleyslaves. The priest explained his friend's mental condition and the officer departed.

Seeing no other means of getting Don Quixote quietly home, his friends disguised themselves and placed the don in a cage mounted on an oxcart. He was later released under oath not to attempt to escape. A canon, joining the party, sought to bring Quixote to his senses by logical argument against books of knight-errantry. The don refuted the canon with a charming and brilliant argument and went on to narrate a typical romance of derring-do. Before the group reached home, they came upon a goatherd who told them a story and by whom Quixote was beaten through a misunderstanding.

Sometime later the priest and the barber visited the convalescing Don Quixote to give him news of Spain and of the world. When they told him there was danger of an attack on Spain by the Turks, the don suggested that the king assemble all of Spain's knights-errant to repulse the enemy. At this time, Sancho entered despite efforts to bar him. He brought word that a book telling of their adventures had appeared. The sight of Sancho inspired the don to sally forth again. His excuse was a great tournament to be held at Saragossa.

Failing to dissuade Don Quixote from going forth again, his friends were reassured when a village student promised he would waylay the flighty old gentleman.

Don Quixote's first destination was the home of Dulcinea in nearby El Toboso. While the don awaited in a forest, Sancho saw three peasant girls riding out of the village. He rode to his master and told him that Dulcinea with two handmaidens approached. Frightened by the don's fantastic speech, the girls fled. Don Quixote swore that Dulcinea had been enchanted.

Benighted in a forest, the knight and his squire were awakened by the arrival of another knight and squire. The other knight boasted that he had defeated in combat all Spanish knights. The don, believing the knight to be mistaken, challenged him. They fought by daylight and, miraculously, Don Quixote unhorsed the Knight of the Wood, who was Carrasco, the village student, in disguise. His squire was an old acquaintance of Sancho. The don declared the resemblances were the work of magicians and continued on his way. Upset by his failure, Carrasco swore vengeance on Don Quixote.

Sancho filled Quixote's helmet with curds which he procured from shepherds. When the don suddenly clapped on his helmet at the approach of another adventure, he thought his brains were melting. This new adventure took the form of a wagon bearing two caged lions. Quixote, ever intrepid, commanded the keeper to open one cage—he would engage a lion in combat. Unhappily, the keeper obeyed. Quixote stood ready, but the lion yawned and refused to come out.

The don and Sancho joined a wedding party and subsequently attended a wedding festival at which the rejected lover tricked the bride into marrying him instead of the rich man she had chosen.

Next, the pair were taken to the Caves of Montesinos, where Quixote was lowered underground. He was brought up an hour later asleep, and, upon awakening, he told a story of having spent three days in a land of palaces and magic forests where he had seen his enchanted Dulcinea.

At an inn Quixote met a puppeteer who had a divining ape. By trickery, the rascal identified the don and Sancho with the help of the ape. He presented a melodramatic puppet show which Don Quixote, carried away by the make-believe story, demolished with his sword. The don paid for the damage done and struck out for the nearby River Ebro. He and Sancho took a boat and were carried by the current toward some churning mill wheels, which the don thought were a beleaguered city awaiting deliverance. They were rescued by millers after the boat had been wrecked and the pair thoroughly soaked.

Later, in a forest, the pair met a huntress who claimed knowledge of the famous knight and his squire. They went with the lady to her castle and were welcomed by a duke and his duchess who had read of their previous adventures and who were ready to have great fun at the pair's expense. The hosts arranged an elaborate night ceremony to disenchant Dulcinea, who was represented by a disguised page. Sancho was told, to his great discomfort, that he would receive five hundred lashes as his part of the disenchantment. Part of the jest was a ride through space on a magic wooden horse. Blindfolded, the pair mounted their steed and servants blew air in their faces from bellows and thrust torches near their faces.

Sancho departed to govern his isle, a village in the domains of the duke and duchess, while the female part of the household turned to the project of compromising Quixote in his worship of Dulcinea. Sancho governed for a week. He made good laws and delivered wise judgments, but at the end of a week he yearned for the freedom of the road. Together he and his master proceeded toward Saragossa. Don Quixote changed their destination to Barcelona, however, when he heard that a citizen of that city had written a spurious account of his adventures.

In Barcelona they marveled at the city, the ships, and the sea. Don Quixote and Sancho were the guests of Moreno, who took them to inspect the royal galleys. The galley which they visited suddenly put out to sea in pursuit of pirates and a fight followed. Sancho was terrified.

There came to Barcelona a Knight of the White Moon, who challenged Don Quixote to combat. After the old man had been overcome, the strange knight, in reality the student Carrasco, sentenced him to return home. Don Quixote went back, determined next to follow a pastoral shepherd life. At home, the tired old man quickly declined. Before he died, he renounced as nonsense all to do with knight-errantry, not realizing that in his high-minded, noble-hearted nature he himself had been a great chivalrie gentleman.

Further Critical Evaluation of the Work:

"For my absolute faith in the details of their histories and my knowledge of their deeds and their characters enable me by sound philosophy to deduce their features, their complexions and their statures," says Don Quixote (II:i), declaring his expertise in knight errantry. This declaration affords a key to understanding Miguel de Cervantes' *Don Quixote de la Mancha,* for it demonstrates both the literal and the symbolic levels of the novel—and the distinction between those levels is crucial to grasping the full import of the story. The literal level, of course, is superficial; it reveals the obvious. The symbolic level, however, probes much deeper; it reveals the significance. In fact, the symbolic level deals, as all good literature must, with values. Thus Don Quixote's declaration must be considered on both levels, and when set in context, it will lend insight into the novel as a whole.

On the literal level, Don Quixote is eminently qualified by his extensive reading to assert familiarity with the history, the deeds, and the character of virtually every knight whose existence was recorded. Indeed, his penchant for reading books of chivalry is established on the first page of the first chapter of the book. Even his niece and his housekeeper refer frequently to his reading habits. Moreover, the inventory of the don's library, made just before the books were burned, reveals the extent of his collection, and earlier mention of his omnivorous reading leads to the assumption that he had read all of them. Further evidence of Don Quixote's erudition is his ready knowledge of the rules of knight errantry and his recalling the legend of Mambrino's helmet in connection with his oath of knighthood as well as elsewhere in the novel. Later, after an encounter with Yanguesan herdsmen, there is evidence, in a very lucid and pragmatic statement for a presumably insane old man, of Don Quixote's having read Machiavelli, followed by the don's citation of the misfortunes which befell his hero, Amadis of Gaul.

Other adventures provide internal evidence of Quixote's knowledge about the history of chivalry. A thrashing by muleteers jogs the don's memory to analogies between his plight and similar outrages visited upon the Marquis of Mantua, Baldwin, Abindarraez, and Don Roderigo de Narvaez. After his lance is broken by a windmill, Don Quixote remembers the makeshift tree-limb weapon used by Diego Perez de Vargas when the latter's weapon was broken in battle. At another time, he explains and defends the code of knight errantry to fellow travelers, citing Arthurian legend, the ever-present Amadis of Gaul, the stricter-than-monastic rules of knight errantry, and the noble families of Italy and Spain who contributed to the tradition. In fact, incredible as it may seem, just before the don attacks the herd of sheep, he attributes to each sheep a title and an estate culled from his reservoir of reading—or from his over-active imagination. In addition, to rationalize his own designation as the Knight of the Sorry Aspect, he recalls the sobriquets of other knights errant. In an attempt to inculcate Sancho Panza with the proper respect for his master, Don Quixote even relates biographical incidents from the lives of the squires of Amadis of Gaul and Sir Galaor. Significantly, almost craftily, he mentions that Gandalin, Amadis's squire, was also Count of the Firm Isle—a blatant inducement for Sancho to remain in the don's service. Yet, all in all, on the literal level, Don Quixote's mastery of chivalric lore seems to serve only as a rationalization for his ill luck.

On the symbolic level, more questions are raised than are answered. Quixote claims to have reached a "sound philosophy." But is reliance on reading alone—as he has done—a valid basis for "sound philosophy," or has the don become so absorbed in his books that he is unable to formulate or express the applicability of his reading? Can, for example, literature serve as a basis for understanding reality as Don Quixote avers? In lieu of a clear-cut answer, Cervantes offers a paradox. Early on, Don Quixote learns from Sancho that the Squire has never read any histories because he is illiterate; but later, trying to divert the don's attention with a story, Sancho, under questioning, admits that although he had not seen the person in question, ". . . the man who told me this story said it was so true and authentic . . . I could swear on my oath that I had seen it all" (I:xx). The issues of verisimilitude and credibility are not really resolved in this novel. Consequently, these issues generate further questions about distinctions between reality and fantasy. Sancho represents empirical, commonsensical reality; the don stands for whimsy and unfettered imagination. Whose view of the world is more accurate? Cervantes is ambiguous, at best, about the answer. However, the question persists, as Luigi Pirandello's *Henry IV* vividly testifies. We are thus left to ponder this paradox which Emily Dickinson has so succinctly described: "Much madness is divinest sense. . . ."

Another issue raised on the symbolic level involves the possible immorality of reading "too many" books. Books, in this sense, are a symbol of education, and this facet of *Don Quixote* may be a veiled protest against the *Index Librorum Prohibitorum*. The literal lesson emphasizes the corruptive power of books (and, therefore, education); however, the symbolic implication—given Cervantes' sympathetic treatment of Don Quixote—is that books and education are liberating influences on the human psyche. Thus the symbolic purport of *Don Quixote* may be a parody of the Church's monopoly of literacy in the Middle Ages, with the uninhibited don a counterfoil to the insensitive, book-burning priest.

To be sure, Don Quixote became a tragic figure toward the end of the novel, but not for failure of his philosophy; rather, it is society's failure to accommodate a deviation from the norm. And herein lies another symbolic level of the novel: society's intolerance of deviance. For Cervantes certainly did not make the don contemptible, nor did he treat him with contempt. Such treatment would have been repellent after the tender tolerance of the first part of the story. Despite the satirical thrust of the novel on the symbolic level, the don himself is a sympathetic character throughout he story. Although he strives to push time back, his efforts are depicted as noble, though nonetheless futile. The sympathy he evokes is that popular sympathy for the underdog who defies all odds and is broken in the attempt in contrast to the protagonist who has everything in his favor and succumbs to a surfeit of success.

Cervantes' novel is a complex web of tangled skeins, subject to many more interpretations than those suggested here. Suffice it to say that *Don Quixote* is unequivocally judged the finest Spanish novel ever written and one of the greatest works in world literature.

Joanne G. Kashdan

DON SEGUNDO SOMBRA

Type of work: Novel
Author: Ricardo Güiraldes (1882-1927)
Type of plot: Regional romance
Time of plot: Late nineteenth century
Locale: Argentina
First published: 1926

> *Principal characters:*
> DON SEGUNDO SOMBRA, a gaucho
> FABIO, a young waif
> DON LEANDRO GALVÁN, a rancher
> PEDRO BARRALES, a gaucho
> PAULA, a pretty young woman, loved by Fabio

Critique:

Don Segundo Sombra: Shadows on the Pampas has been called the South American counterpart of *Huckleberry Finn*. Like the hero of Mark Twain's novel, Fabio wanders on his own through youth in a new country, giving the author a chance not only to tell a story but also to present a vivid and varied documentation of details about the people, the customs, and the countryside. In Argentina itself, the book was immediately popular. It and the earlier gaucho epic, *Martín Fierro*, are the best narratives dealing with the gaucho, the South American cowboy. The hero of Güiraldes' novel was drawn from a real-life gaucho whom the author had known and loved in his own childhood on his father's ranch, La Portena, in the province of Buenos Aires. The novel reflects a pastoral form of life that has all but disappeared in Argentina, and the story will probably fascinate later generations much as Owen Wister's picturesque narrative of the North American cowboy, *The Virginian*, has caught the fancy of post-frontier readers.

The Story:

Fabio was a young lad who lived with his two maiden aunts in a small Argentine village. He disliked his aunts, who felt, in their turn, that he was simply a bother. He was not sure that the two women were truly his relatives, for they paid him little heed as long as he gave them no trouble. Don Fabio Cáceres, a rancher, occasionally came to see the boy and take him into the country for a day, but the man ceased coming about Fabio's eleventh year.

Fabio grew up to be a cheeky youngster who showed off for the worst element of the town. He knew all the gossip and spent most of his time hanging about the saloons; no one seemed to care that he never went to school. The village loafers hinted that he was an illegitimate, unwanted child. At best, he seemed destined to be a ne'er-do-well who carried a chip on his shoulder in defiance of the rest of the world.

One night a gaucho rode into the town as Fabio was going homeward from fishing. The man impressed the boy at sight, and a little later Fabio earned the gaucho's interest by warning him of an ambush laid by a knife-wielding bully. The kind words spoken by the gaucho, Don Segundo, went to the boy's heart, and Fabio immediately decided to follow the man when he left town. Gathering together his meager possessions, which fortunately included a saddle and two ponies, Fabio went quietly away without telling anyone where he was going, in order to escape his hated aunts. He rode to the ranch belonging to Don Leandro Galván, where he knew Don Segundo was going to spend a few days

DON SEGUNDO SOMBRA by Ricardo Guiraldes. Translated by Harriet de Onis. By permission of the publishers, Rinehart & Co., Inc. Copyright, 1935, by Farrar & Rinehart, Inc.

breaking wild horses for riding.

When he arrived, the boy applied for work and was accepted. By the time Don Segundo was ready to leave the ranch on a cattle drive Fabio had convinced Don Leandro and Don Segundo that he was a willing worker, and they let Fabio go with the other gauchos on half pay. At the end of the drive Fabio was well along in his apprenticeship as a gaucho.

For five years Fabio continued under the tutelage of Don Segundo. Traveling from ranch to ranch, they worked for a number of landowners. From the older man Fabio learned to care for himself and his horses, to work cattle under various conditions, to live courageously, to get along with all kinds of people, and to have a good time singing songs, dancing, and telling stories. It was more than a way of making a living that the man passed on to the boy; it was an entier culture, a culture as old as the cattle industry and in some respects even older, going back as it did to the culture of Spain.

There were many incidents in their wanderings, including the time that Fabio won a large number of pesos by picking the winning bird in a cockfight when everyone else bet against the bird. That happened in the town of Navarro, a town which remained a lucky place in young Fabio's mind. He remembered also a long drive with cattle to a ranch on the seashore. There Fabio found a country he detested and a young woman he loved, as well as a great store of bad luck. He had picked up quite a respectable string of horses, the tools of the gaucho's trade, and he was very proud of them. But in working the cattle at the seashore ranch two of the horses were injured, much to the young gaucho's disgust. One of them was badly gored by a bull, and when Fabio came across the bull one evening while exploring with another young man he vowed to break its neck. He lassoed the beast and broke its neck with the shock, but in doing so he injured himself severely, breaking several bones.

While Fabio remained at the ranch convalescing from his injuries he fell in love, he thought, with Paula, a pretty young girl who lived on the place. Unfortunately, she led him on and also the rather stupid son of the rancher. The other lad took advantage of Fabio's crippled arm and attacked him with a knife. Fabio, not wanting to injure the owner's son, to fight over a woman, or to violate the father's hospitality, avoided the other fellow's thrusts until they became deadly. Then with a quick thrust Fabio slashed the boy's forehead slightly, taking the will to fight out of him very quickly. Paula, over whom the fight began, rebuked the crippled Fabio. Disgusted at her and at himself, Fabio, crippled as he was, mounted his horse and rode away to rejoin Don Segundo, who was working at a nearby ranch until Fabio could be ready to travel.

Don Segundo and Fabio happened into a small village on a day when people had gathered from miles around to race horses. Fabio bet and lost a hundred pesos, then another hundred, and finally the third and last hundred he possessed. Still not satisfied that he was a hopeless loser, he gambled five of his horses and lost them as well. He came out of the afternoon's activity a sad young man.

He and Don Segundo were hired to trail a herd of cattle from a ranch near the village to the city to be butchered. It was a long, hard drive, even for experienced gauchos. It was made even more difficult for Fabio by the fact that he had only three horses, for the animals soon became fatigued from the work of carrying him and working the cattle on the road. When the herd stopped to rest one afternoon, Fabio decided to see if he could somehow get another horse or two.

While looking about he found Pedro Barrales, a gaucho who had traveled with him and Don Segundo several times before. Pedro Barrales had a letter addressed to Señor Fabio Cáceres, a letter which he gave to Fabio. The lad looked blankly at the letter, not believing it was addressed to him, for he thought he had no surname. Don Segundo opened the letter to find that the maiden aunts had been truly Fabio's relatives and that Don Fabio Cáceres who had visited him at his aunts' home was really his father, from whom he had inherited a fortune and a large, well-stocked ranch. The news saddened Fabio because he saw that it would take him away from the life he loved. He was angered, too, because he had been left so long under the impression that his parentage was one to be ashamed of.

Acting upon the good advice of Don Segundo, Fabio returned to his native town, however, and from there to the ranch where he had begun work under Don Leandro Galván, who had now become his guardian. When Don Segundo agreed to remain with him for three years on his own ranch, Fabio was willing to settle down. But the three years passed all too swiftly, and at the end of that time Fabio was exceedingly sad when Don Segundo, answering the gaucho's call to wander, rode away.

Further Critical Evaluation of the Work:

This novel is considered the classic novel of the gaucho. It has the clean lines of Hemingway's "The Old Man and the Sea," for Don Segundo Sombra, the patriarchal old gaucho, and Fabio, the boy, are thrown into relief as they ride across the billowing pampa. Don Segundo is introduced into the novel dramatically for, when first seen by the boy, he looms enormously, a giant and almost overwhelming horseman. And when Don Segundo rides off at the novel's end, we see only him, the pampa, and the sky as he disappears, shadow-like, into the distance.

A touch of the American movie "Shane" is present, in the friendship between the boy and the mature man, and the hero worship of the former for the latter. It is almost a fantastic example of youth forming an image of the ideal that it wishes to reach, and at the same time finding an example of this ideal upon which it can concentrate its attention and imitation.

Another theme is the passing of a breed, as represented by Don Segundo himself, the last of the true gauchos. Freedom is still another theme—the wild wandering of the duo across the pampa; the freedom, now disappearing, once enjoyed by the dying gaucho; the gradual smothering of such freedom by civilization. *Don Segundo Sombra* is simultaneously set late in the day of the gaucho's traditional frontier enemy, the wild Indian tribes, who have already been pushed up against the setting sun, into the Andean foothills. Thus, while entertaining, the novel has various social and historical messages.

Güiraldes made unusual use of water imagery. The pampa itself is almost presented as an ocean of land, the reflecting sky overhead being an overhead ocean. Ponds and streams add other touches of water imagery, while Don Segundo and Fabio even reach the Atlantic Ocean itself once and stare raptly at it. Life itself is symbolized by water, for life flows like water, as does the novel's action.

Adventure and travel give another element, in this case Quixotesque. The two riders wander at will, like Don Quixote and Sancho Panza, satiating the human yen to travel and see what lies over the horizon. The appeal to wander-lust is so intense that it has a strong mystic touch. The novel is realistic and true to life, but it can almost be classified as a romance of chivalry since it exalts the virtues of Don Segundo and his adventures with Fabio in the field of struggle of a gaucho's daily labor, and in battle against the inclemencies of weather and nature.

The vocabulary has many Argentinisms, some of colonial vintage brought down centuries before from Jesuit mission lands in Paraguay, but is never difficult. The plot develops serenely to a logical climax; the novel's style is good but not distinctive; the few characters are well done, or deliberately shaded out so as not to distract from the protagonist, Don Segundo, and his young companion, Fabio. The reader thus identifies easily with both.

Güilraldes' use of nature is not equal in some respects to that of, say, Louis L'Amour, but is blended so well into the narration that one can almost hear the rustle of leaves in the trees, the murmuring of the streams, and even the sound of the wind. There is some use of colors and tints—the green ombú trees, the colors of the steers and horses, while gaucho lore is presented extensively and authentically without any touch of "drug-store gauchoism." In general, relatively little of the milk of human kindness or warmth is presented, for Fabio is very much alone in a cold world until he meets Don Segundo.

As genres, the gaucho novel and poetry are extensive. They are important not only because of their intrinsic worth as genuine, regional products of the American hemisphere, but also because they have tinged other aspects of Argentine literature, even the theater and essay. This is true in Argentina it-self—where the core, pampa heartland insinuates itself into other geo-graphical regions of the country—and in "The Purple Land" of Uruguay and the undulating pampa of Southern Brazil. In the latter area an additional, entire gaucho literature exists in Portuguese, forming a natural component to the unique gaucho genre, produced in the River Plate world and its col-lateral systems, such as the Uruguay, Paraná, and Paraguay. To this day one even finds a certain impregnation of gaucho culture in southernmost Para-guay, a little-known and historically isolated area that for long was almost a semi-tropical Tibet.

Although moving even further from the classic gaucho age in time, and despite paved roads and mechanization, Argentina, Uruguay, Southern Brazil, and Paraguay's southernmost tip still have gaucho flavor in dress and speech. In Brazil, for example, as one travels southwards in a bus from gigantic, modernistic São Paulo the first individuals of gaucho dress may board the bus in the mountains of the Brazilian-Germanic state of Santa Catarina. Novels in the tradition of *Don Segundo Sombra* are still being published from Santa Catarina southward, while a faint gaucho tinge has even spread northward into

Brazil's immense "wild west" of Minas Gerais, Goiás, and Mato Grosso. Gaucho novels are still a favorite of the urban Argentine reader in such centers of the true gaucho core-land as Buenos Aires, Rosario, and Bahia Blanca, or in Montevideo, Porto Alegra, Córdoba, and Santa Fe.

The modern gaucho uses barbed wire and rides a jeep, but the average *estancia* still has gauchos in whose hearts beat the spirit of Don Segundo and Martin Fíerro.

William Freitas

DOÑA BÁRBARA

Type of work: Novel
Author: Rómulo Gallegos (1884-1969)
Type of plot: Regional romance
Time of plot: Early twentieth century
Locale: The Arauca Valley of Venezuela
First published: 1929

> *Principal characters:*
> Doña Bárbara, a beautiful, unscrupulous mestiza
> Santos Luzardo, owner of the Altamira ranch
> Marisela, illegitimate daughter of Doña Bárbara and Lorenzo Barquero
> Antonio, a cowboy at the Altamira ranch
> The Wizard, a rascally henchman of Doña Bárbara
> Señor Danger, an American squatter on the Altamira ranch
> Don Balbino, treacherous overseer at the Altamira ranch

Critique:

Seldom is the literary man a political leader, but Rómulo Gallegos is an exception to that rule. He was one of the founders of the Democratic Action Party in Venezuela in 1941 and was nominated by that party for the Venezuelan presidency in 1947. He was elected by the people to office and served until overthrown by a military dictatorship. Gallegos and his party stood for a liberal, social-minded government which would improve living conditions for the masses of Venezuela. Gallegos' national pride in his country and his people is reflected in his fiction. Although his fiction, like most of the books written in Latin America, is little known in the United States, it has a high reputation with readers who have come to know it either in Spanish or in translation.

The Story:

The Altamira ranch was a vast estate in the wildest section of the Arauca River basin of Venezuela, a ranch that had been established early in the history of the cattle business of that South American country. Late in the nineteenth century, however, it had been divided into two parts by the joint heirs of one of the owners. One part retained the old name and went to the male heir of the Luzardo family. The other part, going to a daugh-

ter who had married a Barquero, took its name from the new owner. As the years went by the two families carried on a feud which killed most of the men on both sides. In the years of the Spanish-American War, the owner of Altamira and his elder son quarreled; the father killed the son and then starved himself to death. Doña Luzardo took her only remaining son and went to Caracas, there to rear him in a more civilized atmosphere.

Years went by, and finally the son, Santos Luzardo decided to sell the ranch, which had been allowed to deteriorate to almost nothing under irresponsible overseers. In order to set a price upon his property he went into the back country to see it for himself. On his arrival he found that the neighboring ranch of the Barqueros had fallen into the hands of Doña Bárbara, a mestiza who had been the mistress of the real owner before she ran him off his own property. Doña Bárbara was in the process of taking over Altamira ranch with the help of several henchmen, including Don Balbino, the overseer of Altamira ranch. Santos decided to keep the ranch and try to make it a prosperous business, if he could only keep it out of Doña Bárbara's hands.

To help him, Santos had a handful of loyal cowboys who had known him as a child, including Antonio, a cowboy who had been his playmate years before. Santos Luzardo's first move was to end the feud between himself and the Barqueros. He found Lorenzo Barquero living in a cabin in a swamp, the only land his mistress had not taken from him. After making his peace with Lorenzo and with his illegitimate daughter Marisela, Santos took her to live at Altamira ranch. Marisela was as beautiful as her mother, Doña Bárbara, and Santos wished to retrieve her from barbarity.

Most of the cattle had been stolen from Altamira ranch, until only about a hundred head were left. But Antonio, the loyal cowboy, had seen to it that many hundreds more had been allowed to stray into wild country in order to save them from the depredations of Doña Bárbara and Señor Danger, an American who had begun as a squatter and who was carving his own ranch out of Altamira land. Don Balbino, the treacherous overseer, was immediately discharged. Since he had been working for Doña Bárbara and was her lover, he sought the mestiza's protection.

Santos, who had been trained as a lawyer, decided first to try legal means in order to repossess part of his ranch. He went to the local magistrate and through his knowledge of the law forced that official to call in Doña Bárbara and Señor Danger. They were told to permit a roundup of his cattle and to help him, since their herds were intermingled with those from Altamira. They were also told to take action with respect to fences. Danger had to build fences, for according to the law he had too few cattle to let them run wild. Doña Bárbara was to help build a boundary fence between her ranch and Altamira. Surprisingly, she took the decisions with good grace. Her henchmen were completely surprised, for previously she had ridden roughshod over all opposition. The answer lay in the fact that she was secretly in love with Santos Luzardo, and she thought she could command his love and his property by her beauty.

As weeks of deadening ranch routine passed, Santos was glad that he had brought Marisela to his house, for his efforts to teach her culture kept him from losing touch with civilization. Although his interest in her was only that of a friend and tutor, Marisela had fallen in love with the rancher.

Along the Arauca River there were thousands of herons. When the birds were moulting, the people of Altamira went out to collect the plumes and gathered fifty pounds of the valuable feathers, which were sent with two of the cowboys to market. Santos intended to use the money from the sale to fence his boundaries. On their way to market the cowboys were murdered and the feathers stolen. Their loss and the failure of the authorities to track down the culprit caused a great change in Santos. He determined to take the law into his own hands and to match violence with violence when he found it necessary.

His first act was to have three of Doña Bárbara's henchmen captured and sent off to prison, for they had been long wanted for a number of crimes. A short time later he received word from Doña Bárbara, who was pulled in two ways by her love for him and by her wish for power, that he would find in a certain canyon the thief who had taken the feathers. Santos went in the night and killed the Wizard, Doña Bárbara's most trusted and bloodthirsty henchman. Meanwhile Don Balbino, the treacherous overseen who had been in charge of Altamira and who had been Doña Bárbara's lover, became distasteful to her. She had him killed after discovering that it was he who had stolen the feathers. To aid Santos, she threw on Don Balbino the blame for killing the Wizard.

Recovering the feathers, Doña Bárbara went to town to sell them for Santos. At the same time she had documents made out to transfer the disputed lands to their rightful owner. When she returned to her ranch she found that her people had deserted her; they could not understand why she had turned on her trusted killers. Doña Bárbara rode immediately to Altamira, where she found Santos talking to Marisela, whose father had recently died. Because the girl's love for Santos showed plainly on her face, Doña Bárbara, unseen, drew her revolver to kill her daughter. Her own love for Santos prevented the deed, however, and she rode away without revealing her presence.

Doña Bárbara was not heard from again. The next day a large envelope was delivered to Santos. In it he found a sheaf of documents giving back the property that had been stolen from him, and others transferring the Barquero ranch to Doña Bárbara's daughter Marisela. Shortly afterward Santos and Marisela were married, and thus the two ranches which had been separated for many years were once again joined under one owner.

Further Critical Evaluation of the Work:

Doña Bárbara is *the* novel of the *llanos*. In it is painted the llanos, or tropical grassland bordering the Orinoco River, in the center of Venezuela, a republic almost as large as America's Southwest. Next to the llanos itself, the ranch-woman Doña Bárbara is the most clearly-etched character, symbolizing barbarism, for she is a wild, dreadful, beautiful half-breed from beyond the remotest tributaries of the Orinoco. Her very name reeks of barbarism. Opposed to her is Santos Luzardo, who symbolizes the civilizing energy that is trying to penetrate the llanos' savagery and tame it.

Gallegos uses symbols for barbarism, such as the great *tolvaneras,* or whirlwinds, that periodically flay the llanos. There are also rampaging herds of horses and steers; the power of flowing rivers and currents; a midnight-black stallion as savage as Satan, but tamed by Santos Luzardo; a fire that scorches the plains, leaving blackened embers in its hellish path; and, evoking the violent spirit of the llanos, are the llanero horsemen who almost destroy the tendrils of civilization that come within reach. Gallegos does bring in beauty such as flowers, sunset tints, breezes, white clouds, rains, the pink herons, and other delicacies, but, ever lurking wraith-like in the background is the malaria that had earlier nearly depopulated the llanos, causing its historical decline (the llanos had once supplied the cavalry that had filled General Simón Bolívar's revolutionary army's ranks, giving it victory over Spain's Royalist armies during Venezuela's War of Independence from Spain).

Gallegos uses symbols for barbarism, such as the great *tolvaneras,* or but not overdone—we see the llanero, or cowboy; the boatmen of the Arauca River; a stock military official; ranch owners; and the itinerant Syrian peddlers, both rascally and otherwise. Some of Gallegos' sociological types are presented as clearly as if they inhabited an animated museum. Possibly his only near-caricature is Mister Danger, a one-dimensional villain who over-represents the alleged Yankee rascality that is the compulsive whipping-boy of so many Spanish-American novelists.

Gallegos' plot is logically developed. Coupled with worthy subject matter, and knowledge of his fellow Venezuelans, it produces a near-masterpiece. Human cruelty is not overdrawn, realism is almost never lacking, and there are few distortions, but—as a city-dweller and intellectual, belonging to a professional class not noted for dirtying its hands with physical toil—Gallegos did not give an in-depth study of the llanos' lowest social types. The novel is thus limited at times by an unconscious social prejudice, and the author's perception of the llaneros' religious views, or psychology, or superstitions, is superficial. Human suffering is not presented feelingly, introspection is generally lacking. But most of the characters do live, and are not likely to be forgotten by the reader, for they develop and change subtly but gradually. The reader thus lives with them through the pages of *Doña Bárbara,* and with their llanos grasslands.

The basic themes of *Doña Bárbara* are universal ones. Civilization against barbarism is about as dominant a theme as in Domingo Sarmiento's *Facundo* (the noted masterpiece of Argentine literature). Also present are such themes as man against nature, female against male, cruelty against kindness, justice against oppression, and freedom against bureaucratic government. Nowhere in *Doña Bárbara,* however, is it suggested that hard work and thrift such as practiced not only by Horatio Alger, but by, say, Japanese, Germans, Jews, Mormons, or even Venezuela's Syrian peddlers, could alleviate the llanos' poverty.

Doña Bárbara is rich in Venezuelan expressions, idioms, and flavor of speech, but its vocabulary is not difficult. Gallegos' style moves effortlessly along and reader interest is not sacrificed by excess words or structural disorganization. The plot also moves briskly and is never clouded by deviant subplots or excessive complexity, yet even discerning readers cannot anticipate events, including the climax with its curiously passive finale for Doña Bárbara, the violent woman of the barbaric Venezuelan plains. From the first page, violence hangs over the story like a Sword of Damocles or a nightmare. It either lurks in the background, like a boa constrictor coiled in the llanos grass, or it erupts like a llanos fire.

Doña Bárbara, like various other Venezuelan novels, exposed and spotlighted national ills. Realistic reform could have come earlier to Venezuela, aided by such revelatory writings, but it was slow even when Gallegos himself became president. Gallegos was apparently not strong enough, or perhaps lacked enough political horse sense to accomplish what was accomplished in the nineteenth century by Argentina's two literary presidents, Bartolomé Mitre and Domingo Sarmiento, who were men of action as well as of the pen. As a genre, the novel remains, nevertheless, the most important literary tool not only in Venezuela but in all Latin America. Being the broadest and least restricted literary form, and mirroring social ills, it is a supple tool in the hands of would-be reformers such as Rómulo Gallegos, who are brave enough to risk political persecution for their writings.

William Freitas

DOÑA PERFECTA

Type of work: Novel
Author: Benito Pérez Galdós (1843-1920)
Type of plot: Tragedy of religious bigotry
Time of plot: Late nineteenth century
Locale: Orbajosa, Spain
First published: 1876

Principal characters:
JOSÉ ("PEPE") REY
DOÑA PERFECTA REY, his aunt
ROSARIO, her daughter
DON INOCENCIO, canon of the cathedral
MARÍA REMEDIOS, his sister
JACINTO, María's son

Critique:

Pérez Galdós went to Madrid as a student of law in 1863; however, literature and the theater proved more interesting than the bar. Early in his literary career he wrote several novels about politics and social customs. Then, between 1875 and 1878, Galdós became interested in religion and published three novels dealing with its different aspects: *Doña Perfecta,* the story of a town dominated by the clergy; *Gloria* (1876-1877), a novel about a Jewish-Christian clash, and *The Family of León Roch* (1879), a story of religious fanaticism ruining a happy household. All are classified as belonging to the novelist's early period, though they represent a great technical advance over his first attempts. In *Doña Perfecta,* Galdós describes the clash of modern ideas against the walls of bigotry and prejudice in a small Andalusian town removed from the main current of life. Representative of the new order is the scientifically trained, clear-thinking, outspoken bridge builder. The old is represented by a wealthy woman so fanatically religious that to save her daughter's immortal soul she would even condone murder. The result is a suspense novel that has shown its popularity by translation into eight languages.

The Story:

The city of Orbajosa, with its 7,324 inhabitants, was proud of its religious atmosphere. It boasted a cathedral and a seminary, but it possessed nothing else to make it known to the rest of Spain. It had no manufacturing, and its only agricultural activity was the raising of garlic.

The leading citizen of Orbajosa was Doña Perfecta Rey, a widow whose wealth was the result of legal victories won over her husband's family by her brother, an Andalusian lawyer. Since he had a son, Pepe Rey, and she had a daughter, Rosario, the idea of marriage between the two young people seemed a natural arrangement to their elders. It was for this purpose that Pepe first came to Orbajosa.

In his busy life as a road construction engineer, Pepe had thought little about matrimony, but he began to do so after seeing the lovely Rosario. The girl was in turn attracted to her cousin. Doña Perfecta was also much taken with Pepe, but not for long.

Doña Perfecta, like the other inhabitants of Orbajosa, was under the domination of the Church, and as the town's most exemplary citizen she felt the need to be especially devout. At the same time Don Inocencio, canon of the cathedral, had other plans for Rosario. Urged on by his sister, María Remedios, who desired the Rey fortune for her son Jacinto, Don Inocencio, far less innocent than his name implied, began conniving to end all talk of marriage between the cousins.

Pepe, through his wide travel and training, was unorthodox, though not without regard for religion. Before long, however, Don Inocencio made him appear a heretic, and Doña Perfecta, forgetting her indebtedness to his father and ignoring the feelings of her daughter, refused him permission to see Rosario. The girl, made meek by education and dominated by her mother, lacked the courage to assert herself in declaring her love for her cousin.

Soon all the people of Orbajosa, from the bishop to the working man in the fields, were made to feel it a matter of religious and civic pride to rid their city of the heretic. The unsuspecting Pepe could not conceive of such intolerance. He tried to explain that he had no intention of attacking religion, but his attempts to make clear his position only made matters worse.

Finally, after several stolen interviews with Rosario in the family chapel, Pepe decided to take her away, and Rosario agreed to go with him. But the lovers had failed to reckon with the power of community opinion. While the conscience-stricken Rosario was revealing to her mother her plan to run away that night with Pepe, María Remedios, filled with hatred for the young man who was cheating her Jacinto out of the Rey fortune, arrived to warn Doña Perfecta that the heretic was entering the garden.

Warned now that Pepe was coming to take Rosario away, her mother ordered one of her acquaintances to shoot him. Pepe fell, mortally wounded. His death drove Rosario insane. Don Inocencio felt himself cut off from the world, and Doña Perfecta died of cancer. Nobody gained anything, but Orbajosa felt sure it had won a victory for the faith.

Further Critical Evaluation of the Work:

Jesus Christ warned almost two thousand years ago that his church was like a fisherman's net, containing both good fish and rotten fish. In *Doña Perfecta,* the Spanish novelist Pérez Galdós portrays religious intolerance in a cathedral town of interior Spain; in so doing, he attacks religious hypocrisy and emphasizes Christ's warning. *Doña Perfecta* was the first of four novels that Pérez Galdós wrote in the late 1870's picturing current Spanish life. It graphically presents what Gerald Brennan labeled "the stagnant, stupid, fanatical Spain of the country districts."

The shadow of intolerant Doña Perfecta herself lowers darkly over Orbajosa, just as the cathedral looms over plaza and town. The human beings within the cathedral make it a somber place, rather than the mellow, beautiful, hope-inspiring temple of God that it should have been. Pérez Galdós does not attack religion itself, however, for his purpose in writing *Doña Perfecta* is to reform religion. He thus criticizes Catholicism for its faults, but indirectly acknowledges that it had once given strength to robust, rural Spain. Pérez Galdós also champions the cause of progress, while condemning the abuses of traditionalism, even though aware that traditionalism should be a life-giving flame rather than dead ashes.

The novel's characterization is skimpier than that of the author's later works. Father Inocencio clearly symbolizes one of the many types of rural priests of his time, but other characters are not depicted with finesse. Character motivations are also vague; gorgon-like Doña Perfecta herself is one of Pérez Galdós' weaker female characterizations. Individuals are not strongly etched because Pérez Galdós viewed them as representatives of their class or profession. Atmosphere and setting *are* stressed for the same reason. Gloomy scenes and stock social types thus loom in the reader's memory more than do specific individuals themselves.

An interesting element in *Doña Perfecta* is Pepe's hope that man can be led upward by education, a view which reflects the influence on the author of nineteenth century Spanish intellectuals who held that education can reform man. Pepe Rey also exemplifies accurately the type of impractical idealist always to be found in Spain; hence he is more realistically drawn than many critics have implied.

Perhaps the most genuine praise that can be given to *Doña Perfecta* is that its satire has helped to modernize religious institutions in Spain. The Spanish Church today is not entirely lacking in social consciousness, while it has sometimes been observed that religious old ladies in Spain strive visibly to avoid being branded as Doña Perfectas.

DOSTOEVSKY

Type of work: Critical study
Author: Nicholas Berdyaev (1874-1948)
First published: 1934

Nicholas Berdyaev, one of the foremost religious thinkers of modern Russia, pays homage in *Mirosozertzanie Dostoievskago* (original English title: *The World-Outlook of Dostoievsky*) to the major influence upon his unique interpretation of Jesus Christ and the role of Christianity in the twentieth century. While his critical study throws considerable light on Dostoevsky's philosophy, it admittedly reveals Berdyaev's own religious and ethical concerns to such an extent that critic and subject are inseparable. In the first part of his analysis Berdyaev, beginning with a portrait of the Russian mind, discusses Dostoevsky's conceptions of man, freedom, evil, and love. In the second, he turns more to the implications of these conceptions in terms of modern Russia, politics, and especially their most complete statement, *The Grand Inquisitor,* the famous chapter from *The Brothers Karamazov.* Altogether, the critical study provides a significant key for the understanding of Berdyaev's remarkable intellectual career as well as for Dostoevsky's works.

Asserting that he thinks Dostoevsky Russia's greatest metaphysician, Berdyaev wants to unfold the dynamic ideas that he calls Dostoevsky's *conception of the world.* The Russian mind, he claims as a basis of his study, is an antagonistic dualism, in which the natural tendency is to seek such extremes that the individual is sharply torn by mutually exclusive positions. The "nihilists" avidly seek anarchy, atheism, and self-destruction; the "apocalypsists" want only the most excessive asceticism and a messianic revival. These two sides of the Russian spirit are more fully expressed in Dostoevsky's fiction than in any other philosophy or literature; they create the passion that makes his novels so disturbing. This passion is the tragic view of human destiny, a view

that he was able to communicate because he fully expressed the dualism that he found in himself and also because he saw life in depth, never on the surface. By holding the dualism that he found in himself and also because he saw life in depth, never on the surface, and by keeping the dualism always in its greatest tension, he created the true human spirit as it faces tragedy, undergoes purification through suffering, and finds release in Christ.

Although opposed to Humanism, Dostoevsky's absorbing theme was man and man's destiny; this theme was developed in such an intense manner that the inability of Humanism to solve the tragedy of human destiny is completely undermined. All of his novels are built around a single character who is the center of a whirlpool of passions that drive him away from a social framework; once the character completely alienates himself, he believes that he is emancipated from law and from God. But this "freedom" is the condition through which Dostoevsky plunges into the inner depths of man. According to the Humanistic view of the modern world, this alienated character should be free, but Dostoevsky shows that his freedom is really a descent into Hell, for the character develops an unhealthy self-love that makes him introspective and consequently miserable. Human nature, being extreme, antinomian, and irrational, is overwhelmingly attracted toward lawless freedom, and this lawlessness can end only in the deification of man or the discovery of God. In other words, freedom is a test that leads either to misery or to release; it is the essential condition of tragic suffering.

The justification both of God and of man rests in human freedom; thus, all of Dostoevsky's novels are concerned with the experiment of human liberty. Freedom is an amoral, valueless state out of which the dignity or debasement of man grows, but freedom, being amoral, implies the freedom of evil and the freedom of good, either of which will destroy the other. Thus freedom is essentially tragic, for once it is found, it presents the free man with choices that are beyond his power. Since freedom implies such a choice, Berdyaev believes that it is by nature Christian and that the figure of Christ presents itself as the ultimate and final freedom. The experience of complete freedom, embracing both good and evil, can lead to God, but more often it ends in self-will that cancels freedom by negating God and becoming trapped in compulsion. In fact, the usual mind advocates a freedom that negates evil, and without evil there would be no need for God because the world itself would be divine.

Wherever there is freedom, there must be evil; to reject freedom on the basis that it can bring evil is to make the evil twice as bad. Thus, while freedom can degenerate into evil, goodness cannot exist without it. Dostoevsky here saw clearly into the depths of human nature: evil rests in the depths of man's own personality—it is the sign of his inner profundity and the key to true personality, not a condition caused by society. In other words, evil is the inevitable tragic road that a man must travel before he can discover himself or God; the truly free man learns that evil will defeat and destroy itself and that through this purgation he can rise to spiritual adulthood. Thus, evil is an essential step in the spiritual process: Dostoevsky's heroes go through freedom and evil to redemption. In the state of freedom, the hero believes that everything is allowable; however, he becomes obsessed by some fixed idea, and with this obsession freedom becomes tyranny. He appears to be a maniac. But all things are not allowable, because men, having been created in the image of God, have an absolute value that the hero cannot violate without violating himself and

becoming a slave. Yet if man were not completely free, he could do anything and be responsible for nothing; thus the state of freedom turns the hero into a divided man, able to become either a devil or a saint.

In Dostoevsky's treatment of love, Berdyaev sees the full depth of the novelist's profundity. Love is a Dionysian force that literally tears the individual to pieces. Woman is the dark principle that draws man toward a tragic sensuality or an equally tragic pity; there is no unity or perfection in his treatment of love. Instead it is a power that infects and destroys. Yet the blame rests entirely with the man; he is powerless before the female; she brings out the tragic separation of his own nature. In sexual as well as in social love, man's inner nature yearns for an excess that enslaves him; even pity takes on a violence that is self-destructive. The only kind of love that remains real is Christan love, an affirmation of eternity; all other love is an illusion and a lie.

Having outlined Dostoevsky's conception of human destiny, Berdyaev turns to the larger issues that grow out of this central vision; these issues—revolution, socialism, and modern Russia—place the heroes' struggles in significant frameworks that shape and are shaped by them. Of all of the Russian novelists, Dostoevsky saw clearest that revolution was inevitable; the very nature of the Russian mind dictated the excessive cry for freedom that led to socialism. Socialism, however, wants to displace God and fills itself with messianic spirit; it attempts to create a utopianism that denies evil and hence God. Thus freedom leads to slavery; man loses freedom by asking for too much lawlessness and comes under an unhuman force. In fact, Dostoevsky saw that the only way to end the conditions of nineteenth century Russia was through the Church—to find the freedom of brotherhood in Christ. But before that era, the Russian people must tread the path of evil, of humiliation and despair, that will purge them of their utopianism and allow a national redemption.

In *The Grand Inquisitor*, Berdyaev finds Dostoevsky's greatest statement of his religious views—the untangling of the problem of human freedom. Only two choices are available to man, the alternative of Jesus Christ or that of the Inquisitor; there is no third. Christ, who is silent throughout most of the chapter, offers the true freedom of the spirit; the Inquisitor confronts Him with compulsion, recognizing that people cannot bear the freedom offered by Christ. In one sense, the Inquisitor denies God in the name of man, but he also denies man because he believes that man can be happy only as a slave. What he overlooks is that Christ can be seen only through a free act of faith. Thus the deification of man ends in hopeless misery; Christ offers to the few a love that lifts man from self-destruction, but the freedom of Christ comes only through the renunciation of all claims to earthly power.

In portraying Dostoevsky's philosophy, Berdyaev thus shows that the novelist created a violent and contradictory world in order to describe what he regards as the basic Christian message. The movement through freedom and evil to redemption is to Berdyaev the fundamental theme of Dostoevsky's works and the philosophy that makes him great.

THE DOUBLE-DEALER

Type of work: Drama
Author: William Congreve (1670-1729)
Type of plot: Tragi-comedy
Time of plot: Seventeenth century
Locale: London
First presented: 1694

Principal characters:
MELLEFONT, an earnest young man
LORD TOUCHWOOD, his uncle
LADY TOUCHWOOD, in love with Mellefont
CYNTHIA, Mellefont's sweetheart
MASKWELL, Mellefont's false friend

Critique:

The Double-Dealer, Congreve's second play, failed at the time of its presentation. This failure probably can be explained by the play's departure from the established tradition of Restoration comedy. In spite of its firm construction and witty dialogue, The Double-Dealer contains some repulsive elements not relished by the play-going audience of Congreve's day. Yet its plot, characters, and light dialogue make it one of the best comedies of the period. The play also reflects the dramatic conventions of its time and type: the attack on Puritans and Puritanism, dissolute dandies, devastatingly witty maidens, faithless young wives of old men, rascally servants, and devious intrigue.

The Story:

Lady Touchwood was infatuated with her husband's nephew, Mellefont, who had pledged himself to Cynthia, daughter of Sir Paul Plyant. When she confessed her ardor to him, and he rebuked her, she attempted to end her life with his sword. Prevented in her attempt, she vowed revenge.

Fearing the designs of Lady Touchwood, Mellefont engaged his friend Careless to keep Lady Plyant, Cynthia's stepmother, away from Lady Touchwood. Careless also revealed his distrust of Maskwell, Mellefont's friend, who was under obligations to Lord Touchwood.

From sheer spite, Lady Touchwood gave herself to Maskwell. In return, Maskwell promised to help Lady Touch-

wood by insinuating to Lady Plyant that Mellefont really loved her, not Cynthia.

Lady Touchwood's plan began to work. Old Sir Paul Plyant and Lady Plyant expressed indignation when they were told that Mellefont desired Lady Plyant. Actually, Lady Plyant was flattered and merely pretended anger, but she was nevertheless shocked that Mellefont intended to marry Cynthia for the ultimate purpose of cuckolding Sir Paul. Lady Plyant rebuked him, but at the same time she told the puzzled young man not to despair. Maskwell revealed to Mellefont that he was Lady Touchwood's agent in provoking trouble; Maskwell's real purpose was to create general confusion and to win Cynthia's hand.

Lord Touchwood, refusing to believe that his nephew played a double game, was scandalized when Lady Touchwood recommended cancellation of the marriage on the grounds that Mellefont had made improper advances to her. Maskwell, instructed by Lady Touchwood, ingratiated himself with Lord Touchwood by saying that he had defended Lady Touchwood's honor and had prevailed upon Mellefont to cease his unwelcome attentions.

Maskwell, in his own vicious behalf, told Mellefont that his reward for assisting in the breakup of Mellefont's marriage to Cynthia was the privilege of bedding with Lady Touchwood. Plotting Mellefont's ruin, the fake friend pretended that he wished to be saved from the shame of collecting his reward, and he asked the credulous young man to go to Lady Touchwood's chamber and there surprise Maskwell and Lady Touchwood together.

When Lord Plyant, frustrated by Lady Plyant's vow to remain a virgin, complained to Careless that he did not have an heir, Careless waggishly promised to see what he could do in the matter.

Mellefont, to escape the evil that was brewing, impatiently urged Cynthia to elope with him. Although she refused, she promised to marry no one but him. When she challenged Mellefont to thwart his aunt and to get her approval of their marriage, he promised to get Lady Touchwood's consent that night.

Lady Plyant, meanwhile, had consented to an assignation with Careless. When Lord Plyant appeared, Careless had to give her, secretly, a note containing directions for their meeting. Lady Plyant, anxious to read Careless' letter, asked her husband for a letter which he had received earlier. Pretending to read her husband's letter, she read the one given her by Careless. By mistake she returned her lover's letter to her husband.

Discovering her mistake, she reported it in alarm to Careless. Lord Plyant, meanwhile, had read the letter. Lady Plyant insisted that it was part of an insidious plot against her reputation, and after accusing her husband of having arranged to have it written in order to test his fidelity, she threatened divorce. Careless pretended that he had written it in Lord Plyant's behalf to test his wife's virtue. As foolish as he was, Lord Plyant was not without suspicion of his wife and Careless.

That night Mellefont concealed himself in Lady Touchwood's chamber. When she entered, expecting to find Maskwell, Mellefont revealed himself. Lord Touchwood, informed by Maskwell, then appeared. When her husband threatened his nephew, Lady Touchwood

pretended that the young man was out of his wits.

Not suspecting Maskwell's treachery, Lady Touchwood later told him of her lucky escape. Maskwell, in a purposeful soliloquy, revealed to Lord Touchwood his love for Cynthia. Duped, the old man named Maskwell his heir and promised to arrange a marriage between Cynthia and the schemer.

Lady Touchwood learned of Maskwell's treachery when Lord Touchwood told her that he intended to make Maskwell his heir. Chagrined by her betrayal, Lady Touchwood urged her husband never to consent to Cynthia's marriage with anyone but Mellefont.

Maskwell, still pretending to be Mellefont's friend, made his final move by plotting with the unwary Mellefont to get Cynthia away from her house. His intention being to marry her himself, he privately told Cynthia that Mellefont would be waiting for her in the chaplain's chamber. Careless checked Maskwell's carefully laid plans, however, when he disclosed to the young lovers Maskwell's true villainy. Cynthia and Lord Touchwood, in concealment, overheard Lady Touchwood rebuke Maskwell for his betrayal of her. At last she tried to stab her lover but was overcome with emotion. Maskwell then revealed the meeting place where Mellefont, in the disguise of a parson, would be waiting for Cynthia. Lady Touchwood, planning to disguise herself as Cynthia, hurried away to meet him there.

Lord Touchwood, knowing of her plan, put on a chaplain's habit and confronted his wife when she came to make overtures to the man she supposed was Mellefont. The whole plot uncovered, and Maskwell, the double-dealer, unmasked, Mellefont, cleared of all suspicion, took Cynthia for his own.

Further Critical Evaluation of the Work:

After the great success of his first comedy, *The Old Bachelor,* Congreve was disappointed at the poor reception of *The Double-Dealer,* which he considered a better play on a more serious theme. Serious it was; like other contemporary comedies, it satirizes the follies and vices of the time, but here the emphasis is on the vices rather than the follies. An unusual combination of Restoration comedy and Jacobean melodrama, its action is largely devoted to the intrigues of the "villain" Maskwell. Audiences were no doubt uncomfortable at being forced to take such a long hard look at Machiavellian treachery and romantic knavery at work. As Dryden pointed out, "The women think he has exposed their bitchery too much and the gentlemen are offended with him, for the discovery of their follies, and the way of their intrigues, under the notion of friendship to their ladies' husbands." Maskwell, in the depth of his resourceful villainy, reminds us of Iago; Lady Touchwood compares him to a devil.

Lady Touchwood, of course, is herself a villain, but, as one of the victims of Maskwell's double-dealing, a lesser one. As she reminds Maskwell, her excuse is "fire in my temper, passion in my soul, apt to every provocation, oppressed at once with love, and with despair. But a sedate, a thinking villain, whose black blood runs temperately bad, what excuse can clear?" In any case, the ability of burning love to turn into burning hatred has seldom been shown so powerfully in a work professing to be a comedy. Lady Touchwood, indeed, has struck some critics as an almost tragic figure (she attempts to stab Mellefont and then Maskwell, at different points in the play, after her passion has been thwarted). Other indications of the playwright's striving for tragic effect are the unusual number of soliloquys, and the play's ending with a piece of moralizing, rather than (as was customary for Restoration comedy) a dance.

Congreve's focus of attention being Maskwell, his hero and heroine are given relatively short shrift. Mellefont and Cynthia are an agreeable pair of lovers, but no more than that. Cynthia is shown to be sensible and sincere, but she has none of the sparkling wit that was to make his Millamant so admirable. Nor is there any of the almost obligatory battles of wit between hero and heroine. Indeed, the passive Mellefont appears much of the time to be a dupe and a fool, so much so, that Congreve felt obliged to defend his hero from such charges in the play's dedication.

The plot is original; and Congreve was proud that "the mechanical part of [the play] is perfect." Consciously trying to incorporate the three unities into a classical form, he succeeded at least in molding a work that has unity of time (the action is continuous, over a three-hour period) and place (it all takes place in one "gallery"). As for unity of action, the plot is unusually tight, but there are subplots in the form of the cuckolding of Sir Paul Plyant by Careless, and of Lord Froth by Brisk. Indeed, what levity and wit the play has to offer is largely contained in these sub-plots. The various affectations of the minor characters, the romantic intrigues between the ladies and their gallants, and such brilliantly actable passages as the dialogue between Brisk, Lord Froth, and Careless on whether or not one should laugh at comedies, are ample evidence that Congreve had not forgotten that his prime task as a comic playwright was not to moralize—at least, not overtly—but to entertain.

DOWN THERE

Type of work: Novel
Author: Joris Karl Huysmans (Charles Marie Georges Huysmans, 1848-1907)
Time: Late nineteenth century
Locale: Paris
First published: 1891

> *Principal characters:*
> DURTAL, a writer
> DES HERMIES, his friend and interlocutor
> CARHAIX, bell ringer at Saint-Sulpice
> CHANTELOUVE, a Catholic historian
> HYACINTHE CHANTELOUVE, his wife and Durtal's mistress
> CANON DOCRE, a Satanist
> GILLES DE RAIS (1404-1440), Marshal of France, infamous murderer, sadist, and Satanist

Huysmans began his career as a novelist during the 1870's as a member of the naturalistic school of Zola, whose friend and disciple he then was. But in 1884 he broke with Zola by writing his most famous book, *À rebours (Against the Grain)*, which was vastly admired by the *fin-de-siècle* writers on both sides of the Channel.

Down There (Là-bas) was the first of a series of four novels, the purpose of which was to trace the spiritual autobiography of one Durtal (Huysmans himself) as he struggled from skepticism through spiritual despair to the final goal of faith. It was not the author's intention to "tell a story" but rather to analyze his own reactions to the faith that he had lost, but hoped to regain, and to various aspects of historical and contemporary Roman Catholicism; hence, the plots of the books are very slight, and Huysmans used the novels as a platform from which he could express his very decided views on a number of subjects and display his esoteric learning.

When the story opens, Durtal is engaged in writing a biography of Gilles de Rais, the infamous murderer of children, who lived in the fifteenth century. With his friend Des Hermies, whose sole function is to provide someone for him to talk with, Durtal visits the home of Carhaix, the bell ringer of Saint-Sulpice, in the tower of the church. During these visits the conversation turns to Church history and especially to Satanism, a subject in which Durtal has become interested as part of the background for his study of de Rais. Des Hermies avers that Satanism is being practiced in Paris at that very time and he mentions a certain Canon Docre, a renegade priest. While Durtal is wondering how he can make the contacts necessary to observe modern Satanism at first hand, he receives a series of anonymous love letters. He eventually discovers that the writer is a Madame Chantelouve, whose receptions he has sometimes attended. After a few meetings she becomes his mistress, he learns that she knows Docre, and at length he persuades her to take him to a Black Mass. He witnesses the revolting spectacle, held in an abandoned Ursuline convent; afterwards, in a nearby tavern, Madame Chantelouve tricks him into committing sacrilege. Disgusted with her, he breaks off their relationship, and the novel comes to an end.

There is, however, a story within the story, for large sections of the book are devoted to Durtal's readings from his biography of de Rais. The material for this section Huysmans obtained from a work by the Abbé Bossard, published in 1884, which contained a transcript of the records of de Rais' trial preserved in

DOWN THERE by Joris Karl Huysmans. Translated by Keene Wallis. By permission of the publishers, University Books, Inc. Copyright, 1958, by University Books, Inc.

the archives at Nantes. Although he made a number of mistakes, Huysmans traced, with reasonable accuracy and considerable drama, the career of the sinister marshal. The details are often horrifying, and Huysmans spares his readers none of them; but the ending of the story, with de Rais' trial and final repentance, gave him the opportunity for his most famous passages of description. He was attracted to this unsavory bit of history as others have been (for the literature in French on de Rais is considerable) by the problem in morbid psychology that it presents. De Rais had been in his youth a companion-in-arms of Jeanne d'Arc and had apparently shared the religious exaltation that had affected her followers. How, then, did he change into such a monster of butchery, Satanism, and sexual perversion that his name is remembered after the passage of five hundred years? In addition, Huysmans was a fervent medievalist; and all aspects of the period fascinated him, particularly the religious fervor that had been possible in an age of faith. He never tired of contrasting the ardent Catholicism of the Middle Ages, the splendor of its ritual and the beauty of its architecture, with the vulgar manifestations that he saw in his own day. Faith had been easy in the fifteenth century, he believed; the problem was to find it in the materialistic present.

The parts of the novel dealing with modern Satanism—weird as they appear —were taken from happenings in contemporary Paris. There was apparently a good deal of this disgusting hocus-pocus going on at the time, and several of the characters in *Down There* were drawn from life.

Huysmans, during his later period, never wearied of damning the nineteenth century and all its characteristic works. He begins the novel with an attack on Naturalism, the literary school to which he had once belonged. It has "made our literature the incarnation of materialism . . . 'appetite and instinct' seem to be its sole motivation and rut and brainstorm its chronic states." And throughout the book he continues to attack his own age for its shoddiness, crassness, and vulgarity.

But the core of the book is its contribution to the author's spiritual autobiography. Huysmans had spent his childhood quite literally in a religious atmosphere, under the shadow of Saint-Sulpice, but he confessed later that he had been completely indifferent to religion throughout his youth. He was converted between 1884 and 1892; *Down There* represents the first stage of this conversion. In this work Durtal-Huysmans has reached the stage, familiar enough in such cases, of being attracted by the externals of religion, such as the beauty of the liturgy and the fascination of Church history, and yet unable to accept the essentials. He had the true Romanticist's attitude: he could have been a devout Catholic in any period except the present. Because the Church fell artistically short of what he believed it to have been during the Middle Ages, he had difficulty in understanding that the underlying reality could have remained unchanged. Here his artistic nature interfered with his religious conversion because the undoubted ugliness of much nineteenth-century ecclesiastical art was a stumbling block. He had yet to understand that belief in a materialistic age is a greater triumph than during an age of faith.

THE DOWNFALL

Type of work: Novel
Author: Émile Zola (1840-1902)
Type of plot: Social criticism
Time of plot: 1870-1871
Locale: France
First published: 1892

Principal characters:
MAURICE LEVASSEUR, a private in the French Army
JEAN MACQUART, his corporal
DELAHERCHE, a textile manufacturer
WEISS, his secretary
HENRIETTE, twin sister of Maurice and wife of Weiss
FOUCHARD, a shrewd farmer
HONORÉ, his son
SILVINE, Fouchard's servant

Critique:

Zola's theme in this highly contrived novel would seem to be that France paid in full measure for the indulgences of seventy years in her wretched defeat at the hands of Bismarck and Von Moltke in 1870-71. Each character is a symbol of an economic or social group. Zola's account of Sedan, of the events leading up to Sedan, and of the insurrection in Paris, command admiration for his research. The plot makes even more dramatic the historical facts.

The Story:

Corporal Jean Macquart, a sturdy French peasant, led the squad of infantry of which Private Maurice Levasseur was a member. The squad was a part of the 106th Regiment of the Seventh Corps of the French Army. A state of war existed between France and Prussia; the year was 1870. At the outset it had been felt in France that the war would be nothing more than a quick promenade to Berlin, but shortages of equipment, the rivalry of the French commanders, and quick Prussian success made the outcome of the conflict doubtful.

Maurice, a scapegrace who had enlisted to get away from financial troubles in Paris, believed in the evolutionary necessity of war. As a member of the middle class, he loathed Jean, whose peasant common sense was unendurable to him.

Misinformation and lack of information led the leader of the Seventh Corps to order his divisions to fall back from their positions around Mulhausen, in Alsace. Defeat was in the air. Civilians, having heard that the Prussians were sweeping all before them, were fleeing westward. Demoralized, the troops threw away their packs and rifles. At Belfort the corps entrained for Rheims, where the retreating and disorganized French forces were regrouping.

Prussian victories cost Emperor Napoleon III his command of the French armies. But Napoleon, with his official entourage, remained with the troops. Maurice, in Rheims, learned from battle veterans that the Prussians were young, healthy, well-organized, and well-equipped. He lost all hope for France when he caught sight of the sickly emperor in Rheims.

The army was ordered to march to Verdun. Mendacious ministers and journalists lulled the French forces into a false sense of security. When the troops reached the Ardennes, there were marches and counter-marches, for the positions of the Prussian armies were not known by the French commanders. Regiments became mobs as the French approached Sedan. By that time Maurice had become reconciled to his fate, and had even grown to admire Jean, whose steadiness had kept the squad together.

Near Sedan, Maurice, Jean, and Honoré, an artilleryman, rescued Honoré's father, old Fouchard, from pillaging soldiers. There Honoré also promised to marry Silvine, Fouchard's servant, who had had a baby by Fouchard's hired hand, Goliath. The hired man was suspected of being a Prussian spy, for at the beginning of hostilities he had disappeared from the Fouchard farm.

Sedan was a place of confusion, where men were separated from their units because there was no discipline and no organization. In the confusion, Jean and Maurice met at the house of Delaherche, a Sedan textile manufacturer, whose secretary, Weiss, was the husband of Maurice's twin sister, Henriette. After a rest Jean and Maurice rejoined their regiment. Napoleon III accompanied the troops to Sedan.

As the French poured into Sedan, it became evident that the Prussians were drawing a ring around the fortified town. Weiss and Delaherche went to Bazeilles, a village near Sedan, to check the safety of property which they owned there. Weiss, caught in a battle which took place in the village, joined the French forces against the Prussians. Delaherche hastened back to Sedan. Maurice, in the meantime, experienced his first artillery barrage.

At Bazeilles the Prussians closed in on inferior French forces. Weiss, in his house, was joined by a small group of French soldiers and one civilian to make a last ditch stand. Captured, Weiss was put up against a wall to be shot. Henriette appeared, and despite her plea to be shot with her husband, she was pushed aside while the Prussians shot Weiss. Henriette, nearly out of her mind with grief, wandered about the field where the battle was still going on.

The 106th Regiment was decimated in a futile attempt to retake a strategic hill. When Jean was wounded, Maurice carried him to safety. Honoré Fouchard was killed at his gun. Napoleon had a white flag raised over a city roof, but it was torn down. Delaherche's factory was converted into a hospital, soon filled to overflowing with French wounded. Napoleon sent General Reille to the Prussians with a letter of capitulation.

Maurice, Jean, and several survivors of the 106th made their way into Sedan, where Maurice met Henriette and learned of Weiss' gallant death. They were engaged in a fight with Prussian Guards commanded by an officer whom Maurice recognized to be his cousin Gunther. Henriette kept Maurice from shooting Gunther.

By nightfall all had become silent except for the turmoil created by the movement of thousands of French troops into Sedan. The French were forced to accept the demands of Bismarck and Von Moltke.

The next day Silvine went out to the battlefield and recovered the body of Honoré. Henriette learned that Weiss' body had been consumed in fires started by the Prussians at Bazeilles.

The surrendered French soldiers were herded together to await deportation to Germany. A few French officers who promised never to take up arms again were released. In the camp men were murdered for filthy scraps of bread and spoiled horseflesh. Maurice, who no longer believed in anything, nearly lost control of himself. Jean, a cool veteran of previous campaigns, placed himself and Maurice among soldiers of a regiment leaving for Germany. At a stop along the way, Jean procured civilian clothes from a sympathetic French girl who was selling bread. The pair changed quickly inside a tent and escaped into a forest. When they came to a Prussian outpost, Jean was wounded by rifle fire, but they managed to escape and make their way back to old Fouchard's farm, where they found Henriette. Maurice went on to aid in the defense of Paris; Jean remained with Fouchard to be nursed back to health by Henriette.

The proclamation of the Second Republic was followed by the capitulation of Marshal Bazaine at Metz. Paris was invested by the Prussians while frantic attempts were made to organize new French armies in other parts of France.

Goliath, employed by the Prussians as a spy around Sedan, came to Silvine seeking her good graces. Upon her refusal, he threatened to expose Fouchard's connection with French partisans. When Goliath returned for his answer, two of the partisans, assisted by Silvine, killed him.

In Sedan Delaherche became friendly with Prussian Captain Von Gartlauben, who was billeted in the Delaherche house; he found the captain's friendship to be most advantageous in the matter of reëstablishing his textile works.

Jean, well again, joined the Army of the North. Maurice, meanwhile, took part in the defense of Paris. Sick of the Republic, he deserted after the capitula-tion of Paris and took a room near the boulevards. When the Commune took command in Paris and civil war broke out, Maurice joined the forces of the Commune to fight against the Republican forces, of which Jean's regiment was a part. The insurrectionists fired the city as they were pushed back. Maurice was bayoneted by Jean during night fighting in the streets. Jean disguised Maurice as a Republican soldier and took him to Maurice's lodgings, where Henriette, who had come to Paris to seek Maurice, was waiting. There Maurice passed the crisis safely, but a later hemorrhage killed him. Jean, broken-hearted at having been the cause of his friend's death, told Henriette goodbye, with the feeling that here was a pin-point of the desolation all France must know.

Further Critical Evaluation of the Work:

The Downfall is a part of Zola's compendious social ledger chronicling the fortunes of the Rougon-Macquart family in France during Napoleon the Third's Second Empire (1852-1870). This work, like others of Zola, is an excellent historical-social document; it documents in a way that only literature can the social and intellectual proclivities of one articulate Frenchman.

In *The Downfall,* Zola angrily indicted the pompous and decadent posturings of French society, particularly the imperial court and the upper officer corps. He described an army top-heavy with sallow, aging, and porcine officers who suffered the collective delusion that the French military was as powerfully energetic and capable as it had been throughout the nineteenth century. The Franco-Prussian War (1870-1871) quickly shattered that myth. Zola made an incisive comparison between the two armies when he described the wizened appearance of the French Emperor and that of the young Prussian faces marching toward Paris.

Zola was militantly nonmilitant. When he wrote this book he saw a revival of the same kind of militarism which led to the Franco-Prussian war. By 1890, military circles in France, particularly the dashing General Georges Ernest Jean Marie Boulanger, had gained a zealous following devoted to his program of revenge against Germany and the reclamation of Alsace-Lorraine, provinces taken from the French by the Germans in 1870. In Zola's mind, such sentiments were folly. The key problems begging the attention of the French nation lay within French boundaries, not outside them.

As Balzac hoped to show in his novels, France had to marshall its forces to remedy the many social ills of the Third French Republic. France needed effective social legislation aimed at easing the plight of the urban working classes. *The Downfall*, like Zola's other novels, expressed Zola's sincere concern for the plight of France's social outcasts.

DRACULA

Type of work: Novel
Author: Bram Stoker (1847-1912)
Type of plot: Horror romance
Time of plot: Nineteenth century
Locale: Transylvania and England
First published: 1897

Principal characters:
JONATHAN HARKER, an English solicitor
MINA MURRAY, his fiancée
COUNT DRACULA, a mysterious nobleman
DR. SEWARD, head of a mental hospital
DR. VAN HELSING, a Dutch medical specialist
LUCY WESTENRA, Mina's friend
ARTHUR HOLMWOOD, engaged to marry Lucy

Critique:

This strange tale of vampires and werewolves has worn surprisingly well. It has been presented on the stage and its principal character, Dracula, has become a well-known figure of literary reference. Full of Gothic touches such as mysterious gloomy castles and open graves at midnight, the story is exciting even today. Although *Dracula* is not truly great literature, it is an excellent example of its type. Written with the rhetorical device of letters and diaries, its overall effect is one of realism and horror.

The Story:

On his way to Castle Dracula in the province of Transylvania, in Rumania, Jonathan Harker, an English solicitor, was apprehensive. His nervousness grew when he observed the curious, fearful attitude of the peasants and the coachman after they learned of his destination. He was on his way to transact business with Count Dracula, and his mission would necessitate remaining at the castle for several days.

Upon his arrival at the castle, Harker found comfortable accommodations awaiting him. Count Dracula was a charming host, although his peculiarly bloodless physical appearance was somewhat disagreeable to Harker's English eyes. Almost immediately Harker was impressed with the strange life of the castle. He and the count discussed their business at night, as the count was never available during the daytime. Although the food was excellent, Harker never saw a servant about the place. While exploring the castle, he found that it was situated high at the top of a mountain with no accessible exit other than the main doorway, which was kept locked. He realized with a shock that he was a prisoner of Count Dracula.

Various harrowing experiences ensued. While Harker half dozed in the early morning hours, three phantom women materialized and attacked him, attempting to bite his throat. Then the count appeared and drove them off, whispering fiercely that Harker belonged to him. Later Harker thought he saw a huge bat descending the castle walls, but the creature turned out to be Count Dracula. In the morning Harker, trying frantically to escape, stumbled into an old chapel where a number of coffin-like boxes of earth were stored. Beneath the cover of one which Harker opened lay the count, apparently dead. In the evening, however, the count appeared as usual, and Harker demanded that he be released. Obligingly the count opened the castle door. A pack of wolves surrounded the entrance. The count, laughing hysterically, left poor Harker a prisoner in his room.

The next day Harker, weak and sick from a strange wound in his throat, saw a pack cart loaded with the mysterious boxes drive from the castle. Dracula was gone and Harker was alone, a prisoner with no visible means of escape.

In England, meanwhile, Harker's fiancée, Mina Murray, had gone to visit her beautiful and charming friend, Lucy Westenra. Lucy was planning to marry Arthur Holmwood, a young nobleman. One evening, early in Mina's visit, a storm blew up and a strange ship was driven aground. The only living creature aboard was a gray wolf-like dog. The animal escaped into the countryside.

Soon afterward Lucy's happiness began to fade because of a growing tendency to sleepwalk. One night Mina followed her friend during one of her spells and discovered Lucy in a churchyard. A tall, thin man who was bending over Lucy disappeared at Mina's approach. Lucy, on waking, could remember nothing of the experience, but her physical condition seemed much weakened. Finally she grew so ill that Mina was forced to call upon Dr. Seward, Lucy's former suitor. Lucy began to improve under his care, and when Mina received a report from Budapest that her missing fiancé had been found and needed care, she felt free to end her visit.

When Lucy's condition suddenly grew worse, Dr. Seward asked his old friend, Dr. Van Helsing, a specialist from Amsterdam, for his professional opinion. Van Helsing, examing Lucy thoroughly, paused over two tiny throat wounds which she was unable to explain. Van Helsing was concerned over Lucy's condition, which pointed to unusual loss of blood without signs of anemia or hemorrhage. She was given blood transfusions at intervals, and someone sat up with her at night. She improved but expressed fear of going to sleep at night because her dreams had grown so horrible.

One morning Dr. Seward fell asleep outside her door. When he and Van Helsing entered her room, they found Lucy ashen white and in a worse condi-

tion than ever. Quickly Van Helsing performed another transfusion; she rallied, but not as satisfactorily as before. Van Helsing then secured some garlic flowers and told Lucy to keep them about her neck at night. When the two doctors called the next morning, Lucy's mother had removed the flowers because their odor might bother her daughter. Frantically Van Helsing rushed to Lucy's room and found her in a coma. Again he administered a transfusion and her condition improved. She said that with the garlic flowers close by she was not afraid of nightly flapping noises at her window. Van Helsing sat with her every night until he felt her well enough to leave. After cautioning her always to sleep with the garlic flowers about her neck, he returned to Amsterdam.

Lucy's mother continued to sleep with her daughter. One night the two ladies were awakened by a huge wolf that crashed through the window. Mrs. Westenra fell dead of a heart attack and Lucy fainted, the wreath of garlic flowers slipping from her neck. Seward and Van Helsing, who had returned to England, discovered her half-dead in the morning. They knew she was dying and called Arthur. As Arthur attempted to kiss her, Lucy's teeth seemed about to fasten on his throat. Van Helsing drew him away. When Lucy died, Van Helsing put a tiny gold crucifix over her mouth, but an attendant stole it from her body.

Soon after Lucy's death several children of the neighborhood were discovered far from their homes, their throats marked by small wounds. Their only explanation was that they had followed a pretty lady. When Jonathan Harker returned to England, Van Helsing went to see him and Mina. After talking with Harker, Van Helsing revealed to Dr. Seward his belief that Lucy had fallen victim to a vampire, one of those strange creatures who can live for centuries on the blood of their victims and breed their kind by attacking the innocent and making them vampires in turn. The only way to save Lucy's soul, according to Van Helsing, was to drive a stake through the heart of her corpse, cut off her head, and stuff her mouth with garlic flowers. Dr. Seward protested violently. The next midnight Arthur, Dr. Seward, and Van Helsing visited Lucy's tomb and found it empty. When daylight came they did as Van Helsing had suggested with Lucy's corpse, which had returned to its tomb.

The men, with Mina, tried to track down Dracula in London, in order to find him before he victimized anyone else. Their object was to remove the boxes of sterilized earth he had brought with him from Transylvania so that he would have no place to hide in the daytime. At last

the hunters trapped Dracula, but he escaped them. By putting Mina into a trance Van Helsing was able to learn that Dracula was at sea, and it was necessary to follow him to his castle. Wolves gathered about them in that desolate country. Van Helsing drew a circle in the snow with a crucifix and within that magic enclosure the travelers rested safely. The next morning they overtook a cart carrying a black box. Van Helsing and the others overcame the drivers of the cart and pried open the lid of Dracula's coffin. As the sun began to set, they drove a stake through the heart of the corpse. The vampire was no more.

Further Critical Evaluation of the Work:

Legend is inextricably twined with Bram Stoker's novel *Dracula,* for the novel is based on the legend. It is impossible to separate the two: the reader will inevitably supply legendary associations between the lines of the novel. But more often than not, everyone tends to forget that both legend and novel were based on reality. This is not to say, of course, that vampires do or did roam Transylvania or elsewhere. However, the prototype for the Dracula legend was a verifiable historical figure, Prince Vlad Tepes, ruler of Transylvania and Walachia (now Rumania) in the mid-fifteenth century. Tepes— nicknamed "The Impaler"— earned a bloody reputation by spearing his victims (some 100,000 of them in a six to ten-year reign, so it is reported) on wooden sticks, a tactic which served to deter domestic criminals and potential outside invaders alike. He assumed the name Dracula—variously interpreted as "son of the dragon" and "son of the devil"—as a further reminder of his vicious tendencies. But the subjects of his small kingdom were convinced that such blood lust could be found only in a human vampire. Hence, Vlad Tepes, self-proclaimed Dracula, was the basis for the legend which Stoker captured so well.

Vampirism has been traced by historians, studied by scholars, embellished by artists and writers, and feared by the superstitious. And although vampirism has, in Western culture, been associated mainly with the Transylvania region of Eastern Europe, the vampire phenomenon in one form or another is attested in all parts of the world from ancient times onward. Outside of Europe, the vampire has appeared in the ancient cultures of the Middle East and the Mediterranean, in China as well as throughout Asia, in several African cultures, and in Aztec civilization and later in Mexico. Some references are in allegedly official reports and in religious works on demonology; others occur in folklore and in literature, drama, painting, and sculpture. Clearly, the vampire was no nineteenth century European invention, but the Romantic obsession with Gothic horror certainly stimulated a spate of vampiric literature, among its other supernatural preoccupations. A short story, "The Vampyre," by John Polidori, was published in 1819. The melodrama *Les Vampires*, by Charles Nodier and Carmouche, was first produced in Paris in 1820. *Varney the Vampire, or The Feast of Blood* (authorship is disputed; either John Malcolm Rymer or Thomas Peckett Prest), a long novel, appeared in 1847. And Joseph Sheridan Le Fanu's redoubtable "Carmilla" first saw print in 1871. But it was Stoker's *Dracula,* published in 1897, that surpassed them all and remains the paragon of vampire stories even today.

Drawing primarily upon European sources, Stoker produced a terrifyingly credible tale by eliminating the inconsistencies and the contradictions common to legendary matter. Wisely avoiding some of the more outlandish explanations of vampirism, for example, Stoker portrayed the trait as transmitted from vampire to victim, who in turn became a vampire, and so on. But to evade straining credulity, Stoker required prolonged contact between vampire and victim before the victim was irrevocably enlisted in the ranks. Thus, Jonathan Harker, whose sustenance of Count Dracula was brief, recovered with no lasting ill effects. But Lucy Westenra was literally drained and consequently became a vampire herself. As a result—and given the perilous circumstances—Van Helsing was compelled to restrain forcibly Lucy's erstwhile fiancé Arthur from giving her a death-bed kiss on her frothing fanged mouth. Stoker also conceded the vampire's power to exercise a species of demonic possession, without physical contact, as the affliction of Mina Murray Harker illustrates.

In like manner, Stoker employed only the most conventional techniques for repelling vampires: garlic and the crucifix. And the requirements for vampire survival were equally simplified from the vast complexity of alternatives which accumulated in the legend. Stoker limited his vampires to nocturnal acvtivity; mandated, of course, the periodic sucking of blood (allowing for moderate stretches of hibernation or abstinence); insisted upon daylight repose in a coffin filled with Transylvania soil; and claimed vampiric invulnerability to ordinary human weapons.

Finally, Stoker's methods for the total annihilation of vampires were similarly conventional, without resort to esoteric impedimenta. He stipulated that a wooden stake be driven through the vampire's heart (although Dracula himself was dispatched with a bowie knife); that the vampire's head be cut off; and the vampire's mouth be stuffed with garlic flowers. Again the inconsistency of these remedies accounts for much of the impact of Stoker's horror story.

In fact, Stoker's recounting of the vampire legend has become the "standard version" in Western culture. Short stories and novels have spun off from the Stoker novel—all distinctly imitative and inferior; attempted sequels have been likewise unsatisfactory, never rising above the level of cheap journalism. A number of theatrical and film adaptations have been mounted. But the classic stage and screen performances of Bela Lugosi, based upon Stoker's *Dracula,* have never been equaled. Lugosi's 1932 portrayal of Dracula still spellbinds motion-picture audiences as no other production has been able to do. And in this atmosphere of at least semi-credulity, reported sightings of vampiric activity—much like reported sightings of flying saucers or unidentified flying objects—continue to the present.

In the meanwhile, Vlad Tepes's castles in Walachia and the Carpathians have been refurbished by the Rumanian government as tourist attractions, and the historical Dracula is being hailed as a national hero who strove to upgrade the moral fiber of his subjects. Thus, in many ways, Stoker's Dracula lives on to influence the present as powerfully—albeit in a different manner— as he influenced the past.

Joanne G. Kashdan

DRAGON SEED

Type of work: Novel
Author: Pearl S. Buck (1892-1973)
Type of plot: Social chronicle
Time of plot: World War II
Locale: China
First published: 1942

Principal characters:
LING TAN, a Chinese farmer
LING SAO, his wife
LAO TA,
LAO ER,
LAO SAN, and
PANSIAO, their children
ORCHID, Lao Ta's wife
JADE, Lao Er's wife
WU LIEN, Ling Tan's son-in-law
MAYLI, a mission teacher

Critique:

The plot of this novel as a social chronicle is swiftly paced and convincing until the appearance of Mayli; then the emphasis shifts to the rather improbable love affair of Mayli and Lao San. Background and character remain superior to plot. As a result, the reader absorbs an excellent impression of these people of an alien culture, through colorful details woven into the pattern of the narrative. *Dragon Seed* also tells what World War II meant to the Chinese peasantry.

The Story:

Ling Tan's family all lived together in his ancestral home. Besides Ling Tan and his wife, Ling Sao, there were three sons, Lao Ta, Lao Er, and Lao San, and a daughter, Pansiao. Lao Ta and his wife Orchid had two children. Lao Er and his wife Jade as yet had none.

Jade was a strange woman who cared little for the old rules and customs governing Chinese wives. Her free manners and frank tongue were an embarrassment to Lao Er, for the men chided him about it. Then, too, he felt as if he did not really understand his wife. One evening, after they had both heard how the Japanese had begun war in the north, they unburdened their hearts to each other,

and Lao Er accepted the fact that he was married to a woman who was not like the others. He promised to go to the city and buy her a book so that she could learn what was happening in the world.

While Lao Er was in the city, he visited Wu Lien, a merchant who had married his older sister. Some Chinese students destroyed the Japanese merchandise that Wu Lien had for sale and branded him as a traitor. When Ling Sao heard this bad news, she too went to the city. Wu Lien was sick with worry over what had happened to him; he had also heard that the Japanese had landed on the coast nearby and were pushing inland. Ling Sao comforted him as well as she could and returned home.

The next morning Ling Tan was working in his fields when he saw Japanese aircraft approaching to bomb the city. He and the other farmers watched the planes, curious and unafraid. That night Wu Lien came to his father-in-law's house seeking refuge, for his shop had been hit by a bomb. Only then did Ling Tan's family learn the meaning of what had happened that day.

The next day Ling Tan and Lao San went to the city, where they were caught in the second air raid. Gravely, Ling Tan

DRAGON SEED by Pearl S. Buck. By permission of the author, her agent David Lloyd, and the publishers, The John Day Co., Inc. Copyright, 1941, 1942, by Pearl S. Buck.

asked his family how they were going to resist this enemy. Lao Er and Jade said that they must go westward into the hills, for Jade was now with child. The rest of the family decided to stay and hold the ancestral land at all costs.

Streams of refugees passed along the road toward the west, and Lao Er and Jade joined a group of students who were moving their school inland. Lao Er promised to send word when the baby was born. Other students passed through the village and stopped to tell of the atrocities of the Japanese, but the simple farmers could not believe the stories they heard. After a month or so Ling Tan and his family could hear the roar of the Japanese guns as they approached the city. Chinese soldiers deserted to the hills, leaving the inhabitants at the mercy of the enemy. For a few days after the city was taken all was peaceful. Then some Japanese marched to the village and demanded wine and women. Ling Tan hid his family in the fields. The soldiers discovered Wu Lien's mother, who was too old and fat to flee. When they found no other women, they attacked her and killed her. Then they wrecked the house and left.

Since he knew now that no woman was safe from the Japanese, Ling Tan put all of the women of his family with the white missionary lady in the city. The men remained at the farm, except for Wu Lien. He returned to his shop in the city and advertised for Japanese business.

Meanwhile the soldiers came again to Ling Tan's house in search of women. When they found none, they attacked Lao San, the youngest son. Humiliated and filled with hatred, the boy left to join the hill people who were fighting the Japanese.

Wu Lien ingratiated himself with the conquerors and was appointed to a job in the new city government. He took his family from the mission and moved into spacious quarters provided by the Japanese.

Orchid grew bored in the mission. She thought that the city was quiet now and nothing could happen to her. One day she went for a walk. Five soldiers captured her and killed her while they satisfied their lust. When her body was returned to the mission, Ling Sao sent for Ling Tan and Lao Ta. She could no longer stay in the city. She returned to the farm with Ling Tan, Lao Ta, and the two children of Orchid and Lao Ta. Pansiao was sent westward to a mission school in the hills, where she would be safe.

A message from Lao Er announced that Jade had a son. Ling Tan sent for Lao Er and his family to come and help with the farm. Lao Er obeyed the summons, for he could be useful as a messenger between the village and the guerilla warriors in the hills. He and Jade made a secret cavern under the house where they could store arms for the villagers. Meanwhile the children of Lao Ta died of flux and fever. Despondent, he left for the hills to join Lao San. Ling Tan worked his farm as best he could and held back from the enemy as much grain as he dared.

Lao San and Lao Ta returned from the hills to hide in the secret cavern. Whenever there were no witnesses, the farmers killed Japanese soldiers and secretly buried them. Jade succeeded in poisoning many Japanese leaders at a great feast in the city. A cousin of Ling Tan went to the city and stole a radio from Wu Lien. Afterwards he was able to report to the people the progress of the war. The people took heart from the knowledge that there were others fighting the Japanese.

Lao San had become a ruthless killer and Ling Tan thought that he needed a spirited wife to tame him. Jade wrote to Pansiao, asking her to find a wife for Lao San among the girls at the mission. Pansiao told one of her teachers, the daughter of a Chinese ambassador, about her brother. This girl, Mayli, traveled to see Lao San for herself. The young people fell in love at first sight, but Mayli returned to the hills to wait for Lao San to come after her. Lao Ta also returned home with a new wife. Ling Tan's house was full again, for Jade gave birth to twin boys.

The hardships continued. Losing all hope of conquering the Japanese, Ling Tan began to brood. Then one day Lao Er took the old man to the city to hear the news from the hidden radio. They heard that England and the United States were now fighting on their side. Ling Tan wept for joy. Perhaps some day there would be an end to the war. Once again there was hope.

Further Critical Evaluation of the Work:

Pearl S. Buck's novel *Dragon Seed* was written during the early part of World War II, which partially accounts for its views on the Sino-Japanese conflict of the late 1930's. Miss Buck, the daughter of American missionaries, was raised in China, although she was born in the United States. Many of her works are about China, and she came to have a great affinity for these people. *The Good Earth,* her greatest novel, was written in 1936 about China, and became the major factor in leading her to the Nobel Prize for literature in 1938. *Dragon Seed,* though similar in scope, never demonstrated the power of that great first work. It provides a colorful background to the Chinese people during the Japanese occupation of China prior to World War II, but the story is not a profound one.

The basic plot involves the common people's struggle against the oppression of a tyrannical regime. This is a typical war-oriented story line and one which can only rise above the commonplace if it has good characterization and excellent writing. Pearl Buck's characters are real, which is the saving grace of the book, and her writing style is lucid; thus, readers accepted *Dragon Seed* with fervor, and it was a nationwide best seller. However, the book is seriously limited by its polemical topicality, which borders on the propagandistic. It has not survived the test of time as has her earlier work, *The Good Earth.*

Much of *Dragon Seed*, particularly near the end when great hopes are raised after the announcement that the United States has entered the war on the side of China, is an expression of war-time patriotism, and as such limits the lasting value of the book. One excellent aspect of the book, however, is the characterization of Ling Sao, the female protagonist. Her strong will was atypical for a woman from China, at least in popular fiction. Traditionally Chinese women have been portrayed as silent, subservient creatures. This is not the case in the books of Pearl Buck, however, where females are usually the stronger and therefore deeper characters.

DRAMATIC MONOLOGUES AND LYRICS OF BROWNING

Author: Robert Browning (1812-1889)
First published: Dramatic Lyrics, 1842; *Dramatic Romances and Lyrics,* 1845; *Men and Women,* 1855

Much of Browning's finest writing was done during his thirties, years which comprise most of the poems in the volumes *Dramatic Lyrics, Dramatic Lyrics and Romances,* and *Men and Women.* The intentions and procedures of these three volumes are similar, so that most often one's comments on the first two hold good for the third as well. In fact, Browning himself in a later collected edition reshuffled many of these poems, breaking down the divisions between individual books but preserving always the dominating premise that the poems should be, as he said, "though often Lyric in expression, always Dramatic in principle, and so many utterances of so many imaginary persons, not mine." During his middle years we see Browning striving to write poems at once less sentimental and more objective than those of his early hero, Shelley: he develops his own form of the dramatic monologue in the attempt to overcome subjectivity and vagueness, and his success here is in the nature of an overcompensation. The poems in these volumes, "always Dramatic in principle," are brilliant but somehow chilly.

Browning's verse-play, *Pippa Passes,* published in 1841, immediately precedes *Dramatic Lyrics* and by its superb rendering of the spirit of Italy—a country which is for Browning always the dialectical counterpart of England, a kind of anti-England—the play foreshadows the skeptical attitude conveyed by the poems. In "The Bishop Orders His Tomb at Saint Praxed's Church," in "My Last Duchess," and in the immense narrative poem *The Ring and the Book* the poet was later to draw implicit and explicit contrasts between contemporary England and Renaissance Italy. His habitual approach is in this way argumentative and skeptical, the counterbalancing of opposing countries, times, sexes, and beliefs

which is suggested even by many of the titles in these volumes: "Meeting at Night" against "Parting at Morning," "Love in a Life" against "Life in a Love," "The Italian in England" against "The Englishman in Italy." The method permits Browning to end an elegant dialogue between two Venetian lovers, "In a Gondola," with a vicious stabbing. Alternately, he can present the interior monologue of a warped person, allowing the character to condemn himself by his (or her) words: as is the case of the female poisoner, crossed in love, in "The Laboratory," or the deranged murderer who speaks in "Porphyria's Lover." Perhaps the best of these interior monologues is the "Soliloquy of the Spanish Cloister," in which a splenetic monk grumbles against his abbot:

> GR-R-R—there go, my heart's abhorrence!
> Water your damn flower-pots, do!
> If hate killed men, Brother Lawrence,
> God's blood, would not mine kill you!
> What? your myrtle-bush wants trimming?
> Oh, that rose has prior claims—
> Needs its leaden vase filled brimming?
> Hell dry you up with its flames!

The lines are characteristic: not only does the voice contradict the speaker's appearance and vocation, but the very exclamations and dashes render the punctuation histrionic and serve to define a particular habit of mind.

The monologues which imply a listener are psychologically more complex. "My Last Duchess" and "The Bishop Orders His Tomb at Saint Praxed's Church," appeared in 1842 and 1845, respectively, and are models, in these earlier volumes, of the kind of irony and immediacy which the dramatic method at its best is capable of generating:

That's my last Duchess painted on
the wall,
Looking as if she were alive, I call
That piece a wonder, now: Fra Pan-
dolf's hands
Worked busily a day, and there she
stands.

Browning consciously follows Donne in beginning poems with arresting first lines. Here, much of the Duke's ruthlessness is conveyed at the very outset by his exquisitely casual reference, with the possessive "my", to his dead wife, by his evident pleasure at being able now to consider her as an art object, not as an intractable life-study:

> She had
> A heart—how shall I say?—too soon
> made glad,
> Too easily impressed; she liked what-
> e'er
> She looked on, and her looks went
> everywhere.

Subtly, Browning manages to turn the Duke's criticism of his former wife, his specious yet elegantly phrased "how shall I say?" claim that she was too much alive, too indiscriminately joyous, into an exposure of his own monstrous pride in "a nine-hundred-years-old name." Flexible couplets with unobtrusive rhymes are the fit medium for his self-justifying logic and for the vicious sweetness which informs even his dealings with his present auditor, the envoy of the woman who will probably be Ferrara's next Duchess ("Will't please you rise?" addressed to the envoy is a command in the guise of a question). By tracing a logic of association in the blank verse of "The Bishop Orders His Tomb at Saint Praxed's Church," Browning focuses in a similar way on an incident of crucial importance for the self-revelation of his title character, the delirious churchman whose dying words concern pagan luxury and wordly pomp rather than Christian salvation.

Two dramatic monologues from the *Men and Women* volume, "Fra Lippo Lippi" and "How it Strikes a Contemporary," are explicitly concerned with aesthetics and the process of composition in poetry and painting. If we read between the lines of these poems, looking for the passages which most accord with Browning's actual practice, it is clear that he believes the best art is a universalizing of individual experience; and that to this end the poet or painter must be first of all curious, pre-eminently a noticer. Indeed, the verbs "notice," "mark," "see" are common in Browning's dramatic lyrics, where to notice a unique scene or situation is to exert an individual consciousness, and where to notice intensely is the first step in separating the apparent from the real and in beginning to write, a book that in words from *The Ring and the Book*, "shall mean beyond the facts." Accordingly, a collection of "so many utterances of so many imaginary persons" would escape the charge of subjectivity, yet taken as a whole it would convey a meaning beyond the mathematical sum of the dramatic lyric voices involved. These speakers reveal themselves far beyond what the occasion warrants, and the poems are essentially more dramatic and romantic than lyric. Browning takes definite pleasure in the vivid selfhood of his speakers, and pleasure as well in the multiple vision of the artist who can create and embody conflicting viewpoints while remaining himself uncommitted.

Browning's interest in conflict, incongruity, even in the grotesque, has its natural complement in his dramatic technique. The range of styles and effects is as various as the range of complexity among his characters. "An Englishman in Italy" exhibits a cataloguing, descriptive style, for instance in the request that one observe a fishing skiff from Amalfi, with alien English eyes watching

> . . . Our fisher arrive,
> And pitch down his basket before us,
> All trembling alive
> With pink and gray jellies, your sea-
> fruit;
> You touch the strange lumps,
> And mouths gape there, eyes open, all
> manner
> Of horns and lumps. . . .

In "The Pied Piper of Hamelin," and in "Incident of the French Camp," Browning manages well two very different kinds of narrative. The mode of "Pictor Ignotus," an early monologue which looks ahead to "Andrea Del Sarto" and "Fra Lippo Lippi," is one of ratiocination, following a proud artist's ebb and flux of thought:

O human faces, hath it split, my cup?
   What did ye give me that I have not
     saved?
Nor will I say I have not dreamed
   (how well!)
Of going—I, in each new picture,
   —forth,
As, making new hearts beat and bos-
   oms swell,
   To Pope or Kaiser, East, West,
     South, or North. . . .

There is also the lyric outcry of "Home-Thoughts, From Abroad," with its famous lines, "Oh, to be in England/Now that April's there." Browning's metrical range is diverse and experimental as well; in "Boot and Saddle" and "How They Brought the Good News From Ghent to Aix" he brilliantly turns the difficult anapestic meter to his own purposes, for both poems succeed in conveying by a kind of metrical imitation the excitement of a fast ride on a horse ("I galloped, Dirck galloped, we galloped all three"). Finally, it accords well with Browning's perspectivism, his prizing of unique objects and irreducible selfhood, that he should have created a new metrical or stanzaic form for almost every separate poem.

These earlier poems are a true representation of Browning in that they show him to be intellectually ingenious but no philosopher; an experimenter with both social and literary norms but by no standard a Victorian radical; a writer aware of evil and violence, but for the most part a cautious optimist. The later poems and *The Ring and the Book* bear out one's sense that his major achievement is in fact in these dramatic poems of his middle years, where the view of truth as relative is first impressively demonstrated in dramatic monologues. There is, of course, something deeply subversive in the notion that different points of view are equally valid, in the oblique yet damaging criticisms of Victorian sexual and religious conventions conveyed in some of these poems, in the attacks on bureaucracy such as the telling poem written against the "official" Wordsworth, "The Lost Leader." The dramatic monologue, at once objective and subjective, public and private in its methods, was the main vehicle used by Browning for criticism of Victorian society and manners; the monologue permitted ethical pronouncements to be made through someone else's voice, as it were, ventriloquially.

Thus in "My Last Duchess," in "Bishop Blougram's Apology," in many of his best poems Browning is a public writer with disturbing private tendencies: he never pushes exposure or criticism past the point of pleasure, and his work as a whole gives an effect of hard impersonal brilliance. Browning was typically a man of his age in believing that the poet was a moral agent in his society, a "Maker-see" whose concerns were norms and value, the discovery and presentation of a heightened reality. Yet in wishing to write poems which would mean "beyond the facts" he settled on a method which from the start excluded personal directness. Because all his sincerities and critiques had to be conveyed indirectly, these poems for all their peculiar triumphs will be found to lack the keynote of passionate personal despair which is the most profound theme in the finest Victorian poetry.

DRAMATIS PERSONAE

Type of work: Poetry
Author: Robert Browning (1812-1889)
First published: 1864

When Robert Browning published *Dramatis Personae* he was just beginning to gain a measure of general esteem, both in the eyes of the public and of the critics. The year before its publication a three-volume collection of his earlier works had sold moderately well. *Dramatis Personae* added considerably to his popularity, and a second edition was called for before 1864 was out. It is ironic that this volume, the first that can be said to have achieved popular success, contained the first clear signs of the decline of his poetic powers.

It was his first volume of new poems since *Men and Women,* published in 1855. In the interval the pattern of Browning's life had undergone complete transformation. On June 29, 1861, his wife had died. They had made their home in Italy; after her death, Browning returned to England. For years he had been virtually out of touch with the currents of English thought. Now he plunged into a society that was perplexed by what it had learned and troubled by what it had come to doubt. Browning was soon personally involved in the intellectual and religious controversies of the day.

The changes in his life produced changes in his poetry. His love poems, understandably, became more melancholy. Many of the poems in *Men and Women* had had historical settings; all but a few of those in *Dramatis Personae* have contemporary settings. Even when he gives his version of an old tale, as in "Gold Hair: A Legend of Pornic," he manages to work in discussion of nineteenth century problems. In general, he was becoming more argumentative, more of a preacher. He still preferred the dramatic mode of utterance but the voice of the poet is often heard behind the dramatic mask.

Two of the important themes in the volume are love and death, frequently juxtaposed. The death of Mrs. Browning may have been an influence on his choice of subjects, but it should not be overestimated; a number of the poems antedate her death. "Prospice," however, written in the fall of 1861, is clearly Browning speaking in his own voice. It is an open affirmation of belief in immortality. When death ends his life, he says, as it has ended hers,

> O thou soul of my soul! I shall clasp
> thee again,
> And with God be the rest!

In "Too Late" another man grieves over a dead woman, but with a difference. He had never expressed his love for her and now suffers not grief alone but regret at having missed his opportunity. It is a familiar theme in Browning, love unfulfilled through negligence, expressed earlier in "The Statue and the Bust," and, elsewhere in *Dramatis Personae,* in "Youth and Art," and in "Dîs Aliter Visum; or Le Byron de Nos Jours." If "Too Late" has an autobiographical element it is of an inverse order: Browning, unlike the speaker, had not missed his opportunity for love. The speaker of "Too Late" says it would have been better to

> . . . have burst like a thief
> And borne you away to a rock for us
> two
> In a moment's horror, bright, bloody,
> and brief,
> Then changed to myself again . . . .

Browning, a sedentary man, had stepped out of character once in his life, when he had spirited a middle-aged poetess off to Italy.

Two of the finest poems in *Dramatis Personae*, also love poems, are "Confessions" and "James Lee's Wife" (originally called, misleadingly, "James Lee"). One reason why they are perennially satisfying is that, unlike many poems in the volume, they are free from topical controversy. In "Confessions," one of Browning's shortest dramatic monologues, a dying man recalls, with satisfaction, a love affair of long ago:

How sad and bad and mad it was—
But then, how it was sweet!

In "James Lee's Wife," as in Tennyson's "Maud," the story is that of the death of love. It is a restrained, dignified cry of heartbreak, a skillfully wrought dramatic lyric, the desolate scene and the dying year serving as mute echoes of the speaker's mood.

Of the eighteen poems originally grouped in *Dramatis Personae* (two occasional pieces were later added: "Deaf and Dumb" and "Eurydice to Orpheus"), few are not cluttered with argument. Of these, none besides "James Lee's Wife" and "Confessions" is particularly memorable. "The Worst of It" is mawkish; "May and Death" is pleasant, but slight; "A Face" and "A Likeness" are insignificant. It should not be assumed, however, that the remaining poems, those which do serve as vehicles for Browning's beliefs, can all be dismissed as inferior poems.

"Caliban upon Setebos," for example, is not only a statement of Victorian religious belief; it is as well one of Browning's successful poems of the grotesque. But the controversial element is certainly there, as indicated by the subtitle: "Natural Theology in the Island." Browning is satirizing those who, relying too closely on their own resources, posit God in their own image. And Caliban is not merely a . figure taken from Shakespeare's *The Tempest*; he is also a post-Darwinian figure, a poet's version of the evolutionary "missing link." The topical references in the poem do not, however, prevent it from being rated one of Browning's best dramatic monologues.

"A Death in the Desert," another dramatic monologue, is perhaps more seriously marred by its attempts to promote certain religious ideas. Proponents of the "higher criticism" of the Bible—Strauss in *Leben Jesu* and *New Life of Jesus*, Renan in *La Vie de Jésus*—had attempted, among other things, to prove that the Gospel of St. John had not been written, as had been assumed, by the beloved disciple. Browning's poem, an imaginative re-creation of John's death, is an argument for the authenticity of the Gospel. It contains a number of Browning's religious positions (e.g., a theory about miracles). The fact that it is the dying Apostle who gives expression to these ideas is anachronistic: many of them are clearly indigenous to the middle of the nineteenth century. As a result, the dramatic effect of the poem is appreciably undercut.

The longest poem in *Dramatis Personae*, "Mr. Sludge, 'The Medium,'" its 1525 lines comprising three-eighths of the entire volume, is more successful. It is one of Browning's liveliest character studies, not unworthy of comparison with the great dramatic monologues in *Men and Women*. But it too is tinged by Browning's growing fondness for argument. Browning satirizes spiritualism, quite a fad in the mid-nineteenth century England, by portraying a fraudulent medium whose character is based on an American, Daniel Dunglass Home, whom Browning had met. Moreover, Mr. Sludge, the speaker, gives voice, although inconsistently, to some of Browning's characteristic religious ideas. The propagandizing is done rather subtly, however, and does not strike the reader as being obtrusive.

"Rabbi Ben Ezra" and "Abt Vogler" are similar to "Mr. Sludge" in being good poems as well as statements of opinion with regard to contemporary questions. The first eight sections of "Abt Vogler" are a brilliant tour de force, a lyrical evocation of the exalted spirit of a musician improvising at the keyboard of an organ. The last four sections are not quite so successful, being too flat an exposition of one of Browning's pet theories, the "philosophy of the imperfect":

> On the earth the broken arcs; in the
> heaven, a perfect round.
> And what is our failure here but a
> triumph's evidence
> For the fullness of the days?

But the argumentative element does not predominate; sound and sense are not at odds but in harmony with each other. It was one of Browning's favorites, among his own poems, and it has since been one of the favorites of his readers.

"Rabbi Ben Ezra," another of Browning's most popular poems, is perhaps somewhat less successful than "Abt Vogler." It is unsurpassed, however, as an expression of Browning's own belief in God. Some have suggested that he intended it to be an answer to the hedonism of Edward FitzGerald's *The Rubáiyát of Omar Khayyám*, but if this is true it is less than obvious in the poem itself. The ideas contained in it are typical of Browning. He says, for example:

> What I aspired to be,
> And was not, comforts me. . . .

We are reminded of Andrea del Sarto's dictum in *Men and Women*: "A man's reach should exceed his grasp." Above all, "Rabbi Ben Ezra" is a cogent presentation of Browning's famous and frequently, if too facilely, maligned optimism.

"Gold Hair: A Story of Pornic" is a curious and troubling poem. The body of it relates an old story about the death of a young girl. She had been regarded virtually as a saint; years after her death, however, it is learned that she had been interested in earthly treasure far more than in a heavenly one. Some have objected to the story itself but that, though macabre and a bit cynical, is really unobjectionable. What ruins the poem are the last three stanzas Browning has tacked on:

> Why I deliver this horrible verse?
> As the text of a sermon, which now
> I preach:
> Evil or good may be better or worse
> In the human heart, but the mixture
> of each
> Is a marvel and a curse.

> The candid incline to surmise of late
> That the Christian faith may be false,
> I find;
> For our Essays-and-Reviews' debate
> Begins to tell on the public mind,
> And Colenso's words have weight:

> I still, to suppose it true, for my part,
> See reasons and reasons; this, to
> begin:
> 'Tis the faith that launched point-blank
> her dart
> At the head of a lie—taught Original
> Sin,
> The Corruption of Man's Heart.

Browning makes no bones about his intention to preach, and the value of his stories begins to decline as they become more and more pointedly the texts for sermons.

"Apparent Failure," a lesser poem, again finds Browning speaking in his own voice. The story is merely the occasion for moral instruction; it is in Browning's own words, "the sermon's text."

The final poem in *Dramatis Personae*, "Epilogue," gives brief expression to three religious positions current when Browning wrote. The "First Speaker, *as David*," sums up the High Church, ritualistic position; the "Second Speaker, *as Renan*," expressed the skepticism of one familiar with the "higher criticism." The "Third Speaker," Browning himself, answers the first two, calling ceremony unnecessary and belief tenable. Browning's belief, not unlike Tennyson's, is sustained by personal feeling rather than by a process of the reason. What is really significant about the poem is that it makes no pretense of being dramatic. It sets the pattern for the bulk of his later poems, for Browning's values have changed; controversy now means more to him than writing poems, for poetry has become the vehicle for argument. Inevitably, poetry suffers, as some of the poems in this volume and virtually all of the later poems, save *The Ring and the Book,* clearly testify.

DREAM OF THE RED CHAMBER

Type of work: Novel
Author: Tsao Hsueh chin (c. 1715-1763), with a continuation by Kao Ou
Type of plot: Domestic chronicle
Time of plot: c. 1729-1737
Locale: Peking
First published: 1792

Principal characters:

MADAME SHIH (the MATRIARCH), the living ancestress of the Chia family
CHIA SHEH, her older son, master of the Yungkuofu, or western compound
MADAME HSING, his wife
CHIA LIEN, their son
HSI-FENG (PHOENIX), Chia Lien's wife
YING-CHUN (WELCOME SPRING), Chia-Sheh's daughter by a concubine
CHIA CHENG, the Matriarch's younger son
MADAME WANG, his wife
PAO-YU, their son
CARDINAL SPRING, their daughter, an Imperial concubine
CHIA HUAN, Chia Cheng's son by his concubine
TAN-CHUN (QUEST SPRING), Chia Cheng's daughter by his concubine
TAI-YU (BLACK JADE), the Matriarch's granddaughter, an orphan
HSIANG-YUN (RIVER MIST), the Matriarch's grandniece
PAO-CHAI (PRECIOUS VIRTUE), Madame Wang's niece
HSUEH PAN, Precious Virtue's brother, a libertine
CHIA GEN, master of the Ningkuofu, or eastern compound
YU-SHIH, his wife
CHIA JUNG, their son
CHIN-SHIH, Chia Jung's wife
HSI-CHUN (Compassion Spring), Chia Gen's sister
HSI-JEN (PERVADING FRAGRANCE),
CHING-WEN (Bright Design), and
SHEH-YUEH (Musk Moon), Pao-yu's serving maids

Critique:

Chinese scholars and readers consider the eighteenth century *Hung Lou Meng* (*Dream of the Red Chamber*) the greatest of their novels. Published anonymously in 1792, and for a long time a matter of scholarly reference and dispute, the book is now ascribed to Tsao Hsueh-chin, who completed the first eighty chapters before his death in 1763, and Kao Ou, who added forty more as an expansion of Tsao Hsueh-chin's original notes. There is internal evidence to show that Tsao Hsueh-chin may have drawn on his own experience and family background in creating the character of Pao-yu, the pampered younger son of an aristocratic and powerful family in gradual financial decline at the time of his birth. Like Pao-yu. Tsao Hsueh-chin was petted by his family and spoiled by luxury; unlike Pao-yu, he failed to pass the Imperial Examinations which would have raised him to some official position. *Dream of the Red Chamber* is within a single framework a long and extremely complicated domestic chronicle—the novel contains more than four hundred characters—that is both a lively comedy of manners and a realistic fable of moral seriousness. The title is capable of expressing several meanings. In the view of Professor Chi-Chen Wang, it may be trans-

DREAM OF THE RED CHAMBER by Tsao Hsueh-chin. Translated by Chi-Chen Wang. Published by Twayne Publishers. By permission of the translator. Copyright, 1958, by Chi-Chen Wang.

lated as "Dreams of Young Maidens," since the younger women of the Chia clan lived in the traditional "red chamber" of a palace compound like those which housed wealthy or aristocratic Chinese families until fairly recent times. The term may also be interpreted as a reference to the metaphor "Red Dust," which in Buddhist usage is a designation for the material world with all its pleasures, follies, and vices. Manuscript copies of the first eighty chapters of the novel were apparently circulated before the publication of the complete 120-chapter version in 1792.

The Story:

Ages ago, in the realm of the Great Void, the Goddess Nügua whose task it was to repair the Dome of Heaven rejected a stone which she found unsuited to her purpose. Because she had touched it, however, the stone became endowed with life, so that thereafter it could move as it pleased. In time it chanced on a crimson flower in the region of the Ethereal, where each day it watered the tender blossoms with drops of dew. At last the plant was incarnated as a beautiful young girl. Remembering the stone that had showered the frail plant with refreshing dew, she prayed that in her human form she might repay it with the gift of her tears. Her prayers were to be granted, for the stone, too, had been given life in the Red Dust of earthly existence. At his birth the piece of jade was miraculously found in the mouth of Pao-yu, a younger son of the rich and powerful house of Chia, which by imperial favor had been raised to princely eminence several generations before.

At the time of Pao-yu's birth the two branches of the Chia family lived in great adjoining compounds of palaces, pavilions, and parks on the outskirts of Peking. The Matriarch, an old woman of great honor and virtue, ruled as the living ancestress over both establishments. Chia Ging, the prince of the Ningkuofu, had retired to a Taoist temple some time

before, and his son Chia Gen was master in his place. The master of the Yungkuofu was Chia Sheh, the older son of the Matriarch. Chia Cheng, her younger son and Pao-yu's father, also lived with his family and attendants in the Yungkuofu. A man of upright conduct and strict Confucian morals, he was a contrast to the other members of his family, who had grown lax and corrupt through enervating luxury and the abuse of power.

Pao-yu, the possessor of the miraculous jade stone and a boy of great beauty and quick wit, was his grandmother's favorite. Following her example, the other women of the family—his mother, aunts, sisters, cousins, and waiting maids—doted on the boy and pampered him at every opportunity, with the result that he grew up girlish and weak, a lover of rouge pots and feminine society. The traits of effeminacy he displayed infuriated and disgusted his austere father, who treated the boy with undue severity. As a result, Pao-yu kept as much as possible to the women's quarters.

His favorite playmates were his two cousins, Black Jade and Precious Virtue. Black Jade, a granddaughter of the Matriarch, had come to live in the Yungkuofu after her mother's death. She was a lovely, delicate girl of great poetic sensitivity, and she and Pao-yu were drawn to each other by bonds of sympathy and understanding that seemed to stretch back into some unremembered past. Precious Virtue, warm-hearted and practical, was the niece of Pao-yu's mother. She was a girl as good as her brother Hsueh Pan was vicious, for he was always involving the family in scandal because of his pursuit of maidens and young boys. Pao-yu's favorite waiting maid was Pervading Fragrance. She slept in his chamber at night, and it was with her that he followed a dream vision and practiced the play of cloud and rain.

When word came that Black Jade's father was ill and wished to see her before his death, the Matriarch sent the girl home under the escort of her cousin Chia Lien. During their absence Chin-shih the daughter-in-law of Chia Gen, died after a long illness. By judicious bribery the dead woman's husband, Chia Jung, was made a chevalier of the Imperial Dragon Guards in order that she might be given a more elaborate funeral. During the period of mourning Chia Gen asked Phoneix, Chia Lien's wife, to take charge of the Ningkuofu household. This honor gave Phoenix a position of responsibility and power in both palaces. From that time on, although she continued to appear kind and generous, she secretly became greedy for money and power. She began to accept bribes, tamper with the household accounts, and lend money at exorbitant rates of interest.

One day a great honor was conferred on the Chias. Cardinal Spring, Pao-yu's sister and one of the emperor's concubines, was advanced to the rank of an Imperial consort of the second degree. Later, when it was announced that she would pay a visit of filial respect to her parents, the parks of the two compounds were at great expense transformed into magnificent pleasure grounds, called the Takuanyuan, in honor of the consort's visit. Later, at Cardinal Spring's request, the pavilions in the Takuanyuan were converted into living quarters for the young women of the family. Pao-yu also went there to live, passing his days in idle occupations and writing verses. His pavilion was close to that of Black Jade, who had returned to the Yungkuofu after her father's death.

Pao-yu had a half-brother, Chia Huan. His mother, jealous of the true-born son, paid a sorceress to bewitch the boy and Phoenix, whom she also hated. Both were seized with fits of violence and wild delirium. Pao-yu's coffin had already been made when a Buddhist monk and a lame Taoist priest suddenly appeared and restored the power of the spirit stone. Pao-yu and Phoenix recovered.

A short time later a maid was accused of trying to seduce Pao-yu. Dismissed, she drowned herself. About the same time Chia Cheng was told that his son had turned the love of a young actor away from a powerful patron. Calling his son a degenerate, Chia Cheng almost caused Pao-yu's death by the severity of the beating which the angry father administered.

As Phoenix became more shrewish at home, Chia Lien dreamed of taking another wife. Having been almost caught in one infidelity, he was compelled to exercise great caution in taking a concubine. Phoenix learned about the secret marriage, however, and by instigating claims advanced by the girl's former suitor she drove the wretched concubine to suicide.

Black Jade, always delicate, became more sickly. Sometimes she and Pao-yu quarreled, only to be brought toegther again by old ties of affection and understanding. The gossip of the servants was that the Matriarch would marry Pao-yu to either Black Jade or Precious Virtue. While possible marriage plans were being talked about, a maid found in the Takuanyuan a purse embroidered with an indecent picture. This discovery led to a search of all the pavilions, and it was revealed that one of the maids was involved in a secret love affair. Suspicion also fell on Bright Design, one of Pao-yu's maids, and she was dismissed. Proud and easily hurt, she died not long afterward. Pao-yu became even moodier and more depressed after her death. Outraged by the search, Precious Virtue left the park and went to live with her mother.

A begonia tree near Pao-yu's pavilion bloomed out of season. This event was interpreted as a bad omen, for Pao-yu lost his spirit stone and sank into a state of complete lethargy. In an effort to revive his spirits the Matriarch and his parents decided to marry him at once to Precious Virtue rather than to Black Jade, who continued to grow frailer each day. Pao-yu was allowed to believe, however, that Black Jade was to be his wife. Black Jade, deeply grieved, died shortly after the ceremony. Knowing nothing of the deception that had been practiced, she felt that she had failed Pao-yu and that he had been unfaithful to her. So the flower returned to the Great Void.

Suddenly a series of misfortunes overwhelmed the Chias as their deeds of graft and corruption came to light. When bailiffs took possession of the two compounds, the usury Phoenix had practiced was disclosed. Chia Gen and Chia Sheh were arrested and sentenced to banishment. The Matriarch, who took upon herself the burden of her family's guilt and surrendered her personal treasures for expenses and fines, became ill and died. During her funeral services robbers looted the compound and later returned to carry off Exquisite Jade, a pious nun. Phoenix died also, neglected by those she had dominated in her days of power. Through the efforts of powerful friends, however, the complete ruin of the family was averted, and Chia Cheng was restored to his official post.

But it was the despised son who in the end became the true redeemer of his family's honor and fortunes. After a Buddhist monk had returned his lost stone, Pao-yu devoted himself earnestly to his studies and passed the Imperial Examinations with such brilliance that he stood in seventh place on the list of successful candidates. So impressed was the emperor that he wished to have the young scholar serve at court. But Pao-yu was nowhere to be found. The tale was that he became a bodhisattva and disappeared in the company of a Buddhist monk and a Taoist priest.

Further Critical Evaluation of the Work:

A pattern of downfall dominates *The Dream of the Red Chamber,* a book which is a realistic novel of manners as well as a metaphysical allegory.

On the metaphysical level, the stone and the flower, originally located in the Ethereal, suffer a fall when they enter earthly reality in the Red Dust. Here the novel may be read as an allegory endorsing a Taoist-Buddhist system of other-worldly values (represented by the mysteriously recurring priest and monk) and rejecting the this-worldly view of Confucianism (represented by Chia Cheng). Interestingly enough, this novel's critique of feudalist and Confucian China has won praise from Marxist readers.

The Ethereal stone's fortunes translate into a novel of manners when the stone falls into earthly existence as the protagonist, Chia Pao-yu. In this mode, the novel becomes, through its portrayal of the Chia family, a brilliantly realistic document of upper-class life during the Ching dynasty. It encompasses financial affairs and sexual aberrations, fraternal jealousies and tragic suicides. The Chia fortunes reach their apogee when Cardinal Spring becomes the Emperor's concubine. The Takuanyuan Garden, built to honor Cardinal Spring, symbolizes these halcyon days; it becomes the domain of the younger Chia generation led by Pao-yu. Here their way of life is carefree, innocent, almost Edenic. But, just as Pao-yu must grow into adulthood, so evil invades this Eden. The fall begins when an indecent purse is found. A general search ensues, scandals surface, a tragic death results. Analogous disasters overtake the family. Their financial dealings incur the Emperor's displeasure; Imperial Guards ransack the Chia compound. Then bandits raid the garden itself.

Finally, Pao-yu chooses to deny the folly of this world and join the Buddhist priest and the Taoist monk journeying presumably to the Ethereal.

To Western readers, this novel will seem episodic; Chinese novels, however, did not aim to tell a particular story but to weave a rich tapestry of life. This latter purpose Tsao achieves brilliantly, and his novel remains widely appreciated for its skillful interweaving of philosophical allegory with unblinking realism.

DRINK

Type of work: Novel
Author: Émile Zola (1840-1902)
Type of plot: Naturalism
Time of plot: Second half of the nineteenth century
Locale: Paris
First published: 1877

Principal characters:
GERVAISE, a laundress
COUPEAU, a roofer, her husband
LANTIER, her lover and the father of her first two children
ADÈLE, Lantier's mistress
GOUJET, a neighbor secretly in love with Gervaise
NANA, the daughter of Gervaise and Coupeau
VIRGINIE, Adèle's sister

Critique:

Drink belongs to the series of the Rougon-Macquart in which Zola attempted to apply the methods of the experimental sciences to the social novel. This particular novel depicts with an extremely cruel precision the destructive effects of alcoholism among workers. At the time of publication it was received either with enthusiasm or with indignation, never with indifference. Actually, Drink might well be the one of Zola's novels in which there is the least prejudice and where the bare document is the most effective. Zola's visionary imagination communicates an intense life to the social group he describes as a whole; thus, a certain poetry evolves from the atmosphere of fatality in Drink, and it is this quality which makes the reading bearable.

The Story:

All night Gervaise had been waiting for her lover, Lantier, to come back to their quarters in Paris. When he finally came home, he treated her brutally and did not display the least affection toward Claude and Étienne, their two children. He stretched out on the bed and sent Gervaise off to the laundry where she worked.

When she was thirteen, Gervaise had left her country town and her family to follow Lantier; she was only fourteen when Étienne was born. Her family had been cruel to her, but until recently Lan-

tier had treated her rather kindly. Gervaise knew that Lantier had come under the influence of the dram shop and at the same time of Adèle, a pretty prostitute.

Gervaise herself was rather pretty, but she had a slight limp which, when she was tired, became worse; the hard life she had lived also had put its mark on her face, although she was only twenty-two. She would have been perfectly happy working hard for her own home and a decent life for her children, but all she had ever known was endless hardship and insecurity.

At the laundry she found some relief in confiding her story to Madame Boche, an older woman who had become her friend. Suddenly the children came running in with word that Lantier had deserted the three of them to go away with Adèle and that he had taken with him everything they owned.

Gervaise's first thought was for her children, and she wondered what would become of them. Soon, however she was roused in anger by the insults of Virginie, Adèle's sister; Virginie had come to the laundry for the sadistic pleasure of watching how Gervaise would take the triumph of her rival. Gervaise was quite frail and much smaller than Virginie; nevertheless she jumped toward her, full of rage. A struggle followed, in which the two women used pieces of laundry equipment and wet clothes to beat each other. Surprisingly, Gervaise, who had given all her strength, came out victorious. Virginie was never to forgive her.

Madame Fauconnier, proprietress of a laundry, gave Gervaise work in her establishment. There she earned just enough to provide for herself and her children. Another person interested in Gervaise was Coupeau, a roofer who knew all about her unhappy life. He would have liked to have her live with him. Gervaise preferred to devote herself entirely to her two small boys, but one day, when Coupeau proposed marriage to her, she was overcome by emotion and accepted him.

The situation was not very promising at first because the couple had no money. Coupeau's sister and brother-in-law, who were as miserly as they were prosperous, openly disapproved of his marriage. Slowly, perseverance in hard work made it possible for the Coupeaus to lead a decent life and even to put a little money aside. Gervaise had quite a reputation as a laundress and she often dreamed of owning her own shop. A little girl, Nana, was born to the couple four years later. Gervaise resumed working soon afterward.

This good fortune could not last. While he was working on a roof, Nana diverted her father's attention for a split second and he fell. Gervaise, refusing to let him be taken to the hospital, insisted on caring for him at home. Coupeau somehow survived, but his recovery was very slow. What was worse, inactivity had a bad effect on him. He had no more ambition, not even that of supporting his family. He also went more and more often to the dram shop.

Meanwhile, Gervaise was preparing to give up her dream of a little shop of her own when Goujet, a neighbor secretly in love with her, insisted that she borrow the five hundred francs he offered her as a gesture of friendship. She opened her shop and soon had it running quite well.

Goujet's money was never returned. Instead, the family's debts kept pro-gressively increasing, for Coupeau remained idle and continued his drinking. Gervaise herself had become accustomed to a few small luxuries, and she was not as thrifty as she had once been. Actually, she still felt quite confident that she would be able soon to meet her obligations; she had a very good reputation in the whole neighborhood.

At this point, Virginie returned, pretending that she had forgotten the fight in the laundry. Gervaise was a little startled at first to discover that her old enemy was going to be her neighbor once more. Being unprejudiced, however, she had no objection to being on friendly terms with Virginie.

Then Lantier came back. When Gervaise heard from Virginie that he had deserted Adèle and had been seen again in the neighborhood, she had been badly frightened. So far, however, her former lover had made no attempt to see her and she had forgotten her fears.

Lantier had waited to make a spectacular entrance. He chose to appear in the middle of a birthday party that Gervaise was giving. Most unexpectedly, Coupeau, who by that time was continuously drunk, invited him in. During the weeks that followed the two men became drinking companions. Later on, Lantier suggested that he might live and board with the Coupeaus. Gervaise's husband had reached such a state of degeneration that he welcomed the idea.

Although the agreement was that Lantier was to pay his share of the expenses, he never kept his promise, and Gervaise found herself with two men to support instead of one. Furthermore, Lantier had completely taken over the household and was running it as he pleased. Still a charming seducer, he was extremely popular with the women of the neighborhood.

Gervaise herself began to degenerate. Disgusted by her husband, she could not find the strength to refuse the embraces of her former lover. Before long her work suffered from such a state of affairs, and eventually she lost the shop. Virginie bought it and, at the same time, won the favors of Lantier.

Meanwhile, Nana had almost grown up, and she was placed as an apprentice in a flower shop. When she deicded to leave home for the streets. Gervaise gave up all interest in life and joined Coupeau in the dram shop. After he finally died of delirium tremens, she tried walking the streets, but nobody would have her, wretched as she was. Goujet's timid efforts to help her were useless. Completely worn out by all the demands that had been made on her, she died alone.

Further Critical Evaluation of the Work:

Even if Zola had never written *Drink,* his stature among the pantheon of French writers would have been secure. Only Balzac could rival Zola for sheer literary fecundity. Balzac's epic Human Comedy is continued in spirit in Zola's meticulous, multi-volume chronicle of the trials and tribulations of the Rougon-Macquart family. Zola's fame was guaranteed not only by the volume of works produced but also by the subject matter of the French working classes.

In *Drink,* the author again directed his scalpel-like pen to the most bruised spot on the French social body, the impoverished urban working class. Zola's surgical gaze left no part of the wound unexamined. Indeed, *Drink* is perhaps Zola's most severe and hopeless diagnosis of French society. Trapped by a mean environment as well as by genetic proclivities toward alcohol, the heroine of the story proves no match for the degrading life Zola made her lead.

Zola's bleak depiction of French society stemmed from two scientific influences, one methodological, the other ideological. Zola, like many European intellectuals, was convinced that science held the key to social improvement. If one only remained objective and observed reality, he could establish the truth of a given situation. Zola pressed this scientific method into his literary service. He likened all literature to a scientific experiment, and like the most dogged and objective chemist, Zola recorded all of the seamiest "data" he could observe.

The second expression of Zola's literary tryst with science came from Darwin. The vogue of Darwin's theories reached a climax in the 1870's when Zola was at work on *Drink.* Darwin emphasized the biological nature of man, the influence of environment, and to a lesser degree genetic inheritance on his character. Thus, when Zola described the downfall of a Gervaise, he could claim to be describing a condition for which science had an answer.

Naturally, Zola wrote *Drink* for reasons other than to demonstrate his knowledge of contemporary scientific methods and theories. He was genuinely concerned with the plight of the French working class and wished to bring their baleful state to the attention of his fellow Frenchmen. And with good reason, for throughout the nineteenth century, French social legislation remained the most backward in all of Europe.

DRUMS

Type of work: Novel
Author: James Boyd (1888-1944)
Type of plot: Historical romance
Time of plot: American Revolution
Locale: North Carolina and London
First published: 1925

> *Principal characters:*
> SQUIRE FRASER, a North Carolina planter
> MRS. FRASER, his wife
> JOHN FRASER, their son
> SIR NAT DUKINFIELD, a sportsman
> CAPTAIN TENNANT, Collector of the Port at Edenton
> EVE TENNANT, his daughter
> WYLIE JONES, a plantation owner
> PAUL JONES, a sailor
> SALLY MERRILLEE, a neighbor of the Frasers

Critique:

In *Drums* the author attempted to reproduce the feelings and actions of all classes of Americans during the Revolution, and he accomplished his purpose admirably, sometimes, however, at the expense of the movement of the plot. The episodes at the race track and on the sea stand out in vividness above the rest of the action. The book is a pleasing mixture of history and adventure, with little emphasis upon character.

The Story:

John Fraser lived with his mother and father in the backwoods of North Carolina. Squire Fraser, a strict but kind Scotsman, was determined that his son should have a gentleman's education, and so he sent John to the coastal town of Edenton to be tutored by Dr. Clapton, an English clergyman.

There John made many friends. Sir Nat Dukinfield, a young rake, asked John to go riding with him one afternoon. They parted close friends. Through Dr. Clapton, John met Captain Tennant the Collector of the Port at Edenton. Captain Tennant took John home with him and introduced him to Eve, his daughter, who overwhelmed John and embarrassed him with her coquettish manners. Captain Flood, a river boat

skipper, was another of his friends. The old man taught him some sea lore and on his trips up and down the river acted as a messenger between John and his parents.

John went often to visit Captain Tennant and Eve. One evening two other gentlemen arrived at their house, Mr. Hewes, a shipbuilder, and Mr. Battle, a young lawyer. A bitter argument began among the gentlemen over the new tax on tea. Autumn came, and Squire Fraser sent for John to come home for a short vacation. Captain Flood took John up the river to Halifax. There he stayed overnight at the plantation of Wylie Jones, a rich young landowner.

After three years of schooling from Dr. Clapton, John became a young provincial gentleman. The only cloud on his horizon was the report of troubles with the British in Boston. Many people were angry; some predicted violence. But John thrust dark thoughts aside, for tomorrow was the day of the races. Sir Nat was to match his horse against a thoroughbred from Virginia. Everyone seemed to be excited over the holiday except Mr. Hewes, Mr. Battle, and Wylie Jones. The three sat apart at a table in the tavern and talked seriously among themselves while the rest of the company sang songs. At last Wylie Jones rose and announced that the ministers in Parliament had requested the king to declare the American Colonies in a state of rebellion.

The next day John rode to the races with Sir Nat; Eve was going with fat Master Hal Cherry, a repulsive boy, but rich. Sir Nat's horse was in perfect condition; his jockey, who had been drunk the night before, was not. He lost the first heat to the horse from Virginia. Then Sir Nat turned to John and asked him to ride. John rode the next two heats and won both of them. His friends celebrated the victory he had won for North Carolina.

Spring came. Sir Nat, putting no stock in rumors of war with the Colonies, volunteered for the English cavalry; he wanted to fight the French. The day after Sir Nat left for England, John learned of the battle fought at Lexington.

Squire Fraser sent a letter to his son with instructions to come home at once if British authority were overthrown at Edenton. John went to say goodbye to Captain Tennant and Eve, and then, following his father's instructions, he took leave of Dr. Clapton and went up the river with Wylie Jones. At Wylie's plantation he met Paul Jones, an adventurous seaman who had taken Wylie's last name. Mr. Battle, Paul Jones, and Wylie discussed a naval war against the British. They urged John to decide soon on which side he would be. He rode sadly home from Wylie's, but he brightened when he met Sally Merrillee, an old playmate. He suddenly decided that he liked her backwoods manners, so different from those of Eve Tennant. Later a company of militia camped on the Merrillee property, and the officers were billeted in Sally's house. John became angry at Sally's attentions to the militia officers and ceased courting her. Finally, Squire Fraser sent John to England to put the family money in a safe bank. John was happy at a chance for an honorable escape from his problem. But when he went to say goodbye to Sally, she had

only contempt for him. Her brother had gone with the militia.

In London, John became the clerk of an importing firm and again met Eve and Captain Tennant. He received a letter from Wylie Jones, who asked him to deliver some money to Paul Jones' mother in Scotland. John was staying at an inn on the Scottish coast the night American sailors made a shore raid. Suddenly homesick for America, he went back with them to their ship. The captain was Paul Jones. Grateful for the favor John had done for him in Scotland, he signed John on as a crew member.

After a naval engagement, the ship anchored in the French harbor of Brest. Then came long months of waiting while Paul Jones tried to get a larger ship from the French. Sir Nat arrived from England to visit John. One evening the two became involved in a tavern brawl, and Sir Nat was killed. At last Paul Jones obtained another ship, the *Bonhomme Richard*.

The ship put to sea with a motley crew and captured several British merchant vessels. Then, in a running fight with the Baltic Fleet, John was wounded in the left elbow. No longer fit for active duty and still feverish from his wound, he sailed home to North Carolina on a Dutch ship. As soon as his arm had healed, he volunteered in the militia, but they wanted no stiff-armed men. He helped out Sally's mother on her farm. Sally had gone north to nurse her brother, who had smallpox. Mr. Merrillee had been killed in the war.

When Sally returned, John went to call on her. But when he tried to tell her that he loved her, she wept. Thinking she was rejecting his love, he left disconsolately. He volunteered again for the militia and was accepted. In a skirmish with British troops he was wounded a second time.

His arm now useless, John spent his days sitting on the front porch. One day Sally's mother came to call on him and scolded him for neglecting her daughter. Sally was in love with him; he had mistaken her reason for crying. John suddenly felt much better. He felt better still when his father heard that the British were retreating. As he sat on the porch, General Greene's victorious army passed along the road. John stumbled down to the fence and raised his stiff arm in an Indian salute as the last man of the rear guard came to the crest of a hill. The distant soldier, silhouetted against the sunset, raised his rifle over his head in answer. The war was over. In a few days he would be strong enough to visit Sally.

Further Critical Evaluation of the Work:

At a time when major American novelists like Hemingway and Fitzgerald were involved in expatriate experience for its test of character and enlargement of their social and artistic consciousness, James Boyd sought similar enrichment closer to home. *Drums* was hailed as one of the finest novels yet written about the American Revolution when it appeared in 1925; it launched Boyd, who had been a moderately successful short story writer, on a major career as a historical novelist. *Marching On* (1927), another war novel (this time about the Civil War in the South), was followed by *The Long Hunt* (1930), *Roll River* (1935), and *Bitter Creek* (1939). The later novels continued to explore the evolving American character.

In many ways *Drums* is a conventional historical romance: a morally sound young hero weathers the temptation of superficial but charming aristocrats, lovers, and friends, and discovers his democratic soul in the heat of battle. His bravery in the battle between the *Bonhomme Richard* and the *Serapis* recalls the fictional treatment of the same fight in Melville's *Israel Potter,* and is the kind of ordeal by fire that American youths have endured from Crane to Hemingway.

Boyd was trying to do more than simply write a traditional historical novel with the usual trappings of adventure and romance. He wanted to suggest some of the things that went into the making of the American Revolution itself. John Fraser's assuming of the American cause is the psychological and moral equivalent of the emergence of what Boyd felt was the American identity. The indifference of the English aristocrats to the dying vagabond, and Sir Nat's coming to the defense of American honor despite his basic social detachment, are the kind of examples that gradually educate John Fraser to the strong emotional response to the democratic army that marches across the horizon at the end of the novel.

DRUMS ALONG THE MOHAWK

Type of work: Novel
Author: Walter D. Edmonds (1903-   )
Type of plot: Historical chronicle
Time of plot: 1775-1783
Locale: The Mohawk Valley
First published: 1936

Principal characters:

GILBERT MARTIN, a young pioneer
MAGDELANA BORST MARTIN (LANA), his wife
MARK DEMOOTH, a captain of the militia
JOHN WOLFF, a Tory
BLUE BACK, a friendly Oneida Indian
MRS. MCKLENNAR, Captain Barnabas McKlennar's widow
JOSEPH BRANT, an Indian chief
GENERAL BENEDICT ARNOLD
NANCY SCHUYLER, Mrs. Demooth's maid
JURRY MCLONIS, a Tory
HON YOST, Nancy's brother

Critique:

Drums Along the Mohawk depicts with great clarity the history of those stirring years from 1775 to 1783. Edmonds does not attempt a sweeping picture of the Revolutionary War. Instead, he shows how the times affected the farmers and residents of the Mohawk Valley in upstate New York. Realistically told, the novel gains added authenticity because its people, with some exceptions, actually lived during that period of American history. Edmonds lists his fictitious characters in an Author's Note.

The Story:

Magdelana Borst, the oldest of five daughters, married Gilbert Martin and together they started off from her home at Fox's Mill to settle farther west in their home at Deerfield. The time was July, 1776, and the spirit of the revolution was reaching into the Mohawk Valley, where settlers who sided with the rebels had already formed a company of militia commanded by Mark Demooth. Soon after he came to his new home Gil had to report for muster day. Some Indians had been seen in the vicinity. Also, the militia had decided to investigate the home of John Wolff, suspected of being

a king's man. Finding evidence that a spy had been hidden on the Wolff farm, they arrested John Wolff, convicted him of aiding the British, and sent him to the Newgate Prison at Simsbury Mines.

A few months after their arrival at Deerfield, Gil decided to have a log-rolling to clear his land for farming. The Weavers, the Realls, and Clem Coppernol all came to help with the work. When they were about half finished, Blue Back, a friendly Oneida Indian, came to warn them that a raiding party of Seneca Indians and whites was in the valley. The settlers immediately scattered for home to collect the few movable belongings which they might save, and then drove to Fort Schuyler. Lana, who was pregnant, lost her baby as a result of the wild ride to the fort. The enemy destroyed the Deerfield settlement. All the houses and fields were burned; Gil's cow was killed, and Mrs. Wolff, who had refused to take refuge with the people who had sent her husband to prison, was reported missing. Gil and Lana rented a one-room cabin in which to live through the winter. With spring coming on and needing a job to support himself and Lana, Gil became the hired man of Mrs.

McKlennar, a widow. The pay was forty-five dollars a year plus the use of a two-room house and their food.

General Herkimer tried to obtain a pledge of neutrality from the Indian chief, Joseph Brant, but was unsuccessful. At the end of the summer, word came that the combined forces of British and Indians, commanded by General St. Leger, were moving down from Canada to attack the valley. The militia was called up and set out westward to encounter this army. But the attack by the militia was badly timed and the party was ambushed. Of nearly six hundred and fifty men, only two hundred and fifty survived. The survivors returned in scattered groups. Gil received a bullet wound in the arm. General Herkimer, seriously injured in the leg, died of his wounds.

After the death of General Herkimer, General Benedict Arnold was sent out to reorganize the army and lead it in another attack—this time against General St. Leger's camp.

When Nancy Schuyler, Mrs. Demooth's maid, heard that her brother, Hon Yost, was in the neighborhood with a group of Tories, she decided to sneak out to see him. On the way she met another Tory, Jurry McLonis, who seduced her. Before she was able to see Hon, the American militia broke up the band. Hon was arrested but was later released when he agreed to go back to the British camp and spread false reports of the American strength. As a result of her meeting with Jurry McLonis, Nancy became pregnant. About that same time John Wolff escaped from the prison at Simsbury Mines and made his way to Canada to join Butler and to look for his wife.

The following spring brought with it General Butler's destructives, raiding parties that would swoop down to burn and pillage small settlements or farms. Mrs. Demooth tormented Nancy constantly because of her condition and one night frightened the girl so completely that Nancy, in terror, packed a few of her belongings in a shawl and ran away. Her only idea was to try to get to Niagara and find her brother Hon, but she had not gone far before labor pains overtook her and she bore her child beside a stream. An Indian found her there and took her with him as his wife. Lana had her child in May. The destruction by the raiding parties continued all through that summer, and the harvest was small. Mrs. McKlennar's stone house was not burned, but there was barely enough food for her household that winter. In the spring Colonel Van Schaick came to the settlement with an army, and the militia headed west once again, this time to strike against the Onondaga towns.

Lana had her second child the following August. Because of the lack of food during the winter, she was still weak from nursing her first boy, Gilly, and after the birth of her second boy it took her a long while to recover. The next winter they all had enough to eat but the cold was severe. During that winter Mrs. McKlennar aged greatly and kept mostly to her bed. The destructives continued their raids through the next spring and summer. The men never went out to their fields alone; they worked in groups with armed guards. One day, after all the men had gone to the fort, Lana took the two boys for a walk and then sat down at the edge of a clearing and fell asleep. When she awoke, Gilly was gone. Two Indians were near the house. She put the baby, Joey, into a hiding place and then searched for Gilly. She found him at last and the two of them crawled into the hiding place also. Meanwhile the two Indians had entered the house and set it on fire. Overwhelmed by Mrs. McKlennar's righteous indignation, they carried out her bed for her. They fled when men, seeing the smoke, came hurrying from the fort. Gil and the two scouts, Adam Helmer and Joe Boleo, built a cabin to house them all during the coming winter.

With the spring thaws, a flood inundated the valley. As the waters receded, Marinus Willett came into the Mohawk

Valley with his army, with orders to track down and destroy the British forces under General Butler. Butler's army already was having a difficult time, for British food supplies were running out and tracking wolves killed all stragglers. The militia finally caught up with Butler, harassed his army for several miles, killed Butler, and scattered the routed army in the wilderness. The Mohawk Valley was saved.

Three years later, the war over, Gil and Lana went back to their farm at Deerfield. They now had a baby girl and Lana and Gil felt content with their hard-won security, their home, their children, and each other.

Further Critical Evaluation of the Work:

During the 1930's the historical novel became extremely popular. Most of them followed the same pattern: they were long, had many characters, were full of action and realistic detail, and usually ended happily. *Drums Along the Mohawk* has all of these qualities, but it is one of the best of the genre. In 1936 it was on the best seller list. Edmonds in his author's note defends the genre, noting that the life presented is not a bygone picture, for the parallel is too close to our own. The valley people faced repercussions of poverty and starvation and were plagued by unfulfilled promises and the inevitable red-tape of a central government which could not understand local problems. Thus, the valley farmers, in the typically American tradition, learned to fight for themselves and for the land they had worked so hard to wrench from the wilderness and could not abandon.

Contrary to the patriotic myth, for all American soldiers the war was not a glorious fight for freedom. Many fought only because it was necessary to protect their families. They never thought of the American troops in the South and East; that was too remote, while the ever-present threat of instant disaster was too near. When Captain Demooth says to Gil, "Who gives a damn for the Stamp Tax?" Gil admits that it had not bothered him and asks the key question of most of the farmers: "Why do we have to go and fight the British at all?" The attitude of many of the men conscripted for the militia is "Damn the militia! I need to roof my barn." Yet, as the attacks upon the small settlements begin, they realize that they must band together and fight.

At times the western settlers wonder which side is the enemy. Denied food, munitions, and the protection of regular troops by the government at Albany, their seed grain commandeered, and their fences burned for firewood, the settlers of German Flats become extremely bitter at the indifferent treatment they receive. When the widowed Mrs. Reall with her many children tries to collect her husband's back pay, she is denied because he is not marked dead on the paymaster's list. Even though Colonel Bellinger swears he saw Reall killed and scalped, the money is withheld. The only alternative she is given is to file a claim before the auditor-general which must then be passed by an act of Congress. In the meantime the family must starve or rely on the charity of others who cannot really afford to help. They find that the Continental currency is practically worthless, but the climax of the colonists' disillusionment with the Congress comes when the residents receive huge tax bills for land which has been abandoned, buildings that have burned, and stock that has been killed. The incredulous settlers realize that the tax list is the one formerly used by the king.

The bestiality of what war does to men dominates the book. As the Indian raids become more ghastly, the Continentals grow more brutal. Scalps are taken by both Indian and white, and the atrocities and mutilations committed by both sides become increasingly barbarous.

Yet, in spite of the ever-present atmosphere of horror, fear, and death, Edmonds also presents the forces of life. There is fierce energy in the characters in spite of their hardships. This is seen most clearly in the character of Lana, who, though weakened by starvation, work, and fear, manages to bear and care for her two boys. There is a mystery about her as she nurses and cares for her babies. Although she deeply loves Gil, with the birth of the first child she becomes mother first. Even the rough scout Joe Boleo senses the maternal mystery she exudes. There is also beauty in life itself as seen in the human body and in reproduction. The pregnant Nancy becomes more beautiful as she carries her illegitimate child, and the marriage of young John Weaver to Mary Reall begins another generation when Mary becomes pregnant.

Edmonds' style is free flowing, and he has an excellent ear for natural folk speech. As omniscient narrator, he goes deeply into the minds of the main characters and captures their reactions to the many things going on about them. All of the main characters have individuality and the gift of life.

The praise that is often given the novel is for the realism which Edmonds achieves by minute detail; however, this is also a weakness. His accounts of the many battles and raids become repetitious, for in the interest of historical truth, he does not want to eliminate anything. Thus, the action becomes blurred because there are so many similar accounts.

Structurally the book is well handled with the exception of the last chapter, "Lana," which occurs three years after the preceeding one. It appears to have been tacked on simply to tie up a few loose ends and to give the story a happy ending. In a book which has proceeded slowly season by season for five years, the three year interval startles the reader.

The theme of the novel is the strength of the men who will endure anything to achieve the American dream. Through their own efforts they hope to earn their land, houses, animals, and the material things necessary to make life easier and more beautiful for themselves and particularly for their children. Lana and Gil begin their marriage with a cow, a few pieces of furniture, and Lana's most valued possession—a peacock feather which, with its mysterious beauty, symbolizes the beauty of the dream. All of this is lost in the war, but in the last chapter Gil realizes his ambitions. He is farming his own land, he has built a new house, and he owns a yoke of oxen. Lana has her two boys, a baby daughter, security, and even the now battered but still gorgeous peacock feather which the Indian Blue Back returns to her. She is supremely content and secure as she tells herself, "We've got this place. . . . We've got the children. We've got each other. Nobody can take those things away. Not any more."

Vina Nickels Oldach

THE DUCHESS OF MALFI

Type of work: Drama
Author: John Webster (?—Before 1635)
Type of plot: Romantic tragedy
Time of plot: Sixteenth century
Locale: Amalfi and Milan, Italy
First presented: (?-Before 1635)

Principal characters:
> GIOVANNA, Duchess of Amalfi
> ANTONIO, her second husband
> FERDINAND, Duke of Calabria, jealous brother of the duchess
> THE CARDINAL, another brother of the duchess
> BOSOLA, the brothers' spy and executioner

Critique:

Webster's play is a blood-tragedy typical of the so-called decadent drama of the reign of James I of England. The melodrama of its scenes, however, is not enough to detract from the general dignity and tragedy of the play. A peculiarity of this play is that a year elapses between the first and second acts and another two years between the second and third acts, the passage of time made apparent to the audience by the birth of children to the duchess. As in most of the bloody tragedies, the setting is a Latin country.

The Story:

The Duchess of Malfi was a young widow whose two brothers, one a Cardinal and the other Ferdinand, the Duke of Calabria, were desperately jealous lest she marry again, for they planned to inherit her title and estates. Their spy in her household was Bosola, her master of horse.

In spite of the warnings of her brothers, the duchess fell in love with Antonio, her steward, and married him. Later, unknown to any person in the court except Antonio and Cariola, a servant girl, she had a child, a boy. Unfortunately, the happy father wrote out the child's horoscope according to the rules of astrology and then lost the paper. Bosola found the document and so learned about the duchess' child. He dispatched a letter immediately to Rome to inform the brothers. The duke swore that only her blood could quench his anger and threatened that once he knew for certain the duchess' lover, he would be content only with her complete ruin.

The years passed and the duchess bore Antonio two more children, a second son and a daughter. Antonio told his friend Delio that he was worried because Duke Ferdinand was too quiet about the matter and because the people of Malfi, not aware of their duchess' marriage, were calling her a common strumpet.

Duke Ferdinand had come to the court to propose Count Malateste as a second husband for the duchess. She refused. Meanwhile Bosola had not been able to discover the father of the duchess' children. Impatient with his informer, the duke decided on a bolder course of action. He determined to gain entrance to the duchess' private chamber, and there to wring a confession from her. That night, using a key Bosola had given him, the duke went to her bedroom. Under threats she confessed to her second marriage, but she refused to reveal Antonio's name. After the duke left, she called Antonio and Cariola to her chamber. They planned Antonio's escape from Malfi before his secret became known to the duchess' brothers.

The duchess called Bosola and told him that Antonio had falsified some accounts. As soon as Bosola left, she recalled Antonio and told him of the feigned crime of which she had accused him to shield both their honors, and then bade him flee to the town of Ancona, where they would meet later. In the presence of Bosola and the officers of her guard she again accused Antonio of stealing money, and banished him from Malfi. Antonio replied that such was the treatment of stewards of thankless masters, and then left for Ancona. The duped Bosola upheld Antonio in an argument with the duchess. She then felt that she could trust Bosola with the secret of her marriage, and she asked him to take jewels and money to her husband at Ancona. Bosola, in return, advised her to make her own departure from the court more seemly by going to Ancona by way of the shrine of Loretto, so that the flight might seem a religious pilgrimage.

Bosola immediately traveled from Malfi to Rome, where he betrayed the plans of Antonio and the duchess to Duke Ferdinand and the Cardinal. They had the lovers banished from Ancona.

Bosola met the duchess and Antonio near Loretto with a letter from Duke Ferdinand bidding Antonio report to him, since now he knew Antonio a his sister's husband. Antonio refused and fled with his oldest son toward Milan. After Antonio's departure, Bosola took the duchess back to her palace at Malfi, a prisoner by Duke Ferdinand's command. At Malfi the duke again visited her in her chamber. He presented her with a dead man's hand, implying that it was from Antonio's corpse. Finally Bosola came to the duchess and strangled her. Cariola and the children were also strangled, though not with the quiet dignity with which the duchess was murdered. When Bosola asked Duke Ferdinand for his re-

ward, the hypocritical duke laughed and replied that the only reward for such a crime was its pardon.

In Milan, meanwhile, Antonio planned to visit the Cardinal's chamber during the night to seek a reconciliation with the duchess' brothers. He intended to approach the Cardinal because Duke Ferdinand had lost his mind after causing his sister's murder. The Cardinal ordered Bosola that same evening to seek out Antonio, who was known to be in Milan, and murder him. But when so ordered, Bosola accused the Cardinal of having plotted the duchess' murder and requested his reward. When a reward was again refused, Bosola swore to himself to join forces with Antonio to avenge the duchess' death.

That night all plans miscarried. In the dark Bosola accidentally murdered Antonio, the man he hoped to make an ally in his revenge on Duke Ferdinand and the Cardinal. A few minutes later, Bosola stabbed the Cardinal and was in turn stabbed by the mad Duke Ferdinand, who had rushed into the room. Bosola, with his last strength, stabbed the duke and they both died. Alarmed, the guards broke into the apartments to discover the bodies. Into the welter of blood a courtier led the young son of the Duchess of Malfi and Antonio, whom Antonio had taken to Milan. He was proclaimed ruler of the lands held by his mother and uncles.

Further Critical Evaluation of the Work:

Little is known of John Webster's life, although the title page of his pageant, *Monuments of Honor* (1624), calls him a "merchant-tailor." In the custom of Jacobean playwrights, he often collaborated, probably with Dekker, a practice supported by Philip Henslowe, whose *Diary* gives much information about the theater of the period. Webster's reputation rests almost entirely upon *The White Devil* (c. 1612), and *The Duchess of Malfi* (c. 1613). Both are studies of illicit love, revenge and murder, and intrigues worthy of the Machiavellians so appealing to Elizabethan and Jacobean audiences.

The Duchess of Malfi is a finer play than *The White Devil,* in part due to the noble character of the Duchess herself. Her story has the reputation of being the best poetic tragedy written after Shakespeare. It reveals Webster's powers, often compared to Shakespeare's, to present themes of great moral seriousness in magnificent language while also creating flesh-and-blood characters. Webster and Shakespeare mastered thinking in images so well that the images develop themes and meaning as fully as does plot.

Not all critics find Webster's work excellent, however, partly due to distaste for the violence of revenge and blood tragedies which may obscure finer qualities of the plays. Bernard Shaw referred to Webster as "a Tussaud-laureate." Few critics underestimate Webster's brilliance as a psychologist despite the melodramatic or surrealistic qualities of his work. One can appreciate the psychological insights and also the fact that the dramas reflect their origins: many descended from Kyd's *The Spanish Tragedy,* Senecan tragedy, the medieval morality play with its preoccupation with death. They also reflect the tempestuous Renaissance history. Many of the dramas are set in Italy, the epitome of evil locales to Renaissance Englishmen, a view which history supports.

The Duchess of Malfi was an actual Italian duchess, but Webster's immediate source was Painter's *Palace of Pleasure* (1567), a collection of tediously moral stories. Painter's work was in turn based on twenty-five novellas of Matteo Bandello which provided themes for several plays by Shakespeare and his contemporaries. Painter concentrates on two major "sins" or weaknesses: the Duchess' sensuality and Antonio's excessive ambition. Bosola is referred to only once in Painter's story. Webster does not alter Painter's version so much as he enlarges it by surrounding the limited Romantic-Tragic world of the lovers with other worlds: the corrupt court of Amalfi and the religious state of Rome, thus exposing a universal corruption that expands concentrically beyond the lovers' chambered world. Moving beyond the lovers into other worlds, he enlarges and magnifies the role of the villain Bosola, using him to bind the various worlds together. A "revenge tragedy" results which treats the question of personal honor (still tied to feudal values), the political and moral problems of lawlessness, and the supreme question— human vengeance and Divine or Providential vengeance.

Webster creates this fallen world through the actions of the Duchess, Ferdinand, the Cardinal, Antonio, and Bosola, particularizing the questions mentioned above. First, what does passionate and true love do in the presence of family pride and social taboos; second, how can man rise in an evil, power-dominated world without corrupting himself; and finally, does not man create his own heaven or hell? Free will is implicit and explicit throughout the play: man is responsible for his choices. Webster forces the smaller worlds into collision in the working out of the themes, and tragic destruction ensues. Providence asserts its influence finally through the hope vested in the Duchess' and Antonio's innocent son.

The Duchess of the play is a headstrong but noble woman who says to her executioners: "Pull, and pull strongly, for your able strength/Must pull down heaven upon me. . . ." Nobility notwithstanding, her "passion is out of place," for Antonio is but head steward of her household. She denies the chain of being on its social level in wooing Antonio. Even at the moment when she and Antonio confess their love, they are therefore threatened. She tries to ease his fears:

> Ant.: But for your brothers?
> Duch.: Do not think of them:
> All discord without this circumference
> Is only to be pitied, not fear'd:
> Yet, should they know it, time will easily
> Scatter the tempest.   (I.111.176-181)

Her optimism is that of the pure soul; she misjudges the power of those outside "this circumference." Her willfulness and passion are lust in the eyes of brothers, Church, and society at large. Webster communicates the sweetness of the romance, however, so thoroughly that the lovers are totally sympathetic throughout.

Second to the Duchess in importance is Bosola, a symbol of Webster's disgust with an era which admired ambition excessively, but provided little opportunity for its honest realization. This melancholy scholar perverts his intelligence to "serve" Ferdinand and the Cardinal, representatives of political and ecclesiastical corruption. Bosola's evil actions continue after the Duchess' murder so that Webster can complete the theme of corruption. This accounts for the extended action of Acts IV and V sometimes found objectionable. Ultimately, of course, Bosola recognizes his misplaced devotion and his responsibility for the horrors, a recognition too sudden for some readers. But outside Shakespeare's works, dramatic characters of the period seldom changed gradually, a vestige of the parent morality plays.

Even Ferdinand (who may hide incestuous feelings for his sister) accepts his guilt, saying:

> Whether we fall by ambition, blood, or lust,
> Like diamonds, we are cut with our own dust. (V.v.75-76)

Ferdinand's marvelous image is characteristic of the powerful figurative language of the play. The image refers to all the characters, identifying them as the most precious of jewels, yet paradoxically made of dust. Man's place as a little below the angels, Webster tells us, is secure only so long as he acts in accordance with the moral laws established by Providence. He may rise or fall by his own acts. Delio's words close the play in Webster's imagistic way of a final comment upon the fallen of Amalfi:

> These wretched eminent things
> Leave no more fame behind 'em, than should one
> Fall in a frost, and leave his print in snow:
> (V.v.117-119)

Mary H. Hayden

DUINO ELEGIES

Type of work: Poetry
Author: Rainer Maria Rilke (1875-1926)
First published: 1923

For the reader who must rely on a prose translation of Rainer Maria Rilke's culminating work, the story and the man behind its appearance may overshadow the poem itself. Nothing of the elegiac quality of the original German can be translated which is as deeply affecting as the inspiration which produced the work, or the philosophy of the man who wrote it.

Often ranked with Yeats as one of the great poets of this century, Rilke is also called the great beginner. One might, however, better compare his poetic innovations with those of Gerard Manley Hopkins, though in the case of Rilke experimentation with rhythm and rhyme never took precedence over content. Like Yeats, he more often let the content find the form. Of the three, Rilke was the most intuitive, rhapsodic, and mystical; and he was perhaps the most consummate craftsman.

In October, 1911, the poet visited his friend, Princess Marie von Thurn und Taxis-Hohenlohe, at Schloss Duino, near Trieste. He remained at the castle, alone throughout the winter, until April, and there he composed the first, the second, and parts of several other elegies. The opening stanza, "Who, if I cried, would hear me among the angelic orders?" came to him while walking in a storm along a cliff two hundred feet above the raging sea, a romantic interlude worthy of an atmospheric passage in a Gothic novel. Rilke conceived the plan of all ten elegies as a whole, though ten years elapsed before the poem found its final form.

The First Elegy, like the first movement of a musical work, presents the central theme and suggests the variations that follow. From the opening line to the last, Rilke invokes the Angels, not those of Christianity but of a special order immersed in time and space, a concept of being of perfect consciousness, of transcendent reality. As a symbol appearing earlier in Rilke's poetry, the Angel represents to him the perfection of life in all the forms to which he aspired, as high above man as God is above this transcending one. Nearest to this angelic order are the Heroes—later he praises Samson—and a woman in love, especially one who dies young, as did Gaspara Stampa (1523-1554), whom Rilke celebrates as a near-perfect example. Like the lover, man must realize each moment to the fullest rather than be distracted by things and longings. With this contrast of Man and Angels, of Lovers and Heroes, and with the admission of life's transitoriness, the poet suggests the meaning of life and death as well as words can identify such profound things.

If the introduction or invocation is a praise of life, the Second Elegy is a lament for life's limitations. We moderns must, at best, content ourselves with an occasional moment of self-awareness, of a glimpse at eternity. Unlike the Greeks, we have no external symbols for the life within. In love, were we not finally satiated, we might establish communication with the Angels; but finally our intuitions vanish and we have only a fleeting glance at reality.

Rilke began the Third Elegy at Duino and completed it in Paris the following year; during an intervening visit to Spain he composed parts of the Sixth, Ninth, and Tenth Elegies. In the third section he confronts the physical bases of life, especially love. He suggests that woman is always superior in the love act, man a mere beginner led by blind animal pas-

DUINO ELEGIES by Rainer Maria Rilke. Translated by J. B. Leishman and Stephen Spender. Excerpts reprinted by permission of the publishers, W. W. Norton & Co., Inc. Copyright, 1939, by W. W. Norton & Co., Inc.

sion, the libido a vicious drive. Sublime love is an end in itself, but often human love is a means to escape life. Even children have a sort of terror infused into their blood from this heritage of doubt and fear. From this view of mortality Rilke would lead the child away, as he says in powerful though enigmatic conclusion,

> . . . Oh gently, gently
> show him daily a loving, confident task
>   done,—guide him
> close to the garden, give him those
>   counter-
> balancing nights. . . .
>   Withhold him. . . .

Perhaps the advent of war made the Fourth Elegy the most bitter of all, written as it was from Rilke's retreat in Munich in 1915. The theme of distraction, our preoccupation with fleeting time and time serving, makes of this part a deep lament over the human condition. We are worse than puppets who might be manipulated by unseen forces, Angels. Our attempts to force destiny, to toy with fate, cause us to break from heaven's firm hold. We must be as little children, delighted within ourselves by the world without, and with our attention and energies undivided, alone. Here, we will find our answer to death as the other side of life, a part of life and not the negation or end of it.

The Fifth Elegy, the last from the standpoint of time, written at the Château de Muzot in 1922, was inspired by Picasso's famous picture of the acrobats. Here again the circumstances of the writing overshadow the very real worth of the poem. *Les Saltimbanques* of Picasso was owned by Frau Hertha Koenig, who allowed Rilke the privilege of living in her home in 1915 in order to be near his favorite painting. Either the poet imperfectly remembered the details of the painting when the poem was finally written or else he included recollections of acrobats who had so delighted him during his Paris years. Regardless of influences, however, this poem is remarkable

in its merging of theme and movement with a painting, emphasizing Rilke's conviction that a poem must celebrate all the senses rather than appeal to eye or ear alone.

The acrobats, symbolizing the human condition, travel about, rootless and transitory, giving pleasure neither to themselves nor the spectators. Reality to the acrobat, as to man, is best discovered in the arduousness of the task; but routine often makes the task a mockery, especially if death is the end. If death, however, is the other side of life and makes up the whole, then life forces are real and skillfully performed to the inner delight of performers and spectators, living and dead alike.

The Hero, Rilke asserts in the Sixth Elegy, is that fortunate being whose memory, unlike that of long-forgotten lovers, is firmly established by his deeds. He, being single-minded and single-hearted, has the same destiny as the early departed, those who die young without losing their view of eternity. The great thing, then, is to live in the flower of life with the calm awareness that the fruit, death, is the unilluminated side of life. For the Hero, life is always beginning.

In the Seventh Elegy, the poet as the *we* and the *you* as well as the *I*, no longer worries about transitory decaying or dying. Now he sings the unpremeditated song of existence:

> Don't think that I'm wooing!
> Angel, even if I were, you'd never come.
> For my call
> is always full of 'Away!' Against such a
>   powerful
> current you cannot advance. Like an
>   outstretched
> arm is my call. And its clutching, up-
>   wardly
> open hand is always before you
> as open for warding and warning,
> aloft there, Inapprehensible.

From this viewpoint, Rilke attempts in the Eighth Elegy, dedicated to his friend Rudolph Kassner, to support his belief in the "nowhere without no," the "open" world, timeless, limitless, inseparable "whole." "We," contrasted to animals, are always looking away rather than toward this openness.

The theme of creative existence Rilke continues in the Ninth Elegy, possibly begun at Duino but certainly finished at Muzot. Here he suggests that the life of the tree is superior in felicity to the destiny of man. We should, perhaps, rejoice in spite of the limiting conditions of man by overcoming this negation of the flesh with a reaffirmation of the spirit. Then death holds no fears since it is not opposite to life, not an enemy but a friend. This work possibly represents the author's own transformation from the negating, inhibiting conditions of the Great War to a renewed faith in life.

The Tenth Elegy, the first ten lines of which came to him in that burst of creativity at Duino, contains a satiric portrait of the City of Pain where man simply excludes suffering, pain, death, from his thoughts; where distractions, especially the pursuit of money, are the principal activities. This semi-existence the poet contrasts with that in the Land of Pain, Life-Death, where there is continuous progress through insights of a deeper reality to the primal source of joy.

> And we, who have always thought
> of happiness climbing, would feel
> the emotion that almost startles
> when happiness falls.

Perhaps Rilke means that by complete submission or attunement to universal forces one is suspended or even falls into the "open." This deeply realized philosophy he developed in the *Sonnets to Orpheus* (1923), a work which complements the *Duino Elegies*, though it does not surpass them in deep emotional undertones and sheer power of expression.

THE DUNCIAD

Type of work: Poem
Author: Alexander Pope (1688-1744)
Time: Eighteenth century
Locale: England, the underworld
First published: 1728-1743

> *Principal personages:*
> DULNESS, a goddess
> TIBBALD, hero of the first edition, a Shakespearian scholar
> COLLEY CIBBER, hero of the second edition, playwright, producer, and
> poet laureate

When Alexander Pope set out to criti-cize the general literary climate of his time and to avenge the slights given his own work by other writers, he took the theme of John Dryden's *MacFlecknoe*, in which the poetaster Thomas Shadwell is crowned ruler of the Kingdom of Non-sense, and expanded it to make a true mock epic of three books. He added a fourth book when he rewrote the poem in 1742. *The Dunciad* acclaims the god-dess Dulness, daughter of Chaos and Night, and her chosen prince: the scholar Lewis Theobald (Tibbald) in the first edition, Colley Cibber, playwright and poet laureate, in the second.

This poem lacks the close-knit quality of Pope's other fine mock epic, *The Rape of the Lock.* It is longer, and the fact that the hero appears only at intervals explains a certain disunity. Tibbald-Cib-ber appears at the middle of Book I, is present only as a spectator at the epic games described in Book II, and dreams the trip to the underworld, modeled on that of Aeneas in Book VI of the *Aeneid.* Thus, the action is limited. The impor-tant points in the poem are made in the descriptive passages in these episodes and in conversations which contain criticism of individuals and trends.

The general plan outlined above shows Pope's close reliance on the classical epic as his model. *The Dunciad*, like *The Rape of the Lock,* begins with a parody of the *Aeneid*:

> The mighty Mother, and her Son, who
> brings
> The Smithfield Muses to the ear of
> Kings,
> I sing.

The invocation is appropriately directed not at a muse but at the Patricians, the patrons whose purses inspire dull writing. The dedication to the author's friend Jonathan Swift which follows is an eight-eenth-century, rather than a classic con-vention.

Pope describes in detail the abode of Dulness and the allegorical figures gath-ered around her throne: Fortitude, Tem-perance, Prudence, and Poetic Justice, who is weighing truth with gold and "solid pudding against empty praise." The gods are notoriously interested in the affairs of mortals; Dulness looks out upon the ingredients of dull writing and the numerous creators of it. Her eye lights upon the hero, who is raising to her an altar of tremendous tomes of his writing. She anoints him as king of her realm, and the nation croaks Aesop's line, "God save King Log."

In the second book Pope designs appro-priate contests for his various groups of enemies. The booksellers race to win a phantom poet. A patron is designated for the poet who tickles best, but he is car-ried off by an unknown sycophantic secretary. Journalists swim through the muck of the Thames River:

> Who flings most filth, and wide pollutes
> around
> The stream, be his the Weekly Journals
> bound;
> A pig of lead to him who drives the
> best;
> A peck of coals a-piece shall glad the
> rest.

As a final test the goddess promises her "amplest powers" to anyone who can remain awake as he listens to the verses of "Three College Sophs, and three pert Templars." The book ends with the whole company lying asleep.

Grandiose heroic couplets and numerous parallels with classical visits to the underworld fill the third book. John Taylor, the Water Poet, replaces the ferryman Charon; Elkanah Settle, a Restoration poet, takes Anchises' part in showing the hero the future of Dulness and her offspring. The high point of this book is the crowning of Tibbald-Cibber with a poppy wreath by Bavius, prototype of the worst of poets from ancient times.

The 1742 *Dunciad,* centering on the triumph of Dulness over England, reveals a slightly more mature outlook in the poet than does the earlier version. Tibbald was the object of a vindictive attack, occasioned by his criticism of Pope's edition of Shakespeare. Cibber is representative of the dull poet; as laureate he was well known for his poor occasional verse. The fourth book is far more concerned with the institutions promoting the rise of dullness than with individuals. The more frequent use of classical names, rather than personal ones, indicates the poet's movement toward universality.

The last book is almost an entity in itself. It opens with a new invocation, to Chaos and Night. The pseudo-learned notes, effective satire written by Pope himself, point out the precedents for a second invocation when important new matter is introduced. Evil omens presage the coming destruction as Dulness ascends her throne and Cibber reclines in her lap, making his only appearance in this book.

Around the goddess are Science, Wit, Logic, Rhetoric, and other abstractions in chains, reminiscent of several scenes in *The Faerie Queene.* Various personages appear to tell of Dulness' victory over the many arts and institutions. First to come is a harlot representing the Italian opera; she rejoices in the banishment of Handel to Ireland and the supremacy of chaos in music.

Pope uses an epic simile to describe the nations clustering around the goddess:

> Not closer, orb in orb, congloved are seen
> The buzzing Bees about their dusky Queen.

Present are the passive followers of Dulness and those who lead the advance: pompous editors who make mincemeat of good poets with notes and commentary, patrons who set up a bust of a poet after he has died neglected.

A specter, the head of Westminster School, modeled on Milton's Moloch, speaks on the state of education:

> As Fancy opens the quick springs of Sense,
> We ply the Memory, we load the brain,
> Bind rebel Wit, and double chain on chain,
> Confine the thought, to exercise the breath;
> And keep them in the pale of Words till death.

Pope criticizes the hair-splitting grammarians in Aristarchus' boasts that he has turned good verse into prose again. Science is also satirized as the study which loses itself in detail; but Dulness fears even that condition of affairs, for an object of nature is capable of awakening a mind. Religion does not escape; the poet says that it has degenerated into a belief in a mechanistic God, made in man's image.

Knowing the state of her kingdom, the goddess celebrates her mysteries, reflecting Pope's interest in ceremony. As the rites are concluded a state of dullness encompasses the country, schools, government, army. Truth, philosophy, and religion perish as "Universal Darkness buries All."

The Dunciad contains more of the true heroic spirit than most other mock epics, like Samuel Butler's coarse *Hudibras* or the delicate and sophisticated *The Rape of the Lock.* These poems are directed toward the amusement of the reader, while *The Dunciad* reveals Pope's passionate conviction that the triumph of dullness was a real danger to art, science, and learning. He chose to deliver his warning to England in the humorous mock-epic form, but his seriousness about his subject raises the latter part of the fourth book to the level of real heroic poetry.

There are many fine lines of poetry in *The Dunciad*, but it is more diffuse and less brilliant satire than either *MacFlecknoe* or Pope's own *Epistle to Dr. Arbuthnot*. Missing are the biting, succinct couplets like Dryden's

The rest to some faint meaning make pretense,
But Sh— never deviates into sense . . .

or Pope's lines on Addison:

Damn with faint praise, assent with civil leer,
And without sneering, teach the rest to sneer.

The greatest deterrent to the modern reader of *The Dunciad* is probably the fact that so much of the poet's contemporary criticism is almost unintelligible; few names die faster than those of the fifth-rate writers of an era. Yet the satirical comments on universal conditions remain fresh and pointed. *The Dunciad* is worthy of a high place among mock-heroic poems.

THE DYNASTS

Type of work: Verse drama
Author: Thomas Hardy (1840-1928)
Type of plot: Historical epic
Time of plot: 1806-1815
Locale: Europe
First published: 1903-1908

Principal characters:

NAPOLEON I
JOSEPHINE, his first wife
MARIE LOUISE, his second wife
KING GEORGE III OF ENGLAND
TSAR ALEXANDER OF RUSSIA
EMPEROR FRANCIS OF AUSTRIA
SIR WILLIAM PITT, Prime Minister of England
SPIRIT OF YEARS,
SHADE OF EARTH,
SPIRIT OF PITIES,
SPIRIT SINISTER, and
SPIRIT IRONIC, allegorical figures

Critique:

Written in various types of verse and in poetic prose, *The Dynasts*, a vast epic-drama of the tragedy of Napoleon, marks Hardy's greatest effort to portray Man as completely subject to a disinterested Destiny. Among his manifold points of view, shifting from a point somewhere above the earth to the courts of emperors or the cottager's fireside, that of the rural folk of southern England is the most effective. Long prose stage directions fill out the historical perspective of this sweeping panoramic treatment of the constant turmoil in Europe from 1805 to 1815. The array of allegorical spectators who comment on the events of the drama as they occur, and Hardy's device of switching the point of view, tend to make strikingly trivial the alarums and excursions of earth-bound humanity.

The Story:

The Spirit of Years, Shade of Earth, Spirit Sinister, Spirit Ironic, Spirit of Pities, and their accompanying choruses, forgathered somewhere above the earth to watch the larger movements of men in western Europe in 1805. The design of the Immanent Will manifested itself at the time in Napoleon's preparations for the invasion of England.

Sir William Pitt, in England, contended with isolationist members of Parliament in order to secure proper defense against the invasion. Meanwhile Napoleon went to Milan to be crowned King of Italy. The spirits made light of the chicanery and pomp that attended the coronation. The Spirit of Pities descended to earth and disturbed Napoleon by reminding him of his original intention of championing liberty.

At sea, a Pyrrhic victory of the French and Spanish over the English prevented the support required for the planned invasion. On the south coast of England the Phantoms of Rumor caused great disturbance. A fleet of fishing craft was mistaken for the invasion fleet, and civilians fled from the coastal towns as signal fires flared upon the cliffs and hills.

When Napoleon learned that his admiral, Villeneuve, had returned to Cadiz, he discarded his invasion plan and moved eastward against Austria and Russia, countries which Pitt had enlisted in the English cause. The Spirit of Years remarked that the ensuing campaign would be a model in tactics for all time.

At Ulm, Napoleon defeated the Austrians, who had hoped in vain that the English fleet would hold the French forces in northern France. In London, Pitt, unsuccessful in gaining permission from the king to form a coalition government, visibly declined in health under his terrible burden.

Villeneuve was ordered out of Cadiz. The British under Nelson met the French and Spanish off Trafalgar and defeated them. Nelson was killed in the engagement; Villeneuve subsequently ended his own life in an inn at Rennes.

Napoleon defeated the Austrians and Russians at Austerlitz. Then, hearing of the English victory at Trafalgar, he declared his intention of closing all continental ports to English ships. He dictated peace terms to Emperor Francis of Austria while attendant Austrian officers stood by in disgust at the sight of a nobody dictating to true royalty. In Paris the Spirit of Rumor commented on the way Napoleon was uprooting old dynasties and founding new ones.

Pitt having died and King George III being mentally ill, England, in the person of Charles James Fox, negotiated with Napoleon for peace; but the emperor used the negotiations as a screen for his real plans. He marched on Prussia and defeated the Germans at the Battle of Jena. In Berlin he decreed that all British ships were barred from continental ports. Next, Napoleon and Tsar Alexander of Russia met at the River Niemen, where the two drew up a Franco-Russian alliance. During this meeting Napoleon expressed the desire to cement his various alliances with blood ties. The Spirit of Years remarked ironically that Napoleon was one of the few men who could see the working of the Immanent Will.

Napoleon invaded Spain as a friend to help the Spanish gain Portugal. The Spanish Bourbons abdicated and Napoleon's brother, Joseph, was proclaimed king. When Bourbon partisans enlisted English aid, an English invasion fleet

sailed for Portugal.

Back in Paris, Napoleon told his wife, Josephine, that he wished a divorce. Josephine had borne the emperor no children and he was anxious to perpetuate the dynasty he had founded. The British invasion of the Iberian Peninsula drew the emperor to Spain to direct the campaign there. Preparation for war in Austria caused Napoleon next to invade that country and to defeat its forces at Wagram. The British, under the Duke of Wellington, held their own against the French in Spain. At that point the Spirit Sinister reminded the Spirit Ironic not to sneer for fear Immanent Will would cut short the comedy that was taking place.

A British force was sent to the Scheldt, but the expedition ended disastrously when the army was decimated by miasmal fever. Napoleon, fearful of assassination and still anxious to perpetuate his line, negotiated with the Russians for the hand of a Russian princess, and with the Austrians for the hand of Princess Marie Louise. The tsar accepted the offer, but Napoleon had already arranged, through Metternich, for a marriage with the Austrian princess, Marie Louise. The marriage was performed in the conspicuous absence of many high clergy, and the Russians, incensed, prepared for war. In the meantime the British in Spain under the Duke of Wellington gained a decisive victory at Albuera.

In due time Marie Louise gave birth to Napoleon's heir. The insane King of England died after hearing of British successes in Spain. On the continent war became imminent between France and Russia.

Again on the banks of the Niemen, Napoleon received an evil portent when he was thrown from his horse. The Spirit of Pities foresaw misery for the French Grand Army in the Russian campaign. Wellington in Spain defeated the French at Salamanca. Napoleon gained a costly victory over the Russians at Borodino, and the French entered Moscow to find the city deserted and in flames. There followed a general retreat by the French across snow-covered Russian steppes to Lithuania. Thousands perished from the cold or were killed by harassing Russian cavalry. Napoleon deserted his army and raced back to Paris in order to arrive there before the news of his failure in Russia. His chief task now was to hold his empire together.

As the British continued their successes in Spain, Austria joined the allies. Napoleon met defeat at the hands of the Austrians and Prussians at Leipzig. The allies invaded France. Napoleon, forced to abdicate, was exiled to Elba, an island in the Mediterranean. Marie Louise and the infant King of Rome went to Austria to stay. The Bourbons reassumed the throne of France and a congress to deliberate on general peace in Europe met in Vienna.

Napoleon escaped from Elba and returned to Paris at the head of an army he had picked up on his way. The allies outlawed Napoleon and prepared to overthrow him again.

A private ball in Brussels was broken up by the news that the French army was nearing the Belgian frontier. Almost overnight, Napoleon had organized and put into the field a large army. But he failed to separate the British and Prussians in Belgium, and he was brought to utter defeat on the fields south of Waterloo. The Hundred Days were ended.

The Spirit of Years pointed out to the Spirits assembled that the human beings below them behaved as though they were in a dream, as though they were puppets being drawn by strings manipulated by Immanent Will. The Spirit of Years pointed to Napoleon in defeat and compared him to a tiny insect on an obscure leaf in the chart of the Ages. When the Spirit of Pities asked for what purpose the events below had taken place, the Spirit of Irony answered that there was no purpose, for only a dumb thing turned the crank which motivated and directed human behavior.

Further Critical Evaluation of the Work:

The Dynasts represents Hardy's most ambitious attempt to portray his philosophic fatalism. An epic-drama written for "mental performance," it combines the skills of Hardy, the novelist with those of Hardy, the poet. Hardy's ability to tell a story is nowhere more apparent than here, and his drama, with its scenes of battle, court life, and common life, anticipates the great motion picture spectacles of such directors as D. W. Griffith. At the same time there are powerful lines and much extremely competent verse which make the stuff of poetry.

Unlike the great Victorian long poems, Hardy's poetic drama deals with recent events. As in his novels, Hardy is concerned with the plight of the common man in an indifferent world. But, unlike in his novels, he is concerned also with potentates, whose will often seems to control the lives of common men and women. This, however, is an illusion, for even the great are moved by the Immanent Will, an impassive, unmotivated force, which at one point is described as having "films or brain-tissue" which "pervade all things." In his final defeat, Napoleon himself comes to acknowledge that he has always "passively obeyed" this Will. His gradual physical deterioration symbolizes his spiritual decay.

The Dynasts is also implicitly anti-war in its vivid portrayal of the carnage that always accompanies war. It is a democratic drama, holding up parliamentary government as preferable to rule by monarchical fiat. And it is a very English work, portraying even the typical English xenophobia. In spite of the gloom that pervades *The Dynasts,* there are moments of humor, and Hardy permits the Chorus of the Spirit of Pities to have the last, semi-hopeful word.

THE EAGLE AND THE SERPENT

Type of work: Autobiographical chronicle
Author: Martín Luis Guzmán (1887-   )
Time: 1913-1915
Locale: Mexico and The United States
First published: 1928

Principal characters:
THE NARRATOR
FRANCISCO VILLA, revolutionist, commander of the "Division of the North"
VENUSTIANO CARRANZA, supreme chief of the Constitutionalist army

The Mexican Revolution, perhaps the only one military movement that changed radically the position of a Latin American country after achieving its independence from Spain, affected in different ways the Mexican writers of those days. Some remained indifferent; others defended its motives and facts; a few engaged themselves actively in its vicissitudes. To no one can be attributed greater and more direct participation than that of Martín Luis Guzmán. Executor, witness, chronicler, interpreter, critic, novelist, he embraced all the possible angles of relationship with the Mexican Revolution. For this reason his work about the movement is the closest, most objective and penetrating of all the literary productions written upon the subject.

Guzman wrote three books—at the same time biography, history, and novel —about the Revolution: *El Aguila y la Serpiente* (*The Eagle and the Serpent*), *La Sombra del Caudillo*, and *Memorias de Pancho Villa* (*Memoirs of Pancho Villa*). Of these, the nearest to a work of the creative imagination is the first, published in fascicles in 1926 and as a book in 1928.

The reasons why Guzmán titled his book in such a way may be found in the origins of Mexican nationality. The Aztecs, the main indigenous ancestors of Mexico, had as a legendary core of their nomadic period the belief that they should found their capital city in a spot where they would find an eagle, devouring a serpent, perched upon a nopal. Guzmán took these images and turned

them into symbols for his book, to show the bipolarity of Mexican history, in constant conflict between reptant passions and an ascension of the spirit.

There is no better source to know the genesis and spirit of this book than the speech pronounced by the author at the time of his reception as a member of the Mexican Academy of the Language. Son of his time and his country, Guzmán declared that from his earliest childhood he was accustomed to beauty from having lived in Tacubaya, one of the most charming suburbs of Mexico City, near the Chapultepec Castle, scene of many decisive moments in Mexican history, and that this same environment imposed on him a feeling for history in all its grandeur. Some years later, when he embraced the cause of the Revolution, he had at his disposal raw historical material of the first quality, out of which he took the subject for his most representative books.

For a long time Guzmán hesitated to write about the Revolution. On one side he had been the witness of ruthless crimes, usurpations, disloyalties; on another he had seen in many participants of that movement a great spirit of service, purity of intention, and patriotic goals. This knowledge finally moved him to write about the Revolution, to transform into literary values those violent deeds against the Porfirio Díaz' dictatorship. He finally decided to embody what he had seen or done. He thought that if the chief leaders of the Revolution had not been as faulty as they were, the Revolution would not have been what it became.

To understand some pages of this book, the reader must take into account the fact that the revolutionary movement was not born from a set of ideas but erupted from instinctive forces, submitted to oppression for many centuries.

El Aguila y la Serpiente, a work which brings together literature and history, truth and fiction, is divided into two parts: "Esperanzas Revolucionarias" ("Revolutionary Hopes") and "En la Hora del Triunfo" ("At the Hour of the Triumph"). In the first part, consisting of seven books, Guzmán tells of his revolutionary adventures during the period preceding the peak of the fighting. In the second section, also of seven books, he tells of deeds that occurred during the most turbulent years of the conflict.

The book opens when Guzmán, apparently the narrator of most of the work because of its strong autobiographical structure, escapes from Victoriano Huerta's usurping government and sets sails, incognito, in flight from Veracruz to the United States, with the intention of reaching the northern Mexican states of Sonora or Coahuila and helping Venustiano Carranza in his fight against Huerta. Aboard ship, he meets four Mexicans, one of them a physician who shares his political views. They establish relations with a beautiful American woman who turns out to be a spy of the Huerto government. When this fact becomes known to Guzmán and his associates, the physician, in order to get rid of her, pretends ardent love for the lady and proposes that they marry in Havana, the next stop on the voyage. The trick fails because the ship delays her departure in that port, after landing the Mexicans and the beautiful secret agent. Again aboard ship, the revolutionaries are afraid of being imprisoned upon their arrival in New York. Then the physician feigns intent to kill the spy, but the woman does not appear at any place when they go ashore. The reader glows perplexed over the fate of the woman, but the author does not add to what has already been told.

Guzmán, unable to carry out his plan to contact Carranza, returns to Mexico City. But his enthusiasm for the Revolution causes him to embark again for Havana and later for New Orleans. After traveling to San Antonio, Texas, he meets there José Vasconcelos, a writer and the only great minister produced by the Revolution, according to Guzmán. Finally, in Ciudad Juárez, the author meets Pancho Villa, who is for him the chief hero of the Revolution. The encounter is not as dramatic as could be expected, but an intimate, deep impression about Villa will remain with the writer. Later he is introduced to Venustiano Carranza, first chief of the Constitutionalist Army; the first ideological collision with him ensues because Carranza had the viewpoint that good will is the primary virtue in leading men; Guzmán believed in technique. The author met another revolutionary leader, Alvaro Obregón, whom he considers an impostor. Gradually, Guzmán realizes that sooner or later deep disagreement will arise among the fighters. He thinks that at the very bottom everything could be reduced to the eternal dispute of the Mexicans who are always looking for power and the accomplishment of personal ambitions instead of great, disinterested aspirations.

A good number of episodes are intermingled in this part of the work. Perhaps they are the most interesting and representative material in the novel. Among them, "A Night in Culiacán," "The Murdering Spider," "A Race in the Darkness," and "The Feast of the Bullets," emerge as masterpieces of suspense and narrative vigor. This part of the work ends when the author is again in Ciudad Juárez, under the influence of Villa, after a journey to New York.

The second part of the novel deals with the triumph of the Revolution as a group, but the schism between the leaders of the movement is inevitable, chiefly between Villa and Carranza. Guzmán joins Villa because he thinks that, in spite of the revolutionist's instinctiveness and moral blindness, he is the only possible leader who can give a democratic and impersonal character to the Revolution, in contrast with Carranza, who is too prone to oligarchy. The author arrives again at Veracruz, taken by American soldiers, and finally makes his way to Mexico City. Guzmán, exultantly, writes now the most lyric pages he has ever composed. The sight of the city and the volcanoes, the inhalation of the thin air of the plateau, the bath of clarity, the perfect adequation of person and environment, were some of the unforgettable impressions of the "rebel who returned," as Guzmán calls himself. He goes again to Chihuahua, meets Villa anew, and gets the impression that the legendary warrior could never exist if there were not a gun in the world. Villa and his pistol were a single thing; from his gun all his friendships and enmities were born. To combat now against Carranza, the writer goes to Mexico City again. For him Carranzaism is synonymous with ambition, lack of ideals, systematic corruption, and theft. Imprisoned by Carranza's orders, he is sent to Matamoros, but the Convention of Aguascalientes, a meeting of revolutionists in which was decided the way to future action of the movement, sets him free. Having been appointed Minister of War by President Roque González Garza, Guzmán rejects the post and is threatened with the penitentiary; but he escapes and goes to see Villa, who has been estranged by the Convention of Aguascalientes. The writer, caught between loyalty to the Convention and friendship toward Villa, expatriates himself to the United States.

EARTH

Type of work: Novel
Author: Émile Zola (1840-1902)
Type of plot: Social realism
Time of plot: 1860's
Locale: La Beauce, France
First published: 1887

Principal characters:
 FOUAN, an old peasant farmer
 ROSE, his wife
 HYACINTHE, called Jésus-Christ, his older son
 FANNY, his daughter
 BUTEAU, his younger son
 DELHOMME, Fanny's husband
 LISE, Fouan's niece, daughter of Old Mouche
 FRANÇOISE, Lise's sister
 JEAN MACQUART, a soldier and artisan, later a farm laborer in La Beauce

Critique:

Earth (*La Terre*), the fifteenth volume of the Rougon-Macquart series, is Zola's horrifying vision of the French peasantry before the Franco-Prussian War. In the relationships between Fouan and his family, Zola consciously adopted the theme of Lear, although the farmer drawn with realistic detail has none of the nobility of Shakespeare's king. Zola's introduction of Rabelaisian humor in the character Jésus-Christ was an innovation in literary realism. The earth itself dominates the novel, and its beauty and indifference contrast vividly with the peasants' passionate absorption in possessing the land and with the crimes they commit in order to do so. When the novel appeared, Zola was reproached for his lack of idealism and his lack of understanding of the peasants. Mallarmé, however, did not hesitate to see in it true poetry. *Earth* is now among the most widely read of Zola's novels.

The Story:

As Jean Macquart finished sowing each furrow with grain, he paused and gazed over the wide, rich plain. As far as he could see farmers were scattering their wheat, anxious to finish sowing before the frosts came. He met and talked with Françoise about the coming division of old Fouan's property.

In the notary's office, plans for Fouan's sons and son-in-law to divide and farm his land were angrily made. Fouan could not bear to lose the land which had taken all his strength to work and which he had loved more passionately than his wife. The rent and food he asked in return for his property seemed excessive to his children, who, now that the land was within their grasp, intended to keep as much of its yield as possible. Buteau declared that the old man had money saved in bonds. This claim so enraged Fouan that he exhibited some of his former ferocity and authority. Finally the notary completed the transaction and arranged for the division of land by the surveyor.

Buteau, having drawn the third lot of land, declared it was the worst, and he refused to take that part of the property. His refusal distressed Lise, Françoise's sister, for Buteau had been her lover and she was pregnant. She had hoped that when he got the land he would marry her.

Old Mouche, the sisters' father, had a stroke and died in his home. As the village women watched by his deathbed, a violent hail storm laid waste the village crops. The peasants examined the damage by lamplight, their animosities forgotten in their common anguish at this devastation and their fury at the destructiveness of heaven.

Lise and Françoise stayed in the house

1682

after their father's death. Lise's son had been born and still Buteau had not married her. Jean became a constant visitor in the household. Believing that he was attracted by Lise, he proposed to her. Before accepting him, she decided to consult Buteau because of the child.

At the autumn haymaking Jean and Françoise worked together. While the girl stood atop the growing rick, Jean forked up bales of hay to her. She was flushed and laughing and Jean found her violently attractive. Because he was years older than Françoise, he was greatly upset when he suddenly realized that it was she who had drawn him to the house and not Lise.

Jean and the sisters met Buteau at the market in Cloyes. Because Lise now had property of her own and because he had at last accepted his share of land, Buteau decided to marry Lise. Buteau, delighted now by possession of the land, plowed and sowed with vigor and passion, determined never to relinquish one inch of the earth. As the wheat grew, its rolling greenness covered La Beauce like an ocean. Buteau watched the weather as anxiously as a sailor at sea. Although Françoise wished to have her share of the land decided, Buteau managed to avoid a final settlement.

When Fouan's older son, nicknamed Jésus-Christ, took to buy brandy the money which Buteau had grudgingly given his parents as their allowance, Buteau was so infuriated that he struck his mother to the floor. Rose did not recover and in three days she was dead. Fouan was then left completely alone. Finally, much against his will, he decided to make his home with Delhomme, his son-in-law.

By harvest time the green sea of wheat had turned to a fiery gold, and the whole village worked at the harvest. Jean, meanwhile, was tormented by his desire for Françoise. Finally, exhausted by her struggle to resist the constant attentions of Buteau as well, she yielded to him. Buteau, in his fear of losing both the girl and her land, asserted wildly that

they could never be married while Françoise was under age.

Meanwhile, Fouan was bullied and restricted in Delhomme's home; he had no money for tobacco and he was allowed little wine. Completely miserable, he went to live with Buteau and Lise. There he was appalled by Buteau's pursuit of Françoise, whose resistance made Buteau so angry that even Lise expressed the wish her sister would surrender in order to have peace once more in the household. Françoise, continuing proudly to refuse Buteau, was gradually turned into a domestic drudge.

In desperation Françoise agreed to marry Jean when she was of age. Fouan, drawn into these household quarrels, was no happier than he had been with Delhomme. At last, because Buteau and his wife begrudged every mouthful of food that he ate, he accepted Jésus-Christ's offer of a home. Jésus-Christ was the only one of Fouan's children without a passion for land. Although it distressed Fouan to see his hard-won acres go to buy brandy for Jésus-Christ, he enjoyed the jokes and the occasional excellent meals cooked in the nearly ruined house by Jésus-Christ's illegitimate daughter.

Before the time of the vintage Jésus-Christ discovered that his father was spending his bonds on an annuity by which he hoped to acquire some land of his own once more. Amazed, first Fanny and then Buteau tried to bribe the old man to return to them. Fouan's relationship with Jésus-Christ was never close again after the discovery.

After a final explosion with Lise, Françoise left the house and went to live with her aunt. It was arranged that she should soon marry Jean and claim her full share of the property. The ill will between the sisters was intensified when the land was divided and Françoise secured the house at auction. Buteau and Lise moved to an adjacent house, where Fouan, fearing that Jésus-Christ would steal his bonds, joined them.

Jean and Buteau were forced to work side by side in the fields. One day, while

Jean was manuring the earth, Lise told Buteau that Fouan had had a stroke and that she would bring the doctor. Surprisingly, the old man recovered. During his illness, however, Lise discovered his bonds. When they refused to return them, he left.

Homeless and desperate, Fouan wandered to Delhomme's farm, where he stayed wearily looking into the house. Next he went to Jésus-Christ's hovel, but fear and pride again prevented him from entering. That night, during a terrible storm, Fouan, wretched and exhausted, dragged himself around to look once more at the land he had owned. Finally his hunger became so great that he returned to Buteau, who jeeringly fed him.

Françoise was pregnant. Enraged by the fear that the property might not revert to him and by the fact that Jean's plow had cut into their land, Buteau, aided by Lise, at last raped Françoise. The girl then realized with revulsion that she had always loved him. Jealous, Lise knocked Françoise against a scythe in the field and the blade pierced her abdomen. As she lay dying Françoise refused to will her share of the farm to Jean; although he was her husband, she still regarded him as an outsider. After her death, Jean was evicted from the land.

Greedy for more money, and terrified that the old man would betray the manner of Françoise's death, Lise and Buteau murdered Fouan by smothering him with a pillow and then setting fire to his bed. Jean Macquart, having no further ties with La Beauce, decided again to become a soldier. After a final tour of the land he left the region for good. If he could not cultivate it, he would at least be able to defend the earth of France.

Further Critical Evaluation of the Work:

Zola began as a literary romantic and an idealist. In his youth, he wrote fairy tales and dreamt of perfect beauty and perfect love. But the poverty he experienced early in life and the general Europan literary climate brought him to try to picture an imperfect but real "corner of nature."

Earth, a magnificent example of Zola's groping for the authentic details in life, can be best understood when placed in the literary context of realism and naturalism. Literary realism developed in the nineteenth century partly as a response to the conditions of modern society. It stressed fidelity to the facts of everyday existence. Scenes, characters, motives, conflicts were presumably drawn from experiences in life rather than from dreams of other worlds or of the supernatural. Within the realist tradition are distinct and coherent groupings. Naturalism is one of them. But it is easier to place a work such as *Earth* in the naturalist tradition than it is to define literary naturalism. In general, however, for the purposes of examining *Earth,* we can establish two basic points: first, naturalism attempts to portray the actual and significant details of life and especially (though not exclusively) the life of poor and working people; second, naturalism most often attempts to uncover those forces, in the environment and in the genetic make-up of the individual, that determine the course of life.

Earth tries to give an accurate picture of French rural life in the 1860's; and this picture is not merely a general account, but a brilliantly detailed canvas that conveys the humanity and density of rural life.

The basis of the action of the novel is the division of his land by an old man. Much of the novel, therefore, describes the unending, vicious, implacable hatreds and the unyielding tensions that emerge within the farmer's family. Domestic life appears in the conversations, the cooking and cleaning utensils, the jealous glances, the dirt, the cobwebs, and the small, damp rooms of the peasant households. The smells of the fields, the manure, the sweat, the musky odors of water and age saturate everything.

The life of the countryside is further explored in relation to the fields, skies, and attention to the weather. The division of these fields, the occasional run-down cottage, the seeding and fertilization of the fields are communicated in the most meticulous detail. Pages are devoted to storms of various kinds, including a hail storm. But unlike the romantics, for whom the excesses of the weather are often merely spectacular, these storms are viewed as destructive and, toward the end of *Earth,* in the tradition of *King Lear*, as brutalizing and humbling.

Main events in the harvest are not omitted. A grape harvest, for example, is sketched by Zola. The workers pick these grapes, stuff themselves, and get sick. In fact, sickness, drunkenness, perversity, and violence—all inherent in the life of these times—are examined with special intensity. Fevers, passions, obsessions, jealousies, and the mutual destruction inseparable from the conditions of the life of the peasants are not spared. The reader feels that Zola leaves out nothing, including the sexual aspect. From the beginning of the novel, wherein Zola describes a young man and woman helping a bull and cow to mate, without embarrassment, the sexual theme is established. Rape and incest are not excluded.

Zola's accumulation of detail from real experience becomes more and more powerful as the novel advances. These details—linked through action, character, and theme—become, for the reader, the tightly woven, actual fabric of life. Reading *Earth* is, in fact, to be submerged in this life; and this feeling of submersion accounts, no doubt, for the powerful influence the novel continues to exert. At the same time, the accumulation of these details naturally raises the question of selection. Can Zola be accused of presenting only the sordid side of life, of emphasizing the nasty aspects of life unnecessarily? Has he only selected those details which demonstrate the obscene or degraded features of country life? *Earth* was sharply attacked when it was first published precisely for these reasons. The novel was even thought to be deliberately pornographic. Although a modern reader may tell himself that such an accusation is outdated or humorously quaint, it must be said that the brutality and often unexpected violence and sex remain, to this day, quite literally shocking. But a good argument can be made that these scenes are included not for their shock value but for more serious reasons. These reasons are, strangely enough, connected to Zola's understanding of science.

The second important feature of literary naturalism, its attempt to portray the underlying forces that shape human destiny, is especially evident in the work of Zola. These forces were understood by Zola in a scientific context. They were describable, measurable, and inevitable. In his view, in fact, by understanding the genetic and environmental forces working on his characters, and by altering these forces, he could explain his characters scientifically and, at the same time, actually experiment on them and test them in his fiction. Zola did not carry out this experimental procedure vigorously in his novels.

In *Earth,* the forces that are most evident are those associated with the land. The greed for the land, which is manifest in Buteau, one of the central characters, overcomes all obstacles. Buteau will have the land or destroy it, himself, and his competitors and family. Also connected to the earth is the power of sex. The opening scene of the novel deals with the fertilization of the land. A sexual life "close to the earth" is also described. Sexual activity takes place in the fields as well as in the home.

Finally, there is the genetic composition of the characters. Their strengths and weaknesses, determined by the strengths and weaknesses of their ancestors, provide a spectrum of responses to the conditions of rural France. The family thus helps place *Earth* in its proper position in the massive architecture of Zola's Rougon-Macquart series.

Although Zola may have seen his characters as more or less determined by forces outside their control, *Earth* leaves the impression that men and women can, within limits, choose their course in life. It should be said that some other practitioners of naturalist fiction—such as Frank Norris in the United States—took a much more mechanical approach to the "scientific" forces that shape human life. In Norris' work, the reader is left with the impression that human freedom is simply low farce. But Zola, in the novel *Earth,* does not communicate this sense of a claustrophobic fate. No matter how awful Fouan's end may be, Zola never shifts the responsibility away from Fouan to the abstraction of heredity.

Earth, in the last analysis, certainly demonstrates the limits and the narrowness of the life of the peasant in nineteenth century France. But within those limits Zola shows that freedom survives, and with freedom the refreshing possibilities of birth.

Howard Lee Hertz

THE EARTHLY PARADISE

Type of work: Poetry
Author: William Morris (1834-1896)
First published: 1868-1870

Of all the poems of William Morris, the most successful, in terms of popularity, is *The Earthly Paradise,* published originally in five thick volumes. Following closely the plan of *The Canterbury Tales,* this composition reveals Morris' attraction to Chaucer's method as well as his sense of beauty. Like Chaucer, he found in medieval legends and ancient myths material for his poetic narrative art; and he also found a general plan according to which these unrelated stories could be brought together harmoniously by a technique in which Eastern cultures had long anticipated Chaucer and other Europeans. Unlike Chaucer, whose plan was so large that he could not complete it, Morris, upon an almost equal scale, easily brought his work to a happy conclusion.

The prologue introduces a company of Norsemen who have fled the pestilence and set sail to seek the fabled Earthly Paradise "across the western sea where none grow old." Not having succeeded in their quest, they have returned "shrivelled, bent, and grey," after lengthy wanderings abroad, to a "nameless city in a distant sea" where the worship of the ancient Greek gods has not died out. In this hospitable city they spend the rest of their lives. Twice each month they participate in a feast at which a tale is told, alternately, by one of the city elders and one of the wanderers. The former tell tales on classical subjects, and the latter draw their tales from Norse and other medieval sources. Thus, of the twenty-four stories, twelve are Greek and classical and twelve are medieval or romantic. Each pair of stories corresponds with one of the twelve months, the first two being told in January, the second two in February, and so on. Thus the long poem is neatly partitioned into twelve books with interpolated prologues and epilogues in the form of lyrics about the progressive changes in nature. *The Earthly Paradise* actually revived in England an enthusiasm for long romances. Despite their high cost, many thousands of Morris' books were sold, and the effect was a favorable one for the new revival of romantic feeling which Morris was fostering in art and decoration as well as in literature. Instead of exhausting Morris, this poetic effort inspired him to embark on other vast projects such as the translation of Homer and Vergil and a modern version of a Scandinavian epic, *Sigurd the Volsung.*

Among the tales told by the wanderers in *The Earthly Paradise,* the most striking is "The Lovers of Gudrun," a version of the Icelandic Laxdaela Saga. It tells of Gudrun, daughter of a great lord in Iceland, who was loved by many men but especially by Kiartan, a youth of manly deeds and kindly disposition. Although Gudrun passionately returns his love, Kiartan, before he will marry her, goes with his bosom friend and cousin Bodli to seek fame in Norway, where he remains some years at the court of Olaf Trygvesson. When Bodli returns alone to Iceland, he yields to his passion for Gudrun and tells her that Kiartan has fallen in love with King Olaf's sister Ingibiarg and will marry her. Convinced of Kiartan's unfaithfulness, Gudrun brokenheartedly marries Bodli. When Kiartan returns to claim his bride, Gudrun curses Bodli, and the desolate Kiartan, half in contempt, spares his life. Despairing and taunted by those about him, Bodli participates in an ambush set up by Kiartan's enemies, treacherously slays his friend, and is in turn killed by Kiartan's brothers. Although Gudrun marries again, what remains indelibly with the reader is Morris' picture of her agonized realization of what, in her faithlessness, she has done:

She cried, with tremulous voice, and

eyes grown wet
For the last time, what e'er should happen yet,
With hands stretched out for all that she had lost:
"I did the worst to him I loved the most."

Morris was a natural creator; that his hand could not outspeed his brain is evidenced by his composing seven hundred lines of poetry in a day. Years after the composition of *The Earthly Paradise* he explained the nonchalant attitude toward the writing of poetry which enabled him to race undaunted through that enormous project: "Waiting for inspiration, rushing things in reliance on inspiration, and all the rest of it, are a lazy man's habits. Get the bones of the work well into your head, and the tools well into your hand, and get on with the job, and the inspiration will come to you. . . ."

In spite of its quantity of production, his poetry has a remarkably high quality. Although somewhat lacking in humor, pathos, and rich humanity, it shows none of the crabbed agonies undergone by many poets. His range of subject matter is as broad as his composition was fluent. The very spacious cycle of stories in *The Earthly Paradise* includes these titles: "The Story of Theseus," "The Son of Croesus," "Cupid and Psyche," "The King's Treasure-House," "Orpheus and Eurydice," "Pygmalion," "Atalanta's Race," "The Doom of King Acrisius," "Rhodope," "The Dolphin and the Lovers," "The Fortunes of Gygis," "Bellerophon," "The Watching of the Falcon," "The Lady of the Land," "The Hill of Venus," "The Seven Sleepers," "The Man Who Never Laughed Again," "The Palace East of the Sun," "The Queen of the North," "The Story of Dorothea," "The Writing on the Image," "The Proud King," "The Ring Given to Venus," and "The Man Born to Be King."

These stories are so arranged that, with the revolving calendar, their temper becomes darker and stronger, developing into a sinister tone at the end. The full effect thus depends upon a continuous and consecutive reading. Conversely, the problem which arises as the reader progresses through this lengthy work is that the embroidery becomes too profuse to be sustained by the fabric. The result is the taint of decoration inherent in the Pre-Raphaelites—too much of beauty, love, languor, everything—so that the reader longs for a little substantial simplicity and cheerfulness. One might, therefore, argue for an occasional and selective reading of the stories, so long as their total scope is kept in mind.

The interludes give us glimpses into the poet's mind which are evidence that despite his disapproval of introspective poetry, Morris did not always avoid it. While the stories of *The Earthly Paradise* come from all parts of the medieval world, these poems of the months are unequivocally English; they give an admiring description of the land of Morris' birth and life. With variations, they repeat the keynote of the Prologue in which he characterizes himself as "the idle singer of an empty day" who has no power to sing of hell or heaven or to make death bearable. By "idle" Morris does not mean "useless" but, rather, one who can, by the scenes he presents, distract from "empty," daily cares. In this manner he acknowledged spiritual emptiness in his time.

Throughout this poetic work there runs a strain of despondency, doubt, and mild skepticism which records the poet's genuine pity for mankind. Although there is in the work an elemental vigor, glorying in youth, power, love, and possessions, these aspects of life are presented primarily through old men's memories. Despite the strong swift-moving action, the narrative generally seems grandly slow. Neither the tale-tellers nor the actors in the tales are particularly individualized as characters. Finally we see a vast, intricate tapestry with its panorama of interwoven figures.

EAST OF EDEN

Type of work: Novel
Author: John Steinbeck (1902-1968)
Type of plot: Regional chronicle
Time of plot: 1865-1918
Locale: California
First published: 1952

Principal characters:
ADAM TRASK, a settler in the Salinas Valley
CATHY AMES, later Adam's wife
CALEB and
ARON TRASK, their twin sons
CHARLES TRASK, Adam's half-brother
SAMUEL HAMILTON, a neighbor of the Trasks
LEE, Adam's Chinese servant
ABRA BACON, Aron's fiancée

Critique:

East of Eden is an ambitious but not altogether successful attempt to present three themes simultaneously: a panoramic history of the Salinas Valley (and thus of America itself) around the turn of the century; a melodramatic chronicle of two families in the valley; a symbolic re-creation of the Cain and Abel story. Its expressed concern, however, is philosophic—the nature of the conflict between good and evil. In this conflict love and the acceptance or rejection it brings to the individual plays an important role, yet one has always the opportunity to choose the good. In this freedom lies man's glory. The book's defects stem from the author's somewhat foggy and sentimental presentation of its philosophy and his tendency to manipulate or over-simplify characters and events for symbolic purposes.

The Story:

The soil of the Salinas Valley in California is rich, though the foothills around it are poor and its life shrivels during the long dry spells. The Irish-born Hamiltons, arriving after American settlers had displaced the Mexicans, settled on the barren hillside. There Sam Hamilton, full of talk, glory, and improvident inventions, and Liza, his dourly religious wife, brought up their nine children.

In Connecticut, Adam Trask and his half-brother Charles grew up, mutually affectionate in spite of the differences in their natures. Adam was gentle and good; Charles, roughly handsome with a streak of wild violence. After Adam's mother had committed suicide, his father had married a docile girl who had borne Charles. Adam loved his stepmother but hated his father, a rigid disciplinarian whose fanatic militarism had begun with a fictitious account of his own war career and whose dream was to have a son in the army. To fulfill his dream, he chose Adam, who could gain the greater strength that comes from the conquest of weakness as Charles could not. But Charles, whose passionate love for his father went continually unnoticed, could not understand this final rejection of himself. In violent despair, he beat Adam almost to death.

Adam served in the cavalry for five years. Then, although he hated regimentation and violence, he reënlisted, for he could neither accept help from his father, who had become an important figure in Washington, nor return to the farm Charles now ran alone. Afterward he wandered through the West and the South, served time for vagrancy, and finally came home to find his father dead and himself and Charles rich. In the years that followed he and Charles lived together, although their bickering and inbred solitude drove Adam to periodic wanderings. Feeling that their life was one of pointless industry, he talked of moving west but did not.

Meanwhile, Cathy Ames was growing up in Massachusetts. She was a monster, born unable to comprehend goodness but with a sublimely innocent face and a consummate knowledge of how to manipulate or deceive people to serve her own ends. After a thwarted attempt to leave home, she burned her house, killing her parents and leaving evidence to indicate that she had been murdered. She then became the mistress of a man who ran a string of brothels and used his insatiable love for her to torment him. When he realized her true nature, he took her to a deserted spot and beat her savagely. Near death, she crawled to the nearest house—the Trasks'—where Adam and Charles cared for her. Adam found her innocent and beautiful; Charles, who had a knowledge of evil through himself, recognized the evil in her and wanted her to leave. Cathy, needing temporary protection, enticed Adam into marrying her, but on their wedding night she gave him a sleeping draught and went to Charles.

Feeling that Charles disapproved of Cathy, Adam decided to carry out his dream of going west. He was so transfigured by his happiness that he did not take Cathy's protests seriously; as his ideal of love and purity, she could not disagree. Adam bought a ranch in the richest part of the Salinas Valley and worked hard to ready it for his wife and the child she expected. Cathy hated her pregnancy, but she knew that she had to wait calmly to get back to the life she wanted. After giving birth to twin boys, she waited a week; she then shot Adam, wounding him, and walked out.

Changing her name to Kate, Cathy went to work in a Salinas brothel. Her beauty and seeming goodness endeared her to the proprietress, Faye, and Kate gradually assumed control of the establishment. After Faye made a will leaving Kate her money and property, Kate slyly engineered Faye's death. Making her establishment one which aroused and purveyed to sadistic tastes, she became legendary and rich.

Adam was like a dead man for a year after his wife left him, unable to work his land or even to name his sons. Finally Sam Hamilton woke him by deliberately angering him, and Sam, Adam, and Lee, the Chinese servant and a wise and good man, named the boys Caleb and Aron. As the men talked of the story of Cain and Abel, Lee concluded that rejection terrifies a child most and leads to guilt and revenge. Later, after much study, Lee discovered the true meaning of the Hebrew word *timshel*—thou mayest—and understood that the story meant in part that man can always choose to conquer evil.

Sam, grown old, knew that he would soon die. Before he left his ranch, he told Adam of Kate and her cruel, destructive business. Adam, disbelieving in her very existence, visited her and suddenly knew her as she really was. Though she tried to taunt him, telling him that Charles was the true father of his sons, and to seduce him, he left her a free and curiously exultant man. Yet he could not tell his sons that their mother was not dead.

Caleb and Aron were growing up very differently. Aron was golden-haired and automatically inspired love, yet he remained single-minded and unyielding; Caleb was dark and clever, a feared and respected leader left much alone. When Adam moved to town, where the schools were better, Aron fell in love with Abra Bacon. Abra told Aron that his mother was still alive, but he could not believe her because to do so would have destroyed his faith in his father and thus in everything.

About this time Adam had the idea of shipping lettuce packed in ice to New York, but the venture failed. Aron was ashamed of his father for failing publicly. Caleb vowed to return the lost money to his father.

As they faced the problems of growing into men, Aron became smugly religious, disturbing to Abra because she felt unable to live up to his idealistic image of her. Caleb alternated between wild impulses and guilt. Learning that Kate was his mother, he began following her until she, noticing him, invited him to her house. As he talked to her, he knew with relief that he was not like her; she felt his knowledge and hated him. Kate herself, obsessed by the fear that one of the old girls had discovered Faye's murder, plotted ways to destroy this menace. Although Caleb could accept Kate's existence, he knew that Aron could not. To get the boy away from Salinas, Caleb talked him into finishing high school in three years and beginning college. Adam, knowing nothing of Caleb's true feelings, was extravagantly proud of Aron.

World War I began. Caleb went into the bean business with Will Hamilton and made a fortune because of food shortages. With growing excitement, he planned an elaborate presentation to his father of the money once lost in the lettuce enterprise. First he tried to persuade Aron, who seemed indifferent to his father's love, not to leave college. Caleb presented his money to Adam, only to have it rejected in anger because Adam's idealistic nature could not accept money made as profit from the war. He wanted Caleb's achievements to be like his brother's. In a black mood of revenge, Caleb took Aron to meet his mother. After her sons' visit Kate, who was not disturbed by those she could hurt as she was by someone like Caleb, made a will leaving everything to Aron. Then, overburdened by age, illness, and suspicion, she committed suicide.

Unable to face his new knowledge of his parents' past, Aron joined the army and went to France. Adam did not recover from the shock of his leaving. Abra turned to Caleb, admitting that she loved him rather than Aron, whose romantic stubbornness kept him from facing reality. When the news of Aron's death arrived, Adam had another stroke. As he lay dying, Caleb, unable to bear his guilt any longer, told his father of his responsibility for Aron's enlisting and thus his death. Lee begged Adam to forgive his son. Adam weakly raised his hand in benediction and, whispering the Hebrew word *timshel,* died.

Further Critical Evaluation of the Work:

Compared to other novels by John Steinbeck, *East of Eden* has received relatively little attention, and most of it has been adverse. The primary reason for relegating *East of Eden* to the status of an inferior novel seems to be that it is atypical of Steinbeck's corpus. After all, in most of his other works Steinbeck was concerned with social issues from a realistic or a naturalistic point of view, portraying human travail with relentless accuracy through an intensive examination of a short time span. But in *East of Eden,* Steinbeck departs from his customary literary style to write an epic portrait which ranges less intensively over a much broader time span of about seventy years. Although depictions of characters and events are really no less vivid than in his other novels, Steinbeck's *East of Eden* is certainly less structured, a looser novel than his dedicated readers had come to expect. Thus, despite some quite explicit sex scenes, disappointed reader expectation accounts in large measure for the failure of *East of Eden* to win popular or critical acclaim. It simply was not what people had come to expect of Steinbeck.

But the novel is at least respectable if not brilliant. In fact, it is, in many ways, a historical romance in its panoramic sweep of significant history overlaid with specific human problems. The story ranges from the Civil War to World War I, from the East Coast to the West Coast, over several generations of two families. It displays all of the conventional elements of historical romance. Genuinely historical events and people providing the backdrop, even the shaping forces which mold the fictional characters' lives and determine their destiny. These characters thus appear to have only partial control over their lives, at best; and external factors consequently determine to a large extent what they must cope with in order to survive. They appear to be buffeted mercilessly by fate.

However, Steinbeck's philosophical commitment to free will aborts the naturalistically logical conclusion. As a result, both Charles and Adam Trask appear to select freely their own paths in life, the former indulging fantasies of evil and the latter choosing to disregard everyone's evil inclinations, including his own. So, too, is Cathy made to seem capable of choice and responsible for it. Likewise, the other major characters are depicted as having the capacity for moral choice and for living with the consequences. Yet it is just this aspect of *East of Eden* which flies in the face of the reader's expectations of "typical" Steinbeck and flies in the face of both logic and reality. Finally it is Steinbeck's own ambivalence about free will and determinism which constitutes the major weakness in *East of Eden*. For whatever we or Steinbeck believe about a historical-Biblical Garden of Eden, neither we nor Steinbeck believe that a Garden of Eden exists now—east or west—even in the Salinas Valley.

EASTWARD HO!

Type of work: Drama
Authors: George Chapman (c. 1559-1634) with Ben Jonson (1573?-1637) and John Marston (1576-1634)
Type of plot: Realistic comedy
Time of plot: About 1605
Locale: London
First presented: 1605

> *Principal characters:*
> TOUCHSTONE, a goldsmith
> MISTRESS TOUCHSTONE, his wife
> GERTRUDE, his haughty daughter
> MILDRED, his dutiful daughter
> FRANCIS QUICKSILVER, his idle and prodigal apprentice
> GOLDING, his diligent apprentice
> SIR PETRONEL FLASH, a new-made knight
> SECURITY, an old usurer
> WINIFRED, his young wife
> SINDEFY, Quicksilver's mistress

Critique:

Eastward Ho! is a remarkable example of successful collaboration. For three authors as different in temperament as Chapman, Jonson, and Marston to write together a smooth, unified, and amusing play is almost a miracle. It encompasses the heartwarming theme of the Prodigal Son and satirical thrusts at contemporary society. Scholars have tried to assign specific scenes and lines to the individual authors, but the general reader or playgoer need not trouble himself with problems of authorship. The play's rapid dramatic movement, in keeping with its apparently rapid composition, carries its audience through laughter and sentiment to an appropriate happy ending. The characters are amusing, and even the victims of the satire are treated without the bitterness or savagery that other works of Jonson and Marston might lead one to expect. It is a true comedy which should be as effective on the modern as on the Elizabethan stage.

The Story:

Touchstone, a goldsmith, had two daughters, Gertrude, a flutter-brained social climber, and Mildred, a modest, gentle girl. He also had two apprentices, Francis Quicksilver, a fellow as unstable as his name, and Golding, who was steady and conscientious.

Caught while trying to slip away from the shop, Quicksilver made a spirited defense of his way of life, especially of his prodigality among the town gallants. Touchstone answered with a severe moral lecture and pointed out the exemplary behavior of his fellow apprentice. The lecture was interrupted by a messenger from Sir Petronel Flash, who wished to make arrangements to marry Gertrude. As soon as Touchstone was out of hearing, Quicksilver abused the old citizen; but Golding defended his master and warned and rebuked Quicksilver.

Mildred, with the help of a tailor and a maid, attired Gertrude elegantly to receive her knight, while Gertrude rattled away, full of herself and contemptuous of her bourgeois family. Touchstone brought in Sir Petronel and concluded the arrangements for the wedding, warning both Gertrude and the knight that they need not expect any gifts beyond the agreed dowry. Gertrude impudently flouted him and left with the knight, Mistress Touchstone fluttering in attendance on her soon-to-be-married daughter. After their departure Touchstone proposed a match between Mildred and

Golding.

From the wedding feast Quicksilver returned to the shop drunk, hiccuping and quoting lines from popular plays like *Tamburlaine* and *The Spanish Tragedy.* Touchstone, losing patience with the fellow, released him from his indenture and discharged him. After Quicksilver's defiant and staggering exit, Touchstone told Golding that he too would no longer be an apprentice, but a full-fledged member of the guild and his master's son-in-law.

At the home of old Security, where Quicksilver and his mistress Sindefy lived, the old usurer plotted with them to trap Sir Petronel and to gain possession of Gertrude's property. Quicksilver was to encourage the knight to borrow money for a proposed voyage to Virginia, and both Quicksilver and Sindefy, who was to become Gertrude's maid, were to encourage the bride to put up her land to cover the debt. Before leaving to set his plans in motion, Security delayed to bid farewell to his pretty young wife, Winifred.

Sir Petronel confessed to Quicksilver that he had no castle, but that he intended to send his bride on a wild-goose chase to an imaginary castle in the country in order to get her out of the way while he carried off old Security's young wife on the Virginia voyage. Security brought in Sindefy and placed her with Gertrude as a maid, then took Sir Petronel to his home for breakfast. Captain Seagull, Scapethrift, and Spendall joined Sir Petronel there to make the final plans for the voyage.

As Gertrude prepared for her ride into the country to see her husband's nonexistent castle, Touchstone entered with his other daughter and his new son-in-law, Golding. Gertrude heaped contempt on all three, and Sir Petronel made disparaging remarks about the groom's lack of nobility. Touchstone distributed a few ironical barbs and led away the newlyweds. After their departure, Security presented Gertrude with papers, supposedly to cover a loan for new furnishings

for the country castle. At Sir Petronel's request she signed the papers without even reading them and set out in her coach after urging the knight to follow as soon as possible. Sir Petronel and Quicksilver convinced Security that the knight was planning to elope with a lawyer's wife; and Security, maliciously delighted at the chance to injure another man, promised to lend them his wife's gown as a disguise. He also felt that lending the gown would be a good way to make certain that his wife did not leave home.

Sir Petronel, the disguised Winifred, Quicksilver, and the other adventurers ignored storm warnings and set out in their boats for the ship. Security discovered his wife's absence and tried to follow them. Slitgut, a butcher coming to Cuckold's Haven to set up a pair of horns, saw from his elevated vantage point a boat overturned in the waves. A few minutes later old Security crawled ashore bemoaning the appropriateness of his place of shipwreck. As soon as he had crept away, the butcher saw a woman struggling in the waves and a boy plunging in to save her. The boy rescued a very repentant Winifred, brought her ashore, and offered her shelter and dry clothes. A third victim of the storm was washed ashore at the foot of the gallows—a bad omen, Slitgut thought. The man was Francis Quicksilver, who passed by cursing his fate. Finally, Sir Petronel and Captain Seagull reached shore and met Quicksilver. Sir Petronel, having lost his money in the water, had no hope of saving his ship, which he expected to be confiscated. Winifred, now dry and freshly dressed, convinced Security that she had not left home until she began to worry about him. Slitgut made a few wry remarks about marriage and went home, unobserved by any of the adventurers.

Touchstone, thoroughly angered by the knight's desertion and by his wife's and daughter's foolishness, turned out Gertrude and Sindefy to shift for themselves, but having borne his wife as a cross for thirty years, he felt he should continue to do so. Golding, made an alderman's deputy on his first day in the guild, reported that Sir Petronel and Quicksilver had been arrested and the ship attached.

Mistress Touchstone had learned her lesson; but Gertrude, in spite of her mother's entreaties that she beg forgiveness, treated her father with her customary contempt. Sir Petronel and Quicksilver were brought in by a constable, and Quicksilver was charged with the theft of five hundred pounds, a capital offense. A warrant was also sent out for old Security for his share in the business. Sir Petronel and Quicksilver reached a peak of repentance that made them the talk of the prison. Golding and the jailer joined Mistress Touchstone and her daughters in pleading with Touchstone to show mercy to the offenders; but Touchstone was adamant. Finally Golding had himself arrested, sent for Touchstone to come to release him, and arranged for the latter to overhear Quicksilver's ballad of repentance, sung for the edification of other prisoners to the tune of "I Wail in Woe, I Plunge in Pain." Touchstone's heart was moved, and he offered forgiveness to both prodigal son-in-law and prodigal apprentice. Old Security, hearing that a song of repentance had worked such wonders, rushed up howling a lamentable song in a most lamentable voice; he too received mercy. At Golding's urging, Quicksilver agreed to marry Sindefy. Security returned to Winifred. Even Gertrude forgave her erring husband and asked forgiveness from her father. Thus all differences were reconciled.

Further Critical Evaluation of the Work:

A product of collaboration by three successful playwrights in their own right, *Eastward Ho!* is one of a genre of Jacobean plays called city comedies. As such, the play deals heavily with the domestic imbroglios of merchants and their apprentices and seems designed to appeal to just such individuals in the audience. Those to whom the play would most readily appeal would be those who accepted the conventional morality of the day. It is this morality —a solid aggregate of thrift, hard work, and humility—which forms the foundation on which the play's didactic message is based.

The plot builds upon the timeless and popular exemplum of the Prodigal Son. In this case, the son has been split into an artificial son, the apprentice Quicksilver, and a natural daughter, Gertrude. They are balanced by their virtuous counterparts, the good apprentice, Golding, and the good daughter, Mildred. Quicksilver and Gertrude (with Sir Petronel Flash thrown in for interest) are wasteful, lazy, and proud; Golding is thrifty, hard-working, and humble, as is Mildred. Touchstone, as his name indicates, provides the play with a judgmental intellect, one who tests the various characters and pronounces them false, or good as gold.

But the play transcends its precursor, the medieval morality play, in presenting characters who are more than merely their types. Quicksilver, who had previously been a stealer of unconsidered lines from other plays, becomes something of a didactic poet and is saved through his repentance. Touchstone, embodiment of morality though he is, shows his weakness in willfully denying his own impulses to mercy. Finally, from a position of power gained by his life of virtue, Golding rises above all as the dispenser of impartial justice and selfless mercy.

Eastward Ho! was written to compete with a play of similar title, *Westward Ho!,* produced by a rival company. It is famous in part for a passage (III, iii, 42-47) insulting to Scots, which offended James I, causing Chapman and Jonson to be imprisoned.

EBONY AND IVORY

Type of work: Short stories
Author: Llewelyn Powys (1884-1939)
Time: Early twentieth century
Locale: Africa and Europe
First published: 1923

Llewelyn Powys, the youngest of three brothers to achieve literary fame, was a rather gifted and remarkable British writer. He was educated at Cambridge, worked as a stock farmer in Kenya during World War I, and then moved to New York to work as a journalist for five more years. The stories in *Ebony and Ivory*, many of which were published in the best magazines of the time, were written during his stay in Kenya and New York. They present perhaps the best and most representative examples of his outlook and art.

Powys' outlook and art are very closely related. His vision of life informs every aspect of his art, while his art is an attempt to answer that vision. This tension between outlook and art, truth and style, content and form, provides Powys' stories with their intensity and force.

Powys' vision of life, the spirit that informs these stories, was grounded in pain and death, cruelty and mortality, vanity and doom, for Powys was obsessed with agony and fate, which for him were the sole absolutes of life. His stories dwell overwhelmingly on the tragic soul-destroying aspects of life and have much the same spirit as *Ecclesiastes*, the *Rubáiyát of Omar Khayyám*, and much of the fiction of Joseph Conrad. They show an intimate acquaintance with the terror, cruelties, and savagery that plague men. Powys knew the futility and mortality of humanity. This was the lesson he learned in Africa.

In this collection there are the Ebony stories and sketches, which take place in British East Africa, and the Ivory tales, which take place in Europe. The title obviously contains an ironic play on skin color, on black and white, but beyond this fact and far more important is the reference to the Arab proverb: "On Ebony and Ivory the same dark doom is writ."

The Ebony stories provide the hard core of Powys' vision, for their total effect is that of hopelessness and despair. These sketches show the soul-killing effect of Africa on the European and African alike. The unrelenting sun, the harshness of color and noise, the voraciousness of animal and human life all reduce men to their naked, cruel selves. The European is demoralized and all of his illusions are destroyed. His rule is stripped of its benevolence in Africa and is shown to rest on brutality and cunning. Thus in "Black Parasites" a hard-hearted, mediocre farmer sets fire to his brushland after tying up a native sheep thief in the middle of it. In "How It Happens" a sensitive boy arrives in British East Africa from England, and in his harsh, new surroundings he is demoralized by his mediocre associates, gets syphilis, and commits suicide. Powys' theme, the loss of innocence, was almost inevitable, given his outlook on life. In "Black Gods" he declared that the bottom of the well of life contains no hope, that the surface was all, the depth hollow and empty.

When Powys' heroes undergo any change, it is in the direction of shedding illusions, of descending to the bottom of the well of life and facing life without hope. This does not mean that they necessarily give up; Powys' most memorable heroes face life's savagery with a hopeless defiance. In "Dead Matter in Africa" a zebra guards his dead mate against the vultures, against all hope and reason, and against the universe. Again, in his Ebony story, "The Stunner," a dumb brute of a man rises from his deathbed and staggers miles to his sweetheart solely on strength of his love. But this kind of heroism, however admirable, is essentially futile; it means involving oneself in pain, in death, and in tragedy. Although Powys' stories are not Christian in outlook, the figure of the crucified Jesus runs through the majority of them, for Jesus is the epitome of this futile heroism, of this agonized defiance of fate.

As the Arab proverb suggests, Powys' Ivory tales elaborate the ideas and motifs of the Ebony section. In "Threnody," "Death," and "The Brown Satyr," Powys develops the same theme he used in "How It Happens," namely the loss of innocence and the problem of facing a world devoid of hope. In "Not Guilty," "Un Mufle," and "The Wryneck," Powys shows again the impossibility of love in a cursed and savage world devoid of meaning and full of doom.

In quality the Ebony stories seem slightly superior to the Ivory tales simply because Africa provided a more appropriate background for Powys' despairing vision, even though he does a fine job of conveying that vision in the Ivory section as well. For Powys the world was cursed and damned, and it was damned no matter where one was, whether in the heart of Africa or in the heart of civilization. To him it was as if some evil wizard had desolated the world and left it in agony and despair.

Needless to say, such a vision of life could easily become intolerable to the person who possessed it unless he had some means of protecting himself against it, some means of converting it into something productive. Powys' method of achieving release was through writing, through art which gave a tangible form to that vision. Powys sought his salvation through his stories and through observation. If participation in the world meant pain and tragedy, observation was a way of protecting oneself from pain and tragedy, a way of keeping the world at a distance. Art, for Powys, was a way of re-shaping life's pain and thereby controlling it. Passive observation and active artistic creation were his way of protecting himself against his vision.

As one might expect, Powys wrote about pain and tragedy in a detached style that was both cool and evocative. Powys possessed a happy feeling for the right word, the precise expression, which contributed greatly to the crisp, cold, clear quality of his writing. This detached mode of writing, which at times approached cruelty, considerably heightened the horror of his tales. If Powys had written with sympathy for his characters the effect would have been reduced and the full power of his vision would not have come through.

Powys was essentially an ironist. His irony was engendered by the conflict between his vision and his art. On the one hand he saw the world as irrevocably damned and on the other he tried to escape this damnation through art; thus he wrote about cruelty, pain, and doom with detachment and reserve. Truth, for Powys, was only to be gained through passive observation. Through truth he hoped to gain a kind of salvation, but the truth proved to be just as ironic as himself. What Powys did gain through passive observation was the ability to transform horror into beauty. His stories possess a cruel, evocative beauty, but his beauty, like his truth, was essentially ironic, frigid and sterile in its revelation.

Powys' failings and virtues as a writer arise from his vision of life and his attempt to cope with that vision. He was a fine writer of short stories and sketches and had a remarkable ability to express himself with clarity, beauty, and force, but he paid for this ability in terms of agony and coldness. His stories are comparable with those of Poe, Bierce, and Hemingway in vividness, beauty, and power. One must be prepared to pay for these things.

THE ECCLESIAZUSAE

Type of work: Drama
Author: Aristophanes (c. 448-c. 385 B.C.)
Type of plot: Utopian comedy
Time of plot: Early fourth century B.C.
Locale: Athens
First presented: 392 B.C.

Principal characters:
PRAXAGORA, leader of the revolution
BLEPYRUS, her husband
CHREMES
A YOUNG MAN
THREE OLD WOMEN

Critique:

The *Ecclesiazusae* is not one of Aristophanes' best plays. Written late in his career, it lacks the wit and ingenuity of *Lysistrata*, the play which it most resembles. The scatological humor seems gratuitous, but the satire on the communistic Utopia enforced by the women of Athens is effective and the action moves swiftly, especially since the role of the chorus has been reduced to practically nothing. Although the play appeared some twenty years before Plato's *Republic*, some critics believe that the playwright is here deriding the philosopher's ideas as they circulated in discussion.

The Story:

Praxagora, who had stolen her husband's clothes and escaped from the house before dawn, was waiting in the street for her fellow conspirators to appear. As they arrived she inspected them to see if they had made all the preparations that had been agreed upon at the feast of the Scirophoria. Had they let the hair under their armpits grow? Had they darkened their complexions by rubbing themselves thoroughly with oil and standing all day in the sun? Had they prepared false beards? Had they stolen their husbands' shoes, cloaks, staffs, and clubs? Assured that they had done everything possible to disguise themselves as men, Praxagora opened the discussion of their plot to save Athens by taking over the government from the men. This was to be achieved by invading the assembly disguised as men and dominating the vote. The first problem was to select a spokesman. When woman after woman failed the practice test by invoking goddesses or addressing the audience in feminine terms, Praxagora herself took on the responsibility of speaking for them. At dawn they departed for the assembly.

Meanwhile, Blepyrus, Praxagora's husband, had awakened with a need to relieve himself, only to find both his wife and his clothes missing. His need was so great, however, that he dressed in his wife's saffron robe and rushed outdoors. Before he could return to the house, he was accosted by his friend Chremes, who gave him a detailed account of the strange proceedings at the assembly. He told how, after several citizens had proposed stupid suggestions for curing the economic plight of the city, a rather fair young man had taken the floor to urge that the government be hereafter entrusted to the women. The speaker had been enthusiastically applauded by a large crowd of strange shoemakers. Chremes himself was rather in favor of the idea, since it was the one and only solution that had hitherto not been tried.

After supervising a secret change back to feminine dress among the women, Praxagora returned to her husband with the excuse that she had been called during the night to aid a friend in labor and had taken his clothes for greater warmth. When Blepyrus described the decision of the assembly, Praxagora expressed great surprise and delight and immediately launched into a detailed list of the revolutionary reforms she intended to carry out. Every conceivable kind of private property—land, money, food, and even husbands and wives—was to be common to all. All cheating, bribery, and lawsuits would disappear, since no one would have to engage in such activities to achieve what he wanted. Robbery, gambling, and the exchange of money would be abolished. Prostitutes would be outlawed so that decent women could have the first fruits of the young men. Upon Blepyrus's protest that complete sexual freedom would result in chaos, Praxagora established the rule that all the youth would first have to satisfy the prior claims of the aged before mating with other young people and that all children would look upon the oldest people in the community as their parents. Blepyrus, thrilled, looked forward to the prospect of being known as the dictator's husband.

Chremes, also eager to coöperate, began to pack up all his belongings to contribute to the common store, despite the taunts of a skeptical citizen who reminded him that all previous decrees, such as the reduction of the price of salt and the introduction of copper coinage, had failed. But Chremes insisted that the new reform was thoroughgoing and departed for the common feast, leaving the citizen to devise some scheme whereby he, too, might participate without abandoning all his goods.

The first great test of the new society occurred when a young man, about to enter the house of a voluptuous girl, was stopped by an old woman, a veritable hag, who insisted on her prior claim. The young man tried every conceivable stratagem to avoid relations with the aged flat-nose, but the old woman stubbornly insisted on her legal rights. At first the young man decided to do without sex altogether, rather than yield to the disgusting hag first; but, finding such renunciation impossible, he at last reluctantly submitted. Before the old woman could get him into her house, an even older and uglier hag appeared on the scene to demand her prior right to him. While he quarreled with her, a third and truly horrendous old woman seized him. He was last seen being carried off by two frightful old hags.

Praxagora's maid, returning from the great banquet, met Blepyrus, who had not yet dined, and regaled him with a frenzied account of the delicious viands that were being served there. Taking some young girls with him, Blepyrus hurried off to gorge himself on rich food and drink.

Further Critical Evaluation of the Work:

The Greek title of this play means "Assembly women"—a contradiction to the male-oriented society and politics of ancient Greece. Yet, like the *Lysistrata,* this play must not be seen as a vehicle of feminine protest. In both plays Aristophanes is criticizing the mismanagement of affairs of state and is turning toward women not as the proper alternative but as the last desperation. Both situations and solutions are intolerable, but in the course of each drama the playwright exposes the vanity of power and its consequences.

As Aristophanes' penultimate play, *The Ecclesiazusae* tends away from personal invective and reliance on the chorus. The play contains no *parabasis,* a device essential to Old Comedy, whereby frequently the chorus would address the audience with the playwright's indignation over contemporary or current social or political outrages. This, then, marks the beginning of Middle Comedy, the fourth century transition to New Comedy. In *The Ecclesiazusae* we see the stock types so popular in later comedy—such as the shrewish wife, the hellish hag, the amorous young man, and the lecherous old one. Yet, unlike New Comedy, plays of this period still rely heavily on misrepresentation of philosophic schools. The communism of goods and sex proposed by Praxagora was not Plato's, since in *The Republic* the philosopher aimed at removing from the guardians of the state any temptations to selfish interests; in Aristophanes the motive for shared property is basely selfish. While Socrates wants to manage the breeding of the best class, Praxagora wants sex to be widely available to those who have the least chance for it.

There is little doubt that Aristophanes is cynically warning his fellow Athenians against yearning for Utopia; simplistic solutions bring abominable consequences. Praxagora ("Mrs. Forum-Business") does away with prostitution but dissolves marriage, thereby turning wives into loose women and their husbands into free men. She provides a free dinner for everyone, but only at the expense of one's entire property.

ECLOGUES

Type of work: Pastoral poetry
Author: Publius Vergilius Maro (70 B.C.-19 B.C.)
First transcribed: c. 48-37 B.C.

    Principal characters:
        TITYRUS, an aging shepherd, sometimes thought to represent Vergil
        MALIBOEUS, an exile
        CORYDON, a lovelorn shepherd boy
        DAPHNIS, in the fifth eclogue, a shepherd hero who had recently died
        GALLUS, a poet and military leader, a friend of Vergil

Vergil's ten eclogues made their young author a nationally renowned figure when they were first made public about 39 B.C. Although these poems do not reach the heights of the *Georgics* or the *Aeneid,* they are the work of a master, not the hesitant stumblings of an apprentice writer. Vergil made the pastoral form, first popularized by Theocritus, his own and paved the way for many English poets who imitated him, among them Edmund Spenser, Philip Sidney, John Milton, Percy Bysshe Shelley, and Matthew Arnold.

Vergil's pastoral world is not populated by Dresden-china shepherdesses in a never-never landscape; while his shepherds have their light-hearted moments, they inhabit real Italian hills and farms from which they can be evicted by unjust landlords. Exile, loneliness, and poverty threaten many of the characters in the poems. Even the traditional lovelorn shepherds are tied to Vergil's world by the naturalness of the landscape in which they lament; the heat of the Italian summer, the shade of the willow tree, the rocky hillsides where sheep pasture—all are part of the total effect of the eclogues.

Much scholarly effort has been directed toward proving that these poems are allegories that deal with contemporary events. It seems more fruitful and more realistic to accept the fact that Vergil is commenting on conditions of his age, without searching for disguised poets and government officials. There is no certainty that any shepherd represents the poet's own view, although he has often been identified with Tityrus in the first eclogue.

This poem is one of the most realistic of the group; it reflects the days after Julius Caesar's assassination when residents of northern Italy were dispossessed to provide land for discharged soldiers. Meliboeus, one of the speakers, is among the exiles. He has left his newborn goats on the rocky road as he makes his way toward a new home in Africa, Scythia, or Britain. He laments the fact that the land he has labored to cultivate must fall into the hands of some barbarous veteran, and he inquires how his friend Tityrus has managed to escape the general desolation. Tityrus explains that he went to Rome to plead for his land and that a youth, whom some have identified with Augustus, granted his request, leaving him free to enjoy the humming of the bees on his neighbor's land. He offers his sympathy and his simple hospitality to the unfortunate Meliboeus.

The second eclogue is the disjointed lament of the Sicilian shepherd, Corydon, for his disdainful beloved, Alexis. Vergil conveys the character of Corydon brilliantly in his passionate, illogical outbursts, uttered as the boy wanders in the hot midday sun, when even lizards have sought shelter, recognizing the futility of his love, yet unable to forget the scornful youth and settle down to care properly for his vines.

Among the most vividly conceived personages of the eclogues are the two brash young shepherds who amicably insult each other in the third poem. Damoetas and Menalcas taunt each other with misdeeds they have witnessed; Damoetas has seen his friend slashing at a farmer's grapevines, while Menalcas suspects Damoetas of trying to steal a goat from Damon's flock. Damoetas spiritedly defends himself; he had won the goat legitimately in a singing match, but Damon refused to pay the prize. Menalcas scoffs at the notion of Damoetas' possessing such skill, and he is immediately challenged to a contest. The ensuing song follows the traditional pattern; the challenger sings one verse, then his opponent adds a second in keeping with the first, and the song moves from invocations to Jove and Apollo to tributes to the sweethearts of each singer to realistic comments on the scene. Each singer concludes with a riddle, and Palaemon, who has been brought in as judge, decides that both deserve prizes, as do all who know the joy or bitterness of love.

The most famous of these poems is the fourth, or Messianic, eclogue, in which Vergil prophesies the birth of a child who will usher in a new golden age when peace will prevail, man and nature will become self-sufficient, commerce will cease, and the land will need no further plowing and pruning. The poet laments that he will not survive to see this new age come to fruition, but he rejoices at being able to bid the infant smile at his mother.

The identity of the expected child has been cause for extensive speculation; both Antony and Augustus became fathers about this time, and Vergil may have politically refused to single out one or the other. However, throughout the Middle Ages Vergil was thought to have foreseen the birth of Christ; for this reason he became for later ages a kind of pagan saint.

The pastoral elegy, the form of the fifth eclogue, has been imitated more often than any of the other types of poetry in this collection. Readers of English poetry may find many echoes of Mopsus' lament for Daphnis, who is mourned by nymphs, lions, and by the men whom he taught to celebrate Bacchic rites. Since his death crops have failed, as if the flowers, too, lamented; only thorns and thistles grow where the violet and narcissus were planted. Mopsus' elegy concludes with a request for shepherds to build a mound for Daphnis and to carve an epitaph commending his fame and loveliness.

Menalcas rhapsodizes over his friend's verse, then begins his own elegy, in which he places Daphnis, now deified, at the gate of heaven, bringing peace to all the countryside. The mountains and rocks rejoice and the shepherds worship their new god in joyous rites. The contrasting moods of grief and exaltation remained a part of the pastoral tradition throughout succeeding ages, in poems like Milton's *Lycidas* and Shelley's *Adonais*.

The prologue to the sixth eclogue gives interesting insight into Vergil's poetic ambitions. The speaker, Tityrus, comments that his earliest poetry was in the Sicilian vein, pastoral, but that he had for a time turned to kings and battles until Apollo cautioned him that a shepherd poet should sing of the countryside. Therefore he depends on others to celebrate the great deeds of his friend Varus, while he must be content to dedicate to him his rustic song about the old satyr, Silenus, who tells young satyrs and naiads old tales about the creation, the Golden Age, the fate of Prometheus, and many other mythological legends. The reference within the poem to a scene in which the Muses bestowed a reed pipe upon Gallus, one of the best-known writers of Vergil's time, has led to the suggestion that in this eclogue allusions are made to Gallus' own work. The range of subject matter is wide, and there seems to be little connection between the various episodes in Silenus' narrative.

In the seventh eclogue another singing match is described. The song of Corydon and Thyrsis reflects Vergil's deep love for the countryside and for the simplicity of the life of the shepherds. The reader can almost see the mossy springs, the budding vines of the early spring, and the chestnuts.

The eighth poem is addressed to a Roman hero, variously identified as the consul, Pollio, who is mentioned within the body of the poem, or as Augustus. Vergil will attempt to please this nobleman with the pastoral song he requested, while he waits for a chance to record his heroic exploits. In the lyric itself Damon and Alphesiboeus recite songs for each other. The first is a lament for the infidelity of Nysa, Damon's beloved, who has married Mopsus. The deserted shepherd is both scornful and sentimental, at one moment recalling his first childhood meeting with the girl, at another bitterly berating the bridegroom or mourning the cold cruelty of the god of love. All nature should be upturned, with the wolf fleeing from the lamb and apples growing on oak trees when such a love does not take its natural course. The singer sees no final recourse but death; he will plunge from the mountain top into the waves below.

Alphesiboeus' song is a curious one. He speaks as a young girl who is trying to lure her lover home from town by witchcraft, and the song begins with a number of spells. The ashes on the girl's altar flame spontaneously in the last stanza, and she expresses her hope that the absent shepherd is, indeed, coming.

The mood of the first poem is recreated in the ninth as Moeris tells his friend Lycidas that he has been evicted from his property by a new owner. Lycidas expresses surprise; he had heard that Menalcas' poetry had preserved that land. Moeris, made wise in the world's ways by misfortune, replies that there was such a rumor, but that poetry has no force against the soldiers who are taking over the land. He and Menalcas barely escaped with their lives.

The thought that they might have lost the best of their shepherd poets recalls some of his lines to Lycidas and Moeris, and they quote them as they talk. One passage, referring to the new, beneficent star of "Olympian Caesar," has aroused special interest, since it obviously refers to the recently deceased Julius Caesar. This eclogue ends with an appealing scene, as Lycidas urges Moeris to stop and rest beside the calm lake they are passing and to sing as they watch countrymen pruning their vines.

The final poem is another tribute to Gallus, who was a highly competent military leader, as well as a fine poet; he served as Viceroy of Egypt after the defeat of Antony at the battle of Actium. Unfortunately, his pride led to his political downfall and probably also to the loss of his poetry; we must rely on Vergil's praise for an estimate of his talents.

Gallus' mistress, Lycoris, to whom most of his love poetry had been addressed, had run away to the north of Italy with another soldier. In Vergil's poem her betrayed lover laments her loss, followed by sympathetic shepherds. He resolves to seek what comfort he can in writing pastoral verse and hunting the wild boar, yet he cannot restrain a poignant hope that the sharp glaciers of the Alps will not cut the feet of his lost lady. He realizes, finally, that even poetry and hunting are powerless to mollify the god of love; he can only yield and accept his misery.

Vergil's *Eclogues* brought a new note of personal feeling and a fresh appreciation of nature into the highly artificial and rhetorical poetic tradition of his time. It is in large part this element of humanity that has sustained the appeal of his pastorals to the present day.

EDMUND CAMPION

Type of work: Novelized biography
Author: Evelyn Waugh (1903-1966)
Type of plot: Historical chronicle
Time of plot: Sixteenth century
Locale: Oxford, London, Douai, Rome, Prague
First published: 1935

> *Principal characters:*
> EDMUND CAMPION, an English martyr
> DR. WILLIAM ALLEN, head of the English College at Douai
> ROBERT PERSONS, Campion's classmate at Oxford
> GEORGE ELIOT, a priest-hunter

Critique:

This book is an intelligent, sober, and admirably written biography of a man dear to the hearts of Anglo-Saxon Catholics. Evelyn Waugh has written a fine impressionistic portrait of the English martyr after whom Campion Hall at Oxford was named. Waugh warns that intolerance is a growing evil in our modern world, and martyrs may again be forced to die for their faith.

The Story:

Edmund Campion, born in 1540, was one of the most promising young men at Oxford. When Elizabeth visited the university in 1566, she was so impressed by him that she assured him of her patronage. Although there was a strong Protestant group in the university, Oxford then had a population of students who were mostly Catholic in religion, for laws against Catholics were not rigidly enforced. Campion, who as proctor held a responsible position, was suspected of Catholicism, however, and was asked to make a public declaration of his principles by delivering a sermon in a suitable church. He refused, and when his term was over he left for Dublin, where he was warmly received by the Stanihurst family. A university was to be built in Dublin, and he was waiting to accept a post on its faculty. Then rebellion threatened, and all Catholics were ordered arrested. Campion managed to escape

and make his way to Dousai and the English College there.

The mild restrictions against Catholics turned into persecution when the Pope issued a Bull of Excommunication against Queen Elizabeth. Because of the fear of a French-Spanish alliance against England, the Bull caused grave anxiety in England and led to reprisals against Catholics. It became illegal to hear mass, to harbor a priest, or openly to profess Catholicism.

With the Catholic bishops imprisoned, thereby preventing the ordination of priests, and with all Catholic schools closed, the faith began to die out in England. The college at Dousai sent young English priests into England to perserve the faith of the English Catholics.

Campion went to Douai and became a priest. Then he announced his intention of going to Rome entering the Society of Jesus. Athrough Dr. Allen, the venerable head of the college, did not like to lose him to the Jesuits, he made no objection to Campion's plans. Admitted into the Society, Campion was sent to Bohemia, where he held important posts at the University of Prague.

Dr. Allen wrote Campion a letter informing him that he was to go to England. He and a few others, including Robert Persons, who had been an undergraduate at Oxford during the time of Campion's proctorship, were to be smuggled into England, there to carry on the work of the Church. They all realized that capture meant certain death. Campion demanded that Persons be made his superior before the group departed. Though the English government had learned of the group's intentions and had all the ports guarded, the priests succeeded in getting into England.

In disguise, Campion visited the homes of various Catholics, where he said mass and brought the sacraments to the faithful who had been long without them. He wrote his famous *Campion's Brag,* a defense of himself and his Church, which the best minds of the Anglican Church were called upon to answer. Persons wrote his own *Censure* of the Anglican reply. Later Campion wrote his equally famous *Ten Reasons.*

Persecution grew more intense, with Campion the prize the government most hoped to capture. During one of his tours Campion was persuaded to stop at Lyford Grange, the home of Mr. Yate, a well-known Catholic. He stayed there briefly, warning everyone not to tell the neighbors of his presence. After his departure some neighbors heard of his visit and were distressed that they had missed the visit of Father Campion. Father Ford was sent after him and reluctantly Campion returned.

A certain George Eliot, a professional priest-hunter, stopped at Lyford Grange. He was informed by a servant, who presumed Eliot to be Catholic, that Father Campion was there. He was shown into the room where Campion was saying mass. After receiving communion from Campion, Eliot went to notify the authorities. They came at once, but all evidence of the mass had been destroyed and the priests had been hidden behind a secret panel. The guards found nothing and were preparing to go when one of the searchers happened to tap a hollow-sounding portion of the wall. The priests were discovered in a secret room.

Months of imprisonment followed. Four conferences were held at which Campion and the Anglican clergy disputed points of doctrine. Campion was tortured and finally brought to trial with some other prisoners who were charged with having plotted to murder Queen Elizabeth and with conspiring with foreign powers. But Campion insisted that their only crime was their faith. They were tried by a court that was absolutely biased. Found guilty, they were sentenced to die by hanging, and their bodies to be drawn and quartered. Father Campion and the others went to the scaffold and died the death of martyrs on December first, 1581.

Further Critical Evaluation of the Work:

Evelyn Waugh was awarded the Hawthornden Prize for *Edmund Campion* as a work of marked distinction by an author under forty. Some critics have found Waugh's descriptions of Campion's last Mass and sermon at Lyford, his subsequent hiding with two other priests, and their final discovery and arrest among the most descriptive and dramatic passages in all his writings. Others have pointed out that the story is related with bias, and without any attempt to create a true historical atmosphere. In any case, the short novel is told simply and does relate the tragedy of a martyr in the service of Catholicism.

It is interesting to note that the novel was written shortly after Waugh's own conversion to Catholicism and reflects his search for inner peace and joy which he ultimately found in the martyred Englishman. Waugh reveals in Campion's life what the Catholic faith meant to him personally, and his book is full of reverence and complete affirmation of the Church. He held a nostalgia for the past and his romantic sense of history comes out in this novel. At the time Waugh undertook to write the novel, the Jesuits were rebuilding Campion Hall on a new site at Oxford. Waugh pledged all the royalties he received from the book to the building fund for Campion Hall.

Reviewers of the book, including most of those who were unsympathetic to the general thesis it contained, praised its style and overlooked some of the inaccurate historical details. Throughout *Edmund Campion* there is a sense of historical continuity. The opening pages picture Elizabeth on her deathbed and reflect upon the profits and losses of her reign. Waugh glances forward many years beyond Elizabeth and then returns to the queen's encounter with the scholar, hero, and martyr, Campion. Everything is seen in the light of the "Catholic" perspective. In the last pages, the author looks historically beyond Campion, thirteen years later, and describes another martyr for the Catholic minority in England, Henry Walpole. At times, *Edmund Campion* seems to reach beyond the boundaries of a short novelized biography, and attempt to make a larger statement about Catholicism and its struggle for survival during different periods in various places. Such a task is a large one and Waugh's efforts seem rewarded by a generally well-accepted and respected religious biography.

THE EDUCATION OF HENRY ADAMS

Type of work: Novelized autobiography
Author: Henry Adams (1838-1918)
Type of plot: Intellectual and social history
Time of plot: 1838-1905
Locale: America, England, France
First published: 1907

> *Principal characters:*
> HENRY ADAMS, an American
> CHARLES FRANCIS ADAMS, his father
> JOHN HAY, his friend
> CLARENCE KING, whom he admired

Critique:

The theme of *The Education of Henry Adams* is the process of multiplication and acceleration of mechanical forces which, during his own lifetime, led to the breakdown of moral relationships between men and the degeneration of their pursuits into money-seeking or complete lassitude. The book is, too, an excellent autobiography, tracing Adams' thought processes intimately, and on an intellectual plane not generally achieved by most writers. Both for style and content this book ranks with the finest of American autobiographies.

The Story:

Henry Brooks Adams was born of the union of two illustrious Massachusetts families, the Brookses and the Adamses, and he was, in addition, the grandson and the great-grandson of presidents. His wealth and social position should have put him among the leaders of his generation.

Although the period of mechanical invention had begun in 1838, Henry Adams was raised in a colonial atmosphere. He remembered that his first serious encounter with his grandfather, John Quincy Adams, occurred when he refused to go to school, and that gentleman led him there by the hand. For Henry Adams, the death of the former president marked the end of his eighteenth-century environment.

Charles Francis Adams, Henry's father, was instrumental in forming the Free-Soil party in 1848, and he ran on its ticket with Martin Van Buren. Henry considered that his own education was chiefly a heritage from his father, an inheritance of Puritan morality and interest in politics and literary matters. In later life, looking back on his formal education, he concluded that it had been a failure. Mathematics, French, German, and Spanish were needed in the world in which he found himself an adult, not Latin and Greek. He had opportunity to observe the use of force in the violence with which the people of Boston treated the anti-slavery Wendell Phillips, and he had seen Negro slaves restored to the South.

Prompted by his teacher, James Russell Lowell, he spent nearly two years abroad after his graduation from college. He enrolled to study civil law in Germany, but finding the lecture system atrocious he devoted most of his stay to enjoying the paintings, the opera, the theater in Dresden.

When he returned to Boston in 1860, Henry Adams settled down briefly to read Blackstone. In the elections that year, however, his father became a Congressman, and Henry accompanied him to the capitol as his secretary. There he met John Hay, who was to become his best friend.

In 1861 President Lincoln named Charles Francis Adams Minister to England. Henry went with his father to Europe. The Adams party had barely disembarked when they were met by bad news. England had recognized the belligerency of the Confederacy. The North was her undeclared enemy. The battle of Bull Run proved so crushing a blow to American prestige that Charles Francis Adams felt he was in England on a day-to-day sufferance. The Trent Affair and the second battle of Bull Run were equally disastrous abroad. Finally, in 1863, the tide began to turn. Secretary Seward sent Thurlow Weed and William Evarts to woo the English, and they were followed by announcements of victories at Vicksburg and Gettysburg. Charles Francis Adams remained in England until 1868, for Andrew Johnson had too many troubles at home to make many diplomatic changes abroad.

At the end of the war Henry Adams had no means of earning a livelihood. He had, however, developed some taste as a dilettante in art, and several of his articles had been published in the *North American Review*. On his return to America, Henry Adams was impressed by the fact that his fellow-countrymen, because of the mechanical energy they had harnessed, were all traveling in the same direction. Europeans, he had felt, were trying to go in several directions at one time. Handicapped by his education and by his long absence from home, he had difficulty in adapting himself to the new industrial America. He achieved some recognition with his articles on legal tender and his essays in the *Edinburgh Review*, and he hoped that he might be offered a government position if Grant were elected president. But Grant, a man of action, was not interested in reformers or intellectuals like Henry Adams.

In 1869 Adams went back to Quincy to begin his investigation of the scandals of the Grant administration, among them Jay Gould's attempts to obtain a corner on gold, Senator Charles Sumner's efforts to provoke war with England by compelling her cession of Canada to the United States, and the rivalries of Congressmen and Cabinet members.

He decided it would be best to have his article on Gould published in England, to avoid censorship by the powerful financier. Gould's influence was not confined to the United States, however, and Adams was refused by two publications. His essay on Gould was finally published by the *Westminster Review*.

Adams became assistant professor of Medieval History at Harvard and taught at Cambridge for seven years. During that time he tried to abandon the lecture system by replacing it with individual research. He found his students apt and quick to respond, but he felt that he needed a stone against which to sharpen his wits. He gave up his position in 1871 and went west to Estes Park with a Government Geological Survey. There he met Clarence King, a member of the party, with whom he could not help contrasting himself. King had a systematic, scientific education and could have his choice of scientific, political, or literary prizes. Adams felt his own limitations.

After his flight from Harvard he made his permanent home in Washington, where he wrote a series of books on American history. In 1893 he visited the Chicago Exhibition. From his observations of the steamship, the locomotive, and the newly-invented dynamo, he concluded that force was the one unifying factor in American thought. Back in Washington, he saw the gold standard adopted, and concluded that the capitalistic system and American intervention in Cuba offered some signs of the direction in which the country was heading. During another visit to the Exhibition in 1900 Adams formulated an important theory. In observing the dynamo, he decided that history is not merely a series of causes and effects, of men acting upon men, but the record of forces acting upon men. For him, the dynamo became the symbol of force acting upon his own time as the Virgin had been the symbol of force in the twelfth century.

During the next five years Henry Adams saw his friends drop away. Clarence King was the first to go. He lost his fortune in the panic of 1893 and died of tuberculosis in 1901. John Hay, under McKinley, became American Minister to England, and then Secretary of State. He was not well when he accepted the President's appointments, and the enormous task of bringing England, France, and Germany into accord with the United States, and of attempting to keep peace, unsuccessfully, between Russia and Japan, caused his death in 1905.

Adams considered that his education was continuous during his lifetime. He had found the tools which he had been given as a youth utterly useless and he had to spend all of his days forging new ones. As he grew older, he found the moral standards of his father's and grandfather's times disintegrating, so that corruption and greed existed on the highest political levels. According to his calculations, the rate of change, due to mechanical force, was accelerating, and the generation of 1900 could rely only on impersonal forces to teach the generation of 2000. He himself could see no end to the multiplicity of forces which were so rapidly dwarfing mankind into insignificance.

Further Critical Evaluation of the Work:

As a work of literature, *The Education of Henry Adams* may be read in at least three ways: first, as a conventional autobiography; second, as a work in the mainstream of the European *Bildüngsroman* tradition, a personal narrative of one person's intellectual and emotional coming of age; and third, as a critical treatise on Western civilization and culture. In this latter sense, Adams anticipated the twentieth century preoccupation with the relationship between technological science and humanistic cultural assumptions.

No matter how Adams' work is read, however, the key chapter is "The Dynamo and the Virgin." Here he uses the two symbols of the "Dynamo" and the "Virgin" to spell out his analysis of the shaping forces of civilization, a synthesis of ideas reflecting his entire education, first broached in *Mont-Saint-Michel and Chartres*. This excursion into historiography places Adams in the front rank of nineteenth century historical philosophers, for it is at this point that he posits the thesis that "belief" is the guiding force of socio-political and cultural phenomena.

Just as religious beliefs, the "Virgin," created the great works of the Middle Ages, he says, so also the modern belief in science and technology, the "Dynamo," will shape the major creations of the modern age. At last, though, he views that latter age with trepidation and anxiety, for he realizes that in some ways the humanistic education he received from his forefathers did not suit him for the Age of the Dynamo. Indeed, he sees that moral values of great worth, values which underlie the significant achievements of his grandfather, John Quincy Adams, and his father, are being destroyed by the machine. At last, then, Henry Adams defines for us the major conflict of twentieth century American civilizations, a drama whose denouement still remains undecided.

EDWARD THE SECOND

Type of work: Drama
Author: Christopher Marlowe (1564-1593)
Type of plot: Historical chronicle
Time of plot: Fourteenth century
Locale: England and France
First presented: c. 1590

Principal characters:
EDWARD II, King of England
PRINCE EDWARD, his son
EDMUND, Earl of Kent, half-brother to the king
PIERCE DE GAVESTON, Earl of Cornwall
GUY, Earl of Warwick
THOMAS, Earl of Lancaster
LORD MORTIMER, the elder
LORD ROGER MORTIMER, the younger
HUGH SPENCER, Earl of Gloucester
QUEEN ISABELLA, wife of King Edward

Critique:

The Troublesome Reign and Lamentable Death of Edward the Second, the last play written by Marlowe before his untimely death, is a pre-Shakespearian chronicle in its highest form. In fact, the drama had in the past been assigned to Shakespeare himself. Unlike Marlowe's earlier work, this play is polished in form, sustained in theme, and consistent in characterization. Marlowe's first real success in the field of historical drama, Edward the Second sacrifices for a highly dramatic and tragic ending the lyrical beauty of language and metaphor present in his other plays. A further accomplishment to be noted here is Marlowe's use of a large group of dominant characters; in his earlier plays he had employed only two central figures.

The Story:

King Edward II having recalled his favorite from exile, Pierce de Gaveston joyfully returned to England. While hurrying to Westminster to rejoin his monarch, he came upon the king talking to his courtiers. Secretive, he hid from the royal assemblage and overheard the noblemen discussing his repatriation.

Edward, an immature and weakminded yet stubborn man, nourished for Gaveston an unwholesome and unyielding love, in spite of the fact that Edward's father had originally banished the man.

The noblemen of England, sworn to uphold the decree of exile, hated the royal favorite. Most passionate in his fury was young Mortimer. But others were not far behind Mortimer in lusty dislike, and they threatened the king with revolt if Gaveston were permitted to remain in England. None but the king's brother Edmund would harbor Gaveston.

The fiery discussion ended, the nobles stalked off in haughty displeasure. Gaveston, still in hiding, rejoiced in his knowledge of the king's love, for Edward revealed his pettiness by his unconcern for the welfare of his kingdom as weighed against his desire to clasp Gaveston to his bosom once more. When Gaveston revealed his presence, Edward ecstatically rewarded him with a series of titles and honors, the scope of which caused even Edmund to comment wryly that Edward had outdone himself. Gaveston smirkingly claimed that all he desired was to be near his monarch. To add further salt to the kingdom's wounds, Edward sentenced the Bishop of Coventry, the instigator of Gaveston's exile, to die in the Tower of London.

This action, coupled with the titles and estates lavishly bestowed upon Gaveston, so incensed the rebellious nobility that under the leadership of the two Mortimers, Warwick, and Lancaster, they plotted to kill the favorite. The Archbishop of Canterbury, protesting the damage inflicted upon the Church by the king's folly, allied himself with the plot. Queen Isabella, who professed to love her lord dearly, complained to the noblemen that since Gaveston's return Edward had snubbed her beyond endurance. She agreed that Gaveston must be done away with, but she cautioned the angry noblemen not to injure Edward.

When the rebellious nobility seized Gaveston, Edward, yielding to the archbishop's threat to enforce his papal powers against the king, could do nothing but stand by and allow his beloved friend to be carried off. A bitter exchange of words between the king and his lords was tempered by the gentle sentiments of Gaveston as he bade Edward farewell. Driven by childish anger, perhaps incensed by an intuitive knowledge, Gaveston attacked the queen and accused her of a clandestine association with the younger Mortimer, a charge which she denied. Sensing his advantage, Edward seized upon the accusation as a wedge to undermine his enemies, and he compelled the queen to use her influence to save Gaveston. The queen, because of her love for Edward and her hopes for a reconciliation, resolved to mend the rift by abetting her husband.

At first the nobles disdainfully refused to hear her entreaties. Then, having prevailed upon young Mortimer's sympathy, she disclosed to him a plot whereby Gaveston could be overthrown and the king obeyed at the same time. Mortimer then convinced the other nobles that if Gaveston were allowed to remain in England, he would become so unpopular that the common people would rise in protest and kill him.

There was peace in England once more. Edward affected renewed love for his queen and the lords humbly repledged their fealty to Edward. An undercurrent of meanness prevailed, however, in the bosom of young Mortimer, whose sense of justice was outraged at the fact that Edward had chosen such a baseborn villain as his minion. He still believed that it would be a service to his king and country to unseat Gaveston, and thus he plotted secretly.

But at the ceremonial in honor of Gaveston's return the lords could not stomach the presence of the king's minion. Bitter sarcasm was showered upon Gaveston and young Mortimer tried to stab him. So outraged was Edward at this show of independence by his peers that he vowed vengeance for his dear Gaveston's sake. Even the loyal Edmund could not brook this display on the part of his brother; he deserted Edward to join the nobles.

Edward renewed the smoldering accusation against Isabella that she was Mortimer's lover. Defeated in battle, the king's forces, with Gaveston in flight, were split up to confuse the enemy. Warwick, Lancaster, and others succeeded in capturing the king's minion and ordered his death, but Arundel, a messenger from Edward, pleaded that Gaveston be allowed to say farewell to the king. One of the nobles, unable to scorn the king's wishes, arranged to escort Gaveston to Edward. With a servant in charge, Gaveston was conducted to a hiding place to spend the night. Warwick, driven by blind hatred and an irrational patriotism, kidnaped the prisoner.

Meanwhile Valois, King of France and Isabella's brother, had taken advantage of the revolt in England and had seized Normandy. Edward, displaying the corruption of his statesmanship, dispatched his son Prince Edward and Isabella to negotiate a parley with Valois. Arundel, meanwhile, reported to Edward that Warwick had beheaded Gaveston. Edward, in a wild rage against his lords, swore to sack their lands and destroy their families. Characteristically, having lost his beloved friend, he declared that henceforth young Spencer would be his favorite. He continued to resist the rebels, and before long Warwick, Lancaster, and Edmund were captured and sentenced to death.

In France, the Earl of Gloucester suspected that Isabella was gathering forces to place her son upon the throne. Isabella, in the meantime, had been rejected by Valois. Sir John of Hainault rescued the queen and prince by offering to keep the pair at his estate in Flanders until Edward had matured sufficiently to rule England. The young prince was already showing signs of royal character and a depth and magnitude of personality which promised to make him a suitable monarch.

The condemned Mortimer and Edmund escaped to France, where Sir John agreed to help them in levying forces to aid Isabella and the prince. Landing at Harwich, the forces of Mortimer and Edmund routed the king, who fled toward Ireland. Stalwart, sincere, and intellectually honest, Edmund, who had broken with his brother only after the king had driven him too far, relented in his feelings against Edward; he was further disturbed by a suspicion that Isabella was in love with Mortimer. Mortimer became a despot in his triumph. Edward was captured and sent to Kenilworth Castle, a prisoner. There he was prevailed upon to surrender his crown to the prince.

With the queen's consent Mortimer outlined a crafty scheme to kill Edward. He drew up an ambiguous note which ordered the king's death in one sense and abjured it in another. When Prince Edward, Isabella, Edmund, and Mortimer argued fiercely to decide upon the prince's protector, the prince revealed his distrust for Mortimer. Edmund, fearing greater disunion, resolved to rescue the imprisoned king. His attempt failed.

Prince Edward was crowned by the Archbishop of Canterbury. Shortly after the coronation the deposed Edward, tortured cruelly in a dungeon, was murdered by Mortimer's hireling. Edmund was beheaded. Thereupon Edward III, now monarch in his own right, ordered Mortimer to be hanged and Isabella, who was suspected of being the nobleman's accomplice in plotting her husband's death, to be taken to the Tower of London.

Further Critical Evaluation of the Work:

Marlowe's last drama—the dating of Marlowe's dramas is, of course, conjectural—is regarded by many as his finest work, showing tighter structure and greater clarity and unity than his earlier works. Since it was published almost immediately after his death, the text escaped the corruption which his other works suffered, and there are relatively few problems with establishing an accurate text. We also possess the source material for the work, Holinshed's *Chronicles of England,* in the edition of 1577 or 1587. By comparing this play with others of its genre and with its source, it is possible to arrive at an appreciation of Marlowe's achievement.

Holinshed's account of the reign of Edward II (1307-1327) is relatively unstructured and, though providing much material, does not establish clear relationships or a connected series of events. Marlowe, who worked closely enough with Holinshed's text to incorporate actual phrases from the chronicle, nevertheless set about to structure the story and bring out salient features, developing relationships and characterizations, and compressing the events of over twenty years—from Gaveston's return in 1307 to the execution of Mortimer in 1330—into what seems on stage to be a relatively short span. While this creates some problems in terms of improbably swift shifting of loyalties and changes of policy, it gives the drama a tightness of structure and a forward movement that underscores the alienation of all Edward's associates—his wife, the loyal Kent, and the well-meaning, but outraged barons.

It is this surging wave of hostility that is the central event of the play, which begins with the return of the king's beloved Gaveston from exile. Marlowe makes it quite clear that the two men are lovers, but it is not the homosexual relationship that disturbs the barons—in fact, at one point the Elder Mortimer explains "the mightiest kings have had their minions," and lists famous pairs of male lovers in history. Rather it is the fact that Edward ignores his role as king for the sake of Gaveston that enrages the nobles. Gaveston is lowborn, but Edward elevates him to share the throne, and in his infatuation, he forgets his duties to his realm. He is following his personal will, and shows this weakness in his inability to give up his personal pleasure for the good of his kingdom. He is childlike both in his willfulness and in his stubbornness, and he remains blind to the fact of his own misrule and the justice of the nobles' grievances.

Yet the Tudor world saw rebellion against an annointed king as the most grievous breach of natural law, and the play documents the slow evolution of rebellion. At first it is solely against Gaveston that the hostility is directed. Only gradually does this hostility spread to the king, the more especially after the death of Gaveston, however, when Edward fastens his affections upon new flatterers, primarily Spencer. Whereas the loyalty of Gaveston and Edward, for all its folly, had a touch of nobility about it, Spencer is merely a sycophant, and the king, in listening to him, reveals his irredeemable weakness of character. His early frivolousness turns to vengeance when the barons move to open revolt, and even his loving queen and the loyal Kent slowly turn against him. It is perhaps a weakness of the play that neither party in the conflict can arouse our admiration; there is no moral framework here, no good and evil, or even wisdom to oppose the folly. The misrule of the king is overthrown by a Machiavellian villain, the hypocritical Mortimer. Whereas Shakespeare tended to glorify those who put an end to misrule, as Bolingbroke in *Richard the Second,* which bears many similarities to *Edward the Second,* Marlowe paints a picture of unrelieved gloom, as the rebels, led by the unfaithful queen and the power-grabbing Mortimer, depose the weak and yet bloody king. It is only at the very end, as Edward III comes to the throne, executing Mortimer and imprisoning the queen, that rightful rule is restored. Edward III specifically seeks the counsel of his nobles before he acts and in so doing restores the reciprocity upon which the well-being of the realm rests.

Beyond the concept of divine right, there remains the concept that the king must rule not by whim, but with concern for the welfare of his land, and in concert with his nobles, who, like him, are born to their station. Though the play has strong political overtones, the absence of any developed conflict between right and wrong robs it of the sort of symbolic value that is possessed by Shakespeare's finest history plays. Indeed, the absence of a figure with whom the audience can identify may be in part responsible for the unpopularity of the play, which perhaps because of its historicity lacks the fascination of the powerfully imaginative *The Tragedy of Doctor Faustus* or *Tamburlaine.*

Marlowe's genius was at its best when expressing powerful emotions and characters with extravagant poetic imaginations. In *Edward the Second* there is less opportunity for such luxuriant language, and for many, the play does not really come alive until the downfall of the king, when in spite of his unsympathetic character, the pathos of his situation commands the involvement of the audience. To be sure, Gaveston is also very much a Marlowe character, perhaps much like Marlowe himself—impulsive, poetic, a lover of pleasure and beauty, both irresponsible and passionate—for Marlowe was repeatedly involved in dueling and was killed in a tavern. But it is Edward who sticks in the mind. Though aside from his touching and loyal love for Gaveston he has no redeeming qualities, the extremity of his suffering gives him a nobility that is not destroyed even by his anguish. Even at the end he can still exclaim "I am still king!" Marlowe has constructed one of the most harrowing death scenes to be found in Elizabethan drama—though he actually softened the even more horrible historical fact—and the pathos of Edward's intense emotional suffering elevates the play beyond the level of historical chronicle and assures its place among the world's great dramas.

Steven C. Schaber

EFFI BRIEST

Type of work: Novel
Author: Theodor Fontane (1819-1898)
Type of plot: Domestic tragedy
Time of plot: Second half of the nineteenth century
Locale: Germany, Prussia
First published: 1895

Principal characters:
EFFI VON BRIEST, only child of the Briest family
FRAU VON BRIEST, her mother
RITTERSCHAFTSRAT VON BRIEST, her father
BARON VON INNSTETTEN, Effi's husband, a government official in Kessin
ANNIE, Effi's daughter
MAJOR VON CRAMPAS, District Commander in Kessin
ROSWITHA, Effi's maid

Critique:

Although he had been a writer for most of his life—poet, journalist, historian—Fontane did not begin to write fiction until he had gained a thorough knowledge of Prussian society. He was sixty when he completed his first novel, seventy-five when he wrote *Effi Briest.* His main subject was the human being entangled in a net of strict rules and principles of a society which felt secure in a Prussia stabilized by the "Iron Chancellor," Bismarck. Fontane did not raise a warning pedagogical finger when he described the merciless destruction of human happiness by the rigid rules of that society. He merely introduced his characters and left judgment to his readers. When, after the tragic death of Effi Briest, Effi's mother asks whether they might have done something wrong, the father waves the question aside because it is useless to discuss it. Fontane initiated in Germany the modern realistic novel, and in describing him the term "psychological novel" appears for the first time in German literature. The tragic tale of Effi Briest remains a perennial reprint favorite of German publishers.

The Story:

Effi Briest was sixteen years old when her mother cheerfully announced that Baron von Innstetten had asked for her hand in marriage. Effi had seen Innstetten only once, but she knew he had

vainly tried to marry her mother years before. When Baron von Innstetten was absent for a long period, her mother had married Effi's father; at the time a match with Ritterschaftsrat von Briest had seemed too good an opportunity to forego. Innstetten was now a government official with a promising future.

Half an hour before, Effi had been sitting on a swing enjoying a happy childhood. Suddenly she was a bride to be. The situation seemed to her a new and welcome experience. In a few weeks she would be the wife of an important government official.

After the excitement of preparations, the wedding, and a honeymoon trip to Italy, the couple arrived in Kessin, a small town on the Baltic Sea. At first the completely new surroundings were interesting for Effi, but soon she felt ill at ease in the house. It was a strange house, formerly owned by a seafaring captain; his relics and souvenirs gave the place a bizarre character. A stuffed shark, stories about the captain's mysterious Chinese servant, and a mentally ill maidservant, who sat in the kitchen with a black chicken on her shoulder, brought nightmares to Effi, and she claimed that she heard noises in an unoccupied upstairs room. Considerate toward his young wife, Innstetten never failed to show his devotion, but being a practical-minded man, he paid no attention to Effi's tales of supernatural happenings in the house. He was convinced that his wife's childish imagination would soon return to normal.

The obligatory social visits to the local aristocracy revealed to Effi that she would not have friends in their circle. At first her only friend was the town apothecary. Her second friend was Roswitha, her maid, whom she met in the graveyard where the girl was bemoaning the loss of her former mistress. Effi was pregnant and needed a maid. Learning that Roswitha was Catholic, she was convinced Roswitha's faith would conquer the ghostlike noises in the house. Roswitha never heard ghosts and her straightforward manner was a relief from the formal stiffness of Effi's social world. The birth of a daughter, Annie, gave Effi new activities, but her boredom with Kessin continued.

The new military commander in Kessin, Major von Crampas, was another addition to Effi's social world. The major's carefree behavior and witty conversation were quite a contrast to the well-disciplined and formal Innstetten, but both men respected each other and became friends. Visits to the Innstetten home, horseback riding along the seashore, and participation in community plays brought Effi and Crampas closer together. Effi, realizing the danger of this situation, made efforts to avoid him. During a sleighride Crampas overstepped the boundaries of their friendship.

One day Innstetten informed Effi that he had been promoted to a new post in a Berlin Ministry, a position which would take them to Berlin. Effi was happy to leave the strange house, the boring people, and above all to be separated from Crampas, for their relationship, although a well-kept secret, burdened her conscience increasingly. Innstetten, seeing Effi's great joy when he told her about the transfer to Berlin, felt guilty for not having considered leaving the disliked house sooner.

In Berlin, Innstetten made a special effort to have a cheerful house and an enjoyable social life. Though Innstetten's duties at the Ministry kept them from spending much time together, the years in Berlin were happy ones until Effi went to the Rhine country for recuperation after an illness. Meanwhile, Innstetten and Annie remained in Berlin. One day Annie fell on a stairway and cut her forehead, and Roswitha searched through Effi's belongings to find a bandage. Innstetten, trying to restore order in Effi's room, found a bundle of love letters from Crampas, written six years before. Innstetten did what he considered his duty regardless of his personal feelings: he called a friend to make the necessary arrangements for a duel with Crampas. Although his friend pointed out that the letters were more than six years old, Innstetten, who would have preferred to pardon Effi, decided to go through with the duel because he felt that the insult to his honor had not been diminished by time. In the duel, fought near Kessin, Crampas was shot fatally.

At the time Effi was still in the Rhine country waiting for Innstetten's letters, which used to arrive punctually every day. Instead, a letter from her mother informed her of the duel and of pending divorce. Annie was put in the custody of Innstetten. The Briest family was willing to assist Effi financially, but her conduct had made it impossible for her to return home. Heartbroken, she went back to Berlin and lived in a small apartment. As quickly as she had changed years ago from a child into a woman, she now became a social outcast. Only Roswitha remained faithful to her.

Effi's health declined rapidly. Once she accidentally saw Annie leaving school, but she avoided meeting the child. Finally, moved by a desire to see her daughter again, Effi asked for permission legally to have Annie visit her. When Annie arrived at the apartment, however, she gave only well-rehearsed and evasive answers. Discouraged, Effi sent the child home without the hope of seeing her again. Soon after this incident Effi's health became extremely poor and the family doctor reported her condition to her parents, hinting that their continued rejection could mean her death. Her health improved when she was finally permitted to return home. Aside from her parents and the local minister, however, there was nobody for Effi to speak to. Roswitha, concerned for her mistress' loneliness, wrote to Innstetten asking him to give Effi the family dog. Innstetten was glad to fulfill her desire. His career in the Ministry had been extremely suc-

cessful, but no promotion would lessen the pain in his heart; he still loved his former wife.

After a beautiful summer at her parents' home, Effi died. In her last conversation with her mother she asked Frau von Briest to tell Innstetten that he had done the only correct thing possible for him. She wanted to die as Effi Briest, for she had not honored her married name.

Further Critical Evaluation of the Work:

Theodor Fontane's *Effi Briest* is a novel without passion, in spite of its tale of adultery, dueling, and death. It is, however, precisely in its depiction of basically pleasant, uncomplicated characters, living their lives according to a strict code of behavior, that the work achieved its strength and remarkable subtlety. The novel is generally regarded as Fontane's best, and its classical form is a model of construction and narrative technique. It moves in equal divisions from the Briest estate, through the events at Kessin, in Berlin, and finally back to the family home. Throughout the novel, Fontane describes the psychological state of the characters, revealing their inner life through their gestures and words. He does not take sides, nor moralize, letting both the characters and their society speak for themselves.

The story itself is unremarkable, one of a number of adultery stories popular at the time. But the import of the novel lies beyond the story line. Fontane depicts a class of people—the Prussian Junkers, or old nobility, whose lives have settled into a meaningless prescribed form. Effi's parents married without love, and never question their lives; Effi may break with the code, but not because she questions or rejects. She is merely bored and frivolous.

Her husband, basically a good man, is unable to act otherwise than social convention dictates, and when, after some years, he discovers the adultery, he takes the consequences—duel and divorce—with some vague regret, but no real anger or hurt. Powerful emotion, grief, anger, or happiness seems beyond these people, and father Briest's refusal to go into the matter—"that is too wide a field,"—is typical. The characters are incapable of taking distance from their situation, of seeing the degree to which their lives are impoverished by their adherence to a class code. Fontane, too, does not examine an alternative, but leaves it to the reader to draw his own conclusions.

EGMONT

Type of work: Drama
Author: Johann Wolfgang von Goethe (1749-1832)
Type of plot: Romantic tragedy
Time of plot: Sixteenth century
Locale: Brussels
First presented: 1788

> *Principal characters:*
> COUNT EGMONT, Lord of Gaure
> CLÄRCHEN, his beloved
> BRACKENBURG, a citizen in love with Clärchen
> THE DUKE OF ALVA, emissary of Philip II
> MARGARET OF PARMA, Regent of The Netherlands
> WILLIAM, Prince of Orange

Critique:

This tragic account of the martyrdom of Egmont has remained constantly in favor, partly because of Beethoven's musical setting. Here Goethe has taken for his theme the undying love for liberty of oppressed peoples everywhere, and for his plot an episode in the struggle of The Netherlands to throw off Spanish rule. Egmont is warmly depicted as a brave and generous man, but the other characters are less fully developed. The action of the play is designed to bring out the theme of liberty, and in that design it succeeds admirably.

The Story:

The people of The Netherlands were unhappy in the state of their homeland. Philip II of Spain was tightening his absolute control of the Lowlands, particularly in religious matters, for Philip was the main instrument of the Inquisition. Recently a new regent had been appointed to administer his rule. The populace had hoped the office would go to Count Egmont, who, after his defeat of the French at Gravelines, had become a national hero. Besides, although Egmont was a Catholic, he treated the Protestants with kindness, and he had even gone to Madrid to plead with Philip to lessen the strictures of Catholic repression.

The king, however, had given the office to Margaret, his half-sister. She, like Philip, tolerated no dissidence from the established church, yet by firmness and tact she had pacified the sturdy burghers who stubbornly resisted any laws but their own. She had even managed to conciliate Egmont and William of Orange, so that outwardly at least there was harmony among the nobility.

Margaret summoned Machiavel, her secretary, to hear his account of new uprisings. He told her how throughout Flanders mobs were breaking into cathedrals and despoiling the monuments of the hated foreign religion. He counseled Margaret to be firm but not cruel toward the Protestants. Margaret told him that her efforts toward conciliation would mean little, for it was rumored that the cruel Duke of Alva was on his way to assume control of the provinces. Machiavel reminded her that as regent she would hold the final power, but Margaret was wise in the ways of kings. Officially or not, Alva would rule The Netherlands, and she could hope to circumvent him only by appealing directly to her brother. She was especially fearful of what might happen to Egmont and William of Orange, and the effects of Alva's harsh rule on the people.

Meanwhile, in her humble house, Clärchen was happily singing; that night Egmont would come to her. Brackenburg watched her anxiously, for he loved her and he was certain that no good would come of that love affair between a count and a commoner. When Clärchen, looking from her windows, saw a mob in the street, she asked Brackenburg to learn the cause of the disturbance. During his absence her mother reproached Clärchen bitterly for rejecting Brackenburg's suit. Even now, the mother declared, the burgher would be glad to marry Clärchen. Brackenburg returned to tell them the people had heard of the outbreaks in Flanders, and were heartened by that uprising against their oppressors.

A group of commoners argued about their rights as citizens. One, who could read, told them of their rights under the constitution and of their forefathers' vigilance in protecting their privileges. Egmont, arriving on the scene, advised them to be moderate in their talk but to preserve their ancient liberties. After he left, a keen observer remarked that Egmont's head would make a dainty morsel for the headsman.

In his residence Egmont attended to duties of state. One of his letters came from Count Oliva, his old preceptor, who counseled him to be more circumspect in his behavior and less free in his talk. Egmont threw the letter aside, remarking that every one was different; he himself believed in doing what was right without fear or favor. Let others play the part of fawning courtier.

William of Orange arrived to talk over the coming of Alva. William was in favor of caution; they would do nothing until they knew what Alva had been sent to accomplish. Egmont reminded him that they were both Knights of the Golden Fleece. As members of that order they could not be punished except through a trial by their peers. Prince William was inclined to place little trust in their rights, however, for Philip was a determined and ruthless ruler. William declared that he himself would remain on his own estate and refuse to meet the Duke of Alva. Egmont, on the other hand, decided to speak his mind freely. If he had to be a rebel, he would openly do his best to advance the welfare of The Netherlands.

Margaret, in the meantime, had received a dispatch from Philip. The letter was gentle and considerate in tone, a fact ominous in itself. The king informed her officially of Alva's mission and told in detail of the formidable army the duke was bringing to garrison the recalcitrant towns. Margaret knew that her authority as regent had been superseded.

In the evening Clärchen received Egmont with joy. For a time Egmont was remote in his conduct, even keeping on his mantle. Then he showed her that he was wearing his full uniform, decorated with the emblem of the Golden Fleece, and said that he had come thus attired because she had asked him to do so as a favor. Clärchen, particularly impressed by the decoration of the Golden Fleece, was touched by that evidence of his regard.

The inhabitants of the town grew fearful. Alva's soldiers had been stationed at every strategic point and his spies were everywhere, so that the citizens dared not congregate to discuss their new woes. The ordinary people were afraid for Egmont; it was rumored that he would be killed.

In his palace Alva had made his plans, with his trusted guards forming so tight a cordon around the residence that no one could get in or out. To his natural son Ferdinand he announced his intentions. He was expecting Egmont and William of Orange. At the end of the audience, Alva would detain Egmont on a pretext. Prince William would be arrested outside. As soon as he was safely in custody, Ferdinand, acting as the duke's messenger, was to return to the reception chamber. His arrival would be the signal to arrest Egmont. Ferdinand, uneasy over the success of the plot, was nevertheless flattered by the part he was to play.

William of Orange was too cautious to fall into the duke's trap, however, and he stayed away from the audience. Egmont, who knew no fear, went without hesitation and discussed at great length the troubled situation in The Netherlands. He was a skillful debater. At every point he upheld the dignity of the burghers and wisely counseled patience and tact in dealing with them. At last Alva became impatient and abruptly ordered his arrest. He read a document in which Philip decreed Egmont had been tried and found guilty of treason. Because the King of Spain did not acknowledge the authority of the Knight of the Golden Fleece, Egmont failed in his demand for immunity.

Clärchen was distraught when she heard of Egmont's arrest. Accompanied by faithful Brackenburg, she wandered about the town in an attempt to incite the citizens to rescue Egmont. But Alva had done his work well; the burghers were all afraid even to discuss the matter. Returning to the house, Clärchen thought of the vial of poison that Brackenburg had once shown her when he was disconsolate. Thinking to quiet her temporarily, he gave her the vial. Clärchen immediately drank the poison and left the room to die.

Meanwhile, in the palace prison, Egmont had been wakeful. When he finally dozed off he was wakened by Ferdinand and Silva. The latter read Egmont's sentence; he was to be executed publicly in the market place as a warning to the people. Silva left, but Ferdinand remained behind to condole with the count. Although he had had a part in the plot, he really sympathized with Egmont.

When Egmont slept again, a vision appeared. Freedom was reclining on a cloud. Her features were those of Clärchen. She held above his head a wreath of victory. Egmont awoke at dawn to strains of martial music. The guards were at his door.

Further Critical Evaluation of the Work:

Of Goethe's dramatic works, two are singled out as his "history" plays. One is *Egmont*; the other is *Götz von Berlichingen* (1774). These plays, like many others of the time, not only in Germany but throughout Europe, reflect the growing interest in democratic principles which found its strongest expression in the American Revolution of 1776 and the French Revolution of 1789. The drama was a powerful vehicle for generating revolutionary spirit, and during this period many plays with nationalistic themes were written to encourage patriotic feelings in the fight for liberty from oppression, both internal and external. Goethe's plays certainly fall in the mainstream of this trend, but they share more than historical content.

As literature, *Egmont* and *Götz von Berlichingen* are often discussed in tandem as examples of Shakespeare's influence on Goethe; however, the plays have intrinsic similarities with or without Shakespeare's influence. Looseness of structure typifies both plays, allowing *Egmont*, like *Götz von Berlichingen*, to emphasize character over action. But the character Egmont, unlike the character Götz, tends to balance action with reflection. To be sure, Egmont led an active life, disregarding danger and never fearing the untried. He was also adept at the practical and worldly skills required of a man in his position. He was a competent marksman, firm and equitable in financial matters, familiar with the temperament of the commoners in his provinces, and he knew how to govern them; he could maneuver around devious feminine logic (Margaret) even while he appreciated feminine wiles (Clärchen); and he was both wise and just in the administration of governmental affairs. These combined qualities bespeak a man more temperate than the often impetuous Götz.

Indeed, the hallmark of Egmont's character was dedication to the principle that justice should be tempered with mercy. Toward that end, Egmont sought to obtain justice for The Netherlands and his people from their Spanish rulers. Like Goethe himself, Egmont felt driven by an inner spirit over whom he had no control (Goethe called it his *"Daimon."*) Edmont's consequent bold route of action, however, ran afoul of the Duke of Alva's abuse of power. Yet, in his death cell, Egmont was consoled by a vision in which "Freedom" (closely resembling Clärchen) told him that his death would spark a revolution which would ultimately free his people. Reassured, Egmont accepted his fate as the means to attain his goal.

Egmont's personality thus emerges in the course of the play to contrast with Götz's, as a balance between active and contemplative components: judicious action preceded by thought and impulsive action followed by thought. That balance, in turn, lends untity to the protagonist's personality: Egmont's character is far less melodramatically onesided than that of Götz. As a result, just as Egmont is a more unified character than Götz, so *Egmont* is a more unified play than *Götz von Berlichingen.* Still, it is the demon-driven character of Egmont who dominates the play, insuring for Egmont and the play a special place in Goethe's own demon-driven affections throughout his long life and prolific career.

THE EGOIST

Type of work: Novel
Author: George Meredith (1828-1909)
Type of plot: Social satire
Time of plot: Nineteenth century
Locale: England
First published: 1879

> *Principal characters:*
> SIR WILLOUGHBY PATTERNE, the egoist
> VERNON WHITFORD, his cousin
> COLONEL DE CRAYE, his relative
> LAETITIA DALE, a neighbor
> CLARA MIDDLETON, Sir Willoughby's betrothed
> DOCTOR MIDDLETON, her father
> CROSSJAY PATTERNE, Sir Willoughby's distant kinsman

Critique:

The Egoist creates a fantastic world where, in scenes of subtle comedy, the characters are treated realistically. The effect is one of drollery. Each character is a symbol of some virtue or vice rather than a living individual. All the characters speak alike, and they speak the language of Meredith. This novel stands apart from Meredith's other novels, distinguished as it is by its originality of technique and purpose. It is, to use Meredith's own term, "a comedy in narrative."

The Story:

On the day of his majority Sir Willoughby Patterne announced his engagement to Miss Constantia Durham. Laetitia Dale, who lived with her old father in a cottage on Willoughby's estate, bore her love for him—she thought—secretly, but everyone, including Willoughby himself, knew about it. Ten days before the wedding day Constantia astonished her betrothed by eloping with Harry Oxford, a military man. For a few weeks after that, the proud Willoughby courted Laetitia while the neighborhood gossiped about the poor girl's chances to become his wife. There was great disappointment when he suddenly decided to go abroad for three years. On his return to his estate he brought with him his cousin, Vernon Whitford, as an adviser in the management of his properties, and a young distant kinsman named Crossjay Patterne.

At first Laetitia, the faithful, was overjoyed at Willoughby's return, but soon she saw that again she was to lose him, for he became engaged to Clara Middleton, the daughter of a learned doctor. Middleton and his daughter came to Willoughby's estate to visit for a few weeks. It might have been the controversy over Crossjay or even the existence of Laetitia that caused Clara to see Willoughby for what he really was. In spite of Willoughby's objections, Vernon wanted Crossjay to enter the Marines and the young man was sent to Laetitia to be tutored for his examination. Vernon a literary man, wanted to go to London, but Willoughby overruled him. Noting Willoughby's self-centered attitude toward Crossjay, his complete and selfish concern with matters affecting himself and his attempt to dominate her own mind, Clara began to feel trapped by her betrothal. She reflected that Constantia had escaped by finding a gallant Harry Oxford to take her away, but she sorrowfully realized that she had no one to rescue her.

When Clara attempted to break her engagement, she found Willoughby intractable and her father too engrossed in his studies to be disturbed. Meanwhile, Wiloughby had picked Laetitia Dale as Vernon's wife. This was Willoughby's plan to keep near him both his cousin and the woman who fed his ego with her devotion. Vernon could retire to one of the cottages on the estate and write and study. Asked by Willoughby to aid him in his plan, Clara took the opportunity to ask Vernon's advice on her own problem. He assured her that she must move subtly and slowly.

In desperation, she persuaded Doctor Middleton to agree to take a trip to France with her for a few weeks. From such a trip she hoped never to return to Willoughby. But this wary lover introduced Dr. Middleton to his favorite brand of claret. Two bottles of the wine put the doctor in such an amiable mood that when Clara asked him if he were ready to go to London with her, he told her that the thought was preposterous. Willoughby had won the first round.

Colonel De Craye arrived to be best man at the wedding. Little by little he sensed that Clara was not happy at the prospect of her approaching marriage. In desperation Clara resorted to other means of escape. She wrote to her friend Lucy Darleton in town and received from that young lady an invitation to visit her in London.

Clara gave Crossjay the privilege of accompanying her to the train station. A hue and cry was raised at her absence from the estate, and Vernon, accidentally discovering her destination, followed her to the station and urged her to come back. Only because she believed that her behavior might cause an injury to Crossjay's future did Clara return to her prison. If she were to leave now, Willoughby would have full control of the young boy, for Vernon was soon to go to London to follow his writing career.

Complications resulted from Clara's attempted escape. At the station Vernon had had her drink some brandy to overcome the effects of the rainy weather. The neighborhood began to gossip. Willoughby confronted Crossjay, who told him the truth about Clara's escape. Clara hoped that Willoughby would release her because of the gossip, but he refused. Doctor Middleton seemed ignorant of what was happening. He was determined that his daughter should fulfill her pledge to marry Sir Willoughby. Furthermore, he liked Willoughby's vintage wines and Willoughby's estate.

By this time the Egoist knew that his marriage to Clara would not take place. He decided upon the one move that would soothe his wounded vanity—he asked Laetitia to become his wife. She refused, declaring she no longer loved him.

Colonel De Craye shrewdly surmised what had happened. He told Clara the hopeful news. Clara felt that her only remaining obstacle was her father's insistence that she must not break her promise to Willoughby. Now she could show that Willoughby had broken his promise first by proposing to Laetitia while he was still pledged to Clara.

Willoughby's world blew up in his face. Dr. Middleton announced firmly that Clara need not marry Willoughby. He had decided that he admired Vernon's scholarship more than he liked Willoughby's wines. But the twice-jilted lover had other plans for his own protection. He must even the score. If he could get Clara to consent to marry Vernon, he felt there would be some measure of recompense for himself, for such a marriage would have the ironic touch to satisfy Willoughby. But Clara told him it was already her intention to wed Vernon as soon as her engagement to Willoughby could be broken. The Egoist's selfishness and arrogance had brought them together.

The Egoist was defeated. He went straight to Laetitia, offering her his hand without love. He was willing for her to marry him only for money. Laetitia accepted on the condition that Crossjay be permitted to enter the Marines. Clara and the doctor planned to leave for Europe. Vernon arranged to meet them in the Swiss Alps, where he and Clara would marry.

Further Critical Evaluation of the Work:

George Meredith expressed what he thought were the essential social conditions for successful comedy in his famous essay "On the Idea of Comedy and of the Uses of the Comic Spirit," first delivered as a lecture two years before the publication of *The Egoist*. In the essay Meredith argues that the comic poet cannot function without the stimulus of a clever society, a society sensitive to ideas and witty in its perceptions. A merely fad-conscious period, giddy and emotional, is too primitive to inspire true comedy. Of major importance is at least some intellectual activity and a tolerance of women in society; that is to say, feminine wit is essential to a healthy social climate, one that will permit a society to laugh at itself.

Meredith's curious anti-hero, Willoughby, is devoid of any ideas, totally wrapped up in a giddy love affair with himself, and singularly incapable of any objective perceptions. Clara tells him to his face that he is boring her to death. Immersed in his own ardor, he is so oblivious to insult that he calls her a "sleeping beauty" immediately after she has intimated that he is putting her to sleep. In other words, Willoughby is the incarnation of everything that makes the Comic Spirit impossible. And yet, the irony of the novel is that he is at the same time the ideal subject for Comedy's ridiculing power.

Willoughby's selfishness and egotism are nowhere more clearly revealed than in his insistence on the servility of women to men. This is his primary violation of Meredith's "Social Law" of Comedy, and it is what finally brings about his comic punishment. Laetitia treats him as an object, by agreeing to marry him without love, and caps his downfall by condemning him to the same treatment he extended to others: "I was once a foolish romantic girl; now I am a sickly woman, all illusions vanished. Privation has made me what an abounding fortune usually makes of others—I am an Egoist."

EL SEÑOR PRESIDENTE

Type of work: Novel
Author: Miguel Ángel Asturias (1899-1974)
Time: Early twentieth century
Locale: Central America
First published: 1946

Principal characters:
> THE PRESIDENT, dictator of a Latin American country
> MIGUEL CARA DE ÁNGEL (ANGEL FACE), his crony
> GENERAL EUSEBIO CANALES, a political rival
> CAMILA CANALES, his daughter
> ABEL CARVAJAL, a lawyer and a suspected Canales conspirator
> AUDITOR GENERAL DE GUERRA, a Judge Advocate
> DR. LUIS BARREÑO, the President's physician
> LUCIO VÁSQUEZ, of the Secret Police
> MR. GENGIS, a whiskey-drinking North American
> MAJOR FARFÁN, a hatchet man for the dictator
> CONCEPCIÓN GAMUCINO, ("Chón Gold Tooth"), Madame of El Dulce
>   Encanto (The Sweet Enchantment)
> COLONEL JOSÉ PARRALES SONRIENTE, a killer for the President
> PATAHUECA (FLAT FOOT), a beggar
> EL PELELE (ZANY), another beggar
> MOSCO (MOSQUITO), a blind, legless beggar

Miguel Angel Asturias, born in Guatemala, has spent much of his life elsewhere. Going to France in 1923, after finishing his studies as a lawyer at the University of Guatemala, he remained there for ten years, writing poetry in the French style and completing a novel about a Spanish American dictator that he had started before leaving home. He has also written other fiction and has served as Guatemala's diplomatic representative in France, Argentina, El Salvador, and Mexico. Following the increasing success of his writings, he retired to Buenos Aires with his wife and two sons.

It is chiefly for this bitter picture of a morally sick Latin American nation under dictatorship, a disease suffered by many of them, that he is recognized as an important New World author. The pictures of human misery in this novel make a powerful impression on even those critics who find it aesthetically weak. *El Señor Presidente* is rather like that other picture of Central American dictatorships, an example of *esperpéntica,* a mixture of satire and the grotesque.

The novel provides no clue as to date or locale, beyond the mention, when Cara de Ángel was searching the pages of *El Nacional* for an announcement of his wedding, that he saw mention of the Battle of Verdun, at a time when Manuel Estrada Cabrera was the Guatemalan president. Apparently Asturias had no special target in mind.

As if to lighten the unpleasant pictures of oppression and the exploitation of the poor, the author includes bits of folklore, references to Tohil, Giver of Fire, folk poetry, and descriptions that might have come from Asturias' earlier French impressionist poetry period. Local color and regional words are so numerous in the novel that Asturias felt the need to include a vocabulary and glossary covering eight pages. The French version of the novel was awarded first place in the International Novel Competition in 1952.

The novel is concerned with the unnamed President of an unnamed Spanish American nation. He is a dictator who maintains himself in power by cruelty and ruthlessness, though his portrait, pasted everywhere, with punishment for its removal, makes him appear a youthful charmer wearing huge epaulets and about to be crowned with a laurel wreath by a smiling cherub. Judge Advocate de Guerra summed up the President's theory of control: never let anyone have grounds for hope; make them realize, by brutal beatings and kickings if necessary, that there is none. The President, lamenting the murder of his hatchetman, Colonel Parrales Sonriente, killed by a crazy beggar named Zany whom he had taunted on the cathedral steps, also revealed his philosophy by declaring that he had intended to make Parrales a general because of his ability to trample on the populace and humiliate them.

The killing of the officer provided the President with an excuse for getting rid of a political rival, General Canales, along with a fellow plotter, Lawyer Abel Carvajal. The Advocate General gathered up all the beggars from the cathedral door where the killing had taken place and beat them until they were willing to swear they had seen Canales commit the murder. The only one refusing to sign the accusation, Mosquito, the legless, blind beggar, was beaten to death. To prevent discovery of the true facts, Vásquez, of the secret police, came upon Zany, the real murderer, trying to flee, and silenced him with two bullets.

Further evidence of the merciless nature of the President is revealed as he orders the beating of his personal physician, Dr. Barreño, for uncovering political graft that had caused the death of soldiers at the hospital, poisoned by impure sodium sulphate. Even worse, he has his secretary whipped to death for spilling ink on a document. It is easy to understand how such a man could mark the innocent General Canales for death.

In order to carry out his scheme against General Canales, the President involved his crony, Miguel Angel Face, in an elaborate plot, first ordering the police to shoot the general if he attempted to flee, then sending Angel Face to warn him of his danger and urge him to escape. The crony, in love with the general's daughter, betrayed his master by getting his victim safely across the frontier. However, the general died before he could recruit an army for invasion.

Complications, including acceptance of bribes by the Judge Advocate to put Camila Canales into the Sweet Enchantment brothel, and her rescue by Angel Face, resulted in the arrangement of the marriage of Camila and Angel Face by the President to insure the loyalty of his crony, but through treachery Angel Face was illegally imprisoned and soon died. Other rebels against the President also died. As opposition continued, so did the atmosphere of terror that allowed the dictator's favorites to thrive in a generally corrupt society. With the Secret Police in power El Señor Presidente continued to have his way.

A dictatorship in Spanish America may have several aspects. It is frequently viewed by the outside world as a comic opera sort of thing. O. Henry and others have written of its amusing moments and its romantic and adventurous episodes such as gun-running, but frequently it is much more tragic and cruel. The stakes are high and the financial returns enormous. History records many long-term Latin American dictatorships. Asturias' novel shows how fear and terror can make such longevity possible.

THE ELDER STATESMAN

Type of work: Drama
Author: T. S. Eliot (1888-1965)
Time: The present
Locale: London and Badgley Court, a nursing home
First presented: 1958

Principal characters:
LORD CLAVERTON, the "elder statesman"
MICHAEL CLAVERTON-FERRY, his son
MONICA CLAVERTON-FERRY, his daughter
CHARLES HEMINGTON, her fiancé
"FEDERICO GOMEZ," formerly Fred Culverwell
"MRS. CARGHILL" (Maisie Batterson, alias MAISIE MONTJOY), a woman
out of Lord Claverton's past

At the first production of this play during the Edinburgh Festival in the summer of 1958, it was accorded more praise than had been given to Eliot's earlier dramatic works. It was described as being "warmer," "mellower," and "more human" than *Murder in the Cathedral* or *The Cocktail Party,* which had been received with the respectful attention due the work of a great poet rather than with any genuine enthusiasm. Yet since its publication in England and America, the play has attracted far less notice than might have been expected when one considers the reputation of its author.

In an essay of 1951, "Poetry and Drama," Eliot discussed at some length not only the general question of the poetic drama but also the particular problems that he had encountered in writing his own plays. The crux of this problem was to find a form of verse such that the audience would not be conscious of it. This search led Eliot to reject some of the methods that his predecessors in poetic drama had employed. Blank verse, he felt, would not do, for, through its long use in nondramatic poetry after the Elizabethan age, it had lost the flexibility necessary to give the proper conversational tone; and to the use of blank verse he attributed the failure of nineteenth century poets who had attempted plays in verse. The prose poetry of Synge was too limited to the Aran Islands; the poetry of William Butler Yeats's later plays was

suitable only for mythological kings and queens. For this reason Eliot felt that he had to forge his own tool if he were to write plays of contemporary people, not historical pageants. And so, beginning with *The Family Reunion,* he employed a line varying in length and syllables, with a caesura and three stresses, with one stress on one side of the caesura and two on the other. This versification, Eliot thought, would be close enough to the rhythm of contemporary speech to avoid the obviously "poetic" that would be unacceptable to a modern audience.

As in his later plays, *The Family Reunion, The Cocktail Party,* and *The Confidential Clerk,* Eliot here chose a contemporary setting and an apparently simple plot. But since, in the essay cited above, he slyly confessed that the plot of *The Cocktail Party* had been merely that of the *Alcestis* of Euripides in modern dress and that no one had noticed this fact, we cannot be certain that some Greek play may not be lurking beneath the surface of *The Elder Statesman.* Certainly, however, none is immediately apparent.

Although Lord Claverton, the "elder statesman," does not appear at the opening of the play, he dominates the scene from the rising of the curtain. His daughter's fiancé, Charles, is protesting that, should he stay for tea in the Claverton town house, he will not be able to have any private conversation with Monica because of her father's presence. It is clear that Monica worships her father, who has been a famous man in both the political and financial worlds of England but who has now, on his doctor's orders, retired from public life and is preparing for a rest cure at Badgley Court, a nursing home somewhere in the country. When Lord Claverton enters, we are conscious of a man of great dignity who has always expected deference and who has received it, although now he has become querulous over the emptiness of his future. Like most men of affairs who have been compelled to give up their former activities, he realizes the hollowness of his past eminence, yet cannot endure the prospect of a life devoid of these activities. Life is now a mere waiting for death. He recognizes himself as a ghost and, with dramatic irony, remarks that he smiles when he thinks men are frightened of ghosts.

Hardly has this remark been uttered when the first ghost from his own past arrives in the form of one Señor Gomez from the Latin American Republic of San Marco. Almost immediately Gomez is revealed as Fred Culverwell, a friend of Lord Claverton's Oxford days. The unbearably suave expatriate is in possession of a damaging secret: when, years ago, the two university students were driving at night with two girls, Claverton —then plain Dick Ferry—ran over a man and did not stop because he feared the possible scandal. Culverwell also accuses Claverton of having been the cause of his ruin in England: by taking him up at Oxford and teaching him expensive tastes which he, a poor boy, lacked the means to gratify, Claverton had forced him to resort to theft and finally to forgery which had led to a prison sentence and flight from England. But in San Marco, with its peculiar political situation, he had done well; he is no crude blackmailer and wants only Claverton's friendship, something to give him "reality" after thirty-five years of homesick exile under an assumed name. He is a realist; he knows that, although a worldly

success, he has failed, though not so badly as has Claverton, who has had to keep on pretending to himself that he has succeeded. To Claverton's credit, he stands the attack well, maintains his dignity, and shows no fear of the moral blackmail that Culverwell is so subtly exercising.

Lord Claverton's doctor had ordered him to Badgley Court, a nursing home run in a grimly cheerful fashion, for a complete rest. But hardly has he arrived when there appears another ghost from his past, this time in the form of Mrs. Carghill. A generation before she had been Maisie Montjoy, a star of the music halls; now she is a prosperous widow. The Dick Ferry of those far-off days had been in love with her and she with him —or so she claims. But she had settled her breach of promise suit out of court, and now she retains only sentimental memories and all of his letters, both the originals and photostatic copies. Again Lord Claverton, in spite of her sarcastic comments, maintains his unruffled dignity, even when she points out that there is only a negligible difference between being an elder statesman and posing as one. Twice have these ghosts brought home to him his essential emptiness.

The ultimate trial comes in the form of his son Michael, a spendthrift and ne'er-do-well who, even in his effort to see his father, has become involved in a motor accident, though not a serious one. In a sense, Michael is also a ghost, the ghost of the boy Claverton might have been had he not been possessed by a devil who was prudent as well as wayward. The son, though obviously a weakling, does have his side of the story: he is desperately eager to get out of England into some country where he can have a life of his own, free from the oppressive shadow of his father's great name. It is clear that the father has dominated the son far too much. But just as the situation between the two seems to have reached an impasse, the solution is provided by the two "ghosts"; Mrs. Carghill has suggested to

Gomez that he take Michael back with him to the mysterious business in San Marco. But the price that has to be paid for this solution to the problem is that Claverton must have all his past errors laid bare before his daughter and her fiancé. This is his act of contrition, after which he receives absolution in the form of Monica's forgiveness and understanding. The ghosts from his past are at last exorcised, to return into the darkness whence they came. And so he goes out into the grounds of the nursing home to await death, much as Oedipus left the grove at Colonus sacred to the Eumenides to find his appointed end. The mask of the "elder statesman" has been dropped forever; he has become himself, the real man under the mask.

Aristotle asserted that "A discovery is, as the very word implies, a change from ignorance to knowledge, and thus to either love or hate in the personages marked for good or evil fortune." This feature of the classical drama is perfectly illustrated in Eliot's play, for it is by the discovery of his true self that Claverton is able to achieve love. He realizes at last the real nature of his past mistakes; he had always proceeded by the letter of the law: he has never been technically guilty, for the man he had run over was proved to be dead before the accident,

and Maisie had been paid off handsomely. He had never understood his wife and his son because he had never loved them. Even his affection for his daughter had been mere possessiveness. Now that he understands himself, can understand that his whole career has been a sham, he can love and hence can find peace. The central theme of the play is, thus, the Christian doctrine of redemption; and redemption leads to love.

It is, of course, unfair to judge a play only by reading it. Certainly *The Elder Statesman* was well received when it appeared. It is also certain that Eliot has been more successful in finding the right poetic language for this play than in his previous efforts. It is probable, however, that many readers will find the play essentially undramatic. The pace is too even; there is a lack of suspense and excitement, which may be crude elements but which are necessary to a good play. Exquisitely handled language does not alone make for effective drama. Perhaps Eliot has been on the wrong track in attributing the failure of the poetic drama of the nineteenth century to the choice of a poor poetic medium. Perhaps these poets, like Eliot himself, lacked the real feeling for the theater which is often possessed by greatly inferior writers.

ELECTIVE AFFINITIES

Type of work: Novel
Author: Johann Wolfgang von Goethe (1749-1832)
Type of plot: Philosophical romance
Time of plot: Eighteenth century
Locale: Germany
First published: 1808

Principal characters:
EDWARD, a wealthy nobleman
CHARLOTTE, his wife
OTTILIE, Charlotte's protégée
THE CAPTAIN, Edward's friend
LUCIANA, Charlotte's daughter by a previous marriage
NANNY, a youngster, Ottilie's protégée
HERR MITTLER, a self-appointed marriage counselor

Critique:

Although written late in the author's career, *Elective Affinities (Die Wahlverwandtschaften)* illustrates some of the romantic tendencies usually found in Goethe's earlier works. The emotionalism of Edward, the quasi-scientific theme, and the poetically fitting (if unrealistic) deaths are examples of the romantic elements. At the same time it is only fair to classify the novel as a philosophical piece of fiction. The human relationships (both the actual and the symbolic), the passages discussing education and pedagogical techniques, and the comments found in the passages taken from Ottilie's fictional diary all contribute to the philosophical effect. *Elective Affinities* is a novel in which psychological actions and reactions are important, while of physical action there is so little that one can almost say there is none, just as there is almost no plot as ordinarily defined.

The Story:

Edward, a wealthy nobleman, had long been in love with Charlotte, but each had been forced to wed someone else. Both their first spouses died before many years elapsed, and soon afterward Edward and Charlotte were married. With Charlotte's daughter Luciana placed in a good school, the pair, happily married at last, settled down to an idyllic existence at Edward's rural castle. They spent their time working at pleasant tasks about the castle and its park, leading together the kind of life they had long dreamed about and hoped for.

But one day a letter came to threaten the happy couple. The Captain, long a friend of Edward, was out of a position. Edward immediately suggested that his friend be invited to the castle, where he could help in improving the grounds and buildings. At first Charlotte withheld her consent, but finally she agreed to her husband's earnest desire. She revealed that she, too, had thought of inviting someone to the castle, the daughter of a dead friend. Charlotte had taken the girl, Ottilie, as her protégée because of her friendship for the girl's mother. Ottilie, who was at school with Luciana, was not immediately invited for the visit Charlotte planned.

When the Captain arrived, as he did shortly, his presence soon made marked differences in the household. In order that he and Edward might work together undisturbed and with greater convenience, Edward moved from the wing in which Charlotte's rooms were located to the wing in which the Captain had been placed; and Charlotte saw less and less of her husband. One evening the three read about the elective affinities of chemical elements and fell to speculating on how people were also attracted to one another in different combinations and in varying degrees. The invitation to Ottilie was again discussed. Since the girl was not doing well in school, and because Charlotte obviously needed additional companionship, Ottilie was immediately sent for.

When Edward had seen the girl and been in her company on previous occasions, Ottilie had made no impression on him. Seeing her in the same household, however, he soon became aware of her attractiveness. It became obvious, too, that Ottilie found Edward attractive. The two fitted together strangely well. When they played duets, Ottilie's very mistakes coincided with Edward's. Gradually, as the two spent more and more time together, Charlotte and the Captain often found themselves together, too, much to their delight. After some weeks had passed, Edward realized the extent of his passion and his influence on Ottilie, all of which made him rejoice. Recognizing the force of his passion, he made efforts to cause it to grow, as it did steadily and swiftly. Although Charlotte noticed the attentions he paid the girl, she refused to become upset by them; since she had discovered her own regard for the Captain, she could more easily overlook her husband's behavior.

One day, while Charlotte and the Captain were out boating, their passion for each other could no longer be concealed. Being mature people, however, they immediately controlled their emotions and resolved, after a few kisses, to adhere strictly to the moral path in their conduct. Also, during one of their periods together, Ottilie and Edward discovered their love for each other. Being more easily swayed and emotionally immature, they welcomed the passion and did not try to curb their emotions.

While the relationships among the four were developing, more guests came to the castle. They were a countess and a baron who were spending a vacation as lover and mistress while away from their respective spouses. On the night of their arrival, Edward showed the baron the way to the countess' rooms, that the lovers might be together. While wishing he could enter Ottilie's room with the same freedom as the baron had entered that of his mistress, Edward found himself at his wife's door. He knocked and was admitted. He remained the night with Charlotte, but when he and his wife embraced they did not think of each other, but of Ottilie and the Captain.

The four people had all been working on plans for improving the grounds of the castle, with the hope, especially on Edward's part, that everything might be finished in time for Ottilie's birthday. On the day of the birthday celebration Edward made a public spectacle of himself, proving almost a fool in his ardor for Ottilie. Finally, Charlotte suggested that Ottilie be returned to school or sent to live with other friends. Edward, angry and frustrated in his love, left the castle. When he left he vowed he would have nothing more to do with Ottilie, as Charlotte wished, so long as the girl remained. On the same day the Captain, who had received a position which promoted him to the rank of major, also left the castle.

Shortly after Edward's departure, Charlotte, discovering that she was pregnant as the result of the night her husband had spent in her apartments, called on the services of Herr Mittler, a volunteer marriage counselor. But Herr Mittler was unable even to begin a reconciliation with Edward, whose passion for Ottilie had conquered him completely. Having been accustomed all his life to doing as he pleased, Edward could not see why he should not have his way in this matter. When war broke out, he entered the king's service. He served gallantly and won many honors. He believed that if he lived through the war he was fated to have Ottilie.

Charlotte, meanwhile, endured her pregnancy, but she and Ottilie were no longer so close to each other, for the younger woman had become suspicious of Charlotte. For a time life at the castle was enlivened when Luciana arrived for a visit with a large party of her friends. During the entertainment of the visit,

Luciana pointedly left Ottilie out of the activities arranged for the guests.

Ottilie's friend during the trying weeks after Edward had gone was a young architect hired to supervise the building of a summerhouse. His work completed, Charlotte had kept him on to redecorate the local church. The young man admired Ottilie very much. A young schoolmaster who had taught Ottilie also expressed interest in marrying the girl, but Ottilie could think only of Edward.

At last a son was born to Charlotte. At the christening Ottilie and Herr Mittler, who stood as sponsors for the baby, were surprised to note how much the infant resembled both Ottilie and the Captain, a resemblance soon noted by others. Charlotte, remembering how she had dreamed of the Captain while embracing her husband, guessed that Edward had been dreaming at the same time of Ottilie. In a sense the child, named Otto, was a symbol of the parents' double adultery.

Edward returned to a nearby farm when the war ended. Meeting the Captain, he made a proposal to solve everyone's problems. He suggested that he and Charlotte be divorced, so that he could marry Ottilie and Charlotte could marry the Captain. Although the ethics of the plan did not appeal to him, the Captain agreed to take the suggestion to Charlotte. When the Captain set out for the castle, Edward also visited the grounds in hopes of seeing Ottilie. They met, and Ottilie was much upset, so much so that while returning to the castle alone in a small boat she dropped Charlotte's baby overboard. The child was drowned. When the Captain arrived at the castle, Charlotte showed him the little corpse that was a miniature of himself.

Ottilie decided to go away. Edward, meeting her at an inn, persuaded her to return to the castle with him. There the four—Edward, Charlotte, Ottilie, and the Captain—tried to resume the happy life they had known before. But Ottilie seldom spoke and ate her meals in her rooms. One day she died suddenly, having starved herself to death. It came out that Nanny, her little protégée, had been persuaded to eat the food intended for Ottilie. Edward also began a fast. When he died a short time later, although not as the result of his fasting, he was laid in a tomb beside the girl he had loved. In death for one, in life for the other, the two couples were finally united.

Further Critical Evaluation of the Work:

Goethe's middle years as a classicist were bracketed by early and late years dominated by romantic characteristics. *Elective Affinities* is a product of that late romanticism. As he aged, however, Goethe was less adamant than he was in his younger days about his own adherence to any set of aesthetic principles. As a consequence, *Elective Affinities* contains elements of both classicism—primarily in form—and romanticism—mainly in content. The novel has a classic symmetry of form which complements the symmetrical arrangement of the four protagonists, dividing the married couple, Edward and Charlotte, between their two guests, Ottilie and The Captain. The classic harmonious structure of *Elective Affinities* is created by its cool, formal, generally unemotional style—particularly evident in the distancing between narrator and action evoked by Goethe's use of a third-person narrator. These classical qualities lead to the expectation that the issues with which the novel deals will be rigorously pursued to the necessary logical conclusion.

Such, however, is not the case, because Goethe treats content from a predominantly romantic perspective. In *Elective Affinities*, the absolute moral imperative of the classical social order collides with the irresistible force of romantic natural law. The classical view would mandate that society emerge the victor. Indeed, classic orthodoxy would reject the simultaneous existence of two immutable but antithetical laws in its organically unified universe. Rather than affirm a clear-cut endorsement of either law, however, Goethe concludes the novel ambiguously: although death is the fate of the lovers who defied the moral code of society, those disciples of natural law ironically carry off a moral victory of sorts by wringing sympathetic comments from the narrator, who thinks about the existence of some higher plane where there is no conflict between social order and natural law. The implication—a thoroughly romantic one—is that the two lovers, buried side by side, may yet reach that plane.

In addition to the fusion of classic and romantic elements typical of Goethe's works, *Elective Affinities* also illustrates another of the author's lifelong preoccupations: the nature of the learning process. From *The Sorrows of Young Werther* (1774) to *Faust II* (1832), Goethe was concerned with epistemology and its relation to education, although that concern is most obvious in the two *Wilhelm Meister* novels. The *Bildüngsroman,* as these novels were called, is a tale of character development and the shaping of one's innate endowments. As such, the term applies equally well to *Elective Affinities,* since this novel subtly delineates the evolving mental and emotional qualities of the four protagonists as each one's elective affinity—in chemistry, the irresistible mutual attraction between two elements—changes over the course of the story. To be sure, *Elective Affinities* is much more than a novel about the philosophy of learning or a study in classic versus romantic, but a delicately woven intense psychological drama.

ELECTRA

Type of work: Drama
Author: Euripides (480-406 B.C.)
Type of plot: Classical tragedy
Time of plot: After the fall of Troy
Locale: Argos
First presented: c. 413 B.C.

Principal characters:
ELECTRA, daughter of Agamemnon
ORESTES, her brother
CLYTEMNESTRA, her mother
AEGISTHUS, lover of Clytemnestra

Critique:

The *Electra* of Euripides is a psychological study of a woman's all-consuming hatred for her mother and stepfather on the one hand, and love for her murdered father and exiled brother on the other. The character of Electra clearly dominates the action, for it is she who spurs her brother on to kill those whom she hates. In Electra, her brother, and her mother, Euripides created three characters who are as alive today as they were on the Athenian stage.

The Story:

After Agamemnon, King of Argos, had returned home from the Trojan War, his wife, Clytemnestra, and her lover, Aegisthus, murdered him in cold blood during the home-coming banquet. Afterward Aegisthus and Clytemnestra were married, and Aegisthus became king. Orestes, young son of Agamemnon, was sent by a relative to Phocis before Aegisthus could destroy him. Electra, the daughter, remained, but was given in marriage to an old peasant, lest she marry a warrior powerful enough to avenge her father's death.

One day, after Electra and the peasant had gone out to do the day's work, Orestes came in disguise with his best friend, Pylades, to the farm to seek Electra. They heard her singing a lament for her lot and for the death of her father. A messenger interrupted her lament with word that a festival would be held in honor of the Goddess Hera and that all Argive maidens were to attend. Electra said she preferred to remain on the farm away from the pitying eyes of the people of Argos. The messenger advised her to pay honor to the gods and to ask their help.

Electra mistook Orestes and Pylades for friends of her brother and told them the story of her grief. She urged that Orestes avenge the death of Agamemnon and the ill treatment of himself and Electra. Aegisthus, meanwhile, had offered a reward for the death of Orestes.

The peasant returned from his work and asked Orestes and Pylades to remain as his guests. Electra sent her husband to bring the relative who had taken Orestes away from Argos. On his way to the peasant's cottage, the old foster father noticed that a sacrifice had been made at the tomb of Agamemnon and that there were some red hairs on the grave. He suggested to Electra that Orestes might be in the vicinity, but Electra answered that there was no chance of his being in Argos. When Orestes came out of the cottage, the old man recognized a scar on his forehead; thus brother and sister were made known to each other.

At the advice of the old peasant, Orestes planned to attend a sacrificial feast over which Aegisthus would preside. Electra sent her husband to tell Clytemnestra that she had given birth to a baby. Electra and Orestes invoked the aid of the gods in their venture to avenge the death of their father.

Orestes and Pylades were hailed by

Aegisthus as they passed him in his garden. The pair told Aegisthus that they were from Thessaly and were on their way to sacrifice to Zeus. Aegisthus informed them that he was preparing to sacrifice to the nymphs and invited them to tarry. At the sacrifice of a calf, Orestes plunged a cleaver into Aegisthus' back while Aegisthus was examining the entrails of the beast. Orestes then revealed his identity to the servants, who cheered the son of their former master. Orestes carried the corpse of Aegisthus back to the cottage where it was hidden after Electra had reviled it.

At the sight of Clytemnestra approaching the peasant's hut, Orestes had misgivings about the plan to murder her. He felt that matricide would bring the wrath of the gods upon his head. But Electra, determined to complete the revenge, reminded Orestes that an oracle had told him to destroy Aegisthus and Clytemnestra.

Clytemnestra defended herself before Electra with the argument that Agamemnon had sacrificed Iphegenia, their child, as an offering before the Trojan venture and that he had returned to Argos with Cassandra, princess of Troy, as his concubine. Electra indicted her mother on several counts and said that it was only just that she and Orestes murder Clytemnestra. The queen entered the hut to prepare a sacrifice for Electra's supposed first-born; within, she was killed by Orestes, who moaned in distress at the violence and bloodshed and matricide in which the gods had involved him.

The Dioscuri, twin sons of Zeus and brothers of the half-divine Clytemnestra, appeared to the brother and sister, who were overcome with mixed feelings of hate and love and pride and shame at what they had done. The twin gods questioned the wisdom of Apollo, whose oracle had advised this violent action; they decreed that Orestes should give Electra to Pylades in marriage and that Orestes himself should be pursued by the Furies until he could face a trial in Athens, from which trial he would emerge a free man.

Further Critical Evaluation of the Work:

Electra is a compelling example of Euripides' dramaturgy. But it also affords us a means of comparing his purpose and techniques with those of Aeschylus and Sophocles, for each of them used the same legend and presented roughly the same action. Aeschylus in *The Libation-Bearers* (part of *The House of Atreus* trilogy), Sophocles in *Electra,* and Euripides in his *Electra* all treat Orestes' return to Argos, his presentation of himself to his sister Electra, their planning of the revenge against Aegisthus and Clytemnestra, and the execution of that revenge. But each treatment is individual and unique, showing the distinct temper of mind of these three tragedians.

With Aeschylus the twin murders of Aegisthus and Clytemnestra are the culminating crimes in a family polluted by generations of kin slayings. Regicide and matricide are evils instigated by Apollo to punish and purge the earlier murder of Agamemnon. Orestes alone takes on the burden of these crimes. A minor character, Electra offers him encouragement to the deeds, but her gentle nature shrinks from being an actual accomplice. Aeschylus shows us Orestes' revenge as an act of divine justice, a crime that will in time earn an acquittal.

Sophocles takes a different view of the matter. The regicide and matricide are justifiable for him in human terms mainly, as the proper retribution for Agamemnon's killing. Electra is portrayed as a hard, bitter, determined young woman who aids her brother as a rightful duty. This perspective is similar to that in Homer's *Odyssey*.

Euripides, however, calls both points of view into question. He sees the murders of Aegisthus and Clytemnestra as wholly unmitigated evils that are neither humanly nor divinely justifiable. Euripides says in effect that no killing is permissible for any reason. And he carries this logic to its ultimate conclusion—that killers have as much right to live as anyone else no matter how twisted their psyche or how questionable their motives. This is a radical stand, but it is based on Euripides' firm conviction in the value of every human life. This belief shines through the whole of *Electra* and makes the idea of just retribution a mockery. One has the impression that Euripides would have liked to abolish all courts and prisons, turning justice into a matter of individual conscience. What is interesting is the way he works out these ideas dramatically.

Whereas Aeschylus and Sophocles concentrate on royalty and heroes, Euripides does not hesitate to depict an honorable peasant or to show ignoble blue bloods. In fact, the entire action of *Electra* takes place in front of a peasant's hut. To Euripides each life had worth, but the index to that worth was strength of character. Position, wealth, power, beauty, and physique were nothing to him. He is chiefly interested in an accurate, realistic psychology— a direct consequence of his beliefs.

Each of the main characters is shown as a clearly defined personality in relation to a specific environment. Euripides tends to concentrate on the sordid aspects in *Electra* as the legend would seem to demand, yet it is here that his faith in human dignity reveals its power. We find it easy to love good people, but to love people as warped by circumstances as Electra, Orestes, or Clytemnestra requires moral courage. Euripides had it, and he portrayed their pain as though it were his own.

Electra has fallen from lavish prosperity to squalor in a forced, loveless marriage to a peasant, which is nonetheless chaste and compassionate. She is slovenly and full of self-pity and spite. Further, she envies her mother, Clytemnestra, who lives in luxury and power, and she hates Aegisthus. Her single passion is to kill them both, and when she discovers Orestes, she uses him to obtain revenge. Orestes himself is a neurotic vagabond of no status, with authorization from Apollo to kill his mother and her lover, yet he declaims pompously about nobility of character.

Clytemnestra seems like a housewife in queen's clothing, operating by a retaliatory logic. She takes a lover because her husband had a mistress, and she kills Agamemnon because he killed their daughter Iphigenia. But none of this has made her happy. And when she visits Electra out of motherly concern, she is hacked to death by her two children. Even Aegisthus appears to be decent. It is precisely their ordinariness that makes the realistic descriptions of their murders so hideously sickening. We feel with Euripides that they deserve to live.

Once their passion for revenge is spent, Orestes and Electra are filled with self-revulsion, having arrived at the depths of a nightmarish degradation. Then Euripides brings two gods on stage, Castor and Polydeuces, to settle the matter. This *deus ex machina* ending puts the action in a new light. Apollo is directly responsible for the murders, just as Zeus is responsible for the Trojan War. These are not wise or just gods by human standards, and an individual person has infinitely more worth than their abominable edicts. Euripides is supremely confident in his position, and he does not shrink from judging gods by it.

Consistent with his faith in man's value, he allows Orestes and Electra a good measure of compassion in the end. These two share in the blood guilt and will be exiled. Orestes will even be driven mad by the Furies, which only he can see. But they deserve to live too, Euripides says in essence, and in time they will win forgiveness. The belief in human dignity has rarely had such a steadfast champion as Euripides.

James Weigel, Jr.

THE ELEGIES OF PROPERTIUS

Type of work: Poetry
Author: Sextus Propertius (C. 50 B.C.-before A.D. 2)
First transcribed: Elegies, I, 26 B.C.(?); II, 24-23 B.C.(?); III, 22-21 B.C.(?); IV, not
earlier than 16 B.C.

Sextus Propertius wrote in the poetic genre known as the Roman love elegy, a form first developed and made famous by Gallus (of whose work only one line survives), Tibullus, Ovid, and Propertius himself. The love elegy was written in alternating hexameter and pentameter lines; the pentameter was actually a hexameter shortened by the removal of syllable in the middle and another at the end of the line. The tone of this genre was always personal and passionate, and it was characterized by the first-person lament of the frustrated or grieving lover alternating with erotic joy. It is from the unhappy aspect of the Roman love elegy that our understanding of the word "elegiac" has developed.

Each of the three more or less contemporary early elegists whose work has, at least in part, survived has a distinctive effect. Tibullus is a man of great sensibility who suffers tenderly. Ovid is an erotic cynic who treats love as a game. Propertius is a passionate and tempestuous lover who both loudly complains and exalts in his love. His style, while generally smooth, vivid, and rapid, is sometimes freighted with a heavy load of learning. Love is not the unique subject of Propertius' four surviving books of elegies —the elegiac form was capable of other subjects than love—but it is his love poems that are the most interesting. Making up the greater part of the work, they are what concerns the modern reader.

Propertius was born in the province of Umbria, Italy; his family was of equestrian rank. His father died when he was a boy and the family suffered serious financial reverses. Propertius began to study the law in his youth, but soon left it for poetry. From its beginning the essential subject of his poetry was his grand passion for Cynthia—her real name was Hostia. Cynthia was a loose woman; she was not exactly a prostitute, but a courtesan who made her living by pleasing wealthy men. Propertius' affair with her was marked by frequent infidelities on Cynthia's part and much anger and lament on Propertius' part. But Propertius had a mind of his own and was, if blindly in love, still capable of dealing with the equally strong-minded Cynthia.

Book One contains twenty-three poems. The first is an introduction to his love affair and the last is a brief biographical sketch, though more important biographical information is found in the first poem of Book Four. The remaining poems in the first book are concerned with various aspects of the poet's passion.

The first poem, which gives us the basic outline and describes the specific nature of the poet's relationship to Cynthia, states that she first taught Propertius what it was to love, though he had formerly been involved with one Lycinna. For a year he has suffered an agony of love and has been wholly drawn away from the decent life and any interest in honest women, all this despite the fact that Cynthia has refused to love him and to make his life less painful. Finally, however, Cynthia gave in. In the second poem we find a description of Cynthia's charms. Pointing out that she is wholly beautiful, Propertius tells Cynthia to forget useless adornments and go naked, as does love himself. In the third elegy we get our first really close look at the woman. The poet, home late from a party, speaks over his sleeping mistress. She awakes and petulantly chides him for keeping her awake with worry. Four, five, and six are thematically related in that all have to do with attempts to separate the poet from Cynthia. First he argues with a friend who wants him to

1739

break with her. Then he warns another friend to stop making overtures to her. Later he regretfully tells another friend that Cynthia will not let him travel abroad with the friend. Here we see another dimension of this love affair. Propertius, full of passion, is nevertheless irritated by Cynthia's possessiveness. This and similar paradoxes have much to do with the interest of Propertius' love poetry. The very perversity of the two strong-minded lovers attracts us.

In the seventh poem, Propertius warns the epic poet Ponticus that he will be less satisfied with himself and the epic style if he should ever fall in love. In the eighth a crisis arises. Cynthia has decided that she will go abroad, and with a rival of the poet. Propertius prays for a storm to hold her back, but he wishes her a safe trip if she does go. Then in eight-A, he ecstatically informs us that Cynthia has decided not to go. In nine we find Propertius saying, in effect, "I told you so" to the epic poet of poem seven, and in ten Propertius is happy because a possible rival has been sidetracked. Cynthia, we find in eleven, has gone to the seaside resort of Baiae, and the poet is worried that she will act scandalously and ruin her "good" name; he begs her to come back to Rome. Twelve and thirteen form a pair: in the former Propertius admits that he has been unable to work lately because of his all dominating attachment to the once more estranged Cynthia. In the latter, the poet, speaking to the man who has just accused him of sloth, says that his friend may gloat over Propertius' love troubles, but that he will not retaliate. Next, in number fourteen, we hear of a reconciliation. The pleasures of love, the poet claims, are superior to the joys of wealth. But in fifteen we find that Propertius is again in trouble with Cynthia. Though he must face some danger, Cynthia is unconcerned and takes a new lover. The poet claims that he will nevertheless remain faithful.

Poems sixteen, seventeen, and eighteen are the lover's laments. The first is expressed beside Cynthia's door, now closed to him; the second has for background a storm at sea; and the third poem, a very influencial piece, is set in a wild and lonely forest. Apparently the laments had some effect, for in nineteen the lovers seem to be reconciled. In this piece Propertius contemplates death and urges lovers to love while they may. Neither twenty, twenty-one, or twenty-three (the autobiographical poem) are concerned with Cynthia. Twenty is a version of the myth of the rape of Hylas, and twenty-one contains the final words of a man being murdered by bandits.

The appearance and success of the first book of elegies brought Propertius to the attention of the great Roman patron of letters, Maecenas. Propertius was admitted to his circle, and thus Book Two begins with a dedicatory poem to Maecenas. Here the poet protests he can only write of love, since his being is dominated by Cynthia. Poems two through nine return to the subject of his love. Cynthia's beauty is praised more fully; her perversity and falseness are described; the poet's continued infatuation and his joy at the repeal of a law that might have forced him to abandon the woman are discussed. Just as love was previously seen to be superior to wealth, it is here proclaimed more wonderful than the soldier's glory. In the tenth poem however, the poet momentarily turns from love, claiming that only youth writes of that subject; now he will turn to the more mature subject of war. Then, he immediately reverses himself, and the rest of the rather confused second book discusses various aspects of his affair with Cynthia. In these poems we observe an interesting aspect of the affair and a clever bit of lover's flattery. Propertius emphasizes the intellectual ability and literary judgment of his mistress. In poem thirteen, for example, he claims that he is not impressed with beauty and breeding alone in a woman. His greatest joy is to lie in the arms of Cynthia, reading his poems which she so intelligently appreciates and so judiciously criticizes. As the book proceeds, however, Propertius' recriminations become both more frequent and bitter; the affair is subtly changing for the worse.

This progress comes to its climax in Book Three. Though he writes on several other topics, love is still his important theme. Particularly noteworthy are poems ten, fifteen, twenty-four and twenty-five. Ten is a beautiful and clever elegy on Cynthia's birthday. The poet sensuously describes the awakening of Cynthia, the birthday ceremonies, the rich and happy banquet; then, he suggests, after much joy and many emptied goblets they will retire to the bedroom to conduct those rites appointed by Venus and thus complete the course of her natal day. Fifteen is interesting in that it speaks of his adolescent love, Lycinna (mentioned several other times in the elegies) who was Propertius' introduction to women. He gives some details of the early affair and a description of how Cynthia swept Lycinna from his mind. In poems twenty-four and twenty-five, the poet bitterly proclaims his final break with Cynthia. In the first Propertius says that the too proud Cynthia puts too much trust in the efficacy of her beauty. As for him, after a long time being tossed about in the sea of love, he has now escaped and is cured of his infatuation. Henceforth, good sense will dictate his ways. In the second poem, the poet remains adamant despite the tears of Cynthia, for too often in the past has he been beguiled by her weeping. For five years her domination of him has been a public joke. He ends by cursing her with a wrinkled old age and says that he will relish her inevitable loneliness.

Book Four is almost wholly taken up with more solemn themes than love. Included are a series of aetiological poems on the god Vertumnus (two), on Tarpeia (four), on the anniversary of Actium (six), on the Great Altar of Rome (nine) and on Jupiter Feretrius (ten). Only two poems, seven and eight, are concerned with Cynthia. Both are excellent. Seven is in the form of a striking and touching interview with Cynthia's ghost in which she chides a moved Propertius for his neglect. Eight is an amusing and active retrospective account of a night when Propertius, bitter at Cynthia's harsh treatment, set out to console himself with two other ladies of easy virtue. Suddenly Cynthia shows up. She violently drives off the girls and physically attacks Propertius. He bows to her chastisements and all is made well on the couch so familiar to them.

Book Four closes with a solemn funeral poem which, paradoxically for a poet made famous by his love poems, is commonly accounted Propertius' greatest single elegy. The poem celebrates Cornelia, the daughter of Augustus' wife Scribonia. Noble in tone, the poem praises the virtue of the dead woman to the judges of the dead, to her family, and to the world.

ELMER GANTRY

Type of work: Novel
Author: Sinclair Lewis (1885-1951)
Time: 1915-1925
Locale: Midwest America
First published: 1927

Principal characters:

ELMER GANTRY, a minister

JIM LEFFERTS, Elmer's companion in rowdiness during his days at Terwillinger College

JUDSON ROBERTS, an ex-football star, State Secretary of the Y.M.C.A., and the main reason for Elmer's so-called conversion

FRANK SHALLARD, a minister and Elmer's chief antagonist

EDDIE FISLINGER, during college, theological school, and in life, a minister and distant admirer of Gantry, constantly hoping to convert him

MRS. GANTRY, Elmer's mother

WALLACE, UMSTEAD, the "Director of Physical Culture" at Mizpah Theological Seminary

HORACE CARP, one of the High Churchmen in the seminary

HARRY ZENZ, the seminary iconoclast

JACOB TROSPER, D.D., Ph.D., LL.D., and Dean of Mizpah Theological Seminary

LULU BAINS, Elmer's mistress

AD LOCUST, a traveling salesman for the Pequot Farm Implement Company

SHARON FALCONER, a woman evangelist

CECIL AYLSTON, Sharon Falconer's assistant

ART NICHOLS, player of the cornet and French horn in Sharon Falconer's three-piece orchestra

MRS. EVANS RIDDLE, an evangelist, a New Thought leader

CLEO BENHAM GANTRY, Elmer's wife

T. J. RIGGS, a rich associate of Elmer in Zenith

HETTIE DOWLER, another of Elmer's mistresses

OSCAR DOWLER, Hettie's husband and companion in trying to trap Elmer

Sinclair Lewis wrote *Elmer Gantry* at the height of his fame, in the middle of the remarkable decade of the 1920's that began for Lewis with *Main Street* and ended with *Dodsworth* and that saw not only *Babbitt* and *Arrowsmith* but also their author's refusal of a Pulitzer Prize that had been awarded to him. Yet curiously, *Elmer Gantry* gives us a first hint of the waning of Lewis' powers. Before this novel Lewis had served a long apprenticeship, and had achieved great success. From 1915 to 1920 he wrote fifty short stories and five novels, trying out his themes and characterizations, sketching out his satiric portraits of various types; not the least among these were re-ligious types, though the climax of that kind of portraiture was not to come until *Elmer Gantry* appeared in 1927.

Main Street burst upon the world in 1920, the result of several years Lewis spent perfecting his method of research to establish the realistic foundation upon which his satires were to rest. His book was a sensational best seller, and apparently it occurred to Lewis that he could repeat his success if he would only, in a programmatic way, turn his satiric eye upon the various aspects of American life in sequence. After his exposure of the village he next chose Zenith, a middle-sized city, and George F. Babbitt a middle-class businessman. Then he applied his attention (now in collaboration with Dr. Paul de Kruif) to medicine, public health, and medical experimentation. Other projects flashed through his mind and were rejected, until he at last found a challenging project he could eagerly work upon, the ministry; and he began to consider how he could assemble ideas, plot, character, and especially background for what would later become *Elmer Gantry*. Undertaking an exposure of hypocrisy in religion was a formidable and dangerous task, but Lewis felt confidently ready for it. In *Babbitt* he had written of Mike Monday, the evangelist; Mrs. Opal Emerson Mudge, leader of the New Thought League; and the Reverend John Jennison Drew, author of *The Manly Man's Religion*.

Following his usual method of research, he sought expert advice to provide the background for his novel. Acquainted with a minister in Kansas City, he went there to find some of his material. He gathered a weekly "seminar" of local pastors of many faiths and sects; after luncheon, there might be a session on "The Holy Spirit," with Lewis challenging, pressing, arguing, and thus absorbing material. Gradually, characters and plot took shape. Elmer Gantry was to be Lewis' most extravagant faker, a salesman of religion with no real knowledge of theology and no scruples or morals, a stupid man who would exploit his parishioners as he climbed to success from village to town to city, a seducer of women, a man of greed.

Elmer Gantry, captain of the football team at Terwillinger College, was known as "Hell-cat" to his classmates and especially to his roommate, a drinking and carousing friend, Jim Lefferts. Then something happened to convert Gantry from being the heathen that he was; he was taken up with the moment. He had met Judson Roberts, the ex-football star who had a following among members of the "manly" set. Gantry's mother had been urging him to give his soul to God and so at a prayer meeting Elmer was

swept up and converted with a mob of other "saved" people, while his mother, Judson Roberts, and his disbelieving classmates looked on. From that point on, Lewis exposed Gantry's cheap education, revealed his mistaken, temporary, and even fraudulent initial religious impulses, surrounded him with religionists of neither character nor morality, carried him through several near-catastrophes, only to allow Gantry to recover and rise further still.

Gantry was ordained a minister at Mizpah Theological Seminary. During his time there he was sent to a spur-line town, Schoenheim, with an assistant, Frank Shallard. Shallard, noting Gantry's questionable motives toward Lulu Bains, a deacon's daughter, reproached Elmer and threatened to take the matter to Dean Trosper. Gantry caught Shallard off guard and reminded him that his faith was shaky and that if Dean Trosper were to know of this it would end Shallard's career at the seminary. When Shallard realized that someone else was aware of this problem, he left the post at Schoenheim and devoted his time to added study. But in his effort to set against Gantry some men of good will and genuine religiosity, Lewis' imagination and understanding failed him, and no true opponent, no convincing expression of what religion could mean or be, emerges from the book. Frank Shallard, Elmer's chief antagonist, remains only a shadowy character; finally his doubts get the best of him and he leaves the ministry in order to put his Christian principles into practice—and he is painfully defeated.

But Gantry's troubles with Lulu Bains had just begun; she informed him that they must get married and thus Gantry was forced into announcing his betrothal to her. He finally managed to get Lulu involved with an innocent but willing bystander, and in this way he was able to break the engagement.

Gantry left Schoenheim, supposedly heartbroken, and was sent to a new post in Monarch. On his way to preach the

Sunday sermon he met Ad Locust, a traveling salesman for the Pequot Farm Implement Company. When Gantry became too drunk to show up at the church, he was fired from the seminary, even though he remained an ordained Baptist minister. Elmer then took a job with the Pequot Farm Implement Company and worked for them for two years. While in Sautersville, Nebraska, he met Sharon Falconer, a woman evangelist. He followed her and eventually became her assistant and lover. Everything went well for Gantry until the opening of Sharon's Waters of Jordan Tabernacle, which burned, killing a large number of the attending worshipers and Sharon.

Gantry then took up with Mrs. Evans Riddle, but he was kicked out of her group when she discovered that he was stealing from the collection. He then moved to a Methodist pastorate after teaching his own school of thought for a brief time. At this post he married Cleo Benham. After several successful charges in larger churches, Gantry was given a large church in New York. Gantry had not lived a pious life even after his marriage, and he became involved with his secretary, Mrs. Hettie Dowler. Those who opposed him used this opportunity to get back at him for his hellfire and brimstone sermons in which he spared no one. The newspapers got wind of the scandal and printed it, but T. J. Riggs saved Gantry from ruin. Gantry swore he would never again desire another woman, but as he knelt to pray because of his congregation's faith in him, he noticed at the same time the ankles of a new and attractive choir member.

Lewis has shown us a large gallery of ministerial frauds, such as Mrs. Riddle, the New Thought leader who taught classes in Concentration, Prosperity, Love, Metaphysics, Oriental Mysticism, and the Fourth Dimension, as well as how to keep one's husband. Another example is Judson Roberts, the state secretary of the Y.M.C.A, a young giant with curly hair and a booming voice that he used to bring in the big fellows.

Lewis gave much of his attention to his portrait of Sharon Falconer, the beautiful and somewhat mad female evangelist who preaches in a majestic temple, then leads Gantry to her retreat in the hills where she allows herself to be seduced on an altar she has built to such pagan goddesses as Astarte. Sharon says she has visions and confesses that she hates little vices like smoking and swearing but loves big ones like lust and murder. Yet from some confused notions about God Sharon derives sufficient strength to stand at the pulpit in her burning tabernacle and attempt to quell the panic of the mob of her parishioners, while Gantry knocks aside dozens of helpless people and is able to escape. Into such scenes as these, and into the final episode in which Gantry narrowly is saved from entrapment in the old badger game, Lewis poured all his vitality. But what critics have missed, and what seems to suggest the first waning of Lewis' powers, is the lack of any real opposition, referred to before. In Gantry himself there seems to be no decency, and therefore there are no alternatives contending in his soul. In the "good" characters there is insufficient understanding and fortitude, and they neither supply important alternatives nor force Gantry to any choices. In this book Lewis displayed his virtuosity as a satirist, but he also indulged it and failed to find for it any opposition in positive values. Thus, as a satirist of American life, he was by now really beginning to repeat himself, and it turned out to be essentially true (though not without some occasional exceptions) that he was to go on for about twenty-five years looking here and there for aspects of American life to expose, exploiting as best he could his earlier brilliance at recording the clichés of our lives and language but not advancing to any new understanding either for himself or for his readers. Meanwhile, the world moved on. If he was right that there was hypocrisy and corruption in the religious practices of America, his portrait was also incomplete in not showing us some of the glimmer that would begin to be fanned into the light of leadership that religion is trying to provide in the crises of today.

ÈLOGES AND OTHER POEMS

Author: St.-John Perse (Alexis St.-Léger Léger, 1887-   )
First published: 1910; enlarged edition, 1956

In its present form *Eloges* (*Praises*) is a revised collection made up of poems dating as far back as 1909, to which has been added "Lullaby" ("Berceuse"), first published in 1945.

Alexis St.-Léger Léger, who writes under the name of St.-John Perse, was born in Guadaloupe, and he has had a long and very distinguished career in both the prewar and postwar French diplomatic service, and thus represents the peculiarly French combination of the public servant and the man of letters. Though his *Anabasis* has been translated by so famous a writer as T. S. Eliot, he remains little known to American readers, in spite of his great reputation in Continental literary circles. Because of the obscurity of his poems, it is highly improbable that his work will ever achieve any wide degree of popularity; nevertheless, because of his marked influence on modern poetry, he is an important figure, at least to the literary historian.

"Pictures for Crusoe," the earliest of the poems included in the volume, should be read first; they are the clearest and, when once understood, provide a sort of key to the other sections. In them, the reader is made immediately aware of the author's background of a childhood spent in the tropics—the succession of luxuriant images from the island left behind by Crusoe, the nostalgia for the clean wind and sea and sand, for the brilliant colors of dawn and sunset. It is the theme of this series of short poems that Crusoe's real disaster occurs when he returns to the cities of men and leaves forever the lost tropic island. Everything that he brings with him, every symbol of the island—the goatskin parasol, the bow, the parrot—decays in the sour dirt of the city; the seed of the purple tropic flower that he plants will not grow; even Goodman Friday, as he steals from the

larder, leers with eyes that have become sly and vicious. Crusoe weeps, remembering the surf, the moonlight, and other, distant shores.

The same theme of nostalgia, much less clearly stated, runs through the longer poems entitled "To Celebrate a Childhood" and "Praises." Here the poet tries to recapture, by the same device of a series of pictures, the lost world of a childhood spent against the background of violent contrasts of brilliant light and shining water and crowding vegetation that is in memory the tropics. The lush images succeed one another with bewildering rapidity until a total effect is achieved and the lost childhood is recreated. Indeed, the images are heaped with such profusion that the poems become almost cloying, like over-ripe fruit. There is a shift of emphasis here also, for no longer is there a contrast between two worlds, the island and the city, but rather an almost total recall of the beauty and the squalor of the tropics.

The second section of the book, "The Glory of Kings," consists of four poems, two written in 1910 and two in 1924. These poems are much more obscure than those in the first section. In them, Perse seems to have moved from the background of his childhood in Guadaloupe to the world of some primitive people where nameless speakers address praises to their half-human, half-divine rulers—the Queen, a mysterious Sphinxlike creature, at once the queen and the mother; the Prince, with his towering headdress, the Healer and Enchanter, keeping vigil. It may be that Perse is trying to express something of the spirit in which members of a primitive society identify themselves with their rulers, until the King becomes the symbol, indeed the very soul, of his people and is rejoiced in as such. By implication, this attitude is set against the critical, questioning attitude of modern man, shorn of reverence, cut off from "the sources of the spirit." "The Glory of Kings" seems to develop further a theme implicit in "Pictures for Crusoe"—the modern cult of the primitive that has appeared in the work of so many contemporary writers.

Under the first pen name of their author, these early poems by Perse are referred to by Proust, who, in *Cities of the Plain,* gives an appreciation of them and an indication of the likely reaction of the average reader. Lying on the narrator's bed was a book of the admirable but ambiguous poems of Saint-Léger Léger. Mme. Céleste Albaret picks up the book and asks if he is sure that they are poems and not riddles. It is natural that Proust, preoccupied as he was with the evocation of the past in all of its subtle ramifications in time and place, would have delighted in a poet bent on the same task of recapturing the totality of the experiences of childhood—the sights, the sounds, the odors. Nor is it surprising that these pictures from the tropics, so different from the hothouse, artificial life that Proust knew, should, by their very contrast, have appealed to him.

Yet by including the remark of Mme. Céleste, so distressing to the narrator, Proust succinctly indicates the probable response of most readers of poetry who in this volume approach Perse for the first time. For it cannot be denied that these poems make very difficult reading. T. S. Eliot, in his preface to his translation of Perse's *Anabasis,* tries to defend the author against the charge of willful obscurity by saying that their seeming obscurity is due to the linkage of explanatory and connecting matter, not to incoherence. Eliot's advice to the reader was to allow the images of the poem to fall into the memory with unquestioning acceptance, each contributing to a total effect apparent at the end of the poem. It is an indication of the contribution that Perse has made to the technique of modern po-

etry that this analysis could equally well be applied to much of Eliot's own work.

It is by means of this sequence of images, abruptly shifting into one another, that Perse achieves his total effect. It is this aspect of his technique that has elicited the special praise of Valéry Larbaud, who considers his descriptions far superior to those of Chateaubriand: concrete, exact, precise, and filled with meaning. The result is a blending of the ugly and the beautiful, the whole a passionate rendering of experience. In his descriptions Perse makes full use of a device so characteristic of contemporary poetry: the sudden juxtaposition of the "poetic" and the deliberately ugly or grotesque. A coconut, tossed into the street, "diverts from the gutter/the metallic splendor of the purple waters mottled with grease and urine, where soap weaves a spider's web." It is difficult to realize that such lines were being written in France in 1910, at a time when English poetry was dominated by the Georgians.

No modern poet so little known to the reading public has received from his fellow craftsmen such high praise as has Perse. He has been translated into English, German, Spanish, Italian, Russian, Rumanian. Hugo von Hofmannsthal considers that a direct road leads from Rimbaud to the early work of Stefan George and to that of Perse. Valéry Larbaud maintains that between 1895 and 1925 perhaps a hundred poets appeared in France, of whom at least thirty continue to be worthy of attention; of these thirty, only five—Claudel, Jammes, Valéry, Fargue, and Perse—will survive. To both of these critics, Perse is valuable because of his attempt, through the manipulation of language and his brilliant descriptions, to revivify French lyricism. It may well be, however, that Perse will remain essentially a poets' poet, important to other writers because of what they can learn from his method, rather than a poet for the general reader. It is no longer necessary for the poet to appeal to the community and the wider view. He may now appeal to himself and the urgencies   of his private vision.

THE EMIGRANTS

Type of work: Novel
Author: Johan Bojer (1872-1959)
Type of plot: Regional romance
Time of plot: Late nineteenth century
Locale: Norway and the American West
First published: 1925

Principal characters:

> ERIK FOSS, an emigrant leader
> OLA VATNE, a laborer
> ELSE, his wife
> MORTEN KVIDAL, a joiner
> KAL SKARET, a crofter
> KAREN, his wife
> PER FÖLL, a young workman
> ANNE, his wife
> BERGITTA, Morten's wife; Anne's sister

Critique:

The Emigrants is a saga of the Norwegians who settled the wheat lands of the Dakotas. Bojer is well qualified for his subject. A Norwegian, he knows the stock from which our prairie pioneers came, and his visits to America have made him familiar with the American scene. The result is a lasting novel, an American story written in Norwegian. It is a vital part of our cultural heritage.

The Story:

Erik Foss came back to Norway after some time spent working in America, and to the cramped, class-conscious farmers and laborers of his Norwegian countryside he held out hope for a more free and generous life in the new country. Many resolved to join his party of emigrants to America.

There was Ola, the colonel's hired boy. Ola had a way with people, especially with girls, and Else, the colonel's daughter, looked on him with eager eyes. But Ola was poor and the stories about him did not please the colonel. After his dismissal from the farm, Ola set fire to the barn. He spent a year in prison and came out in time to join the emigrants. Else came too, as Ola's wife. There was Per Föll, a big, hulking man and his new wife, Anne, the most attractive girl in the parish, already carrying a baby who was to be born soon after her marriage. There were Kal Skaret and Karen, a kindly and slow-moving couple. The tax collector took their only cow when they could not pay even the previous year's taxes. There was Morten Kvidal, a skilled joiner.

When the steamer left, the little band sorrowed to leave Norway. But Erik was strong and he knew the way and he had enough money to help them.

That first summer the emigrants reached Wisconsin. They stayed there during the bleak winter, the men working in the sawmills to add to their meager funds. Early the next spring, they started out across the prairie. Erik had been to the Red River Valley before; he had tested the soil and knew it was good. The settlers had wagons and oxen, now, and all their supplies.

Erik said they had arrived when they came to a vast level land covered with a six-foot stand of grass.

Kal took the quarter farthest to the west. There he swung his scythe in sweeping strokes. The children and Karen piled the fodder, enough to feed a cow all winter! Now he would plow. Morten took no heed of the buffalo grass; he set his great breaking plow and turned

THE EMIGRANTS by Johan Bojer. Translated by A. G. Jayne. By permission of Curtis Brown, Ltd. Published by The Century Co. Copyright, 1925, by Johan Bojer.

it under. They built their homes from the grass, too, piling squares of turf for their sod houses.

That summer there was drought and the wheat crop was poor. Ola went into town with one of the loads, and gambled and drank up all his money. Without the help of the others, Ola and Else would never have survived the winter. During a blizzard Erik's feet were frostbitten while he hunted his strayed stock. When gangrene set in, Morten made the long trip to town on skis; but he returned too late with medicine for the sick man.

After Erik's death, the leadership of the small band fell to Morten. Good times and bad followed.

Per thought long and bitterly about Anne, for he could never forget that his first-born boy had come into the world too soon after his marriage. When Morten's young brother visited his house too frequently, Per began to roam the prairie. They had to tie him finally and take him to the madhouse, leaving Anne with her children and a sense of sin.

Although well established, Morten felt compelled to go back to Norway. When he returned to Dakota, he brought with him a wife, Bergitta, Anne's sister. He became an agent for the new railroad. He said that the people should have their own bank and grain elevators

so that they would not be at the mercy of speculators. The Norwegians became Americans. At a party they put up an American flag beside the Norwegian banner.

Kal and Karen built outbuildings of wood, and each son took up another quarter. Before long Kal's fields stretched to the horizon, and he had to ride from one wheat planting to the other. When the steam thresher came, an army of laborers piled up the mounds of grain; it poured too fast to cart away. In his machine shed, in a tiny strong room, Kal stored wheat, so that his family would never be hungry. Under his bed, in his emigrant chest, he kept his money. He and Karen were proud on the day their son came back from school in St. Louis and preached in their own church.

Morten grew old. He still acted for the railroad; he ran the bank; he was elder of the church; he put up buildings for the growing town. Bergitta died. A lamp exploded in Morten's face, blinding him. Now his grandson read to him. The old man thought of Norway often. He went back, blind and old, to his home. His people were dead; only the old land remained. It must be like that, he realized. The old settlers are a part Norwegian always, but their children belong to the new world.

Further Critical Evaluation of the Work:

The moving story of the difficulties of transplanted national loyalties forms the basis of Johan Bojer's *The Emigrants*. The novel is carefully constructed, carrying the principal characters through their lives, from beginnings in Norway to old age in America. Along the way, the characters grow and change as the new land they have adopted is equally transformed and developed. The author begins with a precise delineation of the social structure of nineteenth century Norway, illustrating the many varying reasons that the people have for emigrating. Some want to escape local scandals, others hope to overcome poverty, some are possessed by ambition, many desire to escape what they consider unfair class distinctions.

The subtle psychological transformations among the settlers are sensitively portrayed. From the beginning of the new life, a growing sense of community binds the emigrants together. The relationships among them change; people who had had nothing to do with each other in the old country become friends, and social distinctions dissolve. The new land affects the settlers in different ways; to some the flatness of the land is depressing after the mountains of Norway; others find the work to build a settlement and a new life more difficult than they anticipated. Karen Skaret could adjust only after becoming convinced that a Norwegian brownie had emigrated with them.

The trials of the life on the prairie are dramatically portrayed; the breathless account of the prairie fire that nearly destroys the settlement is a masterpiece of narrative writing. But through the many disasters and years of labor, the settlers cling to their visions of the future. The construction of the first church becomes a touching symbol of their success. Yet they never forget the old country; they seem to possess two souls, as Morten Kvidal says, one Norwegian and the other American. This double vision gives a rich poetry to the book, and a subtle poignancy combined with the joy of the settlers' triumph.

THE EMIGRANTS OF AHADARRA

Type of work: Novel
Author: William Carleton (1794-1869)
Type of plot: Local color romance
Time of plot: 1840's
Locale: Ireland
First published: 1848

Principal characters:
> BRYAN M'MAHON, an honest young farmer
> KATHLEEN CAVANAGH, in love with Bryan M'Mahon
> HYCY (HYACINTH) BURKE, a well-to-do libertine and rascal
> JEMMY BURKE, Hycy's father
> NANNY PEETY, a beggar girl
> KATE HOGAN, Nanny's aunt, a tinker's wife
> PATRICK O'FINIGAN, master of a hedge-school

Critique:

William Carleton's fiction is best known for his realistic pictures of Irish peasant life during the nineteenth century, and *The Emigrants of Ahadarra* is one of his best novels in this respect. The most noteworthy sections are the chapters describing such things as a "kemp" (a spinning contest among the peasant women), a country funeral, an election, and illegal distillation of whiskey. While his treatment of these matters is outstanding, the entire novel is filled with specific and colorful details of peasant life. The speech of the people, the homes they live in, the farm routine, landlord-peasant relations, whiskey smuggling, the character of the people—all these are related with a view to giving the reader a true picture of rural Irish life a century ago. Although Carleton's fiction is now little read, it deserves attention from the student of the novel as an example of early realism well done.

The Story:

Hycy Burke was the son of a well-to-do and respected peasant who had allowed his wife, a woman with social pretensions of her own, to spoil the young man, and Hycy, with his mother's approval, had become a dissolute young man. Because his father, Jemmy Burke, tried to curb him, Hycy entered into partnership with whiskey smugglers to supplement the diminished allowance from his father.

When one of the prettiest girls in the area, Kathleen Cavanagh, caught Hycy's eye, he determined to seduce her. Unfortunately for his plans, he misdirected two letters: one, intended for Kathleen, went to Bryan M'Mahon, who truly loved the girl; another, intended for young M'Mahon, went to Kathleen. Later, publicly snubbed on more than one occasion, Hycy resolved to have revenge on the girl and her true admirer. Any additional villainy could scarcely put him in greater danger, for he had already been an accomplice to burglarizing his father's house, taking a large sum of money, as well as an active accomplice of smugglers. It was through his fellow smugglers that he planned to get his revenge. At the time there was a law in Ireland which required the inhabitants of a township to pay fines for illegal distillation and smuggling of whiskey if the actual culprits were not known. Bryan M'Mahon's farm at Ahadarra covered an entire township; if he were required to pay such a fine by himself he would be ruined. To carry out his plan, Hycy tried to get the help of the nephew of the local gauger. Hycy promised the exciseman's nephew the chance to lease a fine farm if the latter would press Hycy's suit for his sister's hand. The farm, of course, was Bryan M'Mahon's.

Bryan was not the only member of his family facing tragedy. Both his and his father's farm leases had run out, and

1752

death had prevented the absentee landlord from renewing them. The new landlord, a well-meaning but weak and inexperienced young man, was ruled by his agent, who wished to see the M'Mahons lose their farms, leased by the family for generations.

Hycy carefully made his plans. What he failed to realize, however, was that he had made enemies while Bryan had made friends, so that some persons who knew of his villainy were prepared to take measures to thwart him. In his father's house was Nanny Peety, a pretty, virtuous beggar girl who resented Hycy's attempts to seduce her. She knew something of his plans and she had been a witness to the burglary Hycy and his accomplice had committed. Nanny Peety's aunt, Kate Hogan, loved her niece and thought highly of Kathleen Cavanagh. She was willing to help them and could because she was married to one of Hycy's smuggling associates. Also friendly to Kathleen and Bryan was Patrick O'Finigan, the drunken master of the local hedge-school.

The plot against Bryan was put into operation when Hycy's anonymous letter sent the gauger to discover the illicit still at Ahadarra, on Bryan's farm. Faced with financial ruin and his family's loss of their leases, the young peasant did not know what to do. Because his own honesty kept him from believing that Hycy was working against him in that manner, Bryan even took advice from the man who was bent on ruining him. Before long he found himself worse off by his taking that advice. A parliamentary election was about to take place, in which the M'Mahons' landlord was standing for a seat. The voting turned out to be a tie until Bryan, angry with his landlord and following Hycy's advice, voted for his landlord's opponent. By doing so he made himself appear false in everyone's eyes, for his landlord was a liberal who favored the Irish peasantry and religious freedom, while the opponent was a conservative who worked against the peasants and the Roman Catholic Church.

When Hycy sent another letter enclosing a fifty-pound note, it looked as if Bryan had accepted a bribe for his vote. The evidence was so damning that even Kathleen, who loved Bryan sincerely, was forced to believe him guilty. Faced with calamity and disfavor in his community, Bryan and his family planned, like so many unfortunate Irish at the time, to emigrate to America in order to start a new and more successful life.

But Bryan's friends began to work for him. Kate Hogan, displeased at Hycy's treatment of her niece and the troubles facing Kathleen when she lost her fiancé, began investigating Hycy's activities. She, Patrick O'Finigan, Nanny Peety's father, and others gathered additional information and presented it to the magistrates with demands for a hearing. At the hearing it was proved that Hycy had robbed his father, had been an accomplice of the whiskey smugglers, had placed the still at Ahadarra to incriminate Bryan, had plotted to make his victim appear to have taken a bribe, and had also become a counterfeiter. Confronted with these proofs, Jemmy Burke gave his son two hundred pounds to leave the country and stay away. Hycy's accomplices were arrested, convicted, and transported as criminals from Ireland, thus becoming the "emigrants" of Ahadarra. Cleared of all charges, Bryan resumed his rightful place in the community and in the affections of Kathleen.

Further Critical Evaluation of the Work:

By the time that he wrote *The Emigrants of Ahadarra* in 1848, Carleton was considered the truest novelist of Ireland's "awfullest hours," and Yeats was to concede that the Irish novel began with him. *The Emigrants of*

Ahadarra was avowedly written not to amuse, but to reform and inform. Published while the Potato Famine was raging, it is informative and readable. Folkloric value is enhanced by Carleton's exuberance and hyperbole, which are similar to the imaginative flights that created the ancient Celtic wonder tales. The novel loftily defends virtue. Kathleen's simple dignity and virtue are not cloying but almost Biblical, and contrast with the paler virtues of other characters. Bridget M'Mahon is also convincingly admirable, and uniquely graces the story, which expounds human ideals. Landlords are near-ogres, members of secret societies, and Orangemen (although to a less prominent degree than in other of Carleton's works), but many individuals are tenderly etched. The novel is realistic, and in the Spain of the same day would have been classified as *costumbrista,* owing to its museum-like pictures of customs.

Modern critics sometimes flay *The Emigrants of Ahadarra* for allegedly sloppy construction, mushy sentiment, and—curiously enough—vagueness of purpose. Carleton is also accused of inserting excessive scenery and folklore for their own sake rather than to augment the novel's dramatic effect. Carleton did lack the benefit of proof reading by his publishers, but the novel accomplished its obvious objective of dramatizing the life of the Irish of over a hundred years ago. Even its supposedly overdone rhetoric does not bore the reader.

Herbert Kenney maintains that we have a true picture of the famine-ravaged Irish peasants from Carleton alone. Carleton was an enigmatic novelist who hated landlordism and the Penal Laws, and who was a convert to Protestantism in a very Catholic land. But he scarcely owed loyalty only to his own pen, as has been accused, and some critics concede that they did not really know Irish life until they read *The Emigrants of Ahadarra.*

ÉMILE

Type of work: Novel
Author: Jean Jacques Rousseau (1712-1778)
Time: Eighteenth century
Locale: France
First published: 1762

Principal characters:
JEAN JACQUES ROUSSEAU, in the role of tutor
ÉMILE, a French orphan, healthy and intelligent
SOPHIE, a wellborn, warm-hearted young woman

Rousseau's treatise on education—a novel in name only—is addressed to mothers in the hope that, as a result of learning Rousseau's ideas on education, they will permit their children to develop naturally without letting them be crushed by social conditions. Children cannot be left to themselves from birth because the world as it is would turn them into beasts. The problem is to educate a child in the midst of society in such a manner that society does not spoil him.

Rousseau argues that education comes from nature, from men, and from things. The education from men and from things must be controlled so that habits conformable to nature will develop. Children have natural tendencies which should be encouraged, for nature intends children to be adults; the aim of education, according to Rousseau, is to make a boy a man. Yet by swaddling children, by turning them over to wet nurses, and by punishing them for not doing what is said to be their duty, parents turn children from natural ways of acting and spoil them for life.

Rousseau insists that the proper way to bring up a child is to begin by having the mother nurse the child and the father train him. But if substitutes must be found, a wet nurse of good disposition who was lately a mother should be selected; and a young tutor should be chosen, preferably one with the qualities of Rousseau.

In order to explain his theory of education, Rousseau refers to an imaginary pupil, Émile. The child should come from France, since inhabitants of temperate zones are more adaptable and more intelligent than those from other climates. He should be from a wealthy family, since the poor are educated by life itself, and he should be an orphan in order to allow Rousseau free range as tutor. Finally, he should be healthy in body and mind.

Rousseau recommends a predominantly vegetable diet, particularly for the nurse, since the milk would be better if meat were not eaten. The tutor should see to it that the child is taken out to breathe the fresh air of the country, and, if possible, the family should live in the country: "Men are devoured by our towns."

The child should become accustomed to frequent baths, but he should not be softened by warm water or by other pampering which destroys his natural vigor.

The child should not be allowed to fall into habits other than that of having no habits. He should not have regular meal times or bedtimes, and as far as possible he should be free to act as he chooses. He may injure himself or become ill, but it is better for him to learn how to live naturally than to become a weak and artificial adult.

"The natural man is interested in all new things," wrote Rousseau, and he urged that the child be introduced to new things in such a way that he would not be encouraged to fear whatever is not naturally fearful. He offers, as an example of the proper kind of education in this respect, an account of what he would do to keep Émile from becoming afraid of masks. He would begin with a pleasant mask and then proceed to less pleasing and, finally, to hideous ones, all the while laughing at each mask and trying it on different persons. Similarly, to accustom Émile to the sound of a gun, Rousseau would start with a small charge, so that Émile would be fascinated by the sudden flash, then proceed to greater charges until Émile could tolerate even large explosions.

Rousseau maintained that cries and tears are the child's natural expression of his needs. The child should not be thwarted, for he has no other way of learning to live in the world, and education begins with birth. On the other hand, he should not become the master of the house, demanding obedience from his parents.

It was Rousseau's conviction that children must be given more liberty to do things for themselves so that they will demand less of others. A natural advantage of the child's limited strength is that he cannot do much damage even when he uses his power freely. A child will learn to speak correctly, to read and write, if it is to his advantage to do so; threats and coercion only hinder him.

Speaking of a mode of education which burdens a child with restrictions and is, at the same time, overprotective, Rousseau wrote, "Even if I considered that education was wise in its aims, how could I view without indignation those poor wretches subjected to an intolerable slavery and condemned like galley-slaves to endless toil . . . ? The age of harmless mirth is spent in tears, punishments, threats, and slavery. You torment the poor thing for his good; you fail to see that you are calling Death to snatch him from these gloomy surroundings." Instead of torturing children with excessive care, one should love them, laugh with them, send them out into the meadows, and play with them.

"When our natural tendencies have not been interfered with by human prejudice and human institutions, the happiness alike of children and men consists in the enjoyment of their liberty." Here the principle behind Rousseau's theory of education becomes clear. The effort of the tutor or the parent is so to educate the child in such fashion that he will learn through his own efforts to be as free as possible within society. If he is educated by rules and threats he becomes a slave, and once free he seeks to enslave others. The most satisfactory general rule of education, Rousseau argued, is to do exactly the opposite of what is usually done.

Since the child is supposed to learn through his own experience, misdeeds should be punished only by arranging matters so that the child comes to experience the natural consequences of what he has done. If there is any rule which can be used as a moral injunction, it would be, "Never hurt anybody"; only trouble comes from urging children or men to do good to others.

Rousseau rejected the use of tales and fables for children. An amusing analysis illustrates his conviction that even the simplest fable, such as "The Fox and the Crow," strikes the child as ridiculous and puzzling and encourages him to use language carelessly and to behave foolishly.

After the child has reached adolescence, the education of his intellect should begin. Prior to this time the concern of the tutor was to give Émile the freedom to learn the natural limits of his powers. Now he teaches Émile by showing him the natural advantages of the use of the intellect. The tutor answers questions, but just enough to make the child curious. His explanations are always in language the child can understand, and he encourages the child to solve his own problems and to make his own investigations. Interest should lead the child to increase his experience and knowledge; it is a mistake to demand that he learn. Jean Jacques, as the tutor, shows Émile the value of astronomy by gently encouraging him to use the knowledge that he has in order to find his way out of the woods.

Rousseau's accounts of his efforts to teach Émile owe some of their charm to the author's willingness to show himself unsuccessful in some of his efforts. Nevertheless, the pupil Émile never becomes a distinctive character; Émile is merely a child-symbol, just as later in the book Sophie is, even as the author indicates, a woman-symbol devised to enable Rousseau to discuss marriage problems.

By the time Émile is fifteen he has gained a considerable amount of practical and scientific knowledge; he can handle tools of all sorts, and he knows he will have to find some trade as his life's work. In Book IV of *Émile*, Rousseau discusses the most difficult kind of education: moral education, the study of the self in relation to other men.

Rousseau presents three maxims which sum up his ideas concerning human sympathy, the foundation of moral virtue:

> *First Maxim.*—It is not in human nature to put ourselves in the place of those who are happier than ourselves, but only in the place of those who can claim our pity.
> *Second Maxim.*—We never pity another's woes unless we know we may suffer in like manner ourselves.
> *Third Maxim.*—The pity we feel for others is proportionate, not to the amount of the evil, but to the feelings we attribute to the sufferers.

These maxims fortify the tutor, but they are not imparted to Émile. The youth is gradually made aware of the suffering of individuals; his experience is broadened; and he comes to know through personal experience the consequences of various kinds of acts. The important thing is to turn his affections to others.

Émile is given insight concerning religious matters by hearing a long discourse by "a Savoyard priest" who tells of the difficult passage from doubt to faith. He affirms man's natural goodness and the reliability of conscience when uncontaminated by philosophers or by mere convention.

Sophie, "or Woman," is introduced in Book V, since Émile must have a helpmate. Rousseau begins curiously by saying, "But for her sex, a woman is a man"; but when he considers her education it is apparent that sex makes quite a difference. Woman need not be given as many reasons as man, and she can get along with less intellect; but she must have courage and virtue. Rousseau offers a great deal of advice, even concerning Sophie's refusal of Émile's first attempt to share her bed. The book closes, after a charming digression on travel, with Émile's announcement that he is about to become a father and that he will undertake the education of his child, following the example of his beloved tutor.

Émile is as full of good humor as it is of good advice. Rousseau pursued an educational philosophy which is, on the whole, humane and sensible. He desired to make the child neither a noble savage nor a cultivated gentleman, but a man, living fearlessly and forthrightly according to impulses and abilities which were naturally his. Although Rousseau's psychology is sometimes naïve, it is seldom far from the modern view; and that, if anything, is a compliment to the modern view.

EMILIA GALOTTI

Type of work: Drama
Author: Gotthold Ephraim Lessing (1729-1781)
Type of plot: Romantic tragedy
Time of plot: Early eighteenth century
Locale: Guastalla and Sabionetta, two mythical principalities in Italy
First presented: 1771

Principal characters:
EMILIA GALOTTI, a beautiful, middle-class young woman
ODOARDO GALOTTI, her father
CLAUDIA GALOTTI, her mother
HETTORE GONZAGA, Prince of Sabionetta and Guastalla
COUNT APPIANI, betrothed to Emilia
THE MARQUIS MARINELLI, chamberlain to the prince
THE COUNTESS ORSINA, a mistress spurned by the prince

Critique:

This play, romantic though it now seems, was one of the first tragedies which broke from strict adherence to the French neo-classic unities. The best tragedy of Lessing's small group of plays, *Emilia Galotti* takes its theme from classical antiquity, the story of the innocent maiden who dies at the hand of her father in order to prevent the loss of her chastity. A drama of middle-class life, the work is also a problem play, with revolt from the tyranny of the aristocracy presenting in interesting development an underlying social theme.

The Story:

Prince Hettore Gonzaga, once happily in love with and loved in return by Countess Orsina, had unhappily fallen in love with Emilia Galotti. She, the daughter of a soldier who resisted the conquest of Sabionetta by the prince, was to be married to Count Appiani, of the neighboring principality of Piedmont. This desirable union of a nobleman and a beautiful, middle-class woman was the result of her mother's studied plan.

The treacherous Marquis Marinelli proposed that the prince retire to his palace at Dosalo after sending Count Appiani on a mission to the Princess of Massa, soon to be the prince's bride. The absence of her betrothed would leave Emilia open to the designs of the prince. Motivated by lechery, the ruler eagerly agreed to this plan.

Odoardo Galotti, having readied his villa at Sabionetta in preparation for the wedding, returned to his wife in Guastalla in order to accompany the bridal party. A young assassin garnered from a family servant all these facts so that he could plan the abduction of Emilia, who, pursued by the prince, had just returned from church. This action of Prince Hettore's the honest patriot father or the independent husband-to-be would have avenged, but the unsophisticated Emilia did not know how to treat the prince's lustful behavior.

Count Appiani, disturbed by presentiments of evil, rejected the prince's proposal to send him off on his wedding day, and he was killed for his temerity when the bridal party was attacked.

Closely guarded, Emilia was taken to the palace under pretense of a rescue from brigands. There the prince, playing the gallant, allayed the fears of Emilia by apologizing for his former behavior and promising to escort her to her mother. Claudia, in the meantime, had been made frantic by separation from her daughter, and, hysterical over the death of Count Appiani, she accused Marinelli of plotting this deed of treachery and violence.

The prince, now beset by a hysterical mother and a swooning young woman whom he desperately desired, had not reckoned with the wrath of a rejected mistress as well. The Countess Orsina, whose spies had uncovered all the prince's guilty secrets, arrived at the palace in Dosalo and, failing in an attempt at blackmail, revealed Prince Hettore's guilt to Odoardo Galotti when he came in haste and unarmed to the aid of his daughter and wife. The countess, determined to have revenge on her former lover, gave Galotti the dagger she had intended to use on the prince. Galotti insisted on his rights as a father to take his daughter to her home, but his petition was denied by the crafty Marinelli. Meanwhile, the prince, unaware of Galotti's knowledge and purpose, tried to appear as a benefactor who would see justice done in the courts. Until that time, however, he would keep Emilia apart for security's sake. To this arrangement Galotti seemed to agree, ironically commenting on each provision of treachery as it was proposed.

When the anxious father was finally allowed to see his daughter, she told her fears that her virtue might yield where force could never prevail, the arts of seduction being so brilliantly practiced in Prince Hettore's court. To protect her innocence, Galotti stabbed Emilia, presented her body to the lustful prince, threw the dagger at his feet, and went off to give himself up to the authorities.

Further Critical Evaluation of the Work:

Lessing was the first major German dramatist of the eighteenth century and his work provided the foundation on which Goethe and Schiller built. While he strongly advocated rejection of the French classical style in favor of a more Shakespearean approach, his work retains much of the formal balance and classical unity of the French tradition. Each scene is calculated as an indispensable advancement of the plot; the motivation of the characters is made almost painfully explicit. Each character is sharply defined even to the use of individual styles of speech. Later writers of the Romantic school thought the play was admirable for its craft, but excessively rationalistic and cerebral. "A good piece of theatrical algebra," said Friedrich Schlegel.

But the play was also an important development for the German stage. It is a strongly political drama, which places the tragedy in a bourgeois milieu —an innovation in the eighteenth century—and develops the tragedy out of class conflicts. The depiction of the corrupt world of the absolute monarch was the first sounding of a theme that would return in the 1770's and 1780's as a main theme of German drama. Lessing goes beyond the political, however, to search the mysteries of the human personality. The death of Emilia is necessary because she herself recognizes the weakness of her will. It is not force she fears but seduction, and in acknowledging the potential for nonrational behavior, Lessing anticipates those Romantics who would rebel against the one-sidedly rationalistic view of man held by the eighteenth-century Enlightenment. This vulnerability is accentuated by the elaborateness of the plot contrived by the scheming Marinelli. Emilia is enmeshed in a net from which there is no escape except death. Though her father actually kills her, she wills her own death and this moral suicide has something of old Roman virtue. Her will triumphs over her weakness and elevates her above all those who are, like the prince, the prey of their own emotions.

EMINENT VICTORIANS

Type of work: Biography
Author: Lytton Strachey (1880-1932)
Time: Nineteenth century
Locale: England, Scutari, the Sudan
First published: 1918

Principal personages:
 HENRY EDWARD MANNING, a Cardinal of the Roman Catholic Church
 FLORENCE NIGHTINGALE, a nineteenth-century career woman
 DR. THOMAS ARNOLD, an English educator
 CHARLES GEORGE GORDON, a British general

Though possibly controversial, the biographical writings of Lytton Strachey are never dull; and when they address themselves to the Victorian Period they possess a special interest. For the biographer himself was a product of that period, and his feelings about it, while mixed, were far from being vague or uncertain. The Age of Victoria both fascinated and repelled him; he loved it while he hated it. Even though its pretentiousness exasperated the artist in Strachey, he could not help acknowledging its solidity and force, as manifested in many outstanding scientists and men of action.

Four such people, including one woman, are his subjects in *Eminent Victorians*. Not the greatest of their time, these four yet belong among the most appropriate of its decorations. Superficially diverse in their activities, they include an ecclesiastic, a woman of action, an educational authority, and a man of adventure. As drawn by their biographer, they provide a striking illustration of the many-faceted era in which they lived and worked.

This quartet of portraits proved to be a critical and financial success. It became the cornerstone in an increasingly solid career, and after it appeared, Strachey was no longer in need of assistance from family or friends. Yet his treatment of Cardinal Manning, Florence Nightingale, Arnold of Rugby, and General Gordon did not go unchallenged. The author was accused of undue severity with his subjects, of handling facts with carelessness, and of superficiality in his judgments.

Such indictments derived, in general, from people friendly to one or more of the individuals pictured in *Eminent Victorians;* but not infrequently they were joined by critics of influence and standing.

Some of these critics overlooked the point that Strachey's biographical method aimed at verisimilitude instead of photographic realism. It is true that his determination to rise above mere facts sometimes carried him too far—as far as outright and sometimes outrageous caricature—but the writing remained brilliant and stimulating. The intelligent reader is more likely to be diverted than deceived by his prejudices, for his dislike for such targets as Florence Nightingale and Thomas Arnold is hardly disguised. Whatever charges may be brought against Strachey today, his services to biographical writing are generally admitted: he brought to it good proportion, good style, and colorful realism.

For such talents, the life of Cardinal Manning provides ideal material. But Manning, despite his distinction as a churchman, does not escape a touch of the Strachey lash. He is revealed, this representative of ancient tradition and uncompromising faith, as a survival from the Middle Ages who forced the nineteenth century to accept him for what he was. Practical ability, rather than saintliness or learning, was the key to his onward march. In the Middle Ages, says Strachey, he would have been neither a Francis nor an Aquinas, but he might have been an Innocent.

Very early in his life, Manning's hopes became fixed on a position of power and influence in the world. Upon leaving college he aspired to a political career, but its doors were abruptly closed to him by his father's bankruptcy. Next he tried the Church of England as another, perhaps less promising, avenue to fulfillment. By 1851, already over forty, he had become an archdeacon, but such rank was not enough. For some time his glance had been straying to other pastures; finally, he made the break and became a convert to Roman Catholicism. In the process he lost a friend—a rather important one—named Gladstone.

Thereafter his ecclesiastical career was an almost unbroken series of triumphs and advances. One important asset was the ability to make friends in the right places, especially if one of those places was the Vatican. Brooking no rivals, Manning became the supreme commander of the Roman Church in England, then a cardinal. His magnetism and vigor spread his influence beyond Church boundaries; and at his death crowds of working people thronged the route of his funeral procession. At the end of a long and twisted road, his egoism, fierce ambition, and gift for intrigue accomplished some unexpected rewards; not least among them the regard of the poor.

The second of Strachey's eminent Victorians is Florence Nightingale. Here, in his treatment of one of the most remarkable women of any age, the biographer is conspicuously successful in resisting any urge to be gallant. What her friends called calm persuasiveness, he characterized as demoniac fury; it is clear that to him the "Lady with a Lamp" might be extremely capable but she was also tiresomely demanding and disagreeable. Nevertheless, his account does disclose the almost miraculous energy and endurance which carried Miss Nightingale past obstacle after obstacle.

For the sake of convenience, Strachey divides the accomplishments of Florence Nightingale into two phases. The first is her dramatic contribution to the welfare of British wounded during the course of the Crimean campaign; the second deals with her unflagging efforts, after the war, to transform the Army Medical Department, revolutionize hospital services, and even to work much needed reform in the War Office itself. These aims dominated her completely; in the prosecution of them she drove her friends ruthlessly, but she used herself with even less mercy. Enduring to the age of ninety, she became a legend; but, ironically and cruelly, her last years brought senility and softness upon her. They also brought, after consciousness had dulled almost into insensibility, the Order of Merit.

Dr. Thomas Arnold is generally considered the father, not only of Matthew Arnold, poet and critic, but of the British public school system as well. Neither of these products inspires Strachey with much respect, and his bias against the doctor is obvious in *Eminent Victorians*. Dr. Arnold, for instance, was determined to make good Christians, as well as good Englishmen, out of his public school boys, whereas Strachey had little patience for either Christianity or Christian institutions. This fact, incidentally, seems to color his attitude toward all his subjects in *Eminent Victorians*, since the latter are, without exception, religiously employed or inclined to a very strong degree.

Dr. Arnold's prefectorial system, as he instituted it at Rugby, also meets with strong disapproval. Strachey credits it with two dubious, if unexpected, effects on later English education, the worship of athletics and the worship of good form. To some Victorians, Dr. Arnold may have seemed one of their most influential teachers; to Strachey, he is the apostle of ideas obviously harmful and absurd.

With apparent alacrity, the biographer turns to his fourth and final portrait. It is a long step from the educator to the general, involving as it does the distance between the single-mindedness of Arnold and the maddening inconsistencies of Gordon. For Charles George Gordon is unveiled as a mass of contradictions whom no biographer could ever hope completely to unravel. A mischievous, unpredictable boy, he developed into an undisciplined, unpredictable man. A romantic legend wove itself about his early, swashbuckling exploits in China and Africa. His deeds were genuinely heroic—no one has ever questioned Gordon's bravery—but they combined oddly with his passion for religion. He was influenced strongly, and to an approximately equal degree, by brandy and the Bible. Inclined, on the whole, to be unsociable, he maintained an icy reserve, except for fits of ungovernable temper vented upon unlucky servants or trembling subordinates.

This is the man who, in his fifties, was chosen by the English government for a delicate African mission. Strangely, considering the qualifications of the man selected, it was not military in its nature, but diplomatic, requiring the utmost in self-control, tact, and skill of a negotiator. For General Gordon was to arrange for inglorious evacuation of the Sudan by British forces, a project for which he was disqualified by his opinions, his character, and everything in his life. What followed, not surprisingly, was the tragedy at Khartoum, an episode seldom matched in military annals for the mystery and horror with which it enveloped the fate of the principal actor.

Thus, on a dramatic note, ends the biographer's searching glance at four eminent Victorians. Widely differing in background, vocation, and personality, they illustrate different phases of existence in England of the later nineteenth century. Each is bound to the others, however, by the possession of a restless, questing vitality, and each has left a mark upon his age.

EMMA

Type of work: Novel
Author: Jane Austen (1775-1817)
Type of plot: Social comedy
Time of plot: Early nineteenth century
Locale: Surrey, England
First published: 1816

    Principal characters:
        EMMA WOODHOUSE, heiress of Hartfield
        MR. WOODHOUSE, her father
        HARRIET SMITH, Emma's protégée
        MISS BATES, the village gossip
        JANE FAIRFAX, Miss Bates' niece
        MR. GEORGE KNIGHTLEY, a landowner of the neighborhood
        MRS. WESTON, Emma's former governess
        FRANK CHURCHILL, stepson of Emma's former governess
        MR. ELTON, a rector
        ROBERT MARTIN, a yeoman

Critique:

The major problem in the world of Jane Austen's novels is that of getting the characters properly married, and *Emma* is no exception. Its plot is concerned with the complications taking place before the couples are paired off correctly, and with Emma's sometimes unwise attempts to help things along. She is perhaps a less generally appealing heroine than Elizabeth Bennet in *Pride and Prejudice,* but she is excellently done, as are her father and the rest of the Highbury circle. Miss Bates and Mrs. Elton remain unsurpassed in English satire.

The Story:

Emma Woodhouse, rich, clever, beautiful, and no more spoiled and self-satisfied than one would expect under such circumstances, had just seen her friend, companion, and ex-governess, Miss Taylor, married to a neighboring widower, Mr. Weston. While the match was suitable in every way, Emma could not help sighing over her loss, for now only she and her father were left at Hartfield and Mr. Woodhouse was too old and too fond of worrying about trivialities to be a companion for his daughter.

The Woodhouses were the great family in the village of Highbury. In their small circle of friends there were enough

middle-aged ladies to make up card tables for Mr. Woodhouse but no young lady to be friend and confidante to Emma. Lonely for her beloved Miss Taylor, now Mrs. Weston, Emma took under her wing Harriet Smith, the parlor boarder at a nearby boarding-school. Harriet was an extremely pretty girl of seventeen, not in the least brilliant, but with pleasing, unassuming manners, and a gratifying habit of looking up to Emma as a paragon.

Harriet was the natural daughter of some mysterious person, and Emma, believing that the girl might be of noble family, persuaded her that the society in which she had moved was not good enough for her. She encouraged her to give up her acquaintance with the Martin family, respectable farmers of some substance though of no fashion. Instead of thinking of Robert Martin as a husband for Harriet, Emma influenced the girl to aspire to Mr. Elton, the young rector.

Emma believed from Mr. Elton's manner that he was beginning to fall in love with Harriet, and she flattered herself upon her matchmaking schemes. Mr. Knightley, brother of a London lawyer married to Emma's older sister and one of the few people who could see Emma's faults, was concerned about her intimacy with Harriet. He warned her that no good could come of it for either Harriet or herself, and he was particularly upset when he learned that Emma had influenced Harriet to turn down Robert Martin's proposal of marriage. Emma herself suffered from no such qualms, for she was certain that Mr. Elton was as much in love with Harriet as Harriet—through Emma's instigation—was with him.

Emma suffered a rude awakening when Mr. Elton, finding her alone, asked her to marry him. She suddenly realized that what she had taken for gallantries to Harriet had been meant for herself, and what she had intended as encouragement to his suit of her friend, he had taken as encouragement to aspire for Emma's hand. His presumption was bad enough, but the task of breaking the news to Harriet was much worse.

Another disappointment now occurred in Emma's circle. Frank Churchill, who had promised for months to come to see his father and new stepmother, again put off his visit. Churchill, Mr. Weston's son by a first marriage, had taken the name of his mother's family. Mr. Knightley believed that the young man now felt himself above his father. Emma argued with Mr. Knightley, but she found herself secretly agreeing with him.

Although the Hartfield circle was denied Churchill's company, it did acquire an addition in the person of Jane Fairfax, niece of the garrulous Miss Bates. Jane rivaled Emma in beauty and accomplishment, one reason why, as Mr. Knightley hinted, Emma had never been friendly with Jane. Emma herself blamed Jane's reserve for their somewhat cool relationship.

Soon after Jane's arrival, the Westons received a letter from Churchill setting another date for his visit. This time he actually appeared, and Emma found him a handsome, well-bred young man. He called frequently upon the Woodhouses, and also upon the Bates family, because of prior acquaintance with Jane Fairfax. Emma rather than Jane was the recipient of his gallantries, however, and Emma could see that Mr. and Mrs. Weston were

hoping that the romance would prosper.

About this time Jane Fairfax received the handsome gift of a pianoforte, anonymously given. It was presumed to have come from some rich friends with whom Jane, an orphan, had lived, but Jane herself seemed embarrassed with the present and refused to discuss it. Emma wondered if it had come from Mr. Knightley, after Mrs. Weston pointed out to her his seeming preference and concern for Jane. Emma could not bear to think of Mr. Knightley's marrying Jane Fairfax, and after observing them together, she concluded to her own satisfaction that he was motivated by friendship, not love.

It was now time for Frank Churchill to end his visit, and he departed with seeming reluctance. During his last call at Hartfield, he appeared desirous of telling Emma something of a serious naturer; but she, believing him to be on the verge of a declaration of love, did not encourage him because in her daydreams she always saw herself refusing him and their love ending in quiet friendship.

Mr. Elton returned to the village with a hastily wooed and wedded bride, a lady of small fortune, extremely bad manners, and great pretensions to elegance. Harriet, who had been talked into love by Emma, could not be so easily talked out of it; but what Emma had failed to accomplish, Mr. Elton's marriage had, and Harriet at last began to recover. Her recovery was aided by Mr. Elton's rudeness to her at a ball. When he refused to dance with her, Mr. Knightley, who rarely danced, offered himself as a partner, and Harriet, without Emma's knowledge, began to think of him instead of Mr. Elton.

Emma herself began to think of Churchill as a husband for Harriet, but she resolved to do nothing to promote the match. Through a series of misinterpretations, Emma thought Harriet was praising Churchill when she was really referring to Mr. Knightley.

The matrimonial entanglement was

further complicated because Mrs. Weston continued to believe that Mr. Knightley was becoming attached to Jane Fairfax. Mr. Knightley, in his turn, saw signs of some secret agreement between Jane Fairfax and Frank Churchill. His suspicions were finally justified when Churchill confessed to Mr. and Mrs. Weston that he and Jane had been secretly engaged since October. The Westons' first thought was for Emma, for they feared that Churchill's attentions to her might have had their effect. Emma assured Mrs. Weston that she had at one time felt some slight attachment to Churchill, but that that time was now safely past. Her chief concerns now were that she had said things about Jane to Churchill which she would not have said had she known of their engagement, and also that she had, as she believed, encouraged Harriet in another fruitless attachment.

When she went to break the news gently to Harriet, however, Emma found her quite unperturbed by it, and after a few minutes of talking at cross purposes Emma learned that it was not Churchill but Mr. Knightley upon whom Harriet had now bestowed her affections. When she told Emma that she had reasons to believe that Mr. Knightley returned her sentiments, Emma suddenly realized the state of her own heart; she herself loved Mr. Knightley. She now wished she had never seen Harriet Smith. Aside from the fact that she wanted to marry Mr. Knightley herself, she knew a match between him and Harriet would be an unequal one, hardly likely to bring happiness.

Emma's worry over this state of affairs was soon ended when Mr. Knightley asked her to marry him. Her complete happiness was marred only by the fact that she knew her marriage would upset her father, who disliked change of any kind, and that she had unknowingly prepared Harriet for another disappointment. The first problem was solved when Emma and Mr. Knightley decided to reside at Hartfield with Mr. Woodhouse as long as he lived. As for Harriet, when Mr. Knightley was paying attention to her, he was really trying to determine the real state of her affections for his young farm tenant. Consequently Mr. Knightley was able to announce one morning that Robert Martin had again offered himself to Harriet and had been accepted. Emma was overjoyed that Harriet's future was now assured. She could always reflect that all parties concerned had married according to their stations, a prerequisite for their true happiness.

Further Critical Evaluation of the Work:

Jane Austen had passed her fortieth year when her fourth published novel, *Emma,* appeared in 1816, the year before her death. Although *Pride and Prejudice* has always been her most popular novel, *Emma* is generally regarded as her greatest. In this work of her maturity, she deals once more with the milieu she preferred: "3 or 4 Families in a Country Village is the very thing to work on." Having grown to womanhood in her native Hampshire village of Steventon, the seventh of the eight children of the learned village rector, and having spent the remainder of her life, except for brief intervals in Bath and Southampton, in another Hampshire village, Chawton, she was thoroughly familiar with the world she depicted.

The action of *Emma* cannot be properly considered apart from the setting of Highbury, the populous village only sixteen miles from London, its physical attributes presented in such circumstantial detail that it becomes a real entity. London seems far away, not because of the difficulty of travel, but because of the community's limited views. It is a village where a light drizzle keeps its citizens at home, where Frank Churchill's trip to London for the alleged purpose of getting a haircut is foppery and foolishness, where the "inconsiderable Crown Inn" and Ford's "woollen-draper, linen-draper, and haberdasher's shop united" dominate the main street. Emma's view of the busiest part of town, surveyed from the doorway of Ford's, sums up the life of the village:

> Mr. Perry walking hastily by, Mr. William Cox letting himself in at the office door, Mr. Cole's carriage horses returning from exercise . . . a stray letter boy on an obstinate mule . . . the butcher with his tray, a tidy old woman . . . two curs quarrelling over a dirty bone, and a string of dawdling children round the baker's little bow-window. . . .

The novel concerns the interrelationship between such an inconsequential place and Emma Woodhouse, a pretty and clever young lady almost twenty-one who is rich and has few problems to vex her. Ironically, however, her world is no bigger than the village of Highbury and a few surrounding estates, including her father's Hartfield; nevertheless, in that small world, the Woodhouse family is the most important. Therefore, states the author, the real dangers for Emma are "the power of having rather too much her own way, and a disposition to think a little too well of herself."

Moreover, these dangers are unperceived by Emma. Thus, in the blind exercise of her power over Highbury, she involves herself in a series of ridiculous errors, mistakenly judging that Mr. Elton cares for Harriet rather than for herself; Frank Churchill for herself rather than for Jane Fairfax; Harriet for Frank rather than for Mr. Knightley; and Mr. Knightley for Harriet rather than for herself. It is the triumph of Jane Austen's art that however absurd or obvious Emma's miscalculations, they are convincingly a part of Emma's charming egotism. The reader finally agrees with Mr. Knightley that there is always "an anxiety, a curiosity in what one feels for Emma."

Emma's vulnerability to error can in part be attributed to inexperience, her life circumscribed by the boundaries of Highbury and its environs. No mention is made of visits to London, though Emma's only sister lives there. She has never been to the seacoast, nor even to a famous scenic attraction nearby, Box Hill. She is further restricted by her valetudinarian father's gentle selfishness, which resists any kind of change and permits a social life limited to his own small circle, exclusive to the degree of admitting only four people as his closest acquaintances and only three to the second group.

Nonetheless, Emma's own snobbery binds her to the conclusion that she has no equals in Highbury. Mr. Knightley well understands the underlying assumption of superiority in Emma's friendship for Harriet Smith: "How can Emma imagine she has anything to learn herself, while Harriet is presenting such a delightful inferiority?" Emma fears superiority in others as a threat. Of the capable farmer Robert Martin, Harriet's wooer, she observes: "But a farmer can need none of my help, and is therefore in one sense as much above my notice as in every other way he is below it." Her resolution to like Jane Fairfax is repeatedly shattered by the praise everybody else gives Jane's superior attractions.

While Emma behaves in accordance with her theory that social rank is too important to be ignored, she fails to perceive that she is nearly alone in her exclusiveness. Indeed, the Eltons openly assume airs of superiority, and Jane Fairfax snubs Emma. Emma's increasing isolation from Highbury is epitomized in her resistance to the Cole family, good people of low rank who have nevertheless come to be regarded socially as second only to the Woodhouse family. Snobbishly sure that the Coles will not dare to invite the best families to an affair, she finds only herself uninvited. Thus, ironically, she imagines her power in Highbury to be flourishing even as it is already severely diminished.

Emma's task is to become undeceived and to break free of the limitations imposed by her pride, by her father's flattering tyranny, and by the limited views of Highbury. She must accomplish all this without abandoning her self-esteem and intelligence, her father, or society. The author prepares for the possibilty of a resolution from the beginning, especially by establishing Mr. Knightley as the person who represents the standard of maturity which Emma must assume. Emma is always half aware of his significance, often putting her folly to the test of his judgment. There are brief, important occasions when the two, united by instinctive understanding, work together to create or restore social harmony. However, it is not until Harriet presumes to think of herself as worthy of his love that Emma is shocked into recognition that Mr. Knightley is superior to herself as well as to Harriet.

Highbury itself, which seems so confined, also serves to enlarge Emma's views simply by proving to be less fixed than it appears. As John Knightley observes: "Your neighbourhood is increasing, and you mix more with it." Without losing her desire for social success, Emma increasingly suffers from it. She is basically deficient in human sympathy, categorizing people as second or third rank in Highbury or analyzing them to display her own wit. Yet, as she experiences her own humiliations, she begins to develop in sensitivity. Thus, while still disliking Jane, she is capable of "entering into her feelings" and granting a moment of privacy. Her rudeness to Miss Bates is regretted, not only because Mr. Knightley is displeased but also because she perceives that she has been brutal, even cruel to Miss Bates.

Despite her love of small schemes, Emma shares an important trait with Mr. Knightley, one which he considers requisite for his wife—an "open temper," the one quality lacking in the admirable Jane. Emma's disposition is open, her responsiveness to life counteracting the conditions in herself and her circumstances which tend to be constricting. Her reaction to news of Harriet's engagement to Robert Martin is characteristic: she is "in dancing, singing, exclaiming spirits; and till she had moved about, and talked to herself, and laughed and reflected, she could be fit for nothing rational." Too ready to laugh at others, she can as readily laugh at herself. Impulsive in her follies, she is quick to make amends. She represents herself truthfully as she says, in farewell to Jane, "Oh! if you knew how much I love every thing that is decided and open!"

A fully realized character who develops during the course of the action, Emma is never forced by the author to be other than herself, despite her new awareness. Once Harriet is safely bestowed upon Robert Martin, she complacently allows their friendship to diminish. The conniving to keep her father reasonably contented is a way of life. Mr. Knightley, if he wishes to marry her, is required to move into Hartfield. Serious reflection upon her past follies is inevitably lightened by her ability to laugh at them—and herself. The novel is complete in every sense, yet Emma is so dynamic a characterization that one shares Mr. Knightley's pleasure in speculation: "I wonder what will become of her!"

Catherine E. Moore

THE EMPEROR JONES

Type of work: Drama
Author: Eugene O'Neill (1888-1953)
Type of plot: Expressionistic melodrama
Time of plot: Early twentieth century
Locale: West Indies
First presented: 1920

Principal characters:
BRUTUS JONES, Emperor
SMITHERS, a Cockney trader
LEM, a native

Critique:

Eugene O'Neill departed from traditional dramatic writing when he created this play, which concerns itself expressionistically with the forces that make a man what he is. *The Emperor Jones* goes forward and backward simultaneously: Brutus Jones is carried, in the realm of the stage-actual, from his position as emperor to his death from fear; while, in the short, interrelated, and dynamic episodes which symbolize Jones' and his race's history, the action regresses in point of time from the present to several hundred years ago in the Congo jungle. *The Emperor Jones* was first produced by the Provincetown Players, in 1920.

The Story:

Henry Smithers, a Cockney adventurer, learned from a Negro woman that the followers of Brutus Jones, self-styled emperor of a West Indian island, were about to desert their ruler. With Smithers' help, Jones, a former Pullman porter and jail-breaker, had duped the natives into believing he was a magician. The superstitious natives made him emperor of the island. Smithers disclosed to the emperor the disaffection of his subjects, who had been taxed and cheated by the pair beyond human endurance. Jones had judged that he had six more months of power before the natives caught on to his skullduggery. He had had a silver bullet cast for a good luck charm; besides, the

bullet might be useful if he were ever caught by his subjects.

At Smithers' suggestion, Jones rang a bell for his attendants; no one appeared. Jones resigned his position as emperor on the spot and made immediate plans to escape through the jungle to the coast. Drums began to beat in the hills. The ex-emperor gave the palace to Smithers, took up his white Panama hat, and walked boldly out the front door.

At the edge of the jungle Brutus Jones searched unsuccessfully for tinned food he had cached for such an emergency. The drums continued to beat, louder and more insistent. Night fell, and formless fears came out of the jungle to beset Jones. The moon rose. Jones came into a clearing and there in the moonlight he saw Jeff, a Pullman porter he thought he had killed in a razor duel. Jeff was throwing dice. When the kneeling figure refused to answer him, Jones shot at him. The phantom disappeared. Drums still thudded in the distance. Jones, now sick with fright, plunged into the inky jungle.

After a while he came upon a road and paused to rest. A chain gang came out of the forest. The guard of the gang motioned to Jones to take his place in the gang and get to work. When the guard whipped him, Jones lifted his shovel to strike him, but he discovered that he actually had no shovel. In his rage of fear and frustration, he fired his revolver at the guard. The road, the guard, and the chain gang disappeared; the jungle closed in. The louder beat of the tom-toms drove Jones on in frantic circles.

Now in tatters, the terrified Jones repented the murders he had committed and the way he had cheated the islanders. He came next upon a slave auction attended by whites dressed in the costumes of the 1850's. An auctioneer put Jones on the auction block. Frightened, Jones shattered this apparition by firing one shot at the auctioneer and another at a planter. He dashed into the forest, mad with fear. The drums continued to beat.

At three o'clock Jones came to a part of the jungle which strangely resembled the hold of a slave ship. He found himself one of a cargo of slaves who were swaying slowly with the motion of the ship. Jones and the other slaves moaned with sorrow at being taken away from their homeland. Having only the silver bullet left in his revolver, Jones saved it and dashed on again into the black of the night.

Next he came upon an altar-like arrangement of boulders near a great river. He sank to his knees as if to worship. A Congo witch doctor appeared from behind a large tree and began a primitive dance. Jones was hypnotized by the ritual. The witch doctor indicated to Jones in pantomime that the ex-emperor must offer himself as a sacrifice in order to overcome the forces of evil. A great green-eyed crocodile emerged from the river; Jones fired the silver bullet at the monster and the witch doctor disappeared behind a tree, leaving Jones lying on the ground completely overcome by fear.

At dawn Lem, the leader of the rebels, came with Smithers and a group of natives to the edge of the jungle where Jones had entered the night before. Lem had been delayed in pursuing Jones because of the necessity of manufacturing silver bullets, which, Lem believed, were the only means of taking Jones' life. Several of Lem's men entered the jungle. They soon found the prostrate Jones, who had run in circles all the night. One shot him through the chest with a silver bullet. Jones' body was brought back to Lem, who thought that the silver bullet was what had really killed Jones. But Smithers, looking at Brutus Jones' fear-contorted face, knew differently.

Further Critical Evaluation of the Work:

By the time Eugene O'Neill wrote *The Emperor Jones*, he had joined the current of experimental playwrights who were reacting against realism. *The Emperor Jones* employs a technique popularized in Germany called expressionism, a form that employs exaggerated sets and stylized action. It seeks to project feelings and mental states directly, without the intervention of character development and without much concern for the externals of realistic sets, action, and motivation. While a number of such plays were written and produced, few have survived; among the few are *The Emperor Jones* and O'Neill's other completely expressionist play, *The Hairy Ape*. Like Joseph Conrad's *Heart of Darkness,* among other works, *The Emperor Jones* suggests that beneath the surface of civilized existence there is, in each of us, a savagery that marks our true identities. Public masks versus private realities, identity conflicts, and divisions—these are among O'Neill's central concerns. Further, since Jones moves into and is held and controlled by his past, the play suggests another of O'Neill's major themes: that one cannot escape his past.

Jones' physical journey through the jungle becomes a symbol of his mental journey into his past, even an entering into his own subconscious. The first three jungle scenes contain Jones' private past; the last three take us into his racial past. With each step into the jungle, Jones loses bits and pieces of clothing, his cherished bullets, and his composure—all external marks, not only of the stripping away of his civilized self, but of his mental and spiritual reduction. Toward the last—on the auction block, in the slave ship, on his knees before the witch doctor—Jones becomes increasingly passive, merging with the scene, and thus losing his sense of individual being.

There is very little dialogue in the play. But the throbbing of the tom-toms, the shooting of the gun, and the playing of the lights and shadows of the jungle, take the place, quite effectively, of conventional dialogue and action. The play is, in many ways, an exercise in pure theater.

THE END OF THE ROAD

Type of work: Novel
Author: John Barth (1930-   )
Time: 1951-1955
Locale: Wicomico, Maryland
First published: 1958

Principal characters:
JACOB HORNER, a teacher of English, the narrator
JOE MORGAN, a teacher of history
RENNIE MORGAN, his wife
PEGGY RANKIN, a teacher of English
THE DOCTOR, a doubtful M.D.

The End of the Road begins ambiguously with some doubt as to the narrator's, Jacob Horner's, existence. He tells us that he became a teacher of English at Wicomico State Teachers College on the advice of the Doctor, never given a name, who operates a Remobilization Farm for the treatment of functional paralysis. Between this doubtful beginning and the non-ending, Barth examines the problems of existence and identity that began with his first novel, *The Floating Opera.*

Read on a literal level, the story is a rather banal love triangle involving Jacob, Joe Morgan, and Joe's wife. Read on a serious abstract ethical level, it becomes the setting for a duel of opposing points of view, both concerned with the problems of nihilism.

Jacob meets the Doctor in a railroad station, where he has come after finishing his oral examination for his Master's Degree. In trying to decide where to go for a vacation, he has been overcome by paralysis. He is unable to make a choice. No one destination seems better than another; his will to do anything at all is paralyzed. The Doctor takes him to his Remobilization Farm near Wicomico and begins a series of therapies designed to avoid situations involving complicated choices, the point being to make some choice, any choice, in order to keep moving, so that he would not fall into immobility again.

Mythotherapy, based on the existentialist premises that existence precedes essence, and that man is free not only to choose his essence but to change it at will, is the chief therapy prescribed for Jacob. It is a process of assigning a role to himself and carrying it out logically. It is essentially a mask to protect the ego.

At the college, Jacob becomes acquainted with Joe Morgan and his wife Rennie. The relationship quickly develops into a love triangle, but one in which the responsibility is shared equally by all three. Here, as elsewhere, Barth gives us no chance to make any judgments, to fasten onto any solid ethical ground. *The End of the Road* is a short novel with the characters sketched and filled in quickly, with very little background or examination of motivational processes.

Jacob's *modus operandi* is mythotherapy. Joe's is one of ethical positivism; he has a set of consistent, relative values which he is trying to impress on Rennie. It is around Rennie that the action centers. While teaching Jacob to ride horseback, she tells him of her meeting with Joe, their subsequent relationship and marriage. Until she met Joe, she had no philosophy of her own and she willingly erased her own personality to adopt that of Joe. She is still unsure of herself and not quite at ease with her adopted role. Later on she comes to see Jacob as Satan, tempting her to abandon her assumed personality. She sees him as not consistent, but as having nothing but ever-changing masks, donned one after the other as the situation demands. Following logically, she sees Joe as God: consistent, moral, and logically right. Over the battleground of Rennie, Jacob and Joe fight out their opposing points of view, Jacob with the shifting inconsistencies and limited goals of existentialism, Joe with his relative ethical values that denies any absolutes.

After Rennie and Jacob commit adultery, Barth abandons any consideration of Rennie and concentrates on the relationship between Jacob and Joe. The adultery had happened almost casually, while Joe was away. The seeds had been planted for it when Jacob and Rennie, peeking in on Joe after one of their rides, watched him making faces at himself in the mirror and engaging in a series of disgusting sex activities. Rennie is shattered; her god has his inconsistencies, too.

Rennie tells Joe of her infidelity and he confronts Jacob with it. Instead of behaving like an outraged husband, Joe tries to find the reasons behind the deed. All Jacob can say is that he does not know why it happened. Joe's search for causes goes far beyond the point of believibility so that one is forced to view it in abstract terms. Here, as elsewhere, Barth carries action to an extreme and exaggerated point until it becomes parody.

Jacob's relationship with Peggy Rankin is a parody of Joe's and Rennie's relationship. Both fail, Joe's because it is too intellectualized and Jacob's because it is too physical. Barth implies a middle way, one would assume, but he never says so directly. In fact, Barth provides no absolutes, but merely presents a set of actions. He seems to suggest that human involvement is the answer to the problems posed by nihilism.

Under Joe's urging, Rennie visits Jacob several more times. She tells him that she does not know whether she hates or loves Jacob, but she wants to find out. When both Rennie and Joe visit Jacob one evening, it is to tell him that Rennie is pregnant and that they do not know whose child it is. All she knows is that she will commit suicide if she cannot have an abortion. This situation drives Jacob to his hour of concern. Through a series of lies, impersonations, and gall, he convinces one of the local doctors to give Rennie something to make her abort. When he tells Rennie what he has done and that she must give a false name and story, she refuses. She would rather shoot herself than lie. Jacob, by his imperfect realization of his role and his readiness to assume all the responsibility, has become fully involved, but his commitment is the very thing that the Doctor had told him he must avoid. Joe also has failed in his personal absolutism by turning to Jacob for an answer.

In desperation, Jacob goes to the Doctor and asks him to perform an abortion. The Doctor finally agrees on the condition that Jacob will give him all his money and go with him to a new location in Pennsylvania. Jacob agrees and brings Rennie to the Remobilization Farm. While on the operating table, Rennie dies.

Jacob is afraid that Joe will inform the police. Several days later he receives a telephone call from Joe, who tells him that he has taken care of everything. Joe and his convictions have suffered a mortal blow. He is lost and desperate. He turns to Jacob for an explanation, but Jacob has nothing to offer. Both positions, moral nihilism and ethical positivism, have been wrecked in their encounter with reality. Joe is left to reconstruct his life. Jacob returns to the Doctor because he is not yet ready to assume the responsibilities of life.

The End of the Road is a bitter commentary on the plight of man. Barth, in his examination of nihilism, has given us no answers. There are no moments of high good humor, as in The Sot-Weed Factor, only an unrelieved pessimism. On the surface, the novel is akin to the theater of the absurd in its insistence on telling only the observable actions of a story. Barth points no morals and draws no conclusions, but only shows us that nihilism, in its several guises, is not an end in itself.

ENDYMION

Type of work: Drama
Author: John Lyly (c. 1554-1606)
Type of plot: Romantic comedy
Time of plot: Remote antiquity
Locale: Ancient Greece
First presented: 1588

Principal characters:
ENDYMION, a courtier
CYNTHIA, the queen, loved by Endymion
TELLUS, in love with Endymion
EUMENIDES, Endymion's friend
SEMELE, loved by Eumenides
CORSITES, in love with Tellus
DIPSAS, an enchantress
GERON, her long-lost husband
SIR TOPHAS, a fop
FLOSCULA, Tellus' friend

Critique:

Endymion; or, The Man in the Moon, is undeniably an effete, even trivial play: the plot is singularly inconsequential and artificial; the characters are unreal; the dialogue is pedantic. But *Endymion* was important historically for these very reasons, in that Lyly was trying to make the drama an art. Writing for the court rather than the populace, Lyly replaced the earthiness and crudity of earlier English plays with refinement and polish, thereby setting new standards which later dramatists, including Shakespeare, were to emulate.

The Story:

To his friend Eumenides, Endymion declared his love for Cynthia, goddess of the moon. Eumenides chided Endymion, reminding him of the moon's inconstancy, whereupon Endymion extolled inconstancy and change as virtues, attributes of everything beautiful. Convinced that Endymion was bewitched, Eumenides prescribed sleep and rest for the love-sick swain, but Endymion rejected the advice and berated his friend.

In hopes of misleading his friends, Endymion had also professed love for Tellus, a goddess of the earth. Enraged by his apparent perfidy, Tellus swore to take revenge. Since she still loved Endymion, Tellus was unwilling for him to die; therefore she resolved to resort to magic and witchcraft in order to awaken his love for her. Her friend Floscula warned that love inspired by witchcraft would be bitter, but Tellus ignored the warning and left to consult Dipsas, an enchantress.

In contrast to Endymion and Tellus, Sir Tophas habitually scoffed at love and dedicated his life to war—against blackbirds, mallards, and wrens. When mocked by Endymion's and Eumenides' pages, Dares and Samias, Sir Tophas swore to kill them, but pardoned them when they explained that they had been speaking in Latin.

Meanwhile, Tellus had found Dipsas, whom she consulted about the possibility of killing Endymion's love for Cynthia and supplanting it by magic with love for the earth goddess herself. Dipsas declared that since she was not a deity, she could only weaken love, never kill it. At Tellus' request Dipsas agreed to enchant Endymion in such a way that his protestations of love for Cynthia would be doubted. Accompanied by Floscula and Dipsas, Tellus confronted Endymion in a garden and tried to make him confess his love for Cynthia. Though he admitted that he honored Cynthia above all other women, he insisted that he loved Tellus.

Later, the two pages, Dares and Samias, strolled in the gardens with their own lady loves, whom they had shown Endymion and Eumenides in the act of mooning over their loves. As a jest, Dares and Samias asked the two girls to feign love for Sir Tophas, who, as usual, was playing at warfare in the gardens. The girls complied, but Sir Tophas, ignoring them, reiterated his contempt for love and his passion for war.

Still later, Dipsas came upon Endymion asleep in a grove. Assisted by Bagoa, her servant, Dipsas spelled Endymion into a sleep from which he would not awake until he was old and gray. In a dream, three women appeared to Endymion, and one of them started to stab him. She desisted at the importuning of the third, peered into a looking glass, and threw down her knife. At this moment an old man appeared carrying a book which contained only three pages. Endymion refused to read the book until the man had torn up two of the pages.

When informed of Endymion's mysterious slumber, Cynthia agreed with Eumenides that the sages of the world should be consulted about a remedy. Also, angered by the impertinence of Tellus, Cynthia made her a prisoner in Corsites' palace, where she was to weave tapestries depicting stories of people who had been punished for their long tongues.

On the way to Thessaly, where Cynthia was sending him to seek a cure for Endymion, Eumenides met Geron, an old hermit. Geron said that Eumenides, if he were a faithful lover, could learn the cure from a magic fountain nearby. Since Eumenides had always been true to Semele, the fountain promised to grant any single wish he might make. Although tempted to wish that his love for Semele might be requited, dutifully he asked for a cure for his friend. The fountain answered that the cure was a kiss from Cynthia.

In the meantime Tellus, slowly pining away in prison, promised Corsites, her jailer and suitor, that she would marry if he could perform the impossible task of bringing Endymion to a cave, where she might see him once more. Corsites undertook this task but was himself pinched into a slumber by fairies guarding Endymion's body.

And so Cynthia found two sleeping men when she came to the grove accompanied by wise men who she hoped would wake Endymion. But the sages succeeded in waking only Corsites, who freely confessed his love for Tellus and what he had dared to do, inspired by that love.

At last Eumenides returned and persuaded Cynthia to attempt the cure. And so, upon her kiss, Endymion awoke. But his forty-year slumber had withered him: he was so senile that he could not stand. At Cynthia's request, however, he related his strange dream, explaining that in the book which the old man had given him to read, he saw Cynthia being attacked by beasts of ingratitude, treachery, and envy. Cynthia promised to listen later to a fuller account of this vision.

A short time later Bagoa disclosed that Tellus and Dipsas had been responsible for enchanting Endymion. For her pains Bagoa was transformed into an aspen tree by Dipsas.

Cynthia, however, was more lenient than Dipsas. Learning that Tellus had been motivated by unrequited love, Cynthia forgave her and gave her to Corsites as his wife. Dipsas, too, was pardoned on condition that she would be reunited with Geron, her husband, whom she had sent away many years ago. This reunion displeased Sir Tophas, who had discarded his armor out of love for Dipsas; he was content, however, when Cynthia disenchanted Bagoa and gave her to Tophas as his wife. To Eumenides she promised Semele, but Semele objected on the grounds that Eumenides had not asked for her at the magic fountain. She was placated, however, when Geron explained that Eumenides would not have learned the fountain's secret had he not been faithful.

Most important, Cynthia restored the youth of Endymion and bade him persevere in his love.

Further Critical Evaluation of the Work:

Most famous for his novel *Euphues, the Anatomy of Wit,* John Lyly was also a prolific playwright. He was the most fashionable English writer in the 1580's, praised as the creator of a "new English." Certainly *Endymion* made possible such later plays as Shakespeare's *A Midsummer Night's Dream* and *As You Like It.* Lyly's comedies were a great advance over those of his predecessors. He possessed a unique skill in taking the Italian pastoral and Latin comedy of intrigue and adapting them to the English style by combining them with fanciful plot and mythological characters as well as characters from the lower levels of English life. The grace and charm of his witty dialogue and his analysis of love were not surpassed until Shakespeare's later comedies.

Lyly was chief dramatist for the company of boy players attached to St. Paul's Cathedral, the favorite entertainers of Queen Elizabeth's court. The structure and style of *Endymion* would have been appreciated by their educated audience. The play is filled with references and allusions directed especially to this audience. The division of *Endymion* into acts and scenes is molded on Latin precedent, and the stage directions are of the classical pattern also employed by Ben Jonson: at the head of each scene are listed the characters who take part in it. The stage setting, however, is romantic; places separated by vast distances (the lunary bank, castle in the desert, and fountain) were represented by sections of the same platform stage, and the journey visualized by stepping across the stage. The treatment of time in the play was that of a fairy tale.

The story of Cynthia, the moon goddess, and Endymion was probably borrowed from the Roman poet Lucian. Sir Tophas derived his name and mock-epic exploits from Chaucer's *Tale of Sir Tophas*; in his constant hunger and boastfulness, Tophas was a blend of Latin parasite and braggart soldier. To the Elizabethan court, the main interest in the play lay in its reference to contemporary personalities. Cynthia was the Queen, and Tellus—in her jealousy, captivity in a desert castle, and her wiles—must have recalled Mary, Queen of Scots, who was beheaded in 1586. Endymion must have suggested the Earl of Leicester, and Eumenides, the worthy counselor, Lyly's patron, Burghley. Although today we find the play precious, it nevertheless possesses great charm and wit, much beauty and humor, and probably has been unjustly neglected in the centuries since Lyly's death.

AN ENEMY OF THE PEOPLE

Type of work: Drama
Author: Henrik Ibsen (1828-1906)
Type of plot: Social criticism
Time of plot: Late nineteenth century
Locale: Southern Norway
First presented: 1883

Principal characters:
DOCTOR THOMAS STOCKMANN, a medical officer
MRS. STOCKMANN, his wife
PETRA, his daughter
EJLIF, and
MORTEN, his sons
PETER STOCKMANN, his brother, the mayor
MORTEN KIIL, Mrs. Stockmann's father
HOVSTAD, an editor
BILLING, a sub-editor
ASLAKSEN, a printer
CAPTAIN HORSTER, Dr. Stockmann's friend

Critique:

Known as the foremost dramatist of the nineteenth century, Ibsen was in constant conflict with the society of his time. He believed that it was the *majority* who caused people to stagnate. In *An Enemy of the People,* Doctor Stockmann stood alone, far in advance of the majority of the people. He was persecuted and ridiculed by those he tried to serve only because he was in conflict with established institutions of society. Ibsen saw himself as a Doctor Stockmann, and through the doctor gave the world ideas of universal significance.

The Story:

All the citizens of the small Norwegian coastal town were very proud of the Baths, for the healing waters were making the town famous and prosperous. Doctor Stockmann, the medical officer of the Baths, and his brother Peter, the mayor and chairman of the Baths committee, did not agree on many things, but they did agree that the Baths were the source of the town's good fortune. Hovstad, the editor of the *People's Messenger,* and Billing, his sub-editor, were also loud in praise of the Baths. Business was good and the people were beginning to enjoy prosperity.

Then Doctor Stockmann received from the University a report stating that the waters of the Baths were contaminated. Becoming suspicious when several visitors became ill after taking the Baths, he had felt it his duty to investigate. Refuse from tanneries above the town was oozing into the pipes leading to the reservoir and infecting the waters. This meant that the big pipes would have to be relaid, at a tremendous cost to the owners or to the town. When Hovstad and Billing heard this news, they asked the doctor to write an article for their paper about the terrible conditions. They even spoke of having the town give Doctor Stockmann some kind of testimonial in honor of his great discovery.

Doctor Stockmann wrote up his findings and sent the manuscript to his brother so that his report could be acted upon officially. Hovstad called on the doctor again, urging him to write some articles for the *People's Messenger.* It was Hovstad's opinion that the town had fallen into the hands of a few officials who did not care for the people's rights, and it was his intention to attack these men in his paper and urge the citizens to get rid of them in the next election.

Aslaksen, a printer who claimed to have the compact majority under his control, also wanted to join in the fight to get

1777

the Baths purified and the corrupt officials defeated. Doctor Stockmann could not believe that his brother would refuse to accept the report, but he soon learned that he was wrong. Peter went to the doctor and insisted that he keep his knowledge to himself because the income of the town would be lost if the report were made public. He said that the repairs would be too costly, that the owners of the Baths could not stand the cost, and that the townspeople would never allow an increase in taxes to clean up the waters. He even insisted that Doctor Stockmann write another report, stating that he had been mistaken in his earlier judgment. He felt this action necessary when he learned that Hovstad and Billing knew of the first report. When the doctor refused either to change his report or withhold it, Peter threatened him with the loss of his position. Even his wife pleaded with him not to cross his powerful brother; he was sustained in his determination to do right only by his daughter Petra.

Hovstad, Billing, and Aslaksen were anxious to print the doctor's article so that the town could know of the falseness of the mayor and his officials. They thought his words so clear and intelligible that all responsible citizens would revolt against the corrupt regime. Aslaksen did plead for moderation, but promised to fight for what was right.

Peter Stockmann appeared at the office of the *People's Messenger* and cleverly told Aslaksen, Hovstad, and Billing that the tradespeople of the town would suffer if the doctor's report were made public. He said that they would have to stand the expense and that the Baths would be closed for two years while repairs were being made. The two editors and the printer then turned against Doctor Stockmann and supported Peter, since they felt that the majority would act in this way.

The doctor pleaded with them to stand by the promises they had given him, but they were the slaves of the majority opinion which they claimed to mold. When they refused to print his article, the doctor called a public meeting in the home of

his friend, Captain Horster. Most of the citizens who attended were already unfriendly to him because the mayor and the newspaper editors had spread the news that he wanted to close the Baths and ruin the town. Aslaksen, nominated as chairman by the mayor, so controlled the meeting that a discussion of the Baths was ruled out of order.

Doctor Stockmann took the floor, however, and in ringing tones told the citizens that it was the unbelievable stupidity of the authorities and the great multitude of the compact majority that caused all the evil and corruption in the world. He said that the majority destroyed freedom and truth everywhere because the majority was ignorant and stupid. The majority was really in slavery to ideas which had long outlived their truth and usefulness. He contended that ideas become outdated in eighteen or twenty years at the most, but the foolish majority continued to cling to them and deny new truths brought to them by the intelligent minority. He challenged the citizens to deny that all great ideas and truths were first raised by the persecuted minority, those few men who dared to stand out against the prevailing opinions of the many. He said that the real intellectuals could be distinguished as easily as could a thoroughbred animal from a cross breed. Economic and social position had no bearing on the distinction. It was a man's soul and mind that separated him from the ignorant masses.

His challenge fell on deaf ears. As he knew from the beginning, the majority could not understand the meaning of his words. By vote they named him an enemy of the people. The next day they stoned his house and sent him threatening letters. His landlord ordered him to move. He lost his position as medical director of the Baths, and his daughter Petra was dismissed from her teaching position. In each case the person responsible for the move against him stated that it was only public opinion that forced the move. No one had anything against him or his family, but no one would fight the opinion of the majority. Even Captain Horster, a friend who had promised to take the Stockmanns to America on his next voyage, lost his ship because the owner was afraid to give a ship to the man, the only man, who had stood by the radical Dr. Stockmann.

Then the doctor learned that his father-in-law had bought up most of the now undesirable Bath stock with the money which would have gone to Mrs. Stockmann and the children. The townspeople accused the doctor of attacking the Baths so that his family could buy the stock and make a profit, and his father-in-law accused him of ruining his wife's inheritance if he persisted in his stories about the uncleanliness of the Baths. Reviled and ridiculed on all sides, Doctor Stockmann determined to fight back. He could open a school. Starting only with any urchins he could find on the streets, he would teach the town and the world that he was stronger than the majority, that he was strong because he had the courage to stand alone.

Further Critical Evaluation of the Work:

Following the anger and hostility of the public's reaction to *A Doll's House* and *Ghosts,* two realistic and powerful indictments of social convention, Henrik Ibsen wrote *An Enemy of the People,* a play that may be read as a reply to the fiery public response directed at the two earlier dramas. On a deeper level, this drama about the blindness, selfishness, and greed that motivates majority opinion in society reflects those same themes which concerned Ibsen throughout his career.

The most obvious interpretation of *An Enemy of the People* sees Dr. Stockmann as parallel to Ibsen, and the author's mouthpiece. Both author and protagonist have been rebuked by the populace for publicizing the truth which they have discovered; Ibsen has been censured for exposing the falsity of social values through his dramas, while Stockmann is ostracized by his community for campaigning against the pollution of the baths. Through the doctor and his actions, *An Enemy of the People* dramatizes the problem of the idealist: when the entire opinion of the people is against him, even after facts have been made public, should he bow to the will of the majority, or fight for the truth which only he recognizes? Ibsen's answer is clear: the honest man has no choice but to defend the truth, regardless of the personal expense to himself.

The play illustrates the result of this kind of commitment in the course that Dr. Stockmann's affairs take after his stand against the spa's supporters; he is rejected socially and driven out of his medical practice. The play's message is that the idealist must always be an outcast, but his very isolation is a source of strength; as Dr. Stockmann says, "The strongest man in the world is he who stands most alone." Related to this central message is the theme of democracy: *An Enemy of the People* dramatizes the author's belief that in a democratic society, truth and justice are inevitably overruled, since wise men are always in a small minority.

A more in-depth interpretation of the play, however, reveals subtler themes and more complex questions. The foremost of these is the problem Ibsen raises concerning the advisability of many of Stockmann's actions as an ideal-ist. Why is it that society consistently rejects or ignores what the idealist has to say? Why are even the most ardent forms of idealism usually powerless to change the *status quo*? Ibsen poses these questions in the play, and suggests that the reason might be the idealist's impracticality and tendency to remain oblivious of the nature of his foe. Dr. Stockmann's uncompromising behavior not only leads him and his family to ruin, but fails to effect any change in society. Ibsen suggests that the methods of idealism are naïve, and that they would benefit greatly from a less lofty, headstrong attitude and a more common-sense, realistic approach.

ENGLAND UNDER THE STUARTS

Type of work: History
Author: George Macaulay Trevelyan (1876-1962)
First published: 1904

Principal personages:
KING JAMES I
KING CHARLES I
KING CHARLES II
KING JAMES II
QUEEN ANNE
QUEEN MARY
WILLIAM OF ORANGE
OLIVER CROMWELL

The value of Trevelyan's *England Under the Stuarts* is not in its accuracy and its wealth of detail. Its special quality is its art. From the outset of his career Trevelyan wished to write history that was also literature, and he achieved his goal especially in this book.

He became a historian at a time when the claims of "scientific" history were ascendant. He says in his autobiography that he tried to be a traditional kind of historian, relating history to literature, against a current in the other direction. Indeed, he has a style that is a delight to read. He can combine and condense without losing touch with details. He is pleased to pause to give full treatment to the social scene, the landscape, and the character of the persons of his historical period. He informs his reader of purpose, motive, conclusion, and evaluation. These qualities spring from his commitment to liberal democracy, and the reader feels Trevelyan's constant pleasure in watching the development of English Parliamentary government, humane law, and accomplishment in the arts that grace a civilization. It seems undoubtedly true that he played an important part in inspiring historians to write readable history without losing sight of factual accuracy.

The theme of *England Under the Stuarts* is the exploration of England's unique contribution to the history of the world, which came about through her dealings with the House of Stuart. For in a line of development directly contrary

to what was happening elsewhere in Europe, England transferred sovereignty from the Crown to Parliament and thus laid the foundation for modern democratic government. Despotism, Trevelyan says, was entrenched throughout Europe and would have determined the future but for the events in England during the seventeenth century.

To prepare the reader for these confrontations, Trevelyan skillfully sketches the social, economic, and religious life of the various classes in England in 1603, as James I rode from Scotland to take the English throne. He shows us manor house "high-vaulted dining halls . . . hung with tapestry, armour, weapons, and relics of the chase," hunting, dueling, manners and marriages, education, and religion (the rack, the stake, the burning town, and the massacre). He continues with accounts of the middle and lower classes, the open fields, the wilderness as yet unenclosed, disease, manufacturing, the growing towns.

He prepares us further by discussing Puritanism with thoroughness and clarity. He divides the Puritans into three groups: those who wished to modify customs of the Established Church, retaining bishops; "those who wished for Puritan coercion under a Presbyterian regime"; and "men who desired to abolish the coercive power of the church, whether Anglican or Presbyterian," allowing congregations to form freely.

The first of the great antagonists on

the scene was James I, characterized by Trevelyan as a pedant, but human, whose defect was that he "couldn't tell a good man from a rogue, or a wise man from a fool." In the initial three years of his reign, says Trevelyan, King James set into motion the forces that were to drive two Stuart kings from the throne. In such perceptions and phrasings lies the special quality of Trevelyan's history. He views the century broadly and from a high perspective; he establishes a theme, and he frequently reminds his reader of the controlling motives and ideas of the period. Each action is related to the whole pattern. The Puritans petitioned James "not for supremacy, but for security," and James decided against them. "No Bishop, no King," he declared; "I will make them conform themselves, or else will harry them out of the land." But when his Commons supported the Millenary Petition, the struggle was determined. That the alliance of Puritan and Commons was ominous was a matter disregarded by the king.

It is not necessary to detail the events of the century, Trevelyan's sure grasp of fact and theme reveals itself everywhere. His sentences encompass much. There is little documentation in the conventional sense of footnoting, yet evidence everywhere supports generalization. His summary powers can be shown at the conclusion of his chapters on James I. He notes how James, having allowed the debasement of the kingship, was now mocked in the taverns, so that "when at last the Puritan idealists rode out to battle against the King, they were followed by neighbors Pliable and Worldly-wiseman, who had come to imagine by force of long political sympathy that they themselves were Puritans."

When he comes to the climactic event of the century, the execution of King Charles I, though acknowledging that the Commission had no power and that Charles had committed no legal crime, Trevelyan nonetheless sees the action as the event that first ushered into the world of English politics "the sovereignty of the people and the equality of man with man." Yet the people themselves hardly yet knew the significance of the deed, and "when the bleeding head was held up," the multitude groaned. Thus the outrage postponed the kind of democratic success the leadership had hoped for. No man, not even Cromwell, could have held the Commonwealth permanently together, yet Trevelyan praises him for saving the political liberties of the people and for preventing the destruction of the free-thinkers and dissenters.

Trevelyan's narrative moves rapidly and smoothly everywhere, preparing us for such illuminating summary and interpretative passages as those already mentioned. Nor is he less effective in his treatment of the return of Charles II, or in his description of the social picture of the Restoration. This century of crowded events in England leaves little space for Trevelyan to discuss the settlement of the colonies in America—too little, considering that affairs on one continent were reflected on the other.

In 1665 and 1666 the Great Plague and the Great Fire struck London. The fire brought opportunities for rebuilding the outdated city. Not the least of these opportunities was the chance for the reconstruction of churches, wherein the artistry of Christopher Wren was expressed. Trevelyan finds further meaning in the effects of plague and fire. They influenced the atmosphere of politics "for twenty years to come," for they were interpreted superstitiously by the middle and lower classes, who thought them the result of "God's anger against their governors." Simultaneously, they also thought the fire to be the work of the Papists. Thus there was a resurgence of Puritanism not too long after it had suffered political defeat. There was also a temporary setback for rationalism. In this manner Trevelyan draws for us the complex pattern of history.

Then follow the Popish Plots, the terror, and the final flight of James II, completing the action set in motion eighty-five years earlier. In another fifty pages Trevelyan finishes the story of the century by discussing the reigns of Queen Anne and William and Mary. This extension allows him to conclude upon the note of a triumph of religious toleration, though he recognizes that religious equality was yet to come. The whole book is a model of achievement. One is everywhere impressed by the accomplishment of Trevelyan's announced tasks—to write cultural history in a literary manner.

THE ENGLISH NOTEBOOKS

Type of work: Journals
Author: Nathaniel Hawthorne (1804-1864)
First published: 1870; 1941

As a result of Nathaniel Hawthorne's close friendship with President Franklin Pierce for whom he had written a successful campaign biography, he was appointed United States Consul to Liverpool in 1853. Hawthorne eagerly anticipated his first trip abroad, although he hated to leave his pleasant home in Concord.

During the years Hawthorne was in England, 1853-1858, he did no creative writing, largely because he was too busy with his duties as consul and also because he spent much time touring England, Scotland, and Wales. But he did keep an extensive notebook of his English sojourn, and this journal of 300,000 words, comprising seven manuscript volumes, is what has come down to us as *The English Notebooks.*

The English Notebooks has had a curious history. It was first published posthumously in 1870 as *Passages from the English Notebooks,* edited by Hawthorne's wife Sophia. But this edition was a bowdlerized version. To abide by standards of Victorian taste, Mrs. Hawthorne very carefully revised her husband's manuscripts, superimposing an aura of decorum on the whole book. She made stylistic revisions, deleting colloquialisms or substituting genteel language for Hawthorne's more commonplace terminology; she omitted passages in which mundane, unsavory, or crude subjects were treated; she withheld passages which were too harsh on England and on various English contemporaries of Hawthorne; and she struck out those which gave too personal an account of the Hawthorne family. Though Sophia's version of the journals was better than nothing, obviously it cast deceptive shadows on the true personality of her husband.

It was not until the work of the late Randall Stewart that *The English Notebooks* was published in its authentic form. Stewart's edition, made possible by infrared light as well as his own deft scholarly judgment, gives us Hawthorne's own words and thereby not only gives us a more candid look at the author's view of England and its people but also presents us with a Hawthorne who is more human, more worldly in interests—in short, more alive—than the rather stolid personage of Sophia's rendition. The notebooks as edited by Stewart are now the standard edition.

The notebooks are not only a fascinating, detailed account of many aspects of England—its topography, the customs of its people, the splendors of its historic buildings—but also an important disclosure of a nineteenth century American's feelings toward England. Hawthorne's reaction to the mother country was in part unfavorable. As Professor Stewart points out in his introduction, such a bias was not uncommon among Americans of that day, for a strong patriotism augmented by the Revolution and the War of 1812 still lingered in this country. England was still something of a foe. Moreover, there was much supercilious criticism of America by the British in many English books and periodicals that criticized and satirized America and her customs. As a result, in the notebooks Hawthorne asserts America's superiority over England whenever he can. He writes of the superiority of American women over their "gross" English counterparts; he praises the common American man for knowing more of political happenings than the English countryman; he even feels American natural scenery, though not as richly verdant as that in England, is superior. He rarely wearies of lightly scoffing at the diminutive lakes, rivers, and mountains he sees in England. And he notes the relative lack of brooks and streams in England as compared to those found in New England.

But there was also much about England that attracted Hawthorne. He loved the beauties of nature, such as the luxuriant hedge rows, and felt in some ways more akin to this mild, domesticated nature than to his own rugged New England terrain. His romantic appetite for old ruins in picturesque settings was also satisfied. Repeatedly he describes ivy-covered ruins and marvels over the hazy, antiquated atmosphere surrounding them. He also cherishes his visits to homes of famous deceased English authors.

The major attraction England held for Hawthorne, however, is less tangible than the others. Despite the statement he once made that New England was all his heart could hold, he was possessed by the haunting feeling of ancestral bondage to England. He had always had a keen sense of the past, a fact which is evident both in his fiction and in his inherent sense of guilt over the misguided role some of his ancestors had played in the Salem witchcraft trials. Being keenly conscious of ancestry and the past, Hawthorne felt that his going to England was in a way representative of the Hawthorne line returning to its original home, from which his forefathers had departed in 1635. The very thought of finding a gravestone there with his family name on it excited him. This theme of the ancestral tie appears throughout the notebooks and was later to be the subject of two of the fragmentary novels he left at his death, *The Ancestral Footstep* and *Doctor Grimshawe's Secret*.

Thus, *The English Notebooks* shows Hawthorne's feelings toward England to be ambivalent. While criticizing many aspects of England, he also found much to admire in this land which held a mysterious claim on his affections.

Since Hawthorne made it a practice to make notebook entries of practically ev-

erything he noticed, it is impossible in a limited space to cover the wide range of material he included. But four major categories of his jottings may be distinguished and treated in some detail.

First, much of the notebooks is given over to detailed accounts of side trips which Hawthorne and his family took throughout England, Scotland, and Wales. There were the two visits to the Scottish Highlands, the leisurely tours of the Cumberland lake country, the excursions to such well-known attractions as Blenheim, and the frequent journeys to London. Second, and of necessity related to the first, there are many passages describing Hawthorne's visits to homes of famous deceased authors, among them Shakespeare, Scott, Dr. Johnson, and Southey and also encounters with illustrious English personages still living. Many of the latter occasions were simply brief meetings; others developed into fast friendships. He saw Macaulay at a dinner and Disraeli at the House of Commons, and he observed Tennyson at an art exhibition at Old Trafford but was too shy to introduce himself to the redoubtable poet laureate. He became friends, however, with Leigh Hunt, a "beautiful and venerable" old man, and especially with Robert and Elizabeth Barrett Browning. The Hawthornes' friendship with the Brownings was to continue into their Italian days, from 1858 to 1860.

The third category of Hawthorne's recordings in the notebooks is directly related to his published writings. Although he wrote no fiction during his years in England, he was laying the groundwork for later creative work. In the first place, his later collection of essays on England, *Our Old Home*, borrowed heavily from his notebook entries. Such essays as "Leamington Spa," "Lichfield and Uttoxeter," and "Outside Glimpses of English Poverty" closely followed his notebook accounts.

Moreover, many of the observations recorded in the notebooks were later used in *The Marble Faun* and the frag-

mentary novels, *The Ancestral Footstep,
Doctor Grimshawe's Secret, Septimius
Felton,* and *The Dolliver Romance*. For
example, an attractive, exotic-looking
Jewess Hawthorne observed at the Lord
Mayor's banquet in 1856 became the
prototype for the enigmatic Miriam of
The Marble Faun. An imprint in stone
somewhat resembling a footprint at
Smithell's Hall, said to be that of a Protestant martyr who stamped his foot in
protest against religious injustice during
Bloody Mary's reign, became the germ of
The Ancestral Footstep. Fascinated by
the way moss on English tombstones
served to bring out the inscriptions and
thereby prolong the memory of the deceased, Hawthorne used this phenomenon in both *Septimius Felton* and *Doctor
Grimshawe's Secret*. A venerable yew
tree which Hawthorne observed in a
churchyard at Eastham was later used in
Doctor Grimshawe's Secret as a symbol of
the lingering influence of the past on the
present. The luxuriant English gardens
seemed to Hawthorne to tempt man to
withdraw from life and seclude himself
in their protective sanctuaries, an idea he
later introduced into his unfinished novels. A rare flower, supposedly everlasting,
presented to Sophia by a gardener at the
hot houses at Eaton Hall became a symbol of earthly immortality in *Septimius
Felton* and *The Dolliver Romance*. In
short, the notebooks are a storehouse of
raw materials which Hawthorne molded
into characters, settings, plot elements,
and symbols in his later fiction.

Finally, and perhaps ultimately most
important, *The English Notebooks* reveals
Hawthorne the man. Lurking in the
shadows is Hawthorne the romancer; but
in the limelight is the man who loved
playing parlor games with his family on
cold winter nights, who longed to smoke
a cigar with Tennyson, who was simultaneously aroused and repulsed by the
sensuous Jewess, who performed his mundane duties of the consulate with dili-
gence yet weariness, and who was moved
by the grandeur of English cathedrals but
felt strong yearnings for the simpler
church services of his Puritan heritage
stirring within him. This is the Hawthorne who emerges from the notebooks,
a rich portrait which belies the dated picture of him as a brooding, almost un-
worldy recluse.

ENOCH ARDEN

Type of work: Poem
Author: Alfred, Lord Tennyson (1809-1892)
Type of plot: Sentimental romance
Time of plot: Late eighteenth century
Locale: England
First published: 1864

> *Principal characters:*
> ENOCH ARDEN, a shipwrecked sailor
> ANNIE LEE, his wife
> PHILIP RAY, his friend
> MIRIAM LANE, a tavern keeper

Critique:

To some modern readers the language of *Enoch Arden* may seem stilted and the story of his unselfish love mawkishly romantic, but we must remember that it was written during a period when unrequited love and unselfish devotion to one's family were favorite subjects of the reading public of England and America. Tennyson has one virtue not shared by all of his contemporaries; his poems are easily read and understood. He expressed better than any other poet of his time the essential character of the English people of the nineteenth century.

The Story:

Annie Lee, Philip Ray, and Enoch Arden played together as children. Sometimes Philip was the husband, sometimes Enoch, but Annie was always the mistress. If the boys quarreled over her, Annie would weep and beg them not to quarrel and say she would be a wife to both of them.

As they grew older and ceased their childish games, Enoch and Philip grew to love Annie. Enoch told her of his love, but Philip kept silent. Philip was the miller's son and a rich boy; Enoch was a poor orphan. He bought a small boat and became a fisherman. He sailed aboard a merchant ship for a full year before he had enough money to make a home for Annie. When he reached his twenty-first year he asked her to be his wife. While the two lovers talked together, Philip looked down on them as they sat at the edge of the wood. He went away quietly, locking his love for Annie deep in his heart.

For seven years Enoch and Annie lived in health and prosperity. They had two children, a girl and a boy. Then misfortune came. Enoch slipped and fell and lay months recovering. While he was ill, a sickly child was born, his favorite. There was no money and the children were hungry, and Enoch's heart almost broke to see his family in want.

The chance came for him to sail again on a merchantman bound for China. He sold his fishing boat that he might get a small store of goods and set Annie up as a trader while he was gone, so that she and the children might not be in want before his return. Annie begged him for their children's sake not to take this dangerous voyage. But Enoch laughed at her fears and told her to give all her cares to God, for the sea was His as well as the land, and He would take care of Enoch and bring him safely home. Annie cut a lock of hair from the sickly child and gave it to Enoch when he sailed.

For many months Annie waited for word from Enoch. Her business did not prosper; she did not know how to bargain. In the third year the sickly child died and Annie was crushed by grief.

After the funeral Philip broke his silence. He begged to send the children to school and care for them for the sake of his friendship with her and Enoch. Enoch had been gone for ten long years before Philip asked Annie to be his wife. He had not spoken before because he

knew that she still waited for Enoch's
return. Annie asked him to wait one
year more. Six months beyond the year
passed before she and Philip were wed.
But still she feared to enter her own
house and thought that one day she
would see Enoch waiting for her. It was
not until after she bore Philip a child
that she was at peace with herself.

Enoch had been shipwrecked and cast
upon a desert island. Although he did
not lack for food and shelter, his heart
was heavy with loneliness and worry
about his wife and children. One day
a ship came to the island and took him
aboard. When he returned to England
he was old and stooped and no one knew
him. Finding his old house empty, he
took lodging in a tavern kept by a widow,

Miriam Lane. Not knowing who he
was, Mrs. Lane told him of Annie and
Philip and their new baby. Enoch could
only murmur that he was lost. Watching
from a high wall behind Philip's house,
he saw Annie and the children in their
happiness. He knew he could never
shatter that new life.

He lived quietly and did what work
he could and told no one his name or
from where he came. At last, sick and
dying, he called Mrs. Lane to his bedside and told her his story. He asked
her to tell Annie and Philip and the
children that he died blessing them, and
he sent the lock of hair to Annie so she
would know he spoke the truth. His
was a great unselfish love until the end.

Further Critical Evaluation of the Work:

In *Enoch Arden,* Tennyson relies on heavily adorned treatment of rather
simple subjects. The plot as well is relatively straightforward: the problem
of money or the lack of it accounts for much of the action. Enoch fears that
his family will be reduced to a miserable existence because of their financial
situation and Annie comes to know the misery of his fears when she has to
face poverty alone when he goes to sea. Tennyson reaches the height of his
power to evoke pathos and sentiment, however, in two scenes that balance
each other. The first is at the beginning of the poem when Annie rejects the
suit of Philip, the rich boy, for that of Enoch, the poor but noble fisherman.
The second, which reverses the situations, comes near the conclusion: Enoch
experiences Philip's earlier deprivation after he returns from the sea to discover that he has lost his family and his wife. In both scenes, Tennyson is
at his best; they are realistic, restrained, and lacking the sentimentality that
characterizes the majority of the poem.

It was precisely this sentimentality, however, that Tennyson's Victorian
audience clamored for. Living in an age of emotional repression in which
sentiment and feelings were to be masked by dedication and earnestness, the
middle class looked in their literature for unabashed emotionalism. Sharing
their need, Tennyson, along with Dickens, for example, supplied it un-
ashamedly. *Enoch Arden* possesses all the ingredients to supply the feelings
his readers were seeking: the vivid contrast of rich and poor; the pain of unrequited love; the stoical man, Philip, unable to express his love; and, of
course, the sufferings of children. But with all their demand for vicarious
pain, the Victorians also needed to be reassured, and Tennyson, therefore,
offered his bittersweet conclusion: the happiness of the new family is blessed
by the dying husband.

THE ENORMOUS ROOM

Type of work: Novel
Author: E. E. Cummings (1894-1962)
Type of plot: Autobiographical fiction
Time of plot: 1917
Locale: France
First published: 1922

Principal characters:
E. E. CUMMINGS, an American ambulance driver
W. S. B., his American friend
APOLLYON, head of the French prison
ROCKYFELLER,
THE WANDERER,
ZOO-LOO,
SURPLICE, and
JEAN LE NÈGRE, fellow prisoners

Critique:

The *Enormous Room* tells of more than three uncomfortable months in prison; it tells of the outrage and terror and hope and fear of men caught in the mesh of wartime government. E. E. Cummings did not want the book to stand merely as an indictment of the French government; he wanted it to tell of the strange and amazing things he had learned about people while in prison. In reading the book, one gets to know not only the author and his friend B., but all the inmates of the enormous room. Each is a study of some human quality. Abounding with sharply drawn scenes and portraits, the novel is compelling in its vivid detail. The book is not so much a study of the stupidity and brutality of war as it is a quietly passionate vindiction of the animal Man.

The Story:

E. E. Cummings and his friend, B., were unhappy as members of the Norton-Harjes Ambulance Service, a unit sent by Americans to aid the French during World War I. One day they were arrested by French military police. From hints dropped during an investigation Cummings gathered that B. had written some letters suspected by the censor. Because they were good friends, both men were held for questioning. Exactly

what they were suspected of doing they never found out. On one occasion Cummings was asked whether he hated the Germans. He replied that he did not, that he simply loved the French very much. The investigating official could not understand how one could love the French and not hate Germans. Finally Cummings and B. were separated and sent to different prisons. As time went by, Cummings was questioned again and again and moved from one spot to another, always under strict guard.

Late one night he was taken to a prison in the little provincial town of Macé. There he was thrown into a huge darkened room, given a straw mattress, and told to go to sleep. In the darkness he counted at least thirty voices speaking eleven different languages. Early the next morning he was told that B., his friend, was in the same room. The two men were happy to see each other again. B. told him that the prisoners in the room were all suspected of being spies, some only because they spoke no French.

That morning he learned the routine of the prison. The enormous room was lined with mattresses down each side, with a few windows to let in light at one end. It smelled of stale tobacco and sweat. Some of the men in the room were mad; most of them were afraid they might become so. To all of them life consisted of following dull prison routine. At five-thirty in the morning someone went down to the kitchen under guard and brought back a bucket of sour, cold coffee. After coffee, the prisoners drew lots to see who would clear the room, sweep the floors, and collect the trash. At seven-thirty they were allowed to walk for two hours in a small, walled-in courtyard. Then came the first meal of the day, followed by another walk in the garden. At four they had supper. At eight they were locked in the enormous room for the night.

There was little entertainment except fighting and conversation. Some of the men spent their time trying to catch sight of women kept in another part of the prison. Cummings began to accustom himself to the enormous room and to make friends among the various inmates. One of the first of these was Count Bragard, a Belgian painter who specialized in portraits of horses. The count was a perfect gentleman, even in prison, and always looked neat and suave. He and Cummings discussed painting and the arts as if they were at some polite party. Before Cummings left, the count began to act strangely. He withdrew from his old friends. He was losing his mind.

One day Cummings was taken to see the head of the prison, a gross man he called Apollyon, after the devil in *Pilgrim's Progress*. Apollyon had no interest in the prisoners as long as they made as little trouble as possible for him. He questioned Cummings for a considerable time in an effort to learn why the American was there, a circumstance over which the American himself often wondered.

When new inmates arrived in the room, everyone looked them over hopefully, some to find a man with money he would lend, some to find a fellow-countryman, and some to find a friend. One day a very fat, rosy-cheeked man joined the group. He had been a successful manager of a disreputable house. Because he had a large sum of money

with him, he was nicknamed Rockyfeller. He hired a strong man to act as his bodyguard. Nobody liked him, for he bought special privileges from the guards.

During his stay in the room, Cummings met three men, very different from each other, whose personal qualities were such that they made life seem meaningful to him. He called them the Delectable Mountains, after the mountains Christian found in *Pilgrim's Progress*. The first was the Wanderer, whose wife and three little children were in the women's ward of the prison. He was a strong man, simple in his emotions and feelings. Cummings liked to talk with him about his problems. One of the Wanderer's children, a little boy, sometimes came to the enormous room to visit his father. His pranks and games both bothered and amused the men. The Wanderer treated his son with love and the deepest kind of understanding. Until he was sent away he remained Cummings' best friend.

The second Delectable Mountain was called Zoo-loo, a Polish farmer who could speak neither French nor English, but who could communicate by signs. In a short time he and Cummings knew all about each other. Zoo-loo had a knack for hiding money, and despite the fact that the head of the prison had him searched from head to toe, and all his belongings searched, he seemed always able to produce a twenty franc note from his left ear or the back of his neck. His kindnesses to Cummings and B. were innumerable.

The third Delectable Mountain was an amazing little man named Surplice. Everything astonished him. When Cummings had some candy or cheese, Surplice was sure to come over to his cot and ask questions about it in a shy manner. His curiosity and friendly conversation made everything seem more important and interesting than it really was.

One morning Jean Le Nègre was brought to the enormous room, a gigantic, simple-minded Negro whom Cummings was to remember as the finest of his fellow prisoners. Jean was given to practical jokes and tall tales; he had been arrested for impersonating an English officer and had been sent to the prison for psychopathic observation. Because of his powerful body, the women prisoners called their approval and admiration when he walked in the courtyard. His favorite was Lulu, who smuggled money and a lace handkerchief to him. When she was sent to another prison, Jean was disconsolate. When one of the prisoners pulled at Lulu's handkerchief, Jean handled him roughly. A scuffle followed. The guards came and Jean was taken away for punishment. Calls from the women prisoners aroused him so that he attacked the guards and sent them flying until he was quieted and bound by a fellow prisoner whom he trusted. After that experience Jean grew quiet and shy.

Just before Cummings himself was released, B. was sent away. Jean le Nègre tried to cheer Cummings with his funny stories and exaggerated lies, but without much success. Cummings was afraid B. might never get free from the prisons of France, a groundless fear as he learned later. He himself left the enormous room knowing that in it he had learned the degradation and nobility and endurance of human nature.

Further Critical Evaluation of the Work:

The Enormous Room reveals the disillusionment and cynicism characteristic of the writers who emerged after World War I, and Cummings' particular hatred of systems which threaten individualism and freedom. The human capacity to keep feeling alive in a dehumanizing world is Cummings' basic theme. As in his poetry, he seeks to present his characters through their own particular idioms. Though showing the influence of Fielding, Dickens, and (especially) Bunyan, Cummings' highly autobiographical novel is new both in content and technique.

Chapters entitled "I Begin a Pilgrimage," "A Pilgrim's Progress," "Apollyon," and "An Approach to the Delectable Mountains" make clear parallels between the journey of Bunyan's Pilgrim to salvation and Cummings' own metaphorical journey. From the moment of his arrest, Cummings finds himself in the power of an insecure authority administered by a mindless bureaucracy. Intolerant of the smallest deviation from its norms, the French government—ironically representative of the "democracy" the war was fought to preserve—imprisons all nonconformists, derelicts, and misfits who come to its attention. Ironically, the enormous room holds no real traitors, spies, or enemies of the state.

Supreme among the inmates of the prison are those characters Cummings calls the "Delectable Mountains." Though they are widely diverse types, Cummings seems to find in them a wonderful capacity for feeling which sets them apart from their peers. Thus, these "delectable mountains" in particular come to symbolize for Cummings the beauty and honesty of human emotion in contrast to the unfeeling, mindless and cruel institution. Through his pilgrimage, Cummings comes to believe in the indomitable ability of men to preserve the best of their humanity even in the face of dehumanizing oppression. The novel ends with a bright ray of sunshine, symbolizing Cummings' hope for a future founded upon man's best rather than his worst qualities.

AN ENQUIRY CONCERNING HUMAN UNDERSTANDING

Type of work: Philosophical treatise
Author: David Hume (1711-1776)
First published: 1748

"Philosophical decisions," says Hume toward the end of his *Enquiry,* "are nothing but the reflections of common life, methodised and corrected." This simple, homely epigram conceals a great deal. For one thing, the *Enquiry* is actually a sort of popularized revision of ideas that were systematically developed in Book I of his precocious *Treatise of Human Nature* (1739-1740), which, although it was completed before the author was twenty-five, has been characterized as one of the most profound, thoroughly reasoned, and purely scientific works in the history of philosophy. Secondly, Hume's method for correcting the reflections of common life actually involves a thorough attack on the obscurities of metaphysical idealists.

Born in an age of reason, Hume at first shared the optimism of those who were certain that pure reason could unlock the secrets of nature, and as he read Bacon, Newton, Hobbes, and Locke, he longed for fame equal to theirs. But, as he reported in a letter to Sir Gilbert Elliot, though he "began with an anxious search after arguments, to confirm the common opinion; doubts stole in, dissipated, returned; were again dissipated, returned again; and it was a perpetual struggle of restless imagination against inclination, perhaps against reason." That last, "perhaps against reason," is the crucial phrase, for no philosopher before Hume used reason so brilliantly in an attack against the certainties of reason. The twelve essays of the *Enquiry* reflect his three principal attacks: (1) against rationalism, the doctrine of innate ideas, faith in ontological reasoning and an ordered universe; (2) against empiricism, both the kind that led to Lockian dualism and Berkeleyan idealism, on the ground that neither the physical nor the spiritual can be proved; and (3) against deism, based on universal axioms and the law of causality. It is not surprising that since Hume

religions have largely made their appeals to faith rather than to reason.

Considering what remains when such thoroughgoing skepticism rejects so much of the beliefs of rational men, Hume himself readily admitted (in the fourth essay, "Sceptical Doubts Concerning the Operations of the Understanding") that as a man he was quite satisfied with ordinary reasoning processes, but that as a philosopher he had to be skeptical. For reasoning was not based on immediate sense experience. "The most lively thought is still inferior to the dullest sensation," he asserted in his second essay, "The Origin of Ideas." Unless the mind is "disordered by disease or madness," actual perceptions have the greatest "force and vivacity," and it is only on such matters of basic mental fact rather than on the abstract relations of ideas, as in mathematics, that we must depend for certainties about life. For example, no amount of reasoning could have led Adam in the Garden of Eden to believe that fluid, transparent water would drown him or that bright, warm fire would burn him to ashes. "No object ever discovers [reveals], by the qualities which appear to the senses, either the causes which produced it, or the effects which arise from it." In dealing with this idea, Hume is quite dogged and persistent; he backs every argument into a corner, into some "dangerous dilemma." What is more he enjoys himself immensely while doing it—"philosophers that gave themselves airs of superior wisdom and sufficiency, have a hard task when they encounter persons of inquisitive dispositions," he says. Concerning cause and effect, he argues that we expect similar effects from causes that appear similar; yet this relationship does not always exist and, though it is observed, it is not reasoned. Furthermore, it is merely an arbitrary assumption, an act of faith, that events which we remember as having occurred sequentially in the past will continue to do so in the future. Causation thus was merely a belief, and belief he had defined as a "lively idea related to or associated with a present impression."

This seemed to Hume not merely an impractical philosophical idea, but a momentous discovery of great consequence. Since causation was an *a priori* principle of both natural and moral philosophy, and since causation could not be reasonably demonstrated to be true, a tremendous revolution in human thought was in preparation. Only in the pure realm of ideas, logic, and mathematics, not contingent upon the direct sense awareness of reality, could causation safely (because arbitrarily) be applied—all other sciences are reduced to probability. The concluding essay, "Of the Academical or Sceptical Philosophy," reaches grand heights of eloquence, when Hume argues that *a priori* reasoning can make anything appear to produce anything: "the falling of a pebble may, for aught we know, extinguish the sun; or the wish of a man control the planets in their orbits. . . ."

> When we run over libraries, persuaded of these principles, what havoc must we make? If we take in hand any volume; of divinity or school metaphysics, for instance; let us ask, *Does it contain any abstract reasoning concerning quantity or number?* No. *Does it contain any experimental reasoning concerning matter of fact and existence?* No. Commit it then to the flames: for it can contain nothing but sophistry and illusion.

The polemic vigor of the essays stems in large part from the bitter experiences Hume had in the years immediately preceding the publication of the *Enquiry*. In 1744 he had sought to fill a vacancy in the chair of Ethics and Pneumatical Philosophy at Edinburgh University, but to his astonishment his *Treatise* was invoked to prevent the appointment: "such a popular clamor has been raised against me in Edinburgh, on account of Scepticism, Heterodoxy, and other hard names . . . that my Friends find some Difficulty

in working out the Point of my Professorship." Then he was dismissed without full salary as tutor to the mad son of the Marquis of Annandale. These experiences helped sharpen the hard cutting edge of his thought and prose style.

After refining his conception of reason and its modes of function, Hume applies it to four crucial problems: "Liberty and Necessity," "Reason of Animals," "Miracles," and "Particular Providence and a Future State."

Concerning liberty and necessity, Hume argues that since the subject relates to common life and experience (unlike topics such as the origin of worlds or the region of spirits), only ambiguity of language keeps the dispute alive. For a clear definition, he suggests that it be consistent with plain matters of fact and with itself. Difficulty arises when philosophers approach the problem by examining the faculties of the soul rather than the operations of body and brute matter. In the latter, men assume that they perceive cause and effect, but in the functioning of their minds they feel no connection between motive and action. However, we cannot invoke the doctrine of cause and effect without, ultimately, tracing all actions—including evil ones—to the Deity whom men refuse to accept as the author of guilt and moral turpitude in all his creatures. As a matter of fact, freedom and necessity are matters of momentary emotional feeling "not to be controuled or altered by any philosophical theory or speculation whatsoever."

The "Reason of Animals" consists—as it does in children, philosophers, and mankind in general—not so much in logical inferences as in experience of analogies and sequential actions. Observation and experience alone teach a horse the proper height which he can leap or a greyhound how to meet the hare in her tracks with the least expenditure of energy. Hume's learning theory here seems to be based on the pleasure-pain principle and forms the background for some theories of twentieth-century psychology. However, Hume ends this essay with a long qualification in which he cites the Instincts, unlearned knowledge derived from the original hand of nature, and then adds this curious final comment: "The experimental reasoning itself, which we possess in common with beasts, and on which the whole conduct of life depends, is nothing but a species of instinct or mechanical power, that acts in us unknown to ourselves."

The essay on miracles is perhaps the most spirited of the entire collection and it is the one which Hume expected, correctly, would stir the greatest opposition. Nevertheless, he was certain that his argument would be, for the wise and the learned, "an everlasting check to all kinds of superstitious delusion, and consequently . . . useful as long as the world endures." Events can be believed to happen only when they are observed, and all reports of events not directly observed must be believed only to the degree that they conform with probability, experimentally or experientially derived. A miracle is a violation of the laws of nature; therefore it violates all probability; therefore it is impossible. History gives no instance of any miracle personally attended to by a sufficient number of unquestionably honest, educated, intelligent men. Despite the surprise, wonder, and other pleasant sensations attendant upon reports of novel experiences, all new discoveries that achieve credibility among men have always resembled in fundamentals those objects and events of which we already have experience. The most widespread belief in miracles exists among primitive barbarians. Finally, since there is no objective way of confirming miracles, believers have no just basis for rejecting those claimed by all religions. "So that, on the whole, we may conclude, that the *Christian Religion* not only was at first attended with miracles, but even at this day cannot be believed by any reasonable person without one. Mere reason is insufficient to convince us . . . to believe what is most contrary to custom and experience."

In the 1777 posthumous edition of the *Enquiry* appeared the announcement that these unsystematic essays be *alone* regarded as containing Hume's philosophical sentiments and principles. Despite the fact that professional philosophers, especially the logical positivists, still prefer the earlier *Treatise of Human Nature*, it is well that the *Enquiry* with its livelier style and popular appeal stands as his personal testament. In it he said that he would be "happy if . . . we can undermine the foundations of an abstruse philosophy, which seems to have hitherto served only as a shelter to superstition, and a cover to absurdity and error." The irony is that he succeeded so well in undermining reason that he opened the door to the romanticism of the late eighteenth and early nineteenth centuries. But his voice has outlasted that babel and his humanistic skepticism survives. "Be a philosopher," he cautioned himself, "but amidst all your philosophy, be still a man."

THE EPIC OF GILGAMESH

Type of work: Poem
Author: Unknown
Type of plot: Heroic adventure
Time of plot: Remote antiquity
Locale: The ancient world
First transcribed: c. 2,000 B.C.

Principal characters:
GILGAMESH, ruler of Uruk
ENGIDU, his companion
ANU, the chief god
ISHTAR, divinity of fertility
UTNAPISHTIM, a man who found the secret of life
UR-SHANABI, boatman on the waters of death
NINSUN, a goddess
SIDURI, the divine cup-bearer
KHUMBABA, a dragon

Critique:

The idea of the superman is not a new one. Demigods who overcame great obstacles enjoy a long and honored literary tradition. Achilles, Odysseus, Hercules, Samson, Beowulf, Roland and King Arthur all have epic stature. Earlier than any of these, however, is Gilgamesh, the valiant hero of a Babylonian epic written about four thousand years ago. A figure of heroic proportions, Gilgamesh knew love and conflict, friendship and loyalty, joy and sorrow, courage and fear, and ultimately the horror and mystery of death. Thus the Gilgamesh epic embraces the enduring themes of literature, and its hero remains an enduring affirmation of life in all its transience and mystery.

The Story:

Gilgamesh was the wisest, strongest and most handsome of mortals, for he was two-thirds god and one-third man. As king of the city-state of Uruk he built a monumental wall around the city, but in doing so he overworked the city's inhabitants unmercifully, to the point where they prayed to the gods for relief.

The god Anu listened to their plea and called the goddess Aruru to fashion another demigod like Gilgamesh in order that the two heroes might fight, and thus give Uruk peace. Aruru created the warrior Engidu out of clay and sent him to live among the animals of the hills.

A hunter of Uruk found Engidu and in terror reported his existence to Gilgamesh. Gilgamesh advised the hunter to take a priestess to Engidu's watering place to lure Engidu to the joys of civilization and away from his animal life. The priestess initiated Engidu into civilization with her body, her bread, and her wine. Having forsaken his animal existence, Engidu and the priestess started for Uruk. On their arrival she told him of the strength and wisdom of Gilgamesh and of how Gilgamesh had told the goddess Ninsun about his dreams of meeting Engidu, his equal, in combat. Engidu challenged Gilgamesh by barring his way to the temple. An earth-shaking fight ensued in which Gilgamesh stopped Engidu's onslaught. Engidu praised Gilgamesh's strength and the two enemies became inseparable friends.

Gilgamesh informed Engidu of his wish to conquer the terrible monster, Khumbaba, and challenged him to go along. Engidu replied that the undertaking was full of peril for both. Gilgamesh answered that Engidu's fear of death deprived him of his might. At last Engidu agreed to go with his friend. Gilgamesh then went to the elders and they, like

THE EPIC OF GILGAMESH by William Ellery Leonard. By permission of the publishers, The Viking Press, Inc. Copyright, 1934, by William Ellery Leonard.

Engidu, warned him of the perils he would encounter. Seeing his determination, the elders gave him their blessing. Gilgamesh then went to Ninsun and she also warned him of the great dangers, but to no avail. Then she took Engidu aside and told him to give Gilgamesh special protection.

Upon climbing the cedar mountain to reach Khumbaba, Gilgamesh related three terrible dreams to Engidu, who shored up Gilgamesh's spirit by placing a favorable interpretation on them. On reaching the gate to the cedar wood where Khumbaba resided, the pair were stopped by the watchman, who possessed seven magic mantles. The two heroes succeeded in overcoming him. Accidentally, Engidu touched the magic portal of the gate; immediately he felt faint and weak, as if afraid of death. The champions entered the cedar wood and with the aid of the sun god slew Khumbaba.

Upon their return to Uruk after their victory, the goddess Ishtar fell in love with Gilgamesh and asked him to be her consort. But Gilgamesh, being wiser than her previous consorts, recalled all of the evil things she had done to her earlier lovers. Ishtar then angrily ascended to heaven and reported his scornful refusal to Anu. Threatening to destroy mankind, she forced Anu to create a monster bull that would kill Gilgamesh.

Anu formed the bull and sent it to Uruk. After it had slain five hundred warriors in two snorts, Engidu jumped on its back while Gilgamesh drove his sword into its neck. Engidu then threw the bull's thighbone in Ishtar's face, and Gilgamesh held a feast of victory in his palace.

Engidu, still ailing from touching the portal to the cedar wood, cursed those who had showed him civilization. He related his nightmares to Gilgamesh, grew faint-hearted, and feared death. Since he had been cursed by touching the gate, he died. Gilgamesh mourned his friend six days and nights; on the seventh he left Uruk to cross the steppes in search of Utnapishtim, the mortal who had discovered the secret of life.

Upon reaching the mountain named Mashu, he found scorpion men guarding the entrance to the underground passage. They received him cordially when they learned he was seeking Utnapishtim, but they warned him that no one had ever found a way through the mountain.

Gilgamesh traveled the twelve miles through the mountain in pitch darkness, and at last he entered a garden. There he found Siduri, the cup-bearing goddess, who remarked on his haggard condition. Gilgamesh explained that his woeful appearance had been caused by the loss of Engidu, and that he sought Utnapishtim. The goddess advised him to live in pleasure at home and warned him of the dangers ahead.

Gilgamesh went on his way, seeking the boatman Ur-Shanabi, who might possibly take him across the waters of death. On finding Ur-Shanabi's stone coffers, Gilgamesh broke them in anger, but he made up for them by presenting the boatman with huge poles. Ur-Shanabi then ferried Gilgamesh across the waters of death.

Utnapishtim, meeting Gilgamesh on the shore, also spoke of his haggard condition. Gilgamesh told him about the loss of Engidu and his own search for the secret of life. Utnapishtim replied that nothing was made to last forever, that life was transient, and that death was part of the inevitable process.

Gilgamesh then asked how Utnapishtim had found the secret of eternal life, and Utnapishtim told him the story of the Great Flood.

Utnapishtim had been told in a dream of the gods' plans to flood the land. So he built an ark and put his family and all kinds of animals on it. When the flood came, he and those on the ark survived, and when the flood subsided he found himself on Mount Nisser. After the waters had returned to their normal level, he gave thanks to the gods, and in return the god Ea blessed him and his wife with the secret of life everlasting.

After finishing his story Utnapishtim advised Gilgamesh to return home, but before going he had Ur-Shanabi bathe and clothe Gilgamesh in a robe that remained clean as long as he lived. As Gilgamesh was leaving Utnapishtim gave him the secret of life, a magic plant which grew at the bottom of the waters of death. However, as Gilgamesh bathed in a pool on his way home, an evil serpent ate the plant.

On arriving home Gilgamesh went to Ninsun to inquire how he could reach Engidu in the land of the dead. Although Ninsun directed him, he failed in his attempt because he broke some of the taboos that she had laid out for him. Deeply disappointed, he made one final appeal to the god Ea, the lord of the depths of the waters, and Engidu was brought forth. Gilgamesh asked Engidu what happened to one after death, and Engidu laid bare the full terrors of the afterworld. Worms, neglect, and disrespect were the lot of the dead.

Further Critical Evaluation of the Work:

The Epic of Gilgamesh belongs to that group of Ancient Near Eastern myths which may be termed "societal." Each nation had its societal myth to justify and sustain its particular social system and to fulfill several crucial functions: to validate prevailing social patterns, to provide rules and acceptable models for living, to supply divine sanction of the existing power structure, and to prove to the individual that the laws and customs of his country were superior to those of other countries. Thus the myth served the purpose of preserving the *status quo*. Particularly in the case of hero tales like the Gilgamesh epic, the heroes were models of proper and improper behavior whose feats dramatized just what should or should not be attempted. Through the events narrated in this chronicle of the life of King Gilgamesh, therefore, one may make several assumptions concerning the Babylonian social system which the tale was intended to substantiate.

The action in *The Epic of Gilgamesh* falls into three major phases of the hero's development. In the first phase, King Gilgamesh is a proud tyrant who rejects the concept of the king as a loving and concerned shepherd of his people; instead, he drives his subjects so cruelly that they petition the god Anu for relief. Since Gilgamesh is two-thirds god himself, a powerful chastisement is necessary, and Anu commissions the king's mother, the goddess Aruru, to create a foe powerful enough to fight with Gilgamesh and thus redirect his energies and interests. This creation—in many ways the sophisticated king's uncivilized alter ego—is named Engidu. After Engidu and Gilgamesh engage in a colossal battle of strength and endurance, they become inseparable friends, and the hero embarks on the second phase of his career. In this phase Gilgamesh rises above the level of pure selfishness and brute force and goes in search of romantic adventures which will bring meaning to his life and lasting fame to himself and his accepted brother. During the course of his adventures, Gilgamesh mocks and insults the goddess of love, Ishtar, and scornfully rejects her offer to become his lover, but escapes death at her hands because of his own divinity and great strength. Soon after, however,

Engidu dies a slow and painful death, thus precipitating Gilgamesh into the final stage of his travels. In this stage, the hero, horrified at the terrible death of his friend and fearing a similar end for himself, departs on a journey to find immortality. This search ultimately terminates in failure when a serpent eats the plant of everlasting life which the hero has located on the bottom of the sea. After an interview with the spirit of Engidu in which his friend reveals to him that nothing awaits man after death but worms and mud, Gilgamesh reaches the conclusion that the only course left open for him is to return to his city of Uruk and fulfill his role of king and shepherd to his people.

The message conveyed through this societal myth is clear: if a heroic demigod cannot acquire immortality and is led to accept his ordained role, there is nothing for the humble Babylonian citizen to do but acknowledge the inevitability of death and likewise embrace the role assigned to him by the social system, no matter how lowly. And while the myth reinforces the Near Eastern belief that there is no life after death, it also offers some practical advice, through the words of a barmaid whom Gilgamesh meets on his travels, on how to make the most of this life:

> Make every day a day of joy.
> Dance, play, day and night . . .
> Cherish the child who grasps your hand.
> Let your wife rejoice in your bosom
> For this is the fate of man.

EPIGRAMS OF MARTIAL

Type of work: Verse epigrams
Author: Martial (Marcus Valerius Martialis, c. 40-c. 104)
First transcribed: 80-104

The fourteen books of epigrams which were written by Martial during a pivotal period in the history of Rome display a rare form of literary accomplishment, the adoption and complete individual mastery of a literary form by one man. From the time of his arrival at Rome, about the age of twenty-three, until his return to his birthplace in Spain, Martial wrote verse epigrams on a wide variety of subjects and in many different styles.

Almost all that we know of Martial we learn from his epigrams, and a great deal of our present knowledge of Rome from the death of Nero, in A.D. 68, until the end of the first century comes from the same source. What Martial tells us is the sort of information that could not, perhaps, be gained in any other way. One of the most common subject areas of Martial's verse is the everyday life of ancient Rome. He took an active part in that life, and it is realistically mirrored in his writings.

There are roughly five other kinds of epigrams that Martial produced. The first of these, probably the most important to him personally, is the epigram written in praise of the emperor or some other man of wealth and power. This type was written largely as a means of subsistence, patronage being the primary system by which poets lived. The contemplative epigrams, usually addressed to friends, show that Martial was realistic almost to the point of cynicism. He reached no great heights of philosophy, wishing only to be comfortable and peaceful. His desire for peace and solitude is expressed in another type of epigram in which he praises life in the country. In these Martial sees the country with the enthusiasm often found in the city dweller, but he did not write pastoral verse; he saw the Italian countryside as it really existed. The epigrammatic epitaphs, often written on children, or animals, are among his best work, revealing sentiments that are rare in Martial, feeling often leavened by humor. In the epigrams on friendship he comes the closest to real emotion. Romantic love is usually treated satirically, and his discussions of that passion in himself seem devoid of sincere feeling.

Perhaps the chief fault that has been found with his work is found in Martial's personal situation, his toadying to men of position. When he begged the Emperor Domitian, whose name has become synonymous with cruel despotism and wicked licentiousness, for a special position (pleading as the father of three children), for example, his epigram has a self-abasement that may disgust the modern reader:

> Welfare and glory of the earth, while thee
> We safe behold, we gods believe to be;
> If my slight books did e'er thee entertain,
> And oft to read them thou didst not disdain,
> What nature does deny, do thou bestow:
> For *father of three children* make me go.
> When my verse takes not, this will be an ease;
> A high reward, in case it thee do please.

It is important, however, to understand the position poets held in Rome at that time. Only through patronage, from the emperor if possible, could a poet lead a comfortable life. Everyone who hoped to be looked upon as a gentleman wrote verses, and those who wrote to live were compelled to praise and praise highly in order to be heard. Martial was certainly not alone in this respect. Completely a product of his time, he accepted the necessity to praise great men as a part of the literary milieu in which he lived.

Criticism that may carry more weight

today is Martial's lack of poetic vision. He is never profound, seldom lyrically imaginative. His subjects are the people and things around him, and he depicts them as they are. It is this accuracy of portrayal that makes his verse so valuable in understanding his era. Counterbalancing this absence of elevated vision, however, is Martial's technical grasp of the form in which he wrote. Although he did not create the epigram, he is usually considered the first epigrammatist. He adopted the form, wrote exclusively in it, and did with it all that could be done.

The verse epigram customarily has two major parts, the exposition and the conclusion. The parts may vary in length —Martial's epigrams are from two to over thirty verses long—but usually the exposition takes up most of the poem, with the conclusion being short, often containing a sharp twist of meaning. Within this general framework Martial used direct address, questions, brief transition from exposition to conclusion, satire, irony, and sarcasm. Striking exaggerations and sudden surprises are common, as are plays on words and brief aphorisms. Rhetorical devices abound. His epigram "On a Pretender," for example, shows the quick turn of meaning at the close:

He whom you see to walk in so much state,
Waving and slow, with a majestic gait,
In purple clad, passing the nobles' seat,
My Publius not in garments more complete;—
Whose new rich coach, with gilt and studded reins,
Fair boys and grown-men follow in great trains,
Lately his very ring in pawn did lay
For four poor crowns, his supper to defray.

Along with his technical skill goes an animation and a lively perception that make his epigrams often sound like casual conversation. With all the conciseness so necessary for the successful epigram, Martial has an ease that removes from his verses the tenseness that very often causes epigrams to be painful reading.

Although he himself was poor, Martial was the associate of rich men, and so had full opportunity to see Roman life in all its aspects. Slaves as well as emperors are the subjects of his epigrams. Dinner parties are described along with great monuments. Everywhere he shows a sharp eye and a penetrating wit. Hating pretension, he pricks many a pompous bubble. Few elements of physical or human nature escape his attention.

Apart from Martial's clear pictures of Rome at the end of the first century, probably his greatest importance lies in his influence upon later writers of the epigram. Certainly it would be difficult to find any seventeenth- or eighteenth-century writer of this form in England who did not turn to Martial as his inspiration and guide. That there are at least seven French translations of the epigrams testifies to his popularity on the Continent.

Shortly after the accession of the Emperor Trajan, whom Martial flattered in verse with little effect, the poet returned, in 94, to his birthplace, Bilbilis, a Roman colony in Spain, where he lived on a comfortable estate given to him by a woman whom he probably later married. Characteristically, he was given money for the trip by a friend, Pliny, because of some verses written to him. It is equally characteristic that Martial continued his writing in Spain, sending his epigrams to Rome promptly, but now with frequent expressions of longing for the excitements and pleasures of the city that was to be for only a short time longer the capital of the world.

THE EPIGRAMS OF MELEAGER

Type of work: Epigrams
Author: Meleager (c. 140-c. 70 B.C.)
First transcribed: First century B.C.

Meleager is one of the few surviving voices in Greek literature from the early first century B.C. This century, so rich in Roman literature, was perhaps the scantiest of all the classical period for Greek. One's sense of dearth is intensified by the kind of literature which survived. Ancient Greek literature at no time produced seriously realistic writing, and when the mythical core vanished, the remains took the form of history, philosophy, or stereotyped, artificial styles such as New Comedy, Romance, and Epigram. So it is that in this unsettled century, when the details of personality and daily existence would have been so fascinating, the chief creative writer transmits to us some one hundred thirty epigrams consisting chiefly of picturesque variations on standard themes and topics of earlier epigrammatic love poets. The incongruity is all the keener from the fact that Meleager's home until manhood was Gadara in Syria, the very town at which Jesus was to cast devils into swine. These two Semitic figures, when juxtaposed in the imagination, are utterly immiscible, as are the styles of their literary remains.

Meleager might be for us somewhat less the hothouse orchid he is if his juvenilia had been preserved. His earliest writings were satirical dialogues in prose, modeled on the writings of Menippus, the famous Cynic philosopher and teacher at Gadara. Something of their character may be sensed from the later dialogues of Lucian. The subject of one is reported as a comparison of pease-porridge with lentil-soup. But these were lost, and Meleager's remains now consist of the epigrams found in the great collection known as the *Greek Anthology*.

The last of Meleager's literary productions was itself one of the early stages in the development of that anthology: his *Stephanos* (usually translated *Garland*) was a collection of epigrams of some fifty poets, himself included, with a famous verse preface which compares each poet to that flower which most suggests his poetic character. Later anthologists included the *Stephanos* in larger gatherings; the final collection (apart from the additions derived from Planudes) was made in the tenth century. The poetically significant sections of that collection are the love poems, dedicatory inscriptions, epitaphs, declamatory, moralizing, convivial, and satiric epigrams. Only about twenty of Meleager's epigrams, however, are to be found outside the love poems.

There is a tendency in the anthology, even within the major sections, to arrange poems on the same theme in a sequence. This tendency provides the most important clue for the appreciation of Meleager. The innocent reader on first encounter is likely to ascribe to Meleager both a hectic variety of erotic liaisons and a continuous intensity of emotion reflected in the extravagant language both of which in fact distract the reader from the true poetic center of most of the epigrams. The poems are best approached as exercises in various types, attempts at overbidding previous treatments of a topic—overbidding in wit, imagery, and rhetoric. (The case is similar to that of such poets as Herrick and Jonson, many of whose short lyrics are adaptations or emulations of Anacreon, Catullus, and the *Greek Anthology* itself.) To illustrate, here is an epigram by the earlier poet Asclepiades (XII, 166):

> Let this that is left of my soul, whatever it be, let this at least, ye Loves, have rest for heaven's sake. Or else no longer shoot me with arrows but with thunderbolts, and make me utterly into ashes and cinders. Yea! yea! strike me, ye Loves; for withered away as I am by distress, I would have from you, If I may aught, this little gift.

Meleager takes up the notion of the incinerated lover and exploits it in various ways. For instance (XII, 74):

> I am down; set thy foot on my neck, fierce demon. I know thee, yea by the gods, yea heavy art thou to bear: I know, too, thy fiery arrows. But if thou set thy torch to *my* heart, thou shalt no longer burn it; already it is all ash.
>
> If I perish, Cleobulus (for cast, nigh all of me, into the flame of lads' love, I lie, a burnt remnant, in the ashes), I pray thee make the urn drunk with wine ere thou lay it in earth, writing thereon, "Love's gift to Death."

The practice of poetry-as-outcapping comes all the more naturally to Meleager in that he was part of the wave of rhetorical fashion known as the Asianic. Meleager was a Syrian, but Oriental race or culture has nothing to do with Asianism, which is purely a development within classical literature. The Asianic style sought for something like the Baroque: extravagance in diction and imagery, special tricks and effects in word arrangements. Most of this is hard to illustrate outside the Greek, but the use of repetition and fancy compounds in the following may give some of the flavor (VII, 476, 1-4):

> Tears, the last gift of my love, even down through the earth I send to thee in Hades, Heliodora—tears ill to shed, and on thy much-wept tomb I pour them in memory of longing, in memory of affection.

The witty side of Meleager's Asianism brings him close at times to the Metaphysicals' conceits (V, 156):

> Love-loving Asclepias, with her clear blue eyes, like summer seas, persuadeth all to make the love-voyage.

None of the foregoing is meant to deny the existence of genuine emotion in Meleager's poetry. The point is that, where emotion is found, it emerges from, launches, or sets on fire the already existing framework of artificial craft, and artifice is inseparable from the result. In various ways, of course, the same can be said of all poetry, but it is so dominant in Meleager (and other epigrammatists) that it needs special emphasis as a defining characteristic.

As for the quality of the emotional experience in those few poems where emotion is genuinely present, this is no place for a full disquisition on the Meleagrian species of "Love in the Western World." J. W. Mackail has spoken of a mystical, almost medieval strain in Meleager's love poetry. The religious aspect is overstated in this judgment, but there is one way in which Meleager does at times approach a medieval quality: more than the other epigrammatists, he expresses the total subjection, abasement, humiliation of the lover, much as the courtly lover of the Middle Ages conceived himself as the abject servant of his lady (XII, 158, 1-2):

> The goddess, queen of the Desires, gave me to thee, Theocles; Love, the soft-sandalled, laid me low for thee to tread on . . .

Along with the intermittent intensity of his passion, however, there is an element of coyness and sentimentality which pervades Meleager as well as most of the other love-epigrammatists of the *Greek Anthology,* an element absent from the love of poetry of the Lyric Age of Greece (c. 700-500 B.C.), absent even from Anacreon. Perhaps it is possible to account for the change by the fact that the period was Hellenistic, not Hellenic. The great love poetry is written when Eros is integrated within or demonically opposed to a religious framework, and for most educated men of the Hellenistic Age there was no serious religion, only philosophy.

One other feature of Meleager's love poetry which needs simply to be noted, at least for contemporary readers, is the characteristic type of the beloved. Meleager's loved ones fall exclusively into two classes: hetaerae (professional female entertainers or courtesans) and boys in their early teens. Since these two classes account for practically all extant ancient Greek love poetry (Sappho is the major exception), this otherwise rather striking phenomenon needs no special discussion in connection with Meleager.

One should not over-emphasize Meleager as a love poet; nor should one be concerned with seeking out those poems which embody "genuine passion," as if these must necessarily be his best. Sheer flights of linguistic dexterity and brilliant variations of traditional themes can produce fine epigrams. Perhaps the most memorable characteristic of Meleager is an outgrowth of this side of his poetry; his bursts of wit often have an element of sheer playfulness and tender humor. In one poem he sends forth a gnat on the dangerous Herculean mission of rousing Heliodora from the side of her current lover to bring her back: the reward will be Hercules' club and lion skin. In another he asks the dew-drunk cicada to strum in antiphon with Pan's piping at high noon and lull him to sleep. An epitaph he wrote for himself makes fun of his own garrulity. In all this one can see a survival of the Meleager who wrote on pease-porridge and lentil-soup.

Meleager's *oeuvre* is a curious mixture of the complex and the trivial, the passionate and the sophisticated. Connoisseurs of the cameo, exquisites of the Yellow Nineties are ex officio licensed to cherish his work; all others will have done him sufficient justice if they read him, at judicious intervals, as an interesting minor poet.

EPINICIA

Type of work: Poetry
Author: Pindar (c. 522-c. 443 B.C.)
First transcribed: 502-452 B.C.

Pindar, by general consent the supreme lyric poet of Greece, is one of the least read of the world's great writers. A number of reasons have been given by various Greek scholars for the neglect of Pindar by modern readers. His language, based upon the Dorian dialect, poses problems for readers of his poems in the original Greek. Because all his *epinicia* or victory odes (his only complete poems extant) were written for special occasions and for special audiences, today's readers must depend upon scholarly notes for explanations of his many allusions and his abrupt transitions. The nature of the victory odes, too, makes them seem monotonous and even somewhat repetitious if a number of them are read at one time.

Edith Hamilton has said that Pindar is the most resistant of all poets to translation; the intricate form of his poems has never been more than faintly approximated in most of the attempts that have been made. In these odes Pindar achieved a masterly blend of carefully balanced structure and apparent emotional freedom, so that while he seems carried away by his feelings, he is at the same time in full control of his art. Such a fusion is difficult enough, one would suppose, for a poet himself to attain. It is even more so for a scholar or another poet to imitate successfully in translating Pindar's Greek. Ernest Myers and Sir John Sandys simply turned the Greek poems into English prose.

One reason for the tenuous appeal of Pindar was mentioned a half-century ago by Robert Tyrrell. "It is hard," says Tyrrell,

for us to figure to the imagination a form of art which partakes in nearly equal parts of the nature of a collect, a ballad, and an oratorio; or to enter into the mind of a poet who is partly

also a priest, a librettist, and a ballet master; who, while celebrating the victory of (perhaps) a boy in a wrestling match, yet feels that he is not only doing an act of divine service and worship, but preaching the sacred truth of the unity of the Hellenes and their common descent from gods and heroes.

Yet the reader who does make the attempt to imagine the ancient occasions when these odes were first performed and to understand their effect upon the Greeks who watched and listened, even if he reads them only in translation, will be richly rewarded as he becomes familiar with their form and purpose and with the artistry of the poet who wrote them.

The *epinicia* were written on contract to celebrate the winning of such events as chariot races, foot races, boxing and wrestling contests, and the combination pentathlon in four regularly held great "games" or athletic meets. (The Pythian games included competition in singing to the flute and playing on the flute and the lyre, as well as the usual athletic events and horse races.) These games were religious as well as secular, and they honored particular gods: the Olympian and Nemean games were in honor of Zeus, the Pythian of Apollo, and the Isthmian of Poseidon. The events were Panhellenic, open only to contestants from Greece or from such Greek island colonies as Rhodes and Sicily. Any soldier bearing arms to the games, which were held during periods of truce, was liable to arrest and could be freed only by ransom.

The odes were not written at the time of the victories which they celebrated but were composed for presentation at a later time. Exact details are not known but it is believed that the odes, commissioned by the family or patron of the victor, were

---

presented by trained singers at some private entertainment.

Though a close study of all forty-five of the *Epinicia* reveals many individual differences (several, in fact, are not really victory odes), most of them follow a general pattern. Composed in groups of three stanzas—strophe, antistrophe, and epode—they contain an introduction which invokes divine aid to the poet, praises the victor, and may include some reference to the contest itself (which is never actually described); a myth about gods or heroes; and eulogy of the victor, his family, and his city, along with social, moral, or even semi-philosophical commentary on life. Though the moral observations and exhortations are usually reserved for the concluding section of an ode, they often appear in other sections. The odes vary considerably in length: Olympia 12, for example, contains only nineteen lines, whereas Pythia 4 runs to 299. The present order of the odes does not follow the chronology of their composition. They are grouped according to the games in which the victories were won; and even within the four groups chronology is not followed.

Pindar belonged to the aristocracy and in the odes he celebrates the virtues and accomplishments of aristocratic families for whom the poems were composed. This praise is to be expected since he had been paid to write the poems, but one gathers that Pindar had scant interest in the less fortunate classes, whom he rarely mentions. When he says, in Pythia 2, that "wealth, with wisdom allotted thereto, is the best gift of Fortune," he seems to be expressing his own belief. A similar sentiment is found in Nemea 9: "For if with much possession a man win conspicuous honor,/there lies beyond no mark for a mortal to overtake with his feet."

The many lines in which Pindar states his faith in the gods or praises them for their gifts to men suggest the earnest sincerity of his religion. In Pythia 2 he reminds Hieron, tyrant of Syracuse, that

> It is God that accomplishes all term to hopes,

God, who overtakes the flying eagle, outpasses the dolphin in the sea; who bends under his strength the man with thoughts too high, while to others he gives honor that ages not.

In Isthmia 3 he says: "Great prowess descends upon mortals,/Zeus, from you." He often invokes the Graces or indicates his great debt to them. One of the most beautiful of the briefer *Epinicia* is Olympia 14, which is less a victory ode than a hymn in praise of the Graces who bless mankind. It begins:

> You who have your dwelling
> in the place of splendid horses, founded
> beside the waters of Kephisos:
> O queens of song and queens of shining
> Orchomenos: Graces: guardians of the
> primeval Minyai,
> hear! My prayer is to you. By your
> means all delight,
> all that is sweet, is given to mankind.

The poet refers to the Olympian victory itself only at the very end, when he asks that Echo tell Kleodamos that his son has "crowned his youthful locks with garlands won from the ennobling games."

Though there is an air of joyousness in the *Epinicia*, with many references to drinking and feasting and to processional singing to the music of flute or lyre, they are dignified by relating mortal victories of strength and skill to the glorious deeds of the gods or great heroes of the past. The myths either alluded to or told in detail include stories about Zeus, Herakles, Belerophon, Tantalus, Jason, Orestes, Peleus, and Hippolyta. The poems are also elevated by the beauty of Pindar's style, his frequent adjurations to right living, and his reminders that man's life is filled with both lights and shadows. In Pythia 8 he praises the sweetness of life when God's brightness shines on men. Yet he reminds us in Pythia 12:

> Success for men, if it comes ever, comes not unattended with difficulty. A god can end it, even today. That which is fated you cannot escape.

Though the fame of Pindar rests almost entirely upon his *Epinicia,* he is known to have written several other types of lyrics, among them hymns, paeans, dithyrambs, eulogies, and dirges. Of these, more than three hundred fragments have survived, enough to show Pindar's considerable versatility both in form and in style. Among the more beautiful of the fragments are those from the dirges, as in this picture of the dead in Elysium:

For them the sun shineth in his strength, in the world below, while here 'tis night; and, in meadows red with roses, the space before their city is shaded by the incense-tree, and is laden with golden fruits. . . .

THE EPISTLES OF HORACE

Type of work: Letters in verse
Author: Horace (Quintus Horatius Flaccus, 65-8 B.C.)
First transcribed: Book One, c. 19 B.C.; Book Two, c. 13 B.C.

The close and intimate life of the Greek city state gave rise to most of the literary forms of ancient literature, the greater number of which were adopted and adapted by the Romans. However, the epistle, the letter in verse, was a Roman literary invention brought to perfection by Horace during the first days of the Roman imperial period. With Rome administering most of the known world, friends would often be separated in different parts of the empire for years, and even if a citizen remained in Italy he would often, as did Horace, retire to his country estate. Letter writing became not merely a matter of occasional necessity, but often the only means of communication, and it was natural that poets and men of letters should turn the epistle into a literary form so that even at a distance friends could share both poetry and, in some measure, epistolary conversation.

Horace's epistles were published in two books; the first, containing twenty letters, appeared about 20 or 19 B.C.; the second, containing two long letters, probably appeared in 13 B.C. Some scholars argue that the second book of epistles should contain the famous *Epistle to the Pisos,* the *Ars Poetica.* However, this work has traditionally been published separately.

In his first book, Horace is a moralist; in the second, a literary critic. The shorter epistles in the first book, some less than fifteen lines long, are familiar and intimate; one need not doubt that they were written as letters first and poems second. In these shorter letters we see Horace, a man of forty-five who claims his days of writing lyric poetry are finished, interested in the writing of the younger generation, inviting a friend to dinner, or the like. The longer epistles of the first book, however, are much more formal and tend to the didactic; they smack of the *tour de force,* and while

they may well have been sent to the persons to whom they are addressed, they read more like open letters to the poet's entire audience. Typical of these longer letters, and setting the moral tone of the first book, is Epistle One, addressed to the poet's friend and patron, Maecenas. In it the poet bids farewell to poetry and states that in his declining years he will devote himself to philosophic inquiry. But he will be an eclectic, limiting his speculation to the precepts of no one school of philosophy, for his interest is to find what is ultimately and lastingly profitable for the achievement of virtue. The calm pursuit of wisdom, he states, is the highest good, not the frantic pursuit of things. Showing himself to be as much a Stoic as anything else, he claims the secret of happiness is not to value anything too much. Other matters he speaks of in the first epistle are the need to control the passions so as not to ruin enjoyment, the need to train one's character, and the need to adapt oneself to both company and oneself alone. Horace's wish from life, he concludes, is enough books and enough food to keep him comfortable.

With the tone thus set, Horace proceeds to write of the following matters in the successive epistles of the first book. Epistle Two, to Lollius, begins with the old doctrine that important moral lessons are to be learned from the study of Homer. Horace quickly turns to his real subject, however, which is the foolishness of putting off or not exerting the effort requisite for moral self-improvement. Epistle Three, to Julius Florus, was written to a friend who was abroad campaigning with Claudius; the poet inquires about other young friends on Claudius' staff. He is particularly interested in their literary activity. Epistle Four, to Tibullus, the poet, is a short note of warm friendship in which Horace gently recommends the Epicurean idea that one should live each day as if it were his last. Epistle Five to Torquatus is an invitation to a frugal but cheerful and friendly dinner party. Epistle Six, to Numicius, is a lay sermon on the famous Horation phrase, *Nil admirari,* "wonder at nothing." The wise man should love nothing but virtue: live, and be happy. Epistle Seven, to Maecenas, is a note of appreciation for various favors. Horace apologizes for absenting himself from Rome for so long, and he uses the occasion to describe the ideal giver and, with some humor, the ideal receiver. Self-sufficiency, he claims, is preferable to all other blessings. Epistle Eight, to Celsus Albinovanus, is a letter to a member of Tiberius' staff. The poet describes his own ill health and admonishes Celsus to bear up well under prosperity. Epistle Nine, to Claudius Tiberius Nero, is a graceful letter of recommendation for Horace's friend Septimus. Epistle Ten, to Aristius Fuscus, praises the superiority of country life as being more conducive to the contented mind and more favorable to liberty of spirit than the city life of Fuscus.

Epistle Eleven, to Bullatus, is an attempt to call this friend back to Rome from Asia, where he has retired because of his despair over the civil wars. Happiness, Horace says, is not in travel but in the mind and is to be achieved anywhere or nowhere. Epistle Twelve, to Iccius, ironically ridicules miserliness, introduces a friend, and gives news of recent events in the empire. Epistle Thirteen, to Vinnius Asina, cautions Asina, Horace's emissary, to present certain of Horace's writings to Augustus at a propitious and proper moment, and with due decorum. Epistle Fourteen chastises the caretaker of his farm, to whom the letter is written, for missing city life. Horace briefly reminisces about his wild younger years and then advises the wisdom of contentment. Epistle Fifteen, to C. Numonius Vala, asks about the situation and conditions of the town of Velia, where Horace has been advised by his physician to take a

cure. Again he comments on country life. Epistle Sixteen, to Quinctius, describes the situation and advantages of Horace's Sabine farm. His description is detailed enough that its position can be determined. The poet goes on to philosophize on the nature of true virtue and the self-sufficiency and freedom of the virtuous man. Epistle Seventeen, to Scaeva, is a letter of advice to one who would seek advantage by frequenting the company of the great. The friendship of the great, the poet says is a good thing, but one must always solicit favors from them with modesty and caution. Epistle Eighteen, to Lollius, in a more elaborate way treats of the same topic as the seventeenth. Horace discusses the tact and discretion a client of the great must have; he concludes with remarks concerning peace of mind, a quality difficult to achieve when one depends on the favor of the great. Epistle Nineteen, to Maecenas, is a review of the poet's literary career; he decries the folly of slavish imitation, and he attacks his detractors. Epistle Twenty, addressed to his book, is developed as an argument between the poet and his now completed first book of epistles. The book is spoken to as if it were a young slave, a favorite of his master, who wants to be sold out of a quiet country household and into an exciting city house where he can seek advancement. Horace explains all the troubles and chances he must undergo. He ends the poem with remarks on what he expects from posterity. The tone of the nineteenth and twentieth epistles implies that the poet is finished now with his writing career.

The impression we receive from these twenty letters is that middle-aged Horace is feeling old and is in delicate health, and that he will write no more. Perhaps he really did believe he was through with poetry; however, he still had a few more poems to write, and among them, of course, were the two long discourses on literature (companion pieces, in effect, to the *Ars Poetica*) that make up the second volume of epistles.

The first of these two letters is to Augustus. After first paying the emperor the highest kind of compliments, Horace plunges into a consideration of the current state of literature. First he intervenes in the then raging Roman "battle of the ancients and the moderns." He acknowledges the greatness of the earlier Greek poets, but he wants to have the early Latin poets respected more than they usually are. Horace sketches out the history of Latin poetry from the beginnings up through the Greeks "capture" of their captor, Rome, and then on to his own day. Looking at the present state of letters, Horace judges (and history shows him to have been quite correct) that the drama would not reach great heights in Rome: the taste of the people was for spectacle, mimes, and elaborate staging. But non-dramatic poetry, he thinks will do very well; for Augustus, whose taste is impeccable, will encourage poetry and will not be deceived by second-rate poets.

The second epistle of the last book is to Julius Florus, a friend of the poet who apparently wanted also to be a poet. This letter is much more personal in tone than the letter to Augustus and is full of intimate detail. Horace begins by testifying that he is rather lazy and undependable now that he no longer must write poetry in order to stay alive, as he did when he was young. Moreover, poetry is one of the follies of the young and, now that he is growing old, he must give it up as he has his other youthful pastimes. How, he asks, can a man write real poetry amidst the hustle and bustle and distractions of Rome? The real poet must live and write in the quiet countryside. The poets who stay in the city form worthless mutual admiration societies out of which comes no true criticism. A good poet is a good critic too, and he can take and use valid criticism of his own work. Bad poets hate criticism of any kind. Perhaps the happiest writer is the madman who writes very badly, but who thinks he writes divinely. At any rate, Horace concludes, at his age it is proper to think of gaining happiness, which is found in calm and content, not wealth.

EPITAPH OF A SMALL WINNER

Type of work: Novel
Author: Joaquim Maria Machado de Assis (1839-1908)
Type of plot: Philosophical realism
Time: of plot: 1805-1869
Locale: Rio de Janeiro, Brazil
First published: 1880

Principal characters:
BRAZ CUBAS, a wealthy, cultured Brazilian
MARCELLA, his first mistress
VIRGILIA, his fiancée, later his mistress
LOBO NEVES, Virgilia's husband
QUINCAS BORBA, a philosopher and pickpocket

Critique:

This novel, written by one of Brazil's leading men of letters, was not made available in English translation until 1952, even though it had long been a favorite with readers in the original Portuguese and in Spanish translations. Machado de Assis himself was president of the Brazilian Academy of Letters from its foundation in 1897 until his death in 1908. *Epitaph of a Small Winner* is the story of an ordinary man who sums up the profit of living as nothing, except that he had left no children to whom he could pass on the misery of human existence. Because he left no children to endure life, he was, says the author, a small winner in the game of life. Obviously Machado de Assis' attitude is one of complete and ironic pessimism. As the English translator points out, the book combines the twin themes of nature's indifference to man and man's own egoism. Readers familiar with eighteenth century fiction will recognize many stylistic peculiarities similar to those in Sterne's *Tristram Shandy*.

The Story:

Braz Cubas, a wealthy Brazilian, died of pneumonia in his sixty-fifth year. After his death he decided to write his autobiography, to while away a part of eternity and to give mankind some record of his life.

Braz was born in 1805. His childhood was an easy one, for his father was extremely wealthy and indulgent, only pretending to be severe with his child for the sake of appearances. One of the earliest experiences the boy remembered was the elation of the Brazilians over the defeat of Napoleon, an occasion marked in his memory by the gift of a small sword. The sword was the most important aspect of the occasion, and Braz remarked that each person has his own "sword" which makes occasions important.

As a child, Braz Cubas did not like school. In his seventeenth year he had his first love affair with a courtesan named Marcella. Trying to please his mistress, Braz spent all the money he could borrow from his mother, and then gave promissory notes to fall due on the day he inherited his father's estate. His father, learning of the affair, paid off his son's debts and shipped him off to a university in Spain. At first Braz hoped to take Marcella with him. She refused to go.

Graduated from the university and awarded a degree, Braz admitted that he knew very little. He then took advantage of his father's liberality and wealth and spent several years traveling about Europe. Called back to Rio de Janeiro by news that his mother was dying of can-

EPITAPH OF A SMALL WINNER by Joaquim Maria Machado de Assis. Translated by William L. Grossman. By permission of the publishers, The Noonday Press. Copyright, 1952, by William Leonard Grossman.

cer, he arrived home in time to see her before she died. After her death he went into retirement, remaining in seclusion until his father came to him with plans for a marriage and a seat in the Brazilian legislative body. After some vacillation Braz decided to obey his father's wishes. The reason for his hesitation was a love affair with a rather beautiful girl. His discovery that she was lame, however, turned him away from her. On his return to social life he learned that the young woman his father had picked out for him, a girl named Virgilia, had position, wealth, and beauty. It was through her father's influence that the elder Cubas expected his son to get ahead politically. Unfortunately for the schemes of both father and son, Virgilia met Lobo Neves, a young man with more ambition and greater prospects. She decided to marry him, a decision which ended, at least temporarily, prospects of a political career for Braz.

Disappointed and disgruntled with life, he accidentally met Marcella, his former mistress. He found her greatly changed, for smallpox had destroyed her beauty. After losing her looks, she had left her earlier profession to become the keeper of a small jewelry shop.

Disappointment over his son's failure to win Virgilia was too much for his father, who died shortly afterward. There was a great to-do after the father's death, for Braz' brother-in-law turned out to be an avaricious man who wanted his wife, Braz' sister, to have as much of the estate as possible. Braz accepted calmly the selfish and unfortunate aspect of human nature thus revealed and agreed, for his sister's sake, to be reconciled with his greedy brother-in-law.

Not very long after his father's death, Braz learned from Virgilia's brother that Virgilia and her husband were returning to Rio de Janeiro. Braz was pleased; he was still in love with her. A few days after the return of Virgilia and her husband, he met them at a ball. Virgilia and Braz danced several waltzes together and fell more deeply in love than they had ever been while Braz was courting her. They continued to meet and before long Virgilia became his mistress.

One day Braz found a package in which were several bundles of banknotes. He kept the money and later used it to establish a trust fund for Doña Placida, a former servant of Virgilia's family, who maintained the house in which Virgilia and Braz kept their assignations. They managed for several years to keep their affair a secret, so that Braz could be a guest in Virgilia's home as well. In fact, he and Lobo Neves were good friends.

One day Braz met Quincas Borba, an old schoolmate who had been reduced to begging. The man took some money from Braz and, as he discovered later, also stole his watch. That night Braz suggested to Virgilia that they run away. She refused to do so. They had a lovers' quarrel, followed by a tender scene of repentance.

A short time later Lobo Neves was offered the governorship of a province, and he suggested that Braz accompany him as his secretary. The situation was inviting to the two lovers, but they knew that in the smaller provincial capital their secret could not long be hidden. Their problems were unexpectedly solved when superstitious Neves refused the government post because the document appointing him was dated on the thirteenth of the month.

The love affair continued until Virgilia became pregnant. Neither of the lovers doubted that Braz was the father of the child, and he acted very much like a husband who expected to be presented with his first-born. The child, not carried the full time, died at birth, much to the sorrow of Virgilia and Braz, and of the husband as well, who thought the child was his.

One day Braz received a letter from Quincas Borba, the begging schoolmate who had stolen his watch. Having improved his finances, the beggar had become a philosopher, a self-styled humanist. Borba's ideas fascinated Braz, who had always fancied himself an intellectual and a literary man. He was also pleased when Borba sent him a watch as good as the one he had stolen. Braz spent a great deal of time with Borba, for Neves had become suspicious of the relationship between his wife and her lover, and the two were discreet enough to stay away from each other for a time.

At last Virgilia and her husband left Rio de Janeiro after Neves received another political appointment. For a time Braz felt like a widower. Lonely, he himself turned to public life. Defeated for office, he then became the publisher of an opposition newspaper, but his venture was not successful. He also fell in love and finally decided to get married. Once more he was disappointed, for his fiancée died during an epidemic.

The years passed rather uneventfully. Braz grew older, and so did his friends. Not many weeks after the death of Quincas Borba, who had become a close companion, Braz himself fell ill of pneumonia. One visitor during his last illness was Virgilia, whose husband had died, but even her presence was not enough to keep Braz from slipping into delirium. In his dying moments he cast up the accounts of his life and decided that in the game of life he was the winner by only a small margin, in that he had brought no one else into the world to suffer the misery of life.

Further Critical Evaluation of the Work:

Machado de Assis' ancestry is slightly mysterious. His father was supposedly a "son of free mulattos" and a house-painter, and his mother an impoverished white washerwoman, but these versions of his background are open to question. Although John Nist, for example, wrote that Machado de Assis left the slums of Rio de Janeiro to found Brazil's Academy of Letters, after having conquered Brazil with the greatest outpouring of literary talent in that country's history, some persons question the tradition that he grow up in poverty in Rio's slums. While little is known of Machado de Assis until he reached fifteen years of age, he is known to have had only a primary-level education. It is also known that a French bakeshop owner taught him French and that he was an autodidact, acquiring his impressive culture by educating himself. Even though rather finely featured, he was spindly-legged, myopic, rachitic, a stammerer, endured alarming epileptic seizures, and suffered intestinal disorders. He was Caucasian in features, but his African blood was an added problem for him in nineteenth century Brazil. His white wife's brothers strongly opposed her marriage to Machado de Assis on racial grounds.

Machado de Assis has been awarded a unique place in Brazilian literature and is considered its most singular eminence. Brazilians have called him their sphinx, their enigma, their myth. His writings, including *Epitaph of a Small Winner*, have been contradictorily labeled brilliant, dry, rich, colorless, or ironic, refined, intuitive, pure, correct, limpid, balanced, boring and elegant. Some Brazilians smell the scent of Brazilianism exuding from his pages, or a literary nativism so strong as to comprise a natural emanation. But Pedro Calmon wrote that he did not seem Brazilian, and his works were once described as being psychologically French. Besides *Epitaph of a Small Winner* (in Portuguese as *Memórias Pósthumas de Braz Cubas*), three of his novels and fifteen of his other works have been translated into English, while his reading public in the Northern Hemisphere grows each year. Literary critics commonly eulogize him for stylistic purity, perfect linguistic knowledge, and a great inner richness. It was once said that he knew well all the secrets of the art of writing, and that his intuitive insight into man's intimate peculiarities was remarkable.

As is evident in *Epitaph of a Small Winner* and the three novels that chronologically followed it, Machado de Assis became steadily more disillusioned with human beings. It is said that these novels, plus his masterpiece, *Dom Casmurro*, published twenty-eight years after *Epitaph of a Small Winner*, supply the most convincing evidence for his ever-continuing disillusionment. In any event, each of Machado de Assis' most celebrated novels paint a wasted human life.

His disenchantment with human beings became universal, and his soul was ever more strained by inner turmoil. He liked to expose human egotism and believed that all nature revealed man's idiocy, that everything in the universe resented what it was and pined to be something else. He came to view man as always bouncing, ball-like, until his passions destroyed him. Sometimes compared to William Somerset Maugham for his inferiority complex, Machado de Assis deliberately withheld information about his personal life and hinted that it had little to do with his writing. In *Epitaph of a Small Winner*, however, Machado de Assis puts into Braz Cubas' mouth the statement that although many European novelists had made tours of one or more countries, he, Braz Cubas, had made a tour of life. In this tour, added Braz Cubas, he had seen human assininity, human evil, and the sorry vanity of all matter.

Machado de Assis strove for thirty years to master the art of narration. *Epitaph of a Small Winner* as well as his other early works, give a hint of the development to come, for he always experimented with his storytelling skills. He usually used short sentences, brief chapters, and deliberately interrupted narrative. He was eventually credited with brilliant manipulation of language and haunting character analysis through skilled use of symbols and metaphors. Machado de Assis has also been likened to a hard-rock miner delving into the earth to seek man's infernal image. He cautioned his readers to scrutinize his lines for an interlocking pattern that integrated the various parts. He tinged names of characters with significance and color, and derived inspiration from Shakespeare. He withdrew from the Romanticist movement that was literarily dominant during his youth and became a Realist. In 1907, shortly before his death, he noted that thirty years time had separated two editions of one of his works, and that these thirty years illustrated the difference in composition and temper of his writing.

Machado de Assis rarely left his native Rio de Janeiro, entwined in its granite mountains and curving bay, and never journeyed far when he did.

He remained an autodidact in ideas and cultural values to the end of his life. He died as he lived, loathing the idea of being either a bore, spectacle, or hypocrite. As he was dying, attended by Brazil's most famous writers of the day, he wanted to call a priest, but then reflected that it would be hypocritical.

In any event, it can be said that despite Machado de Assis' celebrated pessimism and bleak insight into human nature, none of his novels alleges that it is impossible to view the world in a more cheerful light than he did; they merely state that it would be difficult.

William Freitas

EREC AND ENIDE

Type of work: Poem
Author: Chrétien de Troyes (c.1140-c.1190)
Type of plot: Chivalric romance
Time of plot: Sixth century
Locale: Arthurian England
First transcribed: Before 1164

Principal characters:
KING ARTHUR
QUEEN GUINEVERE
EREC, a knight of the Round Table and son of King Lac
ENIDE, his bride
GUIVRET THE LITTLE, Erec's friend and benefactor

Critique:

Erec and Enide is chronologically the first of a group of metrical romances by a master tale teller of the medieval period about whom very little is known. More important, it is the oldest romance on Arthurian materials extant in any language. In it the more primitive Celtic elements of the writer's sources have been lost or are almost completely obscured; King Arthur and his knights are now models of the highly sophisticated and intricately detailed chivalric code growing out of the courts of love which flourished in France during the Middle Ages. Written in eight-syllable rhyming couplets, and sometimes called the first novel because of its consistent plot, this story is one of four which give us the most idealized expression of the code of chivalry by a single writer of medieval times.

The Story:

One Easter season, while King Arthur held his court in the royal town of Cardigan, he summoned all his knights to a hunt for the White Stag. Sir Gawain, hearing of the king's wish, was displeased and said that no good would come of that ancient custom, for the law of the hunt decreed that the successful hunter must also kiss the lady whom he considered the most beautiful damsel of the court. As Sir Gawain noted, there was likely to be dissension among the assembled knights; each was prepared to defend his own true love as the loveliest and gentlest lady in the land, and he would be angered by the slight put upon her if she were not so chosen.

At daybreak the hunters set out. After them rode Queen Guinevere, attended by Erec, a fair and brave knight, and one of the queen's damsels, a king's daughter. While they waited by the wayside to hear the baying of the hounds or the call of a bugle, they saw coming toward them a strange knight, his lady, and a dwarf who carried a knotted scourge. First the queen sent her damsel to ask who the knight and his fair companion might be, but the dwarf, barring her way, struck the damsel across the hand with his whip. Then Erec rode forward and the dwarf lashed him across the face and neck. Being unarmed, Erec made no attempt to chastise the dwarf or his haughty master, but he vowed that he would follow the strange knight until he could find arms to hire or borrow that he might avenge the insult to the queen.

In the fair town to which the strange knight and his companions presently led him, Erec found lodgings with a vavasor who told him the reason for all the stir and bustle that Erec had seen as he rode through the gates. On the next day a fine sparrow hawk would be given to the knight who could defend against all comers the beauty and goodness of his lady. The haughty knight, who had won the bird in two successive years, would be allowed to keep it if his challenge went unanswered on the morrow. At the home of the vavasor Erec met his host's daughter Enide, who in spite of her tattered garments was the most radiantly beautiful damsel in Christendom. With her as his lady and with arms borrowed from his host, Erec challenged and defeated in single combat the arrogant knight who was defending the hawk. Then Erec dispatched the vanquished knight, whose name was Yder, to Queen Guinevere to do with at her pleasure, along with his lady and his dwarf. With them he sent word that he would return with his beautiful bride, the damsel Enide.

Erec promised Enide's father great riches and two towns to rule in his own land, but he refused all offers to have Enide dressed in robes suitable to her new station: he wished all in King Arthur's court to see that in spite of her humble garments she was the most beautiful lady who ever lived. So great was her beauty that King Arthur, who himself had killed the White Stag, kissed her without a demur from the assembled knights and ladies. The king also granted Eric the boon of a speedy marriage, so eager was the young knight for the love of his promised bride. The ceremony was performed by the Archbishop of Canterbury at the time of the Pentecost before an assemblage of knights and ladies from every corner of the kingdom, and the celebration continued for a fortnight.

A month after Pentecost a great tournament was held near Tenebroc and in the lists there Erec showed himself the most valiant of all the knights assembled. On his return he received from the king permission to visit his own land, and he and Enide set out with an escort of sixty knights. On the fifth day they arrived in Carnant, where King Lac welcomed his son and his bride with much honor. Meanwhile, Erec found so much pleasure in his wife's company that he had no thought for other pastimes. When tournaments were held in the region around, he sent his knights to the forays but he himself remained behind in dalliance with the fair Enide. At last people began to

gossip and say that he had turned a craven in arms. These reports so distressed Enide that one morning while they were still abed she began to lament the way in which the brave and hardy knight had changed because of his love for her. Overhearing her words, Erec was moved to anger, and he told her to rise and prepare herself at once to take the road with him on a journey of knight-errantry in search of whatever perils he might encounter by chance. At the beginning of the journey he gave orders that she was never to tell him of anything she might see, nor to speak to him unless he addressed her first.

As Enide rode ahead, forbidden to speak, she lamented her disclosure and their sudden departure from the life she had enjoyed with her loving husband. She disobeyed him, however, when they were about to be attacked by three robber knights, and again when they were assailed by five recreants. Erec, having overcome all who opposed him, felt no gratitude for her wifely warnings and fears for his safety, but spoke harshly to her because she had disobeyed his command that she was under any circumstance to remain silent until he gave her leave to speak.

That night, since they knew of no town or shelter nearby, they slept in an open field. There the squire of Count Galoin came upon them the next day and conducted them to lodgings in the town where the count was master. That nobleman, going to pay his respects to the strange knight and his lovely lady, was much smitten with Enide's beauty, so much so that, going to the place where she sat apart, he expressed his pity for her obvious distress and offered to make her mistress of all his lands. When Enide refused, he declared that he would take her by force. Fearful for her husband's life, Enide pretended to do his pleasure. It was arranged that on the next day the count's knights were to overtake the travelers and seize Enide by force. Erec, coming to her rescue, would be killed, and she would be free to take the count as her lord. Once more Enide disobeyed her husband and told him of Count Galoin's plan. Forewarned, Erec overcame his assailants and knocked the false count senseless from his steed. When Galoin's followers would have pursued Erec and Enide, the count restrained them, praising Enide's prudence and virtue and the bravery of her knight.

Departing from Count Galoin's lands, the travelers came to a castle from which the lord came riding on a great steed to offer Erec combat at arms. Enide saw him coming but did not dare tell her husband for fear of his wrath. At last she did speak, however, and Erec realized her love for him that made her disobedient to his commands. The knight who challenged Erec was of small stature but stout heart and both were wounded in the fight. Though the doughty little knight lost, he put up such a good fight that he and Erec became friends. Guivret the Little invited Erec to have his wounds dressed and to rest at his castle, but Erec thanked him courteously and rode with Enide on his way.

At length they arrived at a wood where King Arthur had come with a large hunting party. By then Erec was so begrimed and bloodied that Sir Kay the seneschal did not recognize him. When he would have taken the wounded knight to the king's camp, Erec refused and they fought until Sir Kay was unhorsed. Sir Gawain then rode out to encounter the strange knight, and he was able to bring Erec to the place where the king had ordered tents set up in anticipation of their coming. There was great joy in that meeting for the king and Queen Guinevere, but distress at Erec's wounds. Although the king pleaded with Erec to rest there until his hurts were healed, the knight refused to be turned aside or delayed on his journey, and early the next morning he and Enide set out once more.

In a strange forest they heard the cries of a lady in distress. Leaving Enide to await his return, Erec rode in the direction of the sound and found a damsel weeping because two giants had carried

away her knight. Riding in pursuit, Erec killed the giants and rescued the knight, whose name was Cadoc of Tabriol. Later he sent Cadoc and the damsel to King Arthur's camp, to tell the story of how he fared. Meanwhile, Erec's wounds had reopened and he lost so much blood that he fell from his horse in a swoon.

While Enide was weeping over his prostrate body, a count with his suite came riding through the forest. The nobleman gave orders that the body was to be taken to Limors and prepared for burial. On their arrival at the count's palace he declared his intention of espousing Enide at once. Although she refused to give her consent, the ceremony was performed in great haste and guests were summoned to a wedding banquet that night.

Erec, recovering from his deep swoon, awoke in time to see the wretched count strike Enide across the face because her grief was so great that she could neither eat nor drink at her new husband's bidding. Springing from the funeral bier, he drew his sword and struck the count on the head with such force that blood and brains flowed out. While the other knights and squires retreated in fear of the ghostly presence that had so suddenly returned to life, the two made their escape, Erec meanwhile assuring his wife that he was now convinced of her devotion and love.

Meanwhile, Guivret the Little had received word that a mortally wounded knight had been found in the forest and that the lord of Limors had carried off the dead man's wife. Coming to see that the fallen knight received proper burial and to aid his lady if she were in distress the doughty little knight came upon Erec, whom he failed to recognize in the murky moonlight, and struck a blow which knocked Erec unconscious. Enide and Guivret remained by the stricken man all that night, and in the morning they proceeded to Guivret's castle. There, attended by Enide and Guivret's sisters, Erec was nursed back to health. After his recovery, escorted by Guivret and burdened with gifts, the couple prepared to return to King Arthur's court.

Toward nightfall the travelers saw in the distance the towers of a great fortress. Guivret said that the town was named Brandigant, in which there was a perilous passage called the "Joy of the Court." King Evrain welcomed the travelers with great courtesy, but that night, while they feasted, he also warned Erec against attempting the mysterious feat which no knight had thus far survived. Despite the disapproval of his friend and his host Erec swore to attempt the passage.

The next morning he was conducted into a magic garden filled with all manner of fruits and flowers, past the heads and helmets of unfortunate though brave knights who had also braved danger in order to blow the magic horn whose blast would signify joy to King Evrain's land. At the end of a path he found a beautiful damsel seated on a couch. While he stood looking at her, a knight appeared to engage him in combat. They fought until the hour of noon had passed; then the knight fell exhausted. He revealed that he had been held in thrall in the garden by an oath given to his mistress, whose one wish had been his eternal presence by her side. Erec then blew the horn and all the people rejoiced to find him safe. There was great joy also when the knight of the garden was released from his bondage and the beautiful damsel identified herself as the cousin of Enide.

Erec and Enide, with Guivret, continued their journey to the court of King Arthur, where they were received with gladness and honor. When his father died, Erec returned to reign in his own land. There he and Enide were crowned in a ceremony of royal splendor in the presence of King Arthur and all the nobles of his realm.

Further Critical Evaluation of the Work:

Like *Yvain,* by the same author, *Erec and Enide* deals with the conflict between and the attempt to reconcile knightly and marital responsibilities. It is about many other things but this problem is its main theme.

Apparently Chrétien de Troyes himself thought much of the work: in the romance's first paragraph he tells us " . . . and now I shall begin the tale which will be remembered so long as Christendom endures. This is Chrétien's boast."

Perhaps his scarcely modest claim was well-founded, for this romance of Arthurian England in the sixth century, has outlived many other medieval romances. Even today it offers the reader riches of varied sorts. A mélange of real and unreal incidents, exact and exaggerated statistics, logical and implausible motivation, wildly supernatural events in close juxtaposition with homely, concrete ones, mark his poem.

But from all these seemingly warring elements, Chrétien de Troyes manages to devise a well-constructed plot. Perhaps to the casual reader, Erec's surviving all his ordeals, the various adventures that he and Enide, his wife, encounter in their wanderings, the apparently unconnected strangers they meet, as well as assorted dwarfs, giants, Morgan le Fay with a magic plaster —even a knight in "vermillion arms"—appear unlikely to say the least. But the author, in welding diverse and sometimes incongruous factors together, has a serious purpose. He was interested in problems of conscience within the individual: choices he had to make in the face of conflicting loyalties and personal emotions. He was definitely intrigued with how man solves these individually as a member of his social group. All the usual and contrived situations of medieval romance served Chrétien de Troyes as means of setting forth these problems—providing the complicating webs to entrap the protagonists.

Although Erec, a king's son, married the daughter of a poor vavasour, or country squire, Chrétien takes care to make them equal in beauty and gentilesse. However, when because of excessive love of his wife, reports circulate that Erec has permitted himself to desert the tourneys and quests, thus failing to prove his knighthood, the story takes up its serious purpose. For, after all, this is a tale of married love subjected to the pressures of a man's other obligations and duties: those to his code and to proving his own valor. It is also a story of a wife's patient endurance of her husband's eccentricities and abuse. In many respects Chrétien de Troyes intends *Erec and Enide*, for all its comic incidents and exaggerated postures, to be a sober narrative of love-testing. In this it is similar to Chaucer's "Clerk's Tale" on the familiar "patient Griselda" theme.

Enide's unquestioning obedience may disturb the modern reader, who still cannot fault Chrétien's logic of her reasoning and emotions. It is characteristic of the author that he proves himself an expert at love analysis, particularly within the minds of his heroines. Such subtleties of thought are rare in medieval romance, but Chrétien de Troyes' women in love keenly verbalize their considerations in matters of the heart. Enide, for example, reproaches herself for telling Erec that men say his reputation has suffered, that he is a recreant and that they blame her for it. In a soliloquy she upbraids herself for pride and says it is right she must suffer woe: "One does not know what good fortune is until he has made trial of evil." Enide knows, as her author comments: " . . . she had now made her bed, and must lie in it." Not until the fourteenth century in Chaucer's Criseyde does one find a romance heroine engaged in such subtle love analysis.

Chrétien manages to offer convincing characters, not stock types. In *Erec and Enide* that which he wants readers to concentrate on is not the battles or such farcical scenes as the one where Enide must marry the Count against her will, but Erec's gradual realization of the great love his wife has for him. More important perhaps for the story is Erec's own statement at the testing's end: " . . . for I love you now more than ever I did before." He has learned humility and what faithfulness involves.

In a time when *fin amour,* or courtly love, was supposed to be the reigning material for poets and romance writers—in other words, adulterous love— Chrétien de Troyes shows far more concern for love within the marriage bond. As a matter of fact, he seems to stress this kind of love as the ideal union. When he must deal with adulterous love as in his *Lancelot,* he seems ill at ease and handles both plot and characterization with less finesse. Most critics as a result conclude that in this latter work he wrote upon demand, not inclination. But in both *Yvain* and *Erec and Enide* he concentrates on the difficulties in marriage and their solution.

We feel that if it is true as Chrétien de Troyes also said at the beginning of this romance, that "jongleurs were accustomed to garble and mutilate" the story, he himself has ordered such material into a unified, coherent whole. He does this well. And the reader feels Chrétien was not so interested in reviving customs and feats of valor characteristic of Arthurian knights in a time long past, but of involving his French audience in a tale they could understand and with which they could identify.

Chrétien de Troyes not only successfully develops the plot; he also shows progression in character development. He brings together the lavish ornamentation of watered silk, ivory, gold tapestries, red armor; ragged garments of a peasant girl in a poor household; hardships of wayfaring on roads infested with evils of all sorts; and finally a happy ending with the elevation of King Arthur in a brilliant coronation ceremony for the reconciled Erec and Enide. He has managed with consummate artistry to make it all entertaining and at the same time to pose comments upon problems of married love, not only as they might have existed in the sixth century, or in the twelfth, but perhaps always.

Muriel B. Ingham

EREWHON

Type of work: Novel
Author: Samuel Butler (1835-1902)
Type of plot: Utopian satire
Time of plot: 1870's
Locale: Erewhon and England
First published: 1872

Principal characters:
　HIGGS, a traveler in Erewhon
　CHOWBOK, a native
　NOSNIBOR, a citizen of Erewhon
　AROWHENA, his daughter

Critique:

Erewhon is an anagram of nowhere, but the institutions satirized in this story of an imaginary land are unmistakably British. Beginning as an adventure story, the book becomes an elaborate allegory. Some of Butler's satire grows out of the ideas of Darwin and Huxley. In the main the book is original and often prophetic, The "straighteners" of Erewhon are the psychologists of today, and the treatment of Erewhonian criminals is somewhat like that advocated by our own liberal thinkers. The novel is humorous, but it is also serious.

The Story:

Higgs a young man of twenty-two, worked on a sheep farm. From the plains he looked often at the seemingly impassable mountain range that formed the edge of the sheep country and wondered about the land beyond those towering peaks. From one old native named Chowbok he learned that the country was forbidden. Chowbok assumed a strange pose when questioned further and uttered unearthly cries. Curious, Higgs persuaded Chowbok to go on a trip with him into the mountains.

They were unable to find a pass through the mountains. One day Higgs came upon a small valley and went up it alone. He found that it led through the mountains. When he went back to get Chowbok, he saw the old native fleeing toward the plains. He went on alone. After climbing down treacherous cliffs and crossing a river on a reed raft, he finally came to beautiful rolling plain.

He passed by some strange manlike statues which made terrifying noises as the wind circled about them. He recognized in them the reason for Chowbok's performance.

Higgs awoke next morning to see a flock of goats about him, two girls herding them. When the girls saw him they ran and brought some men to look at him. All of them were physically handsome. Convinced at last that Higgs was a human being, they took him to a small town close by. There his clothing was searched and a watch he had with him was confiscated. The men seemed to be especially interested in his health, and he was allowed to leave only after a strict medical examination. He wondered why there had been such confusion over his watch until he was shown a museum in which was kept old pieces of machinery. Finally he was put in jail.

In jail he learned the language and something of the strange customs of the country, which was called Erewhon. The oddest custom was to consider disease a crime; anyone who was sick was tried and put in jail. On the other hand, people who committed robbery or murder were treated sympathetically and given hospital care. Shortly afterward the jailor informed Higgs that he had been summoned to appear before the king and queen, and that he was to be the guest of a man named Nosnibor. Nosnibor had embezzled a large sum of money from a poor widow, but he was now recovering from his illness. The widow, Higgs learned, would be tried and sentenced for allowing herself to be imposed upon.

In the capital Higgs stayed with Nosnibor and his family and paid several visits to the court. He was well received because he had blond hair, a rarity among the Erewhonians. He learned a great deal about the past history of the country. Twenty-five hundred years before a prophet had preached that it was unlawful to eat meat, as man should not kill his fellow creatures. For several hundred years the Erewhonians were vegetarians. Then another sage showed that animals were no more the fellow creatures of man than plants were, and that if man could not kill and eat animals he should not kill and eat plants. The logic of his arguments overthrew the old philosophy. Two hundred years before a great scientist had presented the idea that machines had minds and feelings and that if man were not careful the machine would finally become the ruling creature on earth. Consequently all machines had been scrapped.

The economy of the country was unusual. There were two monetary systems, one worthless except for spiritual meaning, one used in trade. The more respected system was the valueless one, and its work was carried on in Musical Banks where people exchanged coins for music. The state religion was a worship of various qualities of godhead, such as love, fear, and wisdom, and the main goddess, Ydgrun, was at the same time an abstract concept and a silly, cruel woman. Higgs learned much of the religion from Arowhena, one of Nosnibor's daughters. She was a beautiful girl, and the two fell in love.

Because Nosnibor insisted that his older daughter, Zulora, be married first,

Higgs and his host had an argument, and Higgs found lodgings elsewhere. Arowhena met him often at the Musical Banks. Higgs visited the University of Unreason, where the young Erewhonian boys were taught to do anything except that which was practical. They studied obsolete languages and hypothetical sciences. He saw a relationship between these schools and the mass-mind which the educational system in England was producing. Higgs also learned that money was considered a symbol of duty, and that the more money a man had the better man he was.

Nosnibor learned that Higgs was meeting Arowhena secretly. Then the king began to worry over the fact that Higgs had entered the country with a watch, and he feared that Higgs might try to bring machinery back into use. Planning an escape, Higgs proposed to the queen that he make a balloon trip to talk with the god of the air. The queen was delighted with the idea. The king hoped that Higgs would fall and kill himself.

Higgs smuggled Arowhena aboard the balloon with him. The couple soon found themselves high in the air and moving over the mountain range. When the balloon settled on the sea, Higgs and Arowhena were picked up by a passing ship. In England, where they were married, Higgs tried to get up an expedition to go back to Erewhon. Only the missionaries listened to his story. Then Chowbok, Higgs' faithless native friend, showed up in England teaching religion, and his appearance convinced people that Erewhon actually did exist. Higgs hoped to return to the country soon to teach it Christianity.

Further Critical Evaluation of the Work:

Erewhon is Butler's attempt to work into novel form four philosophic papers written between 1860 and 1870; these appear as the chapters in the novel entitled "The Book of the Machines," "The World of the Unborn," "The Musical Banks," and "Some Erewhonian Trials." While apparently dissimilar, these pivotal chapters all treat the theme of free will, thus unifying the book.

In adapting to his environment, man constructs machines which threaten his survival. With prophetic insight, Butler examines this irony. He argues that the laws governing organic evolution also apply to machines and their development. Challenging the distinction between "organic" and "inorganic," Butler reduces all processes to their mechanical basis and shows how machines are evolving independently of human control. Like Marx, he sees man's nature as changing under the impact of a mechanized environment. But unlike Marx, he predicts man's ultimate enslavement by this environment.

Both comic and serious elements mingle in the Erewhonian myth of pre-existence. Because the "unborn" *will* to become humans, they must bear the consequences of their choice. Thus the Erewhonians make babies sign "birth formulae" which absolve parents from responsibility for the deprivations and deficiencies which go with living. The unborn also elect to share man's essential fate: to be "fettered" to free will while knowing that its proper exercise requires such accidental advantages as innate talent and high social position.

In "The Musical Banks," Butler satirizes commercialism's corruption of religion; the Banks symbolize the existence of "a kingdom not of this world" whose laws measure and judge human laws. For Butler, there is a Divine Will which inhabits the subconscious and which all cultures tacitly acknowledge. In the trials of the unfortunate and sick, Butler uses absurdity to examine further the nature of freedom and responsibility. In Erewhon, crime is a disease and disease a crime; Butler accepts the first equation while mocking the second.

ESSAIS

Type of work: Essays
Author: Michel Eyquem de Montaigne (1533-1592)
First published: Books I-II, 1580; I-II, revised, 1582; I-III, 1588; I-III, revised, 1595

Montaigne began his essays as a stoical humanist, continued them as a skeptic, and concluded them as a human being concerned with man. Substantially, this evolution is the one upon which Montaigne scholars are agreed. Surely these three phases of his thought are apparent in his *Essais,* for one may find, in these volumes, essays in which Montaigne considers how a man should face pain and die, such as "To Philosophize Is to Learn to Die"; essays in which the skeptical attack on dogmatism in philosophy and religion is most evident, such as the famous "Apology for Raimond Sebond"; and essays in which the writer makes a constructive effort to encourage men to know themselves and to act naturally for the good of all men, as in "The Education of Children."

Montaigne retired to his manor when he was thirty-eight. Public life had not satisfied him, and he was wealthy enough to live apart from the active life of his times and to give himself to contemplation and the writing of essays. He did spend some time in travel a few years later, and he was made mayor of Bordeaux, but most of his effort went into the writing and revision of his *Essais,* the attempt to essay, to test, the ideas which came to him.

An important essay in the first volume is "That the Taste for Good and Evil Depends in Good Part upon the Opinion We Have of Them." The essay begins with a paraphrase of a quotation from Epictetus to the effect that men are bothered more by opinions than by things. The belief that all human judgment is, after all, more a function of the human being than of the things judged suggested to Montaigne that by a change of attitude human beings could alter the values of things. Even death can be valued, provided the man who is about to die is of the proper disposition. Poverty and pain can also be good provided a person of courageous temperament develops a taste for them. Montaigne concludes that "things are not so painful and difficult of themselves, but our weakness or cowardice makes them so. To judge of great and high matters requires a suitable soul. . . ."

This stoical relativity is further endorsed in the essay "To Study Philosophy Is to Learn to Die." Montaigne's preoccupation with the problem of facing pain and death was caused by the death of his best friend, Etienne de la Boétie, who died in 1563 at the age of thirty-three, and then the deaths of his father, his brother, and several of his children. In addition, Montaigne was deeply disturbed by the Saint Bartholomew Day massacres. As a humanist, he was well educated in the literature and philosophy of the ancients, and from them he drew support of the stoical philosophy suggested to him by the courageous death of his friend La Boétie.

The title of the essay is a paraphrase of Cicero's remark "that to study philosophy is nothing but to prepare one's self to die." For some reason, perhaps because it did not suit his philosophic temperament at the time, perhaps because he had forgotten it, Montaigne did not allude to a similar expression attributed by Plato to Socrates, the point then being that the philosopher is interested in the eternal, the unchanging, and that life is a preoccupation with the temporal and the variable. For Montaigne, however, the remark means either that the soul in contemplation removes itself from the body, so to speak, or else that philosophy is concerned to teach us how to face death. It is the latter interpretation that interested him.

Asserting that we all aim at pleasure, even in virtue, Montaigne argued that the thought of death is naturally disturbing. He refers to the death of his brother, Captain St. Martin, who was killed when he was twenty-three by being struck behind the ear by a tennis ball. Other instances enforce his claim that death often comes unexpectedly to the young; for this reason the problem is urgent. With these examples before us, he writes, how can we "avoid fancying that death has us, every moment, by the throat?" The solution is to face death and fight it by becoming so familiar with the idea of death that we are no longer fearful. "The utility of living," he writes, "consists not in the length of days, but in the use of time. . . ." Death is natural, and what is important is not to waste life with the apprehension of death.

In the essay "Of Judging the Death of Another," Montaigne argues that a man reveals his true character when he shows how he faces a death which he knows is coming. A "studied and digested" death may bring a kind of delight to a man of the proper spirit. Montaigne cites Socrates and Cato as examples of men who knew how to die.

Montaigne's most famous essay is his "Apology for Raimond Sebond," generally considered to be the most complete and effective of his skeptical essays. Yet what Montaigne is skeptical of is not religion, as many critics have asserted, but of the pretensions of reason and of dogmatic philosophers and theologians. When Montaigne asks "Que sais-je?" the expression becomes the motto of his skepticism, "What do I know?"—not because he thinks that man should give up the use of the intellect and imagination, but because he thinks it wise to recognize the limits of these powers.

The essay is ostensibly in defense of the book titled *Theologia naturalis: sive Liber creaturarum magistri Raimondi de Sebonde*, the work of a philosopher and theologian of Toulouse, who wrote the book about 1430.

Montaigne considers two principal objections to the book: the first, that Sebond is mistaken in the effort to support Christian belief upon human reasons; the second, that Sebond's arguments in support of Christian belief are so weak that they may easily be confuted. In commenting upon the first objection, Montaigne agrees that the truth of God can be known only through faith and God's assistance, yet Montaigne argues that Sebond is to be commended for his noble effort to use reason in the service of God. If one considers Sebond's arguments as an aid to faith, they may be viewed as useful guides.

Montaigne's response to the second objection takes up most of the essay, and since the work is, in some editions, over two hundred pages long, we may feel justified in concluding from length alone the intensity of Montaigne's conviction. Montaigne uses the bulk of his essay to argue against those philosophers who suppose that by reason alone man can find truth and happiness. The rationalists who attack Sebond do not so much damage the theologian as show their own false faith in the value of reason. Montaigne considers "a man alone, without foreign assistance, armed only with his own proper arms, and unfurnished of the divine grace and wisdom . . ." and he sets forth to show that such a man is not only miserable and ridiculous but grievously mistaken in his presumption. Philosophers who attempt to reason without divine assistance gain nothing from their efforts except knowledge of their own weakness. Yet that knowledge has some value; ignorance is then not absolute ignorance. Nor is it any solution for the philosopher to adopt the stoical attitude and try to rise above humanity, as Seneca suggests; the only way to rise is by abandoning human means and by suffering, cause oneself to be elevated by Christian faith.

In the essay "Of the Education of Children," Montaigne writes that the only objective he had in writing the essays was to discover himself. In giving his opinions concerning the education of children Montaigne shows how the study of himself took him from the idea of philosophy as a study of what is "grim and formidable" to the idea of philosophy as a way to the health and cheerfulness of mind and body. He claims that "The most manifest sign of wisdom is a continual cheerfulness," and that "the height and value of true virtue consists in the facility, utility, and pleasure of its exercise. . . ." Philosophy is "that which instructs us to live." The aim of education is so to lead the child that he will come to love nothing but the good, and the way to this objective is an education that takes advantage of the youth's appetites and affections. Though his love of books led Montaigne to live in such a manner that he was accused of slothfulness and "want of mettle," he justifies his education by pointing out that this is the worst men can say of him.

Not all of Montaigne's essays reflect the major stages of his transformation from stoic and skeptic to a man of good will. Like Bacon, he found satisfaction in working out his ideas concerning the basic experiences of life. Thus he wrote of sadness, of constancy, of fear, of friendship (with particular reference to La Boétie), of moderation, of solitude, of sleep, of names, of books. These essays are lively, imaginative, and informed with the knowledge of a gentleman well trained in the classics. Yet it is when he writes of pain and death, referring to his own long struggle with kidney stones and to the deaths of those he loved, and when he writes of his need for faith and of man's need for self-knowledge, that we are most moved. In such essays the great stylist, the educated thinker, and the struggling human being are one. It was in the essaying of himself that Montaigne became a great essayist.

AN ESSAY CONCERNING HUMAN UNDERSTANDING

Type of work: Philosophical treatise
Author: John Locke (1632-1704)
First published: 1690

Locke's purpose in *An Essay Concerning Human Understanding* was to inquire into the origin and extent of human knowledge, and his answer—that all knowledge is derived from sense experience—became the principal tenet of the new empiricism which has dominated Western philosophy ever since. Even George Berkeley (1685-1753), who rejected Locke's distinction between sense qualities independent of the mind and sense qualities dependent on the mind, produced his idealism in response to Locke's provocative philosophy and gave it an empirical cast which reflected Western man's rejection of innate or transcendental knowledge.

An Essay Concerning Human Understanding is divided into four books: Book I, "Of Innate Notions"; Book II, "Of Ideas"; Book III, "Of Words"; and Book IV, "Of Knowledge, Certain and Probable."

In preparation for his radical claim that all ideas are derived from experience, Locke began his *Essay* with a careful consideration of the thesis that there are innate ideas, that is, ideas which are a necessary part of man's convictions and are, therefore, common to all men. Locke's attack on this claim is from two directions. He argues that many of the ideas which are supposed to be innate can be and have been derived naturally from sense experience, that not all men assent to those ideas which are supposed to be innate. He maintained that even if reason enables men to discover the truth of certain ideas, those ideas cannot be said to be innate; for reason is needed to discover their truth.

In Book II, "Of Ideas," Locke considers the origin of such ideas as those expressed by the words "whiteness," "hardness," "sweetness," "thinking," "motion," "man," and the like. The second section states his answer:

Let us then suppose the mind to be, as we say, white paper void of all characters, without any ideas. How comes it to be furnished? . . . Whence has it all the *materials* of reason and knowledge? To this I answer, in one word, from *experience*. . . . Our observation, employed either about *external sensible objects, or about the internal operations of our minds perceived and reflected on by ourselves, is that which supplies our understandings with all the materials of knowledge.*

The two sources of our ideas, according to Locke, are *sensation* and *reflection*. By the senses we come to have perceptions of things, thereby acquiring the ideas of yellow, white, cold, for example. Then, by reflection, by consideration of the mind in operation, we acquire the ideas of thinking, doubting, believing, knowing, willing, and so on.

By sensation we acquire knowledge of external objects; by reflection we acquire knowledge of our own minds.

Ideas which are derived from sensation are simple; that is, they present "one uniform appearance," even though a number of simple ideas may come together in the perception of an external object. The mind dwells on the simple ideas, comparing them to each other, combining them, but never inventing them. By a "simple idea" Locke meant what some modern and contemporary philosophers have called a "sense-datum," a distinctive, entirely differentiated item of sense experience, such as the odor of some particular glue, or the taste of coffee in a cup. He called attention to the fact that we use our sense experience to imagine what we have never perceived, but no operation of the mind can yield novel simple ideas.

By the "quality" of something Locke meant its power to produce an idea in someone sensing the thing. The word "quality" is used in the *Essay* in much the same way the word "characteristic" or "property" has been used by other, more recent, writers. For Locke distinguished between primary and secondary qualities. Primary qualities are those which matter has constantly, whatever its state. As primary qualities Locke names solidity, extension, figure, motion or rest, and number. By secondary qualities Locke meant the power to produce various sensations which have nothing in common with the primary qualities of the external objects. Thus, the power to produce the taste experience of sweetness is a secondary quality of sugar, but there is no reason to suppose that the sugar itself possesses the distinctive quality of the sensation. Colors, tastes, sounds, and odors are secondary qualities of objects.

Locke also referred to a third kind of quality or power, called simply "power," by which he meant the capacity to affect or to be affected by other objects. Thus, fire can melt clay; the capacity to melt clay is one of fire's powers, and such a power is neither a primary nor a secondary quality.

Locke concluded that primary ideas resemble external objects, but secondary ideas do not. It is this particular claim which has excited other professional philosophers, with Berkeley arguing that primary qualities can be understood only in terms of our own sensations, so that whatever generalization can be made about secondary qualities would have to cover primary qualities as well, and other philosophers arguing that Locke had no ground for maintaining that primary ideas "resemble" primary qualities, even if the distinction between primary and secondary qualities is allowed.

Complex ideas result from acts of the mind, and they fall into three classes: ideas of modes, of substances, and of relations. *Modes* are ideas which are considered to be incapable of independent existence since they are affections of substance, such as the ideas of triangle, gratitude, and murder. To think of *substances* is to think of "particular things subsisting by themselves," and to think in that manner involves supposing that there is a support, which cannot be understood, and that there are various qualities in combination which give various substances their distinguishing traits. Ideas of *relations* are the result of comparing ideas with each other.

After a consideration of the complex ideas of space, duration, number, the infinite, pleasure and pain, substance, relation, cause and effect, and of the distinctions between clear and obscure ideas and between true and false ideas, Locke proceeded to a discussion, in Book III, of words and essences. Words are signs of ideas by "arbitrary imposition," depending upon observed similarities which are taken as the basis for considering things in classes. Words are related to "nominal essences," that is, to obvious similarities found through observation, and not to "real essences," the actual qualities of things. Locke then discussed the imperfections and abuses of words.

In Book IV Locke defined knowledge as "the perception of the connection of and agreement, or disagreement and repugnancy, of any of our ideas." An example cited is our knowledge that white is not black, Locke arguing that to know that white is not black is simply to perceive that the idea of white is not the idea of black.

Locke insisted that knowledge cannot extend beyond the ideas we have, and that we determine whether ideas agree or disagree with each other either directly, by intuition, or indirectly, by reason or sensation. Truth is defined as "the joining or separating of signs, as the things signified by them do agree or disagree one with another." For example, the proposition "White is not black" involves the separation by "is not" of the signs "white" and "black," signifying the disagreement between the ideas of white and black; since the ideas are different, the proposition is true. Actually to have compared the ideas and to have noted their disagreement is to know the fact which the true proposition signifies.

Locke devoted the remaining chapters

of Book IV to arguing that we have knowledge of our existence by intuition, of the existence of God by demonstration, and of other things by sensation. Here the influence of Descartes is clearly evident. But it is the empiricism of the earlier parts of the book which won for Locke the admiration of philosophers.

AN ESSAY OF DRAMATIC POESY

Type of work: Literary criticism
Author: John Dryden (1631-1700)
First published: 1668

Principal characters:
CRITES, a sharp-tongued gentleman, a stanch classicist
EUGENIUS, a defender of the English theater of his own time
LISIDEIUS, a devotée of the French classical drama
NEANDER, representative of the author, a lover of the great Elizabethans

The period after the restoration of the Stuarts to the throne is notable in English literary history as an age in which criticism flourished, probably in no small part as a result of the emphasis on neoclassical rules of art in seventeenth century France, where many of Charles' courtiers and literati had passed the years of Cromwell's rule. John Dryden's *An Essay of Dramatic Poesy* is an exposition of several of the major critical positions of the time, set out in a semi-dramatic form that gives life to the abstract theories.

Dryden sets his discussion in June, 1665 during a naval battle between England and the Netherlands. Four cultivated gentlemen, Eugenius, Lisideius, Crites and Neander, have taken a barge down the Thames to observe the combat, and, as guns sound in the background, they comment on the sorry state of modern literature; this naval encounter will inspire hundreds of bad verses commending the victors or consoling the vanquished. Crites laments that his contemporaries will never equal the standard set by the Greeks and the Romans. Eugenius, more optimistic, disagrees and suggests that they pass the remainder of the day debating the relative merits of classical and modern literature. He proposes that Crites choose one literary genre for comparison and initiate the discussion.

As Crites begins his defense of the classical drama, he mentions one point which is accepted by all the others: drama is, as Aristotle wrote, an imitation of life, and it is successful as it reflects human nature clearly. He also discusses the three unities, rules dear to both the classicist and the neoclassicist, requiring that a play take place in one locale, during one day, and that it encompass one, and only one, action or plot.

Crites contends that modern playwrights are but pale shadows of Aeschylus, Sophocles, Seneca, and Terence. The classical dramatists not only followed the unities successfully; they also used language more skillfully then their successors. He calls to witness Ben Jonson, the Elizabethan dramatist most highly respected by the neoclassical critics, a writer who borrowed copiously from many of the classical authors and prided himself on being a modern Horace: "I will use no further argument to you than his example: I will produce before you Father Ben, dressed in all the ornaments and colours of the ancients; you will need no other guide to our party, if you follow him."

Eugenius pleads the cause of the modern English dramatists, not by pointing out their virtues, but by criticizing the faults of the classical playwrights. He objects to the absence of division by acts in the works of the latter, as well as to the lack of originality in their plots. Tragedies are based on threadbare myths familiar to the whole audience; comedies revolve around hackneyed intrigues of stolen heiresses and miraculous restorations. A more serious defect is these authors' disregard of poetic justice: "Instead of punishing vice and rewarding virtue, they have often shown a prosperous wickedness, and an unhappy piety."

Pointing to scenes from several plays, Eugenius notes the lack of tenderness in classical drama. Crites grants Eugenius his preference, but he argues that each age has its own modes of behavior; Homer's heroes were "men of great appetites, lovers of beef broiled upon the coals, and good fellows," while the principal characters of modern French romances "neither eat, nor drink, nor sleep, for love."

Lisideius takes up the debate on behalf of the French theater of the early seventeenth century. The French classical dramatists, led by Corneille, were careful observers of the unities, and they did not attempt to combine tragedy and comedy, an English practice which he finds absurd: "Here a course of mirth, there another of sadness and passion, and a third of honour and a duel: thus, in two hours and a half, we run through all the fits of Bedlam."

The French playwrights are so attentive to poetic justice that when they base their plots on historical events they alter the original situations to mete out just reward and punishment. The French dramatist "so interweaves truth with probable fiction that he puts a pleasing fallacy upon us; mends the intrigues of fate, and dispenses with the severity of history, to reward that virtue which has been rendered to us there unfortunate." Plot, as the preceding comments might suggest, is of secondary concern in these plays. The dramatist's chief aim is to express appropriate emotions; violent action always takes place off stage, and it is generally reported by a messenger.

Just as Eugenius devoted much of his discussion to refuting Crites' arguments, Neander, whose views are generally Dryden's own, contradicts Lisideius' claims for the superiority of the French drama. Stating his own preference for the works of English writers, especially of the great Elizabethans, Neander suggests that it is they who best fulfill the primary requirement of drama, that it be "an imitation of life." The beauties of the French stage are, to him, cold; they may "raise perfection higher where it is, but are not sufficient to give it where it is not." He compares these beauties to those of a statue, flawless, but without a soul. Intense human feeling is, Neander feels, an essential part of drama.

Neander argues that tragi-comedy is the best form for drama, for it is the closest to life; emotions are heightened by contrast, and both mirth and sadness are more vivid when they are set side by side. He believes, too, that subplots enrich a play; he finds the French drama, with its single action, thin. Like Samuel Johnson, who defended Shakespeare's disregard of the unities, Dryden suggests that close adherence to the rules prevents dramatic depth. Human actions will be more believable if there is time for the characters' emotions to develop. Neander sees no validity in the argument that changes of place and time in plays lessen dramatic credibility; the theatergoer knows that he is in a world of illusion from the beginning, and he can easily accept leaps in time and place, as well as makeshift battles.

Concluding his comparison of French and English drama, Neander characterizes the best of the Elizabethan playwrights. His judgments have often been quoted for their perceptivity. He calls Shakespeare "the man who of all modern, and perhaps ancient poets, had the largest and most comprehensive soul." Beaumont and Fletcher are praised for their wit and for their language, whose smoothness and polish Dryden considers their greatest accomplishment: "I am apt to believe the English language in them arrived to its highest perfection."

Dryden commends Ben Jonson for his learning and judgment, for his "correctness," yet he feels that Shakespeare surpassed him in "wit," by which he seems to mean something like natural ability or inspiration. This discussion ends with the familiar comparison: "Shakespeare was the Homer, or father of our dramatic poets; Jonson was the Virgil, the pattern of elaborate writing; I admire him, but I love Shakespeare."

Neander concludes his argument for the superiority of the Elizabethans with a close critical analysis of Jonson's *The Silent Woman,* which he believes a perfect demonstration that the English were capable of following classical rules triumphantly. Dryden's allegiance to the neoclassical tradition is clear here; Samuel Johnson could disparage the unities in his *Preface to Shakespeare,* but Dryden, even as he refuses to be a slave to the rules, makes Jonson's successful observance of them his decisive argument.

The essay closes with a long discussion of the value of rhyme in plays. Crites feels that blank verse, as the poetic form nearest prose, is most suitable for drama, while Neander favors rhyme, which encourages succinctness and clarity. He believes that the Restoration dramatists can make their one claim to superiority through their development of the heroic couplet. Dryden is very much a man of his time in this argument; the modern reader who has suffered through the often empty declamation of the Restoration hero returns with relief to the blank verse of the Elizabethans.

Dryden ends his work without a real conclusion; the barge reaches its destination, the stairs at Somerset House, and the debate is, of necessity, over. Moving with the digressions and contradictions of a real conversation, the discussion has provided a clear, lively picture of many of the literary opinions of Dryden's time.

ESSAY ON CRITICISM

Type of work: Verse essay
Author: Alexander Pope (1688-1744)
First published: 1711

Published when Alexander Pope was twenty-two years old, the *Essay on Criticism* remains one of the best known discussions of literary criticism, of its ends and means, in our language. It stands today the source of numerous familiar epigrams known to the reading public. Pope was very young when he wrote the work; existing evidence points to 1708 or 1709 as the probable period of composition. Pope wrote of its composition: "The things that I have written fastest, have always pleased the most. I wrote the *Essay on Criticism* fast; for I had digested all the matter in prose, before I began upon it in verse." Although Pope may seem to rely too heavily upon the authority of the ancient authors as literary masters, he certainly recognizes, as many readers fail to note, the "grace beyond the reach of art" which no model can teach. True genius and judgment are innate gifts of heaven, as Pope says, but many do possess the seeds of taste and judgment that, with proper training, may flourish. The genius of the ancients cannot be imitated but their principles may be. The poem is structured in three parts: the general qualities of a critic; the particular laws by which he judges a work; and the ideal character of a critic.

Part I opens with Pope's indictment of the false critic. He remarks that as poets may be prejudiced about their own merits, so critics can be partial to their own judgment. Judgment, or "True Taste," derives like the poet's genius from nature, but nature provides everyone with some taste, which if not perverted by a poor education or other defects, may enable the critic to judge properly. The first job of the critic then is to know himself, his own judgment, tastes, abilities; in short, to know his personal limitations.

The second task of the critic is to know Nature, which is his standard as it is the poet's. Nature is defined ambiguously as

Unerring Nature, still divinely bright,
One clear, unchanged, and universal
    light,
Life, force, and beauty, must to all im-
    part,
At once the source, and end, the test of
    Art.

Nature thus becomes a universal or cosmic force, an ideal sought by poet and critic alike in the general scheme, things universally approved throughout history by all men. This ideal must be apprehended by the critic through his judicious balance of wit and judgment, of imaginative invention and deliberative reason.

The rules of literary criticism may best be located in those works that have stood the test of time and universal approbation, the works of antiquity. From the ancient authors critics have derived rules of art that are not self-imposed at the whim of the critic, but are discovered justly operating in the writings of the best authors. Such rules are "Nature still, but Nature methodized."

Formerly critics did restrict themselves to discovering rules in classical literature; now, however, critics stray from the principles of these earlier critics whose motive was solely to make art "more beloved," and prescribe their own rules, which are pedantic, unimaginative, and basely critical of literature. Thus what was once a subordinate sister to creative art now replaces or turns against its superior, assuming a higher place in the order of things. Criticism, once destined to teach the "world . . . to admire" the poet's art, today presumes to be master.

The true critic must learn thoroughly the ancients, particularly Homer and Vergil, for "To copy nature is to copy them." But there are beauties of art which cannot be taught by rules; these intangible beauties are the "nameless graces which no methods teach/And which a master-hand alone can reach." But modern writers should avoid transcending, unless rarely, the rules of art first established by the great men of the past.

Part II traces the causes hindering good judgment—that chief virtue of a true critic. Pope advises the critic to avoid the dangers of blindness caused by pride, the greatest source of poor judgment, by learning his own defects and by profiting even from the strictures of his enemies. Inadequate learning is another reason a critic errs: "A little learning is a dangerous thing;/Drink deep, or taste not the Pierian spring." Or if a critic looks too closely at the parts of a poem, he may find himself preferring a poem dull as a whole yet perfect in parts to one imperfect in part but pleasing as a whole. It is the unity of the many small parts in one whole that affects us: " 'Tis not a lip, or eye, we beauty call,/But the joint force and full result of all." Art without any fault at all, moreover, can never be. And finally, any critic errs who condemns a work for failing to achieve that which its author never intended: in short, "regard the writer's End,/Since none can compass more than they intend."

As some critics deviate from nature in judging "by a love to parts," others confine their attention to conceits, images, or metaphors. Poets who dissimulate their want of art with a wild profusion of imagery have not learned to control their imagination; they overvalue mere decoration and paint, not "the naked nature and the living grace," but the external variables of nature. "True Wit," Pope says, "is Nature to advantage dressed,/ What oft was thought, but ne'er so well expressed."

Other critics too highly praise style and language without respect for content; true eloquence clarifies and improves the thought, revealing nature at her finest, but "False Eloquence" imposes a veil upon the face of nature, obscuring with its finery the truths of nature. Proper expression, in addition, should fit with the content; the poet should never attempt to lend false dignity by archaic words. Proper diction is neither too old nor too modern.

Most false critics judge by meter, criticizing according to the roughness or smoothness of the verse. Overfondness for metrics results in the dull clichés of poetry, such as "the cooling western breeze," and the like. Pope avers that rough or smooth verse should not be the poet's ideal; he should aim rather to fit the sound to the sense

> Soft is the strain when Zephyr gently blows,
> And the smooth stream in smoother numbers flows;
> But when loud surges lash the sounding shore,
> The hoarse, rough verse should like a torrent roar.

Lines 344-383 of the poem constitute a digression by Pope to illustrate "representative meter."

The true critic generally abides by rules of tolerance and aloofness from extremes of fashion and personal taste. The critic who indulges in petty predilections for certain schools or kinds of poets sacrifices his objectivity. Be a patron of no separate group, whether ancient or modern, foreign or native, Pope advises. The critic should pledge himself to truth, not to passing cults. Nor should a critic fear to advance his own judgment merely because the public favors other poets and schools; no critic should echo fashion or let a writer's name influence him. Especially reprehensible is that critic who derives his opinions about literature from lords of quality.

The final pitfall of the false critic is subjectivity, measuring by personal preferences. Private or public envy may distort one's evaluation. The critic must put aside personal motives and praise according to less personal criteria. Nor should the critic be led astray by self-love:

"Good-nature and good-sense must ever join." A critic may justly vent his spleen upon more worthy targets, of which many exist in "these flagitious times." Obscenity, dullness, immodesty: all should concern the critic and receive his lash. But the vices of an age should not infect a critic's judgment on other matters.

Finally, Part III outlines the ideal character of a critic. It lists rules for his manners and contrasts the ideal critic with the "incorrigible poet" and "impertinent Critic," concluding with a brief summary of literary criticism and the character of the best critics.

It is not enough for the critic to know, Pope writes; he must also share the qualities of a good man, worthy of respect not only for his intellect but also for his character. Integrity stands at the head of a list of good qualities for a critic. Modesty that forbids both unseemly outspokenness and rigid adherence to erroneous opinion, tact that supports truth without alienating by bluntness, and courage that fears not to pursue truth despite censure are important attributes for the true critic. But as some dull and foolish poets are best not maligned for fear of provoking them to greater folly, so the critic full of pedantry and impertinence should be ignored. Nothing is too sacred for the learned fool, who rushes in "where Angels fear to tread." The true critic is one "Still pleased to teach, and yet not proud to know." Such a man has knowledge both "of books and human kind."

Having outlined the characteristics of true critics, Pope catalogues the most famous critics, "the happy few" of Greece and Rome: Aristotle, Horace, Dionysius, Quintilian, Longinus. Aristotle, "Who conquered Nature" respected by the poets as the lawgiver; Horace, who "still charms with graceful negligence"; Quintilian's "justest rules, and clearest method": such are the true critics who flourished along with the great empires of their nations. With the fall of the empire came the fall of learning, enslavement of mind and body. Erasmus stemmed the barbarian's reign of ignorance and Boileau of France signified the advancement of critical learning in Europe. Except for the Duke of Buckinghamshire's *Essay on Poetry*, England despises and remains untouched by the return to the "juster ancient cause."